D1476197

International Environmental Law

This textbook provides a concise, conceptually clear and legally rigorous introduction to contemporary international environmental law and practice. Written in an accessible style, the book covers all the major multilateral environmental agreements, paying particular attention to their underlying structure, their main legal provisions and their practical operation. The material is structured into four parts: Part I – Foundations, Part II – Substantive Regulation, Part III – Implementation and Part IV – International Environmental Law as a Perspective. The presentation of the material blends policy and legal analysis and makes extensive reference to the relevant treaties, instruments and jurisprudence. All chapters include a detailed bibliography, along with numerous figures to summarise the main components of the regulation and ensure that readers do not lose sight of the 'forest' while focusing on the 'trees'.

Pierre-Marie Dupuy is Emeritus Professor at the University of Paris II (Panthéon-Assas) and at the Graduate Institute of International and Development Studies in Geneva. He has extensive experience in international law practice, in particular as counsel for governments in numerous cases before the International Court of Justice and as international arbitrator in the field of international investment law.

Jorge E. Viñuales is the Harold Samuel Professor of Law and Environmental Policy at the University of Cambridge. He has published extensively in his specialty areas and in public international law at large and has wide experience as a practitioner. He has advised governments, international organisations and private companies and has worked in many inter-State, investor–State and commercial disputes.

International Environmental Law

PIERRE-MARIE DUPUY, UNIVERSITY OF PARIS II
(PANTHÉON–ASSAS)

JORGE E. VIÑUALES, UNIVERSITY OF CAMBRIDGE

CAMBRIDGE
UNIVERSITY PRESS

University Printing House, Cambridge CB2 8BS, United Kingdom

Cambridge University Press is part of the University of Cambridge.

It furthers the University's mission by disseminating knowledge in the pursuit of education, learning and research at the highest international levels of excellence.

www.cambridge.org
Information on this title: www.cambridge.org/9781107673342

© Pierre-Marie Dupuy and Jorge E. Viñuales 2015

First published 2015
Reprinted 2016

Printed in the United Kingdom by TJ International Ltd. Padstow Cornwall

A catalogue record for this publication is available from the British Library

Library of Congress Cataloguing in Publication data
Dupuy, Pierre-Marie, 1948– author.
International environmental law : an introduction / Pierre-Marie Dupuy, Jorge E. Viñuales.
    pages   cm
ISBN 978-1-107-04124-0 (hardback)
1. Environmental law, International.   I. Viñuales, Jorge E., author.   II. Title.
K3583.D87   2015
344.04'6–dc23

2014042969

ISBN 978-1-107-04124-0 Hardback
ISBN 978-1-107-67334-2 Paperback

Contents

Abbreviations

AB	Appellate Body of the WTO Dispute Settlement Body
African Commission	African Commission of Human and Peoples' Rights
African Court	African Court of Human and Peoples' Rights
APEC	Asia Pacific Economic Co-operation
ASMA	Antarctic Specially Managed Areas
ASPA	Antarctic Specially Protected Areas
ATCM	Antarctic Treaty Consultative Meeting
ATS	Antarctic Treaty System
BAT	Best available technology
BCH	Biosafety Clearing House
BIT	Bilateral Investment Treaty
CBDR	Common but differentiated responsibility
CDM	Clean development mechanism
CESCR	UN Committee on Economic, Social and Cultural Rights
CFR	United States Code of Federal Regulations
CMP	Conference of the Parties acting as the Meeting of the Parties
COP (COPs)	Conference(s) of the Parties
CRF	Common reporting format
CSD	Commission for Sustainable Development
ECOSOC	UN Economic and Social Council
ECtHR	European Court of Human Rights
EEZ	exclusive economic zone
EGS	environmental goods and services
EIA	environmental impact assessment
EMEP	European Monitoring and Evaluation Programme
EPA	United States Environmental Protection Agency
ETIS	Elephant trade information system
FAO	UN Food and Agriculture Organisation
FTA	Free trade agreement
GA (or UNGA)	United Nations General Assembly
GAOR	UN General Assembly Official Records

GAW	Global Atmosphere Watch
GDP	gross domestic product
GEF	Global Environmental Facility
GMA	global mercury assessment
GMO	genetically modified organism
HRC	UN Human Rights Committee
IAEA	International Atomic Energy Agency
ICEF	International Court of the Environment Foundation
ICJ	International Court of Justice
ICommHR	Inter-American Commission on Human Rights
ICSID	International Centre for Settlement of Investment Disputes
ICtHR	Inter-American Court of Human Rights
IDI	Institut de Droit International
IIA(s)	International Investment Agreement(s)
IISD	International Institute for Sustainable Development
ILA	International Law Association
ILC	International Law Commission
ILM	International Legal Materials
IMO	International Maritime Organisation
INC	Inter-governmental negotiating committee
IOMC	Inter-organisation Programme for the Sound Management of Chemicals
IPCC	International Panel on Climate Change
IPR	intellectual property rights
ITLOS	International Tribunal for the Law of the Sea
IUCN	International Union for the Conservation of Nature
LMO	living modified organism
MDG	Millennium Development Goal
MEA(s)	Multilateral Environmental Agreement(s)
MIKE	Monitoring the Illegal Killing of Elephants
NAFO	Northwest Atlantic Fisheries Organisation
NCP	Non-compliance procedures
NGO	Non-governmental organisation
NIR	National inventory report
OAS	Organisation of American States
OECD	Organisation for Economic Co-operation and Development
OHCHR	Office of the High Commissioner for Human Rights
PCA	Permanent Court of Arbitration
PES	payment for eco-system services
PIC	prior informed consent
POP	persistent organic pollutants
PPP	public-private partnership

REDD	Reduced Emissions from Deforestation and Forest Degradation
RFMO	regional fisheries management organisation
RIAA	Reports of International Arbitral Awards
SAICM	Strategic Aproach to International Chemicals Management
SC (or UNSC)	United Nations Security Council
SDG	sustainable development goals
SFDI	Société française pour le droit international
SGRP	System-wide Genetic Resources Programme of the Treaty on Plant Genetic Resources
TFDD	www.transboundarywaters.orst.edu
TOMAs	tropospheric ozone management areas
TWC	Reports of Trials of War Criminals
UN	United Nations
UNCC	United Nations Compensation Commission
UNCED	United Nations Conference on Environmental Development
UNCITRAL	United Nations Commission on International Trade Law
UNCTAD	United Nations Commission on Trade and Development
UNDESA	United Nations Department of Economic and Social Affairs
UNDP	United Nations Development Programme
UNECE	United Nations Economic Commission for Europe
UNEP	United Nations Environment Programme
UNHCR	United Nations High Commissioner for Refugees
UNTS	United Nations Treaty Series
VOC	volatile organic compound
WMO	World Meteorological Organisation
WTO	World Trade Organisation
WWF	World Wildlife Fund

Figures

Table of treaties and instruments

(cont.)

Date	Full reference	Abbreviation	Pages
18 October 1907	Convention (No. IV) respecting the Laws and Customs of War on Land and its Annex: Regulations concerning the Laws and Customs of War on Land, 205 CTS 277.	Hague Convention IV	346, 347, 357
7 July 1911	Convention between the United States, Great Britain, Japan and Russia providing for the Preservation and Protection of the Fur Seals, 37 Stat. 1542.	Fur Seals Convention	4, 159
17 June 1925	Protocol for the Prohibition of the Use in War of Asphyxiating, Poisonous or Other Gases, and of Bacteriological Methods of Warfare, 94 LNTS 65.	1925 Geneva Protocol	356, 357, 358, 359
8 November 1927	Convention for the Abolition of Import and Export Prohibitions and Restrictions, 97 LNTS 391.		391
24 September 1931	Convention for the Regulation of Whaling, available at: www.ecolex.org (TRE-000073).		4, 158
12 October 1940	Convention on Nature Protection and Wild Life Preservation in the Western Hemisphere, 56 Stat. 1354, TS 981.	Western Hemisphere Convention	159

(cont.)

(cont.)

Date	Full reference	Abbreviation	Pages
18 August 1948	Convention Concerning the Regime of Navigation on the Danube, available at: www.ecolex.org (TRE-000555).		6
12 August 1949	Geneva Convention Relative to the Treatment of Prisoners of War, 75 UNTS 31.	III Geneva Convention	314
12 August 1949	Geneva Convention Relative to the Treatment of Civilian Persons in Time of War, 75 UNTS 287.	IV Geneva Convention	26, 314, 347, 349
8 April 1950	Protocol to Establish a Tripartite Standing Commission on Polluted Waters, available at: www.ecolex.org (TRE-000493).		6
4 November 1950	Convention for the Protection of Human Rights and Fundamental Freedoms, 4 November 1950, 213 UNTS 221.	ECHR	305, 320, 325
20 March 1952	Protocol to the Convention for the Protection of Human Rights and Fundamental Freedoms, ETS 9.	Protocol I	308

(cont.)

(cont.)

(cont.)

(cont.)

(cont.)

(cont.)

(cont.)

Date	Full reference	Abbreviation	Pages
16 June 1972	'Declaration of the United Nations Conference on the Human Environment', Stockholm, UN Doc. A/CONF 48/14/Rev.1, pp. 2ff.	Stockholm Declaration	9–10, 12, 14, 25, 26, 34, 35, 56, 57, 58, 59, 77, 80, 94, 123, 126, 298, 299, 312
16 June 1972	'Action Plan for the Human Environment', UN Doc. A/CONF 48/14, pp. 10–62.		9, 10
16 November 1972	Convention for the Protection of the World Cultural and Natural Heritage, 1037 UNTS 151.	WHC	11, 40, 85, 158, 161, 162, 177, 178–82, 274, 353, 354
15 December 1972	'Institutional and Financial Arrangements for International Environmental Cooperation', UN Doc. A/RES/2997/XXVII.		9, 29
29 December 1972 (modified on 7 November 1996)	Convention for the Prevention of Marine Pollution by Dumping of Wastes and Other Matter, as modified by the Protocol of 7 November 1996, 1046 UNTS 120.	London Convention	11, 52, 98, 99, 101–3, 204

(cont.)

Date	Full reference	Abbreviation	Pages
3 March 1973	Convention on International Trade in Endangered Species of Wild Fauna and Flora, 983 UNTS 243.	CITES	11, 35, 40, 158, 161, 162, 167–73, 175, 180, 195, 239, 241, 286, 287, 289, 291, 351, 394, 398
2 November 1973 (modified on 17 February 1978)	International Convention for the Prevention of Pollution from Ships, as modified by the Protocol of 1978 relating thereto, 1340 UNTS 184.	MARPOL 73/78 or MARPOL	11, 98, 101–2, 103, 204
19 February 1974	Nordic Convention on the Protection of the Environment, available in English at www.ecolex.org (TRE-000491).	Nordic Convention	125
1 May 1974	'Declaration on the Establishment of a New International Economic Order', Res. 3201 (S-VI).		74
16 February 1976	Protocol for the Prevention and Elimination of Pollution of the Mediterranean Sea by Dumping from Ships and Aircraft, available on www.ecolex.org (TRE-001285).		106
12 June 1976	Convention on the Conservation of Nature in the South Pacific, available at: www.ecolex.org (TRE-000540).	Apia Convention	69, 159

(cont.)

(cont.)

(cont.)

(cont.)

(cont.)

Date	Full reference	Abbreviation	Pages
30 April 1982	HRC, General Comment No. 6: Article 6 (Right to Life), UN Doc. HRI/GEN/1/Rev.9 (Vol.1).		303
27 August 1982	Report of the Governing Council on its Session of a Special Character (10–18 May 1982), UN Doc. A/RES/37/ 219, Annex II	Nairobi Declaration	12
28 October 1982	World Charter for Nature, UN Doc. A/ RES/37/7.	World Charter for Nature	11, 25, 35, 63, 158
10 December 1982	United Nations Convention on the Law of the Sea, 1833 UNTS 396.	UNCLOS	11, 52, 59, 60, 64, 65, 69, 70, 74, 82, 84, 85, 87, 93, 94–101, 102, 103, 104, 115, 116, 162, 163–4, 165, 166, 239, 245, 246, 249, 394
24 March 1983	Convention for the Protection and Development of the Marine Environment of the Wider Caribbean Region, available on www.ecolex.org (TRE-000763).	Cartagena Convention	105
24 March 1983	Protocol Concerning Cooperation in Combating Oil Spills in the Wider Caribbean Region, available on www.ecolex.org (TRE-000764).		105, 106

(cont.)

Date	Full reference	Abbreviation	Pages
22 July 1983	Protocol for the Protection of the South-East Atlantic against Pollution from Land-based Sources, available on www.ecolex.org (TRE-000768).		105
22 July 1983	Supplementary Protocol on the Agreement on Regional Cooperation in Combating Pollution of the South-East Pacific by Hydrocarbons or Other Harmful Substances in Cases of Emergency, available on www.eco lex.org (TRE-000769).		105
19 December 1983	'Process of Preparation of the Environmental Perspective to the Year 2000 and Beyond', UN Doc. A/RES/38/161.		12
28 September 1984	Protocol to the 1979 Convention on Long-Range Transboundary Air Pollution on the Long-term Financing of the Cooperative Programme for Monitoring and Evaluation of the Long-Range Transport of Air Pollutants in Europe (EMEP), 1491 UNTS 167.	EMEP Protocol	40

(cont.)

Date	Full reference	Abbreviation	Pages
22 November 1984	Cartagena Declaration on Refugees, Annual Report of the Inter-American Commission on Human Rights, OAS Doc. OEA/Ser.L/V/II.66/doc.10, rev. 1.		369
22 March 1985	Vienna Convention for the Protection of the Ozone Layer, 1513 UNTS 293.	Ozone Convention	12, 42, 62, 74, 133–4, 146, 147, 224, 245
21 June 1985	Convention for the Protection, Management and Development of the Marine and Coastal Region of East Africa, available on www.ecolex.org (TRE-000821).	Nairobi Convention	105
21 June 1985	Protocol Concerning Cooperation in Combating Marine Pollution in Cases of Emergency in the Eastern African Region, available on www.ecolex.org (TRE-000825).		106
8 July 1985	Protocol on the Reduction of Sulphur Emissions or their Transboundary Fluxes, 1480 UNTS 215.	Sulphur Protocol I	128, 240
9 July 1985	ASEAN Agreement on the Conservation of Nature and Natural Resources, 15 EPL 64.	Kuala Lumpur Agreement	159

(cont.)

(cont.)

Date	Full reference	Abbreviation	Pages
16 November 1988	Additional Protocol to the American Convention on Human Rights in the Area of Economic, Social and Cultural Rights, OAS Treaty Series No. 69.	Protocol of San Salvador	305, 313
22 March 1989	Basel Convention on the Control of Transboundary Movements of Hazardous Wastes and their Disposal, 1673 UNTS 57.	Basel Convention	12, 29, 39, 40, 65, 68, 191, 201, 203, 204, 207, 209, 220, 221–225, 229, 230, 231, 232, 239, 274, 287, 291, 351, 382, 387, 398, 399
25 May 1989	London Guidelines for the Exchange of Information on Chemicals in International Trade, Decision 15/30 of the UNEP Governing Council.		42, 67, 218
29 May 1989	Protocol concerning Marine Pollution resulting from Exploration and Exploitation of the Continental Shelf (ROPME Sea Area), available on www.eco lex.org (TRE-001128).		106
27 June 1989	Convention (No. 169) concerning Indigenous and Tribal Peoples in Independent Countries, 28 ILM 1382 (1989).	ILO Convention 169	67, 326

(cont.)

(cont.)

Date	Full reference	Abbreviation	Pages
30 November 1990	International Convention on Oil Pollution Preparedness, Response and Cooperation, available at www.ecolex.org (TRE-001109).	OPRC Convention	102
30 January 1991	Bamako Convention on the Ban on the Import into Africa and the Control of Transboundary Movement and Management of Hazardous Wastes within Africa, 30 ILM 773.	Bamako Convention	62, 65, 201, 204, 224
25 February 1991	Convention on Environmental Impact Assessment in a Transboundary Context, 1989 UNTS 309.	Espoo Convention	65, 69, 70, 86, 216, 290, 317, 318
13 March 1991	Agreement between the Government of Canada and the Government of the United States of America on Air Quality, available at: www.epa.gov/usca/agreement.html	Air Quality Agreement	124

(cont.)

Date	Full reference	Abbreviation	Pages
19 March 1991	International Convention for the Protection of New Varieties of Plants of December 2, 1961, as revised at Geneva on 10 November 1972, 23 October 1978 and 19 March 1991, available at: www.eco lex.org (TRE-001119).	UPOV Convention	193, 412
4 October 1991	Protocol on Environmental Protection to the Antarctic Treaty, 30 ILM 1455.	Madrid Protocol	69, 106, 114, 159, 162, 173, 182–5, 186
18 November 1991	Protocol concerning the Control of Emissions of Volatile Organic Compounds or their Transboundary Fluxes, 31 ILM 573.	VOC Protocol	128, 129
17 March 1992	Convention on the Transboundary Effects of Industrial Accidents, 2105 UNTS 457.	Convention on Industrial Accidents	65, 201, 204, 206, 209, 214–17
18 March 1992	Convention on the Protection and Use of Transboundary Watercourses and International Lakes, 1936 UNTS 269.	UNECE Water Convention or Helsinki Convention	62, 72, 108, 109, 110, 111, 112, 315
9 April 1992	Convention on the Protection of the Marine Environment of the Baltic Sea Area, available on www.eco lex.org (TRE-001153).		106

(cont.)

(cont.)

(cont.)

Date	Full reference	Abbreviation	Pages
14 August 1992	'Non-legally Binding Authoritative Statement of Principles for a Global Consensus on the Management, Conservation and Sustainable Development of All Types of Forests', UN Doc. A/CONF/151/ 26 (vol. III).	Forest principles	13, 35
17 September 1992	North American Agreement on Environmental Cooperation, 32 ILM 1519.	NAAEC	392
22 September 1992	Convention for the Protection of the Marine Environment of the North-East Atlantic, 2354 UNTS 67.	OSPAR Convention	62, 72, 106, 245
25 November 1992	Terms of Reference for the Multilateral Fund, UNEP/OzL.Pro.4/15.		272, 275
27 November 1992	Protocol amending the International Convention on Civil Liability for Oil Pollution Damage, available at: www.eco lex.org (TRE-001 177).	CLC/92	260–4, 265

(cont.)

(cont.)

Date	Full reference	Abbreviation	Pages
15 April 1994	Agreement establishing the World Trade Organisation, 1867 UNTS 154.	Marrakesh Agreement	392
15 April 1994	Agreement on Sanitary and Phytosanitary Measures, 1867 UNTS 493.	SPS Agreement	63, 250, 403–4, 405
15 April 1994	Agreement on Subsidies and Countervailing Measures, 1867 UNTS 14.	SCM Agreement	399
15 April 1994	Agreement on Trade-Related Aspects of Intellectual Property Trade, 1869 UNTS 299.	TRIPs	187, 193, 407, 408, 410, 411, 412, 413
14 June 1994	Protocol to the LRTAP Convention on Further Reduction of Sulphur Emissions, 2030 UNTS 122.	Sulphur Protocol II	128, 129, 240
17 June 1994	Convention on Nuclear Safety, 1963 UNTS 293.	Convention on Nuclear Safety	201, 227, 228
17 June 1994	United Nations Convention to Combat Desertification in those Countries Experiencing Serious Drought and/or Desertification, Particularly in Africa, UN Doc. A/AC.241/15/Rev. 7 (1994), 33 ILM 1328.	UNCCD	13, 14, 29, 40, 65, 161, 162, 173, 185, 367

(cont.)

(cont.)

Date	Full reference	Abbreviation	Pages
10 June 1995	Protocol Concerning Specially Protected Areas and Biological Diversity in the Mediterranean, available on www.ecolex.org (TRE– 001220).		106
10 June 1995	Convention for the Protection of the Mediterranean Sea against Pollution, 16 February 1976, as amended and later becoming the Convention for the Protection of the Marine Environment and the Mediterranean Coastal Environment, available on www.ecolex.org (TRE-001284).	Barcelona Convention	105
4 August 1995	Agreement for the Implementation of the Provisions of the United Nations Conventions on the Law of the Sea of 10 December 1982 relating to the Conservation and Management of Straddling Fish Stocks and Highly Migratory Fish Stocks, S. Treaty Doc. No. 104–24, 2167 UNTS 3.	Straddling Fish Stocks Agreement	13, 62, 96, 162, 163, 164–5, 166

(cont.)

Date	Full reference	Abbreviation	Pages
3 May 1996	International Convention on Liability and Compensation for Damage in Connection with the Carriage of Hazardous and Noxious Substances, amended by the Protocol of 30 April 2010, available at: www.ecolex.org (TRE-001 245).	HNS Convention 2010	260
1 October 1996	Protocol on the Prevention of Pollution of the Mediterranean Sea by Transboundary Movements of Hazardous Wastes and their Disposal (Hazardous Wastes Protocol), available on www.ecolex.org (TRE-001334).		106
21 May 1997	United Nations Convention on the Law of the Non-Navigational Uses of International Watercourses, 36 ILM 700.	UN Convention on Watercourses	36, 56, 66, 69, 87, 104, 108, 109–12
28 June 1997	'Programme for the Further Implementation of Agenda 21', UN Doc. A/S/19–2, Annex.		17

(cont.)

Date	Full reference	Abbreviation	Pages
5 September 1997	Joint Convention on the Safety of Spent Fuel Management and on the Safety of Radioactive Waste Management, available at: www.eco lex.org (TRE-001273).	Joint Convention	201, 204, 227, 228
12 September 1997	Convention on Supplementary Compensation for Nuclear Damage, IAEA INFCIRC/567.	Complementary Vienna Convention	260, 263
11 December 1997	Kyoto Protocol to the United Nations Framework Convention on Climate Change, Kyoto, 2303 UNTS 148	Kyoto Protocol	27, 28, 30, 37, 38, 39, 42, 45, 53, 74, 135, 144, 145, 146, 147, 148, 149–53, 154, 200, 239, 242, 280, 284, 286, 287, 288, 290, 291, 382, 383, 387, 399
11 February 1998	Guiding Principles on Internal Displacement, UN Doc. E/CN.4/1998/ 53/Add.2 (1998), Annex.		370, 371
17 March 1998	Protocol on the Control of Marine Transboundary Movements and Disposal of Hazardous Wastes and other Wastes (ROPME Sea Area), available on www.ecolex.org (TRE-001298).		103

(cont.)

Date	Full reference	Abbreviation	Pages
24 June 1998	Protocol on Persistent Organic Pollutants to the LRTAP Convention, 2230 UNTS 79.	POP Protocol	128, 130, 211, 251, 388
24 June 1998	Protocol on Heavy Metals to the LRTAP Convention, 2237 UNTS 4.	Heavy Metals Protocol or HM Protocol	128, 130, 201, 229, 230
25 June 1998	Convention on Access to Information, Public Participation in Decision-making and Access to Justice in Environmental Matters, 2161 UNTS 447.	Aarhus Convention	76, 77, 86, 217, 249, 287, 288, 289, 304, 316–19
10 September 1998	Rotterdam Convention on the Prior Informed Consent Procedure for Certain Hazardous Chemicals and Pesticides in International Trade, 2244 UNTS 337.	PIC Convention	43, 65, 67, 201, 203, 204, 217–20, 221, 231, 329, 351, 393, 398
1999	IBRD, Amended and Restated Instrument Establishing the Prototype Carbon Fund, Resolution No. 99–1.	PCF Instrument	273, 274, 280
12 May 1999	General Comment No 12: The Right to Adequate Food, UN Doc. E/C.12/1999/5.		303

(cont.)

(cont.)

(cont.)

Date	Full reference	Abbreviation	Pages
20 November 2001	WTO Ministerial Conference Fourth Session, Ministerial Declaration, WT/MIN(01)/DEC/1.	Doha Declaration	392, 399, 412
12 December 2001	Draft Articles on the Prevention of Transboundary Harm from Hazardous Activities, GA Res. 56/82, UN Doc A/RES/56/82.	ILC Prevention Articles	56–7, 66, 70, 254, 255, 256–7
12 December 2001	Responsibility of States for Internationally Wrongful Acts, GA Res. 56/83, UN Doc A/RES/56/83.	ILC Articles	47, 237, 254, 255, 258, 259, 389
25 January 2002	Protocol Concerning Cooperation in Preventing Pollution from Ships and, in Cases of Emergency, Combating Pollution of the Mediterranean Sea, available on www.eco lex.org (TRE-001402).		105
6 April 2002	ILA New Delhi Declaration of Principles of International Law Relating to Sustainable Development.		72, 79, 81

(cont.)

Date	Full reference	Abbreviation	Pages
21 May 2002	Decision of the Council concerning the revision of Decision (92) 39/FINAL on the Control of Transboundary Movements of Wastes destined for Recovery Operations, C(2001)107/FINAL.	OECD Wastes Decision	224
10 June 2002	ASEAN Agreement on Transboundary Haze Pollution, available in English at www.eco lex.org (TRE-001344).		126
14 June 2002	Black Sea Biodiversity and Landscape Conservation Protocol, available on www.ecolex.org (TRE-154497).		106
4 September 2002	'Political declaration', Report of World Summit on Sustainable Development in Johannesburg (South Africa), 26 August to 4 September 2002. UN Doc. A/CONF.199/20, p. 1, 2002.	Political declaration	17, 20, 79

(cont.)

Date	Full reference	Abbreviation	Pages
4 September 2002	'Implementation Plan', Report of the World Summit on Sustainable Development at Johannesburg (South Africa), 26 August–4 September 2002. UN Doc. A/ CONF.199/20.	Implementation plan	18
26 November 2002	Committee on Economic, Social and Cultural Rights, General Comment No. 15 (2002), The Right to Water (Articles 11 and 12 of the International Covenant on Economic, Social and Cultural Rights), UN ESCOR Doc. E/C.12/ 2002/11.	GC 15	314, 315
16 May 2003	Protocol to the International Convention on the Establishment of an International Fund for Compensation for Oil Pollution, available at: www.ecolex.org (TRE-001 401).	FUND/2003	260, 263
21 May 2003	Protocol on Civil Liability and Compensation for Damage Caused by the Transboundary Effects of Industrial Accidents on Transboundary Waters, Doc. ECE/ MP.WAT/11-ECE/ CP.TEIA/9.	Kiev Protocol	260

(cont.)

(cont.)

(cont.)

Date	Full reference	Abbreviation	Pages
29 May 2007	Regulation (EC) No 1907/2006 of the European Parliament and of the Council of 18 December 2006 concerning the Registration, Evaluation, Authorisation and Restriction of Chemicals (REACH), establishing a European Chemicals Agency, amending Directive 1999/45/EC and repealing Council Regulation (EEC) No 793/93 and Commission Regulation (EC) No 1488/94 as well as Council Directive 76/769/EEC and Commission Directives 91/155/EEC, 93/105/EC and 2000/21/EC, OJ L 136/3.	REACH Regulation	204
2007	UNEP, *Strategic Approach to International Chemicals Management. SAICM texts and resolutions of the International Conference on Chemicals Management*, 2007, available at: www.unece.org	SAICM	204, 205–8

(cont.)

Date	Full reference	Abbreviation	Pages
13 September 2007	'United Nations Declaration on the Rights of Indigenous Peoples', UN Doc. A/RES/61/295, annex.	UNDRIP	67, 326
13 December 2007	Treaty on the Functioning of the European Union, OJ C 83, 30 March 2010.	TFEU	62, 64
7 March 2008	SADC Regional Policy Framework on Air Pollution, available at www.unep.org		
14 March 2008	Bali Plan of Action, Decision 1/CP.13, doc. FCCC/CP/2007/6/Add.1.	Bali Mandate	144, 145, 153
23 October 2008	Eastern Africa Regional Framework Agreement on Air Pollution, available at www.unep.org		126
11 December 2008	'Draft Articles on the Law of Transboundary Aquifers', GA Res. 63/124, UN Doc. A/RES/63/124.	ILC Aquifers Draft	108, 112–13
15 January 2009	*Report of the Office of the United Nations High Commissioner for Human Rights on the Relationship between Climate Change and Human Rights*, UN Doc. A/HRC/10/61.		155, 328, 368

(cont.)

Date	Full reference	Abbreviation	Pages
22 July 2009	West and Central Africa Regional Framework Agreement on Air Pollution, available at www.unep.org.		126
14 August 2009	United Nations High Commissioner for Refugees, *Climate Change, Natural Disasters and Human Displacement: A UNHCR Perspective.*	UNHCR Report	368, 370, 371
23 October 2009	African Union Convention for the Protection and Assistance of Internally Displaced Persons in Africa, 49 ILM 86.	Kampala Convention	371
30 March 2010	Copenhagen Accord, UN Doc. FCCC/CP/2009/L.7.	Copenhagen Accord	35, 145, 147, 276
31 March 2010	'Implementation of Agenda 21, the Programme for the Further Implementation of Agenda 21 and the outcomes of the World Summit on Sustainable Development', UN Doc. A/RES/64/236.	Enabling resolution	19, 20
28 July 2010	'The Human Right to Water and Sanitation', UN Doc. A/64/L.63/Rev.1.		315

(cont.)

Date	Full reference	Abbreviation	Pages
24 September 2010	'Human Rights and Access to Safe Drinking Water and Sanitation', A/HRC/15/L.14.		315
16 October 2010	The Nagoya – Kuala Lumpur Supplementary Protocol on Liability and Redress to the Cartagena Protocol on Biosafety, available at: bch.cbd.int/protocol/NKL_text.shtml		192, 261
29 October 2010	Nagoya Protocol on Access to Genetic Resources and the Fair and Equitable Sharing of the Benefits arising from their Utilization to the Convention on Biological Diversity, available at: www.cbd.int/abs/doc/protocol/nagoya-protocol-en.pdf	ABS Protocol or Nagoya Protocol	67, 158, 162, 188, 193–6, 394, 412, 413
15 March 2011	'The Cancun Agreements: Outcome of the work of the Ad Hoc Working Group on Long-term Cooperative Action under the Convention', Decision 1/CP.16, doc. FCCC/CP/2010/7/Add.1.	Cancun Agreements or Decision 1/CP.16	145, 147, 148, 153, 276, 283, 370

(cont.)

Date	Full reference	Abbreviation	Pages
15 March 2011	The Cancun Agreements: Outcome of the work of the Ad Hoc Working Group on Further Commitments for Annex I Parties under the Kyoto Protocol at its 15th session, Decision 1/CMP.6, doc. FCCC/KP/CMP/2010/12/Add.1.	Cancun Agreements	145
15 March 2011	The Cancun Agreements: Land Use, Land-use Change and Forestry, Decision 2/CMP.6, doc. FCCC/KP/CMP/2010/12/Add.1.	Cancun Agreements	145
October 2011	'Instrument for the Establishment of the Restructured Global Environment Facility'.	GEF Instrument	278–9
9 December 2011	Draft Articles on the Effects of Armed Conflict on Treaties, GA Res. 66/99, UN Doc. A/RES/66/99.	2011 ILC Draft Articles	351, 352, 362
16 December 2011	Office of the High Commissioner on Human Rights ('OHCHR'), *Analytical Study on the Relationship between Human Rights and the Environment*, UN Doc. A//HRC/19/34.	OHCHR Analytical Study	298, 299, 300, 302, 312

(cont.)

Date	Full reference	Abbreviation	Pages
15 March 2012	Establishment of an Ad Hoc Working Group on the Durban Platform for Enhanced Action, Decision 1/CP.17, Doc. FCCC/CP/2011/ 9/Add.1, 2.	Durban Platform	145, 153, 154
15 March 2012	Establishment of the Green Climate Fund, Decision 3/CP.17, Doc. FCCC/CP/2011/ 9/Add.1, Annex: Governing instrument for the Green Climate Fund.	GCF Instrument	276–7, 279
15 March 2012	Outcome of the Work of the Ad Hoc Working Group on Long-term Cooperative Action under the Convention, Decision 2/CP.17, Doc. FCCC/CP/@011/9/ Add.1.		148, 153
2012	UNCTAD, *World Investment Report. Towards a New Generation of Investment Policies* (2012), Chapter IV (Investment Policy Framework for Sustainable Development).	IPFSD	384–5

(cont.)

Date	Full reference	Abbreviation	Pages
24 July 2012	Directive 2012/18/EU of the European Parliament and Council of 4 July 2012 on the control of major-accident hazards involving dangerous substances, amending and subsequently repealing Council Directive 96/82/EC, OJ L 197/1 24 July 2012.	Seveso III	214
11 September 2012	'The Future we Want', UN Doc. A/Res/66/288.		10, 19, 20, 30, 203, 332
19 November 2012	ASEAN Human Rights Declaration, available at: www.asean.org		313
10 October 2013	Minamata Convention on Mercury, available at: www.mercuryconvention.org (last visited on 15 January 2014).	Minamata Convention	201, 229–32, 333, 356

Table of cases

International Court of Justice

International Tribunal for the Law of the Sea and UNCLOS-related arbitral tribunals

WTO Dispute Settlement Body

Other inter-State arbitrations (or assimilated)

Eritrea Ethiopia Claims Commission

United Nations Compensation Commission

Investment disputes

European Court of Human Rights

Inter-American Court of Human Rights

Inter-American Commission on Human Rights

African Commission and African Court of Human and Peoples' Rights

International Criminal Tribunals

European Community Courts

Human Rights Committee

Domestic case-law

Decisions of non-compliance committees

Preface

How to keep – is there any any, is there none such, nowhere known some, bow or brooch or braid or brace, lace, latch or catch or key to keep
Back beauty, keep it, beauty, beauty, beauty, . . . from vanishing away?
The Leaden Echo and the Golden Echo, Gerard Manley Hopkins

This book is an attempt to address two main difficulties we have encountered in our teaching and practice of international environmental law.

One is of a substantive nature and stems from the daunting reach and diversity of the subject matter. No other area of international law gives the newcomer such an impression of dispersion, lack of articulation, even exoticism. The topics gathered under the label international environmental law range from the protection of wetlands or whales or genetic resources to nuclear energy, ozone depletion or hazardous waste control. Each of these topics are worlds in and of themselves and, yet, since the late 1970s, there have been attempts at bringing them together under a single discipline that still calls, after all these years, for robust systematisation. This book is our own humble contribution to such attempts. The conception of international environmental law that underpins the materials discussed here can be concisely stated. We see the international law of environmental protection as both a 'branch' and a 'perspective'. As a branch, international environmental law is based on the ideas of 'prevention' (of environmental harm) and 'balance' (among different considerations and stakeholders), which are themselves expressed in legal form through a small number of principles and concepts discussed in Chapter 3 that, in turn, are spelled out in detail through treaty frameworks analysed in Part II and implemented through the means examined in Part III of this book. This pyramid going from ideas, to principles and concepts, to treaties and their administrative law, is offered as a conceptual narrative articulating the diverse contents encompassed by the expression international environmental law. But the international law of environmental protection cannot be confined within the bounds of a branch. Environmental protection can only be pursued if it is considered not as a separate sphere of activity but as an objective partaking in all other human activities. From this vantage point, the international law of environmental protection is nothing short of public international law in all its forms, as adjusted to take appropriate account of environmental considerations. Part IV develops this perspective, with particular emphasis on the influence of environmental protection on human rights, *jus in bello*, *jus ad bellum*, disarmament law, foreign investment law, international trade law and intellectual property rights. In studying international environmental law as both a branch and a perspective, our purpose is to show that this field of inquiry has some identifying features but also that it cannot be reduced to a mere branch.

The other difficulty is of a pedagogical nature and is related to the one just mentioned. Faced with such a diverse and wide-ranging array of norms, treaties and legally-linked treaties, the newcomer, whether a student, a practitioner or a researcher unfamiliar with the field, can be easily overwhelmed. The specificities of international environmental law create indeed significant barriers to entry. Such barriers are compounded by the constant evolution of the different topics covered in this field, which require textbooks and casebooks to be frequently updated, as well as by the amount of material to be covered. To rise to this challenge, the few existing books encompassing the entire field have grown in scope and volume to a point that they can be considered as true treatises. There is, however, room for a more concise treatment of the subject matter, intended to introduce readers to the different topics, clarifying the location of each topic within the overall pyramid, and highlighting the most important technical aspects of the relevant regulatory regimes. This is the approach followed in this book. It is an attempt to chart the route that goes from utter unfamiliarity with the field to the sophisticated knowledge expounded in existing treatises and other secondary sources, providing an elementary grammar that can hopefully be used as a compass to find one's way in subsequent deeper explorations.

In embarking on this project, we have been encouraged by our experience with several generations of students in Cambridge and Geneva, who have been introduced to international environmental law through this blend of conceptual and technical analysis. Many of them have subsequently become either researchers or practitioners, and they have been kind enough to share with us their own experience in using this training for their activities. Thus, the book condenses the experience of the instructors and, to some extent, that of their students. In addition, the long and patient writing process has greatly benefited from several generations of outstanding teaching and research assistants. Our sincere thanks go in particular to Stephanie Chuffart, Maria de la Colina, Martina Kunz, Magnus Jesko Langer, Jason Rudall and Pablo Sandonato de Leon, whose work between 2009 and 2014 significantly contributed to the preparation of this book. We remain, of course, solely responsible for any mistakes the book may contain.

As a final note, may we add that the book has been a pleasure to write. The two co-authors see eye-to-eye on the content, method and overall understanding of international environmental law as a province of public international law and a perspective increasingly influencing its evolution. The numerous initiatives to protect the environment described in this book witness the efforts of the international community to 'keep back beauty from vanishing away'. They are significant, yet insufficient. Moralising love of beauty may be converging with outright indifference in their end result, namely unrealistic expectations and strategies, a boon to hypocrisy. Lucid environmental regulation, based on the setting of clear priorities, may be the only realistic way to move from norms to practice and to genuine protection. Hopkins' moving poem is a calm yet intense upheaval against ageing and decay, against the loss of beauty. We forfeit the beauty of youth freely, inevitably. No such inevitability applies to the beauty of our environment.

PMD and JV
Cambridge/Geneva

Part I

Foundations

1

Emergence and development of international environmental law

1.1 Introduction

The international regulation of environmental problems is not a recent phenomenon. One can find several precedents of what today would be called international environmental law dating back to the nineteenth and early twentieth century. What characterises modern international environmental law is a focus on protecting the environment *per se* (not only as a useful resource) as well as the sophistication of the legal techniques developed to this effect.

The purpose of this chapter is to provide a concise introduction to the main developments that form the backbone of modern international environmental law.[1] We will not dwell on the historical detail of these developments nor do we intend to conduct a comprehensive analysis of the multiple reasons that led to them. Rather, we will discuss some key developments that, taken together, define an overall trend. From the late nineteenth century to the beginning of the 1970s, the regulation of environmental problems moved from a resource-oriented logic to a more comprehensive one, whereby environmental protection was increasingly valued beyond the immediate economic benefits that the preservation of a resource could bring. Since the 1970s, the need to protect the environment has progressively become one of the most pressing policy issues in the international agenda. Yet, at the same time, newly independent and other developing States have struggled to ensure that environmental regulation does not impose a straitjacket on their ability to pursue developmental policies as they see fit.

Overall, the trend analysed in this chapter can be represented graphically as a line oscillating between economic development and environmental protection considerations. The pull of developmental considerations has become stronger in the last decade, particularly after the 2002 Johannesburg Summit and, more recently, at the 2012 Rio Summit. As we shall see, the 'environment-development equation' is currently in need of significant recalibration and, perhaps, even of a new model, capable of striking a proper balance between development/growth and environmental protection.

---

[1] For a more detailed introduction see L. K. Caldwell, *International Environmental Policy. From the Twentieth to the Twenty-First Century* (Durham: Duke University Press, 3rd edn, 1996).

1.2 Precedents

The initial approach to the international regulation of environmental problems was organised around essentially three issues, namely the rules governing the exploitation of certain resources, transboundary damage and the use of shared watercourses. To illustrate these issues, it is helpful to refer to three classic cases, often cited as precedents of modern international environmental law.[2]

The first case, known as the *Bering Sea Fur Seals Arbitration (United States v. United Kingdom)*,[3] illustrates the difficulties arising from the competing exploitation of a common resource by different States. Following the acquisition of Alaska in 1867, the United States took a series of steps to establish exclusive jurisdiction over sealing activities in the Bering Sea. British vessels were prevented from sealing in the Bering Sea by US patrols. After several years of unsuccessful negotiations between the United States, the United Kingdom and Russia the question was submitted to arbitration by a treaty of 29 February 1892. During the arbitration proceedings, the central argument of the United States was that they had the sovereign rights formerly enjoyed by Russia in this region and, interestingly, that they also had the right and duty to protect fur seals even when they were beyond the limits of US territorial waters. The latter argument was based on the idea, advanced by counsel for the United States, that they had been invested with the responsibility for preventing the over-exploitation of fur seals, which were threatened by the sealing practices of British vessels. In its decision of 15 August 1893, the tribunal rejected the arguments of the United States and sided with the United Kingdom. It should be noted that the second argument of the United States was not intended to protect a species *per se* but rather to preserve its economic exploitation. Thus, the *Fur Seals Arbitration* is a good illustration of the spirit of the time, although the US argument was an innovative one. This same concern underlies certain treaties concluded in the same period for the protection of animal species.[4]

Another important precedent is the *Trail Smelter Arbitration (United States v. Canada)*.[5] This case illustrates the essentially transboundary character of

---

[2] For a selection of early environmental cases, see C. A. R. Robb (ed.), *International Environmental Law Reports*, vol. 1, Early Decisions (Cambridge University Press, 1998).

[3] *Bering Sea Fur Seals Arbitration*, Award (15 August 1893), RIAA, vol. XXVIII, pp. 263–76 ('*Fur Seals Arbitration*').

[4] See, e.g.: Treaty concerning the Regulation of Salmon Fishery in the Rhine River Basin, 30 June 1885, available at: www.ecolex.org (TRE-000072); Convention for the Protection of Birds Useful to Agriculture, 19 March 1902, available at: www.ecolex.org (TRE-000067); Convention between the United States, Great Britain, Japan and Russia Providing for the Preservation and Protection of the Fur Seals, 7 July 1911, 37 Stat. 1542; Convention for the Regulation of Whaling, 24 September 1931, available at: www.ecolex.org (TRE-000073); International Convention for the Regulation of Whaling, 2 December 1946, 161 UNTS 361.

[5] *Trail Smelter Arbitration*, RIAA, vol. III, pp. 1905–82 ('*Trail Smelter Arbitration*').

classical environmental regulation, which has profoundly influenced the development of international environmental law.[6] The United States complained of emissions of sulphur dioxide released by a smelter based on Canadian soil, which caused damage to crops and lands in the neighbouring state of Washington. By a treaty of 15 April 1935, the question was submitted to arbitration. In its award of 11 March 1941, the arbitral tribunal famously concluded that according to the principles of international law:

> no State has the right to use or permit the use of its territory in such a manner as to cause injury by fumes in or to the territory of another or the properties or persons therein, when the case is of serious consequence and the injury is established by clear and convincing evidence.[7]

This principle was later confirmed by the International Court of Justice ('ICJ') in the *Corfu Channel Case* (*United Kingdom v. Albania*)[8] and profoundly influenced the work of the International Law Commission ('ILC') on liability for the injurious consequences arising from lawful activities.[9] As discussed later in this chapter, the principle remains today an essential component of international environmental law.

The third case to be mentioned is the *Lake Lanoux Arbitration* (*Spain v. France*),[10] which illustrates another area of classical environmental regulation, namely the use of shared watercourses. The case concerned certain measures taken by France involving the diversion of the waters of a river tributary of Lake Lanoux. According to Spain, these measures affected the flow of water that would be available to Spain (through the River Carol) in breach of international law. In its award of 16 November 1957, the tribunal rejected this claim noting among others that:

> The Spanish Government endeavoured to establish similarly the content of current positive international law. Certain principles which it demonstrates are, assuming the demonstration to be accepted, of no interest for the problem now under examination. Thus, if it is admitted that there is a principle which prohibits the upstream State from altering the waters of a river in such a fashion as seriously to prejudice the downstream State, such a principle would have no application to the present case, because it has been admitted by the Tribunal . . . that the French scheme will not alter the waters of the Carol. In fact, States are today perfectly conscious of the importance of the conflicting interests brought into play by the industrial use of international rivers, and of the necessity to reconcile them by mutual concessions. The only way to arrive at such

---

[6] See J. E. Viñuales, 'The Contribution of the International Court of Justice to the Development of International Environmental Law' (2008) 32 *Fordham International Law Journal* 232.

[7] *Trail Smelter Arbitration, supra* n. 5, p. 1965.

[8] *Corfu Channel Case*, Decision of 9 April 1949, ICJ Reports 1949, p. 22 ('*Corfu Channel Case*'), p. 22.

[9] See *infra* Chapter 11.

[10] *Lake Lanoux Arbitration (Spain/France)*, Award, (16 November 1957), RIAA vol. XII, pp. 281ff ('*Lake Lanoux Arbitration*').

compromises of interests is to conclude agreements on an increasingly comprehensive basis.[11]

It was common at that time (and it is today) to conclude treaties on the use of shared watercourses.[12] Some of these agreements only contained a few provisions on the protection of waters against pollution while others were mainly devoted to this question.[13]

These three milestones illustrate the existence of international instruments, prior to the 1960s, regulating matters that are today described as falling within the environmental sphere. It must be emphasised that, in general, these were primarily intended to foster the economic exploitation of certain species or resources. As discussed next, this idea was still prevalent in the early 1960s.

1.3 Permanent sovereignty over natural resources

The protection of certain resources or areas has long been inseparable from the concept of State sovereignty. With the exception of the high seas, areas beyond the sovereignty of a State or under colonial or military administration remained scarcely regulated by international law until the second half of the twentieth century.

With the onset of the decolonisation process, newly independent States paid particular attention to their entitlements over their natural resources. As noted by Georges Abi-Saab:

> [i]n applying explicitly the principle of sovereignty – used here in its political sense – to use and freely dispose of natural resources, [it was] intend[ed] to highlight the permanent and intangible link between sovereignty and self-determination, the former serving not only as a legal shield for the political realisation of the latter, i.e. independence, but also as a permanent guarantee of its being exercised in the economic field beyond formal accession to independence.[14]

---

[11] *Ibid.*, para. 13.
[12] See, e.g.: Treaty between the United States of America and Mexico Concerning the Equitable Distribution of the Waters of the Rio Grande, 21 May 1906, 34 Stat. 2953; Treaty between the United States of America and Mexico Relating to the Utilization of the Waters of the Colorado and Tijuana Rivers and of the Rio Grande, 3 February 1944, 3 UNTS 314; Convention Concerning the Regime of Navigation on the Danube, 18 August 1948, available at: www.ecolex.org (TRE-000555); Convention Concerning the Regulation of Lake Lugano and its Additional Protocol, 17 September 1955, 291 UNTS 218.
[13] See e.g.: Protocol to Establish a Tripartite Standing Commission on Polluted Waters, 8 April 1950, available at: www.ecolex.org (TRE-000493); Agreement on the Protection of Lake Constance Against Pollution, 27 October 1960, available at: www.ecolex.org (TRE-000464); Agreement between France and Switzerland on the Protection of Lake Geneva, 16 November 1962, 1974 UNTS 54; Agreement Concerning the International Commission for the Protection of the Rhine against Pollution, 29 April 1963, available at: www.ecolex.org (TRE-000484).
[14] G. Abi-Saab, 'La souveraineté permanente sur les ressources naturelles', in M. Bedjaoui (ed.), *Droit international: bilan et perspectives* (Paris: Pedone, 1989), pp. 638–61, at 639–40 (our translation).

In many ways, and perhaps paradoxically, the principle of permanent sovereignty over natural resources is a building block of modern environmental regulation. Until the 1970s this principle was only intended to protect the resources in view of their economic exploitation by newly independent States. However, over the following decades, this principle was to be linked to the no harm principle and then generalised as the starting-point of the prevention principle, as discussed later.

For present purposes, the historical vicissitudes in the development of this principle are less important[15] than the final result, namely the adoption by the UN General Assembly on 14 December 1962 of Resolution 1803 (XVII) on 'Permanent Sovereignty over Natural Resources'.[16] This landmark resolution, generally regarded as an expression of customary international law,[17] states in its first paragraph that:

> [t]he right of peoples and nations to permanent sovereignty over their natural wealth and resources must be exercised in the interest of their national development and of the well-being of the people of the State concerned.

The main feature of sovereignty over natural resources is its permanence. Sovereignty is indeed the rule, and its limitations are 'necessarily ephemeral and circumscribed in their scope and time'.[18]

The limitations that the drafters of the resolution contemplated were those that could arise from agreements with foreign investors on the exploitation of natural resources. However, starting in the late 1960s, another category of limitations began to emerge, namely the constraints derived from the incipient environmental regulation. This context largely explains the suspicion expressed by developing countries in respect of the first important initiative of industrialised countries in the field of environmental protection.[19] Indeed, as discussed next, tensions between the management of resources from a developmental perspective and environmental protection have characterised international environmental law since its modern inception.

---

[15] See N. Schrijver, *Sovereignty over Natural Resources. Balancing Rights and Duties* (Cambridge University Press, 1997), pp. 36–76.

[16] 'Permanent Sovereignty over Natural Resources', 14 December 1962, UN Doc. A/RES/1803/ XVII, ('Resolution 1803').

[17] Abi-Saab, *supra* n. 14, p. 644; *Texaco Overseas Petroleum Company and California Asiatic Oil Company* v. *The Government of the Libyan Arab Republic*, Arbitral Award (19 January 1977), 17 ILM 1978, para. 87; *Libyan American Oil Company (LIAMCO)* v. *The Government of the Libyan Arab Republic*, Arbitral Award (12 April 1977), 20 ILM 1981, p. 103; *Kuwait* v. *American Independent Oil Company (AMINOIL)*, Arbitral Award (24 March 1982), 21 ILM 1982, para. 1803; *Armed Activities on the Territory of the Congo (Democratic Republic of the Congo* v. *Uganda)*, Judgment (19 December 2005), ICJ Reports 2005, p. 168, paras. 244–5.

[18] Abi-Saab, *supra* n. 14, p. 645 (our translation).   [19] Schrijver, *supra* n. 15, at pp. 231–50.

1.4 The Stockholm Conference on the Human Environment (1972)

During the 1960s, several environmental problems captured the interest of international public opinion and catalysed awareness on the need to act.[20]

In 1962, Rachel Carson published her groundbreaking book *Silent Spring*,[21] highlighting the adverse effects of pesticides (DDT) on the environment and, more specifically, on birds. This book was the first in a series of influential publications on the adverse impact of human activities on the environment, such as Kenneth Boulding's *The Economics of the Coming Spaceship Earth*,[22] Max Nicholson's *The Environmental Revolution*[23] or Barry Commoner's *The Closing Circle*.[24] Similarly, the alarming results of the Meadows Report *The Limits to Growth*,[25] prepared on the initiative of the Club of Rome, also contributed to direct public attention to environmental issues.[26] An additional sense of urgency came from events such as the grounding of the Liberian oil tanker *Torrey Canyon* off the British coast or the poisoning of the population of Minamata, a Japanese village, as a result of mercury spills from a petrochemical company.

In this context, a number of international initiatives were launched. Among others, in December 1968, the UN General Assembly adopted Resolution 2398 (XXIII)[27] entitled 'Problems of the Human Environment' and convening a 'United Nations Conference on the Human Environment'. This conference, which was held from 5 to 16 June 1972 in Stockholm (Sweden), is generally seen as the foundational moment of modern international environmental law. Incidentally, shortly before the start of the conference, a resolution adopted on the initiative of Brazil highlighted the tension between development and environmental protection.[28] This resolution focused on the potential adverse effects of environmental policies on the development of poor countries and 'reiterate[d] the primacy of independent economic and social development as

---

[20] For a review of the main scientific contributions that catalysed the environmental movement, see J. Grinevald, *La Biosphère de l'Anthropocène. Climat et pétrole, la double menace. Repères transdiciplinaires (1824–2007)* (Geneva: Georg, 2007), pp. 115ff.

[21] R. Carson, *Silent Spring* (Boston: Houghton Mifflin, 1962).

[22] K. E. Boulding, 'The Economics of the Coming Spaceship Earth', in H. Jarrett (ed.), *Environmental Quality in a Growing Economy* (Baltimore: Johns Hopkins University Press, 1966), pp. 3–14.

[23] M. Nicholson, *The Environmental Revolution: A Guide for the New Masters of the World* (London: Hodder & Stoughton, 1969).

[24] B. Commoner, *The Closing Circle: Nature, Man, and Technology* (New York: Alfred Knopf, 1971).

[25] D. H. Meadows, D. L. Meadows, J. Randers and W. W. Behrens III, *The Limits to Growth* (New York: Universe Books, 1972).

[26] See R. Guha, *Environmentalism: A Global History* (New York: Longman, 2000); A. Dobson, *Green Political Thought* (New York: Routledge, 4th edn, 2007).

[27] 'Problems of the Human Environment', 3 December 1968, UN Doc. 2398 (XXIII).

[28] 'Development and Environment', 20 December 1971, UN Doc. 2849 (XXVI).

Figure 1.1: The Stockholm Conference (1972)

the main and paramount objective of international co-operation, in the interests of the welfare of mankind and of peace and world security.'[29]

The Stockholm Conference was attended by delegations from more than a hundred States as well as by representatives of major intergovernmental organisations and of over 400 NGOs. The negotiations resulted in three main outcomes, namely a 'Declaration on the Human Environment',[30] also known as the 'Stockholm Declaration', an 'Action Plan for the Human Environment'[31] and, soon after, the establishment of the United Nations Environment Programme or 'UNEP'.[32] Figure 1.1 summarises these outcomes.

The significance of these outcomes warrant some comments. The Stockholm Declaration consists of a preamble and twenty-six principles. There are a number of studies on this important instrument.[33] For present purposes it will suffice to highlight some of its major themes. Principle 1 of the Declaration affirms the fundamental human right to 'adequate conditions of life, in an environment of a quality that permits a life of dignity and well-being'. The debate triggered by this principle over the existence, scope and possible modalities of a right to a healthy environment has continued until today and, as discussed in Chapter 10, this right has now been enshrined in a number of domestic and international instruments. Principles 2 to 26 of the Declaration are devoted, with some overlaps, to (i) the definition of the province of international environmental law (Principles 2 to 8), (ii) an initial statement of the substantive principles guiding efforts in this area and (iii) certain modalities for implementation. The first component involved the preservation of 'the natural resources of the earth, including the air, water, land, flora and fauna and especially representative samples of natural ecosystems' (Principle

---

[29] *Ibid.*, para. 11.

[30] 'Declaration of the United Nations Conference on the Human Environment', Stockholm, 16 June 1972, UN Doc. A/CONF 48/14/Rev.1, pp. 2ff ('Stockholm Declaration').

[31] 'Action Plan for the Human Environment', 16 June 1972, UN Doc. A/CONF 48/14, pp. 10–62.

[32] 'Institutional and Financial Arrangements for International Environmental Cooperation', 15 December 1972, UN Doc. A/RES/2997/XXVII ('Resolution 2997').

[33] See A. Kiss and D. Sicault, 'La Conférence des Nations Unies sur l'environnement (Stockholm, 5–16 June 1972)' (1972) 18 *Annuaire français de droit international* 603; L. B. Sohn, 'The Stockholm Declaration on the Human Environment' (1973) 14 *Harvard International Law Journal* 423.

2), the ability of the earth to generate renewable and non-renewable resources (Principles 3–5) and, more concretely, the need to curb pollution (Principles 6 and 7). Regarding substantive principles, the Declaration provides early formulations of the principles of intergenerational equity (Principle 2), international co-operation for the protection of the environment (Principle 24) or the prevention of environmental damage (Principle 21). The latter is very important for our subject because it summarises the three pillars of environmental protection, namely the *permanent sovereignty* of States over their natural resources, limited by the duty to ensure that activities carried out within the boundaries of their jurisdiction or control *do not cause damage to the environment of other States* or *in areas beyond national jurisdiction*. Finally, the Stockholm Declaration also covers matters of implementation paying particular attention to the situation of developing countries and their specific needs. On several occasions, the Declaration addresses the relationship between development and environmental protection, which had been much debated in the run-up to Stockholm. It recalls the importance of development to ensure access to a healthy environment (Principle 8) or to tackle certain environmental problems (Principles 9 and 10). It also emphasises the need for technical and financial assistance for developing countries (Principle 12) and, significantly, it warns against the possible adverse impact of domestic environmental policies on economic development (Principle 11).

The other two outcomes of the Stockholm Conference are both related to the implementation of environmental policies. The 'Action Plan for the Human Environment' adopted at the Conference includes 109 recommendations organised around three fundamental axes, namely environmental assessment, environmental management and supporting measures. Among the topics covered in this document, Recommendation No. 4 proposed to entrust the coordination of environmental affairs within the United Nations to a single body. Following this recommendation, the UN General Assembly adopted Resolution 2997 (XXVII) establishing the United Nations Environment Programme ('UNEP').[34] This subsidiary body of the United Nations was, until 2012, governed by Council consisting of fifty-eight UN Member States elected for three years by the General Assembly according to geographical distribution.[35] In 2012, membership of the Governing Council was extended to all members of the UN General Assembly. The day-to-day management of UNEP is entrusted to a Secretariat based in Nairobi (Kenya) and headed by an Executive Director. The creation of UNEP was originally intended, *inter alia*, to monitor the Stockholm Programme, including the administration of the 'Environmental Fund' contemplated in section III of Resolution 2997 (XXVII). More generally,

---

[34] See *supra* n. 32.
[35] At the Rio+20 Summit, in June 2012, it was decided to 'establish universal membership in the Governing Council [of UNEP]'. See 'The Future We Want', 11 September 2012, UN Doc. A/Res/66/288, para. 88(a) ('The Future We Want').

the role of UNEP is to promote international co-operation in environmental matters, including initiatives of normative codification. Over the years, normative entrepreneurship has become perhaps the main task of UNEP.

The impact of the Stockholm Conference was considerable, and it can be assessed at three levels.[36] At the domestic level, the conference generated momentum for the creation, in several States, of ministerial structures devoted to environmental problems.[37] At the regional level, it was also at this time that the European Community began to pass environmental legislation. At the international level, the Stockholm Conference not only brought environmental problems within the purview of the United Nations[38] but it also added momentum for the conclusion of many agreements,[39] covering areas such as the protection of habitats and sites,[40] trade in endangered species,[41] marine pollution[42] or the protection of migratory species.[43] These developments were followed by other instruments in the 1980s, such as Resolution 37/7 ('World Charter for Nature') adopted by the UN General Assembly on 28 October 1982[44] and, most importantly, the adoption of the UN Convention on the Law of the Sea, of 10 December 1982,[45] which devotes an entire part (Part XII) as

[36] See P. Galizzi, 'From Stockholm to New York, via Rio and Johannesburg: Has the Environment Lost its Way on the Global Agenda?' (2005/2006) 29 *Fordham International Law Journal,* 952, at 966–7.

[37] See H. Selin and B.-O. Linner, 'The Quest for Global Sustainability: International Efforts on Linking Environment and Development', *CID Graduate Student and Postdoctoral Fellow Working Paper No. 5,* January 2005, at p. 35.

[38] Paragraphs 2–3 of Resolution 2997 (XXVII) express the following recognition: 'Recognizing that responsibility for action to protect and enhance the environment rests primarily with Governments and, in the first instance, can be exercised more effectively at the national and regional levels, [r]ecognizing further that environmental problems of broad international significance fall within the competence of the United Nations system'. See R. Gardner, 'Can the UN Lead the Environmental Parade?' (1970) 64 *American Journal of International Law* 211.

[39] See A. O. Adede, 'The Treaty System from Stockholm (1972) to Rio de Janeiro (1992)' (1995) 13 *Pace Environmental Law Review* 33.

[40] Convention on Wetlands of International Importance especially as Waterfowl Habitat, 2 February 1971, 996 UNTS 245 ('Ramsar Convention'); Convention Concerning the Protection of the World Cultural and Natural Heritage, 16 November 1972, 1037 UNTS 151 ('WHC').

[41] Convention on International Trade in Endangered Species of Wild Fauna and Flora, 3 March 1973, 993 UNTS 243 ('CITES').

[42] Convention on the Prevention of Marine Pollution by Dumping of Wastes and Other Matter, 29 December 1972 ('London Convention'), subsequently modified by the Protocol of 7 November 1996 to the Convention of 1972 on the Prevention of Marine Pollution by Dumping of Wastes and Other Matter, 7 November 1996, 1046 UNTS 120 ('London Convention'); International Convention for the Prevention of Pollution from Ships, 2 November 1973, amended by the Protocol of 17 February 1978, 1340 UNTS 184 ('MARPOL 73/78').

[43] Convention on the Conservation of Migratory Species of Wild Animals, 23 June 1979, 1651 UNTS 333.

[44] World Charter for Nature, 28 October 1982, UN Doc. A/RES/37/7 ('World Charter for Nature').

[45] United Nations Convention on the Law of the Sea, 10 December 1982, 1833 UNTS 396 ('UNCLOS').

well as several other provisions to the protection and preservation of the marine environment.[46] Significantly, starting in the 1980s, environmental treaty-making moved from visible ('first generation') environmental problems, such as pollution and species protection, to more complex ones. Major illustrations of this trend include the adoption of the Vienna Convention on the Protection of the Ozone Layer (1985)[47] and its Montreal Protocol (1987),[48] as well as of the Basel Convention on the Control of Transboundary Movements of Hazardous Wastes (1989).[49]

Despite these important developments, the impact of the recommendations made at the Stockholm Conference on the targeted environmental variables remained well below expectations. As a result, the UN decided to re-examine matters of global environmental governance in the context of another major conference to be held in Rio de Janeiro (Brazil) in 1992.

1.5 The Rio Conference on Environment and Development (1992)

Ten years after the Stockholm Conference, the Governing Council of UNEP met to discuss the implementation of the Stockholm recommendations. This meeting resulted in the adoption of the Nairobi Declaration on 18 May 1982,[50] in which the Council reaffirmed the principles of the Stockholm Declaration (paragraph 1) recognising, at the same time, the insufficient implementation of the Action Plan adopted at Stockholm (paragraph 2). These conclusions were endorsed by the UN General Assembly, which decided to establish a special commission to study the prospects for environmental protection on the horizon for 2000 and beyond.[51] This commission, known as the 'Brundtland Commission' after its chair Gro Harlem Brundtland, issued an influential report entitled 'Our Common Future'.[52] The report introduced the concept of 'sustainable development', defined in the introduction to the second chapter as development 'which implied meeting the needs of the present without compromising the ability of future generations to meet their own needs'.[53] The General Assembly welcomed the Brundtland Report and, shortly thereafter, decided to convene a second international conference, this time

---

[46] See our analysis *infra* at Chapter 4.
[47] Vienna Convention on the Protection of the Ozone Layer, 22 March 1985, 1513 UNTS 293.
[48] Montreal Protocol on Substances that Deplete the Ozone Layer, 16 September 1987, 1522 UNTS 28 ('Montreal Protocol').
[49] Basel Convention on the Control of Transboundary Movements of Hazardous Wastes and their Disposal, 22 March 1989, 1673 UNTS 57 ('Basel Convention').
[50] Report of the Governing Council on its Session of a Special Character (10–18 May 1982), 27 August 1982, UN Doc. A/RES/37/219, Annex II ('Nairobi Declaration').
[51] 'Process of Preparation of the Environmental Perspective to the Year 2000 and Beyond', 19 December 1983, UN Doc. A/RES/38/161.
[52] Report of the World Commission on Environment and Development, 'Our Common Future', 10 March 1987 ('Brundtland Report').
[53] *Ibid.*, para. 49.

not on the human environment but on the relationship between the environment and development.[54] The issue of development was indeed regaining strength on the international agenda.

The United Nations Conference on Environment and Development ('UNCED'), also known as the 'Earth Summit' or simply the 'Rio Conference', was held from 1 to 15 June 1992 in Rio de Janeiro, Brazil.[55] It was attended by delegations from 176 States, often represented by their heads of State or government, as well as from international organisations, NGOs and the private sector. The negotiations resulted in five main outcomes, namely a 'Rio Declaration on Environment and Development',[56] an ambitious long term programme of action called 'Agenda 21',[57] the adoption of two conventions focusing, respectively, on climate change[58] and biological diversity,[59] the creation of a Commission for Sustainable Development ('CSD')[60] under the aegis of the UN Economic and Social Council ('ECOSOC') and, finally, a 'Non-legally Binding Authoritative Statement of Principles for a Global Consensus on the Management, Conservation and Sustainable Development of All Types of Forests'.[61] Furthermore, the Rio Conference created the momentum for the crystallisation, in 1994, of an African initiative to adopt a multilateral convention on the fight against desertification,[62] as well as for the signing in 1995 of an agreement on the issue of highly migratory and straddling fish stocks.[63] Figure 1.2 summarises these outcomes.

---

[54] 'United Nations Conference on Environment and Development', 22 December 1989, UN Doc. A/RES/44/228.

[55] On the conference, see A. Kiss and S. Doumbé-Bille, 'La Conférence des Nations Unies sur l'environnement et le développement (Rio de Janeiro, 3–14 juin 1992)' (1992) 38 *Annuaire francais de droit international* 823; L. A. Kimball and W. Boyd, 'International Institutional Arrangements for Environment and Development: a Post-Rio Assessment' (1992) 1 *Review of Community and International Environmental Law* 295; M. Pallamaerts, 'International Environmental Law from Stockholm to Rio: Back to the Future' (1992) 1 *Review of Community and International Environmental Law* 254; P. H. Sand, 'International Environmental Law After Rio' (1993) 4 *European Journal of International Law* 377.

[56] 'Rio Declaration on Environment and Development', 13 June 1992, UN Doc. A/CONF.151/26. Rev.1 ('Rio Declaration').

[57] Report of the United Nations Conference on Environment and Development, A/CONF.151/26/Rev.l (Vol. l), Resolution 1, Annex 2: Agenda 21 ('Agenda 21').

[58] United Nations Framework Convention on Climate Change, 9 May 1992, 1771 UNTS 107 ('UNFCCC'). This treaty, concluded before the start of the Rio Conference, may still be considered part of the legacy of Rio as its conclusion was supported by the Earth Summit.

[59] Convention on Biological Diversity, 5 June 1992, 1760 UNTS 79 ('CBD').

[60] 'Institutional Arrangements to follow up the United Nations Conference on Environment and Development', 22 December 1992, UN Doc. A/RES/47/191.

[61] 'Non-legally Binding Authoritative Statement of Principles for a Global Consensus on the Management, Conservation and Sustainable Development of All Types of Forests', 14 August 1992, UN Doc. A/CONF/151/26 (vol. III) ('Forest Principles').

[62] United Nations Convention to Combat Desertification in Countries Experiencing Serious Drought and/or Desertification, Particularly in Africa, 17 June 1994, 1954 UNTS 3 ('UNCCD').

[63] Agreement for the Implementation of the Provisions of the United Nations Convention on the Law of the Sea of 10 December 1982 Relating to the Conservation and Management of Straddling Fish Stocks and High Migratory Fish Stocks, 4 August 1995, 2167 UNTS 3.

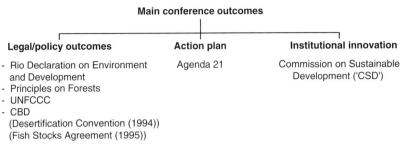

Figure 1.2: The Rio Conference (1992)

The two treaties opened for signature at Rio will be examined in Part II of this book. Here, the analysis focuses on the Rio Declaration, Agenda 21 and CSD. From a legal standpoint, the Rio Declaration is the most important outcome of all three. It consists of a short preamble followed by twenty-seven principles.[64] Since the times of the Stockholm Declaration, the centre of gravity has significantly shifted from environmental protection to the relationship between the latter and the renewed strength gained by development issues, now disconnected from the Communist ideology. In retrospective, however, the Rio Declaration strikes a fair balance between the often competing terms of the environment–development equation. A number of principles (e.g. Principles 3, 5, 6, 7–9, 12, 14, 20–23) present indeed a strong development accent. Yet, at the same time, the Rio Declaration provides the most generally accepted formulation of the main principles of international environmental law, including the principles of prevention (Principle 2), intergenerational equity (Principle 3), co-operation on global issues (Principles 7 and 27), precaution (Principle 15), environmental impact assessment (Principle 17), notification of disasters and activities with significant adverse environmental damage (Principles 18 and 19) and the polluter-pays principle (Principle 16). The Rio Declaration also touches on the issue of individual rights in environmental matters. Principle 1, while less forthright than its Stockholm counterpart, provides that human beings 'are entitled to a healthy and productive life in harmony with nature'. Perceived at the time as a regression, the link between human rights and environmental protection has since then grown in importance overshadowing the fears expressed in the early 1990s. In addition, the Declaration explicitly stated the main components of what can be called 'environmental democracy' in its Principle 10. This principle states that 'each individual shall have appropriate access to information concerning the environment that is held by public authorities, including information on hazardous materials and activities ... as well as ... the

---

[64] On this instrument see J. E. Viñuales (ed.), *The Rio Declaration on Environment and Development. A Commentary* (Oxford University Press, 2015), Preliminary study.

opportunity to participate in decision-making processes'. Moreover, '[e]ffec-
tive access to judicial and administrative proceedings, including redress and
remedy, shall be provided' (Principle 10). Finally, the Rio Declaration
addresses questions of implementation stating the need, *inter alia*, to 'reduce
and eliminate unsustainable patterns of production and consumption and to
promote appropriate demographic policies' (Principle 8), encourage the
transfer technology (Principle 9), ensure the participation of civil society
(Principle 10), avoid using environmental considerations as an excuse to
restrict trade (Principle 12), develop national and international instruments
on compensation for environmental damage (Principle 13) and prevent the
transfer of hazardous wastes to developing countries (Principle 14).

The implementation strategy developed at Rio is specified in the ambitious
Agenda 21,[65] which includes a preamble followed by forty chapters, divided
into four main sections (I. Social and Economic Dimensions; II. Conservation
and Management of Resources for Development; III. Strengthening the Role of
Major Groups; IV. Means of Implementation) over several hundred pages. Of
course we cannot elaborate here on the detail of this lengthy text. Suffice it to
note that the issue of development features regularly throughout. The first two
paragraphs of the preamble set the tone by referring to a 'global partnership for
sustainable development', which must be based on a 'balanced and
integrated approach to environment and development questions'.[66] We find
this emphasis throughout the text, particularly in the first section devoted to
'Social and Economic Dimensions'. From a legal perspective, Chapter 39 of
Agenda 21 further elaborates on this 'integration' policy by formulating the
principles that must guide the negotiation of future treaties in this field:

> The further development of international law on sustainable development,
> giving special attention to the delicate balance between environmental and
> developmental concerns ... and ... [t]he need to clarify and strengthen the
> relationship between existing international instruments or agreements in the
> field of environment and relevant social and economic agreements or instru-
> ments, taking into account the special needs of developing countries.[67]

The impact of this instrument, which seeks to guide the implementation of
integration measures, has varied significantly from one topic to the other,
perhaps due to its over-ambitious nature. However, it has provided a very
useful chart of the vast swathes of environmental policies that could be adopted
in fields as diverse as the protection of oceans, seas (Chapter 17) and water
resources (Chapter 18), the management of chemicals and waste (Chapters 19
to 22), the protection of ecosystems (Chapters 11 to 13 and 15), the planning
and management of land resources (Chapters 10 and 14), or even the management of biotechnology (Chapter 16).

---

[65] See N. A. Robinson (ed.), *Agenda 21: Earth's Action Plan Annotated* (New York: Oceana
Publications, 1993).
[66] Rio Declaration, *supra.* 56, paras. 1.1 and 1.2.   [67] Agenda 21, *supra* n. 57, para. 39.1.

The Rio Conference also led to the creation of a new institution by the ECOSOC, namely the Commission on Sustainable Development ('CSD').[68] Although the CSD has been replaced with a High-Level Political Forum, its twenty years of operation merit some comments. It was composed of representatives of fifty-three UN Member States elected by ECOSOC for a period of three years according to geographic distribution. Its mandate was essentially to monitor the implementation of Agenda 21, the Rio Declaration and the Johannesburg Plan, discussed later. Over time, the CSD restructured this broad mandate, focusing primarily on the consideration of reports by States regarding the implementation of the recommendations of Agenda 21, and on the development of guidelines on institutional co-operation in this area. Between 1993 and 2003, the CSD reviewed the various components of Agenda 21 in general. In 2003 it established a multi-year programme divided into seven periods of two years ('*implementation cycles*'), each focused on specific aspects of its mandate.[69] The first three periods were devoted respectively to water management and human settlements (2004/2005), energy development and the protection of the atmosphere (2006/2007) and the management of land resources in a broad sense (2008/2009). In its last years of operation, the CSD focused on issues related to transportation, resource extraction, the management of chemicals and waste, and models of production and consumption.

1.6 The World Summit on Sustainable Development (2002)

The Rio Conference has become a landmark in the history of global environmental governance, to a point that we refer informally to the conferences held thereafter as 'Rio+5' or 'Rio+10', or more recently, 'Rio+20'. Indeed, the Rio Conference has come to be seen not as an iteration of the Stockholm Conference twenty years on, but rather as a foundational moment in and of itself. If Stockholm symbolised the birth of modern international environmental law, Rio represents its 'coming of age'. Today, global environmental governance still operates within the broad principles developed at Rio, but it is at the World Summit on Sustainable Development held in Johannesburg in 2002 that the focus shifted from normative development to implementation as such.

In 1997, the UN General Assembly held a special session on the implementation of the Rio recommendations and came to the conclusion that, despite

---

[68] By virtue of resolution A/RES.47/191 of 22 December 1992, the UN General Assembly, following the recommendation contained in Chapter 38 of Agenda 21, requested ECOSOC to establish the CSD, while setting the mandate of this body. ECOSOC formally established the CSD by Resolution 1993/207 of 12 February 1993.

[69] Future programme, organisation and methods of work of the Commission on Sustainable Development: Annex. Programme of Work of the Commission on Sustainable Development, 25 July 2003, UN Doc. E/2003/29 and E/2003/L.32.

Figure 1.3: The Johannesburg Summit (2002)

the normative contribution of Rio, the environment had continued to deteriorate.[70] In other words, the main challenge now seemed to be the practical implementation of the recommendations and standards adopted the previous years. It is in this context that, in December 2000, the General Assembly decided to organise a third major conference in Johannesburg (South Africa).[71] Throughout the preparatory work, the emphasis was placed on a selected number of priority issues, with a stronger focus on developmental considerations than on environmental protection. This focus came to be known as the 'WEHAB' agenda, by reference to water and sanitation, energy, health, agricultural productivity and biodiversity.

The Johannesburg Conference, technically known as the 'World Summit on Sustainable Development', took place between August and September 2002. As with the two conferences discussed before, the outcomes of this Summit can be organised in three main categories depicted in Figure 1.3.

Regarding the first category, the contribution of the Summit was rather modest. The delegations adopted a 37-paragraph 'Political Declaration', the 'Johannesburg Declaration on Sustainable Development', which adds little to the normative development of international environmental law.[72] The most notable element of the Declaration is perhaps its emphasis on the social dimension of development as an integral component of sustainable development:

> Accordingly, we assume a collective responsibility to advance and strengthen the interdependent and mutually reinforcing pillars of sustainable development – economic development, social development and environmental protection – at the local, national, regional and global levels.[73]

---

[70] GA Resolution S/19–2, 28 June 1997, Annex, 'Programme for the Further Implementation of Agenda 21', para. 9. See also UNEP, *Global Environment Outlook*, 1997.

[71] See 'Ten-year Review of Progress Achieved in the Implementation of the Outcome of the United Nations Conference on Environment and Development', 20 December 2000, UN Doc. A/RES/55/199.

[72] Resolution 1: 'Political declaration', 4 September 2002, Report of World Summit on Sustainable Development in Johannesburg (South Africa), 26 August to 4 September 2002, UN Doc. A/CONF.199/20, p. 1, 2002 ('Political Declaration').

[73] *Ibid.*, paras. 5 and 18.

In fact, the Declaration is clearly directed towards the question of implementation.[74] Of note is the specific reference to the role of the private sector, particularly in paragraph 27, according to which 'in pursuit of its legitimate activities the private sector, including both large and small companies, has a duty to contribute to the evolution of equitable and sustainable communities and societies'.

The participation of the private sector is further elaborated on in the 'Plan of Implementation' also adopted in Johannesburg.[75] The plan is structured into 11 chapters addressing *tour à tour* the specific areas of the WEHAB agenda (poverty eradication, sustainable consumption/production, natural resource management, health, etc.), regional initiatives (focusing on Africa, Asia and Latin America) and the institutional framework for sustainable development.

The latter chapter expands the purview of the CSD to encompass the monitoring of multi-sectoral partnerships.[76] The issue of multi-sectoral partnerships appears throughout the document, either in connection with poverty eradication,[77] changing unsustainable patterns of production/consumption,[78] the management of natural resources[79] or economic globalisation,[80] to name just a few chapters of the plan. Reflecting the spirit of Johannesburg, these partnerships were seen as a way to implement the objectives of the Millennium Development Goals ('MDGs'), adopted by the UN General Assembly in 2000.[81] Over the years, more than 350 partnerships were set up, mainly in the fields of water, energy and education. From a geographic standpoint, the majority of these partnerships had a global scope (180), while most others had a regional (69) or sub-regional (79) one. However, it is still unclear whether resorting to PPPs has had a meaningful impact in practice.[82] Moreover, as discussed next, the CSD has been recently replaced with a High-Level Political Forum with a different mandate.

1.7 The Rio Summit (2012) and beyond

The adoption of the MDGs in 2000 brought renewed attention to questions of sustainable development. Although the focus of the Millennium Summit was clearly on economic and social development, the 'respect for nature' and the 'protect[ion] of our common environment' were also highlighted, by reference to the outcomes of the Rio Conference.[83] Accordingly, the MDGs included, as 'Goal 7' the need to '[e]nsure environmental sustainability', further specified by four

---

[74] See, notably, *ibid.*, paras. 34–7.
[75] Report of the World Summit on Sustainable Development at Johannesburg (South Africa), 26 August–4 September 2002, UN Doc. A/CONF.199/20 ('Implementation Plan').
[76] *Ibid.*, para. 145.   [77] *Ibid.*, paras. 7(j) and 9(g).   [78] *Ibid.*, para. 20(t).
[79] *Ibid.*, para. 25(g) and 43(a).   [80] *Ibid.*, para. 49.
[81] 'Millennium Declaration', 13 September 2000, UN Doc. A/RES/55/2.
[82] See P. Glasbergen, F. Biermann and A. Mol (eds.), *Partnerships, Governance and Sustainable Development. Reflections on Theory and Practice* (Cheltenham: Edward Elgar, 2007).
[83] See Millennium Declaration, *supra* n. 81, paras. 6 and 21–3.

targets, two with an environmental accent (7A: mainstreaming of sustainable development policies and reversing the loss of environmental resources; 7B: reducing biodiversity loss) and two focusing on social development (7C: improving access to water and sanitation; 7D: improving the lives of slum dwellers).[84]

Since 2000, the UN General Assembly has met several times to review progress on the implementation of the MDGs. The rather modest progress recorded on the environmental protection front (particularly in connection with climate change mitigation and biodiversity loss), together with a Brazilian proposal to host another global conference, led the UN General Assembly to convene a new summit held at Rio de Janeiro in June 2012.[85] According to the enabling resolution, the objective of the 'Rio+20' Summit was

> to secure renewed political commitment for sustainable development, assessing the progress to date and the remaining gaps in the implementation of the outcomes of the major summits on sustainable development and addressing new and emerging challenges.[86]

In addition, the resolution identified two core 'themes to be discussed and refined during the preparatory process: a green economy in the context of sustainable development and poverty eradication and the institutional framework for sustainable development'.[87]

The preparatory process of this summit was largely overshadowed by the excessive media attention paid to the Copenhagen climate conference of December 2009, as well as the subsequent disillusionment caused by its failure. Moreover, the broad themes given to the summit and its elaboration into seven 'priority areas' (decent jobs, energy, sustainable cities, food security and sustainable agriculture, water, oceans and disaster readiness) and sixteen 'issues' ranging from trade to science and technology to population dynamics did not help focus the discussions. The outcome document, 'The Future We Want', confirms the shift, already signalled by the Johannesburg Summit, towards developmental concerns. It is still early to evaluate the impact of the outcome document on global environmental governance. Aside from the strengthening of UNEP, particularly through the extension of UNEP's Governing Council to universal membership (all members of the UN General Assembly) and the commitment to a larger budget,[88] the main contribution of this document concerns the efforts towards 'measuring' progress. 'Measuring' lies indeed at the heart of the three main achievements of the Summit: (i) a call for the development of 'sustainable development goals' for the post-2015 agenda ('SDGs'), which were effectively formulated in late July 2014;[89] (ii) the regular assessment of these goals by a

---

[84] See www.un.org/millenniumgoals/environ.shtml (accessed on 17 December 2012).

[85] 'Implementation of Agenda 21, the Programme for the Further Implementation of Agenda 21 and the outcomes of the World Summit on Sustainable Development', 31 March 2010, UN Doc. A/RES/64/236, para. 20 ('Enabling Resolution').

[86] *Ibid.*, para. 20(a).   [87] *Ibid.*, para. 20(a) *in fine*.

[88] The Future We Want, *supra* n. 35, para. 88.   [89] *Ibid.*, paras. 245–51.

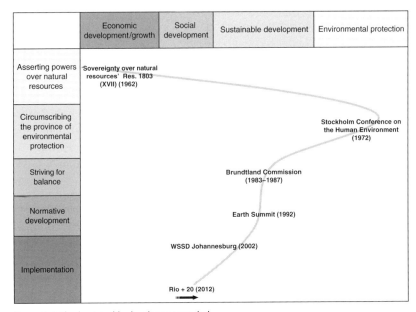

Figure 1.4: The 'sustainable development snake'

'High-Level Political Forum', which was established under the aegis of the UN General Assembly;[90] and (iii) a call for the development of broader measures of progress to 'complement' gross domestic product (GDP), which was still in progress at the time of writing.[91]

Despite the environmental significance of these and other elements, the 2012 Rio Summit tilted the balance between the two terms of the environment–development equation laboriously struck at the 1992 Rio Summit. Social and economic development is no longer seen as 'one' overarching objective of sustainable development,[92] but as 'the' main challenge. As noted by the outcome document, 'poverty eradication is the greatest global challenge facing the world today and an indispensable requirement for sustainable development'.[93] This shift has been confirmed by the SDGs, which places poverty eradication as the first goal out of the seventeen goals identified. The urgent need to fight poverty is, of course, not in question. It is the apparent hierarchy introduced between the pillars of sustainable development that must be carefully assessed. We may recall, in this context, the wording of Resolution 2849 (XXVI) of 1971, one of the early expressions of developing country distrust towards environmental considerations. The last paragraph of this resolution reiterated, indeed, 'the primacy of independent economic and social development as the main and paramount objective of international co-operation, in the interests of the welfare of mankind

---

[90] *Ibid.*, para. 85(e).   [91] *Ibid.*, para. 38.
[92] See e.g. Political Declaration, *supra* n. 72, para 11; Enabling Resolution, *supra* n. 85, preamble, para. 12.
[93] The Future We Want, *supra* n. 35, para. 2.

and of peace and world security'.[94] Figure 1.4 summarises the historical trajectory followed by the environment–development equation since the 1960s.[95]

Sustainable development is turning brownish. We are, of course, not back to square one. The important milestones mentioned in this chapter demonstrate that environmental considerations are far more present in the international and domestic policy agendas today than forty years ago. Yet, the environment–development equation remains unresolved. Fresh thinking is required to move beyond the (transitory) answers provided by the broad concept of sustainable development. This is perhaps the most important intellectual frontier in contemporary international environmental law.

Select bibliography

Abi-Saab, G., 'La souveraineté permanente sur les ressources naturelles', in M. Bedjaoui (ed.), *Droit international: bilan et perspectives* (Paris: Pedone, 1989), pp. 638–61.

Adede, A. O., 'The Treaty System from Stockholm (1972) to Rio de Janeiro (1992)' (1995) 13 *Pace Environmental Law Review* 33.

Boer, B., 'The Globalisation of Environmental Law: The Role of the United Nations' (1995) 20 *Melbourne University Law Review* 101.

Boisson de Chazournes, L., 'Environmental Treaties in Time' (2009) 39 *Environmental Policy and Law* 293.

Bratspies, R. and R. Miller (eds.), *Transboundary Harm in International Law: Lessons from the Trail Smelter Arbitration* (Cambridge University Press, 2006).

Brown Weiss, E., 'The Evolution of International Environmental Law' (2011) 54 *Japanese Yearbook of International Law* 1.

Brunnée, J., 'The Stockholm Declaration and the Structure and Processes of International Environmental Law', in A. Chircop (ed.), *The Future of Ocean Regime-building: Essays in Tribute to Douglas M. Johnston* (Leiden: Martinus Nijhoff, 2009), pp. 41–62.

Caldwell, L. K., *International Environmental Policy. From the Twentieth to the Twenty-First Century* (Durham : Duke University Press, 3rd edn, 1996).

Dobson, A., *Green Political Thought* (New York: Routledge, 4th edn, 2007).

Driesen, D., 'Thirty Years of International Environmental Law: A Retrospective and Plea for Reinvigoration' (2003) 30 *Syracuse Journal of International Law and Commerce* 353.

Dupuy, P.-M., 'Où en est le droit international de l'environnement à la fin du siècle?' (2007) *Revue générale de droit international public* 873.

Ellis, J., 'Unilateral Exercises of Public Authority: Addressing Issues of Fairness in *Teck* v. *Pakootas*, (2012) 25 *Leiden Journal of International Law* 397.

Galizzi, P., 'From Stockholm to New York, via Rio and Johannesburg: Has the Environment Lost its Way on the Global Agenda?' (2005/2006) 29 *Fordham International Law Journal* 952.

Kennet, K., 'The Stockholm Conference on the Human Environment' (1972) 48 *International Affairs* 33.

---

[94] Development and Environment, *supra* n. 28, para. 11.

[95] Source: J. E. Viñuales, 'The Rise and Fall of Sustainable Development' (2013) 22 *Review of Community and International Environmental Law* 3.

Kiss, A., 'Dix ans après Stockholm – une décennie de droit international de l'environnement' (1982) 28 *Annuaire français de droit international* 784–93.

Kiss, A. and S. Doumbé-Bille, 'La Conférence des Nations Unies sur l'environnement et le développement (Rio de Janeiro, 3–14 juin 1992)' (1992) 38 *Annuaire français de droit international* 823.

Kiss, A. and D. Sicault, 'La Conférence des Nations Unies sur l'environnement (Stockholm, 5–16 juin 1972)' (1972) 18 *Annuaire français de droit international* 603.

Maljean-Dubois, S., 'Environnement, développement durable et droit international. De Rio à Johannesbourg: et au-delà?' (2002) 48 *Annuaire français de droit international* 592.

'The making of international law challenging environmental protection', in S. Maljean-Dubois and Y. Kerbrat (eds.), *The Transformation of International Environmental Law* (Oxford: Hart Publishing, 2011), pp. 25–54.

Pallamaerts, M., 'International Environmental Law from Stockholm to Rio: Back to the Future' (1992) 1 *Review of European Community and International Environmental Law* 254.

Rajamani, L., 'From Stockholm to Johannesburg: The Anatomy of Dissonance in the International Environmental Dialogue' (2003) 12 *Review of European Community and International Environmental Law* 23.

Robinson, N. A., *Agenda 21: Earth's Action Plan Annotated* (New York/London: Oceana Publications, 1993).

Sand, P. H., 'International Environmental Law After Rio' (1993) 4 *European Journal of International Law* 377.

'The Evolution of International Environmental Law', in D. Bodansky, J. Brunnée and E. Hey (eds.), *The Oxford Handbook of International Environmental Law* (Oxford University Press, 2007), pp. 31–43.

Sands, P. 'International Environmental Law Ten Years On' (1999) 8 *Review of European Community and International Environmental Law* 239.

'The environment, community and international law' (1989) 30 *Harvard International Law Journal* 393.

Schachter, O., 'The Emergence of International Environmental Law' (1991) 44 *Journal of International Affairs* 457.

Schrijver, N., *Sovereignty over Natural Resources. Balancing Rights and Duties* (Cambridge University Press, 1997).

Selin, H. and B.-O. Linner, 'The Quest for Global Sustainability: International Efforts on Linking Environment and Development', *CID Graduate Student and Postdoctoral Fellow Working Paper No. 5*, January 2005.

Sohn, L. B., 'The Stockholm Declaration on the Human Environment' (1973) 14 *Harvard International Law Journal* 423.

Viñuales, J. E., 'The Contribution of the International Court of Justice to the Development of International Environmental Law' (2008) 32 *Fordham International Law Journal* 232.

'The Rise and Fall of Sustainable Development' (2013) 22 *Review of European Community and International Environmental Law* 3.

2

Main features of international environmental law

2.1 Introduction

In the preceding chapter, we studied the various milestones that shaped the development of international environmental law. Before discussing the technical aspects of this area of international law, it is useful to consider its most salient features. Some comments on these features appear useful at this stage for three main reasons. First, to understand international environmental law as a branch of international law, it is necessary to identify its specific object, namely the environment. Second, the systematic presentation of a number of distinctive features that emerge from the comparative analysis of the main multilateral environmental agreements (MEAs) will help understand their operation, in the same way as grammar facilitates the understanding of a language. Third, the features of international environmental law provide a great deal of information about its dynamics as a legal and social phenomenon, and therefore also about its future evolution.

In other words, understanding the main features of international environmental law is useful both from a theoretical standpoint – to identify the contours of international environmental law as a discipline – and from a practical one – to understand its sources, methods and operation. As regards the theoretical aspects, the relative unity of international environmental law as a discipline comes from its object, the environment, as well as from the principles underlying most of its legal instruments. In this chapter, we analyse the difficulties in the conceptualisation of a reality as broad and multifaceted as the environment (2.2), leaving the study of the unifying principles for Chapter 3. The practical aspects of international environmental law, its distinguishing features as regards its main actors (2.3), sources (2.4) and regulatory techniques (2.5) can, to a large extent, be understood as responses to the political, economic and scientific challenges that this body of law has faced over time, and which will also be discussed. Finally, the last section is devoted to the place of international environmental law within the international legal order (2.6).

2.2 The 'environment' as a legal object

2.2.1 Overview

A first question that arises when we attempt to understand the object of international environmental law is whether the term 'environment' refers or can be pinned down to a single concept or meaning. The term 'environment' pervades scientific, political and media discourse and, yet, its meaning remains unclear. As with the concept of 'time', of which Augustine said that we know what it means so long as we are not asked for a definition, the term 'environment' is as simple to understand intuitively as it is difficult to circumscribe precisely. For present purposes, it will suffice to attempt a characterisation at three levels: scientific, legal and operational.

2.2.2 Scientific level

First, the term 'environment' can be characterised at a scientific level and, more specifically, through the prism of ecology. Different characterisations are provided in the relevant literature.

Broadly speaking, the environment is defined as 'everything which surrounds a spatial entity, abiotic or alive'.[1] Broad definitions dating from the 1970s included a human element as the driving force.[2] Today, the balance of the term has shifted away from a pure human focus and gravitates around an 'organism' (including humans) as its pivotal reference. According to the Oxford Dictionary of Ecology, the 'environment' is:

> [t]he complete range of external conditions, physical and biological, in which an organism lives. Environment includes social, cultural, and (for humans) economic and political considerations, as well as the more usually understood features such as soil, climate, and food supply.[3]

This broad and balanced concept prevails today, and it can be found at the roots of the 'ecosystems approach' increasingly followed by MEAs. The scientific concept seems, however, too broad to determine the province of

---

[1] F. Ramade, *Dictionnaire encyclopédique de l'écologie et des sciences de l'environnement* (Paris: Dunod, 2002), p. 279 (our translation).

[2] At the beginning of the twentieth century, the term 'environment' was used as a synonym for 'geography' in the monumental treatise of E. Reclus, *L'homme et la terre*, 6 vols. (Paris: Librairie Universelle, 1905). See Y. Veyret, 'Environnement', in Y. Veyret (ed.), *Dictionnaire de l'environnement* (Paris: Armand Colin, 2007), p. 133. Ecology was distinguished from 'geography' in the late nineteenth century by its emphasis on biological analysis, but the place of humans between ecology and geography remained a very important question throughout the twentieth century. Some of the first modern accounts of 'ecology' as a science include: W. C. Allee, O. Park, A. E. Emerson, T. Park and K. P. Schmidt, *Principles of Animal Ecology* (Philadelphia: Saunders, 1949); E. P. Odum, *Fundamentals of Ecology* (Philadelphia: Saunders, 1st edn, 1953, 2nd edn, 1959, 3rd edn, 1971). On the history of ecology, see J.-P. Deleage, *Histoire de l'écologie: une science de l'homme et de la nature* (Paris: La Découverte, 1991).

[3] M. Allaby, *Oxford Dictionary of Ecology* (Oxford University Press, 3rd edn, 2005), at 154.

international environmental law as a branch. The social, cultural, economic and political dimensions of the human environment would, indeed, encompass the entire field of international law. This said, the scientific characterisation highlights the need for a balanced approach to environmental protection because the environment is defined not only as the conditions surrounding humans (an 'anthropocentric' view) but also those surrounding any other organism (an 'eco-centric' view).

2.2.3 Legal level

We may also ask whether international law attaches certain legal effects to one or more meanings of the term 'environment'. The answer to this question must be derived from a diverse array of legal instruments.

First, we may look to the founding instruments of international environmental law discussed in Chapter 1. However, such an approach is not entirely satisfactory since none of these instruments has specifically characterised the term 'environment'. They offer, nevertheless, some useful insights. For example, the preamble of the Stockholm Declaration makes reference to two components of the human environment: 'the natural and the man-made, [which] are essential to his well-being and to the enjoyment of basic human rights and the right to life itself'.[4] Further, it refers to '[t]he natural resources of the earth, including the air, water, land, flora and fauna and especially representative samples of natural ecosystems'.[5] The texts of the World Charter for Nature, the Rio Declaration and the Millennium Declaration add little to the characterisation of the term in the Stockholm Declaration.[6] It must be concluded, therefore, that this approach is not, as such, sufficient.

A second possible approach is to refer to the decisions of international courts and tribunals, in particular those of the ICJ. In its well-known Advisory Opinion on the *Legality of Nuclear Weapons*, the ICJ observed that: 'the environment is not an abstraction but represents the living space, the quality of life and the very health of human beings, including generations

---

[1] Declaration of the United Nations Conference on the Human Environment, Stockholm, 16 June 1972, UN Doc. A/CONF 48/14/Rev. 1 ('Stockholm Declaration'), preamble, para. 1.

[5] *Ibid.*, Principle 2.

[6] The World Charter for Nature mentions, in its preamble, that 'Mankind is a part of nature and life depends on the uninterrupted functioning of natural systems which ensure the supply of energy and nutrients', and notes, further on, the need to maintain 'essential ecological processes and life support systems, and … the diversity of life forms'. World Charter for Nature, 28 October 1982, UN Doc. A/RES/37/7 ('Charter for Nature'). The Rio Declaration refers, in its Principle 7, to the 'health and integrity of the Earth's ecosystem', Rio Declaration on Environment and Development, 13 June 1992, UN Doc. A/CONF.151/26 ('Rio Declaration'). As for the Millennium Declaration, it makes reference in para. 6 to 'respect for nature' and 'management of all living species and natural resources', Millennium Declaration, 13 September 2000, UN Doc. A/RES.55/2.

unborn'.[7] However, without questioning the interest of such clarification, this is not enough to give legal content to the term 'environment'.

A third approach is to seek the definition of the term 'environment' within a specific normative context, such as a treaty or a norm. The very strength of this approach, namely the ability to specify the meaning that a term will have in a given treaty context, is also its main weakness because such a meaning will normally be confined to this context. Thus, for example, the characterisation of the term 'environment' that arises from the treaties of the Antarctic Treaty System[8] has little relevance outside that particular context. Similarly, the definition of what amounts to 'environmental' damage in the context of the civil liability regime relating to oil spills[9] or to harm to the 'environment' in the context of Protocol I to the 1949 Geneva Conventions,[10] cannot easily be generalised to the extent that they may exclude certain components of the 'natural' or 'man-made' environment,[11] according to the formula of the Stockholm Declaration.[12] Even a broad characterisation, such as the one provided in Article 1(1) of the UNFCCC,[13] cannot be transposed to other

---

[7] *Legality of the Threat or Use of Nuclear Weapons*, Advisory Opinion, ICJ Reports 1996, para. 29 ('*Legality of Nuclear Weapons*').

[8] E.g. the Convention on the Conservation of Antarctic Marine Living Resources, 20 May 1980, 33 UST 3476 ('CCAMLR'), defines in its Art. 1 its scope as follows: 'This Convention applies to the Antarctic marine living resources of the area south of 60° South latitude and to the Antarctic marine living resources of the area between that latitude and the Antarctic Convergence which form part of the Antarctic marine ecosystem ... The Antarctic marine ecosystem means the complex of relationships of Antarctic marine living resources with each other and with their physical environment.' Similarly, the Protocol on Environmental Protection to the Antarctic Treaty, 4 October 1991, 30 ILM 1455 (1991), defines in Art. 3(1) its scope by reference to the Antarctic Treaty area (the area south of 60° South latitude) specifying the environment within that area as follows 'the Antarctic environment and dependent and associated ecosystems and the intrinsic value of Antarctica, including its wilderness and aesthetic values and its value as an area for the conduct of scientific research, in particular research essential to understanding the global environment'. See P. Birnie, A. Boyle and C. Redgwell, *International Law and the Environment* (Oxford University Press, 2009), p. 6.

[9] See *infra* Chapter 8.   [10] See *infra* Chapter 11.

[11] See United Nations Compensation Commission, *Report and Recommendation made by the Panel of Commissioners concerning the F4 claims*, 22 June 2001, UN Doc. S/AC.26/2001/16, (first instalment); 3 October 2002, S/AC.26/2002/26 (second instalment); 18 December 2003, S/AC.26/2003/31 (third instalment); 9 December 2004, S/AC.26/2004/16 (fourth instalment, part I); 9 December 2004, S/AC.26/2004/17 (fourth instalment part II), and 30 June 2005, S/AC.26/2005/10 (fifth instalment). J.-C. Martin, 'The United Nations Compensation Commission Practice with Regards to Environmental Claims', in S. Maljean-Dubois and Y. Kerbrat (eds.), *The Transformation of International Environmental Law* (Oxford: Hart, 2011), pp. 251–67.

[12] Stockholm Declaration, *supra* n. 4, preamble, para. 1. In addition, international humanitarian law protects civilian objects. See, notably, The (IV) Geneva Convention Relative to the Protection of Civilian Persons in Time of War, 12 August 1949, 75 UNTS 287, Art. 33.

[13] Article 1(1) of the UNFCCC defines '[a]dverse effects of climate change' as 'changes in the physical environment or biota resulting from climate change which have significant deleterious effects on the composition, resilience or productivity of natural and managed ecosystems or on the operation of socio-economic systems or on human health and welfare', United Nations Framework Convention on Climate Change, 9 May 1992, 1771 UNTS 107 ('UNFCCC').

treaty contexts in the absence of a legal relationship (e.g. with the Kyoto Protocol[14]).

2.2.4 Operational level

Finally, the meaning of the term 'environment' can be derived, for purely operational purposes, from the body of instruments referred to as international environmental law. This approach is, of course, unsatisfactory from a theoretical standpoint because of its circularity. It is, however, very useful in practice, especially when it comes to providing a structured overview of international environmental law as a discipline for professional or educational purposes. It helps indeed organise the main contents of this discipline in a manner that is more conducive to their understanding as a whole.

Thus, for example, the physical (air, water, land), biological (species, including the human species, habitats, ecosystems and diversity) and cultural components (the human existence and aesthetic considerations) identified in the aforementioned characterisations of the term 'environment' can be organised analytically in a number of categories or areas of regulation. This is the approach adopted here. For the remainder of this book, we will focus on four 'sub-continents' within the entire 'world' of international environmental law:[15] (i) the marine environment and freshwater;[16] (ii) the protection of the atmosphere;[17] (iii) species, ecosystems and biodiversity;[18] and (iv) the regulation of dangerous substances and activities.[19]

The object of this introduction to international environmental law thus characterised, we can now turn to the main features of this body of law.

2.3 The main actors

2.3.1 From challenges to structures

To understand the main actors shaping the dynamics of international environmental law, we must first recall some of the challenges that the discipline has faced since its modern origins in the 1960s. These challenges can be classified into two main categories.

The first category covers political difficulties at the international level, mainly due to: (i) developing countries' perception of international environmental law as a rich country luxury or a strait-jacket to their development or even a protectionist tactic used by developed countries to regulate trade

---

[14] Protocol to the United Nations Framework Convention on Climate Change, Kyoto, 11 December 1997, 2303 UNTS 148 ('Kyoto Protocol'), Art. 1.

[15] See D. Bodansky, J. Brunnée and E. Hay (eds.), *The Oxford Handbook of International Environmental Law* (Oxford University Press, 2007), part III.

[16] See our analysis *infra* Chapter 4.   [17] See *infra* Chapter 5.   [18] See *infra* Chapter 6.

[19] See *infra* Chapter 7.

from developing countries; (ii) the strategic competition among different countries;[20] and (iii) the need to co-operate and co-ordinate initiatives to tackle transboundary or global environmental problems.

The second category refers to domestic difficulties, mainly as a result of: (i) economic interest groups adversely affected by environmental regulation, with sufficient means to organise themselves and influence the position of their governments on a variety of environmental problems; and (ii) some broader implications of environmental regulation, such as the potential competitive disadvantages arising from it and the risk of outsourcing and job losses, both of which have been often associated, for justified or unjustified reasons, with the adoption of environmental disciplines.[21]

To address these two categories of challenges, international environmental law has developed two features that could be described as 'organisational' in nature insofar as they reflect the organisation of the main actors of global environmental governance.[22] The answer to the first category of difficulties has consisted in creating a number of international structures (or the re-orientation of some existing ones) in order to facilitate State co-operation in environmental matters (2.3.2). As to the second category of difficulties, it has encouraged the organisation of civil society to counterbalance the influence of economic interest groups and to participate in the implementation of environmental norms (2.3.3).

2.3.2 International structures and actors

The problems of trust and efficiency in the relations between States have been managed through the creation of new international organisations or the re-orientation or expansion of existing ones. We do not intend to dwell on the theory of international organisations here[23] nor on their function in international relations.[24] The discussion will be limited to some observations about the types of international organisations active in global environmental governance.

There are broadly four types of international organisations, according to their mode of creation and the scope of their mandate. The first and probably

---

[20] The refusal by the United States Senate to consider the ratification of the Kyoto Protocol is often put down to the fact that some of its strategic competitors, especially China, were not subject to quantified emissions reduction targets. See especially 'Getting Warmer', *The Economist*, 3 December 2009.

[21] See *ibid.*

[22] See generally J. G. Speth and P. Haas, *Global Environmental Governance* (Washington DC: Island Press, 2006).

[23] See M. Virally, *L'organisation mondiale* (Paris: Armand Colin, 1972); H. G. Schermers and N. M. Blokker, *International Institutional Law* (Leiden: Martinus Nijhoff, 5th edn, 2011).

[24] See P. Haas, R. O. Keohane and M. A. Levy (eds.), *Institutions for the Earth: Sources of Effective International Environmental Protection* (Cambridge MA: MIT Press, 1993); Speth and Haas, *supra* n. 22.

most common one encompasses international organisations created by a 'constitutive treaty', which defines the functional scope as well as the principal organs of the organisation. Prominent examples of organisations involved in environmental matters include the World Meteorological Organisation ('WMO'),[25] the United Nations Food and Agriculture Organisation ('FAO')[26] and the International Maritime Organisation ('IMO').[27] The essential function of these organisations is to co-ordinate the efforts of States in a specific area of regulation, often providing a framework for the negotiation of treaties or the adoption of standards.

The second type of organisation is a variation of the first, the main difference being that the basic treaty does not aim to create an organisation with a general purpose in a given area but rather to regulate a specific problem, creating institutions to manage the development of the treaty thus concluded. By way of illustration, most MEAs create organs such as a conference of the parties ('COP') and a secretariat.[28] Examples of this second category include the COP and secretariats established by the Basel Convention, the UNFCCC, the CBD, the Convention on Desertification and the Stockholm Convention, to name a few.[29] The function of these institutions is to facilitate the development of a specific regime by hosting regular negotiations often resulting in new more specific treaties or a wide array of other legal instruments (typically decisions of the COP clarifying the contents and scope of the obligations provided for in the initial treaty).

The third type of organisations, namely the subsidiary bodies established by a principal organ of a treaty, can be seen as a by-product of the previous two types of organisations. For example, the UN General Assembly, one of the principal organs of the UN,[30] has established several subsidiary bodies, two of which are very important in environmental matters, namely the United Nations Environment Programme ('UNEP')[31] and the United Nations

---

[25] Convention of the World Meteorological Organization, 11 October 1947, 77 UNTS 143.

[26] Constitution of the Food and Agriculture Organization of the United Nations, 16 October 1945, 12 UST 980.

[27] Convention of the International Maritime Organization, 6 March 1948, 289 UNTS 4.

[28] See J. M. Lavieille (ed.), *Conventions de protection de l'environnement, Secrétariats, Conférences des parties, Comités d'experts* (Limoges: PULIM, 1999); B. H. Desai, *Multilateral Environmental Agreements. Legal Status of the Secretariats* (Cambridge University Press, 2010).

[29] Basel Convention on the Control of Transboundary Movements of Hazardous Wastes and their Disposal, 22 March 1989, 1673 UNTS 57 ('Basel Convention'), Art. 15; UNFCCC, *supra* n. 13, Art. 7; Convention on Biological Diversity, 5 June 1992, 1760 UNTS 79 ('CBD'), Art. 23; United Nations Convention on Action Against Desertification in Countries Experiencing Serious Drought and/or Desertification, Particularly in Africa, 14 October 1994, 1954 UNTS 3 ('UNCCD'), Art. 22; Stockholm Convention on Persistent Organic Pollutants, 22 May 2001, 2256 UNTS 119 ('POP Convention'), Art. 19.

[30] Charter of the United Nations, 26 June 1945, 1 UNTS XVI, Art .7.1.

[31] 'Institutional and Financial Arrangements for International Environmental Cooperation', 15 December 1972, UN Doc. A/Res/2997/XXVII ('Resolution 2997').

Development Programme ('UNDP').[32] The activities of these subsidiary bodies will be referred throughout this book. It suffices to emphasise at this stage that while UNEP has a function that is in some ways 'entrepreneurial' or 'catalytic' as regards international environmental law,[33] UNDP focuses on the implementation of projects which, in some cases, have environmental components. A third illustration is the Commission on Sustainable Development ('CSD'), created by the Economic and Social Council ('ECOSOC'), another principal organ of the UN.[34] The CSD has been replaced with a High-Level Political Forum, introduced by the outcome document of the 2012 Rio Summit,[35] which is a subsidiary body of the UN General Assembly. COPs are also empowered to create subsidiary bodies. Thus, the COP of the UNFCCC, acting as the Meeting of the Parties to the Kyoto Protocol ('CMP'), has set up bodies to manage the flexible mechanisms under Articles 6 and 12 of the Protocol.[36] In some cases, subsidiary bodies may, in turn, be involved in the creation of a new organisation. For example, in 1991, UNEP and UNDP, together with the World Bank, created the Global Environmental Facility ('GEF'), which became an independent organisation in 1994.[37] This change took place, largely under pressure from developing countries, in order to limit the influence of the World Bank, hence of developed countries, on the allocation of funds by the GEF.

Finally, the fourth type of organisations are characterised by their relative organisational informality insofar as they are not based on a treaty or a decision of an organ but operate as forums for discussion among States and, in some cases, also some other entities. Their composition may therefore need to be expanded depending on the issues that have to be addressed. For example, the G8, which traditionally brings together the heads of State or governments of Germany, Canada, the United States, France, Italy, Japan, Russia and the United Kingdom, has sometimes been expanded to include counterparts in countries like South Africa, Brazil, China, India or Mexico.[38] Another forum linked to the G8, namely the 'Major Economies Forum', brought together leaders of the sixteen States (plus the EU) that emit most greenhouse gases in July 2009.[39] Alongside these forums, there are

---

[32] 'Consolidation of the Special Fund and the Expanded Programme of Technical Assistance in a United Nations Development Programme', 22 November 1965, UN Doc. Resolution 2029 (XX).

[33] On the role of UNEP see M. Ivanova, 'UNEP in Global Environmental Governance: Design, Leadership, Location' (2010) 10 *Global Environmental Politics* 30.

[34] 'Institutional Arrangements to follow up the United Nations Conference on Environment and Development', 22 December 1992, UN Doc. A/Res/47/191.

[35] 'The Future We Want', 11 September 2012, UN Doc. A/Res/66/288, para. 84.

[36] See Doc. FCCC/KP/CMP/2005/8/Add.2, Decisions 3/CMP.1 and 9/CMP.1.

[37] See Instrument for the Establishment of the Restructured Global Environmental Facility (October 2011). The text of the 'Instrument' is reproduced at 9–41 of the 2011 publication.

[38] G8 Summit 2008, Hokkaido, Tokyo (Japan), 7–9 July 2008.

[39] Declaration of the Leaders of the Major Economies Forum on Energy and Climate, see www.g8italia2009.it/static/G8_Allegato/MEF_Declarationl.pdf (3 February 2012).

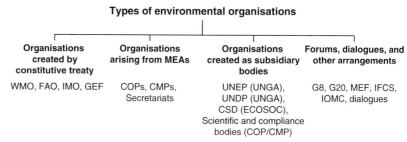

Figure 2.1: Types of environmental organisations

also 'dialogues' on issues such as climate co-operation[40] or chemical management,[41] which may include a variety of stakeholders and allow for the removal of obstacles ahead of formal negotiations. Figure 2.1 summarises the four types of organisations identified so far.

This brief survey highlights one important feature of global environmental governance, namely its decentralisation or, more specifically, the scattered distribution of its governing structures. Referring to one aspect of this scattered landscape, a prominent environmental lawyer spoke of 'treaty congestion'.[42] Indeed, despite several initiatives to this effect, no 'World Environmental Organisation' has been developed so far,[43] unlike areas such as international trade or global health issues. The function of the various organisations active in environmental matters is, in essence, to co-ordinate the efforts of States in this area, seeking as much as possible to avoid duplication as well as to enhance the efficient use of resources. The decentralisation of global environmental governance extends, moreover, well beyond intergovernmental organisations, as discussed next.

2.3.3 Civil society and the private sector

Besides the four types of organisations discussed earlier, private sector organisations and other organisations from civil society play a very important role in shaping international environmental law.[44] It is not an exaggeration to

---

[40] See J. E. Viñuales, 'Du bon dosage du droit international: Les négociations climatiques en perspective' (2010) 56 *Annuaire français de droit international* 437ss.

[41] See *infra* Chapter 7, discussing the 'International Forum on Chemical Safety' (IFCS) and the 'Inter-Organisation Programme for the Sound Management of Chemicals' (IOMC).

[42] See E. Brown Weiss, 'International Environmental Law: Contemporary Issues and the Emergence of a New World Order' (1995) 81 *Georgetown Law Journal* 675.

[43] See F. Biermann and S. Bauer (eds.), *A World Environmental Organization: Solution or Threat for Effective International Environmental Governance* (Aldershot: Ashgate, 2005).

[44] See A. Pomade, *La société civile et le droit de l'environnement. Contribution à la réflexion sur les théories des sources du droit et de la validité* (Paris: LGDJ, 2010).

say that, with the exception of human rights,[45] no other area has experienced such a strong participation from civil society.

The participation of civil society is important to counterbalance the influence of economic interest groups, whose environmental externalities are often insufficiently addressed by State intervention or consumer behaviour. Organisations such as Greenpeace, the World Wildlife Fund ('WWF') or the International Union for the Conservation of Nature ('IUCN'),[46] are but a few prominent examples of a vast and thriving body of environmental NGOs active at both the national and international levels, who have devoted substantial efforts to raise public awareness regarding environmental degradation and to channel public pressure.[47] Indeed, the main functions performed by these NGOs can be classified into three main categories.[48] (i) the formulation of the interests of civil society, (ii) assistance in implementation and (iii) channelling public pressure. Of course, the performance of these functions can follow very different approaches. For example, the adoption of the POP Convention was significantly facilitated by the momentum created by the publication of a report with support from WWF.[49] Another example is the role of IUCN in the development of payment-for-ecosystem-services ('PES') mechanisms, such as reservoirs of biodiversity and of greenhouse gas emissions.[50] Finally, the intervention of NGOs can have significant influence on how a case is managed, as is evidenced by the famous *Brent Spar* case, where the intervention of Greenpeace prevented Shell from sinking an oil platform in the North Sea, by channelling public opinion against this form of decommissioning.[51]

This said, the relations between civil society and the private sector, or between the private sector and environmental protection, are far more complex. In fact, environmental protection can hardly be achieved without the co-operation or even the initiative of the private sector, as has been recognised previously, particularly at the 2002 Johannesburg Summit. The contribution of the private sector is particularly important in connection with (i) project financing, (ii) technology transfer and also (iii) environmental governance. The challenge, therefore, is not only to introduce certain checks on the activities of the private sector (such as corporate social responsibility

---

[45] See e.g. C. Welch (ed.), *NGOs and Human Rights: Promise and Performance* (Philadelphia: University of Pennsylvania Press, 2001).

[46] Note that the IUCN is a mixed organisation with an intergovernmental component.

[47] On the role of NGOs, see A. K. Lindblom, *Non-Governmental Organisations in International Law* (Cambridge University Press, 2006).

[48] See D. Hunter, J. Salzman and D. Zaelke, *International Environmental Law and Policy* (New York: Foundation Press, 2007), Chapter 5.

[49] For a list of detailed examples, see *ibid.*, pp. 255–67.

[50] IUCN UNFCCC Newsletter; Reducing Emissions from Deforestation and Forest Degradation, 09/09, available at: cmsdata.iucn.org/downloads/unfccc_newsletter__september_09.pdf (last visited 3 February 2012).

[51] On the ambiguous results of the intervention of Greenpeace, see Hunter *et al.*, *supra* n. 48, pp. 827–9.

codes or accountability mechanisms[52]) but also to steer private interest in pro-environment projects. One way to do this is to enter into public–private partnerships or PPPs.[53] PPPs have been active in matters such as renewable energy, water purification or waste treatment, as well as in the channelling of financial resources towards environmental projects. The role of the private sector is currently the subject of much discussion, particularly with respect to the financing of projects relating to climate change mitigation and adaptation.[54]

2.4 The sources of international environmental law

The challenges faced by international environmental law have been instrumental in shaping not only its organisational features but also the processes through which environmental norms are generated. The complex aggregation of diverging State interests, the need to institutionalise environmental negotiations or the significant role played by NGOs in the development and implementation of environmental norms have all influenced the sources of international environmental law. Yet, this influence cannot be understood unless we also take into account an additional challenge, which has a much stronger impact on environmental regulation than on any other branch of international law, namely the need to cope with scientific and technological progress.

These difficulties have indeed a significant impact on how traditional methods of creating international law operate in the environmental context. Such impact lies at the roots of three important features of international environmental law: (i) the prevalence of treaties as a source of international environmental law, (ii) the frequent use of instruments of soft law[55] and (iii) the increasing development of a *'droit dérivé'* or administrative law of the environment in the form of decisions adopted by the COPs established by MEAs.

---

[52] OECD Guidelines for Multinational Enterprises: revised in 2000, 11 September 2000, Doc. DAFFE/IME/WPG(2000)9; Tripartite Declaration of Principles Concerning Multinational Enterprises and Social Policy, International Labour Organization, 2006; The Ten Principles of the Global Compact, and more particularly Principles 7 to 9, available at: www.unglobalcom pact.org/aboutthegc/thetenprinciples/index.html (last visited 3 February 2012). See E. Morgera, *Corporate Accountability in International Environmental Law* (Oxford University Press, 2009).

[53] See P. Glasbergen, F. Biermann and A. Mol (eds.), *Partnerships, Governance and Sustainable Development. Reflections on Theory and Practice* (Cheltenham: Edward Elgar, 2007).

[54] See P.-M. Dupuy and J. E. Viñuales (eds.), *Harnessing Foreign Investment to Promote Environmental Protection: Incentives and Safeguards* (Cambridge University Press, 2013); R. Stewart, B. Kingsbury and B. Rudyk, *Climate Finance: Regulatory and Funding Strategies for Climate Change and Global Development* (New York University Press, 2009).

[55] See P.-M. Dupuy, 'Soft Law and the International Law of the Environment' (1990/1991) 12 *Michigan Journal of International Law* 420.

2.4.1 The prevalence of treaties

Perhaps because of its recent vintage, the role of customary international law in international environmental law is still limited, although its importance should not be underestimated.[56] Apart from a few principles, such as those of no harm, prevention, co-operation and regular exchange of information, or equitable utilisation and joint management of shared natural resources, which were developed in the early 1970s in connection with transboundary pollution,[57] or the more recent requirement to conduct an environmental impact assessment or to provide adequate channels for public participation,[58] custom has had limited influence on international environmental law.

In contrast, the role played by treaties has grown steadily since the adoption of the Stockholm Declaration in the 1970s. We have already discussed in Chapter 1 the historical development of international environmental law, and we will analyse in detail the most important environmental treaties in subsequent chapters. Here, we discuss briefly the reasons explaining the prevalence of treaties in this area of international law.

The first reason is the relative 'novelty' of environmental problems and, as a result, the inadequacy of prior customary norms. It is only natural that new problems may call for new rules, better adapted to the regulatory object than norms originally developed for a different purpose. Second, environmental problems know no borders, and their scientific understanding evolves over time. Their regulation therefore has a significant institutional and procedural dimension, which can be better addressed through treaty law. Third, the reluctance of developing countries as regards measures that may hamper their economic development could also explain the appeal of treaties, which allow for some degree of differentiation between developed and developing countries. Differences in the perception of environmental regulation may also explain, to some extent, the attractiveness of non-binding 'soft law' in this area.

2.4.2 The role of soft law

Soft law has played a major role in the development of international environmental law since its modern inception.[59] The two texts that could be described as its founding documents, namely the 1972 Stockholm Declaration and the 1992 Rio Declaration, are instruments of soft law. We could also refer to many other examples, ranging from Resolution 1803 (XVII) on 'Permanent

---

[56] See P.-M. Dupuy, 'Formation of Customary International Law and General Principles' in Bodansky *et al., supra* n. 15, p. 450.

[57] See P.-M. Dupuy, 'Overview of the Existing Customary Legal Regime Regarding International Pollution' in D. Magraw (ed.), *International Law and Pollution* (Philadelphia: University of Pennsylvania Press, 1991), pp. 61–89; J. E. Viñuales, 'The Contribution of the International Court of Justice to the Development of International Environmental Law: A Contemporary Assessment' (2008) 32 *Fordham International Law Journal* 232.

[58] See *infra* Chapter 3.   [59] See Dupuy, *supra* n. 55.

Sovereignty over Natural Resources' of 1962[60] to the 'World Charter for Nature' adopted in 1982,[61] the 'Forests Declaration' adopted at the 1992 Rio Summit[62] or, still, the 'Copenhagen Accord' of December 2009.[63]

To understand the operation of these instruments, it is useful to introduce a classic distinction between the instrument and its content. The use of the adjective 'soft' to describe the legal status of an instrument is intended to stress that the instrument as such is not legally binding, regardless of its content. The contents of the instrument may, however, be legally binding in some other way. In international environmental law, the most striking example of this phenomenon is the principle of prevention enshrined in both the Stockholm Declaration (Principle 21) and the Rio Declaration (Principle 2). This principle, which is currently considered a cornerstone of international environmental law, is not legally binding because of its inclusion in a number of soft law instruments, including the two aforementioned declarations, but by virtue of its customary status recognised by the International Court of Justice ('ICJ') on a number of occasions.[64] However, the ICJ would probably not have affirmed the customary nature of this principle had it not been for its restatement in such soft law instruments. The instruments themselves and the conferences and institutions that create them therefore have an important normative role as catalysts of new international norms. From this perspective, one can distinguish between organisations capable of expressing State practice (e.g. general assemblies of intergovernmental organisations or international conferences) and organisations that seek to influence this practice by adopting various instruments. The General Assembly of the UN or the Rio Conference on Environment and Development are examples of the first category, while the International Law Association ('ILA') and the Institut de Droit International ('IDI') are illustrations of the second category.

The normative role of the latter category of organisations must not be underestimated, both directly as 'entrepreneurs' of legally binding norms, and indirectly, through their influence on the development of legal instruments by the first category of organisations. Regarding the first hypothesis, we can mention, for example, the resolution adopted in 1963 by the IUCN, which later became the basis for the adoption of the Convention on International Trade in Endangered Species ('CITES'). As for the second hypothesis, it can be

---

[60] 'Permanent Sovereignty Over Natural Resources', 14 December 1964, UN Doc. Resolution 1803 (XVII).

[61] World Charter for Nature, *supra* n. 6.

[62] 'Non-Legally Binding Authoritative Statement of Principles for a Global Consensus on the Management, Conservation and Sustainable Development of All Types of Forests', 14 August 1992, UN Doc. A/CONF/151/26 (vol. III) ('Forests Principles').

[63] Copenhagen Accord, 19 December 2009, UN Doc. FCCC/CP/2009/L.7.

[64] *Legality of Nuclear Weapons, supra* n. 7, para. 29; *Gabčíkovo-Nagymaros Project (Hungary v. Slovakia)*, Judgment, ICJ Reports 1997, p. 7 (*'Gabčíkovo-Nagymaros Project'*), para. 53; *Pulp Mills on the River Uruguay (Argentina v. Uruguay)*, Provisional Measures, Order (13 July 2006), ICJ Reports 2006, p. 113, para. 72 (*'Pulp Mills'*).

illustrated by the influence of the 'Helsinki Rules' adopted in 1966 by the ILA[65] on the subsequent work of the UN International Law Commission ('ILC') on this matter, which, in turn, led to the adoption of a treaty under the aegis of the UN General Assembly.[66]

It must be added that even in cases where the contents of a soft law instrument do not become legally binding they may still be influential. For example, a number of financial intermediaries, such as the World Bank, the International Finance Corporation, regional development banks or even private lenders, have adopted environmental and sustainability standards which, because of their impact on the disbursement of funds, command significant authority.[67]

2.4.3 *Droit dérivé*

The French term '*droit dérivé*' refers to the laws and regulations adopted by a body that is empowered to do so by a treaty. In the environmental context, it refers to the law enacted by such intergovernmental bodies as the General Assembly or the Security Council of the United Nations or, more specifically, the COPs and CMPs established by MEAs. The term '*dérivé*' indicates that the legal validity of the resolutions, recommendations and decisions ('regulations') adopted by these bodies depends on the normative powers delegated to them by States parties in the constitutive treaty. As with soft law, these regulations are not strictly speaking a formal source of international law, which in this case would be the constitutive treaty. They remain, nevertheless, a very important technique for the development of international standards.[68]

In international environmental law, these regulations mainly take the form of decisions adopted by the COPs (or CMPs) on various subjects, such as:[69] (i) internal rules (procedural, administrative or financial), (ii) regulations implementing the obligations arising from a MEA or (iii) external regulations (on issues such as compliance, co-operation with other treaties, or the elaboration of a variety of standards intended to guide the conduct of States and other entities). Some examples will help illustrate these types of regulations.

The first is given by Article 2.9(a)(i) of the 1987 Montreal Protocol, which allows for the possibility of introducing 'adjustments' to the ozone

---

[65] Helsinki Rules on the Uses of the Waters of International Rivers; adopted by the International Law Association at its 52nd conference, Helsinki, 20 August 1966, International Law Association, *Report of the Fifty-second Conference*, London, 1967, p. 56.

[66] See United Nations Convention on the Law of the Non-Navigational Uses of International Watercourses, 21 May 1997, 36 ILM 700. This convention entered into force in 2014 but, before, some of its provisions were viewed as a statement of customary international law. See L. Caflisch, 'La convention du 21 mai 1997 sur l'utilisation des cours d'eau internationaux à des fins autres que la navigation' (1997) 43 *Annuaire français de droit international* 751, at 770.

[67] See B. J. Richardson, *Socially Responsible Investment Law* (Oxford University Press, 2008).

[68] See J. Brunnée, 'COPing with Consent: Law-making under Multilateral Environmental Agreements' (2002) 15 *Leiden Journal of International Law* 1.

[69] See G. Ulfstein, 'Treaty Bodies' in Bodansky *et al.*, *supra* n. 15, pp. 880–8.

depleting potentials of regulated substances by means of a decision of the
Meeting of the Parties adopted by a qualified majority and binding on all
the parties (Article 2.9(c)–(d)). The second illustration is given by a set of
decisions of the COP of the UNFCCC known as the 'Marrakesh Accords'
(subsequently approved by the CMP of the Kyoto Protocol), which
govern the details of the three 'flexible mechanisms' provided for in the
Protocol, namely joint implementation,[70] the clean development mechanism[71]
and emissions trading.[72] The third illustration concerns the architecture of
certain implementation mechanisms known as 'non-compliance procedures'
('NCPs') established within the framework of several MEAs.[73] We will discuss
these mechanisms in Section 2.5.4 below and, more generally, in Chapter 9.

Given the importance of the issues managed by way of '*droit dérivé*', it is
not an overstatement to say that such regulations are critical for the operation
of MEAs.

2.5 The implementation of international environmental law

2.5.1 Overview

The implementation of international environmental law presents a number of
specific features that are worth mentioning as part of the overview provided in
this chapter. Several techniques have been developed to cope with such
implementation challenges as resistance from economic interest groups,
political and strategic considerations, or the need to constantly adapt to an
evolving scientific and technological landscape.[74]

Faced with such difficulties, the traditional mechanisms used for the
implementation of international law, i.e. the characterisation of a given conduct as a breach of a legal norm and the determination of the ensuing legal

[70] Decision 2/CMP.1, FCCC/KP/CMP/2005/8/Add.1 ('Decision 15/CP.7'); Decision 9/CMP.1,
FCCC/KP/CMP/2005/8/Add.2 ('Decision 16/CP.7'); Decision 10/CMP.1, FCCC/KP/CMP/
2005/8/Add.2; Decision 2/CMP.2, FCCC/KP/CMP/2006/10/Add.1; Decision 3/CMP.2,
FCCC/KP/CMP/2006/10/Add.1; Decision 3/CMP.3, FCCC/KP/CMP/2007/9/Add.1; Decision
5/CMP.4, FCCC/KP/CMP/2008/11/Add.1.
[71] See Decision 2/CMP.1, FCCC/KP/CMP/2005/8/Add.1 ('Decision 15/CP.7'); Decision 3/
CMP.1, FCCC/KP/CMP/2005/8/Add.1 ('Decision 17/CP.7'); Decision 4/CMP.1, FCCC/KP/
CMP/2005/ 8/Add.1 ('Decision 21/CP.8 and 18/CP.9'); Decision 5/CMP.1, FCCC/KP/CMP/
2005/8/Add.1 ('Decision 19/CP.9'); Decision 6/CMP.1, FCCC/KP/CMP/2005/8/
Add.1 ('Decision 14/CP.10'); Decision 7/CMP.1, FCCC/KP/CMP/2005/8/Add.1; Decision 8/
CMP.1, FCCC/KP/CMP/2005/8/Add.1; Decision 1/CMP.2, FCCC/KP/CMP/2006/10/Add.1;
Decision 2/CMP.3, FCCC/KP/CMP/2007/9/Add.1; Decision 9/CMP.3, FCCC/KP/CMP/2007/
9/Add.1; Decision 2/CMP.4, FCCC/KP/CMP/2008/11/Add.1.
[72] See M. Wara, 'Measuring the Clean Development Mechanism's Performance and Potential'
(2008) 55 *UCLA Law Review* 1759.
[73] See T. Treves *et al.* (eds.), *Non-Compliance Procedures and Mechanisms and the Effectiveness of
International Environmental Agreements* (The Hague: TMC Asser Press, 2009).
[74] See J. E. Viñuales, 'Legal Techniques for Dealing with Scientific Uncertainty in Environmental
Law' (2010) 43 *Vanderbilt Journal of Transnational Law* 437.

consequences,[75] are ill-suited to manage cases of non-compliance resulting from the inability (financial or technical) of a State to abide by a norm. This observation lies at the roots of a new approach to compliance with international law,[76] which considers compliance as a process that must be managed through a variety of non-adversarial methods, such as financial and technical assistance or procedures where the adversarial character of traditional dispute resolution mechanisms is attenuated. In this section, we provide an overview of the types of techniques available to 'facilitate' compliance and 'manage' non-compliance. A more detailed analysis is provided in Chapter 9.

2.5.2 Incentive mechanisms

Incentive mechanisms for the respect of environmental standards have two principal objectives, namely to increase efficiency (by reducing the cost of compliance) and to compensate for the lack of technical and financial capacity in some countries (through assistance mechanisms). The search for efficiency is mostly relevant for developed countries, whereas developing countries are mainly interested in technical and financial assistance.

Examples of techniques that promote *efficiency* may be found in the flexible mechanisms under the Kyoto Protocol and, to some extent, under the Montreal Protocol.[77] To understand how these mechanisms can reduce the costs of compliance with environmental standards, let us take a closer look at some of these mechanisms. Pursuant to Article 3 of the Kyoto Protocol, the countries listed in Annex I to the UNFCCC must limit their average emissions of greenhouse gases during the periods 2008–12 and (when the amendment enters into force) 2013–20 to a certain percentage (set out in Annex B of the Protocol) of their emissions in 1990 (base year). To comply with this obligation, States may adopt 'national' and/or 'international' measures. Within the latter, Article 17 of the Protocol sets up a system of emissions trading to allow Annex B States (or companies based in those States) to meet their obligations more efficiently. The efficiency gain comes from the fact that the ability to emit a tonne of carbon dioxide (or its equivalent of another regulated greenhouse gas) has a different value according to the situation of each State or company. Such variation stems from differences in the production process used by States/companies or from the relative costs (from one State/company to another) entailed by the introduction of cleaner technology or, still, from

---

[75] See *infra* Chapter 8.

[76] See A. Chayes and A. Handler Chayes, *The New Sovereignty: Compliance with International Regulatory Agreements* (Cambridge MA: Harvard University Press, 1995); E. Brown Weiss and H. K. Jacobson (eds.), *Engaging Countries: Strengthening Compliance With International Environmental Accords* (Cambridge MA: MIT Press, 1998).

[77] See Arts. 2.5 (transfers of production) and 2.8(a) (mechanism known as the 'bubble') of the Montreal Protocol on Substances that Deplete the Ozone Layer, 16 September 1987, 1522 UNTS 3 ('Montreal Protocol').

differences in the energy matrix of a country. It has been observed that Canada, which has increased its emissions by 29 per cent compared to the base year (1990), will only be able to fulfil its obligations (reductions of 6 per cent compared to 1990) by acquiring emission credits accumulated by Russia, sometimes referred to as 'Russian hot air'.[78] Flexible mechanisms give Canada, as well as other States such as Spain or Japan, the possibility of acquiring rights to emit owned by or generated in other States, such as Russia, at a lower cost. However, this possibility poses a number of problems that will be discussed in Chapter 5.

Articles 6 and 12 of the Kyoto Protocol contemplate two other flexible mechanisms. We will discuss their operation in Chapter 5, but it may be useful to make a brief reference here to the 'clean development mechanism' ('CDM') provided for in Article 12. The CDM allows an industrialised country (Annex B of the Protocol) to sponsor a project to reduce emissions in a developing country and to obtain, at the end of a verification procedure, an amount of carbon credits equal to the reduction of emissions achieved (i.e. the difference between the level of emissions achieved as a result of the project and those that would have resulted in the absence of the project). These credits can provide some efficiency gains for industrialised countries. Indeed, achieving such reductions in a developing country is normally cheaper than reducing emissions in the industrialised country by other means, such as the introduction of environmental taxes, emissions caps or technology requirements.[79] At the same time, the developing countries where such projects are conducted benefit from a contribution of capital and technology, which constitutes a form of assistance.

The latter point serves as a transition to the discussion of *assistance mechanisms*. Several MEAs recognise the special situation of some of their member States and, in particular, their need for assistance to fulfil their obligations. For example, Article 4(2) of the Basel Convention[80] requires States to set up adequate disposal facilities, if possible located within their territory, allowing for the 'environmentally sound' management of hazardous waste. However, for this requirement to be met, a certain level of technological advancement is necessary. In this regard, Article 14(1) contemplates the establishment of regional and sub-regional financial[81] and technology transfer

---

[78] See 'Carry on Kyoto', *The Economist,* 7 October 2004. Canada has not subscribed to the second commitment period (2013–20) adopted at the Doha Conference, in December 2012.

[79] The economic dimension of efficiency gains that are permitted by this mechanism is analysed in M. A. Toman, R. D. Morganstern and J. Anderson, 'The Economics of "When" Flexibility in the Design of Greenhouse Gas Abatement Policies' in *Resources for the Future Discussion Paper* 99–38-REV, 2–3, 1999.

[80] Basel Convention, *supra* n. 29.

[81] A technical assistance fund has been created to this end, sustained by voluntary contributions. It is known as the 'Trust Fund to Assist Developing Countries and Other Countries in Need of Technical Assistance in the implementation of the Basel Convention on the Control of Transboundary Movements of Hazardous Wastes and Their Disposal'. See 'Enlargement

mechanisms.[82] Similarly, under the CITES, a fund has been established to finance technical assistance activities.[83] These are only two examples of a recurrent feature of MEAs.[84]

In the last years, the question of financial and technological assistance has received sustained attention in climate negotiations. A Green Climate Fund has been set up, based in South Korea, to finance measures for the mitigation of climate change and the adaptation to its effects. Until then, the main source of multilateral climate finance had been the GEF. The GEF also serves as the financial mechanism of other MEAs, such as the CBD, the POP Convention or the UNCCD.[85] In addition, environmental finance is also available from regional development banks[86] as well as from a number of market mechanisms, including the CDM or, potentially the so-called 'REDD' (Reduced Emissions from Deforestation and Forest Degradation).

2.5.3 Managing scientific uncertainty

Some of the techniques mentioned above are also important to tackle one of the main challenges faced by environmental regimes, namely scientific and technological change.[87]

To facilitate the understanding of these techniques, it is useful to distinguish four main stages in the development of an environmental regime.[88] The first stage concerns the identification of an environmental problem, despite the potentially significant scientific uncertainties surrounding the question, as well

---

of the Scope of the Technical Cooperation Trust Fund', Decision V/32, Conference of Parties, 5th meeting, *Report of the Fifth Meeting of the Conference of the Parties to the Basel Convention*, Annex, 10 December 1999, UN Doc. UNEP/CHW.5/29, p. 57.

[82] See *Basel Convention Regional and Coordinating Centres* brochure prepared by the Secretariat of the Convention, available at: www.basel.int (last visited 3 February 2014).

[83] Technical Cooperation, Resolution of the Conference of Parties, Third Session, New Delhi (India), 25 February–8 March 1981, CITES Conf 3.4.

[84] See, in particular: Protocol to the 1979 Convention on Long-range Transboundary Air Pollution, on the Long-term Financing of the Cooperative Programme for Monitoring and Evaluation of the Long-range Transmission of Air Pollutants in Europe ('EMEP'), 28 September 1984, 1491 UNTS 167, the Small Grants Fund of the Ramsar Convention (SGF), www.ramsar.org/SGF/ (last visited 3 February 2014); Multilateral Fund on the Implementation of Montreal Protocol (better known by its acronym 'MFMP'), 29 June 1990, UN Doc. UNEP/OzL.Pro.2/3; World Heritage Fund, Convention for the Protection of the World Cultural and Natural Heritage, 16 November 1972, 1037 UNTS 151, Art. 15ff. On this subject, see L. Boisson de Chazournes, 'Technical and Financial Assistance' in Bodansky *et al.*, *supra* n. 15, pp. 945–73.

[85] Instrument for the Establishment of the Restructured Global Environmental Facility, GEF, October 2011, pp. 7–41, Art. I(6), available at: www.thegef.org (last visited 3 February 2014).

[86] African Development Bank (AFDB) and the African Development Fund, Asian Development Bank (ADB) and the Asian Development Fund, Inter-American Development Bank (IDB) and its Fund for Special Operations.

[87] See Viñuales, *supra* n. 74.

[88] See H. Breitmeier, O. R. Young and M. Zurn, *Analyzing International Environmental Regimes: From Case Study to Database* (Cambridge MA: MIT Press, 2007).

Stage 1: Advocacy	(1) Precautionary reasoning
Stage 2: Design	(2) Framework-protocol approach (3) Advisory scientific bodies
Stage 3: Implementation	(4) Law-making by treaty bodies (5) Managerial approaches to compliance (6) Prior informed consent ('PIC') (7) Environmental impact assessment and monitoring
Stage 4: Reparation	(8) Provisional measures (9) Evidence (10) Facilitated liability

Figure 2.2: Legal techniques for dealing with scientific uncertainty

as the advocacy efforts aimed at the development of a legal regime to manage the problem. The second stage focuses on regime design. In selecting the components of a regime and designing its structure, it is indeed very important to take into account the need to cope with scientific and technological change. The third stage concerns the implementation of the environmental regime thus designed. Over time, the regime will likely have to manage various sources of 'regime stress', either because the political or economic underpinnings of the treaty or the scientific understanding of the problem have changed. The fourth and final stage relates to the scientific uncertainties involved in repairing environmental harm that the regime has been unable to prevent. This distinction is of a purely analytical nature and may not always provide an accurate description of the life of an environmental regime. Moreover, some techniques may operate at more than one stage. Yet, the distinction remains useful to clarify those stages at which a given technique is more likely to operate or, in other words, to understand the critical junctures at which a given technique may be particularly useful.

Figure 2.2[89] links the four stages of regime development to a variety of legal techniques used to manage risk and uncertainty. At the *first stage*, the precautionary 'approach' or 'principle' may be a powerful technique to gather momentum on the need to regulate a given environmental problem.[90] The legal dimensions of this technique will be examined in Chapter 3. Suffice it to mention here that the main objective of precaution as a technique is precisely to encourage action on an environmental problem even when it is still poorly understood from a scientific standpoint. The earliest prominent illustration of the successful use of this technique is the

---

[89] Source: Viñuales, *supra* n. 74, p. 448.
[90] See A. Trouwborst, *Evolution and Status of the Precautionary Principle in International Law* (Dordrecht: Kluwer, 2002).

development of the 'ozone regime' (i.e. the Vienna Convention on the Protection of the Ozone Layer of 1985 and, most importantly, the Montreal Protocol of 1987). Indeed, the stringency of the phase out obligations introduced by the Montreal Protocol contrasts with the scientific uncertainty that (still) prevailed in late 1987 on the causes of stratospheric ozone depletion.[91]

Scientific uncertainty at stage one may significantly influence the regime features negotiated and incorporated in the final treaty at *stage two*. Regimes adopted in a context of scientific uncertainty must be capable of integrating changes in the scientific understanding of the problem regulated. A common technique is to conclude framework treaties laying out an institutional structure to facilitate the subsequent adoption of more specific obligations, usually in the form of protocols.[92] The Vienna Convention (framework) and the Montreal Protocol (specific obligations) offer a good illustration of this technique. Other prominent illustrations include the eight protocols adopted within the framework of the LRTAP Convention,[93] the UNFCCC and the Kyoto Protocol or the Convention on Biological Diversity and the two protocols adopted to specify the CBD's provisions (on Biosafety, in 2000, and on Access and Benefit Sharing, in 2010). Another important design feature of environmental treaties, whether old or new,[94] is the creation of subsidiary scientific bodies, which help adapt the regime to new scientific and technical data.[95] In some cases, scientific bodies are empowered to issue recommendations to the COP for the listing of new substances, as in the case of the POP Convention.[96]

The *third stage*, i.e. the implementation of the regime, involves the use of many techniques. Of particular note are the resort to '*droit dérivé*' and the provision of financial and technical assistance, which have both been discussed earlier. In addition, some treaties set up a system of 'prior informed consent' to ensure that dangerous substances and activities are only sent to countries that are willing and capable of handling them properly.[97] In a similar vein, a number of treaties require the conduct of an environmental impact assessment

---

[91] This point is highlighted in a book by the chief US diplomat who negotiated the Montreal Protocol. See R. E. Benedick, *Ozone Diplomacy* (Cambridge MA: Harvard University Press, 1998).

[92] See on this subject: A. Kiss, 'Les traités-cadre: une technique juridique caractéristique du droit international de l'environnement' (1993) 39 *Annuaire français de droit international* 792.

[93] Convention on Long-range Transboundary Air Pollution, 13 November 1979, 1302 UNTS 217 ('LRTAP Convention'). These protocols are related to long-term financing of the co-operative programme for monitoring and evaluation of the long-range transport of air pollutants in Europe (EMEP), the reduction of sulphur emissions, of nitrogen oxides, of volatile organic compounds (VOCs), and the further reduction of sulphur emissions, of persistent organic pollutants (POPs), of heavy metals, and of acidification, eutrophication in the tropospheric ozone.

[94] See e.g. Convention on Wetlands of International Importance, especially as Waterfowl Habitat, 2 February 1971, 996 UNTS 245 ('Ramsar Convention') and Resolution 5.5 (1993) of the Ramsar COP.

[95] See e.g. the role of the EMEP in the LRTAP Convention, *supra* n. 93, Art. 9.

[96] See POP Convention, *supra* n. 29, Art. 8.

[97] International Code of Conduct on the Distribution and Use of Pesticides, adopted by the FAO Conference in Resolution 10/85, 28 November 1985; London Guidelines for the Exchange of Information on Chemicals in International Trade, Decision 15/30 of the UNEP Governing

to clarify the implications of embarking on a project that may affect the environment.[98] This requirement also arises from customary international law, although its specific contours remain to be specified.[99]

Finally, scientific uncertainty may also pose some difficulties in connection with the reparation of environmental harm. Several techniques have been developed to cope with uncertainty at this *fourth stage*, including some procedural tools used within judicial proceedings and a number of special liability regimes. The scientific uncertainties raised by the complex ecological processes linking a set of acts to the occurrence of environmental damage can be dealt with by shifting the burden of proof to the respondent, by relaxing the applicable standard of proof[100] and/or by making expert assistance more readily available for courts and tribunals.[101] However, even when the claimant has discharged its burden, the author of the conduct under review may show that it took every reasonable step to prevent the damage (and that, therefore, it is neither subjectively at fault nor objectively in breach of an obligation) or that no specific link between its act and the damage can be established. Clarifying this link may be difficult or even impossible in the current state of science. By way of illustration, whereas the link between elements such as emissions of greenhouse gases, climate change and the adverse effects of climate change, is reasonably clear, the link between the specific emissions of a factory and the specific harm suffered by a given community is not. Instead of managing such uncertainty through evidentiary techniques, one could establish a multi-tiered regime focusing on the reparation of the harm arising from some activities involving a certain level of risk. 'Facilitated' liability regimes admit different degrees. Eliminating the need to prove fault or breach (strict liability) would be a way of tackling some forms of scientific uncertainty. Creating a reparation framework applicable to any damage connected (even if the causal link cannot be fully established) with a regulated activity would address other forms of scientific uncertainty. This said, strict liability regimes are exceptional in international law. With the exception of damage caused by space

Council of 25 May 1989; Rotterdam Convention on the Prior Informed Consent Procedure for Certain Hazardous Chemicals and Pesticides in International Trade, 10 September 1998, 2244 UNTS 337 ('PIC Convention'). See P. Barrios, 'The Rotterdam Convention on Hazardous Chemicals: A Meaningful Step towards Environmental Protection?' (2004) 16 *Georgetown International Environmental Law Review* 679.

[98] Convention on Environmental Impact Assessment in a Transboundary Context, 25 February 1991, 1989 UNTS 309. See N. Craik, *The International Law of Environmental Impact Assessment* (Cambridge University Press, 2008).

[99] See *infra* Chapter 3.

[100] On the difficulties of evidence, see C. Foster, *Science and the Precautionary Principle in International Courts and Tribunals* (Cambridge University Press, 2011).

[101] On the recourse to experts, see L. Savadogo, 'Le recours des juridictions internationales à des experts' (2004) 50 *Annuaire français de droit international* 231.

objects,[102] there is no strict liability of States as such in international law. Where a strict liability regime has been introduced,[103] it is one of 'civil liability' whereby liability is channelled towards the economic operator who conducts or benefits from the regulated activity (e.g. the owner of the tanker transporting oil or of the nuclear facility producing electricity). A more innovative framework could potentially arise from the recent climate negotiations on the 'loss and damage' arising from the effects of climate change.[104]

2.5.4 Management of non-compliance

The third type of technique concerns the management of non-compliance.[105] The concept of 'non-compliance' must be distinguished from that of 'breach'. Although there is some overlap between the two concepts, *non-compliance* has a broader scope because it encompasses not only clear 'breaches' but also conduct that is only temporarily inconsistent with an environmental obligation, immaterial breaches (e.g. purely procedural breaches), or even deficiencies that signal a potential breach (e.g. some initial steps of a composite conduct which, taken together, would amount to a breach). In addition, the concept of 'non-compliance' seeks to avoid the adversarial connotations entailed by the concept of 'breach'. It characterises the non-conformity with a standard as a deviation that must be 'contained' and 'managed' until it is corrected.

In this context, it is easier to understand the peculiar features of 'non-compliance procedures' ('NCPs'). First, NCPs can be triggered not only at the request of another State or the Secretariat of a treaty (as other adversarial mechanisms), but also by the State that is in a situation of non-compliance.[106] Second, NCPs are not subject to the same standards of evidence and due process as judicial proceedings.[107] Third, the primary objective of NCPs is not to deter, repair or punish a breach but to manage a deviation, whether voluntary or involuntary. As a result, more often than not, their outcome is the provision of financial or technical assistance rather than an outright sanction.[108] It is only when the body in charge of the procedure detects a

---

[102] See Convention on International Liability for Damage Caused by Space Objects, 29 March 1972, 961 UNTS 187, Art. 2.

[103] See A. Kiss and D. Shelton, 'Strict Liability in International Environmental Law', in T. M. Ndiaye and R. Wolfrum (eds.), *Liber Amicorum Judge Thomas A. Mensah* (Leiden: Martinus Nijhoff, 2007), pp. 1131–51.

[104] 'Approaches to Address Loss and Damage associated with Climate Change Impacts in Developing Countries that are Particularly Vulnerable to the Adverse Effects of Climate Change to Enhance Adaptive Capacity', Draft decision -/CP.18 (December 2012).

[105] See Treves *et al., supra* n. 73.

[106] See F. Romanin Jacur, 'Triggering Non-Compliance Procedures', in Treves *et al. supra* n. 73, pp. 373–87.

[107] See M. Montini, 'Procedural Guarantees in Non-Compliance Mechanisms', in Treves *et al., supra* n. 73, pp. 389–405.

[108] See E. Milano, 'The Outcomes of the Procedure and their Legal Effects' in Treves *et al., supra* n. 73, pp. 407–18.

wilful violation by the State concerned that the outcome may be a sanction. Finally, these sanctions are always internal in that they can only involve the suspension of the benefits arising from the treaty. Thus, the findings of an NCP procedure do not trigger, in principle, the secondary norms of international responsibility[109] but another set of secondary norms specifically designed for each treaty context.

We will explore in more detail the operation of these mechanisms in Chapter 9. Suffice it here to illustrate the transition from assistance to sanction with an example from the Kyoto Protocol.[110] The Kyoto NCP is managed by a Compliance Committee consisting of two 'branches', the 'facilitative' and the 'enforcement' branch. The first seeks to facilitate compliance through the provision of technical and/or financial assistance,[111] whereas the second is empowered to order sanctions, such as restricting access to the flexible mechanisms or even imposing a penalty reducing the overall amount of emissions available under the second commitment period.[112] In practice, however, the enforcement powers of Compliance Committees are very limited. Their main means of pressure seems to be the reputational damage that can be inflicted upon a State.

2.6 The legal environment of international environmental law

To conclude the brief characterisation of international environmental law provided in this chapter, it is worth briefly describing the overall position of this body of law within the international legal order. The specificities of international environmental law reviewed so far constitute in many respects a *lex specialis* derogating from the rules of general international law otherwise applicable.

But this is not to say that international environmental law as a branch or the more specific treaty regimes established by MEAs are to be considered as self-sustaining or self-sufficient regimes cut-off from the international order.[113] Rather, the array of norms and treaties that we refer to as international environmental law are part of international law and, in their historical development, they often had to rely on general international law. Despite their

---

[109] See L. Pineschi, 'Non-Compliance Procedures and the Law of State Responsibility' in Treves *et al, supra* n. 73, pp. 483–97.

[110] See Art. 18 of the Kyoto Protocol, *supra* n. 14 and Decision 27/CMP.1, FCCC/KP/CMP/2005/8/Add.3.

[111] See Decision 27/CMP.1, Annex, Section IV, para. 4 and 6.

[112] *Ibid.*, Section V, para. 6 and Section XV. The Committee has applied sanctions to Sections XV to Greece and Croatia. See Compliance Committee, Final Decision: Greece, 17 April 2008, CC-2007-1-8/Greece/EB; Compliance Committee, Final Decision: Croatia, 19 February 2010, CC-2009-1-8/Croatia/EB.

[113] See generally P.-M. Dupuy, 'L'unité de l'ordre juridique international: cours général de droit international public (2000)', (2002) 297 *Recueil des cours de l'Académie de droit international de La Haye*, 9–489, 428 ss.

specificities, the main actors and formal sources of international environmental law are indeed those of international law. Similarly, some of its principles, such as the principles of no-harm, prevention, co-operation or reasonable utilisation, are in many respects adaptations of broader principles derived from considerations of good neighbourliness.[114] Finally, normative priority among different norms (including norms of international environmental law) is also governed by the general conflict rules arising from international law, in particular the overriding character of *jus cogens*.

One important question in this connection is the relationship between different forms of allocating priority. Some environmental norms could conflict either with another (non-environmental) *lex specialis* or with general norms that command authority as a result of their substance. To understand the relationship between environmental norms and the other two categories of norms, it is necessary to examine the substantial hierarchy of international environmental norms. This is, of course, an exercise that can only be carried out on a norm-by-norm basis. But some general observations appear nevertheless useful to clarify the terms of the inquiry.[115] In international law, the substantive hierarchy of a norm can be expressed in many ways, including through its characterisation as a peremptory norm,[116] an *erga omnes* obligation,[117] or the expression of an essential interest within the meaning of the customary necessity defence.[118] These concepts trigger different hierarchical effects. Whereas the key feature of peremptory norms is that they cannot be derogated from, *erga omnes* obligations are peculiar in that they are owed to all other States and could potentially give a right of action to any State.[119] An 'interest' can be characterised as an 'essential interest', and thus open the gate to the customary necessity defence, through a variety of channels, including by reference to an existing customary norm protecting that interest.[120]

In the current state of international law, it seems difficult to consider that some environmental norms are of a peremptory nature.[121] Although in the

---

[114] See *infra* Chapter 3.

[115] See J. E. Viñuales, 'La protección del medio ambiente y su jerarquía normativa en derecho internacional' (2008) 13 *Revista Colombiana de Derecho Internacional* 11.

[116] See A. Orakhelashvili, *Peremptory Norms in International Law* (Oxford University Press, 2006).

[117] See M. Ragazzi, *The Concept of International Obligations erga omnes* (Oxford University Press, 2000).

[118] In international practice, there are also some adjectives intended to attach particular importance to certain norms by virtue of their substance. See in this regard: R. Kolb, 'Jus cogens, intangibilité, intransgressibilité, dérogation "positive" et "négative"' (2005) *Revue générale de droit international public* 305.

[119] See F. Voeffray, *L'actio popularis ou la défense de l'intérêt collectif devant les juridictions internationals* (Paris: Presses universitaires de France, 2004).

[120] See Viñuales, *supra* n. 57, 248–9.

[121] On this debate, see E. Kornicker, *Ius cogens und Umweltvölkerrecht. Kriterien, Quellen und Rechtsforgen zwingender Völkerrechtsnormen und deren Anwendung auf das*

Gabčíkovo-Nagymaros case, the ICJ left this question open and, therefore, did not rule out this possibility,[122] two further elements suggest the absence of peremptory environmental norms. The first is the withdrawal by the ILC, following opposition from a number of States, of Article 19 of the 1996 Draft Articles on the Responsibility of States for Internationally Wrongful Acts, which characterised wilful and massive environmental damage as a 'crime'.[123] The second element can be derived from the conclusions of the ILC Study Group on the Fragmentation of International Law.[124] The group analysed the difference between the concepts of *jus cogens* (or peremptory norms) and *erga omnes* obligations and concluded as follows:

> It is recognized that while all obligations established by *jus cogens* norms, as referred to in conclusion (33) above, also have the character of *erga omnes* obligations, the reverse is not necessarily true. Not all *erga omnes* obligations are established by peremptory norms of general international law. This is the case, for example, of certain obligations under 'the principles and rules concerning the basic rights of the human person', *as well as of some obligations relating to the global commons.*[125]

Conversely, this observation suggests that certain environmental norms, because of their purpose, have an *erga omnes* character. This conclusion is confirmed by the work of the ILC on State Responsibility. Article 48 of the 2001 ILC Articles[126] mentions the possibility that the responsibility of a State may be invoked by a State other than the injured State, if the obligation that has been breached is owed to a group of States or to the international community as a whole. Paragraph 7 of the commentary to the ILC Articles refers, as an example, to obligations for the protection of the environment.[127]

The importance given to environmental considerations is also reflected in the status of 'essential interest' that the ICJ has granted to the protection of the environment, first in the *Gabčíkovo-Nagymaros* case[128] and then in the *Pulp Mills* case.[129] This significant step was possible thanks to a subtle interaction

---

Umweltvölkerrecht (Basel: Helbing Lichtenhahn Verlag, 1997). This author has summarised her thesis in E. Korniker, 'State Community Interests, Jus Cogens and Protection of the Global Environment: Developing Criteria for Peremptory Norms' (1998–1999) 11 *Georgetown International Environmental Law Review* 101.

[122] *Gabčíkovo-Nagymaros Project, supra* n. 64, para. 112.

[123] See M. Fitzmaurice, 'International Protection of the Environment', (2001) 293 *Recueil des cours de l'Académie de droit international de la Haye,* 9–488, 141.

[124] Conclusions of the work of the Study on the Fragmentation of International Law: Difficulties arising from the Diversification and Expansion of International Law, (2006) 2(2) *Yearbook of the International Law Commission.*

[125] *Ibid.,* conclusion 38 (italics added).

[126] Draft Articles on the Responsibility of States for Internationally Wrongful Acts, (2001) 2(2) *Yearbook of the International Law Commission.*

[127] See Draft Articles on the Responsibility of States for Internationally Wrongful Acts and Commentary, (2001) 2(2) *Yearbook of the International Law Commission* ad Art. 48, para. 7 of the Commentary.

[128] *Gabčíkovo-Nagymaros Project, supra* n. 64, para. 53.   [129] *Pulp Mills, supra* n. 64, para. 72.

between the emergence of a customary norm and the recognition of the importance attached to the interest protected by this norm. This link is spelled out in the paragraph of the *Gabčíkovo-Nagymaros* decision where the ICJ recognises the essential character of environmental protection.[130] Indeed, the Court refers, *inter alia*, to its Advisory Opinion on the *Legality of Nuclear Weapons*,[131] issued the previous year, to emphasise 'the great significance that it attaches to respect for the environment, not only for States but also for the whole of mankind'.[132] The importance attached to environmental protection has also other legal effects. It is mentioned by the Court to buttress its conclusion that new environmental protection norms must be taken into account in implementing the treaty in question.[133]

Overall, the foregoing observations suggest that in the current state of international law some environmental norms can be considered as *erga omnes* obligations. In addition, the protection of the environment may also qualify as an essential interest of a State within the meaning of the customary necessity defence.

Select bibliography

Andonova, L., 'Public-Private Partnerships for the Earth: Politics and Patterns of Hybrid Authority in the Multilateral System' (2010) 10 *Global Environmental Politics* 25.

Boisson de Chazournes, L., 'Le fonds sur l'environnement mondial, recherche et conquête de son identité' (1995) 41 *Annuaire français de droit international* 612.

'Technical and Financial Assistance' in D. Bodansky, J. Brunnée and E. Hey (eds.), *The Oxford Handbook of International Environmental Law* (Oxford University Press, 2007), pp. 945–73.

Breitmeier, H., O. R. Young and M. Zurn, *Analyzing International Environmental Regimes: From Case Study to Database* (Cambridge MA: MIT Press, 2007).

Brown Weiss, E., 'International Environmental Law: Contemporary Issues and the Emergence of a New World Order' (1995) 81 *Georgetown Law Journal* 675.

Brown Weiss, E. and H. K. Jacobson (eds.), *Engaging Countries: Strengthening Compliance With International Environmental Accords* (Cambridge MA: MIT Press, 1998).

Brunnée, J., 'COPing with Consent: Law-making under Multilateral Environmental Agreements' (2002) 15 *Leiden Journal of International Law* 1.

[130] See Viñuales, *supra* n. 57, pp. 248–9.

[131] In its opinion, the ICJ held as follows: 'the environment is not an abstraction but represents the living space, the quality of life and the very health of human beings, including generations unborn. The existence of the general obligation of States to ensure that activities within their jurisdiction and control respect the environment of other States or of areas beyond national control is now part of the corpus of international law relating to the environment', *Legality of Nuclear Weapons, supra* n. 7, para. 29.

[132] *Gabčíkovo-Nagymaros Project, supra* n. 64, para. 53 *in fine.* [133] *Ibid.*, para. 112 *in fine.*

Churchill, R. R. and G. Ulfstein, 'Autonomous Institutional Arrangements in Multilateral Environmental Agreements: A Little-Noticed Phenomenon in International Law' (2000) 94 *American Journal of International Law* 623.

Desai, B. H., *Multilateral Environmental Agreements. Legal Status of the Secretariats* (Cambridge University Press, 2010).

Dupuy, P.-M., 'Formation of Customary International Law and General Principles', in D. Bodansky, J. Brunnée and E. Hey (eds.), *The Oxford Handbook of International Environmental Law* (Oxford University Press, 2007), pp. 449–66.

'Où en est le droit international de l'environnement à la fin du siècle?' (1997) *Revue générale de droit international public* 879.

'Soft Law and the International Law of the Environment' (1990–1991) 12 *Michigan Journal of International Law* 420.

Dupuy, P.-M. and J. E. Viñuales (eds.), *Harnessing Foreign Investment to Promote Environmental Protection: Incentives and Safeguards* (Cambridge University Press, 2013).

Francioni, F. and P.-M. Dupuy, *Preliminary Feasibility Study for the Establishment of a UN Environmental Organisation or Agency* (Florence: European University Institute, 2005).

Haas, P., R. O. Keohane and M. A. Levy (eds.), *Institutions for the Earth: Sources of Effective International Environmental Protection* (Cambridge MA: MIT Press, 1993).

Iovane, M., 'La participation de la société civile à l'élaboration et à l'application du droit international de l'environnement' (2008) *Revue générale de droit international public* 465.

Ivanova, M., 'UNEP in Global Environmental Governance: Design, Leadership, Location' (2010) 10 *Global Environmental Politics* 30.

Kerbrat, Y., 'La Cour internationale de justice face aux enjeux de protection de l'environnement' (2011) *Revue générale de droit international public* 39.

Kiss, A., 'Les traités-cadre: une technique juridique caractéristique du droit international de l'environnement' (1993) 39 *Annuaire français de droit international* 792.

Korniker, E., 'State Community Interests, Jus Cogens and Protection of the Global Environment: Developing Criteria for Peremptory Norms' (1998–9) 11 *Georgetown International Environmental Law* 101.

Lavieille, J. M. (ed.), *Conventions de protection de l'environnement, Secrétariats, Conférences des parties, Comités d'experts* (Limoges: PULIM, 1999).

Martin, J.-C., 'The United Nations Compensation Commission Practice with Regards to Environmental Claims', in S. Maljean-Dubois and Y. Kerbrat (eds.), *The Transformation of International Environmental Law* (Oxford: Hart Publishing, 2011), pp. 251–67.

Morgera, E., *Corporate Accountability in International Environmental Law* (Oxford University Press, 2009).

Pomade, A., *La société civile et le droit de l'environnement. Contribution à la réflexion sur les théories des sources du droit et de la validité* (Paris: LGDJ, 2010).

Richardson, B. J., *Socially Responsible Investment Law. Regulating the Unseen Polluters* (Oxford University Press, 2008).

Romanin Jacur, F., *The Dynamics of Multilateral Environmental Agreements. Institutional Architectures and Law-Making Processes* (Naples: Editoriale Scientifica, 2013).

Savadogo, L., 'Le recours des juridictions internationales à des experts' (2004) 50 *Annuaire français de droit international* 231.

Speth, J. G. and P. Haas, *Global Environmental Governance* (Washington D.C.: Island Press, 2006).

Stewart, R., B. Kingsbury and B. Rudyk, *Climate Finance: Regulatory and Funding Strategies for Climate Change and Global Development* (New York: NYU University Press, 2009).

Streck, C., 'The Global Environmental Facility – A Role Model for International Environmental Governance?' (2001) 1 *Global Environmental Politics* 71.

Treves, T., L. Pineschi, A. Tanzi, C. Pitea, C. Ragni and F. Romanin Jacur (eds.), *Non-Compliance Procedures and Mechanisms and the Effectiveness of International Environmental Agreements* (The Hague: T.M.C. Asser Press, 2009).

Viñuales, J. E., 'The Contribution of the International Court of Justice to the Development of International Environmental Law: A Contemporary Assessment' (2008) 32 *Fordham International Law Journal* 232.

'Legal Techniques for Dealing with Scientific Uncertainty in Environmental Law' (2010) 43 *Vanderbilt Journal of Transnational Law* 437.

'Managing Abidance by Standards for the Protection of the Environment', in A. Cassese (ed.), *Realizing Utopia* (Oxford University Press, 2012), pp. 326–39.

3

The principles of international environmental law

3.1 Introduction

In the preceding chapter, we left open the question of the principles and concepts that underlie international environmental law and define its contours. This chapter can therefore be seen as the continuation of Chapter 2, as it further develops the characterisation of international environmental law outlined there. In addition, the analysis of the principles and concepts of international environmental law is an important step in the study of its substantive aspects, which will be discussed in the second part of this book.

To understand the importance of the principles and concepts of international environmental law, as well as the difference between these two categories, it is helpful to first introduce some analytical distinctions (3.2). These distinctions will allow us to present the fundamental principles and concepts that conform the structure of international environmental law in the light of the two main values advanced by this body of law, namely prevention (3.3) and balance (3.4). The last section will link these principles and concepts to the environmental regimes examined in the second part of this book (3.5).

3.2 Some analytical distinctions

The elements that form the subject matter of this chapter have already been discussed in some detail by legal commentators, although they are often presented in different ways depending on the criteria employed by each author. To facilitate a useful comparison with these other views, distinctions that are sometimes implicit in these analyses should first be made explicit, so as to lay the ground for an introductory discussion of the material.

First, we must distinguish between the use of the term 'principle' to refer to a type of statement or formulation of a norm,[1] and its use to describe the legal

---

[1] See U. Beyerlin, 'Different Types of Norms in International Environmental Law', in D. Bodansky, J. Brunnée and E. Hey (eds.), *The Oxford Handbook of International Environmental Law* (Oxford University Press, 2007), Chapter 18.

foundation of a norm, whether it is a treaty, customary international law or, subsidiarily, a general principle of law.[2] These are two different questions because the formulation of a norm as a principle, for example in a soft-law instrument, says little about its legal grounding in one formal source of international law. The assessment of whether a given principle has a legal character is an exercise that must be performed on a case-by-case basis, as will become evident later.

Second, it is useful to classify environmental norms using three categories (concepts, principles, rules),[3] according to their degree of generality/particularity. Intuitively, this distinction suggests that, as and when a norm becomes more abstract, its practical application in a given case is more prone to controversy, and vice-versa. A norm such as the obligation to prohibit the dumping of waste in the sea ('rule')[4] clearly requires a more specific conduct than the norm prescribing the duty of States to ensure that activities under their control do not cause environmental damage ('principle').[5] The latter is, in turn, more precise than the declaration that the seabed beyond national jurisdiction is a 'common heritage of mankind'[6] or that the conservation of biological diversity is 'a common concern of humankind'[7] ('concepts'). Another way to understand the distinction based on the degree of generality/particularity is to consider concepts as guiding norms that are implemented by principles, which, in turn, are realised by rules.

Third, an alternative approach in the analysis of principles and concepts is to look at the functions they perform. One important function is to provide a certain collective identity for a field of international law. In the same way as administrative law differs from labour law or criminal law by the operation of a number of principles specific to each of these branches of domestic law, the various branches of international law also have some distinctive features. One distinctive feature of international environmental law is the protection of a particular object, namely the environment. This 'identity function' may be performed by principles that are not specifically environmental (e.g. the no harm principle) as long as they have been reformulated in environmental terms. Thus, the function of the no harm principle is no longer to protect the

---

[2] G. Abi-Saab, 'Les sources du droit international: Essai de déconstruction', in *Liber Amicorum en hommage au Professeur Eduardo Jiménez de Aréchaga*, vol. I (Montevideo: Fundación de Cultura Internacional, 1994), pp. 29–49.

[3] This distinction is taken from R. Dworkin, *Taking Rights Seriously* (Cambridge MA: Harvard University Press, 1977), p. 22, and employed in an environmental context by Beyerlin, *supra* n. 1.

[4] Convention for the Prevention of Marine Pollution by Dumping of Wastes and Other Matter, 29 December 1972, as modified by the Protocol of 7 November 1996, 1046 UNTS 120, Art. 4.

[5] The modern formulation of this norm (principle of prevention) is given in Principle 2 of the Rio Declaration. *See* Rio Declaration on Environment and Development, 13 June 1992, UN Doc. A/CONF.151/26.Rev.1 ('Rio Declaration').

[6] United Nations Convention on the Law of the Sea, 10 December 1982, 1833 UNTS 397 ('UNCLOS'), Art. 136.

[7] Convention on Biological Diversity, 5 June 1992, 1760 UNTS 79 ('CBD'), preamble, para 3.

'territory' of other States but rather the environment *per se* both in other States and in areas beyond the limits of national jurisdiction.[8] Second, when seen from the perspective of the relations between international environmental law and other branches of international law, principles and concepts may also perform a 'conciliation function'. For example, the concept of sustainable development serves as a conceptual matrix to articulate the sometimes inconsistent requirements of international environmental law and international economic law.[9] As mentioned by the ICJ in the *Case concerning the Gabčíkovo-Nagymaros Project*: 'This need to reconcile economic development with protection of the environment is aptly expressed in the concept of sustainable development'.[10] Third, concepts and principles can also perform an 'architectural' function in that they can lay the foundations of an environmental regime. For example, the climate change regime has been built upon the principle of common but differentiated responsibilities. The same regime serves to illustrate a fourth function of concepts and principles, namely their interpretation function. The preambles of the Kyoto Protocol as well as certain decisions adopted by the Conference of the Parties ('COP') to the UN Framework Convention on Climate Change or by the Meeting of the Parties ('CMP') to the Kyoto Protocol refer to the principles enshrined in Article 3 of the UNFCCC as a guide to interpretation.[11] The 'interpretive function' also operates beyond the direct application of these environmental norms and instruments, in particular when the application of other international law norms is likely to have an impact on the environment. By way of illustration, the ICJ has held that the principle of prevention of environmental damage must be taken into account when interpreting the terms of the right to self-defence.[12] Lastly, these principles can have a 'decision-making function' or, in other words, operate as 'primary norms'. To cite just one example, the *Trail Smelter Case* – a leading environmental dispute – was decided on the basis of the no harm principle.[13]

Finally, a fourth distinction can be made between principles relevant to the notion of prevention in a broad sense and principles and concepts relevant to considerations of balance. By 'prevention' we refer to the need to avoid, wherever possible, environmental damage or change that would be difficult or impossible

---

[8] See J. E. Viñuales, 'The Contribution of the International Court of Justice to the Development of International Environmental Law: A Contemporary Assessment' (2008) 32 *Fordham International Law Journal* 232.

[9] See P.-M. Dupuy, 'Où en-est le droit de l'environnement à la fin du siècle?' (1997) 101 *Revue Générale de droit international public* 873.

[10] *Gabčíkovo-Nagymaros Project (Hungary* v. *Slovakia)*, Judgment, ICJ Reports 1997, p. 7 ('*Gabčíkovo-Nagymaros Project*'), para. 140.

[11] United Nations Framework Convention on Climate Change, 9 May 1992, 31 ILM 849 ('UNFCCC'); Kyoto Protocol to the United Nations Framework Convention on Climate Change, 11 December 1997, 2303 UNTS 148 ('Kyoto Protocol').

[12] *Legality of the Threat or Use of Nuclear Weapons*, ICJ Reports 1996, p. 226 ('*Legality of Nuclear Weapons*'), para. 30.

[13] *Trail Smelter Arbitration*, RIAA, vol. III, pp. 1905–82 ('*Trail Smelter*'), p. 1965.

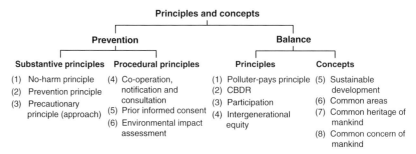

Figure 3.1: The conceptual matrix of international environmental law

to repair. This first category includes both substantive principles, such as the principles of no harm and prevention and the precautionary principle (or approach), as well as some procedural principles, such as the principles of co-operation, notification and/or consultation, the requirement to conduct an environmental impact assessment and the principle of prior informed consent. These principles are unique in that they are applicable to all States in much the same way. As such, they are not intended to introduce any formal differentiation among States or among the many sectors of human activity. In practice, the degree of development of a given State or its financial and technological position may be taken into account to some extent. Yet, the purpose of these principles is not to take such considerations (or other considerations of distributive justice) into account. The expression in international environmental law of these other considerations is channelled through a number of principles, such as the polluter-pays principle, the principle of common but differentiated responsibilities, the principle of participation and the principle of inter-generational equity, as well as concepts, such as those of sustainable development, common area, common heritage of mankind or common concern of mankind. The practical objective of these principles and concepts is to regulate access to certain resources or to distribute, among States and among different sectors of human activity, the burden of managing certain environmental problems.

The latter distinction is, in our view, the most useful one to understand the way in which the principles and concepts that will be analysed in the next paragraphs shape modern international environmental law. It relies on the analytical distinctions made above, as otherwise it would not be possible to distinguish concepts and principles or to understand their operation or legal grounding. Figure 3.1 provides an overview of the conceptual matrix of international environmental law seen from this fourth standpoint.

In what follows, our analysis will be organised around the two main ideas underlying international environmental law, namely the need to prevent environmental harm while striking a satisfactory balance among the different considerations at play.

3.3 Prevention in international environmental law

3.3.1 Introductory observations

The principles expressing the idea of prevention find their source in an older body of general international law concerning the friendly relations between neighbouring States. This older body of principles evolved over the years increasingly reflecting the emergence of transboundary and global environmental concerns. From a historical perspective, the no harm principle was the first to emerge. The adaptation of this principle to cover environmental concerns resulted in an expansion of its scope as well as in a more specific understanding of how it was to be implemented.

An expansion of its scope was necessary to go beyond the limited context of transboundary harm to the territory of another State. It was important to make clear that the environment must be protected as such and not only as part of the territory of another State. States have therefore a positive duty to prevent environmental damage *per se*. This expansion will later result in the emergence of a more comprehensive principle of prevention. An even broader expansion has been attempted, seeking to go beyond prevention to introduce a precautionary principle (or 'approach'). But, as will be discussed later, the status of this principle in general international law is still debated. Regarding the implementation dimension, it is now widely recognised in treaty and customary law that the duty to prevent environmental harm must be performed by reference to several other duties of a procedural nature, including those to co-operate, notify, consult, seek the prior informed consent of the parties concerned or conduct an environmental impact assessment. We will analyse these principles individually, in the order mentioned.

3.3.2 'No harm' principle

In order to understand the origin and content of the 'no harm' principle – and therefore its relationship with the principle of prevention – it is useful to recall its historical development. The classic formulation of the no harm principle in an environmental context appears in the *Trail Smelter Case* (*United States* v. *Canada*). There, the tribunal stated that

> no State has the right to use or permit the use of its territory in such a manner as to cause injury by fumes in or to the territory of another or the properties or persons therein, when the case is of serious consequence and the injury is established by clear and convincing evidence.[14]

The ICJ confirmed the customary nature of this principle in 1949, in the *Corfu Channel Case* (*United Kingdom* v. *Albania*), referring to the existence of 'certain general and well-recognised principles, namely . . . every State's obligation not to

---

[14] *Ibid.*, p. 1965.

allow knowingly its territory to be used for acts contrary to the rights of other States'.[15] In both cases, this principle was used as a primary norm in order to determine the responsibility of a State for damages caused to another State.

This limited understanding of the principle lasted for several decades. In the decade following the adoption of UN General Assembly Resolution 1803 (XVII),[16] the no harm principle came to be regarded as a corollary of the principle of permanent sovereignty over natural resources. The sovereign exploitation of natural resources was therefore limited by the duty not to cause damage to other States. Although this limitation was not mentioned in the text of Resolution 1803 (XVII), it was explicitly recognised in 1972, with the adoption of the Stockholm Declaration on the Human Environment. Indeed, Principle 21 of the Stockholm Declaration specifically linked the 'sovereign right' of a State to exploit its own resources to the responsibility not to cause environmental damage.[17] The scope of such a duty is difficult to circumscribe in the abstract, given that certain measures or activities relating to the use of natural resources, albeit lawful, may have effects on other States. It would be too restrictive to limit such activities for that reason alone. The question becomes, therefore, at what specific point such effects can be said to be causing 'damage' and therefore violating the no harm principle. The Tribunal in the *Trail Smelter Case* used the term 'serious consequences'. In the context of the codification efforts by the UN International Law Commission (ILC) on the 'Law of Non-navigational Uses of International Watercourses', reference was made to the obligation not to cause 'significant harm'.[18] Similarly, the ILC's 'Draft Articles on the Prevention of Transboundary Harm from Hazardous Activities' uses the term 'significant harm'.[19] More recently, in the *Case Concerning Pulp Mills on the River Uruguay* (*Argentina* v. *Uruguay*), the ICJ spoke of a 'significant damage to the environment of another State'.[20] Principle 21 of the Stockholm Declaration does not qualify the term 'damage' with any adjective. It thus suggests that the magnitude of the effect or 'damage' must be assessed *in concreto*, based on criteria such as the likelihood of significant harmful effects on the environment or on the activities carried out in another State, the ratio between prevention costs and potential damage, the impact on other States'

---

[15] *Corfu Channel Case (UK v. Albania)*, ICJ Reports 1949, p. 4 ('*Corfu Channel*'), p. 22.

[16] 'Permanent Sovereignty over Natural Resources', 14 December 1962, GA Res. 1803 (XVII).

[17] Commission on Sustainable Development, Report of the Expert Group Meeting on Identification of Principles of International Law for Sustainable Development, Geneva, Switzerland, 26–28 September 1995 ('Report-Principles'), paras. 51–6.

[18] See United Nations Convention on the Law of the Non-Navigational Uses of International Watercourses, 21 May 1997, 36 ILM 700 ('UN Convention on Watercourses'), Art. 7(1).

[19] Draft Articles on the Prevention of Transboundary Harm from Hazardous Activities, 12 December 2001, GA Res. 56/82, UN Doc. A/RES/56/82 ('ILC Prevention Articles'), Art. 2(a).

[20] *Pulp Mills on the River Uruguay (Argentina v. Uruguay)*, Judgment, ICJ Reports 2010, p. 14 ('*Pulp Mills*'), para. 101.

capacity to use their natural wealth and resources in a similar way, the health of the population of another State, etc.[21]

It is important to underline that Principle 21 went beyond the simple idea of transboundary harm, referring also to the duty not to cause damage 'to the environment of other States *or of areas beyond the limits of national jurisdiction*'. This reference opened the door for a more comprehensive notion of prevention. However, this new conception only became part of positive international law in the 1990s, when the ICJ recognised, in its *Advisory Opinion on the Legality of Nuclear Weapons*, that Principle 21 of the Stockholm Declaration codified customary international law.[22] Over the course of the 1970s and 1980s, a limited conception of the no harm principle seemed to prevail. Two examples taken from international practice illustrate this point. The first example is provided by the *Nuclear Tests* cases.[23] The dispute concerned the consequences of atmospheric nuclear tests conducted by France in the South Pacific. New Zealand made a request for the indication of provisional measures before the ICJ arguing that, because of the potential radioactive fallout from these tests, France violated both the rights of all members of the international community as well as the specific rights of New Zealand. In its Order, the ICJ granted interim relief to safeguard the specific rights of New Zealand only, as opposed to the rights claimed by New Zealand on behalf of the international community.[24] The second example is drawn from the work of the ILC on the International Liability for Injurious Consequences arising out of Acts not Prohibited by International Law. The resolution of the UN General Assembly launching the ILC work on this subject[25] as well as the subsequent reports presented by special rapporteurs between 1978 and 2006 clearly suggest that the focus of this work was on transboundary damage rather than on the prevention of environmental damage *per se*. We find traces of this narrow conception in the final texts adopted by the ILC, respectively on the 'Prevention of Transboundary Harm from Hazardous Activities'[26] and the 'Allocation of Loss in the Case of Transboundary Harm arising out of Hazardous Activities'.[27] In fact, these two instruments only refer to transboundary harm[28] and, despite the emphasis of the former on preventing such

---

[21] Report-Principles, *supra* n. 17, para. 54.   [22] *Legality of Nuclear Weapons, supra* n. 12.

[23] *Nuclear Tests (New Zealand v. France)*, Request for the Indication of Interim Measures of Protection, Order (22 June 1973), ICJ Reports 1973, p. 135 ('*Nuclear Tests – NZ – Order*'); *Nuclear Tests (Australia v. France)*, Request for the Indication of Interim Measures of Protection, Order (22 June 1973), ICJ Reports 1973, p. 99.

[24] *Nuclear Tests – NZ – Order, supra* n. 23, paras. 31–2.

[25] Report of the International Law Commission, UN Doc. Res. 32/151 (1977), 19 December 1977, para. 7.

[26] ILC Prevention Articles, *supra* n. 19.

[27] Draft Principles on the Allocation of Loss in the Case of Transboundary Harm Arising Out of Hazardous Activities, 4 December 2006, GA Res. 61/36, UN Doc. A/RES/61/36 ('ILC Principles').

[28] ILC Prevention Articles, *supra* n. 19, Art. 2(c); ILC Principles, *supra* n. 27, Principle 2(e).

harm, the latter deals specifically with the allocation of the burden of repairing the damage.

The examples provided in this sub-section illustrate the restrictive conception of the no harm principle that prevailed for several decades. As discussed next, the application of this principle to environmental protection led to a significant expansion of its scope, which eventually crystallised into a more comprehensive duty of prevention.

3.3.3 The principle of prevention

The current formulation of the principle of prevention in the environmental context was introduced in 1972 in Principle 21 of the Stockholm Declaration on the Human Environment:

> States have ... the sovereign right to exploit their own resources ... and the responsibility to ensure that activities within their jurisdiction or control do not cause damage to the environment of other States or of areas beyond the limits of national jurisdiction.[29]

As already noted, the content of Principle 21 was both a reflection of general international law (re-affirming the no harm principle) and an attempt at progressive development of this area of law (introducing the responsibility of States not to cause damage to areas outside of State jurisdiction). What Principle 21 seeks to highlight is less the protection of the interests of other States than that of the environment *per se*. Once this caveat has been made explicit, it is easier to understand the difference between no harm and actual prevention. The focus of this new perspective is not on the determination of liability for damage already caused to another State but rather on the obligation to prevent damage to the environment in general. The underlying conception was that prevention was particularly important in the context of environmental protection because environmental damage was often irreversible. This concern for the environment had already started to come into sharp focus in the late 1960s, after disasters such as the sinking of the Liberian oil tanker *Torrey Canyon* near the British coast. But it was nevertheless a new perspective, which required the rethinking – in general – of the relationship between States and different areas of the planet. Such a new perspective needed to be tamed on a case-by-case basis before being admitted into general international law.

It is therefore not surprising that the principle of prevention first featured in soft-law instruments and treaties, before being recognised as a customary principle. It may be useful, in this regard, to refer to a number of international instruments that have provided legal grounding to the principle of prevention.

---

[29] On this principle, see L.-A. Duvic Paoli and J. E. Viñuales, 'Principle 2: Prevention', in Viñuales, J. E. (ed.), *The Rio Declaration on Environment and Development. A Commentary* (Oxford University Press, 2015), pp. 107–38.

For example, Article 193 of the United Nations Convention on the Law of the Sea ('UNCLOS')[30] provides that 'States have the sovereign right to exploit their natural resources pursuant to their environmental policies and in accordance with their duty to protect and preserve the marine environment'. This provision is preceded by a general obligation, under Article 192, to 'protect and preserve the marine environment', and followed by a more specific statement (Article 194(2)), which recalls the formulation of Principle 21 of the Stockholm Declaration. It is noteworthy that the 'marine environment' is not limited to the territory of States or to areas under their control[31] but also includes common areas. Accordingly, measures must be taken to prevent, reduce or control the pollution of the marine environment arising from activities conducted in the 'Area', namely the seabed under the high seas beyond the limits of national jurisdiction.[32] Similarly, the exploitation of the living resources of the high seas must be in accordance with the requirements of conservation and management set out in Articles 116–20 of UNCLOS. Also, the preamble to the United Nations Framework Convention on Climate Change ('UNFCCC')[33] and Article 3 of the Convention on Biological Diversity ('CBD')[34] refer to the prevention principle in its expanded version introduced in the Stockholm Declaration and subsequently taken up by Principle 2 of the Rio Declaration on Environment and Development.

It is in this broad formulation that the prevention principle features in the decisions of international tribunals. As already noted, the transition from a treaty-based principle to a customary one became clear in 1996 when the ICJ, in its *Advisory Opinion on the Legality of Nuclear Weapons*, held that the prevention principle as enshrined in Principle 21 of the Stockholm Declaration and Principle 2 of the Rio Declaration was part of general international law:

> [t]he existence of the general obligation of States to ensure that activities within their jurisdiction and control respect the environment of other States or of areas beyond national control is now part of the corpus of international law relating to the environment.[35]

The ICJ has subsequently confirmed twice the customary nature of the prevention principle. In the *Gabčíkovo-Nagymaros Project* case, the ICJ stated that:

> in the field of environmental protection, vigilance and prevention are required on account of the often irreversible character of damage to the environment and of the limitations inherent in the very mechanism of reparation of this type of damage.[36]

---

[30] UNCLOS, *supra* n. 6.
[31] Such as the exclusive economic zone (Part V, UNCLOS) or the continental shelf (Part VI, UNCLOS).
[32] *Ibid.*, Art. 145(a). See *infra* n. 40.   [33] UNFCCC, *supra* n. 11, preamble, para. 8.
[34] CBD, *supra* n. 7, Art. 3.   [35] *Legality of Nuclear Weapons, supra* n. 12, para. 29.
[36] *Gabčíkovo-Nagymaros Project, supra* n. 10, para. 140.

More recently, in the *Pulp Mills* case, the ICJ further confirmed this principle and spelled out its origins in the no harm principle.[37] In the latter case, the Court also clarified the contours of the obligation of 'due diligence' that flows, for each State, from the prevention principle. Although the Court's analysis relates to the provisions of the Statute of the River Uruguay, its reasoning suggests that the prevention principle requires (i) an obligation of conduct and, more particularly, of co-operation for the implementation and application of appropriate measures for the preservation of the environment,[38] as well as (ii) the obligation to conduct an environmental impact assessment where the proposed activity is likely to have a significant adverse impact in a transboundary context, especially with respect to a shared resource.[39] This understanding has been taken up in the advisory opinion the Seabed Chamber of the International Tribunal on the Law of the Sea ('ITLOS') on the *Responsibilities and Obligations of States sponsoring Persons and Entities with respect to Activities in the Area*.[40] The Seabed Chamber specifically refers to paragraph 187 of the *Pulp Mills* decision in order to characterise the obligation 'to ensure' arising from Article 139(1) of UNCLOS as an obligation 'of conduct' or 'due diligence'.[41] This obligation is subsequently assimilated to the one arising from Article 194(2) of UNCLOS[42] and, more importantly for present purposes, the meaning of 'due diligence' is further specified. Thus, according to the Seabed Chamber, the 'due diligence' obligation encompasses: (i) the obligation of States to adopt appropriate measures and ensure that they are reasonably enforced;[43] (ii) the obligation (based both on the UNCLOS and on customary international law) to conduct an environmental impact assessment;[44] and (iii) the obligation to apply the precautionary approach not only as a requirement of the applicable regulations of the Seabed Authority but also as a component of the 'due diligence' obligation and, possibly, of customary international law.[45]

As discussed next, the *Advisory Opinion on the Area* signals a trend towards the extension of the idea of prevention, at least in treaty law, to cover situations where the impact of an activity on the environment is only hypothetical.

---

[37] *Pulp Mills, supra* n. 20, paras. 101 and 185.   [38] *Ibid.*, paras. 102, 181–9.   [39] *Ibid.*, para. 204.

[40] *Responsibilities and Obligations of States sponsoring Persons and Entities with respect to Activities in the Area*, Case No. 17, ITLOS (Seabed Dispute Chamber), Advisory Opinion (1 February 2011) ('Responsibilities in the Area').

[41] *Ibid.*, para. 110–11.   [42] *Ibid.*, para. 113.

[43] *Ibid.*, paras. 115 (referring to the interpretation of the obligation of 'due diligence' provided by the ICJ in the *Pulp Mills* case), 116 (referring to the ILC Project on Prevention) and 117–20 (referring, in para. 120, to the more detailed answer given by the Chamber in response to the third question put to it).

[44] *Ibid.*, para. 145.   [45] *Ibid.*, paras. 125–35, particularly paras. 131 and 135.

3.3.4 Precaution in international law

Precaution as a legal term has its origins in the '*Vorsorgeprinzip*' introduced by the legislation of the Federal Republic of Germany.[46] The underlying idea is that the lack of scientific certainty about the actual or potential effects of an activity must not prevent States from taking appropriate measures.[47] Beyond this elementary content, the legal implications of precaution are, however, difficult to circumscribe precisely.

Despite numerous attempts at clarifying these implications, the (i) nature, (ii) normative basis and (iii) content of precaution in international law are still debated. This is probably due to the diversity of angles from which precaution can be viewed. While some see precaution as a 'principle',[48] others, including the ICJ, consider precaution as a mere 'approach'.[49] In both cases, the normative basis of precaution is unsettled. Aside from a treaty-based duty of precaution, some commentators argue for the recognition of a precautionary principle based on customary international law[50] or as a general principle of law within the meaning of Article 38(1)(c) of the Statute of the ICJ.[51] Others, including the Dispute Settlement Body of the WTO,[52] refuse to give it any basis in general international law. The difficulties raised by precaution do not stop there. Even if the existence of a customary precautionary principle could be admitted, its content would still have to be defined.[53] Is it an obligation to take action despite the lack of sufficient evidence about the danger that an activity poses to the environment? Or is it, rather, a simple authorisation to take such measures? Or, still, is it a procedural rule shifting the burden of proof (or lowering the standard of proof to facilitate such a shift) when certain activities are potentially harmful to the environment? All of these questions make the task of anchoring the legal concept of precaution in international law difficult. To identify some of the key elements of the debate, it may be useful to review

[46] See K. von Moltke, 'The Vorsorgeprinzip in West German Environmental Policy', in Royal Commission on Environmental Pollution, *Twelfth Report: Best Practicable Environmental Option*, 1988, p. 57.

[47] On this principle, see A. A. Cançado Trindade, 'Principle 15: Precaution', in Viñuales, *supra* n. 29, pp. 403–28.

[48] Report-Principles, *supra* n. 17, paras. 70–4.   [49] *Pulp Mills, supra* n. 20, para. 164.

[50] Public hearing held on Wednesday 16 September 2009, at 10 am, at the Peace Palace, Mr Tomka presiding, Vice-president, Acting-president in the *Case Concerning Pulp Mills on the River Uruguay (Argentina v. Uruguay)*, Pleadings of Mr Sands, p. 58.

[51] See CFI, 26 November 2002, Case T-74/00, *Artegodan GmbH and others* v. *Commission* ECR II-4945, para. 184 (speaking of a 'general principle of Community Law'); *Pulp Mills, supra* n. 20, Separate opinion of A. A. Cançado Trindade, paras. 67–8.

[52] *European Communities – Measures Concerning Meat and Meat Products (Hormones)*, AB Report (16 January 1998) WT/DS26/AB/R, WT/DS48/AB/R, ('*EC – Hormones*'), paras. 123–5; *European Communities – Measures Affecting the Approval and Marketing of Biotech Products*, Panel Report (29 September 2006), WT/DS291/R, WT/DS292/R, WT/DS293/R ('*EC – Biotech Products*'), paras. 7.88–7.89.

[53] Report-Principles, *supra* n. 17, paras. 71–2; D. Bodansky, 'Deconstructing the Precautionary Principle', in D. Caron and H. N. Scheiber (eds.), *Bringing New Law to Ocean Waters* (Leiden: Martinus Nijhoff, 2004), pp. 381–91.

the concept of precaution as it features in treaties, soft-law instruments and decisions of judicial or quasi-judicial bodies.

Regarding, first, treaty law, there are more and more treaties incorporating references to precaution in its various forms.[54] The first treaty regime that explicitly referred to the concept of precaution is the one established by the Vienna Convention for the Protection of the Ozone Layer of 1985,[55] and further developed by its Montreal Protocol of 1987.[56] From 1990 onwards, the number of treaties referring to precaution has increased. Such references may indeed be found not only in the preamble of the CBD,[57] but also in the body of the UNFCCC, in particular Article 3.3, which provides that

> [t]he Parties should take precautionary measures to anticipate, prevent or minimize the causes of climate change and mitigate its adverse effects. Where there are threats of serious or irreversible damage, lack of full scientific certainty should not be used as a reason for postponing such measures.

More recently, the concept of precaution has been incorporated in the text of many other multilateral environmental agreements ('MEAs'), such as the 1995 Agreement on Straddling Fish Stocks ('precautionary approach'),[58] the 2000 Biosafety Protocol to the CBD ('precautionary approach'),[59] or the 2001 Stockholm Convention on Persistent Organic Pollutants ('precaution concern/ precautionary approach').[60] Moreover, the concept of precaution has also featured, to varying degrees, in regional environmental treaties[61] and even in treaties governing other matters.[62]

---

[54] See, generally, A. Trouwborst, *Evolution and Status of the Precautionary Principle in International Law* (The Hague: Kluwer, 2002).

[55] Vienna Convention for the Protection of the Ozone Layer, 22 March 1985, 1513 UNTS 293 ('CPOL'), preamble, para. 5.

[56] Montreal Protocol on Substances that Deplete the Ozone Layer, 16 September 1987, 1522 UNTS 29 ('Montreal Protocol'), preamble, para. 6.

[57] CDB, *supra* n. 7, preamble, para. 9.

[58] Agreement for the Implementation of the Provisions of the United Nations Conventions on the Law of the Sea of 10 December 1982 Relating to the Conservation and Management of Straddling Fish Stocks and Highly Migratory Fish Stocks, 4 August 1995, 2167 UNTS 88 ('Straddling Fish Stocks Agreement'), Art. 6.

[59] Cartagena Protocol on Biosafety to the Convention on Biological Diversity, 29 January 2000, 39 ILM 1027 (2000) ('Biosafety Protocol'), Arts. 1 and 10(6).

[60] Stockholm Convention on Persistent Organic Pollutants, 22 May 2001, 40 ILM 532 (2001) ('POPs Convention'), preamble, para. 8 and Art. 1.

[61] See e.g. Bamako Convention on the ban on the Import into Africa and the Control of Transboundary Movement and Management of Hazardous Wastes within Africa, 30 January 1991, 30 ILM 773 ('Bamako Convention'), Art. 4(3); Convention for the Protection of the Marine Environment of the North East Atlantic, 22 September 1992, 2354 UNTS 67 ('OSPAR Convention'), Annex II, Art. 3(3)(c); Convention on the Protection and Use of Transboundary Watercourses and International Lakes, 18 March 1992, 1936 UNTS 269 ('Helsinki Convention'), Art. 2; Convention on Co-operation for the Protection and Sustainable Use of the River Danube, 29 June 1994, IER 35:0251 ('Danube Convention'), Art. 2(4).

[62] Treaty on the Functioning of the European Union, as amended by the Lisbon Treaty, 13 December 2007, OJ C 83, 30 March 2010 ('TFEU'), Art. 191(2); Agreement on the

Second, as regards the concept of precaution in soft-law instruments, the adoption by the UN General Assembly of the World Charter for Nature in 1982 referred already to precaution in one of its variants: 'where potential adverse effects are not fully understood, the activities should not proceed'.[63] Ten years later, this concept was enshrined in Principle 15 of the Rio Declaration on Environment and Development in the following terms:

> [i]n order to protect the environment, the precautionary approach shall be widely applied by States according to their capabilities. Where there are threats of serious or irreversible damage, lack of full scientific certainty shall not be used as a reason for postponing cost-effective measures to prevent environmental degradation.

This is the most accepted formulation in general discussions about the concept of precaution in international law. However, it raises some difficult issues, such as the determination of the concepts of 'serious or irreversible damage', 'scientific uncertainty' or the distinction between the 'duties' of States 'according to their capabilities'. Faced with such uncertainty, one would have expected that international courts and tribunals clarify the contours of the concept of precaution. Yet, the case law on this question remains divided.

Indeed a survey of the many decisions relevant to this question does not offer a clearer picture. While the Dispute Settlement Body of the WTO ('DSB') seems reluctant to admit the existence of a precautionary principle in general international law,[64] other international courts such as the European Court of Human Rights ('ECtHR') or the International Tribunal for the Law of the Sea ('ITLOS') have given a more favourable reception to the principle. The position of the ICJ is somewhat between these two extremes. In the *Pulp Mills* case, Argentina argued that customary international law recognised the existence of a precautionary principle the effect of which was to shift the burden of proof to Uruguay. However, the ICJ did not follow Argentina's position, and it only observed 'that while a precautionary approach may be relevant in the interpretation and application of the provisions of the Statute, it does not follow that it operates as a reversal of the burden of proof'.[65] This view can be contrasted with that of the ECtHR in its recent jurisprudence. Reversing a long-standing reluctance to accept the precautionary principle, the ECtHR now recognises:

> the importance of the precautionary principle (enshrined for the first time in the Rio Declaration), which 'was intended to apply in order to ensure a level of high

---

Application of Sanitary and Phytosanitary Measures, 15 April 1994, 1867 UNTS 493 ('SPS Agreement'), Art. 5(7).

[63] World Charter for Nature, GA Res. 37/7, 28 October 1982, para. 11(b).

[64] In *EC – Biotech*, the panel noted that 'there has, to date, been no authoritative decision by an international court or tribunal which recognizes the precautionary principle as a principle of general or customary international law', *EC – Biotech, supra* n. 52, para. 7.88. In taking this view, the panel followed the Appellate Body in *EC – Hormones, supra* n. 52, para. 124.

[65] *Pulp Mills, supra* n. 20, para. 164.

protection of health, the safety of consumers and the environment in all Community activities'.[66]

Similarly, the ITLOS noted on two occasions that States must 'act with prudence and caution'[67] or that 'prudence and caution' require States to co-operate to protect the environment,[68] and it has more recently embraced the precautionary approach in its *Advisory Opinion on the Area*:

> [t]he Chamber observes that the precautionary approach has been incorporated into a growing number of international treaties and other instruments, many of which reflect the formulation of Principle 15 of the Rio Declaration. In the view of the Chamber, this has initiated a trend towards making this approach part of customary international law.[69]

At the European Union level, the Court of First Instance ('CFI') and the European Court of Justice ('ECJ') have clearly recognised the normative basis of the precautionary principle as a general principle of European law.[70]

These differences in the recognition of the concept of precaution can be explained, among other factors, by the explicit mention of the precautionary principle in the Treaty on the Functioning of the European Union[71] and, beyond the EU framework, by the nature of the cases that different courts are likely to handle. Indeed, both the ECtHR and the ITLOS are, by their very mandate, likely to hear cases where compliance with certain environmental norms is a major issue, either in connection with the application of human right provisions with environmental content or of the UNCLOS provisions protecting the marine environment. By contrast, in international economic law, environmental protection is still perceived as a limitation to free trade and investment. This divide makes the position of the ICJ all the more important, as the guardian of general international law.

3.3.5 Co-operation, notification, consultation

The existence of a general duty of co-operation is well established in international law. This duty is formulated, *inter alia,* in Principle 4 of General Assembly Resolution 2625 (XXV) on the 'Principles of

[66] *Tatar v. Romania*, ECtHR Application No. 67021/01, Judgment (27 January 2009, Final 6 July 2009) ('*Tatar v. Romania*'), para. 120.

[67] *Southern Bluefin Tuna Cases (New Zealand v. Japan; Australia v. Japan)*, Provisional Measures, ITLOS Case Nos. 3 and 4, Order (27 August 1999) ('*Southern Bluefin Tuna*'), para. 77 (the French text speaks of '*prudence et précaution*').

[68] *MOX Plant Case (Ireland v. United Kingdom)*, ITLOS Case No. 10, Order (3 December 2001) ('*MOX Plant*'), para. 84 (the French text speaks of '*prudence et précaution*').

[69] *Responsibilities in the Area, supra* n. 40, para. 135.

[70] See *Pfizer Animal Health SA v. Council*, CFI Case T-13/99, Judgment (11 September 2002), paras. 114–15. See also *Gowan Comércio Internacional e Serviços L^{da} v. Ministero della Salute*, CJEU Case C-77/09, Judgment (22 December 2010), para. 75.

[71] See TFEU, *supra* n. 62, Art. 191 (formerly EC Treaty, Art. 174).

International Law Concerning Friendly Relations and Cooperation among States'.[72]

In the context of environmental law, however, the duty of co-operation has taken many different forms.[73] The Group of Experts convened by the CSD in 1995 to identify the principles of international environmental law distinguished between a duty to co-operate 'in a spirit of global partnership'[74] and a duty to co-operate in 'a transboundary context'.[75] The first encompasses the relations among States with respect to the 'global commons', and it has crystallised into 'principles' and 'concepts' such as the 'common concern of humankind',[76] the 'common heritage of mankind',[77] the 'common but differentiated responsibilities' of States[78] or, more generally, the 'differential treatment' that may be accorded to States on the basis of their particular situation.[79] The second duty covers, according to this report, some minimal requirements of co-operation in a transboundary context through norms such as the principle of reasonable and equitable use of shared resources,[80] the duty of notification and consultation with States potentially affected by an activity/event having consequences on the environment,[81] the obligation to conduct an environmental impact assessment,[82] the principle of prior informed consent,[83] or the duty to avoid the relocation of activities harmful to the environment.[84]

---

[72] 'Declaration on Principles of International Law concerning Friendly Relations and Co-operation among States in accordance with the Charter of the United Nations', Res. 2625 (XXV), 26 October 1970.

[73] See L. Boisson de Chazournes and K. Sangbana, 'Principle 19: Notification and consultation on activities with transboundary impact', in Viñuales, *supra* n. 29, pp. 492–507; P. Okowa, 'Principle 18: Notification and Assistance in Case of Emergency', in Viñuales, *supra* n. 29, pp. 471– 92; P. H. Sand, 'Principle 27: Cooperation in a Spirit of Global Partnership', in Viñuales, *supra* n. 29, pp. 617–32.

[74] Rio Declaration, *supra* n. 5, Principle 7.   [75] Report-Principles, *supra* n. 17, paras. 75–122.

[76] UNFCCC, *supra* n. 11, preamble, para. 1; CBD, *supra* n. 7, preamble, para. 3.

[77] UNCLOS, *supra* n. 6, Art. 136.   [78] UNFCCC, *supra* n. 11, Art. 3.1.

[79] *Ibid.*, Arts. 3(2), 4(4)–(6) and 4(9); UNCLOS, *supra* n. 6, preamble and Art. 207.4; United Nations Convention to Combat Desertification in those Countries Experiencing Serious Drought and/or Desertification, Particularly in Africa, 17 June 1994, 33 ILM 1328 ('UNCCD'), preamble and Arts. 5–6.

[80] Helsinki Rules on the Uses of the Waters of International Rivers, adopted by the International Law Association at its 52nd Conference, Helsinki, 20 August 1966, Art IV; 'Charter of Economic Rights and Duties of States', Res. 3281 (XXIX), 12 December 1974, Art. 3; UN Convention on Watercourses, *supra* n. 18, Art. 5.

[81] Convention on Long-Range Transboundary Air Pollution, 13 November 1979, 1302 UNTS 217 ('LRTAP Convention'), Art. 5; UNCLOS, *supra* n. 6, Arts. 198 and 206; Convention on the Transboundary Effects of Industrial Accidents, 17 March 1992, 2105 UNTS 457, Arts. 10 and 17; Convention on Early Notification of a Nuclear Accident, 26 September 1986, 1439 UNTS 275; Rio Declaration, *supra* n. 5, Principles 18 and 19.

[82] See Convention on Environmental Impact Assessment in a Transboundary Context, 25 February 1991, 1989 UNTS 310 ('Espoo Convention').

[83] Rotterdam Convention on the Prior Informed Consent Procedure for Certain Hazardous Chemicals and Pesticides in International Trade, 10 September 1998, 2244 UNTS 337 ('Rotterdam Convention' or 'PIC Convention').

[84] Basel Convention on the Control of Transboundary Movements of Hazardous Wastes and their Disposal, 22 March 1989, 1673 UNTS 57 ('Basel Convention'), Arts. 4(5)–(6); Bamako Convention, *supra* n. 61, Art. 4; Rio Declaration, *supra* n. 5, Principle 14.

Thus characterised, the duty of co-operation on environmental matters would seem to be of a substantive (rather than a procedural) nature, in that it would encompass foundational 'principles' and 'concepts'. In fact, the conceptualisation offered by the Expert Group of the CSD is best understood as an attempt to contribute to the progressive development of international environmental law. As such, it may not accurately reflect the nature and content of the duty of co-operation in general international law. Co-operation remains an obligation of conduct whose specific manifestation depends upon what could be expected from a State acting in good faith.[85] Due to the relatively vague nature of such a duty, there are several ways in which it can be spelled out.

As a general rule, States are encouraged to seek, if necessary, the assistance of an international organisation or to conclude a treaty specifically regulating the procedure by which co-operation will take place.[86] And where such arrangements leave room for different interpretations, the duty to co-operate in good faith can be used to specify the content of a treaty obligation. An important consequence is that, in practice:

> as long as the procedural mechanism for co-operation between the parties to prevent significant damage to one of them is taking its course, the State initiating the planned activity is obliged not to authorize such work and, *a fortiori*, not to carry it out.[87]

In some cases, the content of the duty can be defined by an international tribunal. In the environmental context, the duty of co-operation has been construed as requiring the exchange information,[88] the joint evaluation of the environmental impacts of certain activities[89] or, more recently, the consultation of the secretariat of an environmental treaty of particular relevance to the case.[90]

3.3.6 Prior informed consent

The requirement of prior informed consent ('PIC') has two meanings in international law. First, it refers to a duty to consult indigenous peoples who

---

[85] *North Sea Continental Shelf Case*, Judgment, ICJ Reports 1969, p. 3 ('*North Sea Continental Shelf*'), para. 85; *Pulp Mills, supra* n. 20, paras. 145–6.

[86] UN Convention on Watercourses *supra* n. 18, Art. 8; ILC Prevention Articles, *supra* n. 19, Art. 4; *Lake Lanoux Arbitration (Spain v. France)*, Award (16 November 1957), RIAA XII, p. 281 ('*Lake Lanoux Arbitration*'), pp. 22–3; *North Sea Continental Shelf, supra* n. 85, para. 85; *Southern Bluefin Tuna, supra* n. 67, para. 90(e).

[87] *Pulp Mills, supra* n. 20, para. 144.   [88] *MOX Plant, supra* n. 68, para. 89(a).

[89] *See Fisheries Jurisdiction Case (UK v. Iceland)*, Decision on Jurisdiction, ICJ Reports 1974, p. 3 ('*Fisheries Jurisdiction*'), para. 72; *Pulp Mills, supra* n. 20, para. 281; *MOX Plant, supra* n. 68, para. 89(b).

[90] *Certain Activities Carried Out by Nicaragua in the Border Area (Costa Rica v. Nicaragua)*, Provisional Measures, Order of 8 March 2011, ICJ Reports 2011, p. 6 ('*Costa Rica v. Nicaragua*'), paras. 80 and 86(2).

may be affected by the adoption of a measure. This meaning of the PIC requirement would be more appropriately discussed in the context of 'balance', as it seeks to preserve the interests of certain groups. It is recalled here to avoid treating the PIC requirement in two separate sections. The Convention No. 169 of the International Labour Organisation on Indigenous and Tribal Peoples provides for an obligation to consult with and seek the prior informed consent of indigenous peoples as a condition for their exceptional 'displacement' or 'relocation' by the government of a State.[91] Similarly, Resolution 61/295 of the UN General Assembly, entitled 'United Nations Declaration on the Rights of Indigenous Peoples', provides in its Article 10 that '[i]ndigenous peoples shall not be forcibly removed from their lands' and that '[n]o relocation shall take place without the free, prior and informed consent of the indigenous peoples concerned'.[92] A variation of this first meaning appears in the biodiversity regime. Article 8(j) of the CBD requires the 'approval and involvement' of indigenous peoples as a condition for the utilisation of their traditional knowledge.[93] This requirement has been further specified in the Protocol on Access and Benefit Sharing adopted at Nagoya, in October 2010.[94]

Second, the PIC requirement also refers to the obligation assumed by a State not to export certain wastes, substances or products to another State unless the latter has given its prior informed consent.[95] The objective of this requirement is to ensure that such wastes, substances or products are sent only to States who are willing to accept them and have the technical capacity to manage them. In general, there are two ways to implement the requirement of prior informed consent, namely (i) a general PIC procedure (by substance) and (ii) a specific PIC procedure (by shipment). The first approach can be illustrated by reference to the 1998 Rotterdam Convention on the Prior Informed Consent Procedure, also known as the 'PIC Convention'.[96] In force since 2006, the Convention has established a system of product identification[97] and information exchange.[98] For each product subject to the PIC procedure (listed in Annex III), a 'decision

---

[91] Convention (No. 169) concerning Indigenous and Tribal Peoples in Independent Countries, 27 June 1989, 28 ILM 1382 (1989) ('ILO Convention 169'), Arts. 16(2) and 6.

[92] See 'United Nations Declaration on the Rights of Indigenous Peoples', 2 October 2007, UN Doc. A/RES/61/295 ('UNDRIP'), Annex, Arts. 10 and 19.

[93] CBD, *supra* n. 7, Art. 8(j).

[94] Nagoya Protocol on Access to Genetic Resources and the Fair and Equitable Sharing of the Benefits arising from their Utilization to the Convention on Biological Diversity, 29 October 2010, available at: www.cbd.int (visited on 4 January 2013), Arts. 6(2) and 7.

[95] See M. Mbengue, 'Principle 14: Dangerous Substances and Activities', in Viñuales, *supra* n. 29, pp. 383–402.

[96] PIC Convention, *supra* n. 83. The origins of this international instrument can be found in two soft law instruments managed respectively by the FAO and UNEP, namely the 'Code of Conduct on the Distribution and Use of Pesticides' (adopted in 1985 and subsequently revised) and the 'London Guidelines for the Exchange of Information on Chemicals that are the Subject of International Trade' (adopted in 1987 and subsequently revised).

[97] PIC Convention, *supra* n. 83, Arts. 5, 6 and 8.   [98] *Ibid.*, Art. 14.

guidance document' is produced and communicated to the States parties[99] so that each of them can make a decision on the admissibility of such product into its territory.[100] Information about which State accepts the import of a given product is then circulated by the secretariat to the other States parties.[101] Exporting States must take measures to ensure that exporters based in their territories comply with the decision of importing countries.[102]

The foregoing approach may be contrasted with the specific PIC procedure laid out, for example, in Article 6 of the Basel Convention on Hazardous Wastes (Basel Convention).[103] This provision establishes a system whereby the competent authority of the exporting State must notify (respecting certain requirements) its counterpart in the importing State (and any transit States) of any planned shipment of hazardous wastes or other waste, or require private operators do so.[104] Subsequently, the export State may authorise the transboundary movement of wastes if it has received the written consent of the importing State.[105] Article 6(6)–(8) also provides for a facilitated version of this specific PIC procedure, comparable to a general PIC procedure. Under this facilitated procedure waste with similar physical and chemical characteristics may be shipped regularly under the same authorisation over a maximum period of twelve months.[106] Despite these similarities with the general PIC procedure, the procedure of Article 6(6)–(8) remains, however, a specific PIC procedure, as it applies to a particular exporter and is shipment-based.

Regarding the status in general international law of the PIC requirement, in either its general or specific versions, it seems premature to consider it as an international custom. One may observe, however, that the procedural nature of this requirement is not in itself an obstacle to its recognition in general international law, as suggested by the position taken by the ICJ in relation to the legal status of another procedural principle, namely the obligation to conduct an environmental impact assessment.

3.3.7 Environmental impact assessment

The origins of the obligation to conduct an environmental impact assessment ('EIA') can be traced back to the domestic law of some States and, particularly, to the National Environmental Policy Act adopted by the United States as early as 1969.[107] Subsequently, this obligation was introduced into the domestic legislation of many other States[108] as well as into a number of treaties with

---

[99] *Ibid.*, Art. 7.   [100] *Ibid.*, Art. 10.   [101] *Ibid.*, Art. 10(10).   [102] *Ibid.*, Art. 11.
[103] Basel Convention, *supra* n. 84.   [104] *Ibid.*, Art. 6(1).   [105] *Ibid.*, Art. 6(2)–(3).
[106] *Ibid.*, Art. 6(6)–(8).   [107] National Environmental Policy Act, 42 USC ch. 55.
[108] See N. A. Robinson, 'EIA Abroad: The Comparative and Transnational Experience', in S. G. Hildebrand and J. B. Cannon (eds.), *Environmental Analysis: The NEPA Experience* (Boca Raton: Lewis, 1993), pp. 679–702; N. Craik, *The International Law of Environmental Impact Assessment* (Cambridge University Press, 2008); N. Craik, 'Principle 17: Environmental Impact Assessment', in Viñuales, *supra* n. 29, pp. 451–70.

regional[109] and universal scope.[110] It was also incorporated into Principle 17 of the Rio Declaration, which provides that:

> [e]nvironmental impact assessment, as a national instrument, shall be undertaken for proposed activities that are likely to have a significant adverse impact on the environment and are subject to a decision of a competent national authority.

To understand the scope of the obligation to conduct an EIA, three issues must be addressed, namely (i) the formal source from which the obligation derives (treaty, custom, general principles of law), (ii) the spatial scope of the requirement (national, transboundary, global) and (iii) the specific content of the obligation.

Regarding the first point, some treaties provide for an obligation to conduct an EIA. One major example is the Convention on Environmental Impact Assessment in a Transboundary Context ('Espoo Convention') adopted in 1991 as part of the United Nations Economic Commission for Europe ('UNECE').[111] Under this Convention, States parties must introduce into their domestic law the obligation to conduct an EIA before authorising certain activities (listed in Appendix I) that may have a 'significant adverse transboundary impact'.[112] Beyond treaty law, the ICJ has recently recognised, in the *Pulp Mills* case, that the obligation to conduct an EIA has a customary grounding. According to the Court, a practice has developed:

> which in recent years has gained so much acceptance among States that it may now be considered a requirement under general international law to undertake an environmental impact assessment where there is a risk that the proposed industrial activity may have a significant adverse impact in a transboundary context, in particular, on a shared resource.[113]

The statement of the Court takes us directly to the second point identified above, namely the spatial scope of the requirement. Both the Espoo Convention (as well as other conventions) and general international law seem to confine the obligation to conduct an EIA to the transboundary context. This leaves open the question of whether the customary obligation also covers situations where the proposed activity takes place in a purely domestic context or where it concerns areas beyond national jurisdiction.

---

[109] According to Kiss and Beurier, the first international conventions to provide for this requirement was the Kuwait Regional Convention for Cooperation on the Protection of the Marine Environment from Pollution, 24 April 1978, Art. 11(a), and the Apia Convention on the Conservation of Nature in the South Pacific, 12 June 1976, Art. 5(4). They were followed by the Kuala Lumpur (ASEAN) Cooperation Plan on Transboundary Haze Pollution, 9 July 1985, Art. 14. See A. Kiss and J.-P. Beurier, *Droit international de l'environnement* (Paris: Pedone, 2004), para. 324.

[110] See UNCLOS, *supra* n. 6, Art. 206; Protocol on Environmental Protection to the Antarctic Treaty, 4 October 1991, 30 ILM 1455 (1991) ('Madrid Protocol'), Art. 8 and Annex I; UN Convention on Watercourses, *supra* n. 18, Art. 12.

[111] Espoo Convention, *supra* n. 82.   [112] *Ibid.*, Art. 2(3).   [113] *Pulp Mills, supra* n. 20, para. 204.

These questions have not been settled in the case-law yet. It should be noted, however, that the formulation of Principle 17 of the Rio Declaration (which refers to the EIA as a national instrument) or Article 206 of UNCLOS (which aims to prevent 'substantial pollution of or significant and harmful changes to the marine environment' in general) favour the broadening of the spatial scope of the customary obligation to conduct an EIA. Moreover, the ITLOS Seabed Chamber has noted, in its recent *Advisory Opinion on the Area*, that the obligation to conduct an EIA also applied beyond a transboundary context:

> [t]he [ICJ]'s reasoning in a transboundary context may also apply to activities with an impact on the environment in an area beyond the limits of national jurisdiction; and the Court's references to 'shared resources' may also apply to resources that are the common heritage of mankind.[114]

As to the specific content of the EIA, it depends upon the source of the obligation. Whereas, in general, the content of the EIA obligation deriving from a treaty source may be identified quite precisely,[115] the content of the customary rule is set, according to the ICJ, by the domestic law of States.[116] An important question that arises is whether the EIA must necessarily involve consultation with potentially affected populations. In the framework of the Espoo Convention, the question is answered affirmatively in Articles 2(6) and 3(8), and also features as a criterion to determine the significance of the environmental impact of an activity.[117] The Operational Policy on the environment followed by the International Finance Corporation ('IFC') in its project finance activities (IFC OP 4.01) expressly provides for an obligation to consult.[118] Outside the treaty and administrative framework, the question is less clear. The ILC Prevention Articles state, in Article 13, an obligation to provide 'information to the public'.[119] The question arose in the *Pulp Mills* case but the Court merely concluded that no legal duty to consult the affected populations existed for Uruguay on the basis of the 'instruments invoked by Argentina'[120] and that, in any event, a consultation had taken place.[121] This conclusion does not settle the question because the Court avoided the question as to whether an obligation to consult (even with a minimum content) exists in general international law.

---

[114] *Responsibilities in the Area, supra* n. 40, para. 148.

[115] See, e.g., Appendices II and III of the Espoo Convention, *supra* n. 82.

[116] In the *Pulp Mills* case, the Court held that: 'it is for each State to determine in its domestic legislation or in the authorization process for the project, the specific content of the environmental impact assessment required in each case', *supra* n. 20, para. 205.

[117] Espoo Convention, *supra* n. 82, Arts. 2(6), 3(8), and Appendix III, para. 1(b) *in fine*.

[118] International Finance Corporation, Operational Policy 4.01 – Environmental Assessment, October 1998, paras. 12 and 13.

[119] ILC Prevention Articles, *supra* n. 19, Art. 13.   [120] *Pulp Mills, supra* n. 20, para. 216.

[121] *Ibid.*, para. 219.

3.4 Balance in international environmental law

3.4.1 Principles expressing the idea of balance

The principles presented in this section all aim to distribute the efforts involved in protecting the environment among the various stakeholders and to find balance between such protection and other considerations. Among these various principles, the first to emerge in its present form was the so-called 'polluter-pays' principle, which seeks to 'internalise' the cost of pollution or, in other words, to ensure that the financial burden of such pollution is borne by those who caused it. The principle of common but differentiated responsibilities ('CBDR'), also known as 'intra-generational equity', aims to distribute the cost of environmental policies among different States according to their historical responsibilities and respective capabilities. At the level of individuals, the principle of participation performs the function of weighing the interests of various groups and individuals involved in (or affected by) an activity with environmental consequences. As for the principle of 'inter-generational equity', it is intended to distribute the burden of environmental protection efforts between the present and future generations.

3.4.1.1 The polluter-pays principle

The polluter-pays principle can be understood in different ways.[122] At first sight, it would appear as a mere version of the duty to repair the damage caused to others as applied in an environmental context. However, such a limited understanding would deprive this principle of any autonomous content, given that such duty is well-established in customary international law through both the no harm and the prevention principles.

On closer examination, the polluter-pays principle does have a sufficiently distinct content. To grasp such content one must take into account the manner in which industrial operations were conducted before the emergence of environmental protection considerations. The starting-point in this respect is the theory of 'externalities', characterised as the impact of a transaction (or, more generally, of an economic activity) on third parties that do not participate in it.[123] When this impact is negative and is not compensated, one can speak of a 'negative externality'. For example, the pollution of rivers by the normal or 'accidental' operation of a company imposes a cost on society. The question then arises of who should pay the cost: the company, consumers or society at large? If nothing is done, the society at large or those individuals most directly concerned (i.e. a sector of society) will bear the cost. Similarly, if the authorities intervene to treat polluted water, the cost is also borne by society at large (as it is borne by tax-payers). If, however, the cost is borne by the company who

---

[122] On this principle, see P. Schwartz, 'Principle 16: The Polluter-pays Principle', in Viñuales, *supra* n. 29, pp. 429–50.

[123] See R. Coase, 'The Problem of Social Cost' (1960) 3 *Journal of Law and Economics* 1.

causes the pollution or transferred to consumers driving demand for the relevant product, one could speak of an 'internalisation' of the cost. This idea was initially formulated in OECD Council Recommendation, in 1972.[124] According to this instrument 'the cost of [measures adopted by the authorities to fight pollution] should be reflected in the cost of goods and services which cause pollution in production and/or consumption'.[125] The polluter-pays principle is now enshrined in Principle 16 of the Rio Declaration, which provides that:

> [n]ational authorities should endeavour to promote the internalization of environmental costs and the use of economic instruments, taking into account the approach that the polluter should, in principle, bear the cost of pollution, with due regard to the public interest and without distorting international trade and investment.

The specific modalities of this internalisation are difficult to circumscribe because several parameters need to be defined, starting with the social cost itself, the probability (in the case of an accident or when the effects of an activity are not known with certainty), the determination of the share of each polluter (where a negative externality results from the activities of several companies), the compensation modalities (*ex ante* or *ex post*), and many other factors. In the context of certain conventions on civil liability for nuclear accidents or oil pollution damage, cost internalisation is effected through a system consisting of (i) a strict liability regime of the commercial operator, (ii) an obligation to take out adequate insurance and (iii) additional layers of compensation based on State and/or industry contributions.[126] As regards the protection of rivers, certain treaties incorporate the polluter-pays principle as a guiding principle.[127] A number of soft-law instruments, in addition to the Rio Declaration, also mention this principle.[128]

The scope of these instruments is essentially to promote the internalisation of costs at the level of individuals and enterprises. Therefore, it would be difficult to invoke the polluter-pays principle in the distribution of social costs (incurred by the international community) generated by States. It seems more appropriate to refer in this respect either to the no harm principle, the prevention principle or the principle of 'common but differentiated responsibilities', discussed next.

---

[124] OECD Council Recommendation on Guiding Principles concerning the International Economic Aspects of Environmental Policies, C(72)128 (1972), 14 ILM 236 (1975).

[125] *Ibid.*, Annex, para. A.4.   [126] See *infra* Chapter 8.

[127] Helsinki Convention, *supra* n. 61, Art. 2(5)(b); OSPAR Convention, *supra* n. 61, Art. 2(2)(b); Danube Convention, *supra* n. 61, Art. 2(4).

[128] See e.g. 'ILA New Delhi Declaration of Principles of International Law Relating to Sustainable Development', 6 April 2002 ('New Delhi Declaration'), para. 3.1.

3.4.1.2 The principle of common but differentiated responsibilities

The principle of common but differentiated responsibilities ('CBDR') aims to distribute the effort required to manage environmental problems of a global nature, such as the protection of the ozone layer,[129] the fight against climate change[130] or the conservation and use of biodiversity,[131] among States.

Situated at the intersection between development and environmental protection, this principle is intended to reconcile potentially conflicting requirements. On the one hand, developing countries see it as a way to gain recognition for their development needs, their reduced ability to contribute to the management of environmental problems and also their lower contribution to their creation. On the other hand, developed countries consider it as a tool to ensure participation of developing countries in the management of environmental problems and to ensure that the development process takes place within certain environmental bounds.

These considerations underpin the text of Principle 7 of the Rio Declaration, which provides that:

> States shall cooperate in a spirit of global partnership to conserve, protect and restore the health and integrity of the Earth's ecosystem. In view of the different contributions to global environmental degradation, States have common but differentiated responsibilities. The developed countries acknowledge the responsibility that they bear in the international pursuit for sustainable development in view of the pressures their societies place on the global environment and of the technologies and financial resources they command.

This formulation shows both the 'common' dimension of the principle of CBDR, expressed as a duty to co-operate 'in a spirit of global partnership' to protect the environment, as well as the 'differential' dimension, expressed as the recognition by developed countries of their primary responsibility for environmental degradation and their increased ability to deal with its consequences. The origin of these two dimensions of the principle of CBDR can be found in two earlier ideas, namely the idea of a community of interest with respect to certain areas like Antarctica,[132] outer space[133] or the

---

[129] CPOL, *supra* n. 55, Art. 2(2).   [130] UNFCCC, *supra* n. 11, Art. 3(1).
[131] CBD, *supra* n. 7, Art. 20(4).
[132] The Antarctic Treaty, 1 December 1959, 402 UNTS 71, preamble, para. 2.
[133] Treaty on Principles Governing the Activities of States in the Exploration and Use of Outer Space, including the Moon and Other Celestial Bodies, 27 January 1967, 610 UNTS 205 ('Outer Space Treaty'), Art. 1.

seabed,[134] and the idea of differential treatment, present in international trade law[135] or the law of the sea.[136]

Despite its similarities with these two earlier well-established ideas, the principle of CBDR should be considered as a new concept embodied, for the first time, in the ozone regime and further developed in 1992 with the adoption of the Rio Declaration as well as the introduction of this principle in the UNFCCC and the CBD. These three normative contexts (ozone, climate change and biodiversity) can also be seen as three ways to operationalise the principle of CBDR. With regard to the ozone regime, the preamble to the Vienna Convention of 1985 referred to 'the circumstances and particular requirements of developing countries'.[137] This element was also included in the text of the Convention, according to which the parties are to perform their obligations 'in accordance with the means at their disposal and their capabilities'[138] as well as in the form of a duty to co-operate, including in respect of technology transfer.[139] The Montreal Protocol to the Convention went further, providing in Article 5 for differentiated obligations for developing countries.[140] This amounted essentially to the granting of longer time-periods, under certain conditions, to meet their obligations under the Protocol. A second way to operationalise the principle of CBDR is illustrated by the UNFCCC and its Kyoto Protocol. Indeed, Article 3(1) of the UNFCCC explicitly enshrines the principle of CBDR in the following terms:

> The Parties should protect the climate system for the benefit of present and future generations of humankind, on the basis of equity and in accordance with their common but differentiated responsibilities and respective capabilities. Accordingly, the developed country Parties should take the lead in combating climate change and the adverse effects thereof.

The primary responsibility of developed countries (i.e. those listed in Annex I of the UNFCCC) under the UNFCCC has been implemented by the Kyoto Protocol, which requires them to meet quantified emissions targets[141] as provided for in Annex B, while no new obligations are imposed on developing countries (i.e. those not listed in Annex I of the UNFCCC).[142] A third way to operationalise the principle of CBDR is illustrated by the CBD, which seems to

---

[134] 'Declaration of Principles Governing the Seabed and the Ocean Floor, and the Subsoil Thereof, Beyond the Limits of National Jurisdiction', Res. 2749 (XXV), 17 December 1970 ('Seabed Declaration'), preamble, para. 4, Arts. 1–3; UNCLOS, *supra* n. 6, Art. 136.

[135] See R. Prebisch, 'Towards a New Trade Policy for Development', Report of the Secretary General to UNCTAD I, in Proceedings of the United Nations Conference on Trade and Development, UN Doc. E/CONF.46/141, vol. II, 1965, p. 1; 'Declaration on the Establishment of a New International Economic Order', Res. 3201 (S-VI), 1 May 1974, para. 4(n)–(p).

[136] See e.g. UNCLOS, *supra* n. 6, Arts. 69, 254.   [137] CPOL, *supra* n. 55, preamble, para. 3.

[138] *Ibid.*, Art. 2(2).   [139] *Ibid.*, Art. 4(2).   [140] Montreal Protocol, *supra* n. 56, Art. 5(1).

[141] Kyoto Protocol to the United Nations Framework Convention on Climate Change, Kyoto, 11 December 1997, 2303 UNTS 148 ('Kyoto Protocol'), Art. 3(1).

[142] *Ibid.*, Art. 10.

condition compliance by developing countries with their conservation obligations on the prior fulfilment of the financial and technology transfer obligations undertaken by developed countries.[143]

Beyond the grounding of this principle in these or other treaty contexts, its
legal status remains controversial.[144] Such uncertainty does not, for now, pose
any major problems, as this principle has so far been called to perform two
main functions, namely to influence the content of certain agreements and to
assist in the interpretation of their provisions, for which an elucidation of the
principle's current status in general international law is less pressing.

3.4.1.3 The principle of participation

While the principle analysed in the previous section concerns the relations
between States, the principle of participation – or more precisely, the duty of
States to provide various channels of participation to groups and individuals
potentially affected by projects, activities or environmental policies – aims to
consider the interests of these stakeholders in the relations among themselves
(e.g. between the enterprises and individuals affected), or between private
stakeholders and the State.[145] Like the principle of co-operation, the principle
of participation is general in scope, extending beyond the sphere of environmental matters. By way of illustration, Article 25 of the 1966 International
Covenant on Civil and Political Rights provides for a general right to participate in public affairs.[146] It is, however, in the environmental arena that the
principle of participation has come to prominence over the last two decades.
Some aspects of participation have already been discussed in connection with
the principle of prior informed consent of indigenous peoples. The reader is
referred to that section. Here, we focus on two main points, namely (i) the
sources and (ii) the content of this principle.

Concerning the sources, the idea of increased public participation in environmental issues has been affirmed in Principle 10 of the Rio Declaration,
which provides that:

> [e]nvironmental issues are best handled with participation of all concerned
> citizens, at the relevant level. At the national level, each individual shall have
> appropriate access to information concerning the environment that is held by
> public authorities, including information on hazardous materials and activities
> in their communities, and the opportunity to participate in decision-making
> processes. States shall facilitate and encourage public awareness and

---

[143] CBD, *supra* n. 7, Art. 20(4).

[144] See P. Cullet, 'Principle 7: Common but Differentiated Responsibilities', in Viñuales, *supra* n.
29, pp. 229–44; L. Rajamani, *Differential Treatment in International Environmental Law*
(Oxford University Press, 2006).

[145] On this principle, see J. Ebbesson, 'Principle 10: Public Participation', in Viñuales, *supra* n. 29,
pp. 287–309.

[146] International Covenant on Civil and Political Rights, 16 December 1966, 999 UNTS 171.

participation by making information widely available. Effective access to judicial and administrative proceedings, including redress and remedy, shall be provided.

This formulation suggests that public participation is important not only as a distributive instrument (weighing the interests at stake) but also, to some extent, as an instrument of prevention, through the democratic control of decision-making in environmental matters. Other instruments, particularly some treaties,[147] have given a firmer basis to the principle of participation in positive international law, although the question of its customary nature is still debated. In particular, the adoption of the Aarhus Convention[148] under the aegis of the UNECE has given a strong impetus to issues of participation in environmental matters. The influence of this Convention, which is open to accession by any State, can be detected at three levels, namely in States' obligation to adopt internal measures of public participation in environmental matters, in the establishment of a non-compliance procedure open to the public, and in its reception in the case-law of the ECtHR, which has referred to the Aarhus Convention to interpret certain human rights.

As regards the content, Principle 10 of the Rio Declaration introduced the three main components of what can be referred to as 'environmental democracy', i.e. the right to access environmental information, the right to participate in the decision-making process on environmental matters, and a right to judicial recourse, particularly (but not only) in the event the previous rights are denied. As already noted, these rights have subsequently been developed in Articles 4–5 (access to information), 6–8 (decision-making) and 9 (access to justice) of the Aarhus Convention. The interactions between the Convention and other treaties have paved the way for this 'triad' to be taken into account when interpreting a provision such as Article 8 of the European Convention on Human Rights, not only in cases where the respondent State is a party to the Aarhus Convention (Romania) but also where it is not (Turkey).[149] Whereas the latter point would suggest that the principle of participation could have a customary basis, in the *Pulp Mills* case the ICJ seemed to reject such a view, albeit in ambiguous terms. Indeed the Court noted in connection with certain instruments invoked by Argentina (not including the Aarhus Convention) that 'no legal obligation to consult the affected populations [arose]' from these instruments. However, the conclusion of the Court, as it is formulated, does not expressly affirm or deny the existence of a customary principle of participation. The question remains open.

---

[147] See P. Cullet and A. Gowlland-Gualtieri, 'Local Communities and Water Investments', in E. Brown Weiss, L. Boisson de Chazournes and N. Bernasconi-Osterwalder (eds.), *Fresh Water and International Economic Law* (Oxford University Press, 2005), pp. 303–30.

[148] Aarhus Convention on Access to Information, Public Participation in Decision-making and Access to Justice in Environmental Matters, 25 June 1998, 2161 UNTS 447 ('Aarhus Convention').

[149] *Taskın and Others* v. *Turkey*, ECtHR Application no. 46117/99, Decision (10 November 2004), paras. 99–100; *Tatar* v. *Romania*, ECtHR Application no. 67021/01), Decision (27 January 2009), para. 69.

In any event, even in the context of an instrument as progressive as the Aarhus Convention, the requirement of participation does not go as far as to provide the affected groups with a veto over the proposed activities.[150]

3.4.1.4 The principle of inter-generational equity

The principle of inter-generational equity aims to distribute the quality and availability of natural resources and the necessary efforts for their conservation between present and future generations. As such, this principle can be considered as a manifestation of the old idea of nature conservation and the more recent concept of sustainable development.

There are traces of these origins in instruments both old and new. For example, the preamble of the International Convention for the Regulation of Whaling of 1946 contains a reference to the interest of 'nations of the world in safeguarding for future generations the great natural resources represented by the whale stocks'.[151] Similarly, when in 1972 the Stockholm Conference attempted to circumscribe the province of environmental protection through the adoption of the Stockholm Declaration, it noted that: 'Man ... bears a solemn responsibility to protect and improve the environment for present and future generations'.[152] Later, when the Report of the Brundtland Commission introduced the concept of sustainable development in 1987, the focus was on meeting the needs of present generations without compromising those of future ones.[153] It is in this sense that the modern principle of inter-generational equity is expressed in Principle 3 of the Rio Declaration, which states that: '[t]he right to development must be fulfilled so as to equitably meet developmental and environmental needs of present and future generations'. Similarly, in the *Gabčíkovo-Nagymaros Project* case, the ICJ noted that:

> [o]wing to new scientific insights and to a growing awareness of the risks for mankind – for present and future generations – of pursuit of such interventions [in nature] at an unconsidered and unabated pace, new norms and standards have been developed.[154]

However, despite significant efforts to define the contours of the principle in treaties, case-law and commentary,[155] the foundation of the principle in

---

[150] See Aarhus Convention, *supra* n. 148, Arts. 6(8), 7, and 8 *in fine*; Aarhus Convention: An Implementation Guide, pp. 109–110 (available at: www.unece.org).

[151] International Convention for the Regulation of Whaling with Schedule of Whaling Regulations, 2 December 1946, 161 UNTS 361, preamble, para. 1.

[152] Declaration on the United Nations Conference on the Human Environment, 16 June 1972, 11 ILM 1416 (1972) ('Stockholm Declaration'), Principle 1.

[153] Report of the World Commission on Environment and Development: Our Common Future, UN Doc. A/42/427, Annex, 4 August 1987, para. 1.

[154] *Gabčíkovo-Nagymaros Project, supra* n. 10, para. 140.

[155] See E. Brown Weiss, *In Fairness to Future Generations: International Law, Common Patrimony, and Intergenerational Equity* (Dobbs Ferry: Transnational Publishers, 1989); C. Molinari, 'Principle 3: From a Right to Development to Intergenerational Equity', in Viñuales, *supra* n. 29, pp. 139–56.

positive law is still debated. An interesting step in this connection was made by the Supreme Court of the Philippines in the *Minors Oposa* case. There, the principle of inter-generational equity provided the basis for the admissibility of a collective action ('class suit') initiated by a group of Philippine children representing their interests as well as the interests of future generations.[156] The effective use of inter-generational equity as a primary norm in this case should not, however, lead to underestimate the considerable uncertainties surrounding both the principle's status and its content in international law.

3.4.2 Concepts expressing the idea of balance

3.4.2.1 Overview

Since its modern inception, international environmental law has been shaped by a number of concepts or 'programmes', whose function is not to operate as primary norms but, rather, to guide the formulation of such norms and, more generally, the overall structure of certain environmental regimes. In this area, the terminology varies considerably, making it difficult to identify the most relevant concepts or to specify the relations among them. It is therefore necessary to keep in mind the type of programme underlying the use of such concepts in an environmental regime. As a general matter, these concepts are all designed to distribute the benefits and the burden of 'using' the environment, either in the context of a State's growth/development policies or, more specifically, in the sharing of a common resource among States.

In this section, we discuss four 'concepts' selected on the basis of the programmes they seek to express. The first is the concept of 'sustainable development', which aims to integrate, in many ways, the demands of growth and development (both economic and social) with the protection of the environment. Then, we look at three concepts that, despite their terminological proximity, express separate programmes,[157] namely the concepts of 'common area' (free access and prohibition on the appropriation of a resource, accompanied by certain obligations), the 'common heritage of humankind' (joint management of a resource located outside State control) and 'common concern of mankind' (co-operation in the management, by each State, of a resource whose 'common' character is not linked to its location).[158]

---

[156] See *Juan Antonio Oposa and others. v. Fulgencio S. Factoran, Jr., and others*, Supreme Court of the Philippines, Decision (30 June 1993), para. 22.

[157] On the theoretical foundations of these programmes, see P.-M. Dupuy, *Droit international public* (Paris: Dalloz, 2008), pp. 775–7.

[158] See J. Brunnée, 'Common Areas, Common Heritage, and Common Concern', in Bodansky *et al., supra* n. 1, pp. 552–73.

3.4.2.2 Sustainable development

No concept of international environmental law has been used and abused more than the concept of sustainable development. Originally introduced in 1980 in a joint report published by UNEP, the World Wildlife Fund ('WWF') and the International Union for the Conservation of Nature ('IUCN'),[159] the concept of sustainable development gained recognition with the publication of the Brundtland Commission's report 'Our Common Future' in 1987. Subsequently, it featured widely in many texts of all kinds, especially after the Rio Conference in 1992. However, the political use of this concept is less relevant for present purposes than its legal use. For this reason, we focus here on its legal foundation as well as its function in international environmental law.[160] In other words, we analyse the type of legal programme (by contrast with the operational programme expressed in Agenda 21) conveyed by the concept of sustainable development.

The essence of this concept is expressed in Principle 4 of the Rio Declaration, which provides: '[i]n order to achieve sustainable development, environmental protection shall constitute an integral part of the development process and cannot be considered in isolation from it'. This definition was further specified ten years later at the Johannesburg Summit on Sustainable Development. There, a 'Political Declaration' was adopted, the terms of which played an important role in clarifying the components of the concept of sustainable development. According to paragraph 5 of this instrument 'economic development, social development and environmental protection' constitute the 'interdependent and mutually reinforcing pillars of sustainable development'.[161] Shortly before, the International Law Association ('ILA') had adopted the 'New Delhi Declaration on the Principles of International Law Related to Sustainable Development' which, in its preamble, formulated the programme conveyed by the concept of sustainable development as:

> a *comprehensive and integrated approach* to economic, social and political processes, which aims at the *sustainable use of natural resources* of the Earth and the protection of the environment on which nature and human life as well as social and economic development depend and which seeks to realize the right of all human beings to an adequate living standard on the basis of their active, free and meaningful participation in development and in the *fair distribution of benefits* resulting therefrom, with due regard to the *needs and interests of future generations.*[162]

---

[159] IUCN, UNEP, WWF, *World Conservation Strategy. Living Resource Conservation for Sustainable Development* (1980).

[160] See N. Schrijver, 'The Evolution of Sustainable Development in International Law', (2007) 328 *Recueil des cours de l'Académie de droit international de La Haye*, 217–412; V. Barral and P.-M. Dupuy, 'Principle 4: Sustainable Development through Integration', in Viñuales, *supra* n. 29, pp. 157–79.

[161] Report of the World Summit on Sustainable Development, 4 September 2002, A/CONF.199/20, Chapter I, item 1 Political Declaration, para. 5.

[162] New Delhi Declaration, *supra* n. 128, preamble (italics added).

This formulation contains the main components that legal commentators attach to the concept of sustainable development, namely (i) the need to take into account the interests of future generations, (ii) the duty of every State to exploit its natural resources in a 'sustainable' way, (iii) in doing so, the duty of each State to take into account the interests of other States and (iv) the duty of States to incorporate environmental considerations into their development policies.[163] We have already studied the first three components in our analysis of the principles of inter-generational equity, no harm and prevention. However, to understand the programme conveyed by the concept of sustainable development it is necessary to go further because, first, we have not yet developed certain aspects of the programme (including the issue of the integration of environmental considerations in development policies), and, second, legal practice often refers to other principles to express the programme of sustainable development, which also merit attention here.

Regarding the issue of integration, it had been emphasised already at the time of the Stockholm Conference. Principle 13 of the Stockholm Declaration states indeed that:

> [i]n order to achieve a more rational management of resources and thus to improve the environment, States should adopt an integrated and coordinated approach to their development planning so as to ensure that development is compatible with the need to protect and improve environment for the benefit of their population.[164]

The Rio Declaration echoes this view in Principle 4, albeit in more general terms. Thus characterised, however, the issue of integration raises an important practical question: how is the duty of integration to be applied in dispute settlement? In the *Gabčíkovo-Nagymaros Project* case, the ICJ referred to the inclusiveness of the concept of sustainable development, without giving it the character of a primary norm or 'principle'. The Court observed that '[t]his need to reconcile economic development with protection of the environment is aptly expressed in the concept of sustainable development'.[165] However, this conclusion was challenged by the Vice-President of the Court, Judge Weeramantry, in his separate opinion:

> The Court has referred to it as a concept in paragraph 140 of its Judgment. However, I consider it to be more than a mere concept, but as a principle with normative value which is crucial to the determination of this case.[166]

The arbitral tribunal in the *Iron Rhine Arbitration (Belgium/Netherlands)* of May 2005 confirmed the position of Judge Weeramantry noting that:

---

[163] See P. Sands, *Principles of International Environmental Law* (Cambridge University Press, 2003), p. 253. See more generally Schrijver, *supra* n. 160, pp. 339–65.
[164] Stockholm Declaration, *supra* n. 152, Principle 13.
[165] *Gabčíkovo-Nagymaros Project, supra* n. 10, para. 140.
[166] *Ibid.*, Separate Opinion of Judge Weeramantry, p. 85.

where development may cause significant harm to the environment there is a duty to prevent, or at least mitigate, such harm. This duty, in the opinion of the Tribunal, has now become a principle of general international law. This principle applies not only in autonomous activities but also in activities undertaken in implementation of specific treaties between the Parties.[167]

Yet, in the recent decision of the ICJ in the *Pulp Mills* case, the Court reaffirmed the conception of sustainable development expressed by the majority in the *Gabčíkovo-Nagymaros* case, namely that this is a concept or objective that must guide the negotiations between the parties.[168] Under these circumstances, we must conclude that the question of whether sustainable development can operate as a primary norm is still unsettled in general international law.

Concerning the use of other principles to convey the programme of sustainable development, instruments such as the New Delhi Declaration, the Report of the Expert Group convened by the CSD,[169] or the report prepared for the European Commission in 2000,[170] all suggested that other principles do play a role. They refer, for example, to the principles relating to the elimination of poverty,[171] precaution,[172] 'good governance',[173] the 'aesthetic value of nature',[174] the 'obligatory restoration of disturbed ecosystems',[175] the 'development of small and fragile ecosystems',[176] 'cooperation in preventing the relocation of harmful activities and substances',[177] the 'implementation of international obligations'[178] or 'monitoring compliance with international obligations',[179] to name but a few of these 'principles'. It seems clear that at least some of these 'principles' are simply conceptual developments with no actual grounding in international law. This applies, for example, to the

---

[167] *Iron Rhine Arbitration ('Ijzeren Rijn') (Belgium/Netherlands)*, Award (24 May 2005), RIAA XXVII, pp. 35–125, para. 59.

[168] *Pulp Mills, supra* n. 20, paras. 75–7 and 177.   [169] Report-Principles, *supra* n. 17.

[170] European Commission, *The Law of Sustainable Development. General Principles*, 2000 ('EC – General Principles').

[171] 'The Principle of Equity and the Eradication of Poverty', New Delhi Declaration, *supra* n. 128, Principle 2.

[172] 'The Principle of the Precautionary Approach to Human Health, Natural Resources and Ecosystems', *ibid.*, Principle 4.

[173] 'Principle of Good Governance', *ibid.*, Principle 6.

[174] 'Principle of the Aesthetic Value of Nature', *EC – General Principles, supra* n. 170, p. 121.

[175] 'Principle of the Obligatory Restoration of Disturbed Ecosystems', *ibid.*, p. 91.

[176] 'Principle of the Restrained Development of Fragile Ecosystems', *ibid.*, p. 101.

[177] 'Cooperation to Discourage or Prevent the Relocation and Transfer of Activities and Substances that Cause Severe Environmental Degradation or are Harmful to Human Health', Report-Principles, *supra* n. 17, paras. 121–2.

[178] 'National Implementation of International Commitments', Report-Principles, *supra* n. 17, paras. 153–4.

[179] 'Monitoring of Compliance with International Commitments', Report-Principles, *supra* n. 17, paras. 155–60.

'principle of the aesthetic value of nature', which is an attempt to transpose certain instruments of national law upon the international level. Other 'principles' are generalisations of certain obligations arising from environmental treaties or of objectives pursued by these latter or, still, of specific components of well-established principles. This is the case, for example, of the array of principles relating to 'cooperation to discourage or prevent the relocation and transfer of activities and substances that cause severe environmental degradation or are harmful to human health'.[180] Finally, some of these 'principles' are essentially attempts to generalise some processes, such as the 'supervision of international obligations' or the 'national implementation of international obligations', which are found in a number of environmental treaties. While recognising the value of these efforts towards the progressive development of international environmental law and the reorganisation of its concepts or components, greater uniformity seems desirable in order to facilitate the analysis of the legal foundations of certain principles or concepts in international law.

3.4.2.3 Common areas

The concept of 'common area' or 'res communis' is very old. From its ancient sources in Roman law to its development by the jurists of the sixteenth century (Vitoria, Suarez) and its systematisation by Grotius in the seventeenth century, this concept was first used to express the status of the high seas in international law. The programme conveyed by this concept is characterised by two main components, namely free access to a common resource and the impossibility of appropriation. However, this is a programme that could potentially open the door to abuses in the use of common areas by States, especially dominant States.

A possible solution to this problem is to correlate the access and use of the common resource with duties to ensure its protection. This is one of the approaches adopted by UNCLOS,[181] which guarantees free access to and use of the high seas, while imposing restrictions on the use of biological resources[182] and, more generally, some duties relating to the protection of the marine environment[183] and the interests of other States.[184] Freedom of the high seas also includes the freedom to fly over the air space, which is equivalent to the distribution of another 'common area'.[185]

---

[180] See *supra* Section 3.3.5.

[181] UNCLOS has also adopted an approach that is different from the concept of 'common area', but that was deemed more effective as regards the exploitation and protection of marine resources, namely the 'territorialisation' of large areas that previously were part of the high seas. Thus, in accordance with Part V of UNCLOS, coastal States exercise 'sovereign rights' (which should not be equated with the exercise of 'sovereignty') over resources that are located in their 'exclusive economic zone', i.e. an area up to 200 nautical miles from the baselines from which the width of the territorial sea is measured. See UNCLOS, *supra* n. 6.

[182] *Ibid.*, Arts. 116–120.   [183] *Ibid.*, Art. 192.   [184] *Ibid.*, Art. 87(2).   [185] *Ibid.*, Art. 87(1)(b).

A second example of a common area is Antarctica. The preamble to
the Antarctic Treaty, signed in 1959, recognised that it was in 'the
interest of all mankind' that Antarctica be used for peaceful purposes
only.[186] The programme expressed by this concept is relatively similar to
that of the two other common areas mentioned but with some important
nuances. For example, the Treaty 'freezes' all sovereignty claims over the
Antarctic zone during its lifetime,[187] which implicitly suggests that
'appropriation' could become possible at some future point in time. As
for the use of the resources (biological, mineral, other[188]) of Antarctica, it
is subject to a fairly detailed regime set up by a series of treaties of the
'Antarctic Treaty System'.[189]

A third example of a common area is outer space, including the Moon
and other celestial bodies. The principles of free access and non-
appropriation in this context were established by the UN General
Assembly in 1963 with the adoption of the 'Declaration of Legal Principles
Governing the Activities of States in the Exploration and Use of Outer
Space',[190] stressing the 'common interest to all mankind' in the exploration
and exploitation of outer space for peaceful purposes.[191] This was confirmed
by the adoption in 1967 of the Treaty on Outer Space,[192] which provides in
Articles I and II, respectively, for the principle of free access and the prohibition of appropriation. The risks associated with a race to the occupation and
exploitation of outer space have therefore been mitigated to some extent.
In addition, the Treaty on Outer Space introduced some other obligations,
such as the prohibition to place in orbit weapons of mass destruction,[193]
the duty to avoid contamination of outer space or changes in the Earth's
environment,[194] and a regime of liability for damage to another State
party.[195] This legal situation was subsequently modified by the Moon

---

[186] Antarctic Treaty, *supra* n. 132.   [187] *Ibid.*, Art. IV.

[188] Such as the enormous freshwater resources which constitute the icebergs. See J. E. Viñuales,
'Iced Freshwater Resources: A Legal Exploration' (2009) 19 *Yearbook of International
Environmental Law* 188.

[189] This includes, in the area of biological resources, the Convention for the Conservation of
Antarctic Seals ('CCAS'), 1 June 1972, and the Convention for the Conservation of Antarctic
Marine Living Resources ('CCAMLR'), 20 May 1980. In terms of mineral resources, a
Convention on the Regulation of Antarctic Mineral Resource Activities ('CRAMRA') was
concluded in June 1988. However, it has not been ratified, and in any event, it has been
deprived of its object with the adoption, on 4 October 1991, of the Protocol to the Antarctic
Treaty on the Protection of the Environment, Art. 7 providing that '[a]ny activity relating to
mineral resources, other than scientific research, shall be prohibited'.

[190] 'Declaration of Legal Principles Governing the Activities of States in the Exploration and Use
of Outer Space', 13 December 1963, UN Doc. A/18/1962, paras. 2 and 3.

[191] *Ibid.*, preamble.   [192] Outer Space Treaty, *supra* n. 133.   [193] *Ibid.*, Art. IV.

[194] *Ibid.*, Art. IX.

[195] *Ibid.*, Art. VII. This system was completed with the adoption of the Convention on
International Liability for Damage Caused by Space Objects, 29 March 1972 961 UNTS 187.

Treaty, concluded in 1979, which placed the Moon under the status of 'common heritage of mankind'.[196]

3.4.2.4 Common heritage of mankind

The concept of 'common heritage of mankind' conveys a different programme from those we have examined up to now. While excluding the appropriation of a resource (as is the case for common areas), this programme places the exploitation of the resource under common management. As a result, access to the resource is reserved exclusively to the entity in charge of the joint management. However, the joint management is intended for the benefit of all States, both those who have the technical and financial resources to exploit the resource and those who do not. Of course, the details of the programme will vary from case to case.

In the context of the Moon Treaty, where, as noted above, the Moon is conferred the status of 'common heritage of mankind', Article 11(5) provides that:

> States Parties ... undertake to establish an international regime, including appropriate procedures, to govern the exploitation of the natural resources of the Moon as such exploitation is about to become feasible.[197]

However, in the absence of ratification of this treaty by the States most active in the exploitation of outer space, its practical effect is very limited.

The concept of common heritage of mankind has been further developed in connection with the management of the seabed.[198] The first development occurred in 1970 when the UN General Assembly adopted the 'Declaration of Principles Governing the Seabed and the Ocean Floor, and Subsoil Thereof, beyond the Limits of National Jurisdiction',[199] which placed the 'Area' and its resources under the status of common heritage of mankind. This characterisation has been taken up in Part XI of the UNCLOS, which subjects the Area to a regime of international management.[200] In particular, Article 137(2) provides that:

> [a]ll rights in the resources of the Area are vested in mankind as a whole, on whose behalf the Authority shall act. These resources are not subject to alienation. The minerals recovered from the Area, however, may only be alienated in accordance with this Part and the rules, regulations and procedures of the Authority.[201]

The programme conveyed by this provision was very controversial, preventing the entry into force of the Convention for over a decade. It

---

[196] Agreement Governing the Activities of States on the Moon and Other Celestial Bodies, 18 December 1979, 1363 UNTS 3 ('Moon Treaty'), Art. 11(1).
[197] *Ibid.*, Art. 11(5).
[198] See R.-J. Dupuy, 'La notion de patrimoine commun de l'humanité appliquée aux fonds marins', in *Mélanges Colliard* (Paris: Pedone, 1984), pp. 197–205.
[199] See Seabed Declaration, *supra* n. 134.   [200] UNCLOS, *supra* n. 6, Part XI.
[201] *Ibid.*, Art. 137(2).

was only with the adoption in 1994 of the New York Agreement on the application of Part XI of UNCLOS that the entry into force of the latter became possible.[202] While under the New York Agreement the regime of exploration and exploitation of the Area was watered down in response to the concerns of industrialised countries, it nevertheless represents the clearest expression of the programme conveyed by the concept of common heritage of mankind.

Beyond these two examples, references to the concept of common heritage of mankind are rare. Of note are the references to this concept in the 1972 UNESCO Convention on the Protection of the World Cultural and Natural Heritage[203] and, in a different context, in the 'Universal Declaration on the Human Genome and Human Rights', of 1997.[204] However, unlike the previous examples, these references are not linked to a programme of joint management of the object in question. This said, subsequent formulations do include this link, which explains in part why States have been increasingly reluctant to use this concept and have preferred to refer to the concept of 'common concern of humankind'.

3.4.2.5 Common concern of humankind

The concept of common concern of humankind emerged in the 1990s, even though it is possible to find similar earlier ideas. The programme conveyed by this concept is clearly different from that associated with the concept of common heritage of mankind in that the object can be exploited by individual States and is not jointly managed as a common resource. Instead, States are subject to certain requirements regarding the individual exploitation. The specific requirements vary depending on the context, but the emphasis is on cooperation, access regulation and/or protection of a resource. The two main examples of this concept are provided by the CBD and the UNFCCC.

Regarding the first, the reluctance of developing countries (who hold most of the Earth's biological resources) prevented the application of the concept of common heritage of mankind to biological diversity as a resource.[205] As such, the preamble of the CBD merely stated that 'the conservation of *biological diversity* is a common concern of humankind', adding immediately after that

---

[202] See generally, R. R. Churchill and A. V. Lowe, *The Law of the Sea* (Manchester University Press, 3rd edn, 1999), Chapter 11.

[203] Convention Concerning the Protection of the World Cultural and Natural Heritage, 16 November 1972, 1037 UNTS 151 ('World Heritage Convention'). The preamble provides, notably, that 'parts of the cultural or natural heritage are of outstanding interest and therefore need to be preserved as part of the world heritage of mankind as a whole'.

[204] Resolution 29 C/17, UNESCO GC, 29th Sess. (1997), endorsed by UNGA A/RES/53/152. According to Article 1, 'In a symbolic sense, [the human genome] is the heritage of humanity'. See S. Maljean-Dubois, 'Bioéthique et droit international' (2000) 46 *Annuaire français de droit international* 82.

[205] On the origin of the CBD, see M.-A. Hermitte, 'La convention sur la diversité biologique' (1992) 38 *Annuaire français de droit international* 844.

'States have sovereign rights over their own *biological resources*' and that '[they] are responsible for conserving their biological diversity'.[206] Thus, the CBD establishes the duties of conservation for States in respect of biological 'diversity'[207] and a system of (limited) access by other States to biological (and particularly genetic) 'resources'.[208]

As for the UNFCCC, the emphasis is on the duty of co-operation to address the 'adverse effects' of climate change on the planet, which is a 'common concern of humankind'.[209] Thus, unlike the CBD, the UNFCCC focuses on a global resource indirectly defined by Article 2 of the Convention. This resource is, in essence, a stable climatic system, and it must be preserved through the control of anthropogenic interference with the atmospheric composition. Although this 'resource' is global because it transcends the territory of any and all States, its preservation nevertheless requires the adoption of appropriate measures by each State individually (national measures) and/or in co-operation with other States (international measures).

3.5 From principles to regulation

The conceptual matrix of international environmental law analysed in the foregoing paragraphs can be seen, in practice, as a set of 'policies' that are implemented by environmental treaties. Understanding these policies, their operation and their legal grounding thus amounts to learning the underpinnings of the more sophisticated environmental regimes analysed in the next four chapters of this book.

In some cases, a treaty is fully devoted to the advancement of one of these policies. Examples include the Aarhus Convention, which embodies the principle of participation, or the Espoo Convention, which spells out the requirement to conduct an environmental impact assessment. More often, however, environmental regimes implement more than one policy. By way of illustration, the POP Convention is premised both on the precautionary approach and on the prevention principle. Similarly, the ozone and climate change regimes rest upon several principles, including precaution, common but differentiated responsibilities and intergenerational equity.

Different regimes may spell out the same underlying policy in different ways. Thus, as will be discussed in Chapters 5 and 7, the principle of common but differentiated responsibilities is translated in significantly different terms by the ozone regime (all States have similar quantified reduction targets but developing States are given additional assistance and longer deadlines), the climate change regime (some States have quantified reduction targets and others have not) and the POP Convention (differences are managed through a sophisticated system of time-limited exceptions available to all States).

---

[206] CBD, *supra* n. 7, preamble (italics added).   [207] *Ibid.*, Arts. 6–11.
[208] *Ibid.*, Arts. 15 and 19, especially.   [209] UNFCCC, *supra* n. 11, preamble.

There may be cases where a policy is stated as the underlying basis of a treaty but the content of the latter prevents such policy from being effectively translated. This argument could be made either when the treaty is too elementary, such as the 1997 UN Convention on Watercourses, or when it is perhaps too ambitious, such as Part XI of UNCLOS which places the 'Area' under a common heritage regime that, so far, has proved difficult to implement.

For present purposes, what matters most is to keep these considerations in mind when embarking on the study of the specific treaty regimes examined in the following chapters.

Select bibliography

Agius, E. and S. Busuttil (eds.), *Future Generations and International Law* (London: Earthscan, 1998).

Barral, V., *Le développement durable en droit international: Essai sur les incidences juridiques d'un concept évolutif* (Ph.D. dissertation defended at the European University Institute, 2007).

'Sustainable Development in International Law: Nature and Operation of an Evolutive Legal Norm' (2012) 23 *European Journal of International Law* 377.

Barrios, P., 'The Rotterdam Convention on Hazardous Chemicals: A Meaningful Step towards Environmental Protection?' (2004) 16 *Georgetown International Environmental Law Review* 679.

Beyerlin, U., 'Different Types of Norms in International Environmental Law', in D. Bodansky, J. Brunnée and E. Hey (eds.), *The Oxford Handbook of International Environmental Law* (Oxford University Press, 2007), pp. 425–48.

Birnbacher, D., *La responsabilité envers les générations futures* (Paris: Presses universitaires de France, 1994).

Bodansky, D., 'Deconstructing the Precautionary Principle', in D. Caron and H. N. Scheiber (eds.), *Bringing New Law to Ocean Waters* (Leiden: Martinus Nijhoff, 2004), pp. 381–91.

Boisson de Chazournes, L. and S. Maljean-Dubois, 'Les principes du droit international de l'environnement', in *Juris-classeur environnement*, fascicule 146–15 (2011).

Boyle, A., 'Making the Polluter Pay? Alternatives to State Responsibility in the Allocation of Transboundary Environmental Cost', in F. Francioni and T. Scovazzi (eds.), *International Responsibility for Environmental Harm* (London: Graham & Trotman, 1991), pp. 363–79.

Brown Weiss, E., *In Fairness to Future Generations: International Law, Common Patrimony, and Intergenerational Equity* (Dobbs Ferry: Transnational Publishers, 1989).

Brunnée, J., 'Common Areas, Common Heritage, and Common Concern', in D. Bodansky, J. Brunnée and E. Hey (eds.), *The Oxford Handbook of International Environmental Law* (Oxford University Press, 2007), pp. 552–73.

Commission on Sustainable Development, Report of the Expert Group Meeting on Identification of Principles of International Law for Sustainable Development, Geneva, Switzerland, 26–28 September 1995.

Craik, N., *The International Law of Environmental Impact Assessment* (Cambridge University Press, 2008).

Cullet, P., 'Differential Treatment in International Law: Towards a New Paradigm of Inter-State Relations' (1999) 10 *European Journal of International Law* 549.

Differential Treatment in International Environmental Law (The Hague: Kluwer, 2003).

De Sadeleer, N., *Essai sur la genèse et la portée juridique de quelques principes en droit de l'environnement* (Bruxelles: Bruylant, 1999).

Dupuy, P.-M., 'Formation of Customary International Law and General Principles' in D. Bodansky, J. Brunnée and E. Hey (eds.), *The Oxford Handbook of International Environmental Law* (Oxford University Press, 2007), pp. 449–69.

'Où en-est le droit de l'environnement à la fin du siècle?' (1997) *Revue générale de droit international public* 873.

Dupuy, R.-J., 'La notion de patrimoine commun de l'humanité appliquée aux fonds marins', in *Mélanges Colliard* (Paris: Pedone, 1984), pp. 197–205.

Ebbesson, J., 'The Notion of Public Participation in International Environmental Law' (1997) 8 *Yearbook of International Environmental Law* 51.

Epiney, A. and M. Scheyli, *Strukturprinzipien des Umweltvölkerrechts* (Baden-Baden: Nomos, 1998).

European Commission, *The Law of Sustainable Development. General Principles* (2000).

Francioni, F., 'Sviluppo sostenibile e principi di diritto internazionale dell'ambiente', in Società Italiana di Diritto Internazionale, *Il principio dello sviluppo sostenibile nel diritto internazionale ed europeo dell'ambiente* (Naples: Editoriale Scientifica, 2007), pp. 40–61.

Francioni, F. and H. Neuhold, 'International Cooperation for the Protection of the Environment: The Procedural Dimension', in W. Lang, H. Neuhold and K. Zemanek (eds.), *Environmental Protection and International Law* (Dordrecht: Martinus Nijhoff, 1991), pp. 203–26.

French, D., 'Developing States and International Environmental Law: The Importance of Differentiated Responsibilities' (2000) 49 *International and Comparative Law Quarterly* 35.

Gaines, S., 'The Polluter-Pays Principle: From Economic Equity to Environmental Ethos' (1991) 26 *Texas International Law Journal* 463.

Hostiou, R., 'Le lente mais irrésistible montée en puissance du principe de participation' (2003) 112 *Droit de l'environnement* 182.

Kindall, M. P. A., 'UNCED and the Evolution of Principles of International Environmental Law' (1992) 25 *John Marshall Law Review* 19.

Kiss, A., 'The Rio Declaration on Environment and Development', in L. Campiglio, L. Pineschi, D. Siniscalco and T. Treves (eds.), *The Environment after Rio: International Law and Economics* (London: Martinus Nijhoff, 1994), pp. 55–64.

Kovar, J. D., 'A Short Guide to the Rio Declaration' (1993) 4 *Colorado Journal of International Environmental Law and Policy* 119.

Lecucq, O. and S. Maljean-Dubois (eds.), *Le rôle du juge dans le développement du droit de l'environnement* (Bruxelles: Bruylant, 2008).

Lucchini, L., 'Le principe de précaution en droit international de l'environnement: Ombres plus que lumières' (1999) 45 *Annuaire français de droit international* 710.

Maljean-Dubois, S., 'L'accès à l'information et la reconnaissance d'un droit à l'information environnementale', in S. Maljean-Dubois (ed.), *L'effectivité du droit européen de l'environnement: contrôle de la mise en oeuvre et sanction du non respect* (Paris: La documentation française, 2000), p. 25.

Martin-Bidou, P., 'Le principe de précaution en droit international de l'environnement' (1999) *Revue générale de droit international public* 631.

Mbengue, M., *Essai sur une théorie du risque en droit international public. L'anticipation du risque environnemental et sanitaire* (Paris: Pedone, 2009).

McDorman, T., 'The Rotterdam Convention on the Prior Informed Consent Procedure for Certain Hazardous Chemicals and Pesticides in International Trade: Some Legal Notes' (2004) 13 *Review of European Community and International Environmental Law* 187.

Morgera, E. and J. Wingard, *Principles for Developing Sustainable Wildlife Management Laws*, FAO Legal Papers (2008).

Munro, R. D. and J. G. Lammers, Environmental Protection and Sustainable Development, Expert Group on Environmental Law of the World Commission on Environment and Development (1986).

Panjabi, R. K. L., 'From Stockholm to Rio: A Comparison of the Declaratory Principles of International Environmental Law' (1993) 21 *Denver Journal of International Law and Politics* 215.

Paradell-Trius, L., 'Principles of International Environmental Law: An Overview' (2000) 9 *Review of European Community and International Environmental Law* 93.

Porras, I. M., 'The Rio Declaration: A New Basis for International Co-operation' (1992) 1 *Review of European Community and International Environmental Law* 245.

Rajamani, L., *Differential Treatment in International Environmental Law* (Oxford University Press, 2006).

Ramlogan, R., *Sustainable Development: Towards a Judicial Interpretation* (Leiden: Martinus Nijhoff, 2010).

Redgwell, C., 'The International Law of Public Participation: Protected Areas, Endangered Species and Biological Diversity' in D. Zillman, A. Lucas and G. Pring (eds.), *Human Rights in Natural Resource Development – Public Participation in the Sustainable Development of Mining and Energy Resources* (Oxford University Press, 2002), pp. 187–214.

'Regulating Trade in Dangerous Substances: Prior Informed Consent under the 1998 Rotterdam Convention', in A. Kiss, D. Shelton and K. Ishibashi (eds.), *Economic Globalization and Compliance with International Environmental Agreements* (The Hague: Kluwer, 2003), pp. 75–88.

Robinson, N. A., 'EIA Abroad: The Comparative and Transnational Experience', in S. G. Hildebrand and J. B. Cannon (eds.), *Environmental Analysis: The NEPA Experience* (Boca Raton: Lewis, 1993), pp. 679–702.

Romi, R., 'Le principe pollueur-payeur, ses implications et ses applications' (1991) 8 *Droit de l'environnement* 46.

Sands, P., 'International Law in the Field of Sustainable Development' (1994) 65 *British Yearbook of International Law* 303.

Schrijver, N., 'The Evolution of Sustainable Development in International Law' (2007) 329 *Recueil des cours de l'Académie de droit international de La Haye* 217–412.

Schwartz, P., 'The Polluter-pays Principle', in J. E. Viñuales (ed.), *The Rio Declaration on Environment and Development. A Commentary* (Oxford University Press, 2015).

Scovazzi, T., 'Sul principio precauzionale nel diritto internazionale dell'ambiente' (1992) *Rivista di diritto internazionale* 699.

Shelton, D., 'Stockholm Declaration (1972) and Rio Declaration (1992)', *Max Planck Encyclopedia of Public International Law*, www.mpepil.com.

Smets, H., 'Le principe pollueur payeur, un principe économique érigé en principe de droit de l'environnement?' (1998) *Revue générale de droit international public* 85.

Supanich, G., 'The Legal Basis of Intergenerational Responsibility: An Alternative View – The Sense of Intergenerational Identity' (1992) 3 *Yearbook of International Environmental Law* 94.

Trouwborst, A., *Evolution and Status of the Precautionary Principle in International Law* (The Hague: Kluwer Law International, 2002).

Viñuales, J. E., 'The Contribution of the International Court of Justice to the Development of International Environmental Law: A Contemporary Assessment' (2008) 32 *Fordham International Law Journal* 232.

 (ed.), *The Rio Declaration on Environment and Development. A Commentary* (Oxford University Press, 2015).

Virally, M., 'Le rôle des "principes" dans le développement du droit international', *Le droit international en devenir. Essais écrits au fil des ans* (Paris: Presses Universitaires de France, 1990), pp. 195–212.

Voigt, C., *Sustainable Development as a Principle of International Law* (Leiden: Martinus Nijhoff, 2009).

Wirth, D. A., 'The Rio Declaration on Environment and Development: Two Steps Forward and One Back, or Vice Versa' (1995) 29 *Georgia Law Review* 599.

Woods, C., *The Environment, Intergenerational Equity and Long-term Investments* (doctoral dissertation, University of Oxford, 2011).

Xue Hanqin, *Transboundary Damage in International Law* (Cambridge University Press, 2003).

Part II
Substantive regulation

4

Oceans, seas and freshwater

4.1 Introduction

This chapter begins the presentation of sector-specific regulation in international environmental law by focusing on the rules governing oceans, seas and freshwater.

These objects (the marine environment and freshwater), although separate from a regulatory point of view, are closely related in that the main cause of marine pollution originates from land-based sources and is partly carried by rivers. In addition, both the law of the sea and that of watercourses can be traced back very far in the history of international law, even though the regulation of environmental issues within those areas is relatively recent. Another common feature is the customary character of some of the rules governing these two objects. More generally, from an environmental perspective, these different regulatory regimes are all concerned with the 'hydrosphere' or the waterbodies of the planet. For these reasons, it is useful to examine oceans, seas and freshwater in the same chapter.

The first substantive section covers the regulation of the marine environment (4.2). Broadly speaking, the law of the sea protects the marine environment in two principal ways. On the one hand, it distributes the jurisdiction over vast marine areas (and therefore the primary responsibility for their protection) among different States. On the other hand, it introduces a set of duties to protect the marine environment, which are, in turn, specified by other instruments. These instruments are either concerned with specific issues (e.g. a source of marine pollution) or a particular marine area (e.g. the Regional Seas Conventions). Following this structure, we analyse, first, the distribution of jurisdiction under the United Nations Convention on the Law of the Sea ('UNCLOS')[1] (4.2.1) and then turn to the duties of States in the protection of the marine environment, both in general (4.2.2) and in connection with specific sources of pollution (4.2.3) or geographical areas (4.2.4).

---

[1] United Nations Convention on the Law of the Sea, 10 December 1982, 1833 UNTS 397 ('UNCLOS').

The next section of this chapter examines the international regulation of freshwater (4.3). After presenting the overall structure of this body of law (4.3.1), we discuss the law governing international watercourses (4.3.2), groundwater (4.3.3) and freshwater locked in the form of ice (4.3.4). The question of access to water as a human right is left for Chapter 10.

4.2 The international regulation of the marine environment

4.2.1 Environmental jurisdiction over marine areas

4.2.1.1 Overview

The purpose of this section is not to present in detail the different marine areas adjacent to the coasts or the degree of State control over each stretch of water,[2] but only to show how the jurisdiction allocated to States over these areas has an impact on the protection of the environment.

Historically, marine areas have been used primarily for navigation, fishing and more recently the exploitation of mineral resources (e.g. 'offshore' oil and gas). The regulation of these three activities requires a compromise between the interests of the coastal State and other States that wish to use these areas ('flag States'). Furthermore, since the Stockholm Declaration of 1972, the emphasis has gradually shifted towards environmental protection *per se*. To reconcile these considerations, various solutions have been proposed over time, ranging from exclusive use of the sea by a State (*mare clausum*) to total freedom of the sea for all States (*mare liberum*), and many variations in between.[3] Throughout the twentieth century, coastal States have actively sought to increase their control over the marine areas adjacent to their coasts by unilateral declarations, which has often generated political tension.[4] Major codification efforts have since been undertaken under the auspices of the United Nations. However, despite significant advances in the first (1958) and the second (1960) UN Conferences on the Law of the Sea, particularly in respect of the definition of the continental shelf and the recognition of the jurisdiction of the coastal State over its territorial sea and contiguous zone, some fundamental questions remained open, not least as regards the extent of the territorial sea and, more generally, of State powers over marine areas.[5] It was only during the course of the third UN Conference on the Law of the Sea (1974–82) that a general agreement was reached on the extent of the jurisdiction of States over various marine areas, particularly the territorial sea, with the adoption of UNCLOS.[6]

---

[2] See P.-M. Dupuy, *Droit international public* (Paris: Dalloz, 2008), paras. 639–55.

[3] See T. W. Fulton, *The Sovereignty of the Sea* (Clark NJ: The Lawbook Exchange, 1911).

[4] See *Fisheries Case (United Kingdom v. Norway)*, Judgment, ICJ Reports 1951, p. 116.

[5] This question has continued to be a source of international tension. See e.g. *Fisheries Jurisdiction (Federal Republic of Germany v. Iceland)*, Merits, Judgment, ICJ Reports 1974, p. 175; *Fisheries Jurisdiction (United Kingdom v. Iceland)*, Merits Judgment, ICJ Reports 1974, p. 3.

[6] See J. Harrison, *Making the Law of the Sea* (Cambridge University Press, 2011), Chapter 2.

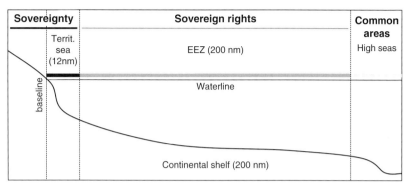

Figure 4.1: Distribution of jurisdiction under UNCLOS

One of the arguments that made the adoption of this 'constitution of the oceans' possible focused on the need to clarify the responsibilities of States regarding the conservation of marine living resources. The granting of 'property rights' to coastal States over these marine areas was therefore concerned as much with conservation as with the right to exploit these resources. Property rights were expected to provide the necessary incentives for the sustainable management of resources.[7] As such, this sense of ownership assumed by coastal States over various marine areas, which was enshrined in UNCLOS, has helped to cultivate duties in respect of conservation. To illustrate this point, it is necessary to examine briefly the three principal areas that were brought within the jurisdiction of coastal States, namely the territorial sea, the exclusive economic zone ('EEZ') and the continental shelf. Figure 4.1 provides an overview of the main areas defined by UNCLOS from an environmental perspective.

4.2.1.2 Territorial sea

The legal regime applicable to the territorial sea is mainly found in Part II of UNCLOS. The territorial sea is defined as an area of sea adjacent to the coast,[8] of a width not exceeding 12 nautical miles[9] from the 'baseline' (normally the low water mark along the coast, as it is shown on a large scale chart officially recognised by the coastal State[10]). The territorial sea is subject to the sovereignty of the coastal State,[11] in the same way as the land territory, except for the requirement that the coastal State must guarantee a 'right of innocent passage' to vessels of other States.[12]

---

[7] On the application of this logic to marine areas, see R. Barnes, *Property Rights and Natural Resources* (Oxford: Hart, 2009), pp. 165–220.
[8] UNCLOS, *supra* n. 1, Art. 2(1).   [9] *Ibid.*, Art. 3.   [10] *Ibid.*, Art. 5.   [11] *Ibid.*, Art. 2(1).
[12] *Ibid.*, Arts. 2(3) and 17 to 32.

With this recognition of sovereignty comes responsibility over the territorial sea. In accordance with Article 21(1) of UNCLOS, the coastal State is required to take certain measures, in particular for the 'conservation of living resources', 'the preservation of the environment' and 'the prevention of pollution'.[13] Furthermore, Article 211(4) specifically provides that, within its territorial sea, the coastal State may take measures for the prevention, reduction and control of marine pollution from foreign vessels, but without impeding their innocent passage. It should be borne in mind that the passage of a vessel causing wilful and serious pollution is not characterised as 'innocent' under the Convention.[14]

4.2.1.3 The exclusive economic zone

As regards the legal regime of the EEZ, it is organised essentially in Part V of UNCLOS. The EEZ is defined as an area beyond and adjacent to the territorial sea[15] up to a maximum of 200 nautical miles from the baselines from which the breadth of the territorial sea is measured.[16] The coastal State does not have sovereignty over the EEZ but only 'sovereign rights for the purpose of exploring and exploiting, conserving and managing the natural resources' found in it.[17]

The provision of more extensive rights accorded to coastal States comes with a correlative duty to protect the living resources and marine environment of the EEZ. Article 56(1)(b)(iii) grants the coastal State jurisdiction in respect of the 'protection and preservation of the marine environment'.[18] Article 61 specifies the obligations of the coastal State as regards the conservation of living resources.[19] When these living resources, owing to their particular characteristics, straddle the EEZ and the high seas, the States concerned (the coastal State and the flag States fishing for such stocks) have a duty to co-operate to ensure conservation.[20]

Ensuring co-operation has not always been easy,[21] but since 1995 an agreement known as the Straddling Fish Stocks Agreement[22] has introduced a more

---

[13] *Ibid.*, Art. 21(1)(d) and (f). Although this Article is not formulated in terms of a duty, this is the interpretation suggested by Arts. 2(1), 192 and 194(1).

[14] *Ibid.*, Art. 19(2)(h).   [15] *Ibid.*, Art. 55.   [16] *Ibid.*, Art. 57.

[17] *Ibid.*, Art. 56(1)(a). There are two primary differences between the exercise of sovereignty and sovereign rights, namely that in the latter case (i) the regime of navigation in the EEZ is similar to that of the high seas, and it is therefore defined more broadly (Art. 58); (ii) the rights of third States, and in particular 'land-locked' and 'geographically disadvantaged States', are more extensive (Arts. 69–70). See Dupuy, *supra* n. 2, para. 654.

[18] UNCLOS, *supra* n. 1, Art. 56(1)(b)(iii).   [19] *Ibid.*, Art. 61.   [20] *Ibid.*, Arts. 63 and 64.

[21] A good illustration is given by the so-called 'turbot war'. In March 1995, a Spanish fishing vessel (the *Estai*), which was fishing near the outer limits of Canada's EEZ, was boarded by a Canadian patrol, causing an international incident between Canada and the European Union. See *Fisheries Jurisdiction (Spain v. Canada)*, Judgment, ICJ Reports 1998, p. 432 ('*Estai*').

[22] Agreement for the Implementation of the Provisions of the United Nations Convention on the Law of the Sea of 10 December 1982 Relating to the Conservation and Management of Straddling Fish Stocks and High Migratory Fish Stocks, 8 September 1995, 2167 UNTS 3 ('Straddling Fish Stocks Agreement').

detailed regime on the conservation of such stocks.[23] Beyond the conservation of biological resources, the coastal State 'may', more generally, adopt laws and regulations for the 'prevention, reduction and control of pollution from vessels'[24] and is also entitled to 'take such measures, including boarding, inspection, arrest and judicial proceedings, as may be necessary to ensure compliance with the laws and regulations adopted by it in conformity with this Convention'.[25]

4.2.1.4 The continental shelf

Regarding the legal regime of the continental shelf, UNCLOS deals with it in Part VI. According to Article 76(1):

> [t]he continental shelf of a coastal State comprises the seabed and subsoil of the submarine areas that extend beyond its territorial sea throughout the natural prolongation of its land territory to the outer edge of the continental margin, or to a distance of 200 nautical miles from the baselines from which the breadth of the territorial sea is measured where the outer edge of the continental margin does not extend up to that distance.[26]

As in the case of the EEZ, the coastal State exercises 'sovereign rights' over its continental shelf for the purposes of exploration and exploitation of natural resources.[27]

Part VI of UNCLOS contains no provision comparable to those on the conservation of the marine environment in respect of the territorial sea and EEZ. However, Article 208(1) of UNCLOS provides that coastal States 'adopt laws and regulations to prevent, reduce and control pollution of the marine environment arising from or in connection with seabed activities subject to their jurisdiction'.[28] As such, one can consider that the environmental jurisdiction of the coastal State does extend to activities carried out in the continental shelf.

4.2.2 Protection of the marine environment: general aspects

The environmental dimension of UNCLOS is not limited to the distribution of jurisdiction among States. On the contrary, Part XII of UNCLOS is devoted entirely to the 'Protection and Preservation of the Marine Environment'.[29] This section includes forty-six articles spread over eleven sections: General Provisions (Section 1); Global and Regional Cooperation (Section 2);

---

[23] See Chapter 6.   [24] UNCLOS, *supra* n. 1, Art. 211(5).   [25] *Ibid.*, Art. 73(1).

[26] *Ibid.*, Art. 76(1). Where the outer edge of the continental margin lies beyond 200 nautical miles, States may claim a longer continental shelf, ranging up to 350 nautical miles from the baselines. See *ibid.*, Arts. 76(4)–(8) and 82.

[27] *Ibid.*, Art. 77(1).   [28] *Ibid.*, Art. 208(1). See also Art. 214 on the implementation of Art. 208.

[29] See: P.-M. Dupuy, 'La préservation du milieu marin', in R.-J. Dupuy and D. Vignes (eds.), *Traité du nouveau droit de la mer* (Paris/Brussels: Economica/Bruylant, 1985), Chapter 20.

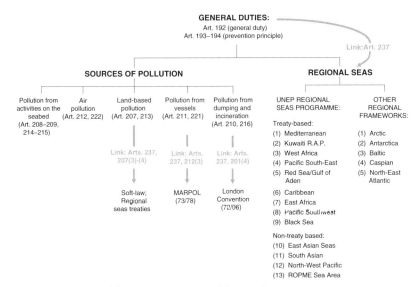

Figure 4.2: Overview of the UNCLOS environmental framework

Technical Assistance (Section 3); Monitoring and Environmental Assessment (Section 4); International Rules and National Legislation to Prevent, Reduce and Control Pollution of the Marine Environment (Section 5); Enforcement (Section 6); Safeguards (Section 7); Ice-covered Areas (Section 8); Responsibility and Liability (Section 9); Sovereign Immunity (Section 10); and Obligations Under the Other Conventions on the Protection and Preservation of the Marine Environment (Section 11). This part of UNCLOS therefore provides a general framework while at the same time formulating substantive obligations for the protection of the marine environment and organisational norms, some of which we have already mentioned in the previous section. To understand how Part XII of UNCLOS works, one must focus on its three main components, namely (i) the duties in respect of environmental protection, (ii) the standards relating to sources of pollution and (iii) the provisions governing the relationship with other conventions. Figure 4.2 provides an overview of the framework set out by UNCLOS for the protection of the marine environment. Only the instruments discussed in this chapter are mentioned.

As regards (i), Article 192 of UNCLOS introduced a general obligation of States to 'protect and preserve the marine environment'.[30] The scope of this provision should not be underestimated. This is the first express statement, contained in a treaty with global coverage, of an obligation to protect and preserve the marine environment.[31] Note that Article 192 does not use the

---

[30] UNCLOS, *supra* n. 1, Art. 192.
[31] See in this regard: M. H. Nordquist, S. N. Nandan and J. Kraska (eds.), *United Nations Convention on the Law of the Sea: A Commentary*, vol. IV (Dordrecht/Boston: Martinus Nijhoff, 1991), pp. 35–43.

term 'States Parties' but only 'States'. Of the various possible interpretations of this terminological choice,[32] we believe that the one that emphasises the customary nature of this obligation is the most persuasive. The contents of this general obligation are formulated with more precision in other contexts. In particular, Article 194 provides for the duty of States (not the 'States Parties') to take measures to 'prevent, reduce and control pollution of the marine environment'[33] and to combat 'all sources of pollution of the marine environment'.[34]

Moving on to (ii), UNCLOS distinguishes between five main forms of marine pollution,[35] namely pollution from land-based sources (including from inland waterways),[36] pollution from vessels,[37] pollution from dumping or incineration,[38] air or trans-atmospheric pollution[39] and pollution resulting from activities on the seabed or in the 'Area'.[40] Articles 207 to 212 lay down the duty of States (in particular, but not limited to, coastal States) to take measures to prevent, reduce and control pollution of the marine environment.[41] Depending on the source of the pollution, the Convention may impose certain minimum requirements or stipulate that certain domestic measures meet international standards. Thus, for example, in terms of pollution by dumping, Article 210 provides that the laws, regulations and measures adopted by States must ensure that dumping is not possible without the authorisation of the competent authorities of the State[42] and that any dumping in the EEZ or the continental shelf requires the prior consent of the coastal State.[43] Moreover, under Article 210(6), the laws, regulations and measures adopted for this purpose should not be less effective than the 'global rules and standards'.[44] However, in terms of land-based sources of pollution, Article 207 only requires States to 'take into account' internationally agreed standards and practices.[45] Article 207(5), on the other hand, requires the adoption of measures 'designed to minimize . . . the release of toxic, harmful or noxious substances, especially those which are persistent', but this duty is qualified by the phrase 'to the fullest extent possible'. These various levels of requirements are explained largely by the presence of treaties specifically addressing some types of pollution.

As for (iii), UNCLOS negotiators were well aware since the beginning of the third codification conference in 1974 of the need to clarify the relationship

---

[32] See ibid., para. 192.8.   [33] UNCLOS, *supra* n. 1, Art. 194(1).   [34] *Ibid.*, Art. 194(3).
[35] The general framework is provided by UNCLOS, Art. 194(3).   [36] *Ibid.*, Arts. 207 and 213.
[37] *Ibid.*, Arts. 211 and 221.   [38] *Ibid.*, Arts. 210 and 216.   [39] *Ibid.*, Arts. 212 and 222.
[40] *Ibid.*, Arts. 208, 209, 214, and 215.
[41] *Ibid.*, Arts. 207(1)–(2), 208(1)–(2), 209(2), 210(1)–(2), 211(1), 212(1).   [42] *Ibid.*, Art. 210(3).
[43] *Ibid.*, Art. 210(5).
[44] *Ibid.*, Art. 210(6). This paragraph should be read as a reference to the London Convention of 1972, which will be discussed. Similar requirements (but referring to international standards and practices) are provided for pollution of the seabed and the Area (Arts. 208(3) and 209(2)) and pollution from ships (Art. 211(2)).
[45] *Ibid.*, Art. 207(1). A similar requirement is stipulated for air and trans-atmospheric pollution (Art. 212(1)).

between the Convention and existing (or future) treaties and agreements on the protection of the marine environment.[46] Article 237 of UNCLOS governs the relationship between Part XII (which is thus distinguished from the relationship between UNCLOS and agreements in general[47]) and other treaties and agreements. Despite a somewhat ambiguous formulation, these relations follow the principle of *lex specialis*. The specific obligations assumed by States under existing (or future) special treaties and agreements prevail over the obligations of States under Part XII, unless they are inconsistent 'with the general principles and objectives of [the] Convention'.[48] The incompatibility must be serious, otherwise it would not reach the threshold required to call into question the 'general' principles and objectives of UNCLOS. The International Maritime Organisation ('IMO'), under the aegis of which many treaties and standards have been adopted, has looked more closely into the relationship between such instruments and Part XII of UNCLOS. Its position is that Article 237 (as well as Article 311) does not hinder the normative activity of the IMO or limit its mandate. On the contrary, UNCLOS seems to rely, in many respects, on the normative role of the IMO in order to achieve its objectives.[49] As discussed next, there are several international instruments concerning the protection of the marine environment and they fit into the framework laid down by Part XII of UNCLOS.[50]

4.2.3 Regulation of sources of pollution

4.2.3.1 Overview
Several instruments have been adopted within the framework of the IMO in order to protect the marine environment against some sources of pollution. The distinction made in UNCLOS between different sources of pollution provides a convenient base to structure the material covered in this section. In this context, we will analyse in turn the main international instruments on pollution by ships (operational or accidental), pollution by dumping or incineration (intentional) and land-based sources of pollution. It should be emphasised that despite the interest that the first two sources of marine pollution have received at the international level, land-based sources are responsible for approximately 70 per cent of marine pollution. This source will be analysed last as its international legal regulation is essentially regional.

[46] On the history of Art. 37, see Nordquist *et al., supra* n. 31, para. 237.2–237.6.
[47] *Ibid.*, para. 237.7(a), referring to UNCLOS, *supra* n. 1, Art. 311.
[48] UNCLOS, *supra* n. 1, Art. 237(2).
[49] See IMO, Implications of the United Nations Convention on the Law of the Sea, 1982, for the International Maritime Organization (IMO), Doc. LEG/MISC/1 (1986 mimeo.), paras. 71–3, cited in Nordquist *et al., supra* n. 31, para. 237.7(e).
[50] See Nordquist *et al., supra* n. 31, para. XII.26.

4.2.3.2 Pollution from vessels

This type of pollution arises from the normal operation of ships for the transportation of goods in a broad sense, as well as from accidents that may occur during transportation.[51] The objective of the international instruments adopted in this regard is essentially (i) to minimise (including by way of prevention) any 'release' of oil or other harmful substances, (ii) in the case of an accident, to facilitate the management of the situation, and (iii) to establish a system of reparation for damage caused. We will focus here on points (i) and (ii), leaving point (iii) for Chapter 8.

Already in 1954, a number of States had adopted an International Convention for the Prevention of Pollution of the Sea by Oil (also known as 'OILPOL').[52] Two decades later, this treaty was replaced through the adoption of the 1973 International Convention for the Prevention of Pollution from Ships and its Protocol of 1978 (collectively known as 'MARPOL 73/78' or 'MARPOL').[53] MARPOL applies to 'discharges'[54] by 'ships'[55] of 'harmful substances'.[56] These terms are broadly defined, with two important nuances. As regards the term 'ship', it may be a vessel, a submarine or a fixed or floating platform, which flies the flag of, or is operated by, a State party to the Convention.[57] However, ships assigned to governmental purposes, such as military ships, are not covered.[58] With respect to the term 'discharge', Article 2(3)(b) excludes from its definition, among other things, 'dumping' within the meaning of the London Convention, which will be discussed later.[59] Regulations under MARPOL to prevent or reduce discharges are included in six annexes.[60] The first two are mandatory, since a State cannot become a party to the Convention without accepting them. MARPOL uses various techniques, depending on the type of pollution. Regarding oil pollution, these techniques are, first, to stipulate a series of requirements that must be met by States (technical requirements for operational discharges; the construction of oil tankers – double hull; the creation of shore installations; the development of emergency plans aboard ships; the definition of special areas in the sea where the requirements for prevention are stricter)

---

[51] See in general, A. K.-J. Tan, *Vessel-Source Marine Pollution* (Cambridge University Press, 2006).

[52] International Convention for the Prevention of Pollution of the Sea by Oil, 12 May 1954, 327 UNTS 3.

[53] International Convention for the Prevention of Pollution from Ships, 2 November 1973, amended by the Protocol of 17 February 1978, 1341 UNTS 3 ('MARPOL 73/78'). See J. Kindt, 'Vessel Source Pollution and the Law of the Sea' (1984) 17 *Vanderbilt Journal of Transnational Law* 287.

[54] MARPOL, *supra* n. 53, Art. 2(3).   [55] *Ibid.*, Art. 2(4).   [56] *Ibid.*, Art. 2(2).   [57] *Ibid.*, Art. 3(1).

[58] *Ibid.*, Art. 3(3).   [59] *Ibid.*, Art. 3(3)(b)(i).

[60] Annex I (Regulations for the Prevention of Pollution by Oil); Annex II (Regulations for the Control of Pollution by Noxious Liquid Substances in Bulk); Annex III (Regulations for the Prevention of Pollution by Harmful Substances Carried at Sea in Packaged Form); Annex IV (Regulations for the Prevention of Pollution by Sewage from Ships); Annex V (Regulations for the Control of Pollution by Garbage from Ships); Annex VI (Regulations for the Prevention of Air Pollution from Ships).

and to establish, on the other hand, a control system for these requirements
(certification, a register of operations and the inspection of ships). In short,
States must adopt technical measures to implement a system that attempts to
reduce discharges and prevent accidents.[61]

If an accident occurs, other sets of rules apply to the management of the
response to that accident. The need to organise such a response has been
underlined by the considerable damage that these accidents can cause. Major
oil spills such as those arising from the grounding of the *Torrey Canyon* (1967),
the *Amoco Cadiz* (1978), the *Exxon Valdez* (1989), the *Erika* (1999), the
Prestige (2002) or the incident on the oilrig Deep Water Horizon (2010) in
the Gulf of Mexico, provide many examples of the magnitude of such risk.
With the adoption of UNCLOS in 1982, a minimum framework for the
management of such accidents was set out.[62] Then, following the sinking of
the *Exxon Valdez*, an International Convention on Oil Pollution Preparedness,
Response and Cooperation[63] ('OPRC Convention') was adopted at the initiative of the IMO. Each State party to this Convention must put in place a
system to respond to oil spills, with a minimum content (notably, identifying
relevant authorities and developing a national contingency plan to deal with
emergencies).[64] States must also require that ships and platforms under their
jurisdiction have an emergency contingency plan to deal with any accidents.[65]
These arrangements are supplemented by notification procedures where an
'event', such as an oil spill, occurs or is likely to occur,[66] as well as obligations to
co-operate in the prevention[67] and management of such an event.[68] In March
2000, a Protocol to the Convention was adopted (OPRC–HNS Protocol),[69]
whereby the scope of the OPRC Convention was extended beyond oil pollution to include hazardous and noxious substances.

4.2.3.3 Dumping and incineration

The dumping of wastes and other materials, which accounts for approximately
10 per cent of marine pollution, has led to the adoption of a treaty with global
scope. Known as the 'London Convention' or 'Dumping Convention', the
treaty was adopted shortly after the Stockholm Conference in 1972 and

---

[61] Other relevant texts in this regard include: the International Convention for the Control and
Management of Ships Ballast Water and Sediments, 16 February 2004, available at www.ecolex.
org (TRE-001412); the International Convention on the Control of Harmful Anti-fouling
Systems on Ships, 5 October 2001, available at www.ecolex.org (TRE-001394) ('AFS
Convention').

[62] UNCLOS, *supra* n. 1, Arts. 198 (Notification of Imminent or Actual Damage), 199
(Contingency Plans against Pollution), and 211(7) (Pollution from Vessels).

[63] International Convention on Oil Pollution Preparedness, Response and Cooperation, 30
November 1990, available at www.ecolex.org (TRE-001109) ('OPRC Convention').

[64] *Ibid.*, Art. 6.   [65] *Ibid.*, Art. 3.   [66] *Ibid.*, Arts. 4 and 5.   [67] *Ibid.*, Arts. 8–10.   [68] *Ibid.*, Art. 7.

[69] Protocol on Preparedness, Response and Cooperation to Pollution Incidents by Hazardous and
Noxious Substances, 15 March 2000, available at: www.ecolex.org (TRE-002482) ('Protocol
OPRC–HNS').

subsequently amended several times, notably with the adoption in 1996 of the 'London Protocol'.[70]

The London Convention has twenty-two articles and three annexes. Its general approach is simple: States parties shall take measures to prohibit or restrict the dumping of certain wastes identified in order of harmfulness, in three annexes. The concept of 'dumping' is defined in Article 3(1)(a) as 'any deliberate disposal at sea of wastes or other matter from vessels, aircraft, platforms or other man-made structures at sea' and, for the avoidance of doubt, 'any deliberate disposal of vessels, aircraft, platforms or other man-made structures at sea'. Excluded from this definition are operational discharges covered by MARPOL.[71] 'Wastes and other materials' are defined broadly,[72] but the precise regime to be applied in respect of particular waste depends on the various annexes. According to Article 3 of the Convention, the dumping of wastes listed in Annex I (e.g. oil, mercury, radioactive waste, etc.) must be prohibited,[73] while the dumping of the substances listed in Annex II (e.g. arsenic, lead, copper, zinc, etc.) and III (other wastes restricted by quantity and/or place of disposal) should be subject to a specific[74] or general permit system.[75]

This general approach (dumping is authorised unless there is a specific prohibition) was amended by the entry into force of the 1996 London Protocol, in March 2006. This Protocol, which is based on the precautionary approach,[76] modifies the fundamental approach of the Convention. The new rule is that dumping and incineration at sea are prohibited[77] unless they are specifically authorised.[78] The Protocol replaces the London Convention for the States parties to both instruments,[79] but it is also open to States that are not a party to the Convention.[80]

4.2.3.4 Land-based pollution

Pollution from land, either directly by urban or agricultural discharges, or indirectly through watercourses or groundwater, accounts for about 70 per cent of marine pollution. The diversity of sources and activities that contribute to this type of pollution make global regulation difficult.[81] As we have seen, UNCLOS

---

[70] Convention on the Prevention of Marine Pollution by Dumping of Wastes and Other Matter, 29 December 1972 ('London Convention'), subsequently modified by the Protocol of 7 November 1996 to the Convention of 1972 on the Prevention of Marine Pollution by Dumping of Wastes and Other Matter, 7 November 1996, 1046 UNTS 120 ('London Protocol'). For an analysis of this system in a concrete case, see C. Warbrick et al., 'The 1996 Protocol to the London Dumping Convention and the Brent Spar' (1997) 46 International & Comparative Law Quarterly 957.

[71] London Convention, supra n. 70, Art. 3(1)(b).   [72] Ibid., Art. 3(4).   [73] Ibid., Art. 4(1)(a).

[74] Ibid., Art. 4(1)(b).   [75] Ibid., Art. 4(1)(c).   [76] London Protocol, supra n. 70, Art. 3(1).

[77] Ibid., Art. 5.   [78] Ibid., Art. 4(1).   [79] Ibid., Art. 23.   [80] Ibid., Art. 24(1).

[81] See M. Qing-Nan, Land-based Marine Pollution: International Law Development (Leiden: Martinus Nijhoff, 1987); T. Mensah, 'The International Legal Regime for the Protection and Preservation of the Marine Environment from Land Based Sources', in A. Boyle and D. Freestone (eds.), International Law and Sustainable Development: Past Achievements and

contains provisions relevant to land-based sources of pollution, including Articles 207 (duty of States to take measures to prevent, reduce and control such pollution) and 213 (duty to implement).[82]

In addition to these, one must mention several other instruments that, despite their non-binding character (except for one of them), have nevertheless exerted some influence on the regulation of land-based pollution, namely the Montreal Guidelines for the Protection of the Marine Environment Against Pollution from Land-based Sources (1985),[83] Chapter 17 of Agenda 21 adopted at the Earth Summit in 1992,[84] two instruments adopted at a Conference held in Washington DC between October and November 1995, namely the Washington Declaration on Protection of the Marine Environment from Land-Based Activities and the Global Programme of Action for the Protection of the Marine Environment from Land-Based Activities[85] and the UN Convention on the Law of Non-navigational Uses of International Watercourses (1997) in force since 2014.[86] Under Article 23 of the latter, States have a duty to take all measures 'with respect to an international watercourse that are necessary to protect and preserve the marine environment'.

Given the magnitude of the problem, these instruments are but a modest response. This said, together with the provisions on land-based pollution in UNCLOS, they provide a general framework for the regulation of the problem.[87] Moreover, the lack of a global treaty is to some extent mitigated by a number of regional treaties and arrangements containing rules for land-based marine pollution.

4.2.4 The protection of regional seas

There are now over forty conventions, agreements and protocols on the protection of regional seas. Most of these have been developed under the 'Regional Seas Programme' ('RSP') established by UNEP in 1974, following the action plan adopted at the Stockholm Conference in 1972.[88]

Future Challenges (Oxford University Press, 1999), pp. 297–324; Y. Tanaka, 'Regulation of Land-Based Marine Pollution in International Law: A Comparative Analysis between Global and Regional Legal Frameworks' (2006) 66 *Zeitschrift für ausländisches öffentliches Recht und Völkerrecht* 535.

[82] See Qing-Nan, *supra* n. 81, Chapter 4.

[83] Reproduced in: H. Hohmann (ed.), *Basic Documents of International Environmental Law* (London, 1992), vol. I, pp. 130–47. See Qing-Nan, *supra* n. 81, Chapter 6.

[84] Report of the United Nations Conference on Environment and Development, A/CONF.151/26/Rev.l (Vol. l), Resolution 1, Annex 2: Agenda 21 ('Agenda 21').

[85] UN Doc. UNEP (OCA) /LBA/IG.2/7.   [86] See *infra* n. 109.

[87] T. Mensah, *supra* n. 81, pp. 310–11.

[88] UNEP, Report of the Governing Council on the Work of Its First Session (12–22 June 1973), New York, Decision 1(I), Section III, para. 12(e): Report of the Governing Council on the Work of its Second Session (11–22 March 1974), New York, Decision 8 (II), Section A I, Chapter 4. See on this subject, the Internet site of the RSP, available on: www.unep.org/regionalseas/about/default.asp (visited on 15 October 2012).

The RSP consists of thirteen action plans on various marine regions world-wide, including nine (the Mediterranean Sea region,[89] the Kuwaiti regional action plan,[90] the West Africa region,[91] the Pacific South-East region,[92] the Red Sea and Gulf of Aden region,[93] the Caribbean region,[94] the East African region,[95] the Pacific Southwest region,[96] the Black Sea region[97]) that are subject to regional conventions. These agreements are, in most cases, supplemented by protocols on specific issues such as land-based pollution,[98] pollution by oil and other substances in the case of accidents,[99] pollution by

[89]   Convention for the Protection of the Mediterranean Sea against Pollution, 16 February 1976, as amended and later becoming the Convention for the Protection of the Marine Environment and the Mediterranean Coastal Environment, 10 June 1995 ('Barcelona Convention'), available at: www.ecolex.org (TRE-001284).

[90]   Regional Convention for Cooperation on the Protection of the Marine Environment from Pollution, 24 April 1978 ('Kuwait Convention'), available at: www.ecolex.org (TRE-000537).

[91]   Convention for Co-operation in the Protection and Development of the Marine and Coastal Environment of the West and Central African Region, 23 March 1981 ('Abidjan Convention'), available at: www.ecolex.org (TRE-000547).

[92]   Convention Concerning the Protection of the Marine Environment and Coastal Area of the South East Pacific, 1981 ('Lima Convention'), available at: www.ecolex.org (TRE-000741).

[93]   Regional Convention for the Conservation of the Marine Environment of the Red Sea and Gulf of Aden, 14 February 1982 ('Jeddah Convention'), available at: www.ecolex.org (TRE-000743).

[94]   Convention for the Protection and Development of the Marine Environment of the Wider Caribbean Region, 24 March 1983 ('Convention'), available at: www.ecolex.org (TRE-000763).

[95]   Convention for the Protection, Management and Development of the Marine and Coastal Region of East Africa, 21 June 1985 ('Nairobi Convention'), available at: www.ecolex.org (TRE-000821).

[96]   Convention for the Protection of Natural Resources and Environment of the South Pacific Region, 25 November 1986 ('Noumea Convention'), available at: www.ecolex.org (TRE-000892).

[97]   Convention on the Protection of the Black Sea against Pollution, 21 April 1992 ('Bucharest Convention'), available at: www.ecolex.org (TRE-001149).

[98]   Protocol of the Protection of the Mediterranean Sea against Pollution from Land-Based Sources, 17 May 1980, available at: www.ecolex.org (TRE-000544); Protocol for the Protection of the South-East Atlantic against Pollution from Land-based Sources, 22 July 1983, available at: www.ecolex.org (TRE-000768); Kuwait Protocol on the Protection of the Marine Environment Against Pollution from Land-based Sources, 21 February 1990, available at: www.ecolex.org (TRE-001129); Protocol on the Protection of the Marine Environment of the Black Sea Against Pollution from Land-based Sources, 21 April 1992, available at: www. ecolex.org (TRE-001392).

[99]   Protocol Concerning Cooperation in Preventing Pollution from Ships and, in Cases of Emergency, Combating Pollution of the Mediterranean Sea, 25 January 2002, available at: www.ecolex.org (TRE-001402); Protocol Concerning Cooperation in Combating Pollution in Cases of Emergency, 23 March 1981, available at: www.ecolex.org (TRE-000548); Agreement on Regional Cooperation in Combating Pollution of the South-East Pacific by Hydrocarbons or Other Harmful Substances in Cases of Emergency, 12 November 1981, available at: www. ecolex.org (TRE-000742); Supplementary Protocol on the Agreement on Regional Cooperation in Combating Pollution of the South-East Pacific by Hydrocarbons or Other Harmful Substances in Cases of Emergency, 22 July 1983, available at: www.ecolex.org (TRE-000769); Protocol Concerning Regional Cooperation in Combating Pollution by Oil and Other Harmful Substances in Cases of Emergency, 14 February 1982 (Red Sea and Gulf of Aden), available at: www.ecolex.org (TRE-000745); Protocol Concerning Cooperation in

dumping of wastes,[100] pollution from the exploration and exploitation of the seabed,[101] the protection of biodiversity in the region,[102] or the transboundary movement of wastes.[103] Beyond the RSP, other seas are also subject to special regimes. Out of the five existing regimes (Arctic, Antarctica, Baltic, Caspian Sea and North-East Atlantic), all but the Arctic have a specific treaty regime for the protection of the marine environment.[104]

A detailed analysis of these texts is beyond the scope of this chapter.[105] Nevertheless, it is important to underline the comprehensive character of the

Combating Oil Spills in the Wider Caribbean Region, 24 March 1983, available at: www.ecolex. org (TRE-000764); Protocol Concerning Cooperation in Combating Marine Pollution in Cases of Emergency in the Eastern African Region, 21 June 1985, available at: www.ecolex. org (TRE-000825); Protocol on Cooperation in Combating Pollution of the Black Sea Marine Environment by Oil and other Harmful Substances in Emergency Situations, 21 April 1992, available at: www.ecolex.org (TRE-001391).

[100] Protocol for the Prevention and Elimination of Pollution of the Mediterranean Sea by Dumping from Ships and Aircraft, 16 February 1976, available at: www.ecolex.org (TRE-001285); Protocol for the Prevention of Pollution of the South Pacific Region by Dumping, 25 November 1986, available at: www.ecolex.org (TRE-000893); Protocol on the Protection of the Marine Environment of the Black Sea Against Pollution by Dumping of Waste, 21 April 1992, available at: www.ecolex.org (TRE-001393).

[101] Protocol for the Protection of the Mediterranean Sea against Pollution Resulting from Exploration and Exploitation of the Continental Shelf and the Seabed and its Subsoil, 14 October 1994, available at: www.ecolex.org (TRE-001206); Protocol concerning Marine Pollution resulting from Exploration and Exploitation of the Continental Shelf (ROPME Sea Area), 29 May 1989, available at: www.ecolex.org (TRE-001128).

[102] Protocol Concerning Specially Protected Areas and Biological Diversity in the Mediterranean, 10 June 1995, available at: www.ecolex.org (TRE-001220); Protocol Concerning Cooperation in Combating Marine Pollution in Cases of Emergency in the Eastern African Region, 21 June 1985, available at: www.ecolex.org (TRE-000825); Protocol for the Conservation and Management of Protected Marine and Coastal Areas of the South East Pacific, 21 September 1989, available at: www.ecolex.org (TRE-001085); Protocol Concerning Specially Protected Area and Wildlife (SPAW), 18 January 1990, available at: www.ecolex.org (TRE-001040); Black Sea Biodiversity and Landscape Conservation Protocol, 14 June 2002, available at: www.ecolex.org (TRE-154497).

[103] Protocol on the Prevention of Pollution of the Mediterranean Sea by Transboundary Movements of Hazardous Wastes and their Disposal (Hazardous Wastes Protocol), 1 October 1996, available at: www.ecolex.org (TRE-001334); Protocol on the Control of Marine Transboundary Movements and Disposal of Hazardous Wastes and other Wastes (ROPME Sea Area), 17 March 1998, available at: www.ecolex.org (TRE-001298).

[104] For the Antarctic: Antarctic Treaty, 1 December 1959, 402 UNTS 71 ('Antarctic Treaty'); Convention for the Conservation of Antarctic Seals, signed in London, 1 June 1972, 1080 UNTS 175 ('Antarctic Seals Convention'); Convention for the Conservation of Marine Living Resources, signed in Canberra, 20 May 1980, 1329 UNTS 47 ('CCAMLR'); Protocol to the Antarctic Treaty on Environmental Protection, signed in Madrid, 4 October 1991, 30 ILM 1455 (1991) ('Madrid Protocol'). For the Baltic Sea: Convention on the Protection of the Marine Environment of the Baltic Sea Area, 9 April 1992, available on www.ecolex.org (TRE-001153). For the North-East Atlantic: Convention for the Protection of the Marine Environment of the North-East Atlantic, 22 September 1992, 2354 UNTS 67 ('OSPAR Convention'). For the Caspian Sea: Framework Convention for the Protection of the Marine Environment in the Caspian Sea, 4 November 2003 ('Tehran Convention'), available at: www. ecolex.org (TRE-001396).

[105] See M. Haward and J. Vince, *Oceans Governance in the Twenty-first Century: Managing the Blue Planet* (Cheltenham: Edward Elgar, 2008), Chapter 3.

regulations adopted. In general, there are three main components in each of the framework agreements mentioned.[106] First, they provide for duties of prevention, reduction and control of marine pollution in the relevant regional sea, distinguishing between various sources of pollution (land-based sources, by dumping, by ships, by the exploration and exploitation of the seabed, by the movement of waste, atmospheric or accidental). Second, some technical and procedural requirements are also provided for monitoring, co-operation and technical assistance, the exchange of information, the environmental impact assessment, etc. Third, these agreements have, as is often the case in environmental matters, an institutional component that allows parties to meet on a regular schedule according to pre-established rules, and the assistance of a secretariat (a function performed by UNEP in six cases[107]).

4.3 The international regulation of freshwater resources

4.3.1 Structure of the regulation

Freshwater resources account for about 2.5 per cent of all water on the planet (the remaining 97.5 per cent is sea water). Most of this 2.5 per cent is locked in the polar ice caps and other ice formations (68.6 per cent). The rest of the freshwater is found mainly in aquifers (30.1 per cent) and, to a much lesser extent, in lakes and rivers (0.3 per cent).[108] Yet, as discussed in the following paragraphs, the international regulation of freshwater resources has mostly focused on international watercourses and, more recently, on groundwater. In other words, international law in this area governs only a small part of the world freshwater resources (particularly rivers and lakes and, to a more limited extent, aquifers). Figure 4.3 summarises this situation.

Traditionally, international law has approached the regulation of freshwater from two fundamental angles, namely (i) the use of international watercourses (including lakes) for navigation, and (ii) the distribution of water resources between riparian States. However, from the 1950s, with the increasing use of freshwater resources for agriculture, power generation and the supply for domestic use, in conjunction with the development of human rights and a growing awareness of the need to protect the environment, efforts to regulate the use of watercourses for purposes other than navigation have multiplied.[109]

---

[106] See P. Sands, *Principles of International Environmental Law* (Cambridge University Press, 2003), pp. 406 ff.

[107] See www.unep.org/regionalseas/programmes/unpro/default.asp (last visited on 12 December 2012).

[108] World Development Report 2010: Development and Climate Change (World Bank), p. 139.

[109] These efforts have been conducted mainly under the aegis of the *Institut de Droit International* (IDI) (particularly: 'Utilization of Non-Maritime International Waters (except for Navigation)', Salzburg, 1961 ('Salzburg Resolution')), of the International Law Association (ILA) (particularly: Helsinki Rules on the Uses of the Waters of International Rivers, adopted at the 52nd conference of the ILA in August 1966 ('Helsinki Rules'); Seoul Complementary

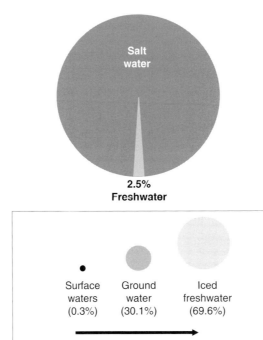

Figure 4.3: Freshwater resources and their international regulation

These efforts include seeking (iii) to preserve water quality and the environment of the affected areas and (iv) to ensure access to water as a human right.

In the following sections, we will leave aside the question of navigation (i)[110] and focus on issues of distribution (ii) and environmental protection (iii). The question of access to water (iv) will be addressed in Chapter 10. The two questions selected will be analysed in the context of international watercourses

Rules, adopted at the 62nd Conference of the ILA in 1986 ('Seoul Rules'); Berlin Rules on Water Resources, adopted by the ILA on 21 August 2004 ('Berlin Rules')), of the United Nations Economic Commission for Europe (UNECE) (Convention on the Protection and Use of Transboundary Watercourses and International Lakes, 18 March 1992, 1936 UNTS 269 ('Helsinki Convention'); Protocol on Water and Health to the 1992 Convention on the Protection and Use of Transboundary Watercourses and International Lakes, 17 June 1999, 2331 UNTS 202 ('Protocol on Water and Health')), and of the United Nations International Law Commission (ILC) (United Nations Convention on the Law of the Non-Navigational Uses of International Watercourses, 21 May 1997, 36 ILM 700 ('UN Convention on Watercourses'); 'Draft Articles on the Law of Transboundary Aquifers', 11 December 2008, GA Res. 63/124, UN Doc. A/RES/63/124 ('ILC Aquifers Draft')). See S. Bogdanovic, *International Law of Water Resources: Contribution of the International Law Association (1954–2000)* (London: Kluwer Law International, 2001); E. Brown Weiss, 'The Evolution of International Water Law', (2007) 331 *Recueil des cours de l'Académie de droit international de La Haye*, 161–404.

[110] See S. McCaffrey, *The Law of International Watercourses* (Oxford University Press, 2nd edn, 2007), pp. 171–97.

(4.3.2), transboundary aquifers (4.3.3) and freshwater locked in the form of ice (4.3.4).

4.3.2 International watercourses

The concept of a 'watercourse' as an object of legal regulation has changed significantly over time. In theory, it is possible to define the concept narrowly (e.g. rivers or lakes crossing an international border – contiguous or successive) or broadly (e.g. a drainage basin and its ecosystems) with a spectrum of definitions in between (e.g. a system of linked or unlinked surface water and groundwater, which either does or does not lead to a common terminus).[111] The definitions used in international practice in the last decades have come increasingly closer to the concept of a drainage basin,[112] although the UN Convention on Watercourses, concluded in 1997 following the work of the ILC, employs a rather restrictive definition. Indeed, the latter defines an 'international watercourse' as a 'system of surface waters and groundwaters constituting by virtue of their physical relationship a unitary whole and normally flowing into a common terminus',[113] which does not include other elements of the affected ecosystems, such as the land (and States) forming part of the drainage basin of the water system or groundwater not related to surface water.

As regards the sharing of resources provided by these watercourses, from a conceptual point of view, there are four main approaches: (i) 'absolute sovereignty', (ii) 'absolute territorial integrity', (iii) 'limited sovereignty' and (iv) 'community interest'.[114] According to (i), the State in whose territory a section of an international watercourse lies can do what it pleases with this section without having regard, under international law, to the consequences of its actions on other States through which the watercourse flows.[115] In contrast, according to (ii), any restriction, however small or reasonable, to the normal flow of water in a State of the watercourse (located downstream) resulting from the activities conducted by another State of the watercourse (located upstream) is prohibited.[116] The distinction between the two intermediate approaches,

---

[111] See L. Teclaff, 'Evolution of the River Basin Concept in National and International Water Law' (1996) 36 *Natural Resources Journal* 359.

[112] See: Helsinki Rules, *supra* n. 109, Art. 2; Helsinki Convention, *supra* n. 109, Art. 1(1)–(2); Protocol on Water and Health, *supra* n. 109, Art. 5(j); *Gabčíkovo-Nagymaros Project (Hungary v. Slovakia)*, Judgment, ICJ Reports 1997, p. 7 ('*Gabčíkovo-Nagymaros Project*'), paras. 53 and 85.

[113] UN Convention on Watercourses, *supra* n. 109, Art. 2(a).

[114] See McCaffrey, *supra* n. 110, pp. 111–70.

[115] This position, known as the 'Harmon Doctrine', after the Attorney General of the United States who asserted the doctrine in a dispute with Mexico over the waters of the Rio Grande in 1895, has since been rejected by the international community, *ibid.*, pp. 76–110.

[116] That position, asserted by Spain in the case of Lake Lanoux between Spain to France, was rejected by the tribunal, *Lake Lanoux Arbitration (Spain v. France)*, Award of 16 November 1957, RIAA, vol. XII, pp. 281ff ('*Lake Lanoux Arbitration*').

(iii) and (iv), is a function of the degree of co-operation between the States concerned. The approach (iii) refers to situations where co-operation is not formalised, but each State of the watercourse abstains from using the water-course in a way that would seriously hamper its use by other States. The approach (iv) would call for a higher level of co-operation, normally reflected by the creation of an institutional framework embodying the community of interest between the various States of the watercourse. Modern international practice is, accordingly, between (iii) and (iv).[117] Relevant to this inquiry is the scope of the customary principles applicable to watercourses (equitable and reasonable utilisation, no harm, prevention of environmental harm and co-operation/notification) and their mutual relationships.

The first principle is that of 'equitable and reasonable utilisation and parti-cipation'. Following previous texts,[118] Article 5 of the New York Convention provides that: '[w]atercourse States shall in their respective territories utilize an international watercourse in an equitable and reasonable manner'.[119] Equitable and reasonable use must be evaluated in light of the (non-exhaustive) criteria listed in Article 6(1) of the Convention (e.g. natural features, including geological features, and economic and broader social, current and potential uses, including alternatives, etc.).[120]

A difficult question is whether 'no harm' is merely a requirement circum-scribing the scope of reasonable utilisation[121] or, rather, a principle in itself, as implied by Article 7 of the UN Convention on Watercourses.[122] This apparently minor point is potentially significant because, depending on the position one adopts, the overall approach could shift from the idea of limited sovereignty to that of absolute territorial integrity. Here we find an issue already raised in Chapter 3 in connection with the specific scope of the no harm principle. The solution to this apparent dilemma between the right to use watercourses and the obligation not to cause harm is, at least in theory, relatively simple. Harm is not always of the same scale. Only harm of certain gravity (qualified as 'serious' or 'significant') will amount to a violation of the second principle (no harm), whereas harm of a lower intensity may only be taken into account as one among other criteria relevant for the assessment of the application of the first

---

[117] M. Kohen, 'Les principes généraux du droit international de l'eau à la lumière de la jurispru-dence de la Cour internationale de Justice', in SFDI, *L'eau en droit international, Colloque d'Orléans* (Paris: Pedone, 2011), pp. 61–78.

[118] See: Salzburg Resolution, *supra* n. 109, Art. 3; Berlin Rules, *supra* n. 109, Art. IV; J. A. Barberis and R. D. Hayton (eds.), *Droits et obligations des pays riverains des fleuves internationaux* (The Hague: Martinus Nijhoff, 1990), see the 'Bilan des recherches' by J. A. Barberis.

[119] UN Convention on Watercourses, *supra* n. 109, Art. 5. See also Helsinki Convention, *supra* n. 109, Art. 2(2)(b); Berlin Rules, *supra* n. 109, Art. 12.

[120] UN Convention on Watercourses, *supra* n. 109, Art. 6(1), 10. Compare with Helsinki Rules, *supra* n. 109, Art. V(2); Berlin Rules, *supra* n. 109, Arts. 13(2) and 14.

[121] As suggested by: Helsinki Rules, *supra* n. 109, Art. IV; Berlin Rules, *supra* n. 109, Art. 13; Helsinki Convention, *supra* n. 109, Art. 2(2)(b); UN Convention on Watercourses, *supra* n. 109, Art. 6(1)(d).

[122] See, more generally, our analysis of the principle of no harm, *supra* Chapter 3.

principle (equitable and reasonable utilisation). Beyond these parameters, the analysis will, of course, be a matter of discretion *in concreto*.

The relationship of these two principles with the requirement to prevent environmental harm also presents some conceptual difficulties. These difficulties have, in essence, been discussed in Chapter 3 as part of our analysis of the relationship between the principle of no harm and the principle of prevention. It should be noted here, however, that the UN Convention on Watercourses, by virtue of Article 20, follows a comprehensive approach to environmental protection by imposing on States, a duty to protect the 'ecosystems' of international watercourses.[123] This approach is confirmed by the prohibition under Article 22 to introduce new species in a watercourse that represent a risk to the ecosystem.[124] In addition, Articles 21 and 23 provide for duties of prevention, reduction and control of pollution of watercourses directly,[125] but also indirectly where they represent a source of marine pollution.[126] As for the foundation, in general international law, of these duties of prevention, we must distinguish between substantive and procedural aspects. With regard to the former, it is now well established that the prevention of environmental harm, including in the context of international watercourses, is a requirement under customary international law.[127] As for the procedural provisions, including how environmental co-operation should unfold under the UN Convention on Watercourses, they include elements of both customary law and progressive development.[128]

This last point raises the question of the duty of co-operation applied to international watercourses. We have analysed the general aspects of this duty in Chapter 3. Here, it will suffice to add two observations. First, the UN Convention on Watercourses is only intended to provide a general framework, which States are free to modify according to their needs in the context of more specific agreements.[129] In this connection, the formulation of the duty of co-operation used in the Convention[130] is less precise than the one found in other instruments. Second, Articles 9 (regular exchange of data and information) and 11 to 18 (notification and consultation) of the Convention provide an accurate description of the co-operation mechanisms regularly adopted in respect of existing uses and planned activities that may have adverse consequences on other watercourse States. The question remains, however, the extent to which these provisions reflect customary law. In practice, the answer lies in the requirement of good faith. While it seems clear that States do not

---

[123] UN Convention on Watercourses, *supra* n. 109, Art. 20. Compare with the more detailed approach of the Helsinki Convention, *supra* n. 109, Arts. 2(2) and 3 and Annexes I–III.

[124] UN Convention on Watercourses, *supra* n. 109, Art. 22.   [125] *Ibid.*, Art. 21.   [126] Art. 23.

[127] See our analysis on the principle of prevention, *supra* Chapter 3.

[128] See L. Caflisch, 'La Convention du 21 mai 1997 sur l'utilisation des cours d'eaux internationaux a des fins autres que la navigation' (1997) 43 *Annuaire français de droit international* 751, 787.

[129] UN Convention on Watercourses, *supra* n. 109, Arts. 3 and 4.

[130] *Ibid.*, Art. 8(2). Compare with: Helsinki Convention, *supra* n. 109, Arts. 9, 11 and 12.

have a veto over the activities of other States,[131] sufficient notice prior to the commencement of activities likely to have significant negative effects on another State is required by good faith, as is allowing a reasonable waiting period before undertaking such activities.[132] In case of disagreement, customary law imposes an obligation to consult in good faith and, during the consultations, a State is not entitled to undertake the activities in question,[133] unless they are urgent and have been declared as such.[134] Similarly, the other State may not, as a matter of good faith, prevent the notifying State from undertaking the planned activities simply by not responding.[135]

4.3.3 Transboundary aquifers

The codification efforts described above concerned essentially surface waters or groundwater linked to them. With the exception of efforts leading to the Helsinki Convention,[136] the other codification efforts did not sufficiently take into account the question of confined groundwater.

This lacuna was eventually filled by two main techniques. The first technique was to supplement the existing instrument in an *ad hoc* fashion, by the adoption of an additional instrument relating to groundwater. Thus, in 1986, the ILA adopted a 'Resolution on Confined Transboundary Groundwater' or 'Seoul Resolution' consisting of four articles, the first of which expressly stated that transboundary aquifers, whether related or not to surface water, formed part of an international basin in the meaning ascribed to this term by the Helsinki Rules.[137] Similarly, in 1994, the ILC adopted a 'Resolution on Confined Transboundary Groundwater'[138] recognising the need to develop rules governing this issue and stating that, in the absence of such rules, States must be guided *mutatis mutandis* by the principles applicable to surface water.[139] The second technique was the adoption of either a general set of provisions incorporating the question of groundwater, as is the case with Chapter VIII of the ILA Berlin Rules of 2004,[140] or a specific set of articles

---

[131] See *supra* n. 117.

[132] This delay is not necessarily six (or twelve) months, as required by the UN Convention on Watercourses, *supra* n. 109, Art. 13.

[133] *Pulp Mills on the River Uruguay (Argentina v. Uruguay)*, Judgment, ICJ Reports 2010, p. 14, para. 144.

[134] See UN Convention on Watercourses, *supra* n. 109, Art. 19.   [135] See *ibid.*, Art. 16(1).

[136] As part of the work of the UNECE, the need for an integrated approach to unconnected surface ground waters was recognised early on in a series of declarations: 'Declaration of Policy on Prevention and Control of Water Pollution', Decision B (XXV), Geneva – 1980; 'Decision on International Cooperation on Shared Water Resources', Decision D (XXXVII), Geneva – 1982; 'Declaration of Policy on Rational Use of Water', Decision C (XXXIX), Geneva – 1984; 'Charter on Groundwater Management', Decision E (44), Geneva – 1989.

[137] Seoul Rules, *supra* n. 109, Art. 1.

[138] 'Resolution on Confined Transboundary Groundwater', (1994) 2(2) *Yearbook of the International Law Commission* 135.

[139] *Ibid.*, para. 1.   [140] Berlin Rules, *supra* n. 109, Arts. 36 and 42(1)(b).

devoted to groundwater, such as the 'Draft Articles on the Law of Transboundary Aquifers' adopted by the ILC in 2008.[141]

As regards the content of these codification efforts, the principles identified are essentially the same in all matters concerning international watercourses (equitable and reasonable utilisation and participation,[142] no harm,[143] prevention of environmental harm,[144] and co-operation[145]). The groundwater instruments place, however, greater emphasis on prevention,[146] joint management,[147] as well as on specific forms of technical co-operation.[148] This is largely due to the greater vulnerability of aquifers (especially those that are confined) to pollution, and the fact that they are located, to a large extent, in developing countries. Another significant difference is the explicit reference to sovereignty in Article 3 of the 2008 ILC Articles: '[e]ach aquifer State has sovereignty over the portion of a transboundary aquifer or aquifer system located within its territory'. The commentary to the Draft[149] notes that the inclusion of this statement was explicitly advocated by a number of States by reference to the principle of permanent sovereignty over natural resources, formulated in General Assembly Resolution 1803.[150]

4.3.4 Iced freshwater resources

4.3.4.1 Overview

As noted above, most of the world's freshwater resources (70 per cent) are locked in the form of ice in the polar or other regions. Despite the significance of these resources, the appropriation, exploitation and transfer (from the place of exploitation to the place of utilisation) have so far received only limited attention.[151] Although a substantial body of scholarship analyses the legal situation of the polar regions,[152] iced freshwater resources are seldom

---

[141] ILC Aquifers Draft, *supra* n. 109.
[142] Seoul Rules, *supra* n. 109, Art. 2; Berlin Rules, *supra* n. 109, Arts. 37 and 40; ILC Aquifers Draft, *supra* n. 109, Arts. 4 and 5.
[143] Berlin Rules, *supra* n. 109, Art. 42(6); ILC Aquifers Draft, *supra* n. 109, Art. 6.
[144] Seoul Rules, *supra* n. 109, Art. 3; Berlin Rules, *supra* n. 109, Arts. 38 and 41; ILC Aquifers Draft, *supra* n. 109, Arts. 10–12.
[145] Seoul Rules, *supra* n. 109, Art. 4; Berlin Rules, *supra* n. 109, Art. 42(2)–(5); ILC Aquifers Draft, *supra* n. 109, Arts. 7–9.
[146] ILC Aquifers Draft, *supra* n. 109, Art. 6(1)–(2).
[147] Berlin Rules, *supra* n. 109, Art. 2(2); ILC Aquifers Draft, *supra* n. 109, Art. 9.
[148] ILC Aquifers Draft, *supra* n. 109, Art. 16.
[149] 'Draft Articles on the Law of Transboundary Aquifers, with commentaries', (2008) 2(2) *Yearbook of the International Law Commission*, Part 2, commentary ad Art. 3, para. 1.
[150] 'Permanent Sovereignty over Natural Resources', 14 December 1962, UN Doc. A/RES/1803/XVII, ('Resolution 1803').
[151] See e.g. F. Quilleré-Majzoub, 'Glaces polaires et icebergs: Quid juris gentium?' (2006) 52 *Annuaire Francais de Droit International* 432; J. E. Viñuales, 'Iced Freshwater Resources: A Legal Exploration' (2009) 20 *Yearbook of International Environmental Law* 188.
[152] On the Antarctic treaty system, see F. Francioni and T. Scovazzi (eds.), *International Law for Antarctica* (Leiden: Martinus Nijhoff, 2nd edn, 1996). On the Arctic, see D. R. Rothwell,

addressed specifically. This is perhaps due to the daunting technological and economic challenges involved in the exploitation of these resources but also to the environmental requirements that such projects would have to meet.

In this section, the discussion is limited to the latter. In order for iced freshwater resources to be put to use or 'exploited', they first must be 'appropriated' by a State or, in other words, subject to the sovereignty or the sovereign rights of a State. The rules governing appropriation are different for resources located in Antarctica or in the Arctic.

4.3.4.2 Antarctica

Regarding Antarctica, one of the fundamental principles established in Article IV of the Antarctic Treaty[153] is the so-called 'freeze' or moratorium of sovereignty claims advanced by a number of countries[154] over sectors of the Antarctic continent and its surrounding seas, as defined in Article VI of the treaty. This basic principle and its implications for the (im)possibility of appropriation of Antarctic resources must be assessed in the light of a relatively complex set of arrangements, referred to as the Antarctic Treaty System (ATS) including both other treaties[155] and numerous resolutions adopted by the governing body of the Antarctic Treaty.[156] The basic picture that arises from these arrangements is that States enjoy some access to marine living resources, regulated *inter alia* by the 1972 Seals Convention and the CCAMLR Convention. The possibility of appropriation of such resources is therefore not barred. The situation of mineral resources is different, as after the failure of the CRAMRA Convention[157] and the adoption of the Protocol on Environmental Protection, activities (other than scientific research) relating to mineral resources are prohibited.[158]

The situation of iced freshwater resources lies somewhere in the middle between these two regimes, as they are not considered to be 'mineral resources'

'International Law and the Protection of the Arctic Environment' (1995) 44 *International and Comparative Law Quarterly* 280; E. Lennon, 'A Tale of Two Poles: A Comparative Look at the Legal Regimes in the Arctic and the Antarctic' (2008) 8 *Sustainable Development Law & Policy* 32.

[153] See *supra* n. 104.

[154] Among the twelve original signatories of the Antarctic Treaty, seven States had territorial claims at the moment of the signature of the Treaty: Argentina, Australia, Chile, France, New Zealand, Norway and the United Kingdom. However, the USSR and the United States maintained a 'basis of claim' protected under Article IV(1)(b).

[155] See *supra* n. 104.

[156] Throughout its thirty-two meetings, the Parties to the Antarctic Treaty have adopted close to 200 resolutions on different issues pertaining to Antarctica. See the website of the Antarctic Treaty Secretariat, at: www.ats.aq/devAS/info_measures_list.aspx (last visited on 12 December 2012).

[157] A Convention for the Regulation of Antarctic Mineral Resource Activities, 2 June 1988, 27 ILM 868 (1988) ('CRAMRA') specifically addressed this issue, but it never entered into force and its objective was subsequently foreclosed by the adoption and entry into force of the Madrid Protocol.

[158] Madrid Protocol, *supra* n. 104, Art. 7.

subject to the prohibition in Article 7 of the Protocol.[159] Moreover, in the meeting of the parties to the Antarctic Treaty held in Paris, in October 1989, the possibility of exploiting these resources (which supposes appropriation) was expressly envisaged. The meeting adopted Recommendation XV-21, which focuses on the 'Exploitation of Icebergs'.[160] The preamble of this Recommendation notes, *inter alia,* that 'technological developments might one day make it possible to utilize icebergs detached from the continent for freshwater requirements, especially in coastal areas',[161] that such possibility raises concerns that 'uncontrolled activities relating to the exploitation of Antarctic icebergs could also have an adverse effect on the unique Antarctic environment and its dependent and associated ecosystems',[162] and that, given the limited information available, it is desirable that 'commercial exploitation of Antarctic ice not occur, in any case, prior to examination by the Contracting Parties to the Antarctic Treaty of the issues posed by such activity'.[163] The Recommendation called essentially for more information on the environmental impact of such potential exploitation.[164] On January 29, 2004, some fifteen years after its adoption, the Recommendation eventually entered into effect when the last party (Belgium) whose approval was required in accordance to Article IX(4) of the Antarctic Treaty approved the text. However, we are not aware of any specific follow-up action taken in subsequent meetings.

4.3.4.3 The Arctic

Unlike Antarctica, the Arctic is not governed by a single treaty or system of treaties, but by a combination of soft-law[165] and hard-law[166] instruments and institutions.[167] The possibility of appropriation of Arctic resources is governed by the basic international rules applicable to the exercise of sovereignty and sovereign rights by States over land and maritime spaces.[168] An apposite

---

[159] The Final Act of the Eleventh Antarctic Treaty Special Consultative Meeting, Madrid, October 1991, states, in para. 6 that: '[t]he Meeting noted that the harvesting of ice was not considered to be an Antarctic mineral resource activity; it was therefore agreed that if the harvesting of ice were to become possible in the future, it was understood that the provisions of the Protocol, other than Article 7, would apply' (available at: www.state.gov/documents/organization/152 91.pdf (last visited on 12 December 2012)).

[160] Recommendation ATCM XV-21, available at; www ats aq (last visited on 12 December 2012).

[161] *Ibid.,* preamble, Recital 2.   [162] *Ibid.,* preamble, Recital 5.   [163] *Ibid.,* preamble, Recital 9.

[164] *Ibid.,* operative part, para. 1–2.

[165] See Arctic Environmental Protection Strategy (AEPS), adopted in Rovaniemi, Finland, June 1991, available at: arctic-council.org/filearchive/artic_environment.pdf (last visited on 12 December 2012).

[166] Most notably UNCLOS, *supra* n. 1. See H. Corell, 'Reflections on the Possibilities and Limitations of a Binding Legal Regime' (2007) 37 *Environmental Policy and Law* 321.

[167] See 'Declaration on the Establishment of the Arctic Council', 19 September 1996, 35 ILM 1382 (1996); E. T. Bloom, 'Establishment of the Arctic Council' (1999) 93 *American Journal of International Law* 712.

[168] See C. Joyner, 'Ice-Covered Regions in International Law' (1991) 31 *Natural Resources Journal* 213.

illustration of how such powers can be deployed for the appropriation of iced freshwater resources as well as of the issues that it may raise is given by the laws and regulations of the provincial government of Newfoundland (Canada), which issues permits for the exploitation of icebergs found in Canadian waters.[169] Such powers have been disputed by Denmark, which claims that Canada has no right to sell the icebergs found in Canadian waters because they come from Greenland's ice sheet.[170]

In addition to the allocation of sovereignty and sovereign rights, UNCLOS also sets environmental standards for the exploitation of these resources. During the negotiation of UNCLOS, Canada proposed the adoption of a provision of particular relevance for the regulation of sea-ice,[171] prompted by the need to introduce in the draft an approach already adopted by the enactment, in 1970, of Canada's Arctic Waters Pollution Prevention Act.[172] The resulting provision, Article 234 of UNCLOS, did not address ice directly as a resource but rather as a risk factor, enhancing the probability of wreck and therefore of pollution of the Arctic environment. There are, however, other provisions in UNCLOS that, although not specifically concerned with sea-ice, have a more direct bearing on the environmental requirements for the potential exploitation of iced freshwater resources. We refer here to our analysis of the environmental standards set, *inter alia,* by Part XII of UNCLOS.[173]

The contours set to such activities in the Arctic region are further influenced by an array of other hard-law and soft-law instruments that have received unequal attention in the analyses devoted to the international law of the Polar Regions. On the one hand, there is a substantial literature on the instruments developed, in particular, under the aegis of the AEPS or of the Arctic Council.[174] On the other, little specific commentary has been devoted to the potential exploitation of iced freshwater resources. In this connection, one may refer to a variety of initiatives adopted under flexible frameworks such as the Arctic Environmental Protection Strategy launched in 1991 and the Arctic Council, created in 1996. The latter is organised in six working groups, one of which ('PAME' – Protection of the Arctic Marine Environment) focuses on policy and non-emergency pollution prevention and control measures related to the protection of the Arctic marine and coastal environment from land and sea-based activities. One of the objectives of PAME's work plan 2009–11 was, for instance, the assessment of the environmental consequences of sea-ice

---

[169] Incident reported by Quilleré-Majzoub, *supra* n. 151, 443.

[170] Although such provenance is as a rule factually accurate, the legal basis of Denmark's claim is unclear. The mere fact that the water forming an iceberg originates in the territory of a State is not sufficient to bar appropriation by other States.

[171] See D. M. McRae, 'The Negotiation of Article 234', in F. Griffiths (ed.), *Politics in the Northwest Passage* (Montréal: McGill-Queens University Press, 1987), pp. 98–114.

[172] See R. M. M. Gonigle, 'Unilateralism and International Law: The Arctic Waters Pollution Prevention Act' (1976) 34 *University of Toronto Faculty of Law Review* 180.

[173] See *supra* Sections 4.2.2 and 4.2.3.

[174] See *supra* n. 151 and the bibliography at the end of this chapter.

reductions and the increasing opportunities arising from such change for the exploitation of natural resources (although iced freshwater resources were not specifically targeted).[175] This is but one example out of many others that could be given to illustrate the 'flexible' initiatives taken for the protection of the environment in the Arctic. However, they all converge in that they seek to influence the national policies of Arctic States as well as other concerned States and groups.

Select bibliography

Arcari, M. and A. Tanzi, *The United Nations Convention on the Law of International Watercourses* (The Hague: Kluwer, 2001).

Barberis, J. A. and R. D. Hayton (eds.), *Droits et obligations des pays riverains des fleuves internationaux* (The Hague: Martinus Nijhoff, 1990).

Barnes, R., *Property Rights and Natural Resources* (Oxford: Hart, 2009).

Bederman, D., 'Antarctic Environmental Liability: the Stockholm Annex and Beyond' (2005) 19 *Emory International Law Review* 1383.

Bloom, E. T., 'Establishment of the Arctic Council' (1999) 93 *American Journal of International Law* 712.

Bogdanovic, S., *International Law of Water Resources, Contribution of the International Law Association (1954–2000)* (London: Kluwer Law International, 2001).

Boisson de Chazournes, L. and S. Salman (eds.), *Water Resources and International Law / Hague Academy of International Law* (Leiden: Martinus Nijhoff, 2005).

Bourne, C., *International Water Law: Selected Writings of Professor Charles B. Bourne* (Boston: Kluwer Law, 1997).

'The Primacy of the Principle of Equitable Utilization in the 1997 Watercourse Convention' (1998) 35 *The Canadian Yearbook of International Law* 215.

Boyle, A., 'The Environmental Jurisprudence of the International Tribunal for the Law of the Sea' (2007) 22 *International Journal of Marine and Coastal Law* 369.

Brown Weiss, E., 'The Evolution of International Water Law', (2007) 331 *Recueil des cours de l'Académie de droit international,* 161–404.

Brunnée, J., 'Environmental Security and Freshwater Resources: The Role of International Law', in Y. Le Bouthillier, D. M. McRae and D. Pharand (eds.), *Selected Papers in International Law: Contribution of the Canadian Council of International Law* (Toronto: Canadian Council of International Law, 1999), pp. 371–83.

Bush, W., *Antarctica and International Law* (Dobbs Ferry NY: Oceana Publications, 3 vols., 1982–8).

Caflisch, L., 'La Convention du 21 mai 1997 sur l'utilisation des cours d'eaux internationaux à des fins autres que la navigation' (1997) 43 *Annuaire français de droit international* 751.

'Règles générales du droit des cours d'eaux internationaux', (1989) 219 *Recueil des cours de l'Académie de droit international,* 9ff.

---

[175] See Arctic Council, PAME Work Plan 2009–11, available at: arctic-council.org/filearchive/pame_work_plan_2009–2011.pdf (last visited on 12 December 2012).

Cohen, H. K. (ed.), *Handbook of the Antarctic Treaty System* (Washington DC: US Department of States, 9th edn, 2002).

Corell, H., 'Reflections on the Possibilities and Limitations of a Binding Legal Regime' (2007) 37 *Environmental Policy and Law* 321.

Dejeant-Pons, M., 'Les Conventions du Programme des Nations Unies pour l'Environnement relatives aux mers régionales' (1984) 33 *Annuaire français de droit international* 689.

De la Fayette, L., 'New Developments in the Disposal of Offshore Installations' (1999) 14 *International Journal of Marine and Coastal Law* 523.

'Oceans Governance in the Arctic' (2008) 23 *International Journal of Marine and Coastal Law* 531.

'The Role of the United Nations in International Oceans Governance', in D. Freestone, R. Barnes and D. Ong (eds.), *The Law of the Sea: Progress and Prospects* (Oxford University Press, 2006), pp. 63–74.

Dellapenna, J., 'The Customary International Law of Transboundary Fresh Waters', in M. Fitzmaurice and M. Szuniewicz (eds.), *Exploitation of Natural Resources in the 21st Century* (Boston: Kluwer Law International, 2003), pp. 143–90.

Dellapenna, J. and J. Gupta (eds.), *The Evolution of the Law and Politics of Water* (Dordrecht: Springer, 2009).

Dupuy, P.-M., 'La préservation du milieu marin', in Dupuy, R.-J. and Vignes, D. (eds.), *Traité du nouveau droit de la mer* (Paris/Bruxelles: Economica/Bruylant, 1985), Chapter 20.

Elferink, A. O. and E. Molenaar (eds.), *The International Legal Regime of Areas beyond National Jurisdiction: Current and Future Developments* (Leiden: Martinus Nijhoff, 2010).

Fitzmaurice, M., 'General Principles Governing the Cooperation between States in Relation to Non-Navigational Uses of International Watercourses' (2004) 14 *Yearbook of International Environmental Law* 3.

Francioni, F. and T. Scovazzi (eds.), *International Law for Antarctica* (Leiden: Martinus Nijhoff, 2nd edn, 1996).

Franckx, E., 'Regional Marine Environment Protection Regimes in the Context of UNCLOS' (1998) 13 *International Journal of Marine and Coastal Law* 307.

Freestone, D. and Z. Makuch, 'The New International Environmental Law of Fisheries: The 1995 United Nations Straddling Stocks Agreement' (1995) 7 *Yearbook of International Environmental Law* 3.

Freestone, D. and S. Salman, 'Ocean and Freshwater Resources', in D. Bodansky, J. Brunnée and E. Hey (eds.), *The Oxford Handbook of International Environmental Law* (Oxford University Press, 2007), pp. 337–61.

Fuentes, X., 'Sustainable Development and the Equitable Utilization of International Watercourses' (1999) 69 *British Yearbook of International Law* 119.

'The Criteria for the Equitable Utilization of International Rivers' (1997) 67 *British Yearbook of International Law* 337.

'The Utilization of International Groundwater in General International Law', in G. S. Goodwin-Gill and S. Talmon (eds.), *The Reality of International Law: Essays in Honour of Ian Brownlie* (Oxford University Press, 1999), pp. 177–98.

Fulton, T. W., *The Sovereignty of the Sea* (Clark NJ: The Lawbook Exchange, 1911).

Gavouneli, M., 'A Human Right to Groundwater?' (2011) 13 *International Community Law Review* 305.

Gonigle, R. M. M., 'Unilateralism and International Law: The Arctic Waters Pollution Prevention Act' (1976) 34 *University of Toronto Faculty of Law Review* 180.

Gupta, J., R. Ahlers and L. Ahmed, 'The Human Right to Water: Moving Towards Consensus in a Fragmented World' (2010) 19 *Review of European Community and International Environmental Law* 294.

Haas, P., 'Save the Seas: UNEP's Regional Seas Programme and the Coordination of Regional Pollution Control Efforts' (1991) 9 *Ocean Yearbook* 188.

Harrison, J., *Making the Law of the Sea* (Cambridge University Press, 2011).

Hassan, D., 'International Conventions Relating to Land-Based Sources of Marine Pollution Control: Applications and Shortcomings' (2004) 16 *Georgetown International Environmental Law Review* 657.

   Protecting the Marine Environment from Land-based Sources of Pollution: Toward Effective International Co-operation (Aldershot: Ashgate, 2005).

Haward, M. and J. Vince, *Oceans Governance in the Twenty-first Century: Managing the Blue Planet* (Cheltenham: Edward Elgar, 2008).

Helal, M. S., 'Sharing Blue Gold: The 1997 UN Convention on the Law of the Non-Navigational Uses of International Watercourses Ten Years On' (2007) 18 *Colorado Journal of International Environmental Law Policy* 337.

Joyner, C., 'Ice-Covered Regions in International Law' (1991) 31 *Natural Resources Journal* 213.

Kindt, J., 'Vessel Source Pollution and the Law of the Sea' (1984) 17 *Vanderbilt* 287.

Koivurova, T., 'Governance of Protected Areas in the Arctic' (2009) 5 *Utrecht Law Review* 44.

Koivurova, T. and D.L. Vanderzwaag, 'The Arctic Council at 10 Years: Retrospect and Prospects' (2007) 10 *University of British Columbia Law Review* 121.

Kramer, L., 'The Contribution of the European Union to Marine Pollution Prevention', in J. Basedow and U. Magnus (eds.), *Pollution of the Sea: Prevention and Compensation* (Dordrecht: Springer, 2007), pp. 63–83.

Lennon, L., 'A Tale of Two Poles: A Comparative Look at the Legal Regimes in the Arctic and the Antarctic' (2008) 8 *Sustainable Development Law & Policy* 32.

McCaffrey, S., 'The 1997 United Nations Convention on International Watercourses' (1998) 92 *American Journal of International Law* 97.

   The Law of International Watercourses (Oxford University Press, 2007).

McRae, D. M., 'The Negotiation of Article 234', in F. Griffiths (ed.), *Politics in the Northwest Passage* (Montréal: McGill-Queens University Press, 1987), pp. 98–114.

Mensah, T., 'The International Legal Regime for the Protection and Preservation of the Marine Environment from Land Based Sources', in A. Boyle and D. Freestone (eds.), *International Law and Sustainable Development: Past Achievements and Future Challenges* (Oxford University Press, 1999), pp. 297–324.

Nordquist, M. H., S. N. Nandan and J. Kraska (eds.), *United Nations Convention on the Law of the Sea: A Commentary,* vol. IV (Dordrecht/Boston: Martinus Nijhoff, 1991).

Qing-Nan, M., *Land-based Marine Pollution: International Law Development* (Leiden: Martinus Nijhoff, 1987).

Quilleré-Majzoub, F., 'Glaces polaires et icebergs: Quid juris gentium?' (2006) 52 *Annuaire français de droit international* 432.

Rayfuse, R., 'Differentiating the Common?: The Responsibilities and Obligations of States Sponsoring Deep Seabed Mining Activities in the Area' (2011) 54 *German Yearbook of International Law* 459.

Rayfuse, R. and R. Warner, 'Securing a Sustainable Future for the Oceans Beyond National Jurisdiction: the Legal Basis for an Integrated Cross-Sectoral Regime for High Seas Governance for the 21st Century' (2008) 23 *International Journal of Marine and Coastal Law* 399.

Redgwell, C., 'From Permission to Prohibition: The 1982 Convention on the Law of the Sea and Protection of the Marine Environment', in D. Freestone, R. Barnes and D. Ong (eds.), *The Law of the Sea: Progress and Prospects* (Oxford University Press, 2006), pp. 180–91.

Rothwell, D. R., 'International Law and the Protection of the Arctic Environment' (1995) 44 *International and Comparative Law Quarterly* 280.

Rothwell, D. R. and T. Stephens, *The International Law of the Sea* (Oxford: Hart Publishing, 2010).

Salman, M. A. S., 'The Helsinki Rules, the UN Watercourses Convention and the Berlin Rules: Perspectives on International Water Law' (2007) 23 *Water Resources Development* 625.

Salman, S., *Regulatory Frameworks for Water Resources Management: A Comparative Study* (Washington DC: The World Bank, 2006).

'The United Nations Watercourses Convention Ten Years Later: Why Has Its Entry into Force Proven Difficult?' (2007) 22 *Water International* 1.

Tan, A. K.-J., *Vessel-Source Marine Pollution* (Cambridge University Press, 2006).

Tanaka, Y., 'Regulation of Land-Based Marine Pollution in International Law: A Comparative Analysis between Global and Regional Legal Frameworks' (2006) 66 *Zeitschrift für ausländisches öffentliches Recht und Völkerrecht* 535.

The International Law of the Sea (Cambridge University Press, 2012).

Tarlock, D., 'The Changing Environment of International Water Management Law' (2001) 12 *Water Law* 351.

'National Water Law: the Foundation of Sustainable Water Use' (2004) 15 *The Journal of Water Law* 120.

'Integrated Water Resources Management: Theory and Practice', in P. Wouters, V. Dukhovny and A. Allan (eds.), *Implementing Integrated Water Resources Management in Central Asia* (Dordrecht: Springer, 2007), pp. 3–21.

'Water Security, Fear Mitigation and International Water Law' (2008) 31 *Hamline Law Review* 704.

Tarlock, D. and P. Wouters, 'Are Shared Benefits of International Waters an Equitable Apportionment?' (2007) 18 *Colorado Journal of International Environmental Law and Policy* 523.

'Reframing the Water Security Dialogue' (2009) 20 *The Journal of Water Law* 53.

Teclaff, L., 'Evolution of the River Basin Concept in National and International Water Law' (1996) 36 *Natural Resources Journal* 359.

Verhoeven, J., P. Sands and M. Bruce (eds.), *The Antarctic Environment and International Law* (London: Graham & Trotman, 1992).

Vidas, D. (ed.), *Protecting the Polar Marine Environment: Law and Policy for Pollution Prevention* (Cambridge University Press, 2000).

Viñuales, J. E., 'Access to Water in Foreign Investment Disputes' (2009) 21 *Georgetown International Environmental Law Review* 733.

'Iced Freshwater Resources: A Legal Exploration' (2009) 20 *Yearbook of International Environmental Law* 188.

Vitanyi, B., *The International Regime of River Navigation* (Alphen aan den Rijn: Sijthoff & Noordhoff, 1979).

Warbrick, C., D. McGoldrick and E. Kirk, 'The 1996 Protocol to the London Dumping Convention and the Brent Spar' (1997) 46 *International and Comparative Law Quarterly* 957.

Watts, A., *International Law and the Antarctic Treaty System* (Cambridge: Grotius Publications, 1992).

Wouters, P., 'National and International Water Law: Achieving Equitable and Sustainable Use of Water Resources' (2000) 25 *Water International* 499.

'The Legal Response to International Water Conflicts: The UN Watercourses Convention and Beyond' (2000) 42 *German Yearbook of International Law* 292.

'Reframing the Water Security Dialogue' (2009) 20 *The Journal of Water Law* 53.

'The International Law of Watercourses: New Dimensions', in *Collected Courses of the Xiamen Academy of International Law*, 2011, pp. 347–541.

Wouters, P. and S. Hendry, 'Promoting Water (Law) For All: Addressing the World's Water Problem: A Focus on International and National Water Law and the Challenges of an Integrated Approach' (2009) 20 *The Journal of Water Law* 44.

Young, O. R., 'Arctic in Play: Governance in a Time of Rapid Change' (2009) 24 *International Journal of Marine and Coastal Law* 423.

5

Protection of the atmosphere

5.1 Introduction

The heading of this chapter might suggest that the Earth's atmosphere is protected as such in international law. However, regulation is generally built around specific problems, rather than in relation to an object such as the atmosphere.[1] The atmospheric issues tackled are as diverse as fumes emissions with transboundary effects, climate change, the acidification of the environment or the depletion of the ozone layer. This said, referring to the protection of the atmosphere remains convenient for pedagogical purposes, as these problems all relate to the composition of the gaseous envelope that extends from the Earth's surface outward into space, retained by gravitational attraction,[2] in particular, that of the two layers closest to the Earth's surface, namely the troposphere (up to about 12 km altitude) and the stratosphere (approximately between 12 and 50 km altitude).

An alternative but complementary way of approaching the protection of the atmosphere is to distinguish the various problems according to the geographical scope of their regulation. From this standpoint, the different regulatory regimes can be organised according to whether they address local, regional or global problems. It is worth recalling that even when dealing with a 'local' problem in international law, we refer to a situation that, due to its transboundary effects, involves two or more States. As for the specific threshold between the categories 'local', 'regional' and 'global', the determination depends, strictly speaking, upon the spatial scope specified in the regulation. Such scope normally coincides with the spatial dimension of the environmental problem tackled by the regulation. However, there is no necessary link

---

[1] However, the International Law Commission decided at its 65th session, in 2013, to include the topic 'protection of the atmosphere' in its programme of work and appointed Professor S. Murase as the Special Rapporteur for the topic. See also S. Murase, 'Protection of the Atmosphere and International Law: Rationale for Codification and Progressive Development' (2012) 55 *Sophia Law Review* 1.

[2] See the entry 'Atmosphere' in M. Allaby (ed.), *Oxford Dictionary of Ecology* (Oxford University Press, 2005); I. H. Rowlands, 'Atmosphere and Outer Space', in D. Bodansky, J. Brunnée and E. Hey (eds.), *The Oxford Handbook of International Environmental Law* (Oxford University Press, 2007), p. 316.

between the two. Global issues, such as certain aspects of climate change or land-based pollution of the marine environment,[3] may be tackled at a local or regional level. Similarly, regional or local environmental problems, such as transboundary air pollution, may be dealt with on a much broader basis. The spatial scope of a regulatory regime very much depends on variables such as the scientific understanding of a problem at a given point in time or, more prosaically, political feasibility. Such variables sometimes account for significant variations between the scope of a regulatory regime and the scope of an environmental problem.

A combination of these two approaches suggests an order of analysis starting with transboundary issues (5.2), then proceeding to regional problems (5.3), such as those addressed by the Convention on Long-Range Transboundary Air Pollution ('LRTAP Convention')[4] adopted in 1979 under the auspices of the United Nations Economic Commission for Europe ('UNECE'), and finally global problems, particularly instruments for the protection of the ozone layer (5.4) and the climate system (5.5).

5.2 'Local' transboundary air pollution

We have already discussed the traditional approach to transboundary pollution in Chapters 1 and 3. This approach is based on the principles of no harm and prevention, as codified in Principle 21 of the Stockholm Declaration and Principle 2 of the Rio Declaration.[5] The historical roots of these principles are to be found in the *Trail Smelter* arbitration, where the arbitral tribunal applied the no harm principle to conclude that Canada was obliged to repair the damages caused to the United States by the emissions of a smelter based on Canadian soil.[6]

As discussed in Chapter 3, this case and its impact on subsequent legal developments provides a useful entry point for the analysis of customary international law in this area. It also serves as an introduction to the way in which transboundary pollution has been regulated between the United States and Canada. The issue is particularly important between these two States because each is responsible for the acidification of the environment of the other. Indeed, acidification of the surface waters in the United States and Canada is largely a consequence of 'acid rain' caused by the emissions of

---

[3] See Chapter 4.

[4] Convention on Long-Range Transboundary Air Pollution, adopted in Geneva on 13 November 1979, 1302 UNTS 217.

[5] *Legality of the Threat or Use of Nuclear Weapons*, Advisory Opinion, ICJ Reports 1996, p. 226, para. 29; *Gabčíkovo-Nagymaros Project (Hungary v. Slovakia)*, Judgment, ICJ Reports 1997, p. 7, para. 53; *Pulp Mills on the River Uruguay (Argentina v. Uruguay)*, Judgment, ICJ Reports 2010, p. 14, para. 101.

[6] *Trail Smelter Arbitration (United States v. Canada)*, Arbitral Award (11 March 1941), RIAA, vol. III, pp. 1905–82. However, the origins of the principles can be traced back much further in the history of law, even to Roman times.

sulphur dioxide (SO_2) and nitrogen oxides (NO_x) from industrial activities.[7] This phenomenon has been known for several decades and, starting in the 1970s, both countries tried to find an agreed solution. The outcome of this process was the Air Quality Agreement, concluded on 13 March 1991.[8] The Agreement sets general and specific objectives as regards air quality, as well as obligations to assess and reduce emissions.[9] Overall, the Agreement has made a positive contribution to the problem, as suggested by the fact that the parties have achieved their goals of reducing emissions of SO_2 and NO_x.[10]

Questions of transboundary air pollution are sometimes regulated through broader bilateral agreements, covering various environmental issues. This is the case of the 1991 Treaty on the Environment between Argentina and Chile,[11] the 1993 Agreement between Ukraine and Hungary,[12] the 1994 Agreement between Russia and Belarus[13] or the 1998 Agreement between Uzbekistan and Ukraine,[14] to cite just a few examples.

The specific content of each bilateral agreement is less relevant for present purposes than the broader point they illustrate, namely that there are different ways to address localised transboundary air pollution. We will see next that, as transboundary air pollution became better understood, regulatory approaches tended to go beyond the bilateral level to become regional.

5.3 Long-range transboundary air pollution

5.3.1 Origins of the regime

The origins of the international regime on long-range transboundary air pollution can be found in the convergence of three processes.

The first process is of a socio-economic nature and concerns the industrial development of Europe from the 1950s until the 1970s, with the resulting air pollution. This is the period known as 'the glorious thirty' in Europe, over the course of which industrial development and, more generally, European economies recovered from the devastation of the Second World War. By the 1960s, however, some scientific publications shed light on the link between emissions of certain substances (notably sulphur dioxide) from Germany, England and

---

[7] Forest fires, volcanoes and bacterial activity in the oceans also contribute to the acidification of precipitation.

[8] Agreement between the Government of Canada and the Government of the United States of America on Air Quality, 3 March 1991, available at: www.epa.og/usca/agreement.html ('Air Quality Agreement'). See J. L. Roelof, 'United States-Canada Air Quality Agreement: A Framework for Addressing Transboundary Air Pollution Problems' (1993) 26 *Cornell International Law Journal* 421.

[9] Air Quality Agreement, *supra* n. 8, Arts. 3 to 5 and Annex I (entitled 'Annex on Acid Rain').

[10] See *Un défi à relever: l'amélioration de la qualité de l'air 2008. Progrès réalisés aux termes de l'Accord Canada – États-Unis sur la qualité de l'air*, available at : www.ec.gc.ca (last visited on 30 October 2012).

[11] See www.ecolex.org (TRE-149484). [12] See www.ecolex.org (TRE-150828).

[13] See www.ecolex.org (TRE-150417). [14] See www.ecolex.org (TRE-150933).

France, and the acidification of surface waters in Scandinavia. Around the same time, a connection was also identified between emissions of sulphur dioxide in the United States and the acidification of lakes in Canada. Disputes between countries that were essentially 'receivers' of pollution (notably the Nordic countries or Switzerland) and countries that were mainly 'emitters' of pollution (e.g. the United States or England) were taken to some international negotiating *fora*.

The first process helped catalyse the second one, namely the emergence of environmental awareness on the international plane. The most salient expression of this awareness is the process leading to the Stockholm Conference of 1972, discussed in Chapter 1. During the Stockholm Conference, the representatives of Scandinavian countries raised indeed the issue of acid rain, albeit with limited success.[15]

The Nordic States' concerns were to fall on fertile ground in the context of a third process, namely attempts at reconciliation between the Western countries and the Soviet bloc during the Conference on Security and Cooperation in Europe held in Helsinki from 1973 to 1975. This Conference dealt with the issue of transboundary air pollution as a ground to explore co-operation[16] and gave decisive impetus to the establishment of the European Monitoring and Evaluation Programme ('EMEP'), which, in turn, provided the scientific basis for the adoption of the LRTAP Convention.[17]

The convergence of these three processes culminated in November 1979 in a conference held in Geneva within the framework of an organisation gathering both Western countries and the Soviet bloc, namely the UNECE. At this conference, the representatives of thirty-four States and the European Communities concluded the Convention on Long-Range Transboundary Air Pollution.[18]

5.3.2 The LRTAP Convention

The LRTAP Convention was the first legally binding instrument concluded at both the continental and transatlantic levels in the fight against transboundary air pollution.[19] In force since 1983, the Convention currently binds over fifty

---

[15] See V. Sokolovsky, 'Fruits of a Cold War', in J. Sliggers and W. Kakebeeke (eds.), *Clearing the Air. 25 Years of the Convention on Long-Range Transboundary Air Pollution* (New York/ Geneva: United Nations, 2004), p. 8.

[16] Final Act of the Conference on Security and Cooperation in Europe, 1975, 14 ILM 1292, p. 32.

[17] See T. Schneider and J. Schneider, 'EMEP – Backbone of the Convention', in Sliggers and Kakebeeke, *supra* n. 15, Chapter 3.

[18] On the origins and function of this treaty see P. Okowa, 'The Legal Framework for the Protection of the Environment Against Transboundary Air Pollution', in H. G. Post (ed.), *The Protection of Ambient Air in International and European Law* (The Hague: Eleven Publishing, 2009), pp. 53–71; Sliggers and Kakebeeke, *supra* n. 15.

[19] Other regional instruments on this issue have been developed over time: the Nordic Convention on the Protection of the Environment, 19 February 1974, available in English at www.ecolex.org

States located not only in Europe (including Eastern Europe), but also in North America and Central Asia.

Although the Convention does not contain any specific substantive obligations (despite attempts in this regard by the Scandinavian States), its structure is of particular interest insofar as it illustrates an important legal technique which came to be known as the 'framework convention/protocol approach'. Indeed, in a context of relative uncertainty and significant political disagreements between 'receivers' and 'emitters' of pollution, the Convention was eventually confined to (i) defining its object; (ii) setting out the fundamental principles; and, importantly, (iii) providing an institutional framework to specify both the objectives and the obligations of States through subsequent instruments (protocols).

Article 1 of the Convention defines 'air pollution' as:

> the introduction by man, directly or indirectly, of substances or energy into the air resulting in deleterious effects of such a nature as to endanger human health, harm living resources and ecosystems and material property and impair or interfere with amenities and other legitimate uses of the environment.

Pollution is therefore to be understood as human interference (as opposed to natural processes causing emissions), which is harmful to humans (anthropocentric element) or the environment (eco-centric element), including the built environment, such as property. Pollution is characterised as 'long-range' when the distance between the source of emission in one State and the adverse effect in another State is such that 'it is generally not possible to distinguish the contribution of individual emission sources or groups of sources'. It should also be noted that both the source and the adverse effect must be under the jurisdiction of a State, which excludes from the definition pollution that would only affect the environment outside of any national jurisdiction, such as the high seas. This reflects the still narrow conception of the principle of prevention prevailing at the time, despite the progressive formulation of Principle 21 of the Stockholm Declaration, which encompasses the environment beyond State jurisdiction.

The Convention establishes certain 'fundamental principles' in Articles 2 to 6. They are of two kinds. On the one hand, each State undertakes to adopt national measures to limit and gradually reduce air pollution (including transboundary pollution) originating within its jurisdiction, subject to a series

---

(TRE-000491); European guidelines in this field (see M. Montini, 'EC Legislation on Air Pollution: From Guidelines to Limit Values' in Post, *supra* n. 18, pp. 73–87); ASEAN Agreement on Transboundary Haze Pollution, 10 June 2002, available in English at www.ecolex.org (TRE-001344); Framework Convention on Environmental Protection for Sustainable Development in Central Asia, 22 November 2006, available in English at www.ecolex.org (TRE-143806); SADC Regional Policy Framework on Air Pollution, 7 March 2008, available at www.unep.org; Eastern Africa Regional Framework Agreement on Air Pollution, 23 October 2008, available at www.unep.org; West and Central Africa Regional Framework Agreement on Air Pollution, 22 July 2009, available at www.unep.org.

of qualifications that render this commitment rather mild.[20] On the other hand, States undertake to co-operate through 'exchanges of information, consultation, research and monitoring'.[21] This may seem modest, but in the context of the East–West confrontation, the fact that receiver States have a legal basis (Article 5) to initiate consultations and, as we shall see later, an institutional architecture for deepening and broadening substantive obligations, was a significant step.

The institutional structure set out by the Convention consists of an Executive Body,[22] comparable to the Conferences of the Parties ('COPs') studied in Chapter 2, a secretariat[23] and a scientific body, a role discharged by the Steering Body of the EMEP but with consolidated and extended functions.[24] This system has grown, over time, through the creation of subsidiary bodies, such as the 'Working Group on Effects', the 'Working Group on Strategies and Review' and an 'Implementation Committee'. The information gathered by the scientific body facilitated, in the decades following the negotiations and within the institutional framework of the Convention, the adoption of no less than eight protocols containing detailed obligations.

Finally, it should be noted that the approach followed by the Convention is to restrict emissions and not to allocate the burden of reparation.[25] This reluctance to address issues of liability, partly due to difficulties in establishing precise causal links between emissions and damage but also a result of political divergences, equally characterises the regimes for the protection of the ozone layer and climate change, as we will see later.

5.3.3 The protocols to the LRTAP Convention

The protocols adopted from the 1980s onwards are of great interest not only because of their practical impact, which is sometimes indeed significant, but also because they provided an important testing ground for the regulation of air pollution. Instead of presenting these protocols in a chronological order, it is more instructive to take a cross-cutting perspective having recourse to three analytical distinctions.

A first distinction concerns the nature of the protocols. While the first Protocol to the LRTAP Convention aimed to strengthen the EMEP,[26] particularly in respect of funding, the subsequent seven protocols were concerned

---

[20] LRTAP Convention *supra* n. 4, Arts. 2, 3 and 6.
[21] *Ibid.*, Art. 3, as well as Arts. 4 and 8 (exchange of information), 5 (consultations between State emitters and State receivers), and 7 (research and development).
[22] *Ibid.*, Art. 10. [23] *Ibid.*, Art. 11. [24] *Ibid.* Art. 9.
[25] In the footnote to Art. 8(f) of the LRTAP Convention, it is expressly stated that 'The present Convention does not contain a rule on State liability as to damage'.
[26] Protocol to the 1979 Convention on Long-Range Transboundary Air Pollution on the long-term Financing of the Cooperative Programme for Monitoring and Evaluation of the Long-Range Transport of Air Pollutants in Europe ('EMEP'), 28 September 1984, 1491 UNTS 167.

with the development of specific obligations in the area of air pollution. Second, the approach of each of these instruments has been to target a certain type of pollutant (sulphur dioxide,[27] nitrogen oxides,[28] volatile organic compounds or 'VOC',[29] heavy metals or 'HM'[30] and persistent organic pollutants or 'POP'[31]). It was only with the adoption of the Gothenburg Protocol in November 1999[32] that the centre of gravity of the regulatory approach shifted from types of pollutants to types of problems (acidification, eutrophication and tropospheric ozone), covering a large number of pollutants and sources of pollution (fixed, mobile, new and existing).[33] Third, the regulatory techniques have become increasingly complex. This last feature sheds light on the legal evolution of these protocols.

The problems of acidification (particularly acid rain) were initially dealt with in a fairly rigid manner, albeit effective in terms of the results the approach achieved.[34] In particular, the first substantive protocol introduced an obligation on each State Party, without differentiation, to reduce sulphur dioxide emissions by a certain percentage (30 per cent) compared to a base year (1980) as soon as possible and no later than 1993.[35]

This rigidity in the approach was largely mitigated following the adoption of the NO_x Protocol, which contemplated a more complex emission reduction system, characterised by three elements: (i) the adjustment of obligations to

---

[27] Protocol to the 1979 Convention on Long-Range Transboundary Air Pollution on the Reduction of Sulphur Emissions or their Transboundary Fluxes by at Least 30 Per Cent, 8 July 1985, 1480 UNTS 215 ('Sulphur Protocol I'); Protocol to the 1979 Convention on Long-Range Transboundary Air Pollution on the Reduction of Sulphur Emissions, 14 June 1994, 2030 UNTS 122 ('Sulphur Protocol II').

[28] Protocol to the 1979 Convention on Long-Range Transboundary Air Pollution Concerning the Control of Emissions of Nitrogen Oxides or their Transboundary Fluxes, 31 October 1988, 28 ILM 212, 216 ('NO_x Protocol').

[29] Protocol to the 1979 Convention on Long-Range Transboundary Air Pollution Concerning the Control of Emissions of Volatile Organic Compounds or their Transboundary Fluxes, 18 November 1991, 31 ILM 573 ('VOC Protocol').

[30] Protocol to the 1979 Convention on Long-Range Transboundary Air Pollution on Heavy Metals, 24 June 1998, 2237 UNTS 4 ('Heavy Metals Protocol').

[31] Protocol to the 1979 Convention on Long-Range Transboundary Air Pollution on Persistent Organic Pollutants (POPs), 24 June 1998, 2230 UNTS 79 ('POP Protocol').

[32] Protocol to the 1979 Convention on Long-Range Transboundary Air Pollution on the Reduction of Acidification, Eutrophication and Ground-Level Ozone, 30 November 1999, Document of the Economic and Social Council EB.AIR/1999/1 ('Gothenburg Protocol').

[33] Initially, the protocol covered emissions of sulphur dioxide, nitrogen oxides, volatile organic compounds and ammoniac. Now it also applies to emissions of fine particles, including black carbon, which is a powerful greenhouse gas that has a short duration and whose effects are localised. See 'Parties to UNECE Air Pollution Convention approve new emission reduction commitments for main air pollutants by 2020', Press release, 4 May 2012, available at: www.unece.org/index.php?id=29858 (last visited on 12 October 2012). Note that this amendment will enter into force after ratification by two thirds of the parties, in the following presentation, we incorporate the amendments into the analysis.

[34] By 1993, emissions had been reduced overall by more than 50 per cent. See P. Sands and J. Peel, *Principles of International Environmental Law* (Cambridge University Press, 2012), p. 249.

[35] Sulphur Protocol I, *supra* n. 27, Art. 2.

reduce emissions tailored to the circumstances of each State (including the possibility of choosing a particular base year),[36] (ii) the adoption of national emission standards for certain sources, both stationary (e.g. power plants) and mobile (e.g. cars, trucks, railways and aircraft), based on the criterion of 'best available technology which is economically feasible' (or 'BAT')[37] and (iii) the use of the concept of 'critical load'. The latter is defined as 'a quantitative estimate of the exposure to one or more pollutants below which significant harmful effects on specified sensitive elements of the environment do not occur according to present knowledge'.[38] Thus, it is necessary to define, for each protected area, the tolerance to a certain type of pollutant. Such an approach, which continues to be used, raises a number of scientific challenges that were already identified at the time,[39] such as the definition of the protected areas, the choice of an indicator to measure their tolerance, or the understanding of the trajectory followed by pollutants from the source to the protected area. It is also important to note that the critical load concept is at odds with the idea of precaution,[40] since it involves polluting up to a critical load determined only by current scientific knowledge.[41] At the same time, this approach provides a scientific basis for introducing a differentiation between the levels of protection required from each State, as in the Sulphur Protocol II, adopted in 1994.

The techniques used to enhance flexibility were further developed by the VOC Protocol. The approach adopted by this protocol is characterised by three elements: (i) the choice offered to States parties of three different sets of emissions reduction obligations, (ii) the adoption of emissions standards for stationary and mobile sources based on the BAT criteria[42] and (iii) the use of the concept of 'critical levels'. The main innovation is to be found in the first and last elements. As regards the first, States parties may, according to their circumstances, choose one of three sets of emissions reduction obligations, namely (i) 30 per cent reduction of national annual emissions (with respect to a base year to be chosen within a certain range) no later than 1999;[43] (ii) 30 per cent reduction of emissions in key areas of the State's territory called 'tropospheric ozone management areas' or 'TOMAs'[44] or (iii) for some States with limited emissions, a less stringent target to keep emissions at the level of the base year (1988).[45] As for the 'critical levels' concept, the idea is similar to that of 'critical loads', but instead of looking at the level of pollution in certain areas

---

[36] NO$_x$ Protocol, *supra* n. 28, Art. 2(1).
[37] *Ibid.*, Art. 2(2) and Technical Annex, paras. 6 and 41.
[38] *Ibid.*, Art. 1(7). See also: J. Nilsson and P. Grennfelt (eds.), *Report: Critical Loads for Sulphur and Nitrogen* (Copenhagen: Nordic Council of Ministers, 1988).
[39] NO$_x$ Protocol, *supra* n. 28, Art. 6.   [40] See Chapter 3.
[41] This caveat is significant to assess the reference to the precautionary approach made in the preamble of the Gothenburg Protocol. Indeed, this instrument also incorporates the critical loads approach.
[42] VOC Protocol, *supra* n. 29, Art. 2(3).   [43] *Ibid.*, Art. 2(2)(a).
[44] *Ibid.*, Art. 2(2)(b) and Annex I.   [45] *Ibid.*, Art. 2(2)(c).

or ecosystems, it is concerned with pollution present in the atmosphere, which may in turn produce 'direct adverse effects on receptors, such as human beings, plants, ecosystems or materials'.[46] Here too, the approach is at odds with the idea of precaution, given that the tolerance levels are estimated on the basis of the 'current state of knowledge'.

The Heavy Metals Protocol adopted in 1998 also contemplates (i) a reduction of emissions of certain heavy metals identified in an annex (cadmium, lead, mercury) as compared to base years specific to each State[47] and (ii) the adoption of emission standards for stationary sources using the BAT criteria as well as the concept of 'limit values'.[48] This concept is the average amount of a given heavy metal emitted per temporal unit (e.g. per hour) during the normal operation of certain facilities. Annex V of the Protocol defines general values and specific values for certain 'major stationary sources'.[49] States must introduce BAT requirements and impose emissions limits within a certain time frame (depending on the type of stationary source) specified in Annex IV. The POP Protocol,[50] adopted the same year, goes a step further. For substances listed in Annex III (e.g. dioxins and furans), the Protocol envisages a system similar to the Heavy Metals Protocol, namely reducing emissions and the imposition of BAT and limit values. Yet, it also provides that the production and use of substances identified in Annex I must be eliminated,[51] while the use of substances listed in Annex II is restricted to the circumstances identified in that annex.[52]

Finally, as regards the Gothenburg Protocol,[53] because of its multiple objectives (curbing acidification, eutrophication and ground-level ozone),[54] it incorporates several regulatory techniques that have already been mentioned. This makes it very complex, but also of particular interest as it offers a summary of the legal experimentation conducted within the framework of the LRTAP Convention. The Protocol provides for (i) quantified obligations – with separate ceilings for each State – for the reduction of emissions of certain pollutants (sulphur, nitrogen oxides, ammonia, VOC and now also particulate matter, such as black carbon);[55] (ii) the use of the 'critical levels' concept in relation to the problem of tropospheric ozone;[56] (iii) the use of the 'critical loads' concept in relation to the problems of acidification and

---

[46] *Ibid.*, Art. 1(8). [47] Heavy Metals Protocol, *supra* n. 30, Art. 3(1) and Annex I.
[48] *Ibid.*, Art. 3(2). An amendment to Annex III (BAT) was introduced in December 2012 and entered into force in 2014. Other amendments are not yet in force.
[49] *Ibid.*, Annexes II and V.
[50] POP Protocol, *supra* n. 31. In December 2009, the protocol was amended to include seven new substances and revise the obligations concerning covered substances, but the amendments are not yet in force.
[51] *Ibid.*, Art. 3(1)(a) and Annex I. See also the additional obligation on how elimination should be carried out as provided for in Art. 3(1)(b).
[52] *Ibid.*, Art. 3(1)(c) and Annex II. For example, the use of the pesticide DDT (whose effects had already been reported by R. Carson in 1962), is exceptionally allowed for the fight against diseases such as malaria and encephalitis.
[53] Gothenburg Protocol, *supra* n. 32. [54] *Ibid.*, Art. 2.
[55] *Ibid.*, Art. 3(1) and Annex II. See *supra* n. 33. [56] *Ibid.*, Art. 2(c) and Annex I (III).

Emission Reduction Objectives		Technical Standards on Emissions structured around:					Pollution Ceilings		Production/Use	
Rigid	Flexible	Type of Source	Type of Standard				Critical Load	Critical Level	Elimination	Restriction on Use
		stationary/ mobile, existing/new	BAT	Limit Values	Specific Measures					
Sulphur-I	NO_x	NO_x	NO_x	Metals	Gothenburg (Annex IX)		NO_x	VOCs	POPs (Annex I)	POPs (Annex II)
	Sulphur-II	Sulphur-II	Sulphur-II	POPs			Sulphur-II	Gothenburg		
	VOCs	VOCs	VOCs	Gothenburg			Gothenburg			
	Metals	Metals	Metals							
	POPs	POPs	POPs							
	Gothenburg	Gothenburg	Gothenburg							

Figure 5.1: Regulatory techniques for atmospheric pollution

eutrophication;[57] and (iv) the adoption, within certain time limits, of emission standards for stationary and mobile sources of some pollutants (sulphur, nitrogen oxides, VOCs and fuels), structured around the BAT criteria[58] and the concept of 'limit values',[59] as well as specific measures to control ammonia emissions from agricultural sources.[60] These techniques are combined in order to achieve the stabilisation and reduction of harmful emissions. Indeed, the requirements governing the emissions of certain pollutants (ceilings and limit values) seek to comply with critical loads and levels.

The four major types of regulatory techniques used by the protocols to the LRTAP Convention (i.e. emissions reduction targets, technical standards on emissions, pollution limits and prohibitions/restrictions) is summarised in Figure 5.1.

The legal experimentation conducted in the framework of the LRTAP Convention is very useful to understand the approaches followed to tackle issues of a global nature, such as the depletion of the ozone layer and climatic change.

5.4 The protection of the ozone layer

5.4.1 The origins of the regime

The international regime developed to address the depletion of the ozone layer[61] shares some aspects with previous efforts in the area of air

---

[57] *Ibid.*, Art. 2 and Annex I.   [58] *Ibid.*, Art. 3(6) and 3(8)(b).

[59] *Ibid.*, Art. 3(2)–(5) (and (7)) and Annexes IV–VI and VIII (as well as X for black carbon and XI for VOC contents of products once the amendment enters into force (limit values), Annex VII (time)).

[60] *Ibid.*, Art. 3(8) and Annex IX.

[61] See O. Yoshida, *The International Legal Regime for the Protection of the Stratospheric Ozone Layer* (The Hague: Kluwer, 2001); R. E. Benedick, *Ozone Diplomacy: New Directions in Safeguarding the Planet* (Cambridge MA: Harvard University Press, 1998).

pollution, but it has distinctive features arising from the global scope of the problem and the scientific uncertainty that characterised its initial understanding.

Regarding the similarities, the protection of the ozone layer had to confront difficulties similar to those faced by long-range transboundary air pollution, namely (i) the science-policy interface (just as EMEP monitors air pollution, UNEP and the WMO – as well as other institutions – periodically assess the state of the ozone layer[62]), (ii) the tension between environmental protection and economic interests (reflected in the difficult negotiations between, on the one hand, the 'Toronto Group' comprising the United States, Canada, Switzerland, the Nordic countries, New Zealand and Australia, who favoured international regulation and, on the other hand, the European Community, itself divided between States reluctant to the idea of strong regulation (France and the UK) and States favouring such regulations (Germany and The Netherlands), and (iii) the legal experimentation necessary to deal with these challenges (e.g. the 'framework convention/ protocol' technique). These difficulties were exacerbated by the unprecedented nature of the problem.

Indeed, the protection of the ozone layer was the first truly global environmental problem that international law had to face. About 90 per cent of the ozone present in the Earth's atmosphere is located in the stratosphere (above 12–50 km above the Earth's surface) and ozone concentrations are greatest at an altitude of about 25 km. This thin layer of ozone that surrounds the planet absorbs an important part of the ultraviolet radiation from the sun, which would otherwise have severe consequences for the environment and human health. It was thus no longer a question of managing a local, regional or even continental problem. The protection of the ozone layer required that the interests of all States as well as of recent and future generations be taken into account. This was particularly difficult because of the significant economic interests involved in the production and use of the main ozone depleting substances, the chlorofluorocarbons ('CFCs'), used in a wide range of industrial activities and products (such as refrigerants, solvents, propellants for aerosols, etc.), as well as scientific uncertainties. From 1974, when the potential danger posed by CFCs to stratospheric ozone was first identified,[63] until the late 1980s when a growing number of scientific publications helped to elucidate the issue, the road was sinuous. Even after the discovery, published in 1985, of a seasonal 'hole' in the ozone layer above

---

[62] Since the early 1980s, UNEP and WMO have at regular intervals published an assessment of the state of the ozone layer. An analogy is possible here with the role of the IPCC and its regular assessment of the state of science on climate change.

[63] See R. S. Stolarski and R. J. Cicerone, 'Stratospheric Chlorine: A Possible Sink for Ozone' (1974) 52 *Canadian Journal of Chemistry* 1610–15; M. J. Molina and F. S. Rowland, 'Stratospheric Sink for Chlorofluoromethanes: Chlorine Atomic Catalyzed Destruction of Ozone' (1974) 249 *Nature* 810–12.

Antarctica of the size of the United States,[64] the causal link between CFCs and the depletion of the ozone layer had still not been understood.[65] This uncertainty marked the regulatory process until a very late stage in the negotiations.[66]

It is in this context that the Vienna Convention on the Protection of the Ozone Layer, adopted in 1985,[67] must be evaluated. Although it does not impose specific substantive obligations, the Convention has provided a framework for the adoption of one of the most ambitious instruments of international environmental law, the Montreal Protocol.[68]

5.4.2 The Vienna Convention of 1985

Like the LRTAP Convention, the Vienna Convention is a framework convention. Despite the efforts of some countries in the Toronto Group to introduce an annex with specific obligations on CFC control, this could not be achieved in 1985.[69] As the LRTAP Convention, the Vienna Convention is limited to (i) a definition of its object, (ii) the formulation of some broad obligations and, most importantly, (iii) the provision of an institutional framework to specify the obligations of States and to develop a differentiated implementation regime. Given the scope of the problem and the significant scientific uncertainty prevailing at that time as regards the link between CFCs and ozone depletion, this outcome should not be underestimated. All the more so because, unlike the LRTAP Convention, the Vienna Convention is based on the idea of precaution, which was not well known in diplomatic circles and, as consequence, was viewed with some suspicion.[70]

The first contribution of the Vienna Convention is to formulate the problem of ozone depletion in terms that highlight its global character and distinguish it from a local or regional problem such as transboundary pollution (notably the issue of ground level ozone). Under Article 1(1), the object of protection is, indeed, 'the layer of atmospheric ozone above the planetary boundary layer'.[71] The protection of the ozone layer is also

---

[64] See B. Farman, G. Gardiner and J. D. Shanklin, 'Large Losses of Total Ozone in Antarctica Reveal Seasonal ClO_x/NO_x International' (1985) 315 *Nature* 207–10. A 'hole' was also found in 2011 above the Arctic.

[65] On the evolution of the problem, see: O. B. Toon and R. P. Turco, 'Polar Stratospheric Clouds and Ozone Depletion' (1991) 264(6) *Scientific American* 68–74.

[66] See Benedick, *supra* n. 61, pp. 19–20.

[67] Vienna Convention on the Protection of the Ozone Layer, 22 March 1985, 1513 UNTS 293 ('Vienna Convention').

[68] Montreal Protocol on Substances that Deplete the Ozone Layer, 16 September 1987, 1522 UNTS 29 ('Montreal Protocol').

[69] Yoshida, *supra* n. 61, pp. 49ff.   [70] Benedick, *supra* n. 61, p. 24.

[71] Yoshida considers that the status of the ozone layer, which is implicit in the text of the Convention, is a 'common concern of mankind'. Yoshida, *supra* n. 61, p. 61.

defined in three other ways, namely by specifying the type of change that should be avoided ('adverse effects'[72]), the source of the modification ('human activities'[73]) and, preliminarily, the substances that cause the damage.[74] It should be noted that both the preamble and Article 1(2) positioned the Convention as an instrument aiming at the prevention of changes in the ozone layer even when the relationship between the activities and substances identified, the modification of the ozone layer and the adverse effects on human health and the environment, was not scientifically settled. This aspect is important to capture the close link between the idea of prevention and the idea of precaution, the latter being in many ways a more ambitious version of the former.

With regard to the obligations assumed by States parties, the Convention merely provides that, on the one hand, parties must take 'appropriate measures' (vertical obligations)[75] and, on the other hand, it encourages States to co-operate among themselves and with competent international bodies (horizontal obligations) in the pursuit of further research on ozone depletion,[76] in order to harmonise their internal policies[77] and develop the international regime, notably by means of protocols to the Convention.[78] For present purposes, it is the system for joint research and for cooperation that merits attention.

As other multilateral environmental agreements ('MEAs'), the Vienna Convention created a permanent institutional framework to spell out the obligations of co-operation and regime development. The COP established by Article 6 performs, *inter alia,* the function of analysing scientific information on the state of the ozone layer, initiating research programmes, maintaining links with international research bodies (including the Global Atmosphere Watch Programme ('GAW') of the WMO),[79] as well as examining and adopting protocols to the Convention.[80] In this context, the COP launched, in late 1986, the negotiations that led to the adoption of the Montreal Protocol. The Secretariat of the Convention[81] is located in Nairobi, Kenya, and is hosted by UNEP. It performs a co-ordination function and has, in practice, significant influence.

---

[72] Vienna Convention, *supra* n. 67, Art. 1(2) defines this term as 'changes in the physical environment or biota, including changes in climate, which have significant deleterious effects on human health or on the composition, resilience and productivity of natural and managed ecosystems, or on materials useful to mankind'.

[73] *Ibid.*, Art. 2(1).

[74] Annex I of the Convention refers to various substances whose effects should be monitored. This is partly a reflection of the significant scientific uncertainties that still surrounded the issue. A more precise definition was introduced by the Montreal Protocol.

[75] *Ibid.*, Arts. 2(1), 2(2)(b), 3 (authorisation to adopt more stringent national measures) and 5 (communication of information).

[76] *Ibid.*, Arts. 2(2)(a), 3, 4 and Annex II.   [77] *Ibid.*, Arts. 2(2)(b) and 4.

[78] *Ibid.*, Arts. 2(2)(c)–(d) and 8.   [79] *Ibid.*, Art. 6(4)(b), (d) and (j).   [80] *Ibid.*, Art. 6(4)(h).

[81] *Ibid.*, Art. 7.

5.4.3 The Montreal Protocol of 1987

In the history of international environmental law, the Montreal Protocol stands as a success.[82] Owing to its ambition and legal sophistication, but also – in retrospect – to its effectiveness,[83] especially when compared to the limited impact of the Kyoto Protocol, the Montreal Protocol has much to teach us. To summarise its contribution in a clear manner, it is necessary to distinguish two dimensions in the architecture of the Protocol, namely the structure of the obligations of the parties and the system designed to ensure compliance with them.

The *obligations of the parties* consist of a complex combination of obligations set out in the Protocol text and specifications introduced in the annexes. The core of the system can be pinned down to four main components: (i) the type of controlled substance (e.g. CFCs, halons, HCFCs, etc.[84]), (ii) the type of party (developing countries have more flexible obligations[85]), (iii) the object of regulation (i.e. the level of 'consumption' and 'production',[86] calculated in a manner defined by the Protocol[87]) and (iv) the structure of the reduction obligations (a timetable scheduling first a production/consumption 'freeze' and subsequently reduction targets of a certain percentage with respect to a base year to be reached within a given period[88]). Reading the text of the Protocol is difficult, among other things because of the various adjustments to the text (six series of adjustments)[89] and the new provisions introduced through amendments (four series of amendments). Despite widespread ratification, these amendments have not yet been uniformly accepted by all States parties to the original Protocol, which makes the system somewhat fragmented. An example may be useful to understand how these four components interact.

Article 2A (and Annex A – Group I) of the Protocol provides for measures to control certain CFCs (CFC-11, CFC-12, CFC-113, CFC-114 and CFC-115). In the initial text, the Protocol governed only two types of substances, namely CFCs and halons (Annex A – Group II). Over time, as the causes of ozone

---

[82] For an overview see D. S. Bryk, 'The Montreal Protocol and Recent Developments to Protect the Ozone Layer' (1991) 15 *Harvard Environmental Law Review* 275.

[83] See D. Kaniaru (ed.), *The Montreal Protocol: Celebrating 20 Years of Environmental Progress* (London: Cameron May, 2007). By 2012, the Montreal Protocol, which now binds all the 197 countries of the world, was able to reduce the production of controlled substances by 98 per cent compared to 1987 levels (1.8 million tonnes in 1987 to 45,000 tonnes in 2010). See the Ozone Secretariat, *Stratospheric Ozone Protection: Progress Report 1987–2012*, available at: www.ozone.unep.org (last visited on 13 August 2012).

[84] Montreal Protocol, *supra* n. 68, Art. 1(4) and Annexes A, B, C and E. The protocol follows a basket approach, whereby the obligations are structured around the type of substance (e.g. focusing on the substances in Annex A, group I, and not on one specific substance within that group. See *ibid.*, Art. 3.

[85] *Ibid.*, Art. 5(1).   [86] *Ibid.*, Art. 1(5) (production) and 1(6) (consumption).

[87] *Ibid.*, Art. 1(7) and 3 (calculated levels).   [88] *Ibid.*, Arts. 2 to 21 and Annexes A, B, C and E.

[89] *Ibid.*, Art. 2(9).

depletion became better understood, the Protocol was extended to other substances, as provided for in Articles 2C to 2I and Annexes B (on fully halogenated CFCs, carbon tetrachloride and methyl chloroform), C (on HCFCs, HBFCs and bromochloromethane) and E (on methyl bromide). For each type of regulated substances, the Protocol provides for two distinct regimes of obligations, one for developed States (those 'not operating under Article 5(1)') and another for developing States (those 'operating under Article 5(1)'). In both cases parties are first required to freeze and then reduce the calculated levels of consumption and production of the regulated substances, but the requirements imposed on States operating under Article 5(1) are less stringent. Production is defined in Article 1(5) as 'the amount of controlled substances produced [in a certain period]' minus the amount destroyed in a certain manner and the amount entirely used in the manufacture of other chemicals. Consumption is defined in Article 1(6) as 'production plus imports minus exports of controlled substances'. As we will see later, the Protocol specifically regulates the possibility of exporting these substances. Pursuant to Article 3, the control levels of production and consumption are the amounts thus defined multiplied by the 'ozone depleting potential' of each substance as specified in Annexes A, B, C and E. The standard used in this regard (or, to use an analogy, the 'currency' used to quantify the value of other currencies) is CFC-11, which is assigned – arbitrarily – a potential of 1. Certain substances that are more harmful (e.g. halons) have a higher value. For instance, Halon-1301 has a depleting potential of 10, which means that a tonne of this substance that reaches the stratosphere depletes the ozone layer ten times more than a tonne of CFC-11. These potentials are regularly adjusted to reflect the advancement of scientific knowledge.

With these remarks in mind, we can return to the structure of the obligations. Take, for example, CFCs. Under Article 2A of the Protocol, industrialised countries committed to first freeze their consumption and production of certain CFCs (Annex A – Group I) during the period from 1 July 1989 to 31 December 1993 with respect to the base year, 1986. Subsequently, they were required to gradually reduce these levels by a certain percentage until achieving the total elimination of the production/consumption of these substances. This reduction is structured in a phased manner, with the year (i.e. the level) of reference remaining 1986. Thus, during the period from 1 January 1994 to 31 December 1995, the annual production/consumption of CFCs was not to exceed 25 per cent of the 1986 level (equivalent to a 75 per cent reduction of the annual production/consumption). Then, from 1 January 1996, production/ consumption was no longer permitted (100 per cent reduction). With regard to developing States, the structure of the obligations is similar, but the base level (being in this case the average of the levels of 1995, 1996 and 1997) and deadlines were more flexible. A freeze was applied for the period from 1 July 1999 to 31 December 2004 followed by a gradual reduction accomplished in three stages: the annual production/consumption in the period from 1 January

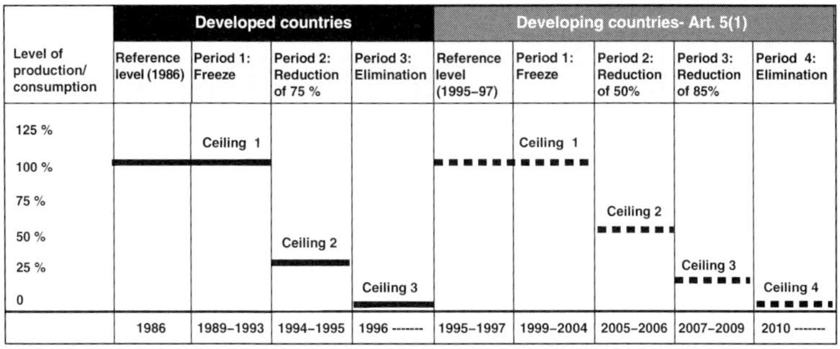

Level of production/ consumption	Developed countries				Developing countries- Art. 5(1)				
	Reference level (1986)	Period 1: Freeze	Period 2: Reduction of 75 %	Period 3: Elimination	Reference level (1995–97)	Period 1: Freeze	Period 2: Reduction of 50%	Period 3: Reduction of 85%	Period 4: Elimination
125 %		Ceiling 1				Ceiling 1			
100 %									
75 %							Ceiling 2		
50 %			Ceiling 2						
25 %								Ceiling 3	
0				Ceiling 3					Ceiling 4
	1986	1989–1993	1994–1995	1996 ------	1995–1997	1999–2004	2005–2006	2007–2009	2010 ------

Figure 5.2: Montreal Protocol – Structure of commitments (CFC)[90]

2005 to 31 December 2006 was not to exceed 50 per cent of the reference level (50 per cent reduction); that in the period from 1 January 2007 to 31 December 2009 was not to exceed 15 per cent of the reference level (85 per cent reduction); and, from 1 January 2010, production/consumption of these substances was no longer permitted (100 per cent reduction). This structure, which is rather difficult to describe in words, is more easily grasped graphically (see Figure 5.2). The demanding nature of these obligations should not be under-estimated, especially as they have been made more and more stringent through a series of adjustments and amendments made to the Protocol.

To *implement* this ambitious system of obligations, the Montreal Protocol has been equipped with mechanisms to encourage participation, facilitate compliance and manage non-compliance in an equally ambitious way. Four mechanisms deserve attention, namely (i) the regulation of trade, (ii) the benefits offered to developing countries, (iii) the flexibility mechanisms and (iv) the procedure for managing non-compliance.

Article 4 of the Protocol governs trade in controlled substances, products containing such substances, and technologies and tools for their manufacture with non-Parties.[91] This provision was important to avoid these substances being imported from third countries (which would have discouraged the search for alternatives) and to control the production/consumption of such substances outside the regime established by the Protocol by reducing demand (the phenomenon known as 'leakage').[92] For these reasons, paragraphs (1) and (2) of Article 4 prohibit the importing and exporting by States parties of

---

[90] Source: this figure is adapted from the one appearing on the website of the Ozone Secretariat. See ozone.unep.org/new_site/en/index.php.

[91] *Ibid.*, Art. 4, paras. (1), (2), (3), (5) and (6). This provision also contemplates trade in products that do not contain such substances but which are produced with them (Art. 4(4)), but the parties agreed in 1993 that it was not possible to restrict trade in these products. See Decision V/ 17, 19 November 1993, Doc. UNEP/OzL.Pro.5/12.

[92] See R. Twum-Barima and L. B. Campbell, *Protecting the Ozone Layers through Trade Measures: Reconciling the Trade Provisions of the Montreal Protocol and the Rules of the GATT* (Geneva: UNEP, 1994), pp. 51ff.

substances from or to third States. Similarly, Article 4(3), supplemented by Annex D in 1991, prohibits the imports of certain products containing controlled substances from third countries. Finally, paragraphs (5) and (6) discourage the export of technologies and tools for the manufacture of controlled substances (or related products) to third countries. These restrictions were first applied to substances in Annex A (CFCs and halons) and were subsequently extended to other substances.[93] The objectives of controlling the proliferation of these substances and of encouraging third States to join the Protocol have been broadly achieved, although, as discussed next, it was necessary to add other incentives to ensure the participation of countries like China and India.

Shortly after its entry into force, the Protocol was amended (at the Meeting of the Parties or 'CMP' in London, 1990) in order to better address the needs expressed by some developing States. Indeed, the additional flexibility offered to States operating under Article 5(1) appeared insufficient to attract some States such as India or China. Through a careful mixture of pressure and concessions, these amendments were finally enough to persuade various developing countries to join the Protocol. Regarding pressure, Article 5 of the Protocol was amended to set a specific date (1 January 1999) beyond which a developing State could not benefit from the grace period of ten years accorded to States operating under Article 5(1). As for concessions, obligations of assistance were substantially strengthened by the amendment of Article 10 of the Protocol (financial assistance) and the introduction of Article 10A (technology transfer). The amended Article 10 created a Multilateral Fund whose main function was to cover the 'agreed incremental costs' incurred by the States operating under Article 5(1) in order to facilitate their compliance with the regulatory measures imposed by the Protocol.[94] This measure was truly innovative at the time. In retrospect, and despite attempts by the United States – the principal contributor – to avoid such a measure becoming a precedent,[95] the establishment of such funds has become a relatively common feature of MEAs. Strengthening the obligation of assistance was particularly important at the London Meeting and Article 5(5) was also amended to introduce a demanding conception of the principle of common but differentiated responsibilities ('CBDR'). The text of the article, which is skilfully drafted, conceals the profound disagreement between industrialised and developing countries:

---

[93] Montreal Protocol, *supra* n. 68, Art. 1*bis*–1*sex* and 3*bis*–3*ter*.

[94] These 'agreed incremental costs' cover the difference between a situation in which industrial development is carried out without environmental constraints (i.e. at a lower economic cost) and a situation where obligations under the Protocol are respected (i.e. at a higher cost). At the time, the agreed incremental costs were estimated at US\$ 160 million during the first three years of the operation of the Fund (plus US\$ 80 million with the accession of China and India). The contribution of the United States, calculated on the basis of the allocation applied in the framework of the UN, was approximately US\$ 40–60 million for this period (25 per cent of the budget). Given that such substantial sums would be required, the US supported the creation of the Multilateral Fund. See Benedick, *supra* n. 61, pp. 187–8.

[95] See *ibid.*, pp. 183–90.

[d]eveloping the capacity ... [for developing States to meet their obligations] ... will depend upon the effective implementation of the financial co-operation as provided for by Article 10 and the transfer of technology as provided by Article 10A.

The term 'depend' introduces some uncertainty about the relationship between the reduction obligations of developing countries and the obligations of assistance of industrialised countries. A close reading shows that the Protocol does not present a relationship of conditionality (i.e. compliance is required only if assistance is provided), but a relationship of justification (i.e. the lack of assistance can justify certain deficiencies in the application of regulatory measures). In other words, a developing country could request assistance at the CMP if it felt it would not be able to apply the regulatory measures.[96]

Besides the benefits accorded to developing countries, the Montreal Protocol also provided two types of 'flexibility' to industrialised nations to help them meet their obligations. First, a State producing a quantity of certain controlled substances below the ceiling set by the Protocol is authorised under paragraphs (5) and (5 *bis*) of Article 2 to transfer its unused production capacity to another Member State, provided that the total 'calculated levels of production' (as defined by Article 3) of the two States for any group of controlled substances do not exceed the production limits specified for that group during the given control period. Such a possibility was recognised, in a more constrained way, in respect of consumption capacity, which was only authorised (i) for industrialised States, (ii) satisfying certain conditions regarding the consumption of controlled substances and (iii) concerning HCFCs (Article 2F). The second type of flexibility, provided for in Article 2(8), was to allow a group of States participating in a regional economic integration organisation to fulfil their obligations jointly, at the group level instead of the individual level. This mechanism, occasionally referred to as the European 'bubble', allowed certain States that were members of a regional organisation to continue to consume controlled substances while other members with lower levels offset such excess in consumption.

Finally, the Montreal Protocol also innovated with respect to the management of 'non-compliance'. We will see in Chapter 9 the more general conception underpinning the term 'non-compliance' (in contrast with that of 'breach') of an obligation. Here it suffices to note that it expresses a more flexible approach to the notion of 'compliance' with the treaty (this compliance is considered as a process with various stages and levels) and takes into account the causes of non-compliance (especially where States wish to fulfil their obligations but do not have the financial and/or technical means to do it). The CMP established a

---

[96] On the compromise in the negotiations, see Benedick, *supra* n. 61, pp. 188–90. In the absence of such a referral (which is basically a manifestation of good faith), the non-fulfilment of obligations under the Protocol, including the obligation to provide data to Protocol bodies, could deprive the State concerned from accessing the Multilateral Fund. See Yoshida, *supra* n. 61, p. 222.

'non-compliance' procedure entrusted to an Implementation Committee, composed of ten representatives of the Parties.[97] The aim of this procedure, which can be triggered by a State party (including the State in non-compliance)[98] or the Secretariat,[99] is not primarily to punish non-compliance[100] but rather to manage it, including through technical and financial assistance to improve the level of compliance of States.[101] Since its inception, the Committee has dealt with many cases.[102] For instance, in 1995 it was faced with the sensitive case of Russia, a State producing and exporting controlled substances, which had declared that it was not able to meet its obligations. The Committee recommended various measures, including a restriction on the export of controlled substances, but the Meeting of the Parties attenuated the latter by introducing some ambiguity.[103] For its part, Russia protested, not least because the export of controlled substances at the time was an important source of foreign currency for the Russian economy.[104] The issue was eventually 'managed' through a combination of monitoring, information disclosure and financial assistance (as well as pressure) by the Global Environmental Facility, which intervened to provide financial aid to Russia because it was not eligible to receive funding under the Multilateral Fund of the Protocol. Finally, in November 2002, the Meeting of the Parties declared that it

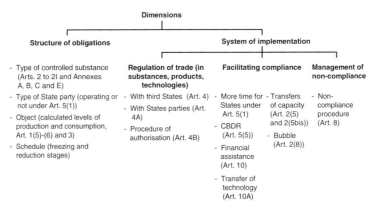

Figure 5.3: Dimensions of the Montreal Protocol

---

[97] See Decision II/5, 29 June 1990, Doc. UNEP/OzL.Pro.2/3; Decision IV/5 and Annexes IV and V, 25 November 1992, Doc. UNEP/OzL.Pro.4/15 ('Annex IV' and 'Annex V'); Decision X/10 and Annex II, 3 December 1998, Doc. UNEP/OzL.Pro.10/9 ('Annex II').

[98] Annex II, *supra* n. 97, paras. 1 and 4.   [99] *Ibid.*, para. 3.

[100] Annex V, *supra* n. 97, paras. B (warning) and C (suspension of rights and privileges under the Protocol).

[101] Annex V, *supra* n. 97, para. A (technical assistance, technology transfer, financial assistance, training, etc.).

[102] See D. G. Victor, *The Early Operation and Effectiveness of the Montreal Protocol's Non-Compliance Procedure* (Laxenburg: IIASA, 1996).

[103] Decision VII/18, 27 December 1995, Doc. UNEP/Ozl.Pro.7/12, para. 8.

[104] Victor, *supra* n. 102, pp. 28–31.

'commend[ed] the efforts made by the Russian Federation to comply with the control measures of the Montreal Protocol'.[105]

The above discussion shows the complexity but also the important innovations introduced by the Montreal Protocol. This complex structure is summarised in Figure 5.3. The Montreal Protocol has had a profound influence beyond the problem of ozone depletion. To the extent that certain controlled substances (CFCs, halons, HCFCs) are also greenhouse gases, the Montreal Protocol has been and remains the primary instrument – in terms of effectiveness – in the fight against climate change. That said, as discussed next, the problem of climate change goes far beyond the emission of industrial gases covered by the Montreal Protocol and challenges, more fundamentally, the principal sources of production of electricity and heat.

5.5 Climate change

5.5.1 Overview of the problem

The problem of climate change is closely linked to the use of fossil fuels, which have been the basis of our civilisation since the Industrial Revolution of the late eighteenth century. To understand this phenomenon, it is necessary to clarify the role of certain gases in the global climate system.

The first layer of the atmosphere, known as the troposphere (up to about 12 km above the Earth's surface), contains concentrations of certain gases that permit the entry of solar ultraviolet radiation and when this radiation is reflected by the Earth's surface into space in the form of infrared radiation, these gases retain part of it. This retention of energy has the effect of maintaining an average global temperature (currently 14° Celsius), which has varied throughout different geological periods (it was about 9° Celsius on average at the time of the great Pleistocene glaciations – between 11,700 and 1,600,000 years ago). A higher concentration of these greenhouse gases or 'GHG' (including carbon dioxide, methane, nitrogen oxides, as well as CFCs, HCFCs, carbon soot, tropospheric ozone and many others) results in a higher retention of energy and thus in an increase of the global temperature.[106] This is what is usually called 'global warming'. However, the term 'climate change' is

---

[105] Decision XIV/35, 5 December 2002, Doc. UNEP/OzL.Pro.14/9, para. 3.

[106] Concentrations of greenhouse gases in the atmosphere are measured in 'parts per million' (dividing one unit of the dry atmosphere into 1 million sub-units and measuring the amount of units represented by greenhouse gas, almost all of which is in units of carbon dioxide). To stabilise the temperature increase to about 2° Celsius at the end of the twenty-first century, it would need to remain below 450 ppm of carbon dioxide. Currently, estimates indicate a concentration of about 400 ppm, and given the increasing level of emissions in many countries, the objective of stabilising the concentration to 450 ppm by the end of the century seems difficult to achieve.

not limited to the issue of global warming. It also refers to greater climate variability or, specifically, to a higher frequency of extreme weather events such as heat waves, heavy rains, violent storms, droughts, and others.

Against this backdrop, we can now better understand the implications of the widespread use of fossil fuels since the Industrial Revolution. Emissions of GHG resulting from human activity ('anthropogenic emissions') have increased the amount of these gases in the troposphere and therefore also the average global temperature.[107] This will in all likelihood result in a number of consequences, which remain for the time being difficult to predict specifically, but could include the melting of glaciers, rising sea levels, extreme droughts and desertification, geographical redistribution of species and diseases, etc.

To address this problem, the international community faces some formidable challenges, both scientific and political.[108] But after sustained efforts for several decades, there is a better understanding of the problem and there now exists an institutional framework to negotiate solutions.

5.5.2 The two pillars of the regime

The current system can be characterised by reference to two key 'pillars', namely the scientific pillar and the political pillar. As we shall see, these two pillars are closely interrelated.

The *scientific pillar* is represented by the Intergovernmental Panel on Climate Change or 'IPCC'.[109] The origins of this body may be found in the research programmes developed in the late 1970s, notably within the WMO. During the 1980s, a series of reports and scientific conferences drew attention to the possibility of human influence on the climate system. In particular, a conference held in Villach, Austria, in 1985, which resulted in a report prepared by Bert Bolin, a leading Swedish expert, emphasised the possibility of an increase in temperature during the first half of the twenty-first century induced by anthropogenic emissions of greenhouse gases.[110] Shortly thereafter, a joint initiative of the UNEP, the WMO and the International Council for Science ('ICSU'),[111] led to the creation of the IPCC in order to cope with the

---

[107] A report issued by a group of 'sceptics' whose objective was to verify measures taken with three thermometer systems distributed around the Earth's surface since the second half of the nineteenth century confirmed that the global average temperature since the first measurements were taken has increased by more than 1° Celsius. See Berkeley Earth Project: www. berkeleyearth.org (last visited on 15 August 2014).

[108] See S. Barrett, *Environment and Statecraft: The Strategy of Environmental Treaty-making* (Oxford University Press, 2005), Chapter 15 and afterword in the latest edition.

[109] On the IPCC and its legal framework, see R. Encinas de Munagorri (ed.), *Expertise et gouvernance du changement climatique* (Paris: LGDJ, 2009), Chapters 1 and 2.

[110] See J. E. Viñuales, 'Legal Techniques for Dealing with Scientific Uncertainty in Environmental Law' (2010) 43 *Vanderbilt Journal of Transnational Law* 437, at 486.

[111] Previously known as International Council of Scientific Unions.

cacophony of scientific views that prevailed in the 1980s, including the so-called 'junk science' financed by interest groups who felt threatened by potential regulation in this area. The IPCC's mission was to examine any serious science on this subject and draw conclusions thereon or, in other words, to assess competing arguments much in the way a tribunal would, facing the evidence and arguments submitted by the parties to the dispute. This review has taken the form of various 'assessment reports', each consisting of thousands of pages organised in three volumes covering, respectively, the physical science basis (volume I), impacts, adaptation and vulnerability (volume II) and mitigation measures (volume III). An important addition to this is the synthesis report containing a 'Summary for Policymakers' of which each line needs to be approved by the representatives of States Parties to the IPCC.[112] During its nearly twenty-five years in existence, the IPCC has produced five assessment reports (1990, 1995, 2001, 2007 and 2013/2014).

Despite fierce criticism in recent years, the IPCC has fulfilled this complex task with great caution. It suffices to mention, in this regard, the slow progress in the understanding of climate change that emerges from the assessment reports published to date. In its first report in 1990, the IPCC came to the conclusion that the 'unequivocal detection of the enhanced greenhouse effect from observations is not likely for a decade or more'.[113] In its second report, published in 1995, it remained very cautious, noting that the balance of evidence 'suggests a discernible human influence on global climate'.[114] Even in its third report, published in 2001, the IPCC was still prudent in asserting that '[t]here is new and stronger evidence that most of the warming observed over the last 50 years is attributable to human activities'.[115] It was not until 2007, with the publication of its fourth assessment report, that the IPCC explicitly confirmed that '[w]arming of the climate system is unequivocal' and that it is 'very likely' that human activities are the cause of '[m]ost of the observed increase in global average temperatures since the mid-20th century'.[116] This conclusion was reaffirmed in even stronger terms in its fifth assessment report. According to the SPM of volume I:

> Warming of the climate system is unequivocal, and since the 1950s, many of the observed changes are unprecedented over decades to millennia ... It is extremely likely that human influence has been the dominant cause of the observed warming since the mid-20th century.[117]

---

[112] See the Principles Governing IPCC Work, Appendix A: Procedures for the Preparation, Review, Acceptance, Adoption, Approval and Publication of IPCC Reports (including the modifications of June 2012), Section 4.6.1.

[113] IPCC, *Climate Change 1990*, General Overview, Section 1.0.5., p. 53.

[114] IPCC, *Climate Change 1995*, Second Assessment Synthesis, para. 2.4, p. 5.

[115] IPCC, *Climate Change 2001*, Synthesis Report, Summary for Policymakers, p. 5.

[116] IPCC, *Climate Change 2007*, Summary for Policymakers, pp. 2 and 5 (the term 'very likely' indicates, in IPCC terminology, a probability of 90 per cent).

[117] IPCC, *Climate Change 2013: The Physical Science Basis*, Summary for Policymakers, section B, at 2, and section D.3, at 15 (the term 'extremely likely' indicates, in IPCC terminology, a probability of 95 per cent).

It is interesting to note that each of the assessment reports can be linked to a significant development in the *political pillar* of the climate change regime. Before analysing the content of the international legal instruments governing the issue of climate change, it is useful to outline their development in relation to evolution in the scientific pillar. The creation of the IPCC and the publication of its first assessment report in 1990 contributed to the adoption of the UN Framework Convention on Climate Change ('UNFCCC') opened for signature in June 1992.[118] The resolution of the UN General Assembly calling for the establishment of an Intergovernmental Negotiating Committee[119] was indeed catalysed by the work of the IPCC, particularly that of the Working Group III on mitigation. Then, in 1995, shortly before the publication of the second assessment report, the IPCC shared its findings with the COP of the UNFCCC. This information influenced the very first decision taken by this body, the so-called 'Berlin Mandate',[120] which laid the groundwork for the adoption of the Kyoto Protocol two years later.[121] The Berlin Mandate also widened the gap between industrialised countries (the so-called UNFCCC Annex I countries) and developing countries, embodied in the wall set up by the Kyoto Protocol. This divide, much deeper than the one found in the Montreal Protocol discussed above (which also imposes obligations on developing countries operating under Article 5(1)), has been at the heart of the negotiations since 2007. The third assessment report, published in 2001, significantly influenced the so-called 'Marrakesh Accords',[122] a series of decisions taken by the COP detailing the regime established by the Kyoto Protocol, even before the entry into force of this instrument.[123] Finally, the fourth assessment report, published in 2007, created momentum for the 'Bali Mandate',[124] which was intended to lead to the adoption of a new protocol in 2009 at the Copenhagen Conference. Despite the failure of this conference, the objective of the Bali Mandate, to reduce or eliminate the gap between the obligations of the developed countries (of Annex I of the UNFCCC) and those of the developing countries, especially emerging economies, remains the priority of current negotiations. Attempts at reducing the gap in the obligations

---

[118] United Nations Framework Convention on Climate Change, 9 May 1992, 1771 UNTS 107 ('UNFCCC').

[119] Protection of the Global Climate for Present and Future Generations of Mankind, Resolution 45/212, 21 December 1990, UN Doc. A/RES/45/212.

[120] The Berlin Mandate: Review of Paragraphs a) and b) of Paragraph 2 of Article 4 of the Convention to Determine if They are Adequate, Plans for a Protocol and Follow-up Decisions, Decision 1/CP.1, 2 June 1995, Doc. FCCC/CP/1995/7/Add.1.

[121] Kyoto Protocol to the United Nations Convention on Climate Change, 11 December 1997, 2302 UNTS 148 ('Kyoto Protocol').

[122] Decisions 2/CP.7 to 14/CP.7, 21 January 2002, Doc. FCCC/CP/2001/13/Add.1.

[123] At the first Meeting of the Parties to the Protocol, in 2005, these decisions were incorporated as decisions of the organs of the Protocol.

[124] Bali Plan of Action, Decision 1/CP.13, 14 March 2008, Doc. FCCC/CP/2007/6/Add.1.

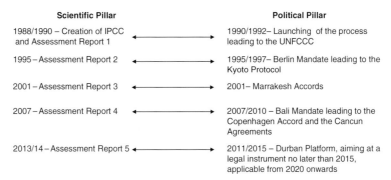

Figure 5.4: The two pillars of the climate change regime

undertaken by the two groups of States, first by the controversial 'Copenhagen Accord'[125] and then the 'Cancun Agreements',[126] are marked by a fundamental ambiguity about the role of the principle of common but differentiated responsibilities.[127] For this reason, during the COP in Durban in December 2011, a new working group (separate from the one created in 2007 in Bali) was mandated to 'develop a protocol, another legal instrument or an agreed outcome with legal force under the Convention applicable to all Parties'.[128] This result must be achieved no later than by 2015, that is to say at the COP following the recent publication of the fifth assessment report of the IPCC. The relationship between science and diplomatic developments can be summarised in Figure 5.4.

Climate negotiations have also been conducted in other *fora*. However, our presentation will focus on the system established by the UNFCCC, bearing in mind nonetheless that other instruments, such as the Gothenburg Protocol or the Montreal Protocol, are also part of the measures taken in the fight against climate change.

---

[125] Copenhagen Accord, Decision 2/CP.15, 30 March 2010, Doc. FCCC/CP/2009/11/Add.1.

[126] The 'Cancun Agreements' include three decisions, one adopted by the Conference of the Parties and the other two by the Meeting of the Parties to the Kyoto Protocol. See 'The Cancun Agreements: Outcome of the work of the Ad Hoc Working Group on Long-term Cooperative Action under the Convention', Decision 1/CP.16, 15 March 2011, Doc. FCCC/CP/2010/7/Add.1; The Cancun Agreements: Outcome of the work of the Ad Hoc Working Group on Further Commitments for Annex I Parties under the Kyoto Protocol at its fifteenth session, Decision 1/CMP.6, 15 March 2011, Doc. FCCC/KP/CMP/2010/12/Add.1; The Cancun Agreements: Land use, land-use change and forestry, Decision 2/CMP.6, 15 March 2011, Doc. FCCC/KP/CMP/2010/12/Add.1.

[127] See L. Rajamani, 'The Durban Platform for Enhanced Action and the Future of the Climate Regime' (2012) 61 *International and Comparative Law Quarterly* 501, 505–6.

[128] Establishment of an Ad Hoc Working Group on the Durban Platform for Enhanced Action, Decision 1/CP.17, 15 March 2012, Doc. FCCC/CP/2011/9/Add.1, 2.

5.5.3 The United Nations Framework Convention on Climate Change

The international law relating to climate change is currently evolving.[129] It is therefore difficult to know which will be the key components of the future regime. However, it is likely that the centre of gravity of such regime will no longer be the Kyoto Protocol but the UNFCCC, as interpreted in the light of the numerous decisions of the COP, as well as the legal instrument that will ultimately result from the process launched at the Durban meeting of December 2011. For this reason, it is necessary to analyse the UNFCCC not only as part of the matrix of the past, but also with an eye to the future.

The negotiation process started by the UN General Assembly in 1990[130] faced two major difficulties, namely the scope that should be given to the Convention and how to handle the differences between developed and developing countries.[131] Regarding the first difficulty, some States (such as the US or certain oil exporting countries) favoured the adoption of a framework convention, like the 1985 Vienna Convention, without specific obligations on emissions. Other States (such as Small Island States or certain European States) considered that the negotiations on climate change were too advanced to settle for a simple framework convention. As to the second difficulty, it is as pressing today as it was then. The question was, and remains, how to take into account the contributions of different countries to the problem of climate change. This meant developing a legal architecture to distribute the burden of the fight against climate change. The negotiators reached a compromise on these two points. To understand this compromise and its implications for the evolution of the regime, it seems useful to distinguish between substantive and institutional aspects of the UNFCCC.

As regards the *substantive aspects*, the UNFCCC sets an objective, certain principles and some procedural as well as substantive obligations. The objective is set out in fairly broad terms in Article 2:

> [t]he ultimate objective of this Convention and any related legal instruments . . . is to achieve . . . stabilization of greenhouse gas concentrations in the atmosphere at a level that would prevent dangerous anthropogenic interference with the climate system.

---

[129] See L. Rajamani, 'The Cancun Climate Change Agreements: Reading the Text, Subtext and Tealeaves' (2011) 60 *International and Comparative Law Quarterly* 499; Rajamani, *supra* n. 127; D. Bodansky, 'The United Nations Framework Convention on Climate Change: A Commentary' (1993) 18 *Yale Journal of International Law* 451; F. Yamin and J. Depledge, *The International Climate Change Regime* (Cambridge University Press, 2004).

[130] See, *supra* n. 119.

[131] See Bodansky, *supra* n. 129; and D. Bodansky, 'The History of the Global Climate Change Regime', in U. Luterbacher and D. F. Sprinz (eds.), *International Relations and Global Climate Change* (Cambridge MA: MIT Press, 2001), pp. 23–40.

This objective has the merit of specifying the source of the emissions that are to be limited – anthropogenic emissions – while remaining open to the further development of the scientific understanding of the problem over the years. Indeed, it was only after the fourth assessment report of the IPCC, published in 2007, that the COP assigned a specific figure to this objective, namely an increase of no more than 2° Celsius by the end of the twenty-first century.[132]

The UNFCCC sets out, in its Article 3, certain fundamental principles of the regime, including the precautionary principle (Article 3(3)), the principle of intergenerational equity (Article 3(1)), and the principle of common but differentiated responsibilities (Article 3(1)). The manner in which the latter principle, which is of considerable importance for current negotiations, has been enshrined in the text of the UNFCCC reflects the approach introduced by the Montreal Protocol.

Indeed, Article 4 of the UNFCCC distributes various obligations of the parties at three levels: (i) obligations of all parties (emissions reduction: Article 4(1); obligations on the gathering and communication of information: Article 12(1)); (ii) obligations for developed States and States undergoing a transition to a market economy ('Parties included in Annex I') (reduction of emissions: Article 4(2), and Article 4(6) regarding flexibilities for countries in transition; communication of supplementary information: Article 12(2)); (iii) obligations of financial and technological assistance undertaken only by developed States ('Parties included in Annex II') (Article 4(3)–(5) and 12(3)). Along the lines of Article 5(5) of the Montreal Protocol, the relation between the assistance obligations of developed States and the emissions reduction obligations of developing States is articulated as one of justification in light of the principle of common but differentiated responsibilities (Article 4(7)).

This system of differentiation could have been implemented in various ways, including in a manner similar to that of the Montreal Protocol, which imposes quantified obligations on both developed and developing States. However, as we will see when discussing the Kyoto Protocol, from the very first COP in 1995 the approach taken was the radicalisation of the gap between the obligations of Annex I and non-Annex I countries.

Regarding *institutional* aspects, the UNFCCC, like the Vienna Convention, is mainly a framework instrument allowing for the progressive development of

---

[132] See Copenhagen Accord, *supra* n. 125, para. 1; and the Cancun Agreements (Decision 1/ CP.16), *supra* n. 126, Chapter V, paras. 138–40 (introducing the requirement to update the objective). As mentioned earlier, this objective corresponds to a concentration of about 450 ppm. Note, however, that such a target seems very demanding. It has been argued, for example, that if all emissions stopped suddenly, the stock of greenhouse gases already in the atmosphere would be enough to cause a temperature increase of more than 2° Celsius. See C. Carraro and E. Massetti, 'The Improbable 2° C Global Warming Target', in *Vox*, 3 September 2009, available at: www.voxeu.org/index.php?q=node/3940 (last visited on 15 August 2012).

its broad obligations. The UNFCCC contemplates indeed the creation of a COP (Article 7), a Secretariat (Article 8), as well as two subsidiary bodies (a scientific body under Article 9 and an implementation body under Article 10) the contribution of which has been very important for the development of treaty mechanisms over the years.

In addition, Article 11 provides for a financial mechanism for the Convention. This provision served as the basis, *inter alia,* for the creation of a 'Green Climate Fund'[133] in December 2010, which will likely mobilise substantial resources (several billions of dollars[134]) and which is empowered not only to cover the 'agreed incremental costs' (as is the case of many other environmental funds, including the Multilateral Fund) but also the 'agreed full costs' of adaptation or mitigation projects undertaken by developing States.[135] Similarly, in 2010, the COP decided to create a 'Technology Mechanism' to both encourage the development of technologies for mitigation and adaptation and to ensure the dissemination of such technology to developing States.[136]

The strengthening of the institutions of the UNFCCC is part of a broader context of a 'return' to the Convention, particularly regarding the rooting of market mechanisms under the Kyoto Protocol. This 'return' was specifically recommended by the COP in 2010 and confirmed in 2011.[137] Two manifestations of such a return are the creation of a mechanism on 'loss and damage'[138] and the adoption of a 'Warsaw framework for REDD-plus'[139] at the COP held in November 2013 in Poland. As discussed next, given the precarious future of the Kyoto Protocol, the return can be seen as a 'rescue operation' of certain regulatory techniques, such as the flexibility mechanisms, for the understanding of which the experience of the Protocol was particularly useful.

---

[133] Cancun Agreements (Decision 1/CP.16), *supra* n. 126, Chapter IV, Section A.

[134] The amounts negotiated in Copenhagen and Cancun were $30 billion for 2010–12 and $100 billion per year by 2020. But some of these amounts will be paid by the private sector and merely facilitated by the Fund, through guarantees or other equivalent financial instruments.

[135] Establishment of the Green Climate Fund, Decision 3/CP.17, 15 March 2012, Doc. FCCC/CP/ 2011/9/Add.1, Annex: Governing instrument for the Green Climate Fund, para. 35. On the concepts of 'agreed incremental costs' and 'agreed full costs', see Chapter 9.

[136] Cancun Agreements (Decision 1/CP.16), *supra* n. 126, Chapter IV, Section B. See also: Technology Executive Committee – Modalities and Procedures, Decision 3/CP.17, 15 March 2012, Doc. FCCC/ CP/2011/9/Add.1.

[137] Cancun Agreements (Decision 1/CP.16), *supra* n. 126, Chapter III, Section D and Outcome of the Work of the Ad Hoc Working Group on Long-term Cooperative Action under the Convention, Decision 2/CP.17, 15 March 2012, Doc. FCCC/CP/2011/9/Add.1, paras. 79–80.

[138] Warsaw International Mechanism for Loss and Damage Associated with Climate Change (Decision –/CP.19).

[139] This framework consists of seven decisions adopted at Warsaw under the UNFCCC, including an important decision on REDD finance: Work Programme on Results-based Finance to Progress the Full Implementation of the Activities Referred to in Decision 1/CP.16, para. 70 (Decision –/CP.19).

5.5.4 The Kyoto Protocol

The future of the Kyoto Protocol[140] is not bright. Following the Durban Conference in December 2011, where States such as Canada, Russia and even Japan refused to accept a new commitment period, it seems clear that the Kyoto Protocol will at best be a minor component of the future climate regime. This notwithstanding, for the purposes of this book, its analysis remains important because the Kyoto Protocol represents a regulatory approach that, despite positive experiences when applied to long-range transboundary air pollution and ozone depletion, no longer seems suitable (time will tell) to tackle climate change. It is this approach that we will present here, as embodied in the Kyoto Protocol, by reference to its four principal dimensions.

The first dimension is familiar. As the other protocols discussed in this chapter, the Kyoto Protocol is an illustration of the 'framework convention/protocol' technique. Article 17 of the UNFCCC explicitly provides for the adoption of protocols with more specific obligations. The conditions for entry into force are determined by each protocol. Article 25(1) of the Protocol required ratification by at least fifty-five States parties to the Convention, including a number of Annex I Parties such that their total carbon dioxide emissions in 1990 represented at least 55 per cent of the carbon dioxide emissions of all Annex I Parties of that year. After the Protocol was disavowed by the United States, this requirement could only be satisfied with the ratification by Russia in November 2004. However, Russia's ratification came too late. As a matter of fact, when the Protocol entered into force in 2005, it was already clear that the reduction targets in Annex B of the Protocol were largely insufficient to control the concentrations of GHG in the atmosphere. The States whose emissions were bound to increase most significantly over the years to come, emerging economies, were indeed not subject to quantified obligations under the Protocol.

This brings us to the second dimension, namely the manner in which the Protocol spells out the principle of common but differentiated responsibilities. After the adoption of the Berlin Mandate in 1995 by the COP, it was very clear that the negotiations (which would lead to the adoption of the Kyoto Protocol) should focus exclusively on strengthening the obligations of States included in Annex I of the Convention and that 'the process [would], *inter alia*: . . . [n]ot introduce any new commitments for Parties not included in Annex I'.[141] The Kyoto Protocol has scrupulously kept to this commitment, making provision only for obligations applicable to States in Annex I (Article 3(1) and Annex B). It is precisely this fact that, fifteen years later, has made it largely obsolete. Indeed, the States whose emission levels are highest (such as the United States, China, India, Brazil and others) are under no quantified obligation. A different

---

[140] On this instrument, see: J. Depledge, 'Tracing the Origins of the Kyoto Protocol: An Article-by-Article Textual History', Technical Paper, FCCC/TP/2000/2 (2000); D. Freestone and C. Streck, *Legal Aspects of Carbon Trading* (Oxford University Press, 2009).

[141] Berlin Mandate, *supra* 120, para. II.2(b).

method, closer to that followed by the Montreal Protocol, could have been adopted, providing for quantified obligations for all States, with a grace period or significant flexibilities for developing countries. It is true that there are critical differences between ozone depletion and climate change as regulatory challenges, which explain the tougher stance adopted by developing countries. In particular, any restrictions on energy production are likely to have a more general impact on economic and social development than restrictions on the production/use of substances covered by the Montreal Protocol. However, the passage of time has only widened the gap. The efforts over the last decade to develop a new system incorporating emerging economies all seek, in essence, to reverse the choice made in 1995.

The quantified obligations undertaken by States in Annex B of the Kyoto Protocol can be characterised by reference to five components: (i) object of regulation (emissions of GHG identified in Annex A of the Protocol from sources within the territory of a State, as opposed to emissions from consumption in another State of products or resources – such as oil – exported by the State concerned); (ii) the base year against which emissions must be measured (subsections (1), (3), (4), (5) and (7) of Article 3 refer to the year 1990, with two exceptions, one for emissions of certain gases for which States can choose the year 1995[142] and the other for transition States, which may choose another base year[143]); (iii) the emissions reduction target (which is expressed in numerical terms in Annex B of the Protocol, with each number representing the percentage of the emissions level to be achieved with respect to the base year – for example, for Germany, the number 92 – and when the amendment for the second commitment period enters into force, the number 80 – means, respectively, a reduction of 8 per cent for the first commitment period and of 20 per cent for the second commitment period, as compared to emissions in 1990); (iv) the commitment period during which the reduction target is to be attained (once the amendment is in force, Article 3(7)–(7bis) of the Protocol will establish two commitment periods – 2008–12 and 2013–20 – during which annual emissions must, on average, be equal to or less than the target number in Annex B); (v) the type of measure to be taken to achieve this goal, prioritising national measures (Article 1(a))[144] over international measures (i.e. the use of flexibility mechanisms under Articles 6, 12 and 17).

---

[142] Kyoto Protocol, *supra* n. 121, Art. 3(8).

[143] *Ibid.*, Art. 3(5). Depending on the trajectory of a State's economy, the choice of a different base year can make obligations more or less demanding. Given that the level of emissions is significantly correlated with the level of economic growth, the choice of a more recent reference year (i.e. with higher emissions) gives greater leeway. Conversely, if the emissions level was higher in 1990 than in subsequent years (e.g. due to an economic recession), a State may want to choose 1990 as a baseline in order to benefit from the greater margin allowed for its development during the commitment period.

[144] Principles, Nature and Scope of the Mechanisms pursuant to Article 6, 12 and 17 of the Kyoto Protocol, Decision 2/CMP.1, 30 March 2006, Doc. FCCC/KP/CMP/2005/8/Add.1, para. 1.

International measures are an area in which the Kyoto Protocol was innovative. The Montreal Protocol had already envisioned market mechanisms, but only in an embryonic manner compared to the Kyoto Protocol, which established in Articles 6, 12 and 17 (supplemented by numerous decisions of the CMP), mechanisms that are much more sophisticated and supported by a complex institutional structure. The three mechanisms are based on the idea of a 'transfer' or 'trade' of emission rights, expressed primarily in Article 17. Indeed, the latter envisages the possibility of transferring the emissions allowances of one country (or private party permitted to engage in emissions trading) to another. This exchange may involve different types of units, the use of which (and therefore their value) varies. For the purposes of this introduction, it suffices to distinguish two kinds.

Some units (the 'assigned amount units' or 'AAUs' and the 'emission reduction units' or 'ERUs') are part of the overall emissions ceiling set out in Annex B for listed States. The exchange of such units between them necessarily implies a reduction of the emissions allowance of the State that sells them and an increase in the emissions allowance of the State that buys them. The transaction can be carried out in an emissions market[145] or may take the form of a project conducted under the terms of Article 6 of the Protocol, in the territory of a State in Annex I.[146] The objective of such projects is to transfer technologies to States undergoing a transition to a market economy, as well as to achieve emission reductions at a lower cost than in the country of origin through the 'greening' of highly polluting facilities in the country of destination. In accounting terms, the State hosting the project (in whose territory the converted facility is located) 'pays' for the technological improvements it receives with emissions units ('AAUs'), which are transferred (in the form of 'ERUs') to the State financing the operation. These transactions often take place between private companies in order to comply with the obligations imposed on them by the relevant Annex I country.

Such projects can also be carried out in the territory of a State which is not included in Annex I, such as China, India and Brazil, as part of the 'clean development mechanism' (or 'CDM') established by Article 12 of the Protocol.[147] The logic remains the same, namely to transfer technologies to developing States and to achieve emission reductions at a lower cost. There is, however, one key difference between the mechanism of Article 6 and that of

---

[145] See, S. Simonetti and R. de Witt Wijnen, 'International Emissions Trading and Green Investment Schemes', in Freestone and Streck, *supra* n. 140, pp. 157–75.

[146] Guidelines for the Implementation of Article 6 of the Kyoto Protocol, Decision 9/CMP.1, 30 March 2006, Doc. FCCC/KP/CMP/2005/8/Add.1. See A. Hobley and C. Roberts, 'Joint Implementation Transactions: An Overview', in Freestone and Streck, *supra* n. 140, pp. 195–212.

[147] Modalities and Procedures for a Clean Development Mechanism as defined in Article 12 of the Kyoto Protocol, Decision 3/CMP.1, 30 March 2006, Doc. FCCC/KP/CMP/2005/8/Add.1. See M. Netto and K.-U. Barani Schmidt, 'The CDM Project Cycle and the Role of the UNFCCC Secretariat', in Freestone and Streck, *supra* n. 140, pp. 213–30.

Article 12. In the former, the emission rights change hands but the total amount of authorised emissions remains the same. By contrast, under Article 12, emission reductions go beyond the emissions available for trade under the overall cap set by the Protocol. The emission rights freshly 'produced' by these projects can be used – to some extent – by the States bound by the cap to fulfil their obligations. For this reason and in order to avoid abuse, the procedure for obtaining such rights ('certified emission reduction units' or 'CERs') is more stringent in the case of Article 12, and it includes a series of certification requirements by independent third parties as well as the participation of an Executive Board responsible for the management of this mechanism. Despite these safeguards, the operation of the CDM has been widely criticised, the main problem being that it induces behaviour contrary to its very purpose. Indeed, insofar as a party (either a developing State or private party situated in such a State) receives more benefits when the reduction of emissions is greater, that party may be tempted to initially increase emissions in order to maximise the reduction potential which in turn attracts CDM projects (and thereby more revenue).[148] In other words, the CDM would penalise low-polluting States and facilities because they do not lend themselves to significant emissions reductions.

Despite these difficulties, a similar mechanism, which also focuses on projects in developing countries and with similar risks as regards its integrity, is currently being set up in order to reduce deforestation. Under the CDM, projects consisting in afforestation or reforestation (increasing the absorption of carbon dioxide by expanding the wooded area) may receive CERs. However, projects to prevent a wooded area from being cleared (typically by fire in order to make way for agricultural uses or for livestock) are not covered by the CDM despite the fact that deforestation causes significant discharges of carbon dioxide into the atmosphere (deforestation is among the top three sources of global emissions[149]) and that it could be prevented at a low cost.[150] This lacuna can be explained by the difficulty in determining which areas would have been burned in the absence of intervention (and therefore the extent to which deforestation has actually been 'avoided' as compared to a business-as-usual situation or 'BAU'). Furthermore, such an approach would face formidable implementation challenges, given the often weak State control over the areas to protect. Despite these difficulties, the idea of establishing a market mechanism consisting essentially in the transfer of resources in exchange for maintaining and improving woodlands (i.e. a reduction of ordinary deforestation) has gained momentum in recent years. In particular, in December 2010, the COP of the UNFCCC adopted guidelines for the establishment of such a

---

[148] For practical applications (including the case of HCFC-23), see M. Wara, 'Measuring the Clean Development Mechanism's Performance and Potential' (2007) 55 *UCLA Law Review* 1759.
[149] See G. R. van der Werf *et al.*, 'CO$_2$ Emissions from Forest Loss' (2009) 2 *Nature Geoscience* 737.
[150] Land Use, Land-use Change and Forestry, Decision 16/CMP.1, 30 March 2006, FCCC/KP/CMP/2005/8/Add.3, para. 13.

mechanism,[151] known by its acronym 'REDD-plus'.[152] This new mechanism, which is likely to come into operation in the near future,[153] will not feature within the framework of the Kyoto Protocol, but will instead be placed under the UNFCCC in line with the 'return' to the Convention, referred to above.

5.5.5 From Bali to Durban and the future of the regime

The material introduced thus far provides sufficient background for the analysis of the three processes that have shaped the evolution of climate change negotiations, namely (i) the process aimed to strengthen the Kyoto Protocol, which came to its end in Doha in December 2012, (ii) the process launched in Bali and ended in Doha aimed at bridging the gap between States listed in Annex I and other States (led by the 'Ad Hoc Working Group for Long-term Cooperative Action under the Convention' or 'AWG-LCA'), and (iii) the process launched in December 2011 known as the 'Durban Platform', which aims to overcome, as far as possible, the principle of common but differentiated responsibilities and to ensure the participation of emerging economies in the effort to reduce emissions.

These three processes of negotiation are interrelated in complex ways of which we can only give an overview here.[154] Processes (i) and (ii) have been linked since their launch in 2005 and 2007. From a political standpoint, the acceptance of a second commitment period by the States of Annex B of the Kyoto Protocol was mostly a concession to the emerging economies in exchange for their acceptance of specific undertakings under the Bali process. However, the latter process did not proceed as developed States had expected. Following the diplomatic failure of Copenhagen, partly compensated for by the Cancun Agreements (which did consider enhanced mitigation measures, including for developing countries),[155] the developed countries agreed that the foundations of the Bali Process had not been clear. As commentators have pointed out, while developing countries interpreted the Bali Process as erecting a 'wall' between their nationally appropriate mitigation actions and mitigation commitments made by developed countries, developed countries viewed the Bali Mandate as something more of a 'bridge' designed to close the gap created by the Berlin Mandate.[156] To avoid any ambiguities on this point, the Durban Platform does not mention the principle of common but differentiated responsibilities at all. Moreover, it makes it explicit that any 'agreed outcome' that

---

[151] Cancun Agreements (Decision 1/CP.16), *supra* n. 126, Chapter III, section C, and appendices I and II.

[152] Which stands for Reduced Emissions from Deforestation and Forest Degradation and (the +) Forest Enhancement.

[153] See Decision 2/CP.17, *supra* n. 137, para. 66.

[154] See Rajamani, *supra* n. 129; Rajamani, *supra* n. 127.

[155] Cancun Agreements (Decision 1/CP.16), *supra* n. 126, Chapter III, section B.

[156] Rajamani, *supra* n. 127, pp. 505–6.

may arise from this new negotiation process must have legal force. The choice of words used to express this commitment led to vivid debates, particularly between European and Indian negotiators.[157] Finally, an agreement was reached on the following terms: 'a protocol, another legal instrument or an agreed outcome with legal force under the Convention applicable to all Parties'.[158] As a result, the compromise leaves open several possibilities, such as the adoption of a new protocol, an amendment of the Convention, the adoption or amendment of annexes to the Convention, and potentially even a set of national laws coordinated by a set of COP decisions.[159]

For our part, although any attempt at forecasting the outcome of a volatile negotiation process is inherently risky, we see three paths open to the future climate regime. The first and most probable path is the return to the UNFCCC, both as a retreat from the Kyoto Protocol and as a prelude to the future instrument to be adopted in the context of the Durban Platform. Regarding the latter, we already know four parameters: (i) the instrument must be adopted no later than 2015; and (ii) it is not expected to come into effect before 2020;[160] (iii) it will impose legal obligations; and (iv) these obligations will likely apply both to developed States and emerging economies. Within these parameters, several options are possible. An important question concerns the type of regulatory technique that will be chosen. The general approach taken by the Kyoto Protocol – setting a quantified cap on emissions – has lost momentum. Alternative approaches would be to set targets for energy efficiency or renewable energy development, rather than a cap on emissions, but this would imply that emissions could still legally rise. We may have to accept that setting a global emissions cap is politically very (perhaps too) difficult.

The latter point suggests a second possible path, namely the emergence of a patchwork of national climate change laws using a variety of regulatory techniques and only loosely co-ordinated at the international level. Despite its greater complexity, the potential of such an approach must not be underestimated. It could create an international market for emission allowances based on two elements: (i) an 'international' cap formed by the aggregation of national caps and (ii) the recognition of foreign emission permits (exchangeable units) or, even better, a unit of exchange recognised by all systems, such as CERs from the Kyoto Protocol, that can be used across the board.[161]

---

[157] *Ibid.*, pp. 506ff.   [158] Decision 1/CP.17, *supra* n. 128, para. 2.

[159] This possibility is mentioned in Rajamani, *supra* n. 127, p. 507. Yet this is a very broad interpretation of Decision 1/CP.17, which speaks of an 'agreed outcome with legal force'. This appears to go beyond the French text, which speaks of '*un texte convenu d'un commun accord ayant valeur juridique*'.

[160] Decision 1/CP.17, *supra* n. 128, para. 4.

[161] See C. Flachslan, R. Marschinski and O. Edenhofer, 'Global Trading versus Linking: Architectures for International Emissions Trading' (2009) 37 *Energy Policy* 1637.

A third and supplementary possibility would be based on the recognition of the human rights implications of climate change.[162] Such a course of action could be explored at several levels: (i) to grant 'rights to emit' to individuals, enabling the calculation of the (national or international) cap of each State;[163] (ii) to facilitate access to justice for cessation, mitigation of effects or reparation of damage caused by private or public emitters; and (iii) to lay the foundations of a system of strict civil liability along the lines of the established regimes on liability for oil spills or nuclear accidents.

These three courses of action are certainly not mutually exclusive. In fact, a combination of the three is not unlikely, since the last two would mostly be useful as a supplement to the first.

Select bibliography

Aldy, J. E. and R. N. Stavins, *Post-Kyoto International Climate Policy. Implementing Architecture for Agreement* (Cambridge University Press, 2010).

Bankobeza, G. M., *Ozone Protection: The International Legal Regime* (Utrecht: Eleven, 2005).

Barrett, S., *Environment and Statecraft: The Strategy of Environmental Treaty-Making* (Oxford University Press, 2005).

Benedick, R. E., *Ozone Diplomacy: New Directions in Safeguarding the Planet* (Cambridge MA: Harvard University Press, 1998).

Bodansky, D., 'The History of the Global Climate Change Regime', in U. Luterbacher and D. F. Sprinz (eds.), *International Relations and Global Climate Change* (Cambridge MA: MIT Press, 2001), pp. 23–40.

 'The United Nations Framework Convention on Climate Change: A Commentary' (1993) 18 *Yale Journal of International Law* 451.

Boisson de Chazournes, L., 'La gestion de l'intérêt commun à l'épreuve des enjeux économiques – Le Protocole de Kyoto sur les changements climatiques' (1997) 43 *Annuaire français de droit international* 700.

Bratspies, R. and R. Miller (eds.), *Transboundary Harm in International Law. Lessons from the Trail Smelter Arbitration* (Cambridge University Press, 2006).

Brunnée, J., *Acid Rain and Ozone Layer Depletion: International Law and Regulation* (Dobbs Ferry: Transnational Publishers, 1988).

Bryk, D. S., 'The Montreal Protocol and Recent Developments to Protect the Ozone Layer' (1991) 15 *Harvard Environmental Law Review* 275.

Caron, D., 'La protection de la couche d'ozone stratosphérique et la structure de l'activité normative internationale en matière d'environnement' (1990) 36 *Annuaire français de droit international* 704.

---

[162] See in this respect the Malé Declaration on the Human Dimension of Global Climate Change, available at: www.ciel.org (last visited on 26 August 2012); *Report of the Office of the United Nations High Commissioner for Human Rights on the Relationship between Climate Change and Human Rights*, 15 January 2009, A/HRC/10/61; Human Rights Council, 'Human Rights and Climate Change', 25 March 2009, A/HRC/10/4.

[163] Access to energy has been recognised as one of the Sustainable Development Goals ('SDGs') that will drive sustainable development efforts in the post-2015 agenda.

Depledge, J., 'Tracing the Origins of the Kyoto Protocol: An Article-by-Article Textual History', Technical Paper, FCCC/TP/2000/2 (2000).

Doumbe-Bille, S. and A. Kiss, 'Conférence des Nations Unies sur l'environnement et le développement (Rio de Janeiro, June 1992)' (1992) 38 *Annuaire français de droit international* 823.

Ellis, J., 'Extraterritorial Exercise of Jurisdiction for Environmental Protection: Addressing Fairness Concerns' (2012) 25 *Leiden Journal of International Law* 397.

Encinas de Munagorri, R. (ed.), *Expertise et gouvernance du changement climatique* (Paris: LGDJ, 2009).

Flachsland, C., R. Marchinski and O. Edenhoffer, 'Global Trading versus Linking: Architectures for International Emissions Trading' (2009) 37 *Energy Policy* 1637.

Freestone, D. and C. Streck, *Legal Aspects of Carbon Trading* (Oxford University Press, 2009).

Gillespie, A., *Climate Change, Ozone Depletion, and Air Pollution: Legal Commentaries within the Context of Science and Policy* (Leiden: Martinus Nijhoff, 2006).

Haas, H., 'Banning Chlorofluorocarbons: Epistemic Community Efforts to Protect Stratospheric Ozone' (1991) 46 *International Organization* 187.

Jaffe, J., M. Ranson and R. Stavins, 'Linking Tradable Permit Systems: A Key Element of Emerging International Climate Policy Architecture' (2009) 36 *Ecology Law Quarterly* 789.

Keohane, R. O. and D. G. Victor, 'The Regime Complex for Climate Change' (2011) 9 *Perspectives on Politics* 7.

Lammers, J. G. (ed.), *Transboundary Air Pollution* (Dordrecht: Martinus Nijhoff, 1986).

Lang, W., 'Is the Ozone Depletion Regime a Model for an Emerging Regime on Global Warming?' (1991) 9 *UCLA Journal of Environmental Law and Policy* 161.

Lawrence, P. M., 'International Legal Regulation for Protection of the Ozone Layer: Some Problems of Implementation' (1990) 2 *Journal of Environmental Law* 17.

Maljean-Dubois, S., 'La mise en route du Protocole de Kyoto à la Convention-cadre des Nations Unies sur les Changements Climatiques' (2005) 51 *Annuaire français de droit international* 43.

Murase, S., 'Protection of the Atmosphere and International Law: Rationale for Codification and Progressive Development' (2012) 55 *Sophia Law Review* 1.

Okowa, P., *State Responsibility for Transboundary Air Pollution in International Law* (Oxford University Press, 2000).
    'The Legal Framework for the Protection of the Environment Against Transboundary Air Pollution', in H. G. Post (ed.), *The Protection of Ambient Air in International and European Law* (The Hague: Eleven Publishing, 2009), pp. 53–71.

Ozone Secretariat, *Handbook for the Montreal Protocol on Substances that Deplete the Ozone Layer* (UNEP, 9th edn, 2012).
    Handbook for the Vienna Convention on the Protection of the Ozone Layer (UNEP, 9th edn, 2012).

Rajamani, L., 'Addressing the Post-Kyoto Stress Disorder: Reflections on the Emerging Legal Architecture of the Climate Regime' (2009) 58 *International and Comparative Law Quarterly* 803.
    'From Berlin to Bali and Beyond: Killing Kyoto Softly?' (2008) 57 *International and Comparative Law Quarterly* 909.

'The Cancun Climate Change Agreements: Reading the Text, Subtext and Tealeaves' (2011) 60 *International and Comparative Law Quarterly* 499.

'The Durban Platform for Enhanced Action and the Future of the Climate Regime' (2012) 61 *International and Comparative Law Quarterly* 501.

'The Making and Unmaking of the Copenhagen Accord' (2010) 59 *International and Comparative Law Quarterly* 824.

Roelof, J. L., 'United States-Canada Air Quality Agreement: A Framework for Addressing Transboundary Air Pollution Problems' (1993) 26 *Cornell International Law Journal* 421.

Rowlands, I. H., 'Atmosphere and Outer Space', in D. Bodansky, J. Brunnée and E. Hey (eds.), *The Oxford Handbook of International Environmental Law* (Oxford University Press, 2007), pp. 315–36.

Skjærseth, J., 'International Ozone Policies: Effective Environmental Cooperation', in E. Lerum Boasson and G. Hønneland (eds.), *International Environmental Agreements: An Introduction* (London: Routledge, 2012), pp. 38–48.

Sliggers, J. and W. Kakebeeke (eds.), *Clearing the Air. 25 Years of the Convention on Long-Range Transboundary Air Pollution* (New York/Geneva: United Nations, 2004).

Tripp, J. T. B., 'The UNEP Montreal Protocol: Industrialized and Developing Countries Sharing the Responsibility for Protecting the Stratospheric Ozone Layer' (1988) 20 *New York University Journal of International Law and Politics* 733.

Twum-Barima, R. and L. B. Campbell, *Protecting the Ozone Layers through Trade Measures: Reconciling the Trade Provisions of the Montreal Protocol and the Rules of the GATT* (Geneva: UNEP, 1994).

Victor, D. G., *The Early Operation and Effectiveness of the Montreal Protocol's Non-Compliance Procedure* (Laxenburg: IIASA, 1996).

Viñuales, J. E., 'Du bon dosage du droit international: Les négociations climatiques en perspective' (2010) 56 *Annuaire français de droit international* 437.

'El Régimen Jurídico Internacional relativo al Cambio Climático: Perspectivas y Prospectivas', in Organisation of American States (OAS), *Course on International Law*, vol. 36, 2009/2010, pp. 233–305.

'Legal Techniques for Dealing with Scientific Uncertainty in Environmental Law' (2010) 43 *Vanderbilt Journal of Transnational Law* 437.

Wara, M., 'Measuring the Clean Development Mechanism's Performance and Potential' (2007) 55 *UCLA Law Review* 1759.

Yamin, F. and J. Depledge, *The International Climate Change Regime* (Cambridge University Press, 2004).

Yoshida, O., *The International Legal Regime for the Protection of the Stratospheric Ozone Layer* (The Hague: Kluwer, 2001).

6

Species, ecosystems and biodiversity

6.1 Introduction

The protection of wildlife was one of the first concerns of international environmental regulation. Although the focus of this regulation has changed significantly over time, from primarily economic considerations to conservation *per se*, this body of norms – tackling issues as diverse as the exploitation of fur seals,[1] whaling,[2] trade in endangered species,[3] the preservation of ecologically, culturally or aesthetically valuable sites[4] or, more recently, the transboundary movement of genetically modified organisms[5] or the access to genetic resources and the sharing of related benefits[6] – has profoundly influenced the development of international environmental law.

The proliferation of international instruments for the protection of animal and plant life[7] makes any attempt to capture the major axes of this area of regulation a challenging exercise. In the early 1980s, the UN General Assembly tried to provide an umbrella for this diverse array of instruments with the adoption of a 'World Charter for Nature'.[8] This instrument was not binding

---

[1] Convention between the United States, Great Britain, Japan and Russia Providing for the Preservation and Protection of the Fur Seals, 7 July 1911, 37 Stat. 1542, TS 564.

[2] Convention for the Regulation of Whaling, 24 September 1931, available at: www.ecolex.org (no. TRE-000073); International Convention for the Regulation of Whaling, 2 December 1946, 161 UNTS 72 ('Whaling Convention'); Convention on the Conservation of Migratory Species of Wild Animals, 23 June 1979, available at: www.ecolex.org (no. TRE-000495).

[3] Convention on International Trade in Endangered Species of Wild Fauna and Flora, 3 March 1973, United Nations, 993 UNTS 243 ('CITES').

[4] Convention on Wetlands of International Importance especially as Waterfowl Habitat, 2 February 1971, 996 UNTS 245 ('Ramsar Convention'); Convention Concerning the Protection of the World Cultural and Natural Heritage, 23 November 1972, 1037 UNTS 151 ('WHC').

[5] Cartagena Protocol on Biosafety to the Convention on Biological Diversity, 29 January 2000, 2226 UNTS 208 ('Biosafety Protocol').

[6] The Nagoya Protocol on Access to Genetic Resources and the Fair and Equitable Sharing of Benefits Arising from their Utilization to the Convention on Biological Diversity, 29 October 2012, available at: www.ecolex.org (TRE-155959) ('Nagoya Protocol').

[7] See generally M. Bowman, P. Davies and C. Redgwell, *Lyster's International Wildlife Law* (Cambridge University Press, 2nd edn, 2010).

[8] World Charter for Nature, 28 October 1982, UN Doc. A/RES/37/7. See H. W. Wood, 'The United Nations World Charter for Nature: The Developing Nations' Initiative to Establish Protections for the Environment' (1984/1985) 12 *Ecology Law Quarterly* 977.

and its strong conservationist focus proved to be an obstacle rather than an advantage in reaching the initial goal. Other attempts with the same purpose were made in the course of the 1980s. The initiative taken by UNEP in 1987 to explore the feasibility of adopting a framework convention in this area deserves particular attention.[9] In November 1988 the task was entrusted to an Expert Panel on Biological Diversity, which in February 1991 became the Intergovernmental Negotiating Committee leading to the adoption of the Convention on Biological Diversity ('CBD') opened for signature at the Rio Summit in June 1992.[10]

The trajectory followed by international environmental law in this area since the early conventions on the protection of specific species until the adoption of the CBD and its aftermath can be analysed by reference to the degree of complexity of the regulatory objects. These objects were first species or, more generally, the fauna and/or flora of a particular region.[11] As the understanding of ecological processes progressed, the regulatory focus shifted to the environment of these species or, more specifically, to their habitat,[12] or to the ecosystem formed by the complex interactions among various species.[13] Finally, the focus of international regulation turned to the variability within species, between species, and between ecosystems, or, in other words, biodiversity[14] and the biological and genetic resources underpinning it.[15]

The foregoing distinction between species, spaces and biodiversity provides, despite some risk of oversimplification, a useful basis for structuring our presentation of the main axes of international environmental regulation in this area. In this chapter, after some observations on the broad approaches pursued by different instruments, we analyse the international protection of species, spaces, and biodiversity, focusing on the increasingly complex regulatory techniques that have been developed in this area.

---

[9] See Governing Council of UNEP, Res. 14/26 (1987).

[10] Convention on Biological Diversity, 5 June 1992, 1760 UNTS 79 ('CBD'). On the developments that led to the adoption of the CBD, see L. Glowka, F. Burhenne-Guilmin, H. Synge, J. A. McNeely and L. Gundling, *Guide de la Convention sur la diversité biologique* (Gland: IUCN, 1996), pp. 2ff.

[11] See Convention on Nature Protection and Wild Life Preservation in the Western Hemisphere, 12 October 1940, 56 Stat 1354 ('Western Hemisphere Convention'); African Convention on the Conservation of Nature and Natural Resources, 15 September 1968, amended 11 July 2003, 1001 UNTS 3 ('African Conservation Convention'), available at: www.ecolex.org (TRE-001395); Convention on the Conservation of European Wildlife and Natural Habitats, 19 September 1979, ETS No 104 ('Bern Convention'); ASEAN Agreement on the Conservation of Nature and Natural Resources, 9 July 1985, 15 EPL 64 ('Kuala Lumpur Agreement'); Convention on the Conservation of Nature in the South Pacific, 12 June 1976, available at: www.ecolex.org (TRE-000540) ('Apia Convention'); Protocol to the Antarctic Treaty on Environmental Protection, 4 October 1991, 30 ILM 1455 ('Madrid Protocol').

[12] One of the first instruments to adopt this approach was the Ramsar Convention, *supra* n. 4. This treaty was subsequently reinterpreted to accommodate an ecosystem approach.

[13] The first instrument to have explicitly adopted this approach was the Convention on the Conservation of Antarctic Marine Living Resources, 20 May 1980, 1329 UNTS 47 ('CCAMLR').

[14] See CBD, *supra* n. 10, Art. 2, para. 5. [15] *Ibid.*, Art. 2, para. 13–14.

6.2 Regulatory approaches

The diversity of legal objects has resulted, over time, in a variety of approaches to their regulation. Among them, three main approaches merit attention: (i) the regulation of resource exploitation, (ii) the protection of spaces and (iii) the regulation of trade in certain species.[16]

Each of these approaches is based on different considerations, which are in turn expressions of the age-old equation opposing the profitable use of a resource (or, in today's terms, 'development' or 'growth') to environmental protection. Broadly speaking, approaches (i) and (iii) generally attribute more weight to the first term of the equation, whereas approach (ii) favours the second. Of course, on closer examination, a more nuanced picture arises. By way of illustration, a resource exploitation regime such as the 1946 Whaling Convention, which initially favoured economic considerations over conservation, later became very protective. The shift came as a result of the use of a specific regulatory technique, namely a moratorium that suspends whaling as a commercial activity to foster whale preservation.[17] The reference to 'approaches', 'considerations' and 'regulatory techniques' in this discussion is intended to provide a broad conceptual chart useful to keep the bigger picture in mind when analysing the intricacies of specific norms and instruments.

Resource exploitation as an approach can be characterised by reference to a number of features: it targets resources shared by two or more countries or located in common areas (conversely, resources solely within the jurisdiction of one State are subject to the latter's sovereignty or sovereign rights); it is concerned with the distribution of a particular resource and/or the protection of an endangered resource; it usually intervenes at a stage where exploitation is already ongoing; and it occasionally conveys a superficial understanding of resource management in that it does not necessarily take into account the interactions between the resource and its ecosystem.[18] The legal techniques implementing this approach include setting exploitation quotas (by species, country, region, fishing fleet, etc.), regulating the methods and technologies allowed for resource exploitation, limiting the time periods and the areas where these activities can be conducted,[19] the conclusion (in the area of genetic resources) of agreements on access and benefit sharing, and many others.

The protection of spaces as a regulatory approach embodies a more complete understanding of the interaction between one or more species and their ecosystem. However, the definition of the relevant 'space' may be challenging

---

[16] See R. Rayfuse, 'Biological Resources', in D. Bodansky, J. Brunnée and E. Hey (eds.), *The Oxford Handbook of International Environmental Law* (Oxford University Press, 2007), pp. 362–93, 374ff.

[17] See Bowman *et al., supra* n. 7, pp. 165ff.   [18] Rayfuse, *supra* n. 16, pp. 374ff.

[19] See K. M. Wyman, 'The Property Rights Challenge in Marine Fisheries' (2008) 50 *Arizona Law Review* 511.

because there are significant differences between the concepts of 'site', 'habitat' and 'ecosystem'. A 'site' can be protected as such, regardless of its value for one or more plant or animal species. This applies, for example, to cultural sites as well as certain natural sites protected under the World Heritage Convention.[20] 'Habitat' is a difficult concept to define from a legal standpoint. It may refer to the conditions necessary for the preservation of certain species or for the protection of a particular population of a species with a specific geographical location. Although such conditions are normally identified by reference to a group of species, a species and/or a population, they can also be characterised in a more generic manner. Thus, the Ramsar Convention defines the protected wetlands to be included in the Ramsar list not only as waterfowl habitat but also, more generally, by reference to their 'ecology, botany, zoology, limnology or hydrology'.[21] These areas are therefore protected both as sites and as habitats. Even more complex is the concept of 'ecosystem', which goes beyond the reference to one or more specific species and seeks to capture a broader functional unit, a set of interactions among plant, animals and micro-organisms as well as their non-living environment.[22] The contours of the protected ecosystem could also be defined in both geographical and functional terms, as is Article 1 of CCAMLR.[23] The legal techniques used to implement this approach are quite diverse, but particular importance is given to the creation of protected areas, as well as to some complementary techniques such as establishing buffer zones or conducting environmental impact assessments and monitoring.[24] Less frequently, a participatory or 'bottom-up' approach has also been used, particularly in relation to desertification, as discussed later.[25]

Finally, the regulation of trade in species or resources may be used as a way of reducing their exploitation (in particular when the demand for a species or specimens is located abroad) or in order to prevent the risks resulting from the introduction of invasive species or species capable of upsetting the ecological balance of an ecosystem.[26] This approach differs from the two previous ones in the type of legal techniques used to achieve the policy objective, namely restrictions on the export[27] and/or import of specimens of regulated species

---

[20] WHC, *supra* n. 4, Art. 1. Of course one can still argue that this protection is based on the value of such sites for the human species.

[21] Ramsar Convention, *supra* n. 4, Arts. 1 and 2(2).   [22] CBD, *supra* n. 10, Art. 2, para. 6.

[23] See CCAMLR, *supra* n. 13, Art. 1.

[24] See A. Gillespie, 'The Management of Protected Areas of International Significance' (2006) 10 *New Zealand Journal of Environmental Law* 93.

[25] See United Nations Convention to Combat Desertification in those Countries Experiencing Serious Drought and/or Desertification, Particularly in Africa, 17 June 1994, 1954 UNTS 3 ('Convention to Combat Desertification' or 'UNCCD'), Art. 10(2)(f).

[26] Rayfuse, *supra* n. 16, pp. 384ff.

[27] See WTO/CTE, Matrix on Trade Measures pursuant to Selected Multilateral Environmental Agreement, 14 March 2007, WT/CTE/W/160/Rev.4, TN/TE/S/5/Rev.2, Section II. More specifically, see CITES, *supra* n. 3, Art. III.

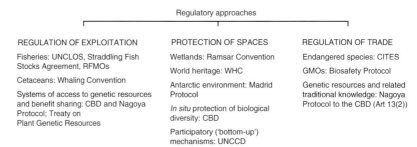

Figure 6.1: Broad regulatory approaches

or of certain types of organisms (i.e. genetically modified organisms or 'GMOs').[28]

As discussed later in this chapter, the choice of a particular regulatory approach largely depends on the object of regulation. 'Resources' or 'species' are generally regulated via approaches (i) and (iii), while approach (ii) is better suited for the regulation of 'sites', 'habitats' and 'ecosystems'. Figure 6.1 provides an overview of what will be covered in the remainder of this chapter. As shown by the case of the CBD, various regulatory approaches and techniques are sometimes combined in a single legal regime to capture the complexity of the object or to take into account the close relationship between the protection of a resource/species and the protection of sites/habitats/ecosystems.

6.3 Protection of species

6.3.1 Regulation of exploitation: fisheries

Fisheries management is a very important issue in practice, not only because of the amounts involved (the value of the fisheries and aquaculture market in 2010 amounted to some $217 billion[29]) but also because of the significant risks of depletion of some resources, and even the extinction of certain species.

At the outset, it is useful to introduce some distinctions regarding objectives and regulatory approaches. Concerning the first element, fisheries management has historically been one of the prime examples of the preservation of a resource for commercial purposes. More recently, however, the object of the regulation has ceased to be viewed solely as a 'resource' but also as 'species' requiring protection. The associated regulatory approaches have evolved in three major stages over time: (i) freedom of fishing by any State in marine areas (except in the narrow stretch considered to be the territorial seas of coastal States); (ii) the creation of extended jurisdictional areas (territorial sea and

---

[28] Cartagena Protocol, *supra* n. 5.

[29] Food and Agriculture Organization, *The State of World Fisheries and Aquaculture 2012*, part I, 3.

exclusive economic zone or 'EEZ') within which coastal States exercise sovereignty or sovereign rights of exploitation together with a duty to regulate (see Chapter 4); and (iii) increasingly institutionalised co-operation on the exploitation and conservation of resources located in areas beyond national jurisdiction, particularly through regional fisheries management organisations ('RFMOs').

Of course, this evolution has not followed a linear trajectory. A number of RFMOs were established well before the adoption of the UN Convention on the Law of the Sea ('UNCLOS') in 1982.[30] However, one can notice a certain convergence between the objectives pursued (increasingly sensitive to environmental considerations) and the techniques used within the general approach to the regulation of exploitation, as illustrated by developments within some institutional frameworks, such as the Whaling Convention and the Northwest Atlantic Fisheries Organization ('NAFO').[31]

It is this trajectory that we will highlight in our discussion of the general framework underlying the regulation of fisheries, the 1995 UN Straddling Fish Stocks Agreement,[32] and, finally, two specific examples of institutionalised co-operation, namely NAFO and the Whaling Convention.

6.3.1.1 The UNCLOS

The general framework governing the rights and obligations of States with respect to marine areas has been presented in Chapter 4. It is however useful to introduce two additional observations here to better understand the issue of fisheries and, more generally, the regime applicable to biological resources located in these areas.

The first observation concerns the location of these resources. Estimates suggest that 90 per cent of the commercially exploited fisheries are within the 200 nautical miles from the baselines, a stretch of water encompassed by the territorial sea and the EEZ.[33] Pursuant to Article 61(1) of UNCLOS, the coastal State 'shall determine the allowable catch of the living resources in its exclusive economic zone'. This provision introduces thereafter the duty to 'ensure through proper conservation and management measures that the maintenance of the living resources in the exclusive economic zone is not endangered by over-exploitation'.[34] Such duty can be broken down into three main components: (i) a limitation on unilateral action (by way of a duty to co-operate with competent international organisations, whether subregional, regional or

---

[30] United Nations Convention on the Law of the Sea, 10 December 1982, 1833 UNTS 397 ('UNCLOS').

[31] Convention on Future Multilateral Cooperation on Northwest Atlantic Fisheries, 24 October 1978, available at : www.nafo.int ('NAFO').

[32] Agreement for the Implementation of the Provisions of the United Nations Convention on the Law of the Sea of 10 December 1982 relating to the Conservation and Management of Straddling Fish Stocks and Highly Migratory Fish Stocks, 4 August 1995, 2167 UNTS 88 ('Straddling Fish Stocks Agreement').

[33] Bowman et al., supra n. 7, p. 125.   [34] UNCLOS, supra n. 30, Art. 61(2).

global,[35] as well as to 'tak[e] into account fishing patterns, the interdependence of stocks and any generally recommended *international minimum standards*, whether subregional, regional or global'[36]); (ii) some minimum content (measures must 'maintain or restore populations of harvested species at levels which can produce the *maximum sustainable yield*' taking into consideration 'associated or dependent species'[37]); and (iii) the availability of a non-adversarial dispute settlement mechanism, i.e. conciliation instead of judicial settlement, unless the coastal State has consented to the latter.[38]

A second point concerns the biological resources located beyond the EEZ. UNCLOS provides for general obligations to protect and preserve the marine environment (Part XII) and contains some more specific provisions relating to biological resources, including fisheries. The principle of the freedom of fishing[39] is articulated in Part VII, Section II, which sets out a protection framework largely similar to the one in Article 61. The duty to preserve applies to all States (not only coastal States).[40] States also have an obligation to co-operate, including through regional or subregional fisheries organisations,[41] and they must take into account minimum content requirements similar to those of Article 61.[42] One can therefore conclude that the requirement of co-operation is firmly enshrined in the framework laid down by UNCLOS. This co-operation has taken various forms. In some cases, there were pre-existing instruments on particular species, as in the case of the Whaling Convention, or on specific regions, such as NAFO. In other cases, new instruments have been adopted, such as the Straddling Fish Stocks Agreement.[43]

6.3.1.2 The Straddling Fish Stocks Agreement

This agreement is of particular interest[44] as an illustration of the foregoing observations because it establishes a specific link between the UNCLOS regime and RFMOs regarding fisheries beyond the EEZ. In addition, in line with the developments at the Rio Conference, the agreement adopts a precautionary and ecosystems approach to fisheries regulation.[45] The essence of this agreement lies in the co-operation and implementation mechanisms it establishes, first by encouraging co-operation between coastal States and flag States, particularly through the RFMOs (preferred mechanism), and second, if such co-operation does not materialise, by providing a subsidiary co-operation and implementation mechanism. To understand its operation, we will briefly discuss the mechanisms set out for both co-operation (preferred and subsidiary) and implementation (preferred and subsidiary).

---

[35] *Ibid.*, Art. 61(2) *in fine* and (5).   [36] *Ibid.*, Art. 61(3) *in fine* (emphasis added).
[37] *Ibid.*, Art. 61(3)–(4) (emphasis added) and 62.   [38] *Ibid.*, Art. 297(3).   [39] *Ibid.*, Art. 87(1)(e).
[40] *Ibid.*, Art. 117.   [41] *Ibid.*, Art. 118.   [42] *Ibid.*, Art. 119.
[43] Other instruments have also been adopted. See Bowman *et al.*, *supra* n. 7, pp. 134–5.
[44] See J. Harrison, *Making the Law of the Sea* (Cambridge University Press, 2011), pp. 99–113.
[45] Straddling Fish Stocks Agreement, *supra* n. 32, Art. 5(c)–(e) and 6.

As regards co-operation, the preferred system aims to strengthen RFMOs.[46] Article 8(3) is particularly important in this regard. It requires States parties to the Agreement to join the relevant RFMO (and requires RFMOs or, more precisely, States parties to such arrangements that are also parties to the Agreement, to accept the initiative whenever a State has a 'real interest', even if the State could not normally become a member) or, alternatively, to apply the conservation and management measures adopted by that organisation. In addition, Article 8(4) provides that only the States that comply with the obligation laid down in Article 8(3) have access to the fishery resources in question. One may wonder whether this requirement concerns only States parties to the Straddling Fish Stocks Agreement or also other States. Article 17 suggests that, in line with the *res inter alios acta* principle, only the first would be subject to such a ban.[47] However, the language used by this provision could also be interpreted more broadly to the extent that it refers not only to conservation obligations of the Agreement but also to those provided for in the UNCLOS, some of which are customary in nature.[48] In cases where an RFMO does not already exist, the subsidiary mechanism comes into play. However, this mechanism is only broadly articulated. States parties to the Agreement have an obligation to co-operate in order to create an organisation or similar arrangements with a certain minimum content.[49]

With respect to implementation, the preferred mechanism distributes powers between the fishing vessel's flag State[50] and the other States,[51] which must ensure compliance with the conservation and management measures adopted by the relevant RFMO. In particular, Article 21(1) provides that any State party to the RFMO (normally this will be the nearest coastal State) may board and inspect on the high seas a ship flying the flag of another State party to the Straddling Fish Stocks Agreement, even when the latter State is not itself party to the RFMO in question. In cases where the RFMO has not adopted boarding and inspection procedures, Article 22 provides for a subsidiary mechanism of 'basic procedures'. As we can see, the framework established by the Straddling Fish Stocks Agreement relies heavily on the existence of RFMOs or other specific arrangements. In what follows, we examine two primary examples of this type of institution.

6.3.1.3 The NAFO

The first example is the NAFO, an RFMO established in 1978, and successor to a much older arrangement dating from 1949. This is an interesting example to illustrate how an RFMO operates in the field of conservation, management and implementation, but it also helps to better understand the relationship

[46] *Ibid.*, Art. 8(1)–(2). The reinforcement objective is expressly provided for in Article 13 of the Agreement.
[47] *Ibid.*, Art. 17(1).   [48] See Chapter 4.
[49] Straddling Fish Stocks Agreement, *supra* n. 32, Art. 8(5)–(6) and 9.   [50] *Ibid.*, Art. 19.
[51] *Ibid.*, Arts. 20 and 21.

between UNCLOS and RFMOs envisioned in the Straddling Fish Stocks Agreement.

The NAFO has various organs, including a Fisheries Commission responsible for the adoption of conservation and management measures, including catch quotas of certain stocks.[52] The measures adopted by the Commission are binding and enter into force simultaneously for each State party, unless the latter has lodged an 'objection' pursuant to Article XII(1). The frequent use of these objections has posed difficulties for the proper functioning of the system.[53] For instance, in March 1995, the European objections to certain catch quotas adopted by the Commission led Canada to board a Spanish vessel, the *Estai*, fishing near the outer part of the Canadian EEZ. This incident gave rise to an action brought by Spain before the ICJ against Canada.[54] It also gave a sense of urgency to the conclusion of an agreement on straddling fish stocks, on which negotiations had been initiated two years earlier.

The conclusion of this Agreement based on the idea of precaution and the ecosystem approach influenced in turn the functioning of NAFO. Indeed, between 2005 and 2007, a reform process was undertaken within NAFO leading to an amendment of its constitutive treaty. This amendment, which is not yet in force,[55] adds in Article XIV(5) an obligation for States that have issued an objection to provide an explanation and to set out alternative measures they intend to apply for the conservation and management of the fishery resources in question.

6.3.1.4 The Whaling Convention

The second example of a specific arrangement is the Whaling Convention. Following two earlier initiatives, in 1931 and 1937, the Whaling Convention was adopted in 1946.[56]

Originally, this Convention had established a system for the exploitation of whales as a resource, but since 1982 a moratorium suspended whaling for commercial purposes. From a technical standpoint, the moratorium took the form of an amendment to paragraph 10, section (e), of the 'Schedule' of the Convention, according to which:

> catch limits for the killing for commercial purposes of whales from all stocks for the 1986 coastal and the 1985/86 pelagic seasons and thereafter shall be zero. This provision will be kept under review, based upon the best scientific advice.

---

[52] NAFO, *supra* n. 31, Art. XI.   [53] Bowman *et al, supra* n. 7, p. 137.

[54] *Fisheries Jurisdiction (Spain v. Canada)*, Judgment, ICJ Reports 1998, p. 432.

[55] In January 2012, only three parties (Norway, Canada, and the European Union) had ratified this amendment; it requires ratification by at least three quarters of the parties to enter into force. See: NAFO, *supra* n. 31, Art. XXI.

[56] See P. Birnie, *International Regulation of Whaling: From Conservation of Whaling to Conservation of Whales and Regulation of Whale Watching*, 2 vols. (Oceana Publications, 1985); Bowman *et al, supra* n. 7, Chapter 6.

This controversial amendment has profoundly changed the approach of the Whaling Convention, which has become a genuine conservation instrument rather than one geared towards exploitation. In the terms famously coined by Patricia Birnie, the regime has moved from the 'conservation of whaling' to the 'conservation of whales'.

Some States, especially Japan, have expressed reservations. At first, Japan lodged an objection under Article V(3) of the Convention, but subsequently withdrew it. However, Japan has launched a series of programmes ('JARPA I and II') concerning the catch of whales for what Japan considers as research purposes, rather than commercial ones, which is authorised under Article VIII(1) of the Convention. The real purpose of these programmes has been the subject of much debate, and it led Australia to bring a claim against Japan before the ICJ for breach of the Whaling Convention. In its 2014 judgment, the Court sided with Australia, concluding that JARPA II was not covered by the research exemption provided for in Article VIII(1) of the Convention and, as a result, whaling activities conducted under it were in breach of paragraph 10(e) of the Schedule.[57]

6.3.2 Regulation of trade: CITES

6.3.2.1 The structure of CITES

The exploitation of one or more species may be regulated indirectly by artificially reducing demand for a resource. This is the approach followed by the Convention on International Trade in Endangered Species of Wild Fauna and Flora Threatened with Extinction, better known by its acronym 'CITES'.[58]

This instrument is important for several reasons. First, the international trade of wildlife species is valued in the billions of dollars. Second, CITES has been reasonably successful in reaching its stated goal of protecting endangered species.[59] Third, in the same vein, the relative effectiveness of the regime established by CITES has prompted a number of initiatives attempting to extend it to species which are subject to other, more specific but less effective regimes. Fourth, CITES exemplifies a distilled version of a regulatory technique that is used quite frequently in international environmental law and that can be referred to as the 'list technique'. To understand the basic structure of CITES, it is useful to start with a characterisation of this technique. Figure 6.2 shows its essential components.

---

[57] *Whaling in the Antarctic (Australia v. Japan: New Zealand intervening)*, Judgment, ICJ, 31 March 2014, not yet reported, available at www.icj-cij.org (last visited on 12 May 2014).

[58] CITES, *supra* n. 3. On CITES see W. Wijnstekers, *L'évolution de la CITES* (Budakeszi: CIC, 9th edn, 2011); Bowman *et al.*, *supra* n. 7, Chapter 15.

[59] Some authors argue, however, that CITES may have engaged in a declining trend. See O. R. Young, 'Effectiveness of International Environmental Regimes: Existing Knowledge, Cutting-Edge Themes, and Research Strategies' (2011) 108 *Proceedings of the National Academy of Sciences* 19853.

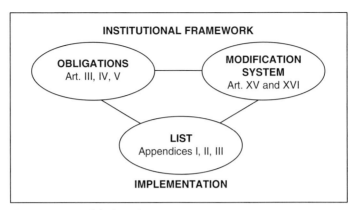

Figure 6.2: CITES and the list technique

The structure described by this diagram is simple. Obligations under the treaty apply to certain species and/or spaces (or another object, e.g. substances), which are usually listed in an appendix to the agreement. The list modification system allows for the updating of the list to reflect the evolving understanding and/or circumstances of a particular problem. This basic structure may be made more complex through different channels, such as the adoption of different lists and/or obligations applicable to different species or spaces. In addition, the modification system often gives States the possibility of objecting to the inclusion of a given species or space in the list. Despite its simplicity, the three components of the list technique help to capture the fundamental architecture of many environmental treaties, including CITES.

This treaty, which in May 2013 had 178 States parties, contains three lists in Annexes I, II and III respectively. The obligations relating to trade in specimens of species[60] listed in each appendix are not the same. Trade in species listed in Annex I (about 600 animal species and 300 plant species characterised as 'endangered') is essentially prohibited with a few exceptions,[61] whilst trade in the species of Annex II (approximately 4,800 animal species and 30,000 plant species that are likely to become endangered if trade is not regulated) is permitted but subject to strict controls.[62] As for the species listed in Annex III (some 135 animal species and fifteen plant species regulated unilaterally by a State party), CITES establishes a system facilitating the assistance of other States parties in the implementation of this unilateral regulation.[63] The list modification system is tightly regulated (Articles XV and XVI) and includes the possibility of emitting

---

[60] The terms 'trade', 'species' and 'specimen' are broadly defined in Article 1 of CITES. A 'specimen' of a species can be (i) a whole animal/plant, living or dead, (ii) a readily recognisable part of an animal/plant or (iii) a readily recognisable derivative of an animal/plant. 'Trade' includes not only import and export but also 're-export' (export of a specimen previously imported) and 'introduction from the sea' (transportation into a State of specimens taken in the high seas). Certain adjustments are made regarding the type of permit required for each category.

[61] *Ibid.*, Art. III.   [62] *Ibid.*, Art. IV.   [63] *Ibid.*, Art. V.

'reservations' (Article XV(3), XVI(2) and XXIII). This basic structure of CITES is complemented by an institutional framework and a system of implementation,[64] an important component of which is the regulation of trade with non-parties to CITES.[65] But the cornerstone of CITES is its system of export/import permits.

6.3.2.2 The permits system

To understand this system we must examine its five main components. First, the stringency of the requirements for the issuance of a permit is a function of the threat to the species in question. Trade in specimens of species listed in Annex I[66] is only authorised in exceptional circumstances. It requires both a permit issued by the exporting State (based not only on administrative considerations – for example, whether the specimen was obtained legally – but also on ecological considerations – whether the trade is detrimental to the survival of the species)[67] and a permit issued by the importing State (again, based on administrative – the specimen is not to be used for 'primarily commercial' purposes – and ecological considerations).[68] By contrast, the trade in a species included in Annex II[69] only requires an export permit based on administrative and ecological considerations.[70] For species in Annex III,[71] an export permit based on administrative considerations is sufficient.[72] CITES provides for 'exemptions' where the cross-border movement of a specimen is not subject to the permit system.[73] This is the case, for example, in respect of specimens in transit[74] or transhipment, or specimens that are personal or household effects,[75] specimens that are part of travelling exhibitions[76] or, still, specimens used for scientific research.[77] This first component is summarised in Figure 6.3.[78]

Figure 6.3 also mentions a second component, namely that the permit system can be extended by domestic law. Indeed, Article XIV(1) expressly reserves the possibility for States parties to go further in their domestic

---

[64] See *infra* Chapter 9. [65] CITES, *supra* n. 3, Art. X. See also *infra* Chapter 12.
[66] See Wijnstekers, *supra* n. 58, Chapter 10. [67] CITES, *supra* n. 3, Art. III(2).
[68] *Ibid.*, Art. III(3). The requirement that the specimen is not used for 'primarily commercial purposes' has been further specified by a resolution of the COP (Resolution Conf. 5.10 (1985), revised in 2010). According to this resolution 'all uses whose non-commercial aspects do not clearly predominate shall be considered to be primarily commercial in nature, with the result that the import of specimens of Appendix-I species should not be permitted.' Due to differing interpretations by some importing States (see e.g. *Born Free USA* v. *Norton*, 278 F. Supp 2d 5 (DDC 2003)), the resolution was recently revised to give a detailed treatment of certain uses that had previously been relatively ambiguous, such as research by the biomedical industry or breeding in captivity for commercial purposes.
[69] See Wijnstekers, *supra* n. 58, Chapter 11. [70] CITES, *supra* n. 3, Art. IV(2).
[71] Wijnstekers, *supra* n. 58, Chapter 12. [72] CITES, *supra* n. 3, Art. V(2).
[73] CITES, *supra* n. 3, Art. VII. See Wijnstekers, *supra* n. 58, Chapter 15.
[74] *Ibid.*, Art. VII(1) and resolution Conf. 9.7 (1994), revised in 2010.
[75] *Ibid.*, Art. VII(3) and resolution Conf. 13.7 (2004), revised in 2007.
[76] *Ibid.*, Art. VII(7) and Resolution Conf. 12.13 (2002), revised in 2007. [77] *Ibid.*, Art. VII(6).
[78] Source: D. Hunter, J. Salzman and D. Zaelke, *International Environmental Law and Policy* (New York: Foundation Press, 4th edn, 2011), pp. 1071–2.

	EXPORT PERMITS		IMPORT PERMITS	
	Administrative considerations	Ecological considerations	Administrative considerations	Ecological considerations
APPENDIX I	required	required	required	required
APPENDIX II	required	required	[optional-domestic law]	[optional-domestic law]
APPENDIX III	required	[optional-domestic law]	[optional-domestic law]	[optional-domestic law]

Figure 6.3: CITES permits system

legislation and impose additional requirements for the issuance of permits (indicated in Figure 6.3 by 'optional – domestic law').

The third component is the minimum content that permits must have in accordance with CITES. Article VI of the Convention lists a number of requirements intended to standardise the content of permits and ensure the reliability of the system.[79]

The fourth component is the institutional structure that States must establish, under Articles VIII and IX of the Convention, to implement and manage the permit system. States must designate or set up a 'Management Authority' responsible for issuing permits, a 'Scientific Authority' capable of advising on environmental considerations relevant to the issuance of a permit and a 'Rescue Centre' responsible for taking care of living specimens, particularly in the case of confiscation, as well as maintain records of permits granted in respect of species included in Annexes I, II and III of the Convention.

The fifth component is the system governing the listing of species in one of the appendices to the Convention. The COP adopted, as a supplement to the text of the Convention, ecological and economic criteria to identify species that may be included in Annexes I and II.[80] However, listing is subject to a vote, which introduces some political volatility in the application of these criteria. To be amended, Annexes I and II require a majority of two thirds of the parties 'present and voting'.[81] Only parties that express a positive or negative vote are taken into account when calculating the required two thirds majority. When such a majority is met, the amendment enters into force for all States parties, including those who voted against it, but any State may lodge a reservation in writing within ninety days and, in this way, avoid being bound by the amendment.[82] As regards Annex III, any State party may list a species by a simple communication to the Secretariat.[83] This amendment enters into force for all States parties within ninety days of the notification thereof by the

---

[79] See Wijnstekers, *supra* n. 58, Chapter 13.

[80] Resolution Conf. 9.24 (1994), revised in 2010. Note that this resolution urges States parties to take due account of the precautionary principle when considering proposals for the amendment of Annexes I and II. See Wijnstekers, *supra* n. 58, Chapters 6–7.

[81] CITES, *supra* n. 3, Art. XV(1)(b).   [82] *Ibid.*, Art. XV(3).   [83] *Ibid.*, Art. XVI(1).

Secretariat, except for those which make a reservation, but contrary to what holds for Annexes I and II, this reservation may be made at any point in time, allowing States to opt-out from an amendment even after its entry into force.[84]

The interpretation of the effect of reservations raised some controversy, which led the COP to adopt a resolution in 1983, revised in 2007, clarifying this point. This resolution 'recommends' that 'any Party having entered a reservation with regard to any species included in Annex I treat that species as if it was included in Annex II for all purposes, including documentation and control'.[85] Another feature of this system is the ability to make amendments in the interval between two sessions of the COP (these take place every two to three years) through a postal voting procedure.[86]

6.3.2.3 CITES in practice

To understand the operation of these arrangements, it is useful to examine two cases more closely.

The first is the case of the African elephant (*Loxodonta africana*). This example serves to illustrate both the effectiveness of CITES and the diversity of considerations and societal forces influencing the amendment system. During the 1980s, the hunting of elephants in some African countries such as Kenya, Tanzania, Zambia and the then Zaire (now DRC) decimated the populations of African elephants.[87] This phenomenon, mainly due to exports of ivory to developed States, led in the late 1980s to a call by States such as Kenya, the United States, the United Kingdom, France and Germany for a ban on ivory trade. Despite the reluctance expressed by other importing countries, in particular Japan, as well as by some exporting countries, including Zimbabwe, Botswana and South Africa, the COP eventually agreed to include the African elephant in Annex I of CITES. This inclusion (or more precisely, the transfer from Annex II to Annex I) had a significant impact on the recovery of elephant populations, to the point that between 1997 and 2000, some populations located in Zimbabwe, Botswana, Namibia and South Africa were downgraded to Annex II under certain conditions.[88] One of the main arguments used to justify the downgrading was that the revenue from ivory trade would benefit local people and that the government could use it to finance conservation measures. At the roots of these debates lies the recurrent tension between the management of a 'resource' from an economic perspective and the conservation of a 'species'.

---

[84] *Ibid.*, Art. XVI(2).   [85] Resolution Conf. 4.25 (1983), revised in 2007.

[86] CITES, *supra* n. 3, Art. XV(2).

[87] See M. Glennon, 'Has International Law Failed the Elephant?' (1990) 84 *American Journal of International Law* 1, 4.

[88] During the session in Harare in 1997, the COP established two monitoring programmes, namely the MIKE (Monitoring Illegal Killings of Elephants) and ETIS (Elephant Trade Information System) to ensure monitoring of the environmental impact of this re-transfer to Annex II and, more generally, the situation of elephant populations. See Resolution Conf. 10.10 (1997), revised in 2010.

Also in 1997, during its Harare session, the COP adopted measures to protect sturgeon, a species from which caviar is derived. Following the dissolution of the Soviet Union, the stocks of this species in the region of the Caspian Sea were decimated by uncontrolled overfishing and illegal trade in caviar. Some species of the order *Acipenseriforms* had already been listed in Annexes I and II of CITES. But it was not until 1997, at the initiative of the United States and Germany, that approximately twenty species of this order were included in Annex II. In addition, the COP adopted a series of other measures, including a labelling system to control the trade of the main product of these species (caviar specimens) and specific rules regarding catch and export quotas (by country, species, and specimen).[89] In 2011, as several States in the range of the species concerned had not followed the rules on quotas, the Secretariat recommended a temporary quota of zero for these States, in accordance with Resolution Conf. 12.7.[90] States parties to the CITES were required not to accept imports from States that do not follow the rules on setting quotas.[91]

In both cases, CITES had positive effects on the evolution of the regulated populations. In the case of the African elephants, two one-off auctions of government-owned, lawfully gathered ivory from Botswana, Namibia, South Africa and Zimbabwe (excluding seized ivory and ivory of unknown origin) have been authorised and conducted under the scrutiny of the Secretary-General of CITES, but no more sales will be allowed before 2017. As for caviar, the regulatory void that followed the dissolution of the USSR has been largely filled. While some States have not complied with the catch and export quotas, and illegal fishing and trade have not been eliminated, the increasingly strict system set up by CITES nevertheless represents an improvement. Other examples also highlight the impact of CITES, in particular the case of vicuñas, which was described in the 2008–9 annual report of the Secretariat as a 'shear success'.[92] This species, whose wool is highly sought after, was close to extinction in the 1970s. It was listed in Annex I (and Annex II for some populations in Argentina, Chile and Peru) and, as a result of the joint efforts of countries and local populations, stocks have now recovered.

These cases demonstrate the effectiveness of CITES as a multilateral instrument for the protection of the environment. However, CITES does not address

---

[89] Resolution Conf. 12.7 (2002), revised in 2004 ('Resolution Conf. 12.7'). This resolution incorporates and repeals the resolutions adopted between 1997 and 2000 (in Harare and Gigiri). For more information, see the website of CITES: www.cites.org/eng/prog/sturgeon.php (last visited on 21 October 2012).

[90] According to this resolution: 'if the quotas have not been communicated to the Secretariat by the deadline indicated in subparagraph iv) above, the relevant range States have a zero quota until such time as they communicate their quotas in writing to the Secretariat and the Secretariat in turn informs the Parties. The Secretariat should be informed by the range States of any delay and shall in turn inform the Parties'.

[91] *Ibid.*, second recommendation, para. (a), chapeau.

[92] *Activity Report of the CITES Secretariat* 2008–2009 (Geneva: Secretariat CITES, 2010), p. 6.

the important threat to the preservation of wildlife posed by other factors, such as the destruction or deterioration of habitats.

6.4 Protection of spaces (sites, habitats, ecosystems)

6.4.1 'Top-down' and 'bottom-up' regulation

The protection of spaces as a regulatory approach has found legal expression in two main ways. The first and most common way is what is often called the 'top-down' approach or, in other words, the vertical approach. States undertake treaty obligations that they must fulfil by adopting domestic laws and regulations. The contents of these laws and regulations may vary from one State to another, but international law often imposes particular techniques, such as the adoption of strategic plans or the creation of protected areas. In this chapter, this approach will be analysed in the light of three major treaties, namely the Ramsar Convention, the World Heritage Convention and the Madrid Protocol on the Antarctic Environment.

The second way to proceed is less frequently used and consists in situating the elaboration of strategies at the level of different groups of stakeholders likely to be affected by the problem at hand. This approach, often called 'bottom-up', is embodied in participatory mechanisms that allow stakeholder groups to express their views or even take part in the decision-making process. It aims to integrate considerations of social and economic development with environmental protection strategies at the stakeholder level. The main illustration is UN Convention to combat Desertification.

6.4.2 The 'top-down' approach: the creation of protected areas

6.4.2.1 The protection of wetlands: the Ramsar Convention

The Ramsar Convention was concluded in 1971, i.e. the year before the Stockholm Conference on the Human Environment. It is therefore one of the first modern environmental instruments. Originally designed as a treaty on waterfowl habitat, the focus of the Convention has shifted over time to the protection of wetlands as an ecosystem and, more recently, to the ecosystem services provided by wetlands, particularly in relation to the water cycle. This evolution cannot be analysed in detail in the context of this book.[93] The discussion will instead concentrate on two aspects of the Convention, namely (i) its specific regulatory object and (ii) its basic structure, characterised by the list technique.

Regarding the *regulatory object* of the Convention, Article 1(1) provides a broad definition of 'wetlands':

---

[93] On this treaty, see Bowman *et al., supra* n. 7, Chapter 13; Ramsar Convention Secretariat, *The Ramsar Convention Manual* (Gland: Ramsar Convention Secretariat, 6th edn, 2013).

areas of marsh, fen, peatland or water, whether natural or artificial, permanent or temporary, with water that is static or flowing, fresh, brackish or salt, including areas of marine water the depth of which at low tide does not exceed six metres.[94]

Various criteria can be applied to the definition of a wetland, both from a scientific point of view or a descriptive one (marine, estuarine, lacustrine, riverine, palustrine).[95] We will focus on four main components of this definition.

First, the definition of protected wetlands in the Convention is very broad and covers both natural and artificial wetlands (e.g. irrigated farmland, rice paddies and even aquaculture ponds), of freshwater or saltwater. What matters above all is that in such areas 'water is the primary factor controlling the environment and the associated plant and animal life'.[96]

Second, the reason why these wetlands deserve protection is increasingly characterised by reference to the services they provide.[97] If we use the current terminology to understand the origins of the Convention, it could be said that, originally, the main (although not the only) 'service' of these wetlands was to provide a habitat for certain species (waterfowl). Today the various ecosystem services provided by wetlands are much better understood and documented. They range from the aesthetic or recreational value to the protection against flooding or even the storage of greenhouse gases. In recent years, the emphasis has been placed on the role of wetlands in the water cycle.[98] Should this focus be fully expressed in the criteria for identifying wetlands, it could transform the Ramsar Convention into the first global treaty on freshwater.

Third, the Convention introduces a distinction between wetlands having 'international significance in terms of ecology, botany, zoology, limnology or hydrology'[99] and other wetlands. As we shall see, the obligations of States in each case are not the same.

---

[94] Ramsar Convention, *supra* n. 4. See also Art. 2(1).

[95] The Ramsar Convention has a classification system for wetlands that distinguishes between forty-two types of wetlands, grouped into three categories: marine and coastal wetlands, inland wetlands, and human-made wetlands. See the *Ramsar Convention Manual, supra* n. 93, pp. 7 and 55–6.

[96] *Ibid.*

[97] This terminology, which aims to clarify the economic value of ecosystems in order to facilitate their protection, was introduced, *inter alia*, in the Millennium Ecosystem Assessment, an initiative launched in 2000 by former UN Secretary General Kofi Annan. See in particular the *Synthesis Report of the Millennium Ecosystem Assessment* (2005), p. 13. A reinterpretation of the older Ramsar terminology with regard to the one introduced by the Millennium Ecosystem Assessment is contained in Resolution IX.1 (2005), Appendix A.

[98] At the 11th COP held in Bucharest in 2012, the definition of the 'Mission of the Convention' as it was stated in the Strategic Plan 2009–15 was modified to include the following paragraph: 'To achieve this Mission it is essential that the vital ecosystem services, and especially those related to water and those that wetlands provide to people and nature through their natural infrastructure, are fully recognized, maintained, restored and wisely used', Resolution XI.3 (2012), para. 4.

[99] Ramsar Convention, *supra* n. 4, Art. 2(2). The COP developed a set of criteria for the identification of wetlands having an international importance. See *Ramsar Convention Manual, supra* n. 93, pp. 52–4.

Fourth, Article 2(3) states that the inclusion of a wetland of international importance in the list maintained by the Secretariat 'does not prejudice the exclusive sovereign rights of the Contracting Party in whose territory the wetland is situated'. This term should not be confused with the concept of 'sovereign rights' used to describe the powers of the States over their exclusive economic zone and continental shelf.[100] It refers instead to the territorial sovereignty of the State, with all its attributes and limitations. The transboundary nature of a wetland has no bearing on this point. In such a case, Article 5 of the Convention urges States to co-operate, including through the creation of bilateral or regional arrangements.[101] A number of such arrangements have been made by States and communicated to the Ramsar Secretariat.[102] However, the territorial status of these sites remains subject to the sovereignty of the relevant States, with a number of obligations deriving, *inter alia*, from the law of international watercourses and transboundary aquifers.[103]

The protection of the regulatory object just described is organised following the *list technique* discussed in the context of CITES. To understand the basic architecture of the Ramsar Convention, it is therefore useful to look at the three components of this technique: the list, the obligations attached thereto, and the system through which the list can be modified.

The Convention provides in Article 2(1)[104] for the establishment of a List of Wetlands of International Importance maintained by the Secretariat (Article 8(2)). This list currently contains more than 2,000 wetlands located all around the world. The list mentions the name of the site, the date of designation, the geographical position within the country, the surface area and the co-ordinates (latitude and longitude) of the centre-points of each site. This list is organised by country, but it can also be consulted by order of designation of each site. In addition, an 'Annotated Ramsar List' providing a short description (200 words) of each site is also available at the Secretariat. Moreover, a second list, the 'Montreux Record',[105] is kept by the Secretariat and includes the sites of the Ramsar list 'where an adverse change in ecological character has occurred, is occurring, or is likely to occur, and which are therefore in need of priority conservation attention'.[106] The inclusion of a site in the Montreux Record (currently this list contains forty-eight sites) has some legal implications, triggering assistance but also an increased level of protection.

Regarding the obligations arising from the Convention, three levels can be identified. The first level applies to all wetlands on the territory of States parties

---

[100] See Chapter 4.
[101] See Resolution VII.19 (1999) 'Guidelines for International Cooperation under the Ramsar Convention' Annex.
[102] *Ramsar Convention Manual, supra* n. 93, pp. 60–4.   [103] See Chapter 4.
[104] See also Resolution VII.11 (1999).
[105] This list was created by the Conference of the Parties that took place in Montreux, Switzerland, in 1990. See Recommendation 4.8 (1990) 'Changes in the Ecological Character of Ramsar Sites'.
[106] See Resolution VI.1 (1996), Annex 3, 'Operating Principles of the Montreux Record', para. 3.1.

to the Convention, whether listed or not. In Article 3(1) States undertake to 'formulate and implement their planning so as to promote the conservation of the wetlands included in the List, and as far as possible the wise use of wetlands in their territory'. The obligation of 'wise use' therefore applies to wetlands in general, whether listed or not. Any potential ambiguity on this point is eliminated by Article 4(1), under which States have an obligation to 'promote the conservation of wetlands and waterfowl by establishing nature reserves on wetlands, whether they are included in the List or not'. Wetlands that are not listed are thus not excluded from the scope of the Convention. The requirements are more demanding, however, with respect to the sites that qualify as 'wetlands of international importance' and are included in the list. On the one hand, the obligation of wise use has a broader scope, insofar as it does not just concern States where the wetland is located, but also other States parties.[107] On the other hand, inclusion in the List entails additional monitoring and reporting obligations (Articles 3(2) and 8(2)(c)–(d)),[108] which, in turn, may trigger an obligation to take measures to deal with a threat or damage to the site.[109] Finally, sites on the Montreux Record benefit in practice from a priority regime, involving the obligation for States to report on the evolution of the site but also, depending on the circumstances, better access to technical and financial assistance.[110]

With regard to the designation of sites and the modification of the List, it pertains to each State individually. This is a particular feature of the Ramsar Convention, which leaves very limited room for the views of third States and treaty bodies. The system is organised around listing and delisting. Article 2 is the main legal basis. Under this provision, each State must designate at least one wetland when joining the Convention (Article 2(4)) and subsequently has:

> [the] right to add to the List further wetlands situated within its territory, to extend the boundaries of those wetlands already included by it in the List, or, because of its urgent national interests, to delete or restrict the boundaries of wetlands already included (Article 2(5)).

It is, in each case, a unilateral decision of the State, but if the decision entails less protection (delisting or reduction of surface area), it is more constrained insofar as the State is required to justify its decision in terms of its 'urgent national interests',[111] inform the Secretariat (which must notify the other parties and 'arrange for these matters to be discussed at the next

---

[107] See Bowman et al., *supra* n. 7, pp. 424–6.
[108] See also Resolution IX.1 (2005), Annex A, paras. 15–21.
[109] See Recommendation 4.8 (1990), according to which States parties are urged, in case of threat or damage, to take quick and effective action to prevent these changes or remedy.
[110] Bowman et al, *supra* n. 7, pp. 443–8.
[111] This point has been clarified by Resolution VIII.20 (2002) 'General Guidance for Interpreting "Urgent National Interests" under Article 2.5 of the Convention and Considering Compensation under Article 4.2'.

conference' (Art. 8(2)(d)–(e)), and take appropriate compensatory measures (Article 4(2)).[112] In addition, the Secretariat may also take the initiative to include a site in the Montreux Record, even if the last word belongs to the State where the wetland in question is located.[113] Difficulties can arise when territorial sovereignty over the site is contested or when it is located in areas beyond national jurisdiction. The first scenario falls under the duty of co-operation stated in Article 5 of the Convention. This obligation applies primarily to transboundary sites, whether listed or not, and it would also apply to wetlands located on a disputed territory. Given the legal consequences that may arise from acquiescence to inclusion in the List of a contested site by one of the States parties to a territorial dispute,[114] the best solution in such a case may be to encourage States to co-operate and agree on a common protective regime, even if the site is not included in the List. As regards wetlands outside State territory, such as those located in Antarctica, Switzerland submitted a proposal to the COP in Kampala (Uganda) in 2005, inviting the 'Antarctic Treaty' to submit a list of sites that meet the criteria for inclusion in the Ramsar List.[115] However, this proposal was very controversial, and it was eventually withdrawn.

The basic structure of the system is summarised in Figure 6.4.

This system has raised awareness of the importance of wetlands, and it has positively influenced their level of protection at the national and international level. The number of sites on the List (currently over 2,000, equivalent to an area of over 200 million hectares) is but one indication of such impact. More

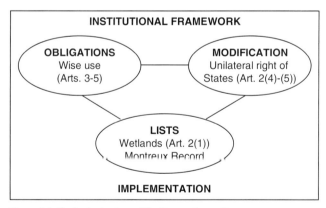

Figure 6.4: The basic structure of the Ramsar Convention

---

[112] In practice, while reductions were made (often offset by expansion elsewhere), no deletion from the main list has been recorded so far. See Bowman *et al., supra* n. 7, p. 412.
[113] 'Operating Principles', *supra* n. 106, para. 3.2.1.
[114] As discussed later, the WHC specifically addresses this problem by providing in Art. 11(3), that '[t]he inclusion of a property situated in a territory covered by claim of sovereignty or jurisdiction of more than one State does not prejudice the rights of the parties to the dispute'.
[115] See Ramsar COP9 DR 23, Rev.1, 7 November 2005, para. 8.

importantly, perhaps, is the effective implementation of protection policies at the national level.[116] As discussed next, the international protection of world heritage follows a similar pattern, albeit in a more institutionalised way.

6.4.2.2 The protection of world heritage: the World Heritage Convention

The WHC[117] is, in many ways, a hybrid instrument. It protects both cultural monuments and certain portions of the natural environment. It also embodies the tension between the interests of all humanity to protect these sites, conveyed by the concept of 'world heritage', and their location in the territory of one or more States. Finally, unlike other environmental treaties concluded in the 1970s, it also explicitly takes into account the interests of future generations to benefit from world heritage. These three dimensions, which, from the outset, gave the WHC an innovative character, underlay the many difficulties that this treaty has faced over time. A detailed description of the evolution of the Convention is beyond the scope of this book.[118] As in the case of the Ramsar Convention, we will only analyse the WHC's specific regulatory object and its basic structure.

The *object protected* by the WHC is the world's cultural and natural heritage. This complex expression has three components: cultural heritage, natural heritage and the 'outstanding universal value' that elevates parts of this heritage to the level of world heritage.

The environmental dimension of the WHC concerns the natural heritage portion of its object. The characterisation of 'natural heritage' given in Article 2 is somewhat rigid. Indeed, drawing upon the concept of cultural heritage defined in Article 1 (monuments, groups of buildings, sites), Article 2 views natural heritage mostly as natural monuments (natural features, geological and physiographical formations, sites). The spatial dimension prevails.[119] By way of illustration, a species as iconic as the great blue whale (*Baleanoptera musculus*) could not be considered natural heritage under the Convention because it is movable.[120] This feature highlights the regulatory approach taken by the Convention, focusing on space, and distinguishes it from other approaches to the protection of species or resources previously studied.

As for the attribute of having 'outstanding universal value', some clarification is provided in the 'Operational Guidelines' adopted and regularly updated by the World Heritage Committee:

---

[116] See M. Bowman, 'The Ramsar Convention on Wetlands: Has it Made a Difference' (2002) *Yearbook of International Co-operation on Environment and Development* 61, 63–5.

[117] WHC, *supra* n. 4.

[118] See F. Francioni and F. Lenzerini (eds.), *The 1972 World Heritage Convention: A Commentary* (Oxford University Press, 2008); Bowman *et al., supra* n. 7, Chapter 14.

[119] Bowman *et al., supra* n. 7, p. 457. See also the *Operational Guidelines for the Implementation of the World Heritage Convention*, July 2012, WHC 12/01 ('Operational Guidelines'), paragraph 48 ('Nominations of immovable heritage which are likely to become movable will not be considered').

[120] *Ibid.*

> 'Outstanding universal value' means cultural and/or natural significance which is so exceptional as to transcend national boundaries and to be of common importance for present and future generations of all humanity.[121]

This definition is further specified by the criteria adopted by the World Heritage Committee and explained in the Operational Guidelines. Three types of criteria must be met: the interest of the site (natural heritage[122] must be of exceptional beauty, symbolically represent a geological phase or ecological process, or be of particular importance for *in situ* conservation of biological diversity or certain species); integrity and/or authenticity[123] (for natural heritage, it is the integrity, understood as 'a measure of the wholeness and intactness of the natural and/or cultural heritage and its attributes',[124] which is relevant); and the existence of a system of protection of the site, expressing the commitment of the State to preserve the value of the site[125] (including the existence of appropriate legislation, a clear delineation of the site, and a management system).

Assigning 'outstanding universal value' to a site raises a number of legal difficulties. For example, one may ask what consequences follow the recognition of such a value and hence of the 'world heritage' status as regards the exercise of State sovereignty over the site concerned. We saw in Chapter 3 that the concept of 'common heritage of mankind' embodies an approach that excludes ownership by a State of the resource in question and organises joint management. However, the WHC takes a different stance. Article 6(1) expressly reserves 'sovereignty of the States on whose territory the cultural and natural heritage . . . is situated' while stressing the duty of States to co-operate in order to ensure its protection and the obligation to take no deliberate action 'which might damage directly or indirectly the cultural and natural heritage . . . situated on the territory of other States Parties' (Article 6(3)). Nonetheless, in some cases, the intervention of the World Heritage Committee has met with strong opposition from national authorities, particularly when the Committee seeks to move a site to the List of World Heritage in Danger to counter threats from economic development projects.[126] One may also wonder whether the characterisation of 'outstanding universal value' is reserved to listed sites or whether this status can be conferred to a site that is not listed, or even a site that has been denied registration. The WHC clearly opts for the latter approach. Article 12 provides, in effect, that:

> [t]he fact that a property belonging to the cultural or natural heritage has not been included in either of the two lists mentioned in paragraphs 2 and 4 of Article 11 shall in no way be construed to mean that it does not have an

---

[121] Operational Guidelines *supra* n. 119, para. 49.   [122] *Ibid.*, para. 77(vii)–(x).
[123] *Ibid.*, paras. 78–95.   [124] *Ibid.*, para. 88.   [125] *Ibid.*, paras. 78 and 96–118.
[126] See N. Affolder, 'Mining and the World Heritage Convention: Democratic Legitimacy and Treaty Compliance' (2007) 24 *Pace Environmental Law Review* 35.

outstanding universal value for purposes other than those resulting from inclusion in these lists.

This raises another question, namely whether the inclusion in the list is of constitutive or declaratory nature. Before addressing this problem, however, it is necessary to explain the basic structure of the Convention.

Much like the CITES and the Ramsar Convention, the WHC follows the *list technique*, with its three components: the list, the obligations under the Convention and the list modification system.

Regarding the list, Article 11 of the Convention sets out two different lists. The 'World Heritage List' provided for in Article 11(2) includes over 980 sites, 193 of which are natural heritage. Some of these may be placed on a second list, the 'List of World Heritage in Danger', when the site is:

> threatened by serious and specific dangers, such as the threat of disappearance caused by accelerated deterioration, large-scale public or private projects or rapid urban or tourist development projects; destruction caused by changes in the use or ownership of the land; major alterations due to unknown causes; abandonment for any reason whatsoever; the outbreak or the threat of an armed conflict; calamities and cataclysms; serious fires, earthquakes, landslides; volcanic eruptions; changes in water level, floods and tidal waves (Article 11(4)).[127]

This list currently contains forty-four sites, eighteen of which are natural heritage. Note that the transfer to this second list falls within the remit of the World Heritage Committee, a feature that has sometimes led to tensions with the State where the site is located.

Regarding the protection obligations undertaken by States, one must distinguish between those applicable to all sites falling under the concept of cultural or natural heritage as defined by the Convention, whether listed or not, and those applicable to listed sites only. The first category includes a 'vertical' obligation to take measures at the domestic level to ensure 'the identification, protection, conservation, presentation and transmission to future generations of the cultural and natural heritage referred to in Articles 1 and 2 and situated on its territory' (Article 4).[128] The scope of this obligation and its effects require some clarification. Commentators consider, on the basis of a contextual reading of Articles 4 and 5 in the light of Articles 6(1)–(2) and 12, that the duty of protection is not limited to listed sites.[129] Thus, listing would only have a declaratory effect.[130] As regards the effects of the obligation, Articles 4 and 5 have been interpreted by domestic courts as conferring

---

[127] Operational Guidelines, *supra* n. 119, para. 177.
[128] See also WHC, *supra* n. 4, Art. 5 (listing specific measures that States are urged to adopt).
[129] Bowman *et al., supra* n. 7, p. 454 (and cited references). See also F. Francioni and F. Lenzerini, 'The Destruction of the Buddhas of Bamiyan and International Law' (2003) 14 *European Journal of International Law* 619, 631.
[130] See, however, *Southern Pacific Properties (Middle East) Limited (SPP)* v. *Arab Republic of Egypt*, ICSID Case No. ARB/84/3, Award (20 May 1992), para. 154.

a discretionary power to the State on whose territory the site is located.[131] This view is not necessarily relevant for other treaty contexts as the courts of other countries have granted direct effect to treaty provisions as broad or broader still than Articles 4 and 5 of the WHC.[132] Also in the first category of obligations, the Convention provides for 'horizontal' obligations, in particular a duty to co-operate, both generally (e.g. through the creation of institutions such as the World Heritage Committee[133]) and more specifically (e.g. through the mechanism of financial and technical assistance[134]), and the abovementioned duty:

> not to take any deliberate measures which might damage directly or indirectly the cultural and natural heritage referred to in Articles 1 and 2 situated on the territory of other States Parties to this Convention (Art. 6(3)).

This is an early formulation of the prevention principle. Regarding the second category of obligations, Article 6(2) provides for an obligation of assistance applicable only to sites included in the list. The scope of this obligation is explicitly restricted to the 'cultural and natural heritage referred to in paragraphs 2 and 4 of Article 11' (as opposed to that referred to in Articles 1 and 2). Listing can also extend the possibilities of obtaining assistance available to States, in particular when the site in question is placed on the List of World Heritage in Danger.

As regards the listing system, unlike the Ramsar Convention, the WHC does not grant States a unilateral right to have a site listed. It establishes a system of nominations that the World Heritage Committee can accept (thereby placing the site on the list) or deny (Article 11(6)).[135] This system is based on Article 11 of the Convention and on various sections of the Operational Guidelines, in particular Section III (paras. 120–68). A distinction must be made between the 'World Heritage List' and 'List of World Heritage in Danger'. The initiative of proposing a site for the former must come from the State where the site is located (Article 11(1) and (3)). Article 11(3) states that the inclusion in this list requires the consent of the State concerned. This has caused problems when sovereignty over a site is contentious. The case of the *Temple of Préah Vihéar*

---

[131] See Bowman *et al.*, *supra* n. 7, pp. 455–6 (referring to Australian jurisprudence in particular: *Richardson* v. *Forestry Commission* [1988] HCA 10, (1988) 164 CLR 261). See also B. Boer and G. Wiffen, *Heritage Law in Australia* (Oxford University Press, 2006), Chapter 3.

[132] See *Netherlands Crown Decision (in Dutch) in the case lodged by the Competent Authority for the Island of Bonaire on the annulment of two of its decisions on the Lac wetland by the Governor of the Netherlands Antilles*, 11 September 2007, Staatsblad 2007, 347 ('*Bonaire*'). J. Verschuuren, 'Ramsar soft law is not soft at all' (2008) 35 *Milieu en Recht* 28 (English translation of a text in Dutch, available on www.ssrn.com, discussing the case of *Bonaire*, in which an administrative authority in the Netherlands granted direct effect to Art. 3 of the Ramsar Convention).

[133] See WHC *supra* n. 4, Arts. 6(1) and 8–14.

[134] See *ibid.*, Parts IV (Fund for the Protection of the World Heritage) and V (terms and conditions of international assistance).

[135] *Operational Guidelines, supra* n. 119, para. 158.

illustrates this point. In 1962, a territorial delimitation dispute between Cambodia and Thailand was brought before the ICJ, which concluded in favour of Cambodia.[136] Since 2001, Cambodia has proposed the inclusion of the temple on the World Heritage List sparking protests from Thailand, in particular because of the precise area Cambodia sought to include. In 2008, Cambodia made a new proposal, with the agreement of Thailand, in which the boundaries of the site were more narrowly defined. This proposal led to the inclusion of the site in the list, despite a last minute change of heart by Thailand. The ICJ subsequently confirmed Cambodia's claim to the surrounding temple grounds.[137] The inclusion of a site in the list is not definitive. Under certain circumstances, entries can be modified[138] or even removed (e.g. if the site has deteriorated to the point that it no longer has outstanding universal value).[139] The system applicable to the List of World Heritage in Danger presents a significant difference from the system we have just described, namely that the listing is in the hands of the World Heritage Committee and the State concerned has no veto (Article 11(4)). While the Committee should wherever possible consult and co-operate with the State in which the site is situated,[140] the requirement of State consent of Article 11(3) for inclusion in the list does not apply in this case. In practice, given the crises that such a procedure can generate,[141] the Committee seeks to act with the consent of the State concerned.

The basic structure of the system is shown in Figure 6.5.

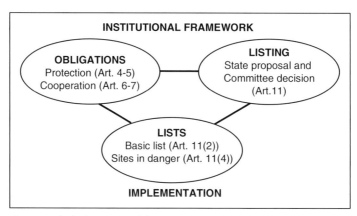

Figure 6.5: The basic structure of the WHC

[136] *Preah Vihear Case (Cambodia v. Thailand),* Judgment of 15 June 1962, ICJ Reports, p. 6.
[137] *Request for Interpretation of the Judgment of 15 June 1962 in the case concerning the Temple of Preah Vihear (Cambodia v. Thailand),* Judgment (11 November 2013), still unreported, available at: www.icj-cij.org (visited on 20 May 2014).
[138] Operational Guidelines *supra* n. 119, paras. 163–7.
[139] *Ibid.,* paras. 192–8 (the withdrawal is made by a decision of the World Heritage Committee adopted by a majority of two thirds of the members present and voting, in accordance with Art. 13(8) of the Convention).
[140] Operational Guidelines *supra* n. 119, para. 183–4.   [141] See Affolder, *supra* n. 126.

The WHC provides another illustration of the list technique in an environmental treaty. However, the WHC focuses only secondarily on the protection
of the natural environment given its practical emphasis on cultural heritage
sites. That said, the WHC is perhaps the most representative international
instrument relating to the protection of spaces as a regulatory approach.

6.4.2.3 Protection of the Antarctic environment: the Madrid Protocol

Antarctica, as a common area, has been governed since the late 1950s by the
'Antarctic Treaty system'.[142] Within this system, the 1991 Madrid Protocol is
the centrepiece of the environmental protection strategy.[143] While other
instruments have been adopted over the years, including treaties on the
protection of seals[144] and on the marine flora and fauna,[145] the Madrid
Protocol covers the entire Antarctic environment as an ecosystem and makes
it a 'natural reserve' (Article 2).[146] It is, in fact, one of the most advanced
environmental regimes, and the first to create a protected area that is truly
international.

The structure of the Madrid Protocol is similar to that of a framework
convention, with two significant differences. First, the instruments specifying the framework agreement in this case are annexes to the Protocol,
while the Protocol itself is also a further refinement of a broader framework
agreement, i.e. the Antarctic Treaty. The Madrid Protocol currently has
six annexes: Annex I (Environmental Impact Assessment), Annex II
(Conservation of Antarctic Fauna and Flora), Annex III (Waste Disposal
and Waste Management), Annex IV (Prevention of Marine Pollution),
Annex V (Management of Protected Areas) and Annex VI (Liability for
Environmental Emergencies). Second, from a substance perspective, the
text of the Protocol is more specific than the framework agreements we have
studied so far. Some additional comments will help to clarify this point.

The text of the Protocol introduces a distinction between activities involving
mineral resources, which are prohibited (Article 7), and other activities, which
may be permitted subject, *inter alia*, to the conduct of an environmental
impact assessment (Articles 3(2)–(3), 8 and Annex I). Regarding mining, the
Madrid Protocol overturns a regime adopted in 1988 on the exploitation of

---

[142] Antarctic Treaty, 1 December 1959, 402 UNTS 71.
[143] Madrid Protocol, *supra* n. 11. See J.-P. Puissochet, 'Le Protocole au Traité sur l'Antarctique
       relatif à la protection de l'environnement – Madrid' (1991) 37 *Annuaire français de droit
       international* 755.
[144] Convention on the Protection of Antarctic Seals, 1 June 1972, 1080 UNTS 175.
[145] Convention on the Conservation of Antarctic Marine Living Resources, 20 May 1980, 1329
       UNTS 47.
[146] The area of the Antarctic Treaty is defined as 'the area south of 60° South Latitude, including all
       ice shelves' (Antarctic Treaty, Art. VI, referred to by the Madrid Protocol, Art. 1(b)). Note that
       Arts. 2 and 8(1) extend protection to 'dependent and associated ecosystems' of the Antarctic
       environment.

mineral resources and introduces a moratorium on all mining activities for a period of fifty years (Articles 7 and 25).[147] As for other activities (research, tourism, other governmental or non-governmental activities),[148] they are conditioned by the obligation to conduct an environmental impact assessment ('EIA'), the scope of which depends on the risk posed by the activity considered. In this regard, Article 8(1) and Annex I distinguish three levels, depending on whether the activity has 'less than a minor or transitory impact' (EIA not required),[149] 'a minor or transitory impact' (obligation to conduct a 'preliminary assessment of impact on the environment'),[150] or 'more than a minor or transitory impact' (obligation to conduct a 'comprehensive evaluation of environmental impact').[151] Activities below the threshold may be undertaken without further delay whereas those considered to have a minor or transitory impact may only be undertaken if the preliminary EIA confirms the limited impact, and they will be subject to the establishment of appropriate monitoring procedures.[152] As for activities that are likely to have more than a minor or transitory impact, they may be authorised on the basis of a comprehensive EIA, which involves, *inter alia*, a review by the Antarctic Treaty Consultative Meeting ('ATCM'). From a practical perspective, one may ask which authority is competent to decide whether a given activity falls under one of the three categories, to conduct the EIA when applicable and, as the case may be, to authorise the activity. The Protocol leaves such decisions to States[153] and, more specifically, to the State of origin of the activity.[154] However, the ATCM has adopted a set of guidelines, last revised in 2005, to guide State practice on this question.[155]

In addition to this general regime there are special restrictions that apply to certain areas, designated in accordance with Annex V of the Madrid Protocol. This Annex, which replicates an older system developed within the Antarctic Treaty System, provides for the designation of 'Antarctic Specially Protected Areas' (or 'ASPA') and 'Antarctic Specially Managed Areas' ('ASMA'). These areas are subject to 'management plans' that define the applicable regime. While the creation of an ASPA pursues a protection objective (environmental, as well as scientific, historical or aesthetic),[156] the establishment of an ASMA is

---

[147] For a detailed discussion of the amendment system in light of the negotiations, see Puissochet *supra* n. 143, pp. 764ff.

[148] Madrid Protocol, *supra* n. 11, Arts. 3(4) and 8(2). Note that the Final Act excludes certain activities from the obligation to conduct an EIA, namely fishing, whaling, and sealing, Puissochet, *supra* n. 143, p. 766.

[149] Madrid Protocol, *supra* n. 11, Annex I, Art. 1(2).   [150] *Ibid.*, Annex I, Art. 2.

[151] *Ibid.*, Annex I, Art. 3.   [152] *Ibid.*, Annex I, Art. 2(2).

[153] *Ibid.*, Art. 8(2) and Annex I, Art. 2(1).

[154] Antarctic Treaty, *supra* n. 142, Art. VII (5) (a). Where several States participate in the activity, Art. 8(4) of the Protocol provides for an obligation to designate the State to co-ordinate the activity.

[155] Resolution 4 (2005): Updating of Guidelines for Environmental Impact Assessment in Antarctica.

[156] Madrid Protocol, *supra* n. 11, Annex V, Art. 3.

mainly concerned with improving co-ordination between the parties, includ-ing control over the cumulative impact of various activities, in order 'to minimize the impact on the environment'.[157] The procedure for the designa-tion of these areas is set out in Article 6 of Annex V. The decision is taken by the ATCM.[158] However, the authorisations to access these areas or to under-take activities are issued by the competent national authorities in accordance with the conditions established by the applicable management plan.[159]

This overview of the regime established by the Madrid Protocol concludes the presentation of the 'top-down' approach to the protection of spaces. We now turn to the less frequent 'bottom-up' approach as illustrated by the UNCCD.

6.4.3 The 'bottom-up' approach: the Convention to Combat Desertification

Mirroring the Ramsar Convention, which targets the protection of wetlands, the 1994 Convention to Combat Desertification ('UNCCD')[160] aims to protect drylands from further 'desertification', which is defined in Article 1(a) as 'land degradation in arid, semi-arid and dry sub-humid areas resulting from various factors, including climatic variations and human activities'.[161] This Convention, the origins of which can be traced back to the 1970s, was adopted as the result of the impulsion given by the 1992 Rio Summit. It entered into force in 1996 and achieved universal participation in 2012. In this section, we focus on how the Convention seeks to protect large areas of high economic and social importance.[162]

To understand the core of this treaty, one must keep in mind the type of problem it is intended to address. Arid areas cover about 40 per cent of the world's land and are inhabited by some two billion people.[163] The vast majority of these people live in developing countries and their livelihoods depend upon the productivity of the land they work. The loss of productivity due to desertification drives these people into poverty. Therefore, the under-lying motivation for the fight against desertification is not land degradation as such, but mostly its socioeconomic consequences. In this context, the creation of protected areas did not seem a suitable technique to address the problems posed by desertification. The Convention does not, however, exclude this technique (Article 5 provides for a 'top-down' strategy, even if it does not expressly mention the creation of protected areas) but it focuses on a participatory approach, the key element of which is the development of

---

[157] *Ibid.*, Annex V, Art. 4.   [158] *Ibid.*, Annex V, Art. 6(1).   [159] *Ibid.*, Annex V, Art. 7.
[160] UNCCD, *supra* n. 25.
[161] See also World Resources Institute, *Ecosystèmes et bien-être humain: Synthèse sur la désertification* (Washington: Island Press, 2005) ('Synthesis on Desertification')
[162] See A. Tal and J. A. Cohen, 'Bringing "Top-Down" to "Bottom-Up": A New Role for Environmental Legislation in Combating Desertification' (2007) 31 *Harvard Environmental Law Review* 163.
[163] Synthesis on Desertification, *supra* n. 161, p. 1.

regional, sub-regional and especially national action programmes (Articles 9 and 10). These programmes, which can be seen as a technique for the localised management of the problem, must integrate the various stakeholder groups, including those that conduct activities placing significant pressure on drylands (Article 10(2)(e)–(f)).

As in many framework agreements, the obligations under the Convention are formulated in a broad manner. However, they are specified in Annexes to the Convention that operate as protocols, as in the Madrid Protocol. The Desertification Convention currently has five annexes (Annex I: Africa; Annex II: Asia; Annex III: Latin America and the Caribbean; Annex IV: Northern Mediterranean; Annex V: Central and Eastern Europe) that all follow the same logic, namely specifying the way national, subregional and/or regional action programmes must be adopted and prescribing a certain minimum content. Annex I on Africa is the most detailed one. The reason for this is both historical (African States led the treaty-making initiative) and empirical (Africa is the continent most affected by desertification). In practice, the development of these action programmes has taken longer than expected, although now there are around a hundred national programmes and some regional and sub-regional ones. Moreover, the practical impact of these programmes and, more generally, of the 'bottom-up' approach remains to be proved.[164] This observation is at the origin of the UNCCD's '10-Year Strategy' adopted at the eighth meeting of the COP in 2007,[165] aimed at strengthening the implementation of the Convention.

The UNCCD is, unfortunately, not the only instrument facing serious implementation challenges. As discussed next, the Convention on Biological Diversity faces similar difficulties despite its important role in normative development.

6.5 The protection of biodiversity

6.5.1 A complex regulatory object

Beyond the protection of species and spaces (sites, habitats, ecosystems), the diversity of these biological resources as such had not been subject to explicit protection until the conclusion in 1992 of the Convention on Biological Diversity ('CBD').[166] The protection of this complex object was already contemplated in some soft-law instruments in the 1980s, including the World Conservation Strategy prepared by IUCN in 1980 and revised in 1991,[167] and

---

[164] See Tal and Cohen, *supra* n. 162, pp. 178–80. These authors thus propose a return to a top-down approach.

[165] See Decision 3/COP.8, 'The 10-year strategic plan and framework to enhance the implementation of the Convention', 23 October 2007, ICCD/COP(8)/16/Add.1.

[166] CBD, *supra* n. 10.

[167] See IUCN, UNEP, WWF, *World Conservation Strategy. Living Resource Conservation for Sustainable Development* (Gland: IUCN, 1980), Section 6 ('Priority Requirements: Genetic

the work of the Brundtland Commission.[168] But it was only specifically
targeted with the adoption of the CBD.[169]

Article 2 of the CBD defines biodiversity as:

> the variability among living organisms from all sources including, inter alia,
> terrestrial, marine and other aquatic ecosystems and the ecological complexes of
> which they are part: this includes diversity within species, between species and of
> ecosystems.

This definition identifies three levels at which biodiversity must be preserved,
namely (i) genetic diversity within species, (ii) species diversity, and
(iii) diversity of ecosystems. Conservation and management of these three
levels of biodiversity requires the protection of the species and habitats that
make this diversity possible. It is for this reason that the CBD is considered as
a hub that provides a common basis for many (global, regional, bilateral)
instruments for the protection of species and spaces.[170]

As for how this complex object has been approached, the CBD combines
conservation with economic considerations. The difference between these two
dimensions of biodiversity is embodied in the CBD's distinction between, on
the one hand, the 'conservation of biological diversity', which is a 'common
concern of humankind'[171] and on the other hand the 'sustainable use' of
'biological resources' under the sovereignty of the State where they are located
but subject to a system of access and benefit sharing.[172]

6.5.2 The regulation of biological diversity

The general framework described above also expresses the two main areas of
normative activity of the CBD, namely the conservation of biodiversity and
sustainable use of biological resources, in particular the management of genetic
resources. These areas are so interconnected in practice that presenting them

---

Diversity'); IUCN, *Caring for the Earth: A Strategy for Sustainable Living* (Gland: IUCN, 1991),
Chapter 4.

[168] See R. D. Munro and J. G. Lammers, *Environmental Protection and Sustainable Development:
Legal Principles and Recommendations adopted by the Experts Group on Environmental Law of
the World Commission on Environment and Development* (London: Graham & Trotman,
1987).

[169] See M.-A. Hermitte, S. Maljean-Dubois and E. Truilhé-Marengo, 'Actualités de la convention
sur la diversité biologiques: science et politique, équité, biosécurité' (2011) 57 *Annuaire
français de droit international* 399; Bowman *et al.*, *supra* n. 7, Chapter 17; E. Morgera and
E. Tsioumani, 'Yesterday, Today, and Tomorrow: Looking Afresh at the Convention on
Biological Diversity' (2010) 21 *Yearbook of International Environmental Law* 3.

[170] This explains also the various COP decisions aimed at clarifying the relationship between the
CBD and other instruments, both in the field of the protection of the life and in other matters
(e.g. UNFCCC or TRIPS).

[171] CBD, *supra* n. 10, Preamble, paras. 3 and 5, and Art. 1.

[172] *Ibid.*, Preamble, paras. 4 and 5, and Art. 1, 3 and 15. Access and benefit sharing is often
presented as a separate objective. However, from a regulatory standpoint, it is perhaps the key
component of the resource management regime set out by the CBD.

CONSERVATION OF BIODIVERSITY	SUSTAINABLE USE OF BIOLOGICAL RESOURCES		
	In general	Management of genetic resources	
- National plans (Art. 6 CBD) - Identification and monitoring (Art. 7 CBD) - Conservation *in situ* (art. 8 CBD) and *ex situ* (Art. 9 CBD) - Invasive species (Art. 8(h) CBD and Guiding principles, decision CP.VI/23)	- National plans (Art. 6 CBD) - Sustainable use (Art. 10 CBD and Guiding principles) - Incentive measures (Art. 11 CBD) - EIA (Art. 14)	- Access and benefit sharing (Art. 15, 16 and 19 CBD and Nagoya Protocol (2010))	- Biosafety risk management - (Protocol of Cartagena (2000) and Protocol of Kuala Lumpur-Nagoya on liability (2010))

Figure 6.6: The basic structure of the CBD

separately would obscure rather than clarify the operation of the treaty. From an analytical standpoint, it is therefore preferable to distinguish three axes along which the Convention and its evolution can be studied.

The first axis takes up the distinction mentioned above between the conservation of biological diversity and the sustainable use of biological and genetic resources. This first perspective helps to understand the basic structure of the text of the Convention as well as of the instruments that have been developed under its aegis. Figure 6.6 shows the basic structure, highlighting some important provisions under the Convention.

It is difficult to determine whether one of the objectives of the Convention has taken precedence over another, whether from a normative standpoint or in practice. As noted earlier, the two objectives are closely linked. For example, the risks associated with certain uses of genetic resources, such as biotechnology, are covered by the Cartagena Protocol on Biosafety, but this instrument is located at the intersection between conservation and sustainable use. It takes as a starting-point that genetic resources can indeed be put to use but, at the same time, it seeks to reduce the risks associated with genetically modified organisms ('GMOs'). A similar analysis could be conducted in respect of the Nagoya Protocol or of several guiding principles adopted over the years by the COP. To understand the relationship between the two objectives and the normative work of the CBD, one must use analytical categories that are more specific than the broad objectives of conservation and sustainable use.

The second axis focuses on a number of 'thematic' questions that the COP has addressed over time, as well as on 'multisectoral' questions that cut across these themes. It is at this level that we can understand the normative practice of the CBD. Work on these issues is approached in a largely similar manner. The COP can decide to engage in a work programme which, depending on the case, has some degree of institutionalisation (permanent working groups, *ad hoc* group of experts, informal groups) and is often linked to the scientific subsidiary body under the Convention or the working group on the review of implementation, itself created by a decision of the COP. In order to find one's way in this dense administrative 'forest', it is important to distinguish between, on the one hand, thematic work programmes, each focusing on one type of biome (marine and coastal biodiversity, forestry, arid lands, inland waters, islands or mountains) or on the key issue of agriculture and, on the other hand, cross-cutting or multisectoral programmes, some of which are in charge of permanent working groups (e.g. the groups on Article 8(j) or on protected areas). The picture that emerges is quite different and covers very general questions, such as the sustainable use of biodiversity and the ecosystem approach, and more specific issues such as invasive alien species, the transfer of technology or impact assessment. It is through these programmes that the CBD has developed its important normative activity. Indeed, at the risk of oversimplification, one could call the system created by the CBD a 'normative factory', insofar as both the Convention and the bodies established under its aegis focus on the development of numerous standards, guidelines and other measures to guide the adoption of domestic measures.[173]

The latter is also the starting-point of the third axis, which goes from a conception of the CBD as a normative factory to a model where the obligations under the Convention and its protocols are effectively implemented by a control system. A first attempt to develop a system of implementation monitoring was made in 2002, following the adoption of the Strategic Plan, including the establishment of the Working Group on the Review of Implementation.[174] However, these first steps are far from sufficient, as demonstrated by the failure to achieve the '2010 target' of reducing the rate of biodiversity loss. A second attempt was launched at the tenth COP held in Nagoya. A significant part of the work focused on the creation of structures to monitor the implementation (and thus harden) the obligations of the Convention, such as a non-compliance procedure,[175] specific indicators allowing for the assessment of progress towards the 'Aichi Targets on Biological Diversity' adopted at this meeting,[176] regional workshops to develop strategies for biodiversity management,[177] or a system of accountability.[178]

---

[173] See the section of the CBD website on guidelines and tools: http://www.cbd.int/guidelines/ (last visited on 10 December 2013).

[174] See Decision CP VII/30 'Strategic Plan: Future Evaluation of Progress', 13 April 2004, UNEP/CBD/COP/DEC/VII/30.

[175] CP decision X/2 'Strategic Plan 2011–2020 and the Aichi Targets on Biological Diversity', 27 October 2010, UNEP/CBD/COP/DEC/X/2, subsections 14 ('Decides that future meetings of the COP shall review progress in the implementation of the strategic plan for biodiversity 2011–2020') and 15 ('Decides to consider, at its eleventh meeting, the need for and possible development of additional mechanisms or enhancements to existing mechanisms . . . to enable parties to meet their commitments under the convention and to implement the Strategic Plan for Biodiversity 2011–2020').

[176] Decision CP XI/3 'Monitoring Progress in Implementation of the Strategic Plan for Biodiversity 2011–2020 and the Aichi Biodiversity Targets' (advanced version), Annex.

[177] Morgera and Tsioumani, *supra* n. 169, p. 10.   [178] See Section 6.5.3.

6.5.3 The regulation of GMOs

The potential risks posed by GMOs had already been identified when the CBD was concluded. Articles 8(g) and 19(3) provided indeed for the adoption of a protocol:

> setting out appropriate procedures, including, in particular, advance informed agreement, in the field of the safe transfer, handling and use of any living modified organism resulting from biotechnology that may have adverse effect on the conservation and sustainable use of biological diversity (Article 19(3)).

At the second COP, a special working group was established on this issue.[179] The work of this group took several years because of the tensions between exporting countries (the so-called 'Miami Group') and importers of GMOs (including the majority of developing countries but also the European Community). Finally, in January 2000, during an extraordinary meeting of the COP, the Cartagena Protocol on Biosafety was signed.[180] Despite the large number of States parties to the Protocol (currently over 160), some major exporters of GMOs (such as Argentina, Australia, Canada or the United States) are not bound. This element must be emphasised, since it has a significant impact on the operation of the Protocol.

The system established by the Protocol is relatively simple: the transboundary movement of two categories of GMOs is subject to two control procedures.[181] To understand this system, it is necessary to clarify these two elements. Regarding the categories of GMOs, the issue was much debated during the negotiation of the Protocol. Two views, one restrictive (supported by the exporting countries) and the other expansive (supported by the importing countries), were expressed. The solution is a compromise between these two positions. The Protocol is not limited to the regulation of living modified organisms ('LMOs',[182] including seeds), which are intended for intentional introduction as such into the environment, with the ensuing risks for biodiversity. It also covers LMOs intended for food or feed (unprocessed agricultural products) or processing in the importing country (flours, oils, etc.). Conversely, the Protocol does not govern goods produced from LMOs in the exporting country (e.g. tomato sauce, flour, oils), pharmaceuticals,[183] LMOs in transit,[184] or those intended for 'contained' use.[185]

As to the second element, the two categories of LMOs governed by the Protocol are subject to two separate procedures. Transboundary movements

---

[179] CP. II/5, 'Consideration of the Need for and Modalities of a Protocol for the Safe Transfer, Handling and Use of Living Modified Organisms', UNEP/CBD/COP/2/19.

[180] Biosafety Protocol, *supra* n. 5. See C. Bail *et al.* (eds.), *The Cartagena Protocol on Biosafety – Reconciling Trade in Biotechnology with Environment and Development?* (London: Earthscan, 2002).

[181] Biosafety Protocol, *supra* n. 5, Art. 3(k).   [182] *Ibid.*, Art. 3(g).   [183] *Ibid.*, Art. 5.

[184] *Ibid.*, Art. 6(1).   [185] *Ibid.*, Art. 6(2) and 3(b).

of LMOs for intentional introduction into the environment of the importing State are subject to a detailed procedure of 'advance informed agreement' (Articles 7–10, 12).[186] This system can be compared to that established by the Basel Convention,[187] although unlike the Cartagena Protocol on Biosafety, the Basel Convention identifies regulated waste in lists drawn up internationally. The main features of this procedure can be summarised in seven points: (i) consent must be obtained prior to the transboundary movement (the object of regulation is the 'transboundary movement' and not a type of GMO which subsequently becomes authorised); (ii) the notification initiative falls on the economic operator who intends to export the LMO (which must be subject to regulation in accordance with the Protocol by the exporting State);[188] (iii) the importing State must acknowledge receipt of the notification within a certain time, and indicate the regime (Protocol regime or the regime established by domestic law) that will govern the transboundary movement;[189] (iv) within the same timeframe set for the acknowledgment, the importing State must inform the exporter of its decision to allow the transboundary movement[190] in writing,[191] which can either lead to the authorisation (if applicable, under specific conditions) or the prohibition of the intended movement;[192] (v) the decision can be taken even in the absence of clear scientific evidence about the effects of the LMO in question, according to the precautionary principle, and it may be reconsidered at any time;[193] (vi) it must be communicated to the exporter as well as to States parties to the Protocol (through the Biosafety Clearing House ('BCH')); (vii) the Protocol states, finally, that the silence of the importing State shall not constitute consent.[194] This procedure is potentially burdensome, especially if it were to apply to all LMOs without distinction, including agricultural products from major exporting countries. An essential component of the compromise reached in negotiations was to submit LMOs intended for human or animal consumption (including agricultural products) to a simplified procedure provided for in Article 11 of the Protocol. This procedure is similar to the general PIC procedure (by substance) set out by the Rotterdam Convention.[195] The focus of the procedure is not on the transboundary movement but on the LMO in question and States must communicate to the BCH the permissions granted to their importers, including the conditions under which imports are permitted (such as the validity period of authorisation or stipulations made in respect of product labelling). In practice, this procedure is less burdensome because one permit can be used for multiple imports of the same product. Note that the Protocol offers the possibility to

---

[186] See Chapter 3. [187] See Chapter 7. [188] Biosafety Protocol, *supra* n. 5, Art. 8 and Annex I.
[189] *Ibid.*, Art. 9(2)(c). [190] *Ibid.*, Art. 10(2)(b). [191] *Ibid.*, Art. 10(2)(a). [192] *Ibid.*, Art. 10(3).
[193] *Ibid.*, Art. 10(6) and 12(1). Article 15 and Annex III of the Protocol provide a framework for risk assessment as a basis for decisions pursuant to Article 10. Note that the risk assessment can be incumbent upon the exporter or the notifier.
[194] *Ibid.*, Art. 9(4) and 10(5). [195] See Chapter 7.

apply a simplified procedure to other LMOs through a communication by each importing country to the BCH identifying the LMOs it does not intend to submit to the advance informed agreement or the cases where a transboundary movement may proceed on the basis of a simple notification.[196]

One may ask whether these measures concerned with the prevention of GMOs-related risks are sufficient and, in particular, what happens when the introduction of such organisms results in harm to biological diversity or human health. Article 19 of the Protocol urged States parties to consider the question of liability and to develop international rules and procedures. This process took longer than expected and only led to a modest instrument with minimal impact on domestic law. Indeed, the Kuala Lumpur Supplementary Protocol, signed in October 2010, does not establish an international regime of liability for damage caused by transboundary movements of LMOs, whether intentional or not, as some had hoped. Strongly influenced by the companies that produce these organisms as well as by major exporting countries, the Protocol delegates most of the measures of intervention to a compensatory regime to be established by the domestic law of each State (Article 12).[197]

6.5.4 Access to genetic resources and benefit sharing

6.5.4.1 The 'seed wars'

The issue of access to genetic resources is very important both as a major regulatory challenge and, more generally, as an illustration of the key role of the CBD in one of the great debates of our time, namely food security.[198]

For centuries, varieties of seeds with a greater yield, identified by a slow process of intergenerational selection of the best specimens, were considered part of the 'common heritage of mankind'[199] in that access to these varieties and subsequent use was free. This approach was not necessarily the result of a shared vision, but the consequence of the practical challenges involved in restraining access to seed varieties. Indeed, seeds are sources of life. They turn into plants and generate new seeds that may be sold (for an end-use such as consumption or processing) or replanted. Farmers only needed to

---

[196] Biosafety Protocol, *supra* n. 5, Art. 13(1).

[197] See Hermitte *et al.*, *supra* n. 169, pp. 426ff; S. Jungcurt and N. Schabus, 'Liability and Redress in the Context of the Cartagena Protocol on Biosafety' (2010) 19 *Review of European Community and International Environmental Law* 197.

[198] See J. Kloppenburg, *First the Seed: The Political Economy of Plant Biotechnology, 1492–2000* (Cambridge University Press, 1988); J. Kloppenburg, 'Impeding Dispossession, Enabling Repossession: Biological Open Source and the Recovery of Seed Sovereignty' (2010) 10 *Journal of Agrarian Change* 367.

[199] Note that the programme conveyed by the concept of the 'common heritage of mankind' is not always the same. In respect of the seabed beyond the jurisdiction of States (the 'Area'), the regulation of access and exploitation are very different. See Chapter 3.

acquire a better variety of seed once. Thereafter, they could simply keep some of the seeds from the harvest and replant them, since these seeds were able to reproduce indefinitely. However, during the twentieth century this initial situation underwent profound changes driven by two main factors.

The first factor is the development of technologies to limit the reproducibility of seeds and, hence, the ability to replant. Whether through hybridisation (modification of seeds to limit subsequent reproduction), sterilisation (genetic modification of a variety of seed to make it sterile after its first use or conditioning reproducibility on the use of certain chemical components that are easier to control by the industry) or marking (a system to identify plants from a variety of marketed seeds), the possibility of replanting has been severely restricted. In addition, for a variety of reasons ranging from the impact of modified seeds on less resistant seeds, the weakening of public research in this field and very aggressive marketing strategies adopted by the industry, the use of modified seeds led to the development of monocultures or, in other words, to a situation where only a small number of seeds were used everywhere. A reduced number of seeds make plants more vulnerable to pests because the latter can more quickly adapt to the characteristics of the new variety and become capable of drastically reducing yields after a few years. The ensuing result is that new varieties of seeds can only provide high yields for a limited period of time (a few years) after which a new variety is needed on the market.

The second factor is of a legal nature. As it was now technically possible to limit the ability to replant, the next step was to formulate this limitation in legal terms. The vehicle used for this purpose was the granting of intellectual property rights ('IPRs') on seeds commercialised at the national[200] and international[201] levels. These rights (breeders' rights) came into direct collision with the rights of farmers. The replanting of seeds had thus become a breach of the IPRs protecting the varieties of seeds commercialised. Of course, these developments were extremely controversial. The developing countries that had allowed, under the common heritage approach, the collection of genetic resources in their territory now faced the need to respect proprietary rights on seed varieties held by multinational companies based in developed countries.

It is in this confrontational context that a number of international instruments were negotiated, including the CBD and the Nagoya Protocol. It must be

---

[200] See TRIPS Council, Review of the Provisions of Article 27.3 b): Illustrative List of Questions Prepared by the Secretariat – Revision, Document IP/C/W/273/Rev.1, 18 February 2003.

[201] International Convention for the Protection of New Varieties of Plants of December 2, 1961, as revised at Geneva on 10 November 1972, 23 October 1978 and 19 March 1991 ('UPOV Convention'), available at: www.ecolex.org (TRE-001119), Agreement on Trade-Related Aspects of Intellectual Property Trade, 15 April 1994, 1869 UNTS 299 ('TRIPS'), Art. 27(3)(b).

noted that the controversy concerns not only the status of genetic resources ('common heritage of mankind' vs. 'sovereignty and ownership') or its legal consequences ('access', 'patentability', 'right to replant') but also the different forms in which a given status can be spelled out. Indeed, a possibility explored in the FAO in the early 1980s was to extend the status of 'common heritage' to products derived from the use of genetic resources, including plant varieties developed by multinationals.[202] At the other extreme, a second option was to subject not only plant varieties but also genetic resources to a system of appropriation. This is the approach that has been followed by the CBD (and its Nagoya Protocol) and, more specifically, by the International Treaty on Plant Genetic Resources,[203] as discussed next.

6.5.4.2 The role of international law

What is the role of international law in the 'seeds war'? As is often the case, the shaping of the law was one of the main battlegrounds.[204] In the late 1980s, it became increasingly clear that the model of ownership had better chances to prevail and the frontline shifted to specific arrangements governing access to genetic resources and the sharing of benefits. In this context, two main questions must be examined, namely (i) the object concerned by the regulation and (ii) the arrangements governing access.

The direct object of the system embodied in Article 15 of the CBD are the 'genetic resources', which Article 2 defines as 'any material of plant, animal, microbial or other origin containing functional units of heredity ... with actual or potential value'. This object is the broad *genus* within which a specific category, the 'Plant Genetic Resources for Food and Agriculture',[205] is subject to special regulations (the 'ITPGR'). The characterisation of 'genetic resources' as the object of protection must also take into account another related object of the CBD, namely 'knowledge, innovations and practices of indigenous and local communities embodying traditional lifestyles relevant for the conservation and sustainable use of biological diversity' (Article 8(j)). The link between 'genetic resources' and 'traditional knowledge' is explained in Article 3 of the Nagoya Protocol, which covers 'traditional knowledge associated with genetic resources'. In practice, this

[202] See J. R. Kloppenburg and D. L. Kleinman, 'Seeds of Controversy: National Property vs Common Heritage', in J. R. Kloppenburg (ed.), *Seeds and Sovereignty: The Use and Control of Plant Genetic Resources* (Durham, NC: Duke University Press, 1988), p. 174.

[203] International Treaty on Plant Genetic Resources for Food and Agriculture, 3 November 2001, 2400 UNTS 379 ('ITPGR').

[204] See M.-A. Hermitte, 'La construction du droit des ressources génétiques – Exclusivismes et échanges au fil du temps', in M.-A. Hermitte and P. Kahn (eds.), *Les ressources génétiques et le droit dans les rapports Nord-Sud* (Brussels: Bruylant, 2004).

[205] ITPGR, *supra* n. 203, Art. 1. It must be noted that genetic resources of animal origin or those of plant origin used for medicinal purposes are not covered by the ITPGR.

link concerns the knowledge of traditional medicine, agricultural practices and, more generally, the fight against insects or personal care.[206] Thus, as suggested by the foregoing observations, the negotiations have gone beyond the context of seeds to apply to other controversial areas, especially traditional medicinal knowledge and the genetic resources that are used for this purpose.[207]

The second aspect concerns the arrangements governing access to the regulated object. The general scheme provided for in Article 15 of the CBD has been further specified by the Nagoya Protocol and the ITPGR. The bedrock of this system is the right of the State where the resources are located to regulate access, either to grant it or to deny it.[208] More specifically, access is conditional on the consent of the State of origin of the genetic resources[209] and, where appropriate, of the 'indigenous and local communities' involved.[210] In turn, this depends on the arrangements regarding the sharing of the benefits arising from the use of the resources accessed (with the State of origin and, where appropriate, also with indigenous and local communities).[211] In practice, the terms of the benefit sharing, which may include monetary rebates, licences to use IPRs or even co-ownership, are determined by agreement on a case-by-case basis with minimal contents often prescribed by law. Plant genetic resources for food and agriculture are subject to a special regime structured around a 'Multilateral System of Access and Benefit-sharing' (ITPGR, Article 10). This system, which applies to a list of resources identified in an Annex to the ITPGR (representing approximately 80 per cent of human consumption), aims to facilitate transactions relating to these resources by limiting the transaction costs involved in negotiating, on a case-by-case basis, access and benefit sharing agreements.

Such are the compromises reached within the overall framework of the resource appropriation model. It is difficult to assess specifically the performance of the systems thus established. Some studies suggest mixed or unsatisfactory results,[212] but there are also cases where true synergies

---

[206] Hermitte *et al.*, *supra* n. 169, p. 415.

[207] See S. Safrin, 'Hyperownership in a Time of Biotechnological Promise: The International Conflict to Control the Building Blocks of Life' (2004) 98 *American Journal of International Law* 641.

[208] See CBD, *supra* n. 10, Art. 15(1); Nagoya Protocol, *supra* n. 6, Art. 6(1), ITPGR, *supra* n. 203, Art. 10(1).

[209] CBD, *supra* n. 10, Art. 15(5); Nagoya Protocol, *supra* n. 6, Art. 6(1).

[210] Nagoya Protocol, *supra* n. 6, Arts. 6(2) and 7.

[211] CBD, *supra* n. 10, Arts. 15(7), 16 and 19; Nagoya Protocol, *supra* n. 6, Art. 5. Article 13(2) of the Protocol introduced a written certification of the legality of access to regulated resources.

[212] See *When Nature Goes Public: The Making and Unmaking of Bioprospecting in Mexico* (Princeton University Press, 2003); S. Greene, 'Indigenous People Incorporated? Culture as Politics, Culture as Property in Biopharmaceutical Bioprospecting' (2004) 45 *Current Anthropology* 211.

have been achieved.[213] For present purposes, it is above all the role played by the CBD with respect to food security as well as the close links between biodiversity conservation and resource exploitation that must be highlighted.

Select bibliography

Affolder, N., 'Mining and the World Heritage Convention: Democratic Legitimacy and Treaty Compliance' (2007) 24 *Pace Environmental Law Review* 35.

Anvar, S. L., *Semences et droit*, Doctoral dissertation (University of Paris I, 2008).

Bail, C., R. Falkner and H. Marquard (eds.), *The Cartagena Protocol on Biosafety – Reconciling Trade in Biotechnology with Environment and Development?* (London: Earthscan, 2002).

Batisse, M. and G. Bolla, *L'invention du patrimoine mondial. Cahiers du Club d'Histoire No. 2* (Paris: AAFU, 2003).

Bekhechi, M., 'Une nouvelle étape dans le développement du droit international de l'environnement: la Convention sur la desertification' (1997) 101 *Revue générale de droit international public* 5.

Birnie, P., *International Regulation of Whaling: From Conservation of Whaling to Conservation of Whales and Regulation of Whale Watching, 2 vols.* (Oceana Publications, 1985).

Boer, B. and G. Wiffen, *Heritage Law in Australia* (Oxford University Press, 2006).

Bourrinet, J. and S. Maljean-Dubois (eds.), *La régulation du commerce international des OGM* (Paris: La Documentation française, 2002).

Bowman, M., 'The Ramsar Convention on Wetlands: Has it Made a Difference' (2002) *Yearbook of International Co-operation on Environment and Development* 61.

'"Normalizing" the International Convention for the Regulation of Whaling' (2008) 29 *Michigan Journal of International Law* 293.

Bowman, M., P. Davies and C. Redgwell, *Lyster's International Wildlife Law* (Cambridge University Press, 2nd edn, 2010).

Chandler, M., 'The Biodiversity Convention: Selected Issues of Interest to the International Lawyer' (1993) 4 *Colorado Journal of International Law and Policy* 141.

Coughlin, M. D., 'Using the Merck-INBio Agreement to Clarify the Convention on Biological Diversity' (1993) 31 *Columbia Journal of Transnational Law* 337.

Davis, P. G. G. and C. Redgwell, 'The International Legal Regulation of Straddling Fish Stocks' (1996) 67 *British Yearbook of International Law* 199.

Farrier, D. and L. Tucker, 'Wise Use of Wetlands under the Ramsar Convention: A Challenge for Meaningful Implementation of International Law' (2000) 12 *Journal of Environmental Law* 21.

---

[213] See M. D. Coughlin, 'Using the Merck-INBio agreement to clarify the Convention on Biological Diversity' (1993) 31 *Columbia Journal of Transnational Law* 337. See also R. Lewis-Lettington and S. Mwanyiki, *Case Studies on Access and Benefit Sharing* (Rome: International Plant Genetic Resources Institute, 2006).

Francioni, F., 'The Madrid Protocol on the Protection of the Antarctic Environment' (1993) 28 *Texas International Law Journal* 47.

Francioni, F. and F. Lenzerini (eds.), *The 1972 World Heritage Convention: A Commentary* (Oxford University Press, 2008).

'The Destruction of the Buddhas of Bamiyan and International Law' (2003) 14 *European Journal of International Law* 619.

Gillespie, A., 'The Management of Protected Areas of International Significance' 10 *New Zealand Journal of Environmental Law* 93.

Glennon, M., 'Has International Law Failed the Elephant?' (1990) 84 *American Journal of International Law* 1.

Glowka, L., F. Burhenne-Guilmin, H. Synge and J. A. McNeely, *A Guide to the Convention on Biological Diversity* (Gland: IUCN, 1996).

Goodwin, E. J., 'The World Heritage Convention, the Environment and Compliance' (2009) 20 *Colorado Journal of International Law and Policy* 157.

Hagen, P. E. and J. Wiener, 'The Cartagena Protocol on Biosafety: New Rules for International Trade in Living Modified Organisms' (2000) 12 *Georgetown International Environmental Law Review* 697.

Harrison, J., *Making the Law of the Sea* (Cambridge University Press, 2011).

Hermitte, M.-A., 'La construction du droit des ressources génétiques – Exclusivismes et échanges au fil du temps', in M.-A. Hermitte and P. Kahn (eds.), *Les ressources génétiques et le droit dans les rapports Nord-Sud* (Brussels: Bruylant, 2004).

'La convention sur la diversité biologique' (1992) 38 *Annuaire français de droit international* 844.

Hermitte, M.-A., I. Doussan, S. Mabile, S. Maljean-Dubois, C. Noiville and F. Bellivier, 'La convention sur la diversité biologique a quinze ans' (2006) 52 *Annuaire français de droit international* 351.

Hermitte, M.-A., S. Maljean-Dubois and E. Truilhé-Marengo, 'Actualités de la convention sur la diversité biologiques: science et politique, équité, biosécurité' (2011) 57 *Annuaire français de droit international* 399.

Iles, A., 'The Desertification Convention: A Deeper Focus on Social Aspects of Environmental Degradation?' (1995) 36 *Harvard International Law Journal* 205.

Jungcurt, S. and N. Schabus, 'Liability and Redress in the Context of the Cartagena Protocol on Biosafety' (2010) 19 *Review of European Community and International Environmental Law* 197.

Kimball, L., 'Institutional Linkages between the Convention on Biological Diversity and Other International Agreements' (1997) 6 *Review of European Community and International Environmental Law* 239.

Kloppenburg, J., *First the Seed: The Political Economy of Plant Biotechnology, 1492–2000* (Cambridge University Press, 1988).

'Impeding Dispossession, Enabling Repossession: Biological Open Source and the Recovery of Seed Sovereignty' (2010) 10 *Journal of Agrarian Change* 367.

Kloppenburg, J. and D. L. Kleinman, 'Seeds of Controversy: National Property vs Common Heritage', in J. R. Kloppenburg (ed.), *Seeds and Sovereignty: The Use and Control of Plant Genetic Resources* (Durham: Duke University Press, 1988), pp. 172–203.

Konate, A., 'L'Afrique et la Convention des Nations Unies sur la lutte contre la desertification' (2000) 12 *African Journal of International and Comparative Law* 718.

Lewis-Lettington, R. and S. Mwanyiki, *Case Studies on Access and Benefit Sharing* (Rome: International Plant Genetic Resources Institute, 2006).

Matthews, V. T., *The Ramsar Convention on Wetlands: Its History and Development* (Gland: Ramsar Convention Secretariat, 1993).

McConnel, F., *The Biodiversity Convention. A Negotiating History* (The Hague: Kluwer, 1996).

McGraw, D., 'The CBD: Key Characteristics and Implications for Development' (2002) 11 *Review of European Community and International Environmental Law* 17.

Momtaz, D., 'L'Accord relatif à la conservation et la gestion des stocks de poissons chevauchants et grands migrateurs' (1995) 41 *Annuaire français de droit international* 676.

Morgera, E. and E. Tsioumani, 'Yesterday, Today, and Tomorrow: Looking Afresh at the Convention on Biological Diversity' (2010) 21 *Yearbook of International Environmental Law* 3.

Orrego Vicuña, F., *The Changing International Law of High Seas Fisheries* (Cambridge University Press, 2005).

Peyroux, E., 'La chasse à la baleine dans le droit international public actuel' (1975) 79 *Revue générale de droit international public* 92.

Puissochet, J.-P., 'Le Protocole au Traité sur l'Antarctique relatif à la protection de l'environnement – Madrid' (1991) 37 *Annuaire français de droit international* 755.

Ramsar Convention Secretariat, *The Ramsar Convention Manual* (Gland: Ramsar Convention Secretariat, 6th edn, 2013).

Rayfuse, R., 'Biological Resources', in D. Bodansky, J. Brunnée and E. Hey (eds.), *The Oxford Handbook of International Environmental Law* (Oxford University Press, 2007), pp. 362–93.

Redgwell, C., 'Environmental Protection in Antarctica: The 1991 Protocol' (1994) 43 *International and Comparative Law Quarterly* 599.

Safrin, S., 'Hyperownership in a Time of Biotechnological Promise: The International Conflict to Control the Building Blocks of Life' (2004) 98 *American Journal of International Law* 641.

Sand, P. H., 'Wither CITES? The Evolution of a Treaty Regime in the Borderline between Trade and the Environment' (1997) 8 *European Journal of International Law* 29.

Tal, A. and J. A. Cohen, 'Bringing "Top-Down" to "Bottom-Up": A New Role for Environmental Legislation in Combating Desertification' (2007) 31 *Harvard Environmental Law Review* 163.

Verschuuren, J., 'The Case of Transboundary Wetlands Under the Ramsar Convention: Keep the Lawyers Out!' (2008) 19 *Colorado Journal of International Environmental Law and Policy* 49.

Wijnstekers, W., *L'évolution de la CITES* (Budakeszi CIC, 9th edn, 2011).

Wood, H. W., 'The United Nations World Charter for Nature: The Developing Nations' Initiative to Establish Protections for the Environment' (1984/1985) 12 *Ecology Law Quarterly* 977.

Wyman, K. M., 'The Property Rights Challenge in Marine Fisheries' (2008) 50 *Arizona Law Review* 511.

Young, O. R., 'Effectiveness of International Environmental Regimes: Existing Knowledge, Cutting-Edge Themes, and Research Strategies' (2011) 108 *Proceedings of the National Academy of Sciences* 19853.

7

Dangerous substances and activities

7.1 Introduction

As discussed in previous chapters, the regulation of the sources of atmospheric, water and soil pollution has been one of the primary concerns of international environmental law, from the perspective of both customary and treaty law.[1] This 'first generation' of environmental problems has, in fact, led to the adoption of many domestic laws and international instruments. In general, we can consider this body of law from two different angles, namely the protection of a specific object[2] and the regulation of a particular source of pollution. A combination of these two angles is also possible (for example, the protection of a specific object from a specific source of pollution). A few examples will illustrate this point.

An important aspect of the instruments that we have studied in previous chapters is that they are designed to protect a certain object against various threats, including pollution (e.g. as a factor in habitat degradation). This applies, in particular, to many conventions on the protection of species, spaces and biodiversity. Conversely, other instruments are structured in such a way as to regulate specific sources of pollution (e.g. operational discharges, oil spills, dumping or the incineration of wastes, emissions of certain substances that pollute the atmosphere, the production and consumption of certain substances that deplete the ozone layer, or the emission of certain substances that have an adverse effect on the climate). The goal pursued by these instruments is often to protect a specific object (e.g. the marine environment, the ozone layer, the climate system). However, their focus is on some (not all) threats to such objects,[3] which have often been added progressively at a pace dictated by the understanding of their environmental implications as well as by political

---

[1] See P.-M. Dupuy, 'Overview of the Existing Customary Legal Regime Regarding International Pollution', in D. B. Magraw (ed.), *International Law and Pollution* (Philadelphia: University of Pennsylvania Press, 1991), pp. 61–89. See also Chapters 1 and 3.

[2] See K. Kummer, *International Management of Hazardous Wastes* (Oxford University Press, 1995), pp. 25–6 and Chapter 5.

[3] See, e.g., the Montreal Protocol on Substances that Deplete the Ozone Layer, 16 September 1987, 1522 UNTS 28 (which provides for specific substances in Annexes A, B, C, and E in order to protect the environment) or the Kyoto Protocol to the UN Convention on Climate Change, 11

feasibility. Alternatively, the regulation of these pollutants may be aimed at the protection of various objects simultaneously, whether they are clearly identified or not.[4]

This chapter focuses on the regulation of certain substances and activities with specific hazards or risks, not as regards a specific object but, more broadly, the environment and/or public health. Among the many instruments potentially relevant in this connection, we focus only on those aimed at the prevention and control of these substances and activities. Instruments providing for compensation for damages resulting from the use of these substances or the conduct of such activities will be studied in Chapter 8. First, we discuss the type of problems addressed by the international regulation of dangerous substances and activities as well as the overall structure of such regulation (7.2). At present, there is no comprehensive global regulation, despite many attempts, over the last twenty years, to achieve some co-ordination and harmonisation at the international level (7.3). Notwithstanding the fragmented nature of the international regulation in force, which targets substances (chemicals,[5] heavy metals[6] and certain types of waste[7]) or specific risks (industrial accidents[8] and nuclear energy[9]), the existing instruments encompass the entire life cycle (production, use, consumption, storage, transport, disposal) of the regulated substances (7.4).

December 1997, 2302 UNTS 148 (which provides for specific substances in Annex A with a view to protecting the climate).

[4] The Protocols to the Convention on Long-Distance Transboundary Air Pollution, 13 November 1979, 1302 UNTS 217 ('LRTAP Convention') target specific substances, but the object of protection is not always clearly identified. Even the Gothenburg Protocol (30 November 1999, available at www.ecolex.org (TRE-001328)), which is arguably the most sophisticated protocol to the LRTAP Convention, follows a structure that combines the regulation of specific substances to combat several problems – acidification, eutrophication, tropospheric ozone – affecting various specific objects. See Chapter 5.

[5] See, in particular, the Rotterdam Convention on the Prior Informed Consent Procedure for Certain Hazardous Chemicals and Pesticides in International Trade, 10 September 1998, 2244 UNTS 337 ('Rotterdam Convention' or 'PIC Convention'); Stockholm Convention on Persistent Organic Pollutants, 22 May 2001, 2256 UNTS 119 ('Stockholm Convention' or 'POP Convention').

[6] Protocol to the 1979 Convention on Long-Range Transboundary Air Pollution on Heavy Metals, 24 June 1998, 2237 UNTS 4; Minamata Convention on Mercury, 10 October 2013, available at: www.mercuryconvention.org (last visited on 15 January 2014).

[7] Basel Convention on the Control of Transboundary Movements of Hazardous Wastes and their Disposal, 22 March 1989, 1673 UNTS 57 ('Basel Convention'); Bamako Convention on the Ban on the Import into Africa and the Control of Transboundary Movement and Management of Hazardous Wastes within Africa, 30 January 1991, 30 ILM 773 ('Bamako Convention').

[8] Convention of the United Nations Commission for Europe on the Transboundary Effects of Industrial Accidents, 17 March 1992, 2105 UNTS 457 ('Convention on Industrial Accidents').

[9] Convention on Early Notification of a Nuclear Accident, 26 September 1986, 1439 UNTS 275 ('Convention on Early Notification'); Convention on Assistance in Case of a Nuclear Accident or Radiological Emergency, 26 September 1986, 1457 UNTS 133 ('Convention on Assistance'); Convention on Nuclear Safety, 17 June 1994, 1963 UNTS 293; Joint Convention on the Safety of Spent Fuel Management and on the Safety of Radioactive Waste Management, 5 September 1997, available at: www.ecolex.org (TRE-001273) ('Joint Convention').

7.2 Object and structure of the international regulatory framework

The production and large-scale use of chemicals is one of the hallmarks of our time. During the second half of the twentieth century, such production increased exponentially. Valued at approximately 171 billions of dollars in 1970, it amounted to approximately 4.12 trillion by 2010.[10] In other words, in some forty years, the value of this production multiplied by a factor of twenty-four. Moreover, chemical products pervade our contemporary economies. These products are not only increasingly present in industrial processes and consumer products but, more generally, their function as a component of economic development has become essential.[11] In this context, one may ask whether the right structures are in place to ensure that the risks posed by this growing production and use are minimised and kept under control. The answer to this question must take into consideration, among other things, the following three observations.

A first observation concerns the way we assess these risks. In this context, a distinction must be made between 'risk assessment' and 'risk management'. The former is the evaluation of the potential hazard a substance may pose to human health or the environment. Over time, the range of effects that have been taken into account in assessing the level of risk has become wider. Early on (during the 1940s and 1950s), regulation essentially dealt with the toxicity of a substance (i.e. the adverse effects caused – in the short term – by exposure to a substance). During the 1960s and 1970s, risk assessments began to take into account the carcinogenicity of a substance resulting from exposure over the long term.[12] More recently, the understanding of risk has evolved towards the consideration of the combined effects of exposure to several substances (even at levels considered as acceptable for a single substance) as well as the potential endocrine disruption of some of these substances (their ability to behave like hormones – 'hormone mimicking' – and therefore influence various processes such as sexuality, reproduction, growth or behaviour).[13] This trend suggests two conclusions. On the one hand, our understanding of risk is nowadays more sophisticated than in the middle of the twentieth century, which is undoubtedly reassuring. On the other hand, one cannot underestimate the challenges presented (the risks still not understood) by the proliferation of chemicals in the economy. We cannot rule out the emergence, in the future, of other adverse effects that were not anticipated when a given chemical was released. At present, however, our understanding rests on the

---

[10] UNEP, *Global Chemical Outlook: Synthesis Report (2012)* ('GCO Report'), p. 9.

[11] *Ibid.*, p. 13.

[12] Carcinogenicity was the dominant element in the understanding of the toxicity of a chemical product until the 1990s. See T. Colborn, D. Dumanoski and J. Peterson Myers, *Our Stolen Future* (New York: Dutton, 1996), p. 19.

[13] The three steps are identified in D. Hunter, J. Salzman and D. Zaelke, *International Environmental Law and Policy* (New York: Foundation Press, 2011), p. 911; GCO Report, *supra* n. 10, pp. 19ff.

limited evidence that we have regarding the impact on the environment and human health of this proliferation of chemicals.[14] An important question is whether there is a sufficient case for stopping the production of these substances? The answer, in some cases, is clearly yes and, as we shall see, a treaty such as the POP Convention prohibits the production and consumption of certain substances. However, the risks posed by many substances currently in circulation (more than 248,000)[15] are not as such sufficient to ban their production. Such risks must be evaluated in light of other factors, including the services these substances are likely to render. This type of assessment is referred to as 'risk management'. The elements to consider in this regard are of a socio-economic nature. For example, Annex E to the POP Convention[16] specifies several elements (such as the practical feasibility of a restriction, the social and economic costs, and many others) that must be weighed at this stage of the regulatory process.

A second observation is that the challenges arising from the uncertainties about the effects of chemicals as well as from the socio-economic dimensions of their regulation are amplified by the increasing relocation of the production and consumption (by way of trade) of these substances to developing countries, including Brazil, Russia, India, Indonesia, China and South Africa (the so-called 'BRIICS')[17] and the potential gaps in the applicable legal framework.

As a third and final observation, it is important to note that the regulation of chemicals has developed on a case-by-case basis, often in a reactive way, when a new risk was identified or unexpectedly materialised. To understand this difficulty, it is useful to compare the number of chemicals currently in circulation (more than 248,000) with the products subject to international regulation (some sixty substances are listed in the annexes to the POP and PIC Conventions, in addition to the sixty types of hazardous waste identified in Annex VIII to the Basel Convention). Of course, one must not overlook the fact that many substances are regulated at the domestic or regional level. Yet, the gap between the abovementioned figures highlights the increasingly pressing need to achieve a certain level of harmonisation in the regulation of these substances.

As discussed in this chapter, two main strategies have been followed in this respect, one aimed at a general regulation of chemicals (as opposed to regulation on a substance-by-substance basis) and the other seeking to develop synergies between treaties on specific substances but covering all phases of the life cycle of chemicals. There are also important interactions between these two strategies, notably where they are mutually reinforcing. Figure 7.1 presents the structure of the international regulatory framework in a schematic way.

As shown in Figure 7.1, most treaties in this area concern specific substances or processes. We have already studied some of these instruments in Chapters 4

---

[14] UNEP, *Global Environmental Outlook 5. Environment for the Future We Want* (UNEP, 2005), pp. 168 and 172ff.
[15] *Ibid.*, p. 170.   [16] POP Convention, *supra* n. 5.
[17] *Ibid.*, p. 174; GCO Report, *supra* n. 10, pp. 13–14.

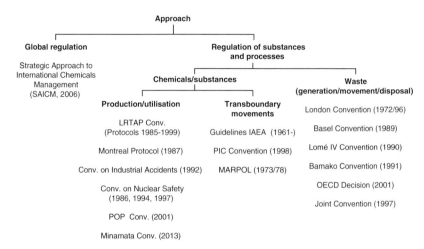

Figure 7.1: The international regulatory framework of dangerous substances/activities

and 5. This chapter focuses on some of the remaining ones. To gain a more complete view of the normative 'forest', it would be necessary to add several codes and standards,[18] as well as national and regional[19] instruments the relevance of which may in practice be higher than that of some treaties.

7.3 Attempts to develop a global regulatory framework

7.3.1 The political impulsion

The regulation of chemicals was a major component of the discussions at the Rio Summit in 1992. The action plan adopted there, Agenda 21,[20] refers in

---

[18] See e.g. below the discussion of the origins of the PIC and Basel Conventions as well as, among others: FAO, Guidelines for Legislation on the Control of Pesticides (1989); FAO, Guidelines for the Registration and Control of Pesticides (1985); ILO, Code of Practice on Prevention of Major Industrial Accidents (1991); ILO, Code of Practice concerning the Use of Chemicals at Work (1993); OECD, Council Decision on the Mutual Acceptance of Data in the Assessment of Chemicals (1981) (including Guidelines for the Testing of Chemicals and GLP, Guidelines on Accidents (1992), and others; UNEP, Code of Ethics on the International Trade of Chemicals (1994).

[19] See e.g. Regulation (EC) No 1907/2006 of the European Parliament and of the Council of 18 December 2006 concerning the Registration, Evaluation, Authorisation and Restriction of Chemicals (REACH), establishing a European Chemicals Agency, amending Directive 1999/45/EC and repealing Council Regulation (EEC) No 793/93 and Commission Regulation (EC) No 1488/94 as well as Council Directive 76/769/EEC and Commission Directives 91/155/EEC, 93/105/EC and 2000/21/EC, OJ L 136/3 (29 May 2007) ('REACH' Regulation). On this instrument see J. Scott, 'REACH: Combining Harmonization and Dynamism in the Regulation of Chemicals', in J. Scott (ed.), *Environmental Protection: European Law and Governance* (Oxford University Press, 2009), pp. 56–91.

[20] Report of the United Nations Conference on Environment and Development, A/CONF.151/26/Rev.l (Vol. l), 13 June 1992, Resolution 1, Annex 2: Agenda 21 ('Agenda 21').

Chapter 19 to six priority areas in order to achieve the 'environmentally sound management' of chemicals, namely:

a) Expanding and accelerating international assessment of chemical risks; b) Harmonization of classification and labelling of chemicals; c) Information exchange on toxic chemicals and chemical risks; d) Establishment of risk reduction programmes; e) Strengthening of national capabilities and capacities for management of chemicals; f) Prevention of illegal international traffic in toxic and dangerous products.[21]

Despite its non-binding character, this chapter has significantly influenced the work of international organisations, coordinated through joint programmes, such as the 'International Forum on Chemical Safety' ('IFCS')[22] or the 'Inter-Organisation Programme for the Sound Management of Chemicals' ('IOMC').[23]

Additional impetus was provided in 2000 with the adoption by the IFCS of the Bahia Declaration on Chemical Safety,[24] and in 2002, at the Johannesburg Summit on Sustainable Development, of a Plan of Implementation reiterating:

the commitment, as advanced in Agenda 21, to sound management of chemicals throughout their life cycle and of hazardous wastes for sustainable development as well as for the protection of human health and the environment, *inter alia*, aiming to achieve, by 2020, that chemicals are used and produced in ways that lead to the minimization of significant adverse effects on human health and the environment.[25]

As discussed next, the impulsion given by these instruments led to the adoption of a number of soft structures for the global regulation of chemicals.

7.3.2 The main outcomes: the GHS and the SAICM

Agenda 21, the Bahia Declaration and the Johannesburg Plan contributed to the development of various initiatives, of which two must be recalled here.

---

[21] *Ibid.*, para. 19.4.
[22] Combining various international organisations, national governments, as well as civil society and the private sector.
[23] Consisting of nine international organisations, namely the United Nations Food and Agriculture Organization ('FAO'), the International Labour Organization ('ILO'), the United Nations Development Programme ('UNDP'), the United Nations Environment Programme ('UNEP'), the United Nations Industrial Development Organization ('UNIDO'), the United Nations Institute for Training and Research ('UNITAR'), the World Health Organization ('WHO'), the World Bank, and the Organisation for Economic Cooperation and Development ('OECD').
[24] Bahia Declaration on Chemical Safety, 20 October 2000, IFCS/FORUM III/23w.
[25] Report of the World Summit on Sustainable Development, Johannesburg, South Africa, 26 August–4 September 2002, Resolution 2, Plan of Implementation of the World Summit on Sustainable Development, Annex, UN Doc. A/CONF.199/20, para. 23.

First, during the ten-year period from the Rio Summit until the aftermath of the Johannesburg Summit, a 'United Nations Globally Harmonised System of Classification and Labelling of Chemicals'[26] was gradually developed. The basis for this important effort may be found in Chapter 19 of Agenda 21, which called specifically for a 'globally harmonised hazard classification and compatible labelling system, including material safety data sheets and easily understandable symbols, [which] should be available, if feasible, by the year 2000'.[27] The work was co-ordinated by the IOMC and, although the text was formally approved after the Johannesburg Summit, it was made available already in 2001. Taking stock of this initiative, the Johannesburg Plan of Implementation explicitly 'encourage[d] countries to implement the new globally harmonised system for the classification and labelling of chemicals as soon as possible with a view to having the system fully operational by 2008'.[28] The practical impact of the GHS is important both for the regulatory instruments existing at the time and for newly developed ones.[29] For example, the European Commission reformed the European system of classification,[30] which led, among other things, to a revision of the Seveso II (now III) Directive on Industrial Accidents[31] and, at the international level, that of the Convention on Industrial Accidents.[32]

Second, the Johannesburg Plan of Implementation called for the development of a 'Strategic Approach to International Chemicals Management' or 'SAICM'.[33] This call led a number of international organisations acting through the IOMC and IFCS to develop a global regulatory framework on chemicals of a 'soft', non-binding nature. This instrument is of particular interest because of its similarities to framework conventions. Indeed, the negotiations leading to the adoption of the SAICM[34] were conducted through

---

[26] United Nations Globally Harmonized System of Classification and Labelling of Chemicals, 2003, ST/SG/AC.10/30 (GHS). See S. Smith, 'GHS: A Short Acronym for a Big Idea' (2007) 69 *Occupational Hazards* 6.

[27] Agenda 21, *supra* n. 20, Chapter 19, para. 27.

[28] Plan of Implementation, *supra* n. 25, para. 23(c).

[29] On the implementation of the GHS see: www.unece.org/trans/danger/publi/ghs/implementa tion_e.html (last visited 31 January 2013).

[30] See Regulation (EC) No. 1272/2008 of the European Parliament and of the Council of 16 December 2008 on the classification, labelling and packaging of substances and mixtures, amending and repealing Directives 67/548/EEC and 1999/45/EC, and amending Regulation (EC) No 1907/2006, OJ L 353/2, 31 November 2008. This regulation complements the REACH Directive, *supra* n. 19.

[31] Directive 2012/18/EU of the European Parliament and Council of 4 July 2012 on the control of major-accident hazards involving dangerous substances, amending and subsequently repealing Council Directive 96/82/EC, OJ L 197/1, 24 July 2012.

[32] 'UNECE aligns its Industrial Accidents Convention with United Nations Globally Harmonized System of Classification and Labelling of Chemicals', 19 November 2012, available at: www. unece.org (last visited 31 January 2013).

[33] Plan of Implementation, *supra* n. 25, para. 23(b).

[34] UNEP, *Strategic Approach to International Chemicals Management. SAICM Texts and Resolutions of the International Conference on Chemicals Management*, 2007, available at: www.unece.org (last visited 31 January 2013).

a negotiation committee comprising representatives of civil society and the private sector, in addition to representatives of States and international organisations, much in the same way as framework conventions. In addition, the outcomes of these negotiations were adopted at an 'International Conference on Chemical Management' ('ICCM') held in February 2006 in Dubai (United Arab Emirates). These include the 'Dubai Declaration on International Chemicals Management', an 'Overarching Policy Strategy' and a 'Global Plan of Action'.[35]

The objective of SAICM is:

> to achieve the sound management of chemicals throughout their life-cycle so that, by 2020, chemicals are used and produced in ways that lead to the minimization of significant adverse effects on human health and the environment.[36]

A series of more specific objectives and actions are then identified and, what is more, the ICCM is entrusted the task of regularly monitoring their implementation.[37] On this point, one can make an analogy between the ICCM and the role of the Conferences of Parties (COPs) of environmental treaties.[38] More specifically, the question arises whether, despite the absence of political consensus for the adoption of a binding global instrument on chemicals, the path followed by the SAICM would not be likely to achieve the same result, while alleviating the legal formalities.

The answer to this question must necessarily be of an empirical nature. At the meeting of the ICCM in September 2012, a first report on the progress in the implementation of the SAICM was presented.[39] This report concludes, in essence, that some progress on this issue has indeed been observed.[40] However, such progress is at present being measured by reference to the number of activities reported for each of the objectives of SAICM and not by the actual impact of these activities (which is more difficult to assess). Furthermore, as noted by the SAICM Secretariat in a summary report, the intense level of activity in terms of risk reduction has probably been influenced by measures adopted to implement the POP Convention as well as by the negotiations towards a treaty on mercury.[41] The existence of binding treaties, such as the POP Convention, the Montreal Protocol or the Basel Convention, has also influenced the level of activity in respect of other objectives, such as governance, technical co-operation or illegal international trafficking.[42] This suggests

---

[35] The latter has not been formally adopted.   [36] SAICM, *supra* n. 34, para. 13.
[37] *Ibid.*, para. 24(a)–(b).   [38] Hunter *et al., supra* n. 13, p. 937.
[39] Progress in Implementation of SAICM Reported for 2009–2010, 18 August 2012, SAICM/ICCM.3/INF/6.
[40] *Ibid.*, p. 3.
[41] Secretariat Summary Report on Progress in Implementation of the Strategic Approach, 7 June 2012, SAICM/ICCM.3/4, para. 13.
[42] *Ibid.*, para. 16–22.

that the most promising approach is to look at the development of synergies between various types of instruments.

As discussed next, despite the purpose/substance-specific character of the treaties in force in this area, there is currently a trend towards the institutional integration of the three major treaties. Such integration could provide a model for a new approach to international environmental governance.

7.4 The regulation of specific substances and activities

7.4.1 Regulatory objects and techniques

Despite its fragmented nature, the international regulation of hazardous substances and activities covers the entire life cycle of chemicals. From a legal standpoint, we can distinguish three phases in this cycle.

The first phase concerns the 'production' and 'use' of chemicals. These terms should be understood broadly. For example, the term 'production' also includes the generation of waste, which, as a result of its composition, must be treated with the same caution as chemicals. Similarly, the term 'use' also applies to the consumption of chemicals, as defined in Article 1(6) of the Montreal Protocol. Overall, the terms 'production' and 'use' also cover the various industrial processes for generating a chemical (for a variety of uses) or the use of a product for another purpose (e.g. electricity production by means of nuclear fission or, more generally, the use of a substance in a production process).

The second phase focuses on the movements of these substances. Such movements can take place within the territory of a State, as well as across borders or through areas beyond national jurisdiction (such as shipping). Internal movements are regulated by domestic law, which is often in accordance with international guidelines and standards. Environmental treaties are mostly concerned with transboundary movements and maritime transportation. The term 'transboundary movement' must also be understood in a broad sense, covering a variety of activities subject to control, such as the export, storage, transportation, transit and import of controlled substances. This understanding of 'movements' aims at capturing the regulatory angles used by international legal instruments.

The third phase focuses on the disposal of chemicals or products containing them, considered as 'waste'. From an analytical standpoint, this phase includes a variety of activities, in addition to the actual elimination of such substances. Indeed, strictly speaking, it would be more appropriate to speak of the 'management' of waste, since the generation and transboundary movement of waste are also targeted. But the term disposal remains useful to highlight the specific objectives of the various activities relating to 'waste'.

As discussed in the following sections, these three phases of the life cycle of chemicals provide a useful basis for discussion of the international regulation of dangerous substances and activities. They also introduce a parallel with the regulatory techniques discussed in the preceding chapters. In particular, we see that the lists technique, with its three components (lists, obligations, modification system),[43] is widely used for the regulation of substances and dangerous activities, as illustrated by the sophisticated architecture employed in the POP Convention. In the context of this book we cannot, however, provide a detailed analysis of all relevant instruments.[44] The following presentation will therefore focus on the four most important treaties, namely the POP Convention (with its regulation of the production/use of persistent organic pollutants), the Rotterdam Convention (with its system of information exchange), the Basel Convention (with its various techniques for the environmentally sound management of hazardous wastes) and the Minamata Convention on Mercury (covering the entire life cycle of mercury). In addition, we will also show how two systems were created to ensure the safety of certain industrial processes, namely the Convention on the Transboundary Effects of Industrial Accidents and the integrated approach to nuclear power.

7.4.2 The regulation of production and use

7.4.2.1 The regulation of substances: the POP Convention

The emergence of the Stockholm Convention on Persistent Organic Pollutants or 'POP Convention'[45] must be analysed in the context of some initiatives taken in the 1990s, namely: (i) the outcomes of the 1992 Rio Summit in the area of chemical regulation, particularly chapter 19 of Agenda 21,[46] (ii) a better understanding of the characteristics of POP (persistency, ability to travel long distances, bio-accumulative nature and, as a result, their ability to move up the trophic chain to the final predator, man), their dynamics (the so-called 'grasshopper' effect, i.e. their volatilisation in temperate regions, their wide circulation through atmospheric winds, and their condensation and deposition in cold areas, especially the poles, in the form of rain) and the risks they pose in terms of endocrine disruption[47] and, finally, (iii) the adoption in the regional context of the LRTAP Convention of a Protocol on POP.[48]

In this context, UNEP initiated a negotiation process, first asking the IFCS[49] to address the issue and make recommendations, and then adopting in 1997 a

---

[43] See Chapter 6.

[44] See Kummer, *supra* n. 2; M. Pallemaerts, *Toxics and Transnational Law: International and European Regulation of Toxic Substances as Legal Symbolism* (Oxford: Hart Publishing, 2003); S. Tromans, *Nuclear Law: The Law Applying to Nuclear Installations and Radioactive Substances in its Historic Context* (Oxford: Hart Publishing, 2010); M. Montjoie, *Droit international et gestion des déchets radioactifs* (Paris: LGDJ, 2011).

[45] See P. Lallas, 'The Stockholm Convention on Persistent Organic Pollutants' (2001) 95 *American Journal of International Law* 692; M. A. Olsen, *Analysis of the Stockholm Convention on Persistent Organic Pollutants* (Dobbs Ferry NY: Oceana, 2003).

[46] See *supra* Section 7.2.1.   [47] See *supra* Section 7.1.   [48] See Chapter 6.

[49] See *supra* Section 7.2.1.

formal mandate for the conclusion of a treaty on POP. This mandate led by an Intergovernmental Negotiating Committee, as is the case for many other environmental treaties, resulted in the adoption of the POP Convention in 2001.[50] The negotiation process faced a number of challenges, such as the definition of the objective of the treaty (elimination v. management), the need for the subsequent inclusion of chemicals other than the twelve most dangerous POPs (known as the 'dirty dozen'), the interactions between the treaty and the obligations of States under international trade or the funding and assistance provided to developing countries.[51] It is useful to keep in mind these issues as we move forward, as they help to understand the underlying compromises reached, which are sometimes obscured by the final text of the Convention.

As noted in the previous section, the POP Convention follows the list technique, as described in Chapter 6 of this book. In reality, the POP Convention is one of the most sophisticated examples of the use of this technique in the regulation of hazardous substances and activities. Such sophistication may be seen not only in the structure of the lists or the scope of the obligations undertaken by States but also in the complex system of checks and balances reminiscent of a genuine constitutional architecture. Figure 7.2 summarises the basic structure of the Convention.

The Convention contains three lists, i.e. Annexes A, B and C. Annex A (Elimination) currently contains, following two amendments in 2009 and 2011, eighteen substances (pesticides and industrial chemicals).[52] Annex B (Restriction) contains only two substances,[53] including the pesticide DDT,

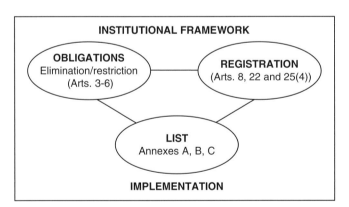

Figure 7.2: The basic structure of the POP Convention

---

[50] POP Convention, *supra* n. 5.   [51] These issues are addressed by Lallas, *supra* n. 45, 696.

[52] Annex A contains the following substances: aldrine; alpha-hexachlorocyclohexane; beta-hexachlorocyclohexane; chlordane; chlordecone; dieldrin; Technical endosulfan and its related isomers; endrin; heptachlor; hexabromobiphenyl; hexabromodiphenyl ether and heptabromo-diphenyl ether; hexachlorobenzene; lindane; mirex; pentachlorobenzene; polychlorinsted biphenyls; tetrabromodiphenyl ether and pentabromodiphenyl ether; toxaphene.

[53] Annex B contains: DDT (1,1,1-trichloro-2, 2-bis (4-chlorophenyl) ethane); Perfluorooctane sulfonic acid, its salts and perfluorooctane sulfonyl fluoride.

which was the target of the famous book by Rachel Carson 'Silent Spring' in 1962.[54] Annex C (Unintentional Production) focuses on POPs that are produced or released unintentionally by human activity and contains five substances,[55] three of which (e.g. polychlorinated biphenyls or 'PCBs') also appear on Annex A (regarding the intentional production/use of these substances).

The substances listed in each of these annexes are subject to specific obligations. To understand the structure of these obligations, two observations are in order. First, unlike the POP Protocol to the LRTAP Convention,[56] which was concluded in a predominantly North-Atlantic context, the POP Convention also aimed to integrate many developing countries. Therefore, it was necessary to allow for some degree of differentiation in the elimination/progressive restriction of these substances in very different socio-economic contexts. Instead of formulating different obligations in the text of the Convention, 'specific exemptions' were added in the text of the annexes for each listed substance. States wishing to avail themselves of any such specific exemption must register with the Secretariat. Specific exemptions can only be used for a limited period of time (normally five years, unless an extension is granted).[57] Thus, the obligations for substances listed in Annexes A and B are subject to a variety of flexibilities, including these specific exemptions. Second, it would be inaccurate to characterise the POP Convention as requiring only the elimination/restriction of the production/use of substances listed in its annexes. The Convention contains, in addition, requirements for the regulation of trade in these substances (Article 3(1)(a)(ii) and 3(2)), as well as an attempt to control certain by-products (Article 5 and Annex C) and even waste management (Article 6). From this standpoint, the regime of the Convention covers the entire life cycle of controlled substances, although its main focus is on the elimination or restriction of these substances.

Article 3 contains the core obligations of the parties. A distinction can be made between obligations relating to *production/use* and obligations relating to *trade*. Regarding the first, each State party has the obligation to take the necessary measures to eliminate the production and use of substances listed in Annex A (Article 3(1)(a)(i)) and restrict the production and use of substances listed in Annex B (Article 3(1)(b)). As for trade obligations, the regime provided for in Article 3(2) is organised on the basis of the status of the substance and the purpose of trade. The import of a substance is allowed only if the proposed use is permitted under an exception or for the purpose of

---

[54] R. Carson, *Silent Spring* (Boston: Houghton Mifflin, 1962).

[55] Annex C contains: hexachlorobenzene; pentachlorobenzene; polychlorinated biphenyls; polychlorinated dibenzo-*p*-dioxins and dibenzofurans.

[56] Protocol to the 1979 Convention on Long-Range Transboundary Air Pollution on Persistent Organic Pollutants (POPs), 24 June 1998, 2230 UNTS 79 ('POP Protocol').

[57] See Lallas, *supra* n. 45, 700. This technique of differentiation can be implemented in conjunction with the provision of technical and financial assistance, see POP Convention, *supra* n. 5, Art. 11(2)(c) and 12 to 14 as well as Chapter 9.

'environmentally sound disposal' as defined by the Convention (Article 3(2)(a)). Similarly, the export of a substance is allowed only for a specific purpose. Depending on whether or not an exception has been added for a particular substance, this goal will be more or less restrictive. Whereas substances for which no exception is made can only be exported for the purpose of their 'environmentally sound disposal', other substances can also be exported for the purposes contemplated in the applicable exceptions. These restrictions also govern exports to States that are not parties to the Convention. Such exports require, in addition, that certain guarantees be provided by the importing State.[58]

The foregoing observations highlight the importance of the system of exceptions for the understanding of the obligations contemplated in the Convention. In fact, the main difference between the obligations governing, respectively, the substances listed in Annex A and Annex B lies in the types of exceptions available in each case. There are two main types of exceptions: specific exceptions (called '*specific exemptions*') and *general exceptions*, which each have several variations. Specific exemptions are available for substances in Annexes A and B. They introduce, for each substance, some specific 'types' of exemptions to the production and/or the use of the substance. As already discussed, each State must declare its intention to avail itself of one or more specific exemptions mentioned for a given substance (only from the exemptions explicitly identified for each substance, as a State could not seek to rely on a type of exemption that is not mentioned). The time duration of this flexibility is limited in principle to five years (Article 4(7)). A 'Register' of specific exemptions used by each State is established by the Secretariat. The advantage of this Register is that it can be modified without going through the cumbersome procedure for the amendment of the Convention or its annexes. Where a 'type' of specific exemption is not (or no longer) used, it is removed and no party may rely on it in the future (Article 4(9)). An example will help to understand this technique and to distinguish specific exemptions from other exceptions. Annex A contains a footnote (note 1) which indicates that a specific exemption for hexachlorobenzene (used as a 'closed system site-limited intermediate') is no longer available from 17 May 2009 as no party has registered for it. However, as indicated by another footnote (note 2), the expiration of this specific exemption does not affect the possibility for a State party to avail, without the need for registration, of a *general exception* envisaged under note (iii) of Annexes A and B. In other words, a largely similar activity was contemplated by a specific exemption and a general exception. The first expired (time limitation is part of any specific exemption), while the general exception remains valid. There are also other general exceptions. Article 3(5) provides, for example, that '[e]xcept as otherwise provided in this Convention, paragraphs 1 and 2 shall not apply to quantities of a chemical

---

[58] POP Convention, *supra* n. 5, Art. 3(2)(b)(iii).

to be used for laboratory-scale research or as a reference standard'.[59] A particular class of general exceptions, which is the essential distinction between Annexes A and B, are said to constitute 'acceptable purposes' for the production or use of a substance in Annex B. As an illustration, DDT can be produced and used for '[d]isease vector control ... in accordance with Part II of [Annex B]', which refers to uses recommended by the World Health Organisation in the fight against malaria. General exceptions, formulated in terms of 'acceptable purposes' or other formulations, do not require special registration and can therefore be used by any State party. Moreover, unlike specific exemptions, general exceptions are not time-barred.

The list technique, where each list is linked to a set of obligations and exceptions, has been designed for treaties to evolve over time. Article 1 of the Convention places the system under the logic of the precautionary approach, as set out in Principle 15 of the Rio Declaration.[60] In addition, the Convention calls upon the COP to create a 'Persistent Organic Pollutants Review Committee', consisting of members nominated by governments and taking its decisions by a majority of two thirds of the members present and voting (Article 19(6)). This Committee plays an important role in the gradual *process of updating the lists* provided for in Article 8 of the Convention. A party wishing to register a new substance in one of the lists of the Convention must submit a proposal which, after a preliminary verification by the Secretariat, will be considered by the Committee. The Committee must assess, first, whether some selection criteria specified in Annex D are respected, and it can, at this stage, reject the proposal. If, however, the Committee considers that these criteria are met, it elaborates a draft 'risk profile' that is then circulated to States parties for comment. On the basis of the parties' submissions, a final risk profile is prepared, in accordance with Annex E. At this stage, and drawing upon the risk profile thus elaborated, the Committee may again decide to proceed or not with the proposal. If it proceeds, the next step consists in carrying out a 'risk management evaluation' taking into account any regulatory measures and socio-economic implications (Annex F). On this basis, the Committee makes a recommendation to the COP regarding the inclusion of the substance in one of the annexes (Article 8(9)). The COP takes its decisions by a majority of three quarters of those parties present and voting (Article 22(4)). The process of registering a new substance is subject to several qualifications. First, it should be noted that the Committee may take decisions in the absence of scientific certainty, in accordance with the precautionary approach. If the Committee decides not to proceed with a proposal (at the stage of Annex D or Annex E), this decision may be appealed to the COP, which can decide otherwise. An important issue is the effect of the adoption by

---

[59] See also the notes in Roman numerals in Annexes A and B.

[60] Rio Declaration on Environment and Development, 13 June 1992, UN Doc. A/CONF.151/26 ('Rio Declaration'), Principle 15.

the COP of an amendment to Annexes A, B or C. Given that such amendments can be adopted at a qualified majority vote, one may ask whether the States that are in disagreement are bound by the amendment nevertheless. The approach of the Convention in this respect is nuanced. In principle, in order not to be bound by the amendment, a State must notify, within one year following notification of the amendment, that it does not wish to be bound by it (Article 22(3)(b)). In the absence of such notification, the amendment will enter into force for that State. But this 'opt-out' system can be transformed into a system of 'opt-in' (where silence does not constitute acceptance) if, at the time of ratifying the Convention, a State specifies that it will not be bound unless it expressly ratifies the amendment in question (Article 25(4)).

The complex system of the POP Convention is the result of a legal experiment that allowed the development of regulatory techniques for dealing with scientific considerations (the precautionary approach and the creation of the Committee) but also that takes into account socio-economic considerations (risk management evaluations, specific exemptions and general exceptions). Despite its sophistication, the POP Convention only applies to a limited number of substances, although in recent years this number has increased. In addition, the Convention does not capture another important risk arising from industrial processes, namely the occurrence of industrial accidents. As discussed next, the prevention and management of industrial accidents has been addressed at the regional level.

7.4.2.2 The regulation of activities: the Convention on Industrial Accidents

The origins of the UNECE Convention on the Transboundary Effects of Industrial Accidents can be found in a series of events which, from the 1970s onwards, highlighted the risks posed by certain industrial processes involving large quantities of highly or moderately dangerous substances. A prominent illustration is the accident that took place in the chemical factory Icmesa (belonging to the Givaudan group) in Northern Italy, in July 1976. A cloud of highly dangerous toxins (2, 3, 7, 8-tetrachlorodibenzo-p-dioxin or TCDD) was released by one of the reactors and spread over towns in Lombardy (in the municipality of Seveso) affecting hundreds of people. Subsequently, the European Community adopted a Directive on industrial accidents, known as 'Seveso', which has since then been revised twice ('Seveso II' and 'Seveso III').[61] Over the years, other industrial accidents also attracted significant public attention. Leaving aside the major oil spills and nuclear disasters, which are often the epicentre of attention, several industrial accidents have occurred both in developing countries, such as the tragedy of Bhopal (India) in 1984 or the explosion of the pesticide plant in Anaversa (Mexico) in 1991, as well as in developed nations, such as the fire at the Sandoz plant in Basel (Switzerland) in 1986 or the PEPCON plant explosion in Nevada (United States) in 1988.

---

[61] See *supra* n. 31.

In all of these (and many other) incidents the main concerns were the industrial processes involving the use and/or aimed at the production of certain hazardous substances. International law has an important role to play in this context because such accidents may have a significant impact on the health and/or the environment of neighbouring States. In some cases, especially when the accident results in the pollution of rivers, transboundary impacts can be felt very far from the place where the event occurred. The type of regulatory techniques most suited to prevent such accidents and, when an accident does occur, to minimise damage, differ significantly from those introduced by the POP Convention. While the latter prohibits or restricts the production and use of certain substances, the regulation of industrial accidents is not intended to ban the regulated activities but only to set certain requirements for the prevention and management of industrial accidents. Such is the approach followed in connection with useful but hazardous activities, such as oil transportation[62] or the production of nuclear energy.[63]

This is also the approach followed by the Convention on Industrial Accidents.[64] To understand its operation, one must examine (i) its object and (ii) the system of identification, prevention and management of information established by the Convention. Regarding the first, the Convention refers to 'industrial accidents capable of causing transboundary effects' (Article 2(1)). This term is characterised in several ways. First, the term is defined by Article 1(a) as 'an event resulting from an uncontrolled development in the course of any activity involving hazardous substances'. This preliminary characterisation calls for some further clarification. The accident must occur in a facility (which may include transport within the industrial site)[65] and the activities must involve 'hazardous substances'. The definition of industrial accidents thus depends upon the type of substance. These substances are, in turn, characterised by their nature and quantity (Annex I). The 'hazardous' nature of substances is defined in relation to the relevant 'category' (e.g. 'flammable' or 'highly flammable', 'toxic' or 'very toxic', etc.) or to the substance itself (e.g. ammonium nitrate or potassium, chlorine, petroleum, etc.). In both cases, Annex I sets the quantities that must be present for a substance to be dangerous enough to be regulated by the Convention. The 'effects' (defined broadly[66]) of the accident must, in addition, be 'cross-border', i.e. 'serious'[67] and resulting from an accident in another State. It is sufficient for an activity to be considered as dangerous if it is 'capable' of causing

---

[62] See Chapter 4.   [63] See *infra* Section 7.3.5.2.

[64] Convention on Industrial Accidents, *supra* n. 8. Commentary on this instrument can be found in the manuals prepared by the United Nations Economic Commission for Europe: *UNECE Industrial Accident Notification System* (Geneva: ECE, 2005); *Safety Guidelines and Good Practices for Pipelines* (Geneva: ECE, 2008). See also, ECE, *The Convention on the Transboundary Effects of Industrial Accidents: Twenty Years of Prevention, Preparedness and Response* (Geneva: ECE, 2012).

[65] Convention on Industrial Accidents, *supra* n. 8, Art. 1(a) and 2(2)(d)(ii).   [66] *Ibid.*, Art. 1(c).

[67] *Ibid.*, Art. 1(d).

transboundary effects (Article 1(b)). Finally, Article 2(2) excludes from the scope of the Convention some accidents, which are subject to specific regulatory systems (nuclear accidents, oil spills, releases of genetically modified organisms) or which, generally speaking, are inappropriate for regulation in this context (military installations).

This complex object (place/activity/substance/accident/effect) is subject to a regulatory framework consisting of four main components: (i) the identification of hazardous activities; (ii) the prevention of accidents; (iii) their management when they occur; and (iv) information exchange and participation.[68] Each component is addressed generally in the text of the Convention and specified in the annexes or by decisions of the COP. The *identification* of the relevant industrial activities is governed by Article 4. The COP has established guidelines to assist the parties in this process.[69] Each State party must establish a list of hazardous activities that take place on its territory, inform potentially affected parties and enter into consultations. The identification process can also be triggered by another State party, when it considers that an activity conducted in the territory of another State is dangerous and should be subject to the regime of the Convention.[70] In the event the parties are unable to reach an agreement, the matter can be submitted by either party to an inquiry commission in accordance with Annex II. In addition, the parties may agree to treat activities that do not fall under Annex I of the Convention as subject nevertheless to the Convention's regulatory framework.[71] The *prevention* of industrial accidents is the main objective of the Convention. Article 6 provides for an obligation of a 'vertical' nature: States parties must take appropriate measures (Annex IV proposes some measures, such as setting specific safety objectives, adopting safety standards, conducting inspections, etc.) for the prevention of industrial accidents. These include measures aimed at inducing action by operators to reduce the risk of industrial accidents,[72] requiring economic operators to provide accurate information about how the safety of industrial processes is ensured in their sites[73] or regulating the location of industrial sites to reduce impact in case of accident.[74] In other words, the Convention requires the adoption of a national regulatory framework as well as a specific prevention framework at the industrial site level. Of course, the prevention framework cannot guarantee that accidents will not occur under any circumstance. In this respect, the Convention sets some parameters for the *management* of such accidents or, more specifically, to ensure an adequate

[68] *Ibid.*, Art. 3.
[69] See 'Decision 2000/3 Guidelines to facilitate the identification of hazardous activities for the purposes of the convention', 22 February 2001, ECE/CP.TEIA/2.
[70] Convention on Industrial Accidents, *supra* n. 8, Art. 4(2).   [71] *Ibid.*, Art. 5.
[72] *Ibid.*, Art. 4(4). This provision refers to the Convention on Environmental Impact Assessment in a Transboundary Context, 25 February 1991, 1989 UNTS 309 ('Espoo Convention').
[73] Convention on Industrial Accidents, *supra* n. 8, Art. 6(2).
[74] *Ibid.*, Art. 7 and Annexes V(1)–(8) and VI.

response so as to minimise damage. In addition to disclosure obligations, the Convention requires the establishment of a system of emergency response (at the site,[75] national[76] and regional[77] levels) as well as obligations of co-ordination[78] and mutual assistance.[79] The *disclosure obligations* apply both during the identification phase (especially with regard to consultations with other States[80] and populations likely to be affected[81]) and thereafter, during the course of the activity[82] or when an accident has occurred (notification and exchange of information). In the latter respect, the Convention provides for the establishment of systems for the exchange of information, including the identification of relevant authorities[83] and requires that some minimal amount of information be provided to other States parties.[84]

The practical importance of the Convention on Industrial Accidents must be assessed in the context of the four other environmental conventions adopted by UNECE.[85] Taken together, the five treaties provide indeed a sophisticated and balanced framework.[86] The Convention itself has guided the adoption of a number of domestic laws relating to the prevention and management of industrial accidents. Notwithstanding, the synergies between the five conventions could be improved.[87] A synergy process is also being pursued at the global level among the Secretariats of the three major chemical and waste treaties,[88] although there is no global treaty on industrial accidents at this level.

7.4.3 The regulation of trade: the PIC Convention

As discussed earlier, the POP Convention not only covers the production and use of POPs identified in the annexes, but it also regulates their exports and imports. However, the purpose of trade regulation in this context is to strengthen the obligations regarding production and use. The Rotterdam Convention or 'PIC Convention'[89] adopts a different perspective. It is

---

[75] *Ibid.*, Art. 8(1)–(2) and Annex 7(4).   [76] *Ibid.*, Art. 8(3) and Annex 7(5).
[77] *Ibid.*, Art. 8(3) *in fine*.   [78] *Ibid.*, Art. 11.
[79] *Ibid.*, Art. 12 and Annex X. See also Art. 18(4) and Annex XII.
[80] *Ibid.*, Art. 4 and Annex III.
[81] *Ibid.*, Art. 9 and Annex VIII. These requirements are now strengthened by the adoption of the Convention on Access to Information, Public Participation in Decision-Making and Access to Justice in Environmental Matters, 25 June 1998, 2161 UNTS 447 ('Aarhus Convention').
[82] Convention on Industrial Accidents, *supra* n. 8, Art. 15 and Annex XI.   [83] *Ibid.*, Art. 17(2).
[84] *Ibid.*, Art. 10(2) and Annex IX.
[85] See W. Schrage, K. Bull and A. Karadjova, 'Environmental Legal Instruments in the UNECE Region' (2007) 18 *Yearbook of International Environmental Law* 3.
[86] *Ibid.*, 3.   [87] *Ibid.*, 4.   [88] See *infra* Section 7.4.5.1.
[89] PIC Convention, *supra* n. 5. See R. W. Emory, 'Probing the Protections in the Rotterdam Convention on Prior Informed Consent' (2001) 12 *Colorado Journal of International Environmental Law and Policy* 47; P. Barrios, 'The Rotterdam Convention on Hazardous Chemicals: A Meaningful Step towards Environmental Protection?' (2004) 16 *Georgetown International Environmental Law Review* 679.

primarily intended to regulate trade in chemicals. More specifically, it seeks to ensure a sufficient level of information to enable States (especially developing countries) to understand the risks posed by certain chemicals and make informed decisions about their import. To understand the purpose and structure of this system, it is useful to recall the historical reasons for its emergence.

Over the course of the 1970s and 1980s, the export of certain pesticides banned in developed countries to developing countries was strongly criticised. This controversy involved primarily *two problems*.[90] On the one hand, the movement known as 'environmental justice', which had focused on the link between the geographical location of pollution sources and the issue of race in the United States, was expanded to cover transboundary movements of hazardous substances. Damage to the environment and the health of people in importing countries was even more outrageous since the exported pesticides had been banned in the legal systems of exporting countries. It seemed necessary, at the very least, to provide importing countries with sufficient information about the risks of pesticides to make an informed decision. On the other hand, the domestic regulations of importing countries (or their insufficient implementation) did not always tackle these risks adequately. It was better, once the position of the developing State on the import of the substance was known, to use the domestic legal system of the exporting (developed) States to control the activities of exporters. This is not only in order to protect the developing countries but also to avoid the so-called 'circle of poison', namely the return of pesticides banned in the global North in the food imported from developing countries. These two problems led to the adoption of two non-binding instruments developed under the aegis of the FAO and UNEP, namely the 'International Code of Conduct on the Distribution and Use of Pesticides' (1985) and the 'London Guidelines for the Exchange of Information on Chemicals in International Trade' (1987). These instruments were revised in 1989 to introduce a general procedure for prior informed consent, which provided the basis for the adoption of the PIC Convention.[91]

The PIC Convention follows the lists technique, with its three components (list, obligations, modification system). Figure 7.3 summarises its basic structure. Annex III to the Convention[92] lists a number of 'banned or severely restricted chemicals'[93] and 'severely hazardous pesticide formulations'.[94] This *list* currently includes thirty-nine substances, most of which are pesticides.

---

[90] See Barrios, *supra* n. 89, 709ff.

[91] See A. M. Mekouar, 'Pesticides and Chemicals – The Requirement of Prior Informed Consent' in D. Shelton (ed.), *Commitment and Compliance* (Oxford University Press, 2000), pp. 146–63.

[92] The Convention also sets out a notification system (specific PIC procedure) for banned or severely restricted substances (Art. 12). This system, which is not applicable when the substance is listed in Annex III (because from that moment on, the general PIC procedure applies), must be understood in the light of the abovementioned problem, namely that of exports to developing countries of banned or restricted products.

[93] PIC Convention, *supra* n. 5, Art. 2(b)–(c).   [94] *Ibid.*, Art. 2(d).

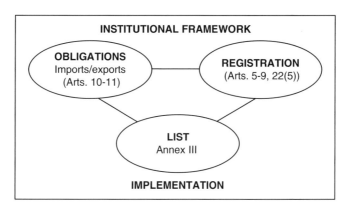

Figure 7.3: The basic structure of the PIC Convention

Among these substances, one finds the majority of POPs listed in the Annexes of the Stockholm Convention. For each substance listed in Annex III, the Chemical Review Committee established by the Convention prepares a 'decision guidance document',[95] which is communicated to all States parties.[96] This document provides the basis for an information exchange system established by the Convention.

The *obligations* attached to the listed substances relate to both the import and export of substances. Regarding the first, States parties undertake to implement the necessary measures to make decisions on the import of a particular product within a certain time (usually less than nine months after they have received the decision guidance document) as well as to communicate this decision to other States parties through the Secretariat of the Convention.[97] This decision, whether final or provisional, may (i) authorise imports, (ii) prohibit imports or (iii) authorise imports under certain conditions.[98] The importing State may also request further information or assistance in evaluating the chemical.[99] When a State decides to prohibit or restrict imports of a given chemical, it also has the obligation to apply this prohibition/restriction to all imports from other countries, as well as to prohibit/restrict domestic production.[100] This is because, in the absence of clauses making provision for 'most favoured nation treatment' and 'national treatment', a State could decide to reject/restrict imports in a discriminatory or protectionist manner, which the PIC Convention seeks to avoid. Article 11 strengthens the system by requiring exporting countries to adopt the measures necessary to ensure compliance – by any private party seeking to export the listed products – with the decisions of the importing countries. Note that in certain exceptional circumstances,[101] the absence of a response from the importing State does not preclude the exporting State from

---

[95] This document must contain certain information about the substance in question specified in Annexes I and IV of the PIC Convention.
[96] *Ibid.*, Art. 7.   [97] *Ibid.*, Art. 10.   [98] *Ibid.*, Art. 10(4)(a) and (b)(i).
[99] *Ibid.*, Art. 10(4)(b)(iii)–(iv).   [100] *Ibid.*, Art. 10(9).   [101] *Ibid.*, Art. 11(2).

authorising the export of a substance. This is the case where there is evidence that the substance is not banned in the importing State, despite the lack of response (hence the need for the importing State to give an interim reply stating that a decision is still pending). Overall, this system can be seen as a compromise between free trade and tight (precautionary) environmental protection and health. This is at the discretion of the importing State, but if it decides to restrict trade, it must also restrict domestic production and imports from other countries. Such 'trade discipline' does not apply to substances that are not included in the list, which shows the implications of such a registration.

Given these implications, the parties have structured the *procedure for registration* of new substances in Annex III of the PIC Convention in a detailed manner. Articles 5 (chemicals) and 6 (severely hazardous pesticide formulations) provide the conditions under which a nomination for registration may be submitted. These include (i) a proposal involving a geographical dimension[102] and (ii) the evaluation of certain criteria (Annexes I, II or IV) by the Secretariat (preliminary) as well as by the Chemical Review Committee, which makes a recommendation[103] to the COP members present and voting.[104] The COP then decides on the basis of this recommendation (Article 7). It adopts its decisions by consensus (Article 22(5)(b)). This provision, which is more demanding than the three quarters majority provided for under the POP Convention, explains why the inclusion in Annex III of the PIC Convention of the politically controversial pesticide endosulfan initially failed. A new attempt was not made until this substance had been included within Annex A of the POP Convention.

It is, moreover, not the only feature where the PIC Convention falls short of the sophisticated legal system laid out in the POP Convention. Among the criticisms often levelled against the PIC Convention is the absence of adequate assistance and capacity building for developing countries to truly understand and manage the information exchanged by the general PIC system[105] or the absence of restrictions on exports to third countries.[106] As discussed next,[107] these deficiencies could be addressed, at least in part, through synergies between the PIC Convention and other instruments, such as the POP Convention or the Basel Convention.

[102] For chemicals, it is necessary that at least two countries from two different regions (Africa, North America, Latin America and the Caribbean, Asia, Europe, South-West Pacific, Middle East) have adopted (and communicated) a regulatory measure in relation to the substance in question. By contrast, for severely hazardous pesticides, the proposal of a developing country or countries in transition is enough to trigger the procedure. See *Ibid.*, Arts. 5(5) and 6(1).
[103] *Ibid.*, Arts. 5(6) and 6(5).   [104] *Ibid.*, Art. 18(6)(c).
[105] Barrios, *supra* n. 89, 743ff. The Secretariat has provided some technical and financial assistance acting under Art. 16 of the Convention, mostly for the organisation of meetings and seminars. But it is only as part of the ongoing process to create synergies with the Stockholm Convention and the Basel Convention ('delivering as one') that strategic priorities have been identified, including the provision of technical assistance to certain countries and on certain issues.
[106] Emory, *supra* n. 89, 54ff.   [107] See *infra* Section 7.4.5.

7.4.4 The regulation of waste: the Basel Convention

Like the PIC Convention, the Basel Convention[108] is also rooted in the environmental justice movement, and its predecessor was also a non-binding instrument.[109] At the origin of this treaty lies a controversial factual configuration characterised by the generation of large amounts of waste in developed countries (or their richest regions) and the transfer of that waste to developing countries (or poor regions) for elimination or simply discharge. This phenomenon, largely induced by the high costs of waste disposal in the countries that generate such waste, came under much criticism, especially because of the impact on the environment and health of the people in receiving States and regions. Although the question is far from settled, the debate has been influenced in recent years by a change in the perception of waste, which is increasingly seen as a 'resource' (e.g. to generate electricity or simply for recycling into certain items) or, at least, as a profitable business 'opportunity' (the waste industry is now present in many countries in the developing world). These considerations are useful to understand not only the text of the Basel Convention but, more generally, the problem it was intended to regulate.

The general approach of the Basel Convention is summarised by K. Kummer,[110] former Executive Secretary of the Convention, as follows: (i) the reduction of hazardous waste generation to a minimum ('principle of waste minimisation', Article 4(2)(a)); (ii) the disposal in an environmentally sound manner by facilities located as near to the source of generation as possible ('principle of proximity of disposal', Article 4(2)(b)–(c)); (iii) absolute prohibition of exports of hazardous waste in some cases (to States which are not parties to the Convention,[111] to Antarctica,[112] to States which have prohibited imports or do not have the capacity to manage them in an environmentally sound manner,[113] or from an OECD State to a non-OECD State[114]); (iv) in all other cases, the exports of hazardous waste must comply with the system established by the Convention, namely the disposal must be carried out in an environmentally sound manner in the country of import and the transboundary movement must meet certain conditions, mainly a specific PIC procedure (Article 6); (v) hazardous waste which is exported illegally or which is not disposed of in an environmentally sound manner must be re-imported into the State of

---

[108] Basel Convention, *supra* n. 7. See Kummer, *supra* n. 2.

[109] UNEP, *Environmental Law Guidelines and Principles no. 8: Environmentally Sound Management of Hazardous Wastes* (Nairobi: UNEP, 1987). See Kummer, *supra* n. 2, p. 39.

[110] Kummer, *supra* n. 2, pp. 47–8.   [111] Basel Convention, *supra* n. 7, Art. 4(5).

[112] *Ibid.*, Art. 4(6).   [113] *Ibid.*, Art. 4(2)(e) and (g).

[114] See Decision III/1, 'Amendment to the Convention', 28 November 1995, UNEP/CHW.3/35. This amendment has not yet entered into force, although in practice it is widely respected. The amendment was adopted by three quarters of those members present and voting but it does not come into effect unless, in addition, at least three quarters of the parties having adopted or accepted (in essence, three quarters of the previous three quarters) subsequently ratify it (Article 17(3)–(5) of the Convention).

origin (Article 8). This system covers all phases of the management of hazardous wastes, from their generation to their transboundary movement to their disposal. In this section, we focus on three main components of the Basel Convention, namely the characterisation of 'waste' as a regulatory object, the control system (the specific PIC procedure), and the relationship between the Convention and other instruments focusing on a similar object.

The system established by the Convention provides for significant restrictions on transactions involving regulated waste. It is therefore important to determine the waste to which it applies. Initially, the Convention followed a rather unpractical approach, merely characterising regulated waste as 'types' of waste (Annex I) with certain characteristics (Annex III).[115] This characterisation introduced some uncertainty as to the object targeted by the Convention. The Convention also applied to waste considered as hazardous by one party (whether the exporting, importing or transit State),[116] a feature that required the establishment of a system of identification of these wastes and the dissemination of information among other States parties. Moreover, as a result of a compromise reached when the text was negotiated, the Convention makes a distinction between 'hazardous waste' and 'other waste' (Annex II), although these two categories are treated in a similar manner from a regulatory standpoint. The ambiguity in the characterisation of regulated waste was tackled at the fourth COP in 1998, with the adoption of Annexes VIII and IX to the Convention. Annex VIII contains a list of waste (with 60 entries) deemed hazardous under Article 1(1)(a) of the Convention. Conversely, Annex IX provides a list of waste presumed to be non-hazardous and, therefore, falling outside the scope of the Convention, unless they contain any of the substances listed in Annex I in a quantity or concentration sufficient to exhibit one of the hazardous characteristics listed in Annex III. Annexes VIII and IX introduced greater clarity on the characterisation of regulated waste. Since their adoption, they have been amended several times, a process that has helped the 'list' of the Convention to be updated. In addition, the Secretariat of the Convention has entered into two partnerships with the private sector to develop specific guidelines in relation to two categories of waste that are very important in practice, namely mobile telephones and computer parts that are no longer in use.[117] It is worth noting in passing that the development of technical guidelines has become a very important part of the Convention's activity,[118] even if its main component remains the procedure for the control of transboundary movements.

The latter remark leads to the core of the system established by the Basel Convention. As for other treaties in this area, the list technique provides a

---

[115] Basel Convention, *supra* n. 7, Art. 1(1)(a).   [116] *Ibid.*, Art. 1(1)(b).

[117] Mobile Phone Partnership Initiative (2003–2008) and Partnership for Action on Computing Equipment (2008).

[118] See www.basel.int/Implementation/TechnicalMatters/tabid/1335/Default.aspx (last visited 10 December 2013).

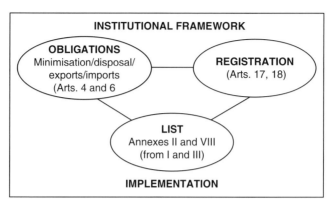

Figure 7.4: The basic structure of the Basel Convention

useful analytical grid to understand this system. Figure 7.4 summarises the main components of the system (list, obligations, updating system).

The complex structure of the list established by the Basel Convention has already been discussed. It involves the interaction between five annexes (I, II, III, VIII and IX) for the identification of regulated waste, although the substances concerned are more directly referred to in Annex II ('other wastes') and VIII (waste deemed to be hazardous). The *amendment of these lists*, as set out in Article 18(3) (which in turn refers to the system of Articles 17 and 18), requires a three quarters majority of the members present and voting (Article 17(3)). Unlike amendments to the Convention itself, amendments to the Annexes enter into force for a State party automatically, unless a written notification (objection) is sent within a certain period (Article 18(2)(b)–(c)). The *obligations* applicable to regulated waste focus, as already noted, on the minimisation of waste generation, disposal close to the source by an environmentally sound method and, where transboundary movements are permitted, the application of a specific PIC procedure. This procedure is mainly described in Article 6 of the Convention. According to this provision, the competent authority of the exporting State must notify (respecting certain requirements) the competent authority of the importing State (and transit States) of the transboundary movement of regulated waste, or require the private operator concerned to make this notification.[119] The exporting State can only authorise transboundary movements of waste when the importing State has given its written consent as well as some assurances, particularly in connection with the environmentally sound management of the relevant waste.[120] Regulated waste that has the same physical and chemical characteristics and is shipped regularly through the same route within a twelve-month period can be subject to a simplified procedure governed by Article 6(6)–(8).

An important dimension of the Basel Convention is its relationship with other instruments, including regional instruments concerning the

---

[119] Basel Convention, *supra* n. 7, Art. 6(1).   [120] *Ibid.*, Art. 6(2)–(3).

management and transboundary movement of wastes. This dimension has been analysed in detail in the literature,[121] but the essentials are worth mentioning here, as they help to understand the general purpose of the Convention with respect to the international regulation of hazardous waste. During the negotiations, the idea to aim for a framework agreement – similar to the LRTAP Convention[122] or the Vienna Convention on the Protection of the Ozone Layer[123] – was put forward but soon discarded in favour of a treaty with specific obligations.[124] The main remnant of the initial approach is Article 11, which governs the relationship between the Convention and other 'agreements' or 'arrangements' addressing the main target of the Convention, namely the transboundary movement of hazardous waste. Such agreements or arrangements may have been made before or after the agreement on a bilateral, regional or even global basis, with other States parties to the Convention or with third States. Such agreements or arrangements may be considered as *lex specialis* with respect to the Convention, provided that they establish a system for the environmentally sound management of waste no less demanding than the one set out in the Convention (Article 11(2)). There are currently several agreements or arrangements of this type,[125] such as the Bamako Convention[126] or the Decision adopted by the OECD on this issue.[127] To understand the operation of this provision, three aspects must be clarified. First, one may ask who should assess whether an agreement or arrangement has environmental standards similar to those of the Convention. It is not a merely academic question, because the answer can have significant repercussions on the outcome of an international dispute.[128] The question was discussed by a working group established at the first COP. The working group preferred to leave this evaluation in the hands of States and merely offered some criteria for guiding their

---

[121] See Kummer, *supra* n. 2, Chapters 3 (The Basel Convention as an Umbrella for Regional Hazardous Waste Treaties), 4 (The Relationship Between the Basel Convention and the Waste Management Systems of the EU and the OECD) and 5 (The Basel Regime and Sectoral Pollution Control Treaties).

[122] LRTAP Convention, *supra* n. 4.

[123] Vienna Convention on the Protection of the Ozone Layer, 22 March 1985, 1513 UNTS 293.

[124] Kummer, *supra* n. 2, p. 87.

[125] A list of agreements and arrangements is available at: www.basel.int (last visited 10 December 2013).

[126] Bamako Convention, *supra* n. 7. See W. F. Jones, 'The Evolution of the Bamako Convention: An African Perspective' (1993) 4 *Colorado Journal of International Environmental Law and Policy* 324.

[127] Decision of the Council concerning the revision of Decision (92)39/FINAL on the control of transboundary movements of wastes destined for recovery operations, 21 May 2002, C(2001) 107/FINAL. On the OECD regime see Kummer, *supra* n. 2, Chapter 4; OECD, *Manuel d'application pour la mise en œuvre de la Décision de l'OCDE C(2001)107/Final modifiée concernant le contrôle des mouvements transfrontières de déchets destinés à des opérations de valorisation* (Paris: OECD, 2009).

[128] See e.g. the case *S. D. Myers Inc.* v. *Canada*, NAFTA Arbitration (UNCITRAL Rules), Award (13 November 2000).

decision.[129] Second, the Convention operates as a *lex generalis* only for transboundary movements of regulated waste between States that are both parties to those agreements or arrangements. Movements between two States parties to the Convention, only one of which is also a party to an agreement or special arrangement, remain regulated by the Convention. Third, one may ask what type of agreements or arrangements are specifically targeted by Article 11. In fact, there are several treaties, such as those for the transportation or dumping of certain substances in the sea (or in regional seas),[130] which are also relevant for the transboundary movement of waste.[131] Article 11 applies only to agreements or arrangements establishing a regulation on the core element of the Basel Convention, namely transboundary movements (between two States) of hazardous waste. Therefore, the relationship between the Convention and agreements that address other aspects of the waste cycle or that, despite their focus on the transboundary movements of waste, do not satisfy the conditions of Article 11, are regulated by the law of treaties, in particular Article 30 of the Vienna Convention on the Law of Treaties.[132]

Of course, the relationships between different treaties are not necessarily conflicting. As discussed next, important synergies between the Basel, PIC and POP Conventions are currently being developed. Eventually, the three instruments could be managed by a single structure with activities extending to the entire life cycle of at least some chemicals. Other integrated approaches are also possible, as suggested by the international regulation of nuclear energy and the more recent Convention on Mercury.

7.4.5 Integrated approaches

7.4.5.1 Synergies between the Basel, PIC and POP Conventions

As mentioned earlier, the POP, PIC and Basel Conventions taken together encompass the entire life cycle of chemicals (production/use, transboundary movement and disposal). Moreover, the obligations arising from these instruments often apply to similar activities and substances. Thus, it appeared useful to co-ordinate the work undertaken under the aegis of these three instruments by exploring synergies, particularly organisational synergies to take advantage of the strengths of each treaty.

In 2005, the COPs of the three conventions created a joint working group[133] in order to analyse the potential synergies and make recommendations. The findings

---

[129] Kummer, *supra* n. 2, p. 89.   [130] See Chapter 4.   [131] See Kummer, *supra* n. 2, Chapter 5.
[132] Vienna Convention on the Law of Treaties, 23 May 1969, 1155 UNTS 331.
[133] Decision SC-2/15 'Synergies', 15 May 2006, UNEP/POPS/COP.2/30; Decision RC-3/8, 'Cooperation and Coordination between the Basel, Rotterdam and Stockholm Conventions', 5 January 2007, UNEP/CHW.8/16.

of this group[134] were discussed and approved by the COPs of the three conventions in 2008.[135] The objective of this synergetic process, which is still in progress, is primarily the search for organisational efficiency. An initial step in the co-ordination of the work of the three secretariats involved the nomination of a common Executive Secretary and the simultaneous organisation of the three COPs. A possible next step would involve the merger of the three secretariats as well as of their contact points operating at the domestic level. This synergy process is expected to result in higher efficiency (cost reduction) and effectiveness (an impact increase and an improvement in the services provided to States).

The organisational experiment conducted in this context has, understandably, attracted the attention of environmental governance circles. Indeed, global environmental governance faces a major problem, namely the proliferation of different environmental regimes, each based on a treaty providing for the establishment of permanent institutions. The diversity of legal and administrative structures tackling the same problem may generate inconsistencies as well as much higher costs. Strengthening the institutional framework for sustainable development was one of the main themes of the 2012 Rio Summit. On this occasion, the Executive Secretary of the Basel, PIC and POP Conventions presented the first lessons to be derived from the synergies process involving the three conventions. Of course, the search for such synergies poses challenges beyond organisational or legal aspects. Occasionally, the bodies established under multilateral environmental agreements may have competing interests with respect to some questions, although this phenomenon is not always noticeable.[136] There are some alternatives that could help address these challenges, such as the creation of a world environment organisation, strengthening an organisation such as UNEP or further developing the piecemeal synergy process in other areas. In practice, only the last two options have been seriously explored so far, although, as discussed next, a more centralised solution has also emerged in connection with nuclear energy and mercury.

7.4.5.2 Integrated regulation: nuclear energy

The international law of nuclear energy provides a good illustration of a more centralised integrated approach to the regulation of dangerous substances and

---

[134] Report of the Ad hoc Joint Working Group on Enhancing Cooperation and Coordination among the Basel, Rotterdam and Stockholm Conventions on the Work of its Third Meeting, 29 March 2008, UNEP/FAO/CHW/RC/POPS/JWG.3/3.

[135] Decision SC-4/34, 'Enhancing Cooperation and Coordination among the Basel, Rotterdam and Stockholm Conventions', 8 May 2009, UNEP/POPS/COP.4/38; Decision RC-4/11, 'Enhancing Cooperation and Coordination among the Basel, Rotterdam and Stockholm Conventions', 31 October 2008, UNEP/FAO/RC/COP.4/24; Decision BC-IX/10, 'Cooperation and Coordination between the Basel, Rotterdam and Stockholm Conventions', 27 June 2008, UNEP/CHW.9/39.

[136] See, e.g., K. Rosendal and S. Andresen, *UNEP's Role in Enhancing Problem-Solving Capacity in Multilateral Environmental Agreements: Co-ordination and Assistance in the Biodiversity Conservation Cluster* (Lysaker: Fridtjof Nansen Institute, 2004), p. 29.

activities. This form of energy and the activities relating to it are subject to a regime consisting of treaties (bilateral and multilateral) as well as of a variety of standards and guidelines. However, the main component of this approach is the creation of a multilateral institution with a global reach and some measure of normative power, normally through the adoption of technical standards or recommendations, namely the International Atomic Energy Agency ('IAEA'). Over the years, the original regime of the IAEA set up in 1956 has been supplemented by the Treaty on the Non-Proliferation of Nuclear Weapons of 1968 ('NPT')[137] as well as some other treaties adopted in 1980,[138] after the Chernobyl disaster in 1986,[139] and then in 1994 and 1997.[140]

To understand the environmental dimensions of this complex system,[141] one must distinguish three different 'layers': (i) a sort of 'common law' or '*droit commun*' consisting of standards and technical norms issued by the IAEA; (ii) a system of multilateral treaties applicable to the main phases of these activities (protection of materials, creation and operation of facilities, including the prevention and management of accidents, movements of radioactive materials and waste management);[142] (iii) a dense array of bilateral agreements on nuclear co-operation, addressing issues such as technology transfer, notification and assistance or, more generally, the prevention of the risks posed by nuclear facilities.[143] These layers of regulation are interconnected, and they also interact with the systems established at the national or European level. This complex structure raises two types of questions. On the one hand, one may ask what is the substance (beyond the diversity of legal instruments) of this multi-layered regulation. On the other hand, it is necessary to clarify the relationship between the 'common law', which consists essentially of soft-law (non-binding) instruments, and the relevant binding instruments (multilateral/bilateral treaties and national/European law).

Regarding the substance of the regime, it covers all phases of civil nuclear activities, from the creation of a nuclear installation and the monitoring of its operations to the regulation of transboundary movements of radioactive substances to the management of waste. It is therefore an integrated approach to nuclear energy. Initially based on non-binding standards issued by the IAEA, this approach was strengthened by the adoption of several treaties in 1979 (physical protection of nuclear materials), 1986 (regarding co-operation and assistance in

---

[137] Treaty on the Non-Proliferation of Nuclear Weapons, 1 July 1968, 729 UNTS 161.

[138] Convention on the Physical Protection of Nuclear Material, 3 March 1980, 1458 UNTS 125.

[139] Convention on Early Notification, *supra* n. 9; Convention on Assistance, supra n. 9.

[140] Convention on Nuclear Safety, *supra* n. 9; Joint Convention, *supra* n. 9.

[141] See IAEA, *Safeguards Legal Framework*, available at: www.iaea.org (last visited 3 January 2014). See P. Birnie, A. Boyle and C. Redgwell, *International Law and the Environment* (Oxford University Press, 2009), Chapter 9; O. Jankowitsch-Prévor, 'La compétence normative de l'AIEA, Bases juridiques et sources du droit', in OECD, *Le droit nucléaire international: Histoire, évolution et perspectives* (Paris: OECD, 2010), pp. 15–34; Tromans, *supra* n. 44; Montjoie, *supra* n. 44.

[142] To this should be added a liability regime in case of nuclear accident discussed in Chapter 8.

[143] See the agreements identified by Birnie *et al.*, *supra* n. 141, pp. 511–15 (notes 149, 150, 164, 175).

the case of an accident),[144] 1994 (regarding the creation and operation of facilities)[145] and 1997 (in relation to the management of spent fuel and waste).[146] However, this layer of multilateral treaties is largely based on the substance of the IAEA standards. Moreover, while stating general principles, these instruments delegate specific modalities (authorisation, regulation and inspection of facilities, or the control of transboundary movements of radioactive substances) to States, whose domestic regulation is also based on IAEA standards. It is therefore important to clarify the legal standing of these international standards.

The legal source of the IAEA's normative power is Article III.A.6 of its Statute, according to which the Agency may:

> [E]stablish or adopt, in consultation and, where appropriate, in collaboration with the competent organs of the United Nations and with the specialized agencies concerned, standards of safety for protection of health and minimization of danger to life and property (including such standards for labour conditions), and to provide for the application of these standards to its own operation as well as to the operations making use of materials, services, equipment, facilities, and information made available by the Agency or at its request or under its control or supervision; and to provide for the application of these standards, at the request of the parties, to operations under any bilateral or multilateral arrangements, or, at the request of a State, to any of that State's activities in the field of atomic energy.[147]

The Agency may, therefore, adopt various types of technical norms and standards, but it is unclear whether they are legally binding for States parties. This question deserves a detailed analysis that goes beyond the limited scope of this section.[148] Suffice it to note here that not only do these technical norms enjoy a wide acceptance in practice but they can also acquire binding force through their incorporation into some agreements[149] as well as through

---

[144] See Convention on Early Notification and Convention on Assistance, *supra* n. 9 and G. Handl, 'Après Tchernobyl: Quelques réflexions sur le programme législatif multilatéral à l'ordre du jour' (1988) 92 *Revue générale de droit international public* 5.

[145] See Convention on Nuclear Safety *supra* n. 9; G. Handl, 'The IAEA Nuclear Safety Conventions: an Example of Successful "Treaty Management"?' (2003) 72 *Nuclear Law Bulletin* 7.

[146] See Joint Convention, *supra* n. 9; Montjoie, *supra* n. 44.

[147] Statute of the International Atomic Energy Agency, 26 October 1956, as amended on 28 December 1989, available at www.iaea.org (last visited 5 March 2013), Article III.A.6.

[148] See Jankowitsch-Prévor, *supra* n. 141; Birnie *et al.*, *supra* n. 141, pp. 495ff; Montjoie, *supra* n. 44, pp. 45ff.

[149] Jankowitsch-Prévor, *supra* n. 141, pp. 32ff (referring e.g. to the Convention on Early Notification (containing the 'Guidelines on Reportable Events, Integrated Planning and Information Exchange in a Transboundary Release of Radioactive Materials', INFCIRC/ 321) and the Convention on Assistance (containing the 'Guidelines for Mutual Emergency Assistance Arrangements in connection with a Nuclear Accident or a Radiological Emergency', INFCIRC/310)). See also Birnie *et al.*, *supra* n. 141, p. 497 (referring e.g., to the Convention on Nuclear Safety and the Joint Convention, which includes the following standards: 'The Safety of Nuclear Installations', IAEA Safety series No. 110, 1993; 'The Principles of Radioactive Waste Management', IAEA Safety series No. 111-F, 1995;

safeguards agreements concluded between States and the IAEA. Indeed, States parties to the NPT that do not have nuclear weapons are required to conclude a specific safeguard agreement with the Agency, which can also incorporate certain standards. However, the primary focus of these agreements is the obligation not to use the assistance provided by the Agency for military purposes[150] and, only subsidiarily to comply with the technical standards of the Agency.[151]

7.4.5.3 Integrated regulation: mercury

Another important development in the search for integrated approaches to the regulation of chemicals is the Minamata Convention on Mercury[152] concluded in October 2013. Despite the fact that, at the time of writing, this treaty had only received one ratification, albeit an important one (the United States), some brief observations on its overall approach and structure are warranted because the Convention (i) has a global scope, (ii) it seeks to encompass the entire life cycle of mercury, and (iii) it relies on the techniques developed in the POP, PIC and Basel Conventions (as well as in the protocols to the LRTAP Convention) to address the different phases of such cycle. Let us discuss these three issues in turn.

Regarding the first, it must be noted that the regulation of a heavy metal such as mercury had already been undertaken at a regional level (the UNECE). As discussed in Chapter 5, one of the protocols to the LRTAP Convention is specifically devoted to heavy metals as a source of transboundary air pollution.[153] The adverse effects of mercury on human health and the environment are well established, and they may be felt both locally and very far from the source (long-range transboundary depositions). UNEP has monitored the mercury cycle since 2001 in the context of its Global Mercury Assessments ('GMA').[154] The GMA and other UNEP initiatives, combined with regulatory developments in domestic law (particularly in the United States), helped gain momentum for the establishment of an Intergovernmental Negotiation Committee ('INC').[155] The INC concluded its work in its Geneva meeting in early 2013 approving the text of the Mercury Convention, which was formally

---

'Radiation Protection and the Safety of Radiation Sources', IAEA Safety series No 120, 1996, 'Code of Practice on the Transboundary Movement of Radioactive Waste', IAEA GC (XXXIV)/939 (1990)).

[150] Even though, in practice, the role of the Agency is most often to facilitate the provision of assistance by States with nuclear technology and material through agreements with suppliers and recipients.

[151] Where a State that is not a party to the NPT, safeguards agreements remain subject to the IAEA Statute, which provides, *inter alia*, the possibility for the Agency to inform the Security Council and the General Assembly of the United Nations in the event of a breach of the undertaking given in accordance with Article XI.F.4 not to use aid for military purposes (Art. XII.C).

[152] See *supra* n. 6.   [153] See *supra* n. 6.

[154] See e.g. UNEP, *Global Mercury Assessment* (2013) (hereafter 'GMA 2013').

[155] See H. Selin, 'Global Environmental Law and Treaty-Making on Hazardous Substances: The Minamata Convention and Mercury Abatement' (2014) 14 *Global Environmental Politics* 1, 4–7.

adopted in Minamata in October 2013 to commemorate the mercury poison-ing tragedy that had taken place in that Japanese town several decades earlier. Unlike the Heavy Metals Protocol, the Minamata Convention has a global scope and is open to the ratification of any State or regional economic integration organisations, even when the members of such organisation are not themselves parties to the Minamata Convention.[156]

Another significant feature of the Minamata Convention is its wide coverage of the mercury cycle, from mercury mining, to its use and release, to trade, storage and finally its disposal. This is in line with the broad objective of the Convention, set out in Article 1, namely 'to protect the human health and the environment from anthropogenic emissions and releases of mercury and mercury compounds'. The Convention only targets 'anthropogenic' emissions of mercury or mercury compounds, and not naturally occurring mercury, much in the same way as climate change agreements focus on anthropogenic (and not naturally occurring) emissions of greenhouse gases. Anthropogenic releases of mercury stem primarily from artisanal and small-scale gold mining (37%), fossil fuel burning (25%), the production of non-ferrous metals (10%), cement production (9%) and several other processes.[157] These sources are governed by the Convention through a variety of regulatory tools borrowed from the other treaties discussed in this chapter and Chapter 5.

Indeed, the Convention brings together the instruments of the POP, PIC and Basel Conventions and some other treaties and applies them to the regulation of mercury, mercury compounds, mercury-added products and mercury-related processes. As such, it is a complex instrument that can only be briefly outlined in the context of this introduction.[158] In this regard, it is useful to distinguish five main phases of regulatory intervention, namely extraction (or mining), use and release, trade, storage and disposal. The Minamata Convention provides a different framework for each phase.

Mercury *mining* is regulated in Article 3. According to this provision, mercury mining that was not conducted at the time of entry into force of the Convention for the party in question (i.e. new mercury mining) must be prohibited, whereas existing mining can only continue for fifteen years after ratification.[159] Regarding other significant sources for extracting mercury (called 'secondary' by contrast with 'primary' mining), they must be identified and in some cases the available mercury must be eliminated following envir-onmentally sound management guidelines.[160]

The *use and release* of mercury is regulated following the model of the POP Convention. Articles 4 to 9 provide for a detailed framework focusing on products and processes (including gold mining and other processes – e.g.

---

[156] Minamata Convention, *supra* n. 6, Art. 30. The term 'regional economic integration organisa-tion' is specifically defined in Art. 2(j) of the Convention.
[157] GMA 2013, *supra* n. 154, p. 9.   [158] For a more detailed discussion see Selin, *supra* n. 155.
[159] Minamata Convention, *supra* n. 6, Art. 3(3)–(4).   [160] *Ibid.*, Art. 3(5).

coal burning – that lead to emissions or the release of mercury into the environment). For some products and processes, which are identified in a 'list' (Annexes A, part I and B, part I), there is a *phase out* obligation,[161] with some exclusions (comparable to the 'general exceptions' of the POP Convention)[162] and country-specific time extensions (comparable to the 'specific exemptions' of the POP Convention).[163] Some other products and processes are only *restricted* (e.g. the use of mercury in dental amalgam or in the production of vinyl chloride monomer)[164] whereas some products are specifically *allowed* (e.g. the use of mercury compounds to extend the lifespan of some vaccines, in accordance with WHO recommendations).[165] Three other types of processes are also addressed. The first, i.e. *artisanal and small-scale gold mining* using mercury, must be tackled through 'national plans' in accordance with Annex C of the Convention.[166] The second, i.e. 'point sources' identified in Annex D that *emit mercury into the atmosphere*, are subject to some control measures. 'New' point sources must be subject to 'best available technologies'[167] and 'best environmental practices'[168] standards in order 'to control and, where feasible, reduce emissions, as soon as practicable but no later than five years [from ratification]'[169] whereas 'existing' point sources are only to be addressed through 'national plans' including some measures mentioned in Article 8(5). Finally, a default provision focuses on other processes ('point sources') whose operation *releases mercury into the environment*. For these sources, there is an obligation to identify and to take measures to reduce such releases.[170]

Regarding *trade*, Article 3(6)–(7) allows exports of mercury both to parties and non-parties on the condition that a prior-informed-consent (PIC) procedure, modelled on the PIC Convention, is respected to ensure that the receiving party is capable of managing mercury properly.[171] As for exports from non-parties to a State party to the Convention, the importing country can only allow the transaction to proceed if it receives assurances that the mercury comes from a source permitted under the Convention.[172]

Article 10 targets the *interim storage* of mercury or mercury-compounds intended for a use allowed in the Convention (other than waste mercury). States parties are required to take measures to ensure that such storage is made in an 'environmentally sound manner'. This standard is to be defined by reference to guidelines issued by the COP, which, in turn, must be based on the relevant guidelines adopted under the aegis of the Basel Convention.[173]

---

[161] *Ibid.*, Art. 4(1) (in addition, Arts. 4(2) provides a more flexible obligation which is only available under strict conditions) and 5(2).

[162] *Ibid.*, Annex A.   [163] *Ibid.*, Art. 6.   [164] *Ibid.*, Annex A, part II, and Annex B, part II.

[165] *Ibid.*, Annex A.   [166] *Ibid.*, Art. 7.   [167] *Ibid.*, Art. 2(b).   [168] *Ibid.*, Art. 2(c).

[169] *Ibid.*, Art. 8(4).   [170] *Ibid.*, Art. 9(3)–(5).

[171] *Ibid.*, Art. 3(6) (requiring written consent and some assurances, more demanding in the case of exports to non-parties) and 3(7) (setting out a facilitated system based on a general notification).

[172] *Ibid.*, Art. 3(8) and 3(9) (setting out a facilitated system based on a general notification).

[173] *Ibid.*, Art. 10(3).

Finally, the Basel Convention also provides the foundations of the approach followed in Article 11 of the Minamata Convention in connection with the *disposal* of mercury waste. Mercury waste is characterised in paragraphs (1) and (2) of Article 11 by direct reference to the Basel Convention. States have three types of obligations with respect to this object, namely: to take measures to ensure the disposal of mercury waste in an environmentally sound manner, taking into account the relevant guidelines of the Basel Convention;[174] not to allow the recovery, reclaim or direct re-use of mercury waste unless it is for a use permitted under the Convention or for its environmentally sound disposal;[175] and to apply the PIC system of the Basel Convention to transboundary movements of mercury waste.[176] Where a State is not a party to the Basel Convention, Article 11 requires it to take into account this instrument and the standards arising from it to shape its legal framework.[177]

As other multilateral environmental agreements, the Minamata Convention has a significant institutional and compliance component, including a financial mechanism that led to much discussion during the negotiations.[178] Such components are analysed in a cross-cutting manner in Chapters 2 and 9 of this book. However, for present purposes, it is the focus on the entire life cycle of a substance such as mercury and the combined use of phase-outs, PIC procedures or BATs/BEPs standards, borrowed from its predecessors, which deserve attention.

Select bibliography

Andrews, A., 'Beyond the Ban – Can the Basel Convention Adequately Safeguard the Interests of the World's Poor in the International Trade of Hazardous Waste?' (2009) 5 *Law, Environment and Development Journal* 167.

Barrios, P., 'The Rotterdam Convention on Hazardous Chemicals: A Meaningful Step towards Environmental Protection? (2004) 16 *Georgetown International Environmental Law Review* 679.

Bitar, F., *Les mouvements transfrontières de déchets dangereux selon la Convention de Bâle. Etude des régimes de responsabilité* (Paris: Pedone, 1997).

Bombier, N., 'The Basel Convention's Complete Ban on Hazardous Waste Exports: Negotiating the Compatibility of Trade and the Environment' (1997) 7 *Journal of Environmental Law and Practice* 325.

Brown Weiss, E., 'International Environmental Law: Contemporary Issues and the Emergence of a New World Order' (1995) 81 *Georgetown Law Journal* 675.

Caron, D. and C. Leben (eds.), *Les aspects internationaux des catastrophes naturelles et industrielles – The International Aspects of Natural and Industrial Catastrophes* (The Hague/Leiden: Académie de droit international/Martinus Nijhoff, 2001).

Clapps, J., *Toxic Exports: The Transfer of Hazardous Wastes from Rich to Poor Countries* (Ithaca NY: Cornell University Press, 2001).

---

[174] *Ibid.*, Art. 11(3)(a).   [175] *Ibid.*, Art. 11(3)(b).   [176] *Ibid.*, Art. 11(3)(c).
[177] *Ibid.*, Art. 11(1) and (3)(c).   [178] Selin, *supra* n. 155, pp. 14–15.

Cox, J., 'The Trafigura Case and the System of Prior Informed Consent Under the Basel Convention – A Broken System?' (2010) 6 *Law, Environment and Development Journal* 263.

Dupuy, P.-M., 'Overview of the Existing Customary Legal Regime Regarding International Pollution', in D. B. Magraw (ed.), *International Law and Pollution* (Philadelphia: University of Pennsylvania Press, 1991), pp. 61–89.

Edvokia, M., 'La Convention de Bâle sur les mouvements transfrontières de déchets dangereux (22 March 1989)' (1989) 93 *Revue générale de droit international public* 899.

Emory, R. W., 'Probing the Protections in the Rotterdam Convention on Prior Informed Consent' (2001) 12 *Colorado Journal of International Environmental Law and Policy* 47.

Grosz, M., *Sustainable Waste Trade under WTO Law* (Leiden: Martinus Nijhoff, 2011).

Handl, G., 'Après Tchernobyl: Quelques réflexions sur le programme législatif multilatéral à l'ordre du jour' (1988) 92 *Revue générale de droit international public* 5.

'The IAEA Nuclear Safety Conventions: an Example of Successful "Treaty Management"?' (2003) 72 *Nuclear Law Bulletin* 7.

Jankowitsch-Prévor, O., 'La compétence normative de l'AIEA, Bases juridiques et sources du droit', in OECD, *Le droit nucléaire international: Histoire, évolution et perspectives* (Paris: OECD, 2010), pp. 15–34.

Jones, W. F., 'The Evolution of the Bamako Convention: An African Perspective' (1993) 4 *Colorado Journal of International Environmental Law and Policy* 324.

Kummer, K., *International Management of Hazardous Wastes* (Oxford University Press, 1995).

Lallas, P., 'The Role of Process and Participation in the Development of Effective International Environmental Agreements: A Study of the Global Treaty on Persistent Organic Pollutants' (2002) 19 *UCLA Journal of Environmental Law and Policy* 83.

'The Stockholm Convention on Persistent Organic Pollutants' (2001) 95 *American Journal of International Law* 692.

Lonngren, R., *International Approaches to Chemicals Control: A Historical Overview* (Stockholm: Kemi, 1992).

McDorman, T., 'The Rotterdam Convention on the Prior Informed Consent Procedure for Certain Hazardous Chemicals and Pesticides in International Trade: Some Legal Notes' (2004) 13 *Review of European Community and International Environmental Law* 187.

Mekouar, A. M., 'Pesticides and Chemicals – The Requirement of Prior Informed Consent', in D. Shelton (ed.), *Commitment and Compliance. The Role of Non-Binding Norms in the International Legal System* (Oxford University Press, 2000), pp. 146–63.

Mintz, J., 'Two Cheers for Global POP's: A Summary and Assessment of the Stockholm Convention on Persistent Organic Pollutants' (2001) 14 *Georgetown International Environmental Law Review* 319.

Montjoie, M., *Droit international et gestion des déchets radioactifs* (Paris: LGDJ, 2011).

Olsen, M. A., *Analysis of the Stockholm Convention on Persistent Organic Pollutants* (Dobbs Ferry NY: Oceana, 2003).

Ouguergouz, F. 'La Convention de Bamako sur l'interdiction d'importer en Afrique des déchets dangereux et sur le contrôle des mouvements transfrontières et la gestion des déchets dangereux produits en Afrique' (1992) 38 *Annuaire français de droit international* 871.

Pallemaerts, M., *Toxics and Transnational Law: International and European Regulation of Toxic Substances as Legal Symbolism* (Oxford: Hart Publishing, 2003).

Redgwell, C., 'Regulating Trade in Dangerous Substances: Prior Informed Consent under the 1998 Rotterdam Convention', in A. Kiss, D. Shelton and K. Ishibashi (eds.), *Economic Globalization and Compliance with International Environmental Agreements* (The Hague: Kluwer, 2003), pp. 75–88.

Riley, P., *Nuclear Waste: Law, Policy and Pragmatism* (Aldershot: Ashgate, 2004).

Rosendal, K. and S. Andresen, *UNEP's Role in Enhancing Problem-Solving Capacity in Multilateral Environmental Agreements: Co-ordination and Assistance in the Biodiversity Conservation Cluster* (Lysaker: Fridtjof Nansen Institute, 2004).

Scott, J., 'REACH: Combining Harmonization and Dynamism in the Regulation of Chemicals', in J. Scott (ed.), *Environmental Protection: European Law and Governance* (Oxford University Press, 2009), pp. 56–91.

Selin, H., 'Global Environmental Law and Treaty-Making on Hazardous Substances: The Minamata Convention and Mercury Abatement' (2014) 14 *Global Environmental Politics* 1.

Smith, S., 'GHS: A Short Acronym for a Big Idea' (2007) 69 *Occupational Hazards* 6.

Söderholm, P., 'The Political Economy of a Global Ban on Mercury-Added Products: Positive versus Negative List Approaches' (2013) 53 *Journal of Cleaner Production* 287.

Szasz, P., *The Law and Practice of the International Atomic Energy Agency* (Vienna: IAEA, 1970) and *Supplement* (1970–1980).

Tromans, S., *Nuclear Law: The Law Applying to Nuclear Installations and Radioactive Substances in its Historic Context* (Oxford: Hart Publishing, 2010).

Winder, C., R. Azzi and D. Wagner, 'The Development of the Globally Harmonized System (GHS) of Classification and Labelling of Hazardous Chemicals' (2005) 125 *Journal of Hazardous Materials* 29.

Winter, G., 'Dangerous Chemicals: A Global Problem on its Way to Global Governance', in M. Fuhr, K. Bizer and P. H. Feindt (eds.), *Umweltrecht und Umweltwissenschaft: Festschrift für Eckard Rehbinder* (Erich Schmidt Verlag: 2007), pp. 819–33.

Wirth, D. A., 'Hazardous Substances and Activities', in D. Bodansky, J. Brunnée and E. Hey (eds.), *The Oxford Handbook of International Environmental Law* (Oxford University Press, 2007), pp. 394–422.

'Trade implications of the Basel Convention Amendment banning North–South Trade in Hazardous Waste' (1998) 7 *Review of European Community and International Environmental Law* 237.

Young, G., J. Garman and S. Tupper, 'A Long Way from Basel Clarity: Implications of the Basel Convention for the Consumer Electronics Sector' (2000) 9 *European Environmental Law Review* 71.

Part III
Implementation

8

Implementation: traditional approaches

8.1 Introduction

In the preceding chapters, we have discussed the substantive regulation of environmental problems at the international level. In particular, we have analysed the obligations imposed on States in fields such as the protection of the marine environment, the atmosphere and wildlife as well as the control of dangerous substances and activities. We now turn to the processes through which these obligations are implemented.

The traditional approach in this area assumed that compliance with international obligations only depended upon a State's will to comply. From a substantive law perspective, the main mechanism to encourage compliance was to make any violation costly for the State, notably through the application of secondary norms of State responsibility.[1] From a procedural standpoint, breaching a norm could have several consequences, ranging from the first allegations of non-compliance, often followed by negotiations and consultations between the States concerned, to judicial mechanisms of dispute settlement and, where appropriate, alternative dispute settlement, such as mediation, conciliation or inquiry.[2]

The transition from compliance to non-compliance with the requirements of a norm is however better understood as a process, which admits degrees. Such degrees provide a useful basis for the discussion in this chapter because they help to locate the different implementation mechanisms at the stage where they are most likely to intervene. Four 'stages' may be distinguished along the compliance axis.[3] Figure 8.1 summarises this understanding graphically.

---

[1] States may also adopt countermeasures, although this is infrequent. See Responsibility of States for Internationally Wrongful Acts, GA Res. 56/83, UN Doc. A/RES/56/83, 12 December 2001 ('ILC Articles'), Art. 22 and Arts. 49–54.

[2] Article 33 of the UN Charter, 24 October 1945, 1 UNTS 16, shows the range of traditional methods for the peaceful settlement of disputes between States. See J. Merrills, *International Dispute Settlement* (Cambridge University Press, 2011).

[3] See P.-M. Dupuy, 'Où en est le droit international de l'environnement à la fin du siècle?' (1997) *Revue générale de droit international public* 873 in particular 893–95; J. E. Viñuales, 'Managing Abidance by Standards for the Protection of the Environment', in A. Cassese (ed.), *Realizing Utopia* (Oxford University Press, 2012), pp. 326–39.

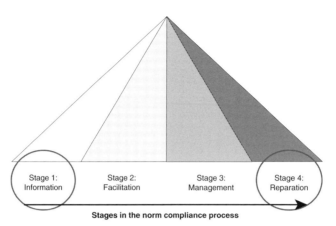

Stage 1:
Information

Stage 2:
Facilitation

Stage 3:
Management

Stage 4:
Reparation

Stages in the norm compliance process

Figure 8.1: Stages in the compliance process

Some mechanisms only play a role 'upstream' before allegations of non-compliance emerge (Stage 1). The main mechanism at this stage is the reporting and communication of information showing a State's behaviour in relation to its international obligations (8.2). By contrast, 'downstream' (Stage 4), we find the more formal mechanisms for the characterisation of a breach by third parties (arbitration and permanent courts) and the determination of the ensuing consequences attached by the law of State responsibility (8.3). Between these two extremes lies a grey area where the level of compliance is unclear. This area has traditionally been the preserve of so-called diplomatic or political mechanisms for the peaceful settlement of disputes. We will see, however, in Chapter 9, that in international environmental law, this area has been populated by new methods of facilitating compliance (Stage 2) and managing non-compliance (Stage 3) with environmental standards.

8.2 Monitoring and reporting

8.2.1 Types of obligations

A series of mechanisms can be utilised to seek compliance with environmental obligations. In this section, we analyse a technique that plays a role upstream of the breach of an obligation, namely the collection of information (monitoring) and the submission of reports in relation to the implementation of an obligation (reporting). To understand how this mechanism works, it is useful to look first at the types of obligations to be implemented.

A first distinction, which we will explore in more depth later in this chapter, can be made between 'primary norms' and 'secondary norms'. Primary norms prescribe specific behaviour to be adopted by States (e.g. to reduce the emissions of certain substances, establish protected areas, communicate reports, etc.) or define conditions that, if met, trigger certain legal consequences. On the other hand, secondary norms spell out the consequences attached to a breach or, more specifically, to the fulfilment of the conditions set by a primary norm ('reparation' in a broad sense). We will see in Section 8.3 of this chapter that the distinction is much more complex than it may appear.

Within primary norms, a further distinction can be made between 'substantive obligations' and 'procedural obligations'. The first category covers various types of obligations. An example is the duty to prevent environmental damage, which is enshrined in both customary[4] and treaty law.[5] Other examples include treaty obligations to reduce emissions[6] or to control the transboundary movement of certain substances.[7] These substantive obligations reflect the intuitive idea that there is an inter-State or 'horizontal' obligation. However, the first category also includes another type of obligation that is important in international environmental law, namely a 'vertical' obligation assumed by a State to adopt domestic measures implementing the provisions of a treaty. Vertical obligations organise the implementation of horizontal obligations. Examples include the obligation to take domestic measures to implement the international trade regulation of species or substances or to adopt national plans for the conservation of biodiversity.[8]

As to the category of procedural obligations, they in turn contribute to the implementation of vertical substantive obligations. Indeed, their main objective is to encourage States not only to take national measures and to communicate these, but also to establish institutions to collect the necessary information[9] and, thereby, to lay the foundations for the creation of a sufficient database for monitoring the evolution of the environmental problem that the regulation is intended to control. As such, these procedural requirements are at the origin of mechanisms for information gathering and reporting.

[4] See *Legality of the Threat or Use of Nuclear Weapons*, Advisory Opinion, ICJ Reports 1996, p. 226 ('*Legality of Nuclear Weapons*'), para. 29.

[5] See United Nations Convention on the Law of the Sea, 10 December 1982, 1833 UNTS 3 ('UNCLOS'), Art. 194.

[6] See e.g. the Montreal Protocol on Substances that Deplete the Ozone Layer, 16 September 1987, 1522 UNTS 29 ('Montreal Protocol'), Arts. 2 to 2I and Annexes A, B, C and E; Kyoto Protocol to the United Nations Framework Convention on Climate Change, 11 December 1997, 2302 UNTS 148 ('Kyoto Protocol'), Art. 3 and Annex B; Stockholm Convention on Persistent Organic Pollutants, 22 May 2001, 2256 UNTS 119 ('Stockholm Convention' or 'POP Convention'), Art. 3(1).

[7] See Convention on International Trade in Endangered Species of Wild Fauna and Flora, 3 March 1973, 993 UNTS 243 ('CITES'), Arts. III–IV; Basel Convention on the Control of Transboundary Movements of Hazardous Wastes and their Disposal, 22 March 1989, 1673 UNTS 57 ('Basel Convention'), Arts. 4 and 6; Rotterdam Convention on the Prior Informed Consent Procedure for Certain Hazardous Chemicals and Pesticides in International Trade, 10 September 1998, 2244 UNTS 337 ('PIC Convention'), Arts. 10 and 11; POP Convention, *supra* n. 6, Art. 3(2).

[8] See Convention on Biological Diversity, 5 June 1992, 1760 UNTS 79 ('CBD'), Art. 6.

[9] See CITES, *supra* n. 7, Art. VIII(1).

8.2.2 Types of mechanisms

In general, environmental treaties provide mechanisms for gathering information and reporting on the implementation of obligations.[10] In the context of
this book, rather than conduct an individual analysis of the numerous treaties,
we will focus on identifying the types of mechanisms used in practice. In this
respect, we can distinguish two main types, depending on the scope of the
power conferred by the relevant treaty.

The *first type of mechanism* is relatively unambitious. States have the
obligation to submit reports to a treaty body (the Conference of the Parties
('COP'), the Secretariat or another organ) on the measures they have taken to
implement the obligations under the treaty. Among these measures, it
is often required that States establish a system to monitor certain environmental variables (e.g. emissions of certain substances). Monitoring systems
provide the basis for the appropriate discharge of reporting obligations. This
mechanism can be illustrated by reference to Articles 4 and 6 of the Protocol
on the Reduction of Sulphur Emissions to the LRTAP Convention.[11] Article
6 provides that States parties shall 'develop national policies, programmes
and strategies which shall serve as a means of reducing sulphur emissions or
their transboundary fluxes, by at least 30% as soon as possible and at the latest
by 1993'. They also have to 'report on progress towards achieving this goal to
the Executive Body.' The 30 per cent reduction stems from the substantive
obligation in Article 2 of the Protocol. The obligation to report on the
measures and progress is confirmed by Article 4, which states that '[e]ach
Party shall provide annually to the Executive Body its levels of national
annual sulphur emissions, and the basis upon which they have been calculated'. These arrangements are also useful to illustrate the articulation of
substantive obligations, horizontal and vertical, and procedural obligations
on monitoring and communication.

The *second type of mechanism* is quite similar to the first, but with two
significant differences. On the one hand, the procedural obligations are more
precise. They pose specific deadlines and formats for the communication of
information. On the other hand, the treaty body that receives communications
has greater powers which, depending on the treaty, may include (i) the
possibility to verify the information submitted, (ii) the ability to request
additional information, or even (iii) the ability to collect information *proprio
motu* by other means.

---

[10] R. Wolfrum, 'Means of Ensuring Compliance with and Enforcement of International
Environmental Law', (1998) 272 *Recueil des cours de l'Académie de droit international de La
Haye*, 9–154, in particular 36–55.
[11] Protocol to the Convention on Long-Range Transboundary Air Pollution 1979 on the
Reduction of Sulphur Emissions or their Transboundary Fluxes by at Least 30 per cent,
8 July 1985, 1480 UNTS 215 ('Sulphur Protocol I'). See also Protocol to the Convention on
Long-Range Transboundary Air Pollution 1979 on Further Reduction of Sulphur Emissions,
14 June 1994, 2030 UNTS 122 ('Sulphur Protocol II'), Art. 5.

For example, the COP of the Ramsar Convention[12] established in 1990 a mechanism for the communication and verification of information concerning protected sites.[13] This mechanism implements Article 3, paragraphs 1 (vertical substantive obligation) and 2 (procedural obligation of monitoring and communication). Annex II to the Decision establishing this mechanism requires the use of a particular format for the communication of information ('Information Sheet on Ramsar Sites' and 'Classification System for Wetland Type').[14] Annex I sets up a procedure whereby States must inform the Bureau of the Convention where the ecological characteristics of a site on the list are changing (or may change) due to human intervention.[15] The Bureau may request additional information to assess the situation and, if it considers that the site characteristics are changing (or may change), it can collaborate with the State in question to find an acceptable solution. The procedure then becomes a political means of dispute resolution, including the elevation of the case to the Standing Committee (which also tries to find a solution) or to the COP. We will return to these procedures in Chapter 9.

Another example is the system established by CITES.[16] Horizontal substantive obligations which may be found *inter alia* in Articles II–IV are to be implemented through vertical substantive obligations (Article VIII(1)). Article VIII(7) provides a procedural obligation for each Party to establish and communicate to the Secretariat reports on the implementation of the Convention. These reports must be submitted within a specified time (depending on the case, either annually or biennially) and in a specific format. In this regard, the Secretariat transmitted to States parties two 'notifications' introducing the standard format for the presentation of annual[17] and biennial reports.[18] The Secretariat, which is the body in charge of reviewing these reports, can also 'request from Parties such further information with respect thereto as it deems necessary to ensure implementation of the present Convention' (Article XII(2)(d)).

A third example is the more complex system established by the UNFCCC.[19] Article 12 of the UNFCCC structures the procedural obligation (monitoring of emissions and absorptions, as well as the adoption of national measures) on

---

[12] Convention on Wetlands of International Importance especially as Waterfowl Habitat, 2 February 1971, 996 UNTS 245 ('Ramsar Convention').

[13] Recommendation 4.7. (1990) 'Mechanisms for Improved Application of the Ramsar Convention' ('Recommendation 4.7'). This mechanism had been established earlier by the Standing Committee of the Convention, but it was not until 1990 that the COP endorsed this measure (see Recommendation 4.7, first paragraph of the operative part).

[14] This format has been revised over time.

[15] Recommendation 4.7, *supra* n. 13, Annex I, para. 1.   [16] CITES, *supra* n. 7.

[17] Notification to the Parties 2011/019, 17 February 2011. This notification refers to the guidelines for the submission of annual reports, which were adopted in 2000 and revised to introduce adjustments adopted at subsequent COPs.

[18] Notification to the Parties 2005/035, 6 July 2005.

[19] United Nations Framework Convention on Climate Change, 9 May 1992, 1771 UNTS 107 ('UNFCCC').

the basis of the substantive obligations studied in Chapter 5 (obligations of all States, obligations of States listed in Annex I, obligations of States listed in Annex II). Depending on the situation of a State, the frequency of reporting, their content and the degree of verification by the treaty bodies will differ. We cannot explain here the details of the rules applicable to each category of States.[20] To grasp the extent and complexity that such a system entails, it suffices to recall briefly the regime applicable to those States listed in Annex I, who are also parties to the Kyoto Protocol.[21] These States must submit annual reports on their emissions of greenhouse gases in accordance with a specific format ('common reporting format' or 'CRF' and 'national inventory report' or 'NIR')[22] and, for Kyoto parties, including additional information required by the Kyoto Protocol.[23] In addition, they must submit regular 'national communications' on measures they have taken to reduce their emissions.[24] These reports may be subject to 'in-depth reviews' by teams of experts coordinated by the Secretariat.[25] The possibility for these teams of experts to visit a country was considered at the first COP and subsequently confirmed.[26] Moreover, this review includes exchanges between the team and the State in question, including the provision of additional information by the latter.[27] Note that, although the data is provided primarily by the States, the COP has acknowledged the possibility that data from other sources also be taken into account.[28]

These various illustrations of monitoring mechanisms provide a representative picture of the evolution of these systems, characterised by a higher level of institutionalisation and more detailed verification. As we will see in Chapter 9, these mechanisms often operate together with other procedures designed to facilitate compliance or manage cases of 'non-compliance'.

---

[20] See unfccc.int/national_reports/items/1408.php (last visited on 28 January 2013).

[21] Kyoto Protocol, *supra* n. 6.

[22] Decision 3/CP.5, 'Guidelines for the Preparation of National Communications by Parties included in Annex I to the Convention, Part I: UNFCCC Reporting Guidelines on Annual Inventories', 16 February 2000, Doc. FCCC/CP/1999/7, revised several times.

[23] UNFCCC Secretariat, *Kyoto Protocol Reference Manual on Accounting of Emissions and Assigned Amount* (2008).

[24] Decision 4/CP.5, 'Guidelines for the Preparation of National Communications by Parties included in Annex I to the Convention, Part II: UNFCCC Reporting Guidelines for National Communications', 16 February 2000, Doc. FCCC/CP/1999/7, revised several times.

[25] See in particular Decision 2/CP.1, 'Review of First Communications from the Parties referred to in Annex I of the Convention', 2 June 1995, Doc. FCCC/CP/1995/7/Add.1; Decision 6/CP.3, 'Communications from Parties included in Annex I of the Convention', 6 March 1998, Doc. FCCC/CP/1997/7/Add.1; Decision 11/CP.4, 'National Communications from Parties included in Annex I to the Convention', 25 January 1999, Coc. FCCC/CP/1998/16/Add.1; Decision 6/CP.5, 'Guidelines for the Technical Review of Greenhouse Gas Inventories from Parties included in Annex I to the Convention', 2 February 2000, Doc. FCCC/CP/1999/6/Add.1, adopting the document FCCC/CP/1999/7* ('Examination Guidelines').

[26] See Decision 2/CP.1, *supra* n. 25, para. 2 (c); Decision 6/CP.3, *supra* n. 25, para. 3 (a); Examination Guidelines, *supra* n. 25, para. 20.

[27] Examination Guidelines, *supra* n. 25, para. 19.

[28] See Decision 6/CP.3, *supra* n. 25, para. 2 (b), allowing the release of inventory data '[with] relevant data from authoritative sources'.

8.3 Dispute settlement and legal consequences

8.3.1 Preliminary remarks

An increasingly common method for the implementation of international law in the second half of the twentieth century has been via the characterisation of a breach through adjudication or quasi-adjudication (e.g. a committee) and the determination of the legal consequences attached to it (responsibility for internationally wrongful acts). This method has a number of difficulties in international environmental law.[29] We will discuss such difficulties in due course but it seems useful, by way of introduction, to identify some of them at this stage.

First, the logic of reparation is not suited to the particularities of environmental damage, which is much more difficult and/or expensive to repair or sometimes simply irreversible. The definition of what constitutes repairable environmental damage (in particular the question of 'pure ecological damage'), the establishment of a causal link between an act and its environmental consequences (e.g. for climate change-related damage), and the determination of appropriate reparation (payment of compensation, compensation in kind, rehabilitation, etc.) are all issues that international law is still struggling to solve. Moreover, articulating prevention and reparation is particularly challenging in international environmental law because some economically desirable activities (e.g. energy generation or industrial processes) necessarily have effects on the environment. Often, it is not possible to eliminate these effects without stopping the activity itself. In such cases, international law seeks to minimise them and, depending on the cases, to provide some form of reparation.

Second, even when reparation is possible, developing rules defining its specific modalities is particularly challenging. Such reparation may, for example, be organised at the international level through rules on State responsibility for breach of horizontal obligations. However, it may also be organised at the national or transnational level, with international law requiring compliance with certain parameters, such as the granting to aggrieved individuals of access to the courts of the State where the damage originated, or the prohibition of discrimination, or, alternatively, a compensation scheme based on a combination of strict liability rules and insurance.

Third, some violations do not result from a lack of State willingness to comply with international law, as assumed by the general theory of international responsibility, but rather a technical or financial inability to do so. In this context, the characterisation of a breach and of the ensuing legal consequences may not be a suitable remedy, as further discussed in Chapter 9.

---

[29] See P.-M. Dupuy, 'A propos des mésaventures de la responsabilité internationale des Etats dans ses rapports avec la protection internationale de l'environnement', in M. Prieur (ed.), *Etudes en hommage à Alexandre Kiss* (Paris: Frisson-Roche, 1998), pp. 269–82, para. 2.

In the following paragraphs, we discuss how these difficulties have been addressed in international law. After a brief discussion of the role of adjudication in international environmental law (8.3.2), we analyse how the consequences of environmental damage are managed under international law (8.3.3).

8.3.2 International environmental adjudication

8.3.2.1 The fora of international environmental law

Despite its important normative development over the past four decades, international environmental law has not undergone the growing judicialisation experienced in other areas. Indeed, specialised international adjudication has significantly developed in areas such as human rights, international criminal law, international trade law, foreign investment law and increasingly the law of the sea, but not on environmental matters.[30] To understand the extent to which environmental disputes have been brought nevertheless before international courts and tribunals, it is useful to distinguish between specialised courts in environmental law and what might be called 'borrowed fora', i.e. specialised courts in other branches of international law, but facing disputes having environmental components. Figure 8.2 introduces these two categories.

These two broad categories will be analysed in the following sections. A general feature that should be noted at this stage is that most international environmental disputes take place outside the jurisdiction and procedures created specifically to address environmental issues. The reasons for this

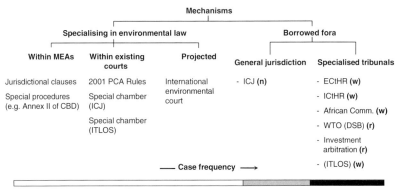

Figure 8.2: The fora of international environmental law

---

[30] On international environmental adjudication see C. Romano, *The Peaceful Settlement of International Environmental Disputes: A Pragmatic Approach* (The Hague: Kluwer, 2000); O. Lecucq and S. Maljean-Dubois (eds.), *Le rôle du juge dans le développement du droit de l'environnement* (Brussels: Bruylant, 2008); J. E. Viñuales, 'The Contribution of the International Court of Justice to the Development of International Environmental Law' (2008) 32 *Fordham International Law Journal* 232; T. Stephens, *International Courts and Environmental Protection* (Cambridge University Press, 2009).

phenomenon are unclear. It could be due to the reluctance of States to describe a dispute as 'environmental' or to use new structures or even to have their dispute subject to a body of rules that are relatively new and poorly understood. One may also refer to the fact that claims have often been brought by individuals (and not States) before international courts to which they have access. Be it as it may, this phenomenon has implications for the development of international environmental law, as discussed in Section 8.3.2.3.

8.3.2.2 Courts specialising in environmental matters

Efforts to create procedures and specialised tribunals in environmental law have followed three main approaches. The first is the development of a procedure for settling disputes in the context of an environmental treaty. Several treaties have dispute settlement clauses[31] although, in most cases, such clauses fall short of consenting to judicial dispute settlement.[32] The Convention on Biological Diversity goes a step further and offers a specific arbitration procedure to States parties. Pursuant to Article 27(3), States may express their specific consent to submit their disputes to the International Court of Justice ('ICJ') or to an arbitration procedure organised by Annex II. However, very few States have consented to this possibility (Austria, Cuba, Georgia and Latvia) and, in any event, this procedure has not been used yet.

A second possibility is to develop special procedures within existing institutions. This approach has taken two main forms. On the one hand, the Permanent Court of Arbitration ('PCA') adopted in 2001 'Optional Rules for Arbitration of Disputes Relating to Natural Resources and/or the Environment'.[33] This instrument, which has been used only rarely, explicitly provide for some procedural powers, such as the possibility for the tribunal to request non-technical summaries of scientific matters (Article 24(4)), the power to grant interim measures to protect the environment (Article 26(1)) or to appoint experts to assist a tribunal (Article 27(1)). On the other hand, special chambers have been established within the ICJ and the International Tribunal for the Law of the Sea ('ITLOS') to address environmental issues. The 'Chamber for Environmental Matters'[34] was established in 1993 in response to

---

[31] Some treaties provide for a so-called 'opt-in' option, i.e. the dispute settlement mechanism is only applicable if the State explicitly consents when it becomes party to the treaty. See e.g. Vienna Convention for the Protection of the Ozone Layer, 22 March 1985, 1513 UNTS 293, Art. 11(3), UNFCCC, *supra* n. 19, Art. 14(2), CBD, *supra* n. 8, Art. 27(3). Other treaties provide an option to 'opt-out', i.e. the dispute settlement mechanism applies unless otherwise notified by the State when it becomes a party to the treaty. See e.g. Convention on the Physical Protection of Nuclear Material, 26 October 1979, 1456 UNTS 124, Art. 17(3). For a more detailed typology see Stephens, *supra* n. 30, p. 25.

[32] See UNCLOS, *supra* n. 5, Art. 287, Convention for the Protection of the Marine Environment of the North-East Atlantic, 22 September 1992, 2354 UNTS 67 ('OSPAR Convention'), Art. 32.

[33] The PCA Rules are available at: www.pca-cpa.org (last visited on 31 January 2013).

[34] See R. Ranjeva, 'L'environnement, la Cour internationale de justice et sa chambre spéciale pour les questions d'environnement' (1994) 40 *Annuaire français de droit international* 433.

certain cases then pending before the ICJ, namely the case concerning *Gabčíkovo-Nagymaros*,[35] the requests for an advisory opinion on the *Legality of Nuclear Weapons*[36] and the case of *Certain Phosphate Lands in Nauru*.[37] More generally, the aftermath of the 1992 Rio Summit was a period of intense normative development at the domestic and international level and brought high hopes for environmental dispute settlement. However, these hopes were dashed. The ICJ chamber was never used and, eventually, the ICJ decided not to reconvene it. The ITLOS also established a special 'Chamber for Marine Environment Disputes' in 1997. The jurisdiction of this chamber is subject to the agreement of States in certain legal matters, including disputes over the interpretation or application of 'any provision' of the Convention on the Law of the Sea[38] 'for the protection and preservation of the marine environment', but also treaties relating to the protection of the marine environment referred to in Article 237 of UNCLOS or conferring jurisdiction on the ITLOS.[39] This is a potentially important jurisdictional scope but, again, the practical relevance of the chamber remains to be demonstrated.

The third approach is to create an international environmental court. A project to this effect was developed in the late 1980s, particularly by Amedeo Postiglione,[40] who was a judge at the Italian *Corte di Cassazione* and the founder of the International Court of the Environment Foundation ('ICEF').[41] Aside from the rather low likelihood that such a project might get off the ground, the issue of a specialised environmental court raises two main questions. The first concerns the technical difficulties that such an initiative would need to overcome, in particular the definition of its jurisdictional scope (which treaties or provision? customary environmental law?) and the potential tensions with other international courts arising from the significant environmental dimension of disputes relating to human rights, trade, investment or other matters. Moreover, the formulation of environmental norms in treaties are often broad or even vague ('soft'),[42] a feature that poses an additional challenge for environmental tribunals. However, the argument could be reversed: it is due to the relative vagueness of environmental norms (which

---

[35] *Case Concerning the Gabčíkovo-Nagymaros Project (Hungary v. Slovakia)*, Judgment, ICJ Reports 1997, p. 7 ('*Gabčíkovo-Nagymaros Project*').

[36] *Legality of the Use by a State of Nuclear Weapons in Armed Conflict*, Advisory Opinion, ICJ Reports 1996, p. 66 ('*Legality of Nuclear Weapons – WHO*'); *Legality of Nuclear Weapons, supra* n. 4.

[37] *Certain Phosphate Lands in Nauru (Nauru v. Australia)*, Preliminary Objections, Judgment, ICJ Reports 1992, p. 240.

[38] UNCLOS, *supra* n. 5.

[39] Resolution on the Chamber for the Settlement of Disputes relating to the Marine Environment, 6 October 2011, ITLOS/2011/RES.2, para. 3.

[40] See A. Postiglione, 'A More Efficient International Law on the Environment and Setting up an International Court for the Environment within the United Nations' (1990) 20 *Environmental Law* 321. For a critique by the former president of the ICJ, see R. Jennings, 'Need for an Environmental Court' (1992) 20 *Environmental Policy and Law* 312. On this debate, see: Stephens, *supra* n. 30, pp. 56–61.

[41] See www.icef-court.org (last visited on 31 January 2013). [42] Dupuy, *supra* n. 3, 892.

are no vaguer than broad standards routinely applied in great detail by other tribunals such as the fair and equitable treatment standard in investment law) that would make specialised environmental adjudication useful.

The second question concerns the function that such an institution should fulfil. In this regard, the limited use of procedures and specialised environmental chambers suggests that there is, at present, no urgent need to create a new institution. General (e.g. ICJ and arbitration tribunals) and specialised courts and tribunals (e.g. human rights, trade, investment) would seem sufficient to accommodate the demand for environmental adjudication. Conversely, it could be argued that specialised environmental adjudication would be useful to release the pressure on 'borrowed fora' and to give more room to environmental law. Indeed, as discussed next, the importance given to environmental protection varies significantly from one jurisdiction to another.

8.3.2.3 Borrowed fora
8.3.2.3.1 Overview
Most environmental adjudication has taken place before borrowed fora. One could certainly argue that these fora are not being 'borrowed' since there are no 'environmental disputes' but only 'disputes with environmental components', and such disputes are heard by the relevant specialised courts. This argument is technically correct. Yet, the term 'borrowed fora' seems useful to underline the fact that environmental adjudication takes place essentially in the fora specialising in other branches of international law or, to a lesser though increasing extent, before the ICJ. This is in turn important to understand the dynamics and prospects of international environmental adjudication. Indeed, specialised courts tend to formulate these disputes in terms that suit their specialisation, sometimes to the detriment of international environmental law. Another consequence is the need to 'formulate' claims of an environmental nature in terms specific to other branches of international law so that they are heard by the respective tribunals. An apposite illustration is provided by what is often called 'human rights approaches' to environmental protection.[43] Due to jurisdictional and admissibility constraints, such approaches cannot protect the environment in the absence of a direct link between environmental degradation and an impairment of a human right.[44] Moreover, attempts to introduce environmental content into international obligations pursuing other purposes are not always well received. Like an immigrant in a foreign country, the protection of the environment is sometimes subject to tight controls within other branches of international law, such as international trade law and foreign investment law.[45]

---

[43] See A. Boyle and M. R. Anderson (eds.), *Human Rights Approaches to Environmental Protection* (Oxford: Clarendon, 1998).

[44] See F. Francioni, 'International Human Rights in an Environmental Horizon' (2010) 21 *European Journal of International Law* 41. See also Chapter 10.

[45] See J. E. Viñuales, 'The Environmental Regulation of Foreign Investment Schemes under International Law', in P.-M. Dupuy and J. E. Viñuales (eds.), *Harnessing Foreign Investment*

In this section, we briefly analyse the development of international environmental law in borrowed fora. The literature often discusses these fora one after the other or organises the discussion on the basis of their jurisdictional scope (see Figure 8.2 *supra*). Here, we will follow a different approach attempting to capture the differing degree of openness to environmental considerations of international courts and tribunals. This approach will highlight a different fault-line in the case-law that can be conceptually pinned down to whether a body is: (i) welcoming, (ii) neutral, (iii) reluctant to integrate environmental considerations.[46] Before undertaking the discussion, two caveats are in order. First, our distinction is a preliminary attempt to get closer to the reality on the ground that can be useful in addition to the approaches commonly used. Second, the assessment of the degree of openness will be on the basis of two criteria or indicators, namely the treatment of the precautionary principle and the use of the interpretation rule codified in Article 31(3)(c) of the VCLT,[47] which takes into account external norms in order to facilitate systemic integration.

8.3.2.3.2 Welcoming jurisdictions

Regarding the most welcoming jurisdictions, human rights courts provide the clearest example. The openness of these bodies has changed significantly over time, suggesting that it is not the formal requirements of their mandate, but their attitude towards environmental considerations that drives change. Thus, the European Court of Human Rights ('ECtHR') was for a long time reluctant to refer to the precautionary principle in its case-law, but it now recognises

> the importance of the precautionary principle (formulated for the first time in the Rio Declaration), which 'is to be applied to ensure a high level of protection to health, the safety of consumers and the environment, in all the activities of the Community'.[48]

Similarly, in its jurisprudence on provisional measures the ITLOS has noted that States must 'act with prudence and caution',[49] which requires that States co-operate to protect the environment.[50] More recently, it has confirmed its commitment to the precautionary approach in its Opinion on the

---

to Promote Environmental Protection: Incentives and Safeguards (Cambridge University Press, 2013), pp. 273–320, at 278–85.

[46] The letters (w), (n) and (r) are used to emphasise this distinction in Figure 8.2 *supra*.

[47] Vienna Convention on the Law of Treaties, 23 May 1969, 1155 UNTS 331 ('VCLT').

[48] *Tatar v. Romania*, ECtHR Application No. 67021/01 (27 January 2009), para. 120.

[49] *Southern Bluefin Tuna Cases (New Zealand v. Japan, Australia v. Japan)*, ITLOS Case Nos. 3 and 4, Order of 27 August 1999 ('*Bluefin Tuna*'), para. 77. See also the dissenting opinion of Judge T. Treves, who points out that the precautionary approach is the basis of paragraph 77 of the Order (Dissenting Opinion, para. 8).

[50] *MOX Plant Case (Ireland v. United Kingdom)*, ITLOS Case No. 10, Order of 3 December 2001 ('*MOX Plant Case*'), para. 84.

Responsibilities and Obligations of States Sponsoring Persons and Entities with Respect to Activities in the Area.[51]

A significant degree of environmental openness is also suggested by the use of systemic integration techniques. Thus, the ECtHR has referred to the Aarhus Convention[52] in interpreting Article 8 of the European Convention on Human Rights in disputes involving States parties to the Aarhus Convention (e.g. Romania[53]) but also States that are not parties to it (e.g. Turkey[54]). Similarly, ITLOS saw no obstacle to the interpretation of UNCLOS and the regulations issued by the International Seabed Authority in the light of other instruments (treaties or instruments of 'soft law') and customary law.[55] A similar analysis can be conducted with regard to the jurisprudence of the Inter-American Court of Human Rights and the African Commission on Human and Peoples' Rights. We return to this issue in Chapter 10.

8.3.2.3.3 A neutral ICJ

The generous reception given to international environmental law by these tribunals can be contrasted with the more *neutral* stance of the ICJ. As the guardian of general international law, the ICJ must be particularly careful since its law-making function (*juris-dictio* in the etymological meaning) is just as important, if not more so, as its dispute settlement function. It is therefore unsurprising that after the significant progress made in the 1990s, the ICJ has returned to a conservative approach. This approach has been discussed in some detail in Chapter 3, in connection with each of the principles of international environmental law. Suffice it to recall two points here.

First, the ICJ has given a mild reception to the precautionary principle. In the *Pulp Mills* case, Argentina referred to this principle to request a reversal of the burden of proof. The Court merely replied that 'while a precautionary approach may be relevant in the interpretation and application of the provisions of the Statute, it does not follow that it operates as a reversal of the burden of proof'.[56] Thus, the ICJ accepts the idea of precaution, but only as an 'approach' potentially useful for interpretation, and without clarifying its content.

---

[51] *Responsibilities and Obligations of States Sponsoring Persons and Entities with Respect to Activities in the Area*, ITLOS (Seabed Disputes Chamber), Case No. 17 Advisory Opinion, 1 February 2011 ('*Responsibilities in the Area*'), para. 125–35.

[52] Convention on Access to Information, Public Participation in Decision-making and Access to Justice in Environmental Matters, 25 June 1998, 2161 UNTS 447 ('Aarhus Convention').

[53] *Tatar* v. *Romania, supra* n. 48, para. 120, para. 118.

[54] *Taskin and others* v. *Turkey*, ECtHR Application No. 46117/99 (10 November 2004, Final 30 March 2005), para. 99–100.

[55] *Responsibilities in the Area, supra* n. 51, paras. 135 and 148.

[56] *Pulp Mills on the River Uruguay (Argentina* v. *Uruguay)*, Judgment, ICJ Reports 2010, p. 14 ('*Pulp Mills*'), para. 164. The reluctance of the Court has been criticised by Judge Cançado Trindade in his separate opinion, paras. 62–92 and 103–113.

Second, the Court resolutely applies the systemic integration technique codified in Article 31(3)(c),[57] including in environmental matters. In the *Gabčíkovo-Nagymaros Project* case, the Court held that the applicable treaty had to be interpreted in the light of environmental standards arising after its entry into force.[58] *In casu* the treaty included a specific provision to this effect, but this is not a necessary condition. Indeed, in the *Pulp Mills* case, the Court recalled the need to take into account some external instruments invoked by Argentina as 'relevant rules of international law applicable to relations between the parties'.[59] We see, therefore, that of the two indicators of openness, the ICJ has only embraced one.

8.3.2.3.4 Reluctant tribunals

Tribunals specialising in international economic law have shown some *reluctance* to entertain international environmental law. This general statement, however, must be qualified since, first, the investment jurisprudence is mixed and, second, indicators different from those selected could possibly lead to different conclusions. That said, the Dispute Settlement Body of the WTO ('DSB') as well as a number of investment tribunals have adopted a restrictive approach. The position of the DSB on the two indicators is summarised in *EC – Biotech*, where the Panel stated '[that] there was so far no authoritative decision made by a court or tribunal which recognizes the precautionary principle as a principle of general or customary international law'.[60] This view can be seen as a continuation of the position taken by the Appellate Body in the first case concerning the SPS Agreement,[61] namely the *EC – Hormones* case.[62] *EC – Biotech* also illustrates the restrictive approach adopted by the DSB on systemic integration. The narrow conception of this interpretation method expounded by the Panel would require, for an external treaty norm to be taken into account to interpret trade law, that all WTO Members (not just the parties to the dispute) be also parties to the external treaty.[63] In practice, the environmental treaties that could satisfy this requirement are rare. It must be highlighted, however, that the Panel referred to the decision of the Appellate Body in

---

[57] *Oil Platforms (Islamic Republic of Iran v. United States of America)*, Judgment, ICJ Reports 2003, p. 161, para. 41.

[58] *Gabčíkovo-Nagymaros Project, supra* n. 35, para. 112.

[59] *Pulp Mills, supra* n. 56, para. 65 (paraphrasing Article 31(3)(c) of the VCLT). See also para. 66, which clarifies the type of standards that can be taken into account.

[60] *European Communities – Measures Affecting the Approval and Marketing of Biotech Products*, Panel Report, 29 September 2006, WT/DS291/R, WT/DS292/R, WT/DS293/R ('*EC – Biotech*') para. 7.88.

[61] Agreement on the Application of Sanitary and Phytosanitary Measures, 15 April 1994, 1867 UNTS 493 ('SPS Agreement').

[62] *EC – Measures Concerning Meat and Meat Products (Hormones)*, AB Report, (16 January 1998), WT/DS26/ABR, WT/DS48/AB/R ('*EC – Hormones*'), para. 124.

[63] *EC – Biotech Products, supra* n. 60, para. 7.70.

Shrimp-turtle[64] in support of its conclusion that a customary norm or even a general principle of law can be taken into account under Article 31(3)(c) of the VCLT.[65] But the value of such an opening depends on the position that the DSB will take with regard to the legal status (custom or general principle of law) of certain environmental principles, which brings us back to square one.

Regarding investment tribunals, the volatility of the case-law makes any transversal analysis of the reception of the precautionary principle or of the use of systemic integration quite challenging. In a jurisprudential context where decisions are highly fact and tribunal-dependent, the value of an award welcoming or rejecting the application of an environmental principle is not representative. However, it is possible to get an idea of the openness of investment tribunals to environmental considerations by reference to three possible approaches followed in practice.[66] The first approach treats domestic environmental measures as manifestations of unilateral and protectionist policy. It neglects the fact that there may be national measures adopted pursuant to an environmental treaty. In contrast, evidence of a favourable reception for international environmental law requires a consideration of the relationship between national measures and international environmental obligations. Such an approach seems too progressive for the time being. The influence of international environmental law in investment disputes is thus limited to an intermediate approach such that the interpretation of investment law is influenced to varying degrees by environmental considerations. For example, the requirements of environmental treaties such as the Aarhus POP Protocol[67] and the POP Convention have been taken into account in the interpretation of the investment chapter of the NAFTA.[68] However, this more welcoming approach coexists with another, more restrictive approach, under which environmental protection has no practical impact on the outcome of an investment dispute.[69]

We return to the interactions between international environmental law and other branches of international law in Chapters 10–12. The above remarks are, however, useful to understand why evolving in the context of welcoming, neutral and reluctant fora has significant implications for the development of

---

[64] *United States – Import Prohibition of Certain Shrimp and Certain Products Containing Shrimp*, Appellate Body, 12 October 1998, WT/DS58/AB/R ('*Shrimp-turtle*'), para. 158 and note 157.

[65] *EC – Biotech Products*, *supra* n. 60, para. 7.67.   [66] See *Viñuales*, *supra* n. 45.

[67] Protocol to the 1979 Convention on Long-Range Transboundary Air Pollution on Persistent Organic Pollutants (POPs), 24 June 1998, 2230 UNTS 79.

[68] North American Free Trade Agreement, 17 December 1992, 32 ILM 296. See *Chemtura Corporation (formerly Crompton Corporation) v. Government of Canada*, UNCITRAL, Award (2 August 2010) ('*Chemtura v. Canada*'), para. 138.

[69] *Compañía del Desarrollo de Santa Elena SA v. Republic of Costa Rica*, ICSID Case No. ARB/96/1, Award (17 February 2000) ('*CDSE v. Costa Rica*'), para. 71. More recently see *Marion Unglaube and Reinhardt Unglaube v. Costa Rica*, ICSID Cases No. ARB/08/1 and ARB/09/20, Award (16 May 2012), paras. 218–21.

international environmental law, particularly with regard to the slow recognition of customary norms and the clarification of what broadly formulated environmental norms require in practice.

8.3.3 The consequences of environmental damage

8.3.3.1 Types of consequences

International law attaches certain legal consequences in the case of 'fault', 'damage' or both. The analysis of responsibility/liability for environmental damage has taken 'fault' as its pivotal concept, making a distinction between responsibility (reparation arising from fault) and liability (reparation in the absence of fault but following damage). This is problematic for two main reasons.

First, a 'primary' or 'triggering' norm may define a situation carrying legal consequences in different ways. Typically, it will state a conduct to be followed with some degree of diligence (e.g. States shall – or shall not – do X). If this conduct is not followed, the norm will be deemed 'breached' and will trigger effects defined by another set of norms that can be referred to as 'secondary' or 'reparation' norms (e.g. in case of breach, the following consequences will apply). However, there are cases where the primary norm attaches certain consequences irrespective of fault (e.g. reparation will be due if event X occurs). This is normally called strict liability. There are reparation norms attaching consequences to the situation defined by such a primary norm (e.g. reparation for the occurrence of X will be organised according to the following principles). But this hypothesis is not technically a 'breach' of a primary norm but simply a case where all the conditions required by this norm to trigger reparation are met. This is where the second problem comes in. The subjective idea of 'fault' applied to an abstract entity like a State or an international organisation is confusing. 'Fault' in this context means 'illegality'. This conception easily fits the context of responsibility for 'breach', but it is difficult to apply to the consequences (liability) of acts without fault or illegality. Indeed, if a norm defining a hypothesis triggering legal consequences does not require illegality, the term 'breach' would be misplaced. One would more appropriately speak of the 'occurrence' of the triggering hypothesis or the fulfilment of the conditions for reparation. This terminological difficulty is further compounded by the fact that the content of such triggering norms may overlap to some extent with that of secondary norms organising reparation. Yet, the conceptual articulation between primary (triggering) and secondary (reparation) norms applies both to responsibility for breach and to liability for occurrence of certain events.

This is the conceptual context where the legal consequences of environmental damage must be analysed. Much like 'fault' (illegality), 'damage' is but a condition set by a primary norm. Depending on the cases, 'fault', 'damage' and/or other conditions will be required to trigger the legal consequences of a norm. Fault (illegality) is always required to trigger the *responsibility of States for breach*. Damage may also be required (e.g. for a breach of the prevention principle), but this is not always the case (e.g. for a breach of procedural obligations, such as reporting or the conduct of an environmental impact assessment). When the situation concerns the *action of an economic operator* (private or public), the occurrence of damage is necessary to trigger the liability system laid out in some specific treaties (focusing on nuclear power or oil pollution damage) or called for by some general instruments.[70] Conversely, fault is not required, although it may trigger additional consequences. As to cases where the *actions of international organisations* are concerned, international law is still in its infancy. We will only note in this regard that international organisations are subject to primary norms that may trigger a system of international responsibility. In addition, some organisations, such as the World Bank or regional development banks, must comply with internal standards (including environmental standards) in the conduct of their activities. They must ensure that the projects they finance comply with these standards and a number of procedures open to civil society (e.g. the one before the World Bank Inspection Panel) have been set up to review compliance with such standards. This type of compliance review must be distinguished from traditional forms of 'responsibility' and 'liability'. The terms used in this regard are 'accountability', much like for procedures established to review compliance with human rights or environmental treaties or with corporate social responsibility standards. The foregoing distinctions are summarised in Figure 8.3.

Figure 8.3 shows that the nature of primary (triggering) and secondary (reparation) norms relevant to environmental protection changes according to the *debtor of the obligation*. An important element that emerges from this figure is the absence, in contemporary international law, of a strict ('no-fault') liability system for States.[71] Such liability has been established, however, with regard to private and public economic operators. We use the term 'liability' to refer to it, even though the term has a broader meaning

---

[70] The Commentary to the ILC Principles, *infra* n. 76, states that it concerns 'primary norms' (commentary to Art. 1, para. 2). To avoid misunderstandings this reference must be clarified. Whereas the ILC Principles set certain parameters regarding the organisation of civil liability (at the domestic level: Arts. 4 and 6; at the international level: Art. 7) that could be interpreted as 'primary' norms or obligations addressed to States to adopt certain domestic measures (vertical) or negotiate some treaties (horizontal), the content of these obligations is, in essence, to organise a system of reparation. Thus, the core provisions of the ILC Principles (defining the parameters of strict liability of economic operators) are best understood as a set of 'reparation' or 'secondary' norms. An exception to this conclusion would be principle 5 (obligation to cooperate in case of accident), which is closely related to prevention and due diligence.

[71] The only exception is Art. 2 of the Convention on International Liability for Damage Caused by Space Objects, 29 March 1972, 961 UNTS 187 ('A launching State shall be absolutely liable to pay compensation for damage caused by its space object on the surface of the earth or to aircraft flight').

	States	Economic operators	International organisations
Primary norms ('triggering')	- (Damage) - Lack of due diligence (ILC Prevention Articles, 2001)	- Damage - (Lack of due diligence)	- (Damage) - Lack of due diligence
Secondary norms ('reparation')	- Customary rules on State responsibility for internationally wrongful acts (ILC State Responsibility Articles, 2001) - Accountability mechanisms, e.g. non-compliance procedures	- Treaty rules on civil liability (e.g. nuclear power and oil pollution) - General parameters (ILC Principles on allocation of loss, 2006) - Accountability mechanisms, e.g. CSR control	- Rules on international responsibility of IOs (ILC Articles on IO Responsibility, 2011) - Accountability mechanisms, e.g. inspection panels

Figure 8.3: Types of legal consequences

in domestic law. Note that when a State entity acts as an economic operator, it may also be subject to the relevant strict liability treaties. Such schemes have been established for a number of activities, all characterised by a tension between the benefits and the risks they entail. We will explore some of these schemes in Section 8.3.3.3. But before discussing this particular form of liability, it is necessary to analyse the operation of the rules on State responsibility for internationally wrongful acts in an environmental context.

8.3.3.2 The international responsibility of the State
8.3.3.2.1 Overview of the system
Clarifying the obligations of States to prevent and repair damage to the environment has raised significant legal challenges since the 1960s.[72] The main problem is how to account for the particular or 'extraordinary' risks posed by certain activities (e.g. nuclear electricity generation or certain industrial processes) that are useful for the State in which they are conducted, but that may cause adverse effects to other States or to the environment beyond national jurisdiction, either as a result of their normal operation (effects) or an accident (risk).

Regarding the *effects of such activities*, the approach followed in international law has already been described in Chapter 3 in connection with the principles of no-harm and prevention. In sum, the State has an obligation of

---

[72] For early manifestations see W. Jenks, 'Liability for Hazardous Activities' (1966) 117 *Recueil des cours de l'Académie de droit international de La Haye*, 102–200; L. F. E. Goldie, 'Liability for Damage and the Progressive Development of International Law' (1965) 14 *International and Comparative Law Quarterly* 1189; P.-M. Dupuy, *La responsabilité internationale des Etats pour les dommages d'origine technologique et industrielle* (Paris: Pédone, 1976). See also T. Scovazzi, 'State Responsibility for Environmental Harm' (2001) 12 *Yearbook of International Environmental Law* 43; C. Nègre, 'Responsibility and International Environmental Law', in J. Crawford, A. Pellet and S. Olleson (eds.), *The Law of International Responsibility* (Oxford University Press, 2010), pp. 803–13.

conduct ('due diligence') to ensure that its territory is not used so as to cause significant damage to the environment of other States or beyond national jurisdiction. Leaving aside a number of grey areas in the scope of this principle (see Chapter 3), the basic obligation imposed on States is breached if three conditions are met: (i) the occurrence of harm (mere risk is not sufficient); (ii) the magnitude of damage (damage below the required threshold is not enough to trigger liability) and its spatial scope (in principle, it must go beyond the territory of the State of origin) and, most importantly, (iii) a duty of due diligence (which implies that even when the damage meets the conditions of scale and scope, the State would not incur liability if it acted with due diligence). It is important to note that the exercise of such diligence is not a circumstance precluding wrongfulness or a '*cause d'exoneration*' but is part of the definition of the triggering or primary norm. In other words, in order to show that the prevention principle has been violated, the injured State must establish (i) damage, (ii) its size and scope, (iii) lack of diligence of the State of origin and (iv) a causal relationship between negligence and the injury. The State of origin has thereafter the option to invoke customary circumstances precluding wrongfulness, including necessity as codified in Article 25 of the ILC Articles on State Responsibility.

With regard to the regulation of *activities that entail potentially serious risks*, two main approaches were possible. On the one hand, some authors suggested the creation of a strict liability regime. Under this system, any damage caused by a high-risk activity would be borne by the State of origin irrespective of the diligence shown by the latter. On the other hand, some authors considered that approach unrealistic and argued that a better way to capture the characteristics of high-risk activities was to extend the basic approach (responsibility for wrongful acts) while requiring a higher level of diligence, in particular through international standards.[73] The latter approach eventually prevailed, at least as regards to the responsibility of States. Indeed, since the early 1970s, the prevention principle has been increasingly recognised in treaty and customary law,[74] and it has also found expression in 'soft law' standards, which specify the content of the due diligence obligation. The work of the ILC, which initially sought to develop a strict liability regime applicable to States, had to admit the impossibility of moving forward without reformulating the subject, in particular by distinguishing two components. The first led to the adoption, in 2001, of 'Draft Articles on the Prevention of Transboundary Harm from Hazardous Activities',[75] which must be seen as an effort to spell out the contents of the prevention principle (a triggering norm) in a transboundary context. The

---

[73] See Scovazzi, *supra* n. 72, p. 49. See also R. Pisillo Mazzeschi, 'The Due Diligence Rule and the Nature of the International Responsibility of States' (1992) 35 *German Yearbook of International Law* 9.

[74] See Chapter 3.

[75] Draft Articles on the Prevention of Transboundary Harm from Hazardous Activities, GA Res. 56/82, UN Doc. A/RES/56/82 ('ILC Prevention Articles')

second continued the work on an international strict liability regime with two important modifications, i.e. the regime targets the liability of economic operators (not States) and the text ultimately adopted in 2006 merely proposes a set of parameters in the form of 'Draft Principles on the Allocation of Loss in the case of Transboundary Harm arising out of Hazardous Activities' ('ILC Principles').[76] The ILC Principles will be discussed in the next section. Here, it suffices to note that these two components are not strictly speaking 'halves' of the original fruit but only what realistically could be preserved from the initial approach. Indeed, the core of the initial project, i.e. a strict liability regime applicable to States, was lost in the process.

In the light of these clarifications, we can now better understand how the general system of State responsibility for internationally wrongful acts covers both responsibility for damages as well as responsibility for risk. In both cases, the State has a duty to prevent. It must conduct itself with 'due diligence' in all circumstances. To elaborate upon this point, two additional comments seem apposite.

8.3.3.2.2 Primary norms: prevention and due diligence

The first comment concerns the obligation that could trigger the system of responsibility. So far, we have only made reference to the customary principle of prevention. However, other obligations of a customary nature (e.g. the obligation of notification/consultation or to conduct an environmental impact assessment) or treaty-based (e.g. reporting obligations) may be violated by the action of the State from whom the damage originates. These obligations stipulate the terms of their compliance or, alternatively, breach,[77] which may be different from those mentioned above (i.e. damage of a certain size and scope, negligence). This said, many obligations arising from treaties must be interpreted in the broader context provided by the duty of 'due diligence'.

In the last two decades, this duty has received increasing attention in the literature,[78] as well as being the subject of jurisprudence and codification efforts. In addition to the recognition of the customary basis of the prevention principle by the ICJ[79] and ITLOS,[80] one may refer to the

---

[76] Draft Principles on the Allocation of Loss in case of Transboundary Harm from Hazardous Activities, GA Res. 61/36, UN Doc. A/RES/61/36 ('ILC Principles').

[77] *Pulp Mills, supra* n. 56, para. 79.

[78] For two book-length studies, see R. Pisillo Mazzeschi, *Due diligence e responsabilità internazionale degli Stati* (Milan: Giuffrè, 1989); A. Ouedraogo, *La diligence en droit international. Contribution à l'étude d'une notion aux contours imprécis* (PhD dissertation, The Graduate Institute, Geneva, 2011).

[79] *Legality of Nuclear Weapons, supra* n. 4, para. 29; *Gabčíkovo-Nagymaros Project, supra* n. 35, para. 140; *Pulp Mills, supra* n. 56, para. 110. See also the discussion of the concept in *Responsibilities in the Area, supra* n. 51.

[80] See *Responsibilities in the Area, supra* n. 51, in particular paras. 99 to 120 (content of the duty of due diligence), 123 (relationship with other so-called direct obligations), 131–2 (link with the precautionary approach), 136 (link with obligation to adopt the 'best

contributions of the Institut de droit international ('IDI')[81] and the ILC.[82] These contributions give a rather detailed idea of what 'due diligence' means in positive international law. Such content can be summarised in five points: (i) the duty of due diligence is an obligation of conduct (the occurrence of damage does not entail *ipso facto* the violation of this obligation),[83] (ii) due diligence standards are defined by States within the discretion left to them under international law (which is exercised within the bounds of 'reasonableness' and is not absolute),[84] (iii) the duty of due diligence may vary according to various criteria, especially as regards the time,[85] the type of activity[86] and the capacity of the State in question,[87] (iv) due diligence concerns both the adoption of measures as well as reasonable efforts to implement them,[88] and (v) the exercise of such diligence involves not only the minimisation of transboundary impacts or risks but also the minimisation of effects or risks that may affect areas beyond any State jurisdiction.[89]

8.3.3.2.3 Secondary norms: addressing complex scenarios

The second comment concerns the operation of secondary norms in the context of responsibility for harm (damage and risk) to the environment. Indeed, environmental problems pose quite unique challenges, particularly with regard to the determination of the responsible State and the injured State.[90] In addition to the basic scenario involving damage to a State resulting

---

environmental practices') and 141–2 (link with the obligation to conduct an environmental impact assessment).

[81] See Institut de Droit International, Resolution on 'Environment' (Rapporteur L. Ferrari Bravo) ('IDI – Environment'), Resolution on 'Responsibility and Liability under International Law for Environmental Damage' (Rapporteur F. Orrego Vicuña) ('IDI – Responsibility'), Resolution on 'Procedures for the Adoption and Implementation of Rules in the Field of Environment) (Rapporteur F. Paolillo) ('IDI – Procedures'), all adopted at the Strasbourg Session (1997).

[82] ILC Prevention Articles, *supra* n. 75, in particular Art. 3 and its commentary.

[83] *Pulp Mills*, *supra* n. 56, para. 187; *Responsibilities in the Area*, *supra* n. 51, para. 110; ILC Prevention Articles, *supra* n. 75, commentary to Art 3, para. 7.

[84] See IDI – Responsibility, *supra* n. 81, Art. 3, para. 2; ILC Prevention Articles, *supra* n. 75, comment to Art 3, paras. 9, 11 and 12, referring to the *Alabama* case where the court rejected the proposition of the UK that 'due diligence' was a national standard. But see *Pulp Mills*, *supra* n. 56, para. 205 (where the ICJ suggests that the content of a component of the duty of care, namely the customary obligation to conduct an environmental impact assessment, would be left to States).

[85] *Responsibilities in the Area*, *supra* n. 51, para. 117.

[86] There is no doubt that 'the degree of care required is proportional to the degree of risk involved in the business,' ILC Prevention Articles, *supra* n. 75, comment to Art. 3, para. 18; *Responsibilities in the Area*, *supra* n. 51, para. 117.

[87] ILC Prevention Articles, *supra* n. 75, commentary to Art. 3, para. 18; *Responsibilities in the Area*, *supra* n. 51, paras. 158–9.

[88] *Pulp Mills*, *supra* n. 56, para. 197; *Responsibilities in the Area*, *supra* n. 51, paras. 115 and 239; ILC Prevention Articles, *supra* n. 75, commentary to Art. 3, para. 10.

[89] *Responsibilities in the Area*, *supra* n. 51, paras. 142–8 (considering the obligation of environmental impact assessment as a component of the duty of care and affirming its application to the Area, that is to say to the environment outside State jurisdiction).

[90] Scovazzi, *supra* n. 72, 61–3.

from the negligence of another State, one must also consider another more difficult scenario, namely damage to the environment caused in a progressive and cumulative manner by the action of a plurality of States the effects of which are felt by many or even all States. The examples abound: climate change, marine pollution (including from land-based sources) or biodiversity loss. These difficulties are compounded by the potentially irreversible character of environmental damage and the inability to establish a causal link between the damage and the individual action of a specific State. The ILC Articles on State Responsibility can accommodate some of these specificities, but not always satisfactorily.

As regards the responsible States, the ILC Articles include the possibility that an internationally wrongful act consist of 'a series of actions or omissions defined in aggregate as wrongful' (Article 15(1)) and that it may be committed by a 'plurality of responsible States' (Article 47(1)) whose individual responsibility would be engaged. However, these provisions imply that one can establish a causal link between a series of acts attributable to several States and (insofar as the primary norm so requires) the occurrence of damage. This is not a simple step. For example, if a regional sea has five riparian States which, at different times and to different extents have discharged pollutants into the sea, the fifth State could consider its four co-riparians responsible for an internationally wrongful act of a composite nature. But each co-riparian could argue that the causal link between its specific actions and the damage has not been established. If causality is difficult to prove in a rather simple scenario as the one just described, one can imagine how difficult it may be in connection with climate change,[91] which results from two centuries of greenhouse gas emissions by economic operators acting with the authorisation of the countries where they are based. A possible approach in this regard can be found in the IDI Resolution, which, as noted by T. Scovazzi, proposes the introduction of a causality presumption for certain activities[92] and the use of joint and several liability regimes[93] as well as of collective reparation.[94]

Regarding the State that is entitled to invoke the responsibility of another State, the ILC Articles introduce a distinction based on whether the obligation breached is owed to a particular State, a group of States or the international community as a whole. The two latter categories can accommodate breaches to environmental obligations (customary or treaty-based) that go beyond the bilateral (synallagmatic) relationship between two States and are generally

---

[91] For an overview, see R. Lord, S. Goldberg, L. Rajamani and J. Brunnée (eds.), *Climate Change Liability: Transboundary Law and Practice* (Cambridge University Press, 2011). The question was asked in the context of international climate negotiations, but in a terminology that avoids the idea of reparation and emphasises the idea of assistance. Draft decision –/CP.18 see 'Approaches to Address Loss and Damage associated with Climate Change Impacts in Developing Countries Vulnerable to the Adverse Effects of Climate Change' ('Decision – loss and damage').

[92] IDI – Responsibility, *supra* n. 81, Art. 7.   [93] *Ibid.*, Art. 11.   [94] *Ibid.*, Art. 12.

owed either to all States parties to a treaty (obligations *erga omnes partes*) or to the community of States as a whole (*erga omnes*). Responsibility for breach of these obligations can be invoked by 'injured States' (a category encompassing States 'individually' or 'specially' affected as well as other States to whom the obligation is owed if the breach radically changes their position)[95] or by 'other' States (where the entitlement to act follows from the mere position of a State within a collective interest treaty or as a member of the international community).[96] It must be emphasised, however, that with respect to the latter category (Article 48), the ILC Articles are not necessarily a codification of customary law.[97] Moreover, even if the system were applicable to hypotheses such as climate change or marine pollution from land-based sources, including for environmental damage to areas beyond State jurisdiction, it is unclear how such damage should be repaired. As noted by Scovazzi, where restoration of the environment is not possible, any compensation paid by the responsible States would make sense only in respect of injured States and not of 'other' States. Yet, there may be cases of environmental damage for which there is no injured State. It is unclear whether and how such damage should be compensated. Article 28 of the IDI Resolution makes a useful proposal in this regard calling for States to identify or create entities entitled to make claims and receive compensation in such cases.[98] This proposal is a conceptual extension of solutions adopted in the context of certain civil liability regimes.

8.3.3.3 The liability of the economic operator
8.3.3.3.1 Overview of treaty systems

Treaties regulating the liability of the economic operator (public or private) can be understood as what in private international law is often called 'uniform law' (*'droit uniforme'*), namely substantive law common to several States and established by treaty.[99] Indeed, the use of international law in this area is primarily intended to establish some parameters for the harmonised or at least equivalent operation of laws relating to compensation for certain damages resulting from regulated activities.

The first treaties or treaty systems were adopted in respect of damages resulting from the production of nuclear energy and oil pollution damage. As regards nuclear energy, two separate but related systems have been developed, one among OECD States[100] and the other under the aegis of the International Atomic Energy

---

[95] ILC Articles, *supra* n. 1, Art. 42(b).   [96] *Ibid.*, Art. 48.

[97] On the existence of an *actio popularis* in international law, see F. Voeffray, *L'actio popularis ou la défense de l'intérêt collectif devant les juridictions internationales* (Paris: Presses Universitaires de France, 2004).

[98] IDI – Responsibility, *supra* n. 81, Art. 28, noted by Scovazzi, *supra* n. 72, 63.

[99] On strict liability for environmental damage, see L. Bergkamp, *Liability and Environment: Private and Public Law Aspects of Civil Liability for Environmental Harm in an International Context* (The Hague: Kluwer, 2001).

[100] Convention on Third Party Liability in the Field of Nuclear Energy, 29 July 1960, 956 UNTS 251 ('Paris Convention'). The regime established by the Paris Convention was supplemented

Agency ('IAEA').[101] These systems are linked via a common protocol adopted in 1988, which seeks to harmonise the situation of persons affected by the effects of a nuclear accident governed by one of the two systems.[102]

As for oil pollution damage, a system was developed in the context of the International Maritime Organisation ('IMO') in response to the grounding of the Liberian oil tanker *Torrey Canyon* near the British coast in March 1967. This incident led to the adoption of the two pillars of the system, namely the 'Convention on Civil Liability' of 1969 ('CLC') and the Convention known as 'FUND' of 1971. The current system results from the overhaul of these two pillars via two protocols, which gave rise to the 'CLC/92'[103] and the Convention 'FUND/92'.[104] The regime was supplemented by two instruments addressing a case not covered in the original regime[105] and adding an additional layer of compensation.[106]

More recently, civil liability regimes have also been adopted in respect of damages resulting from industrial accidents[107] or the movement of certain substances, such as hazardous waste[108] or genetically modified

by another treaty, the Convention Supplementary to the Paris Convention of 29 July 1960 on Third Party Liability in the Field of Nuclear Energy, 31 January 1963, 1041 UNTS 358 ('Brussels Supplementary Convention'). The 'Paris/Brussels' system was amended in 1964, 1982 and 2004. The latter amendment, which is the result of a process initiated following the Chernobyl accident, is a major overhaul of the original, but it is not yet in force. See M. Montjoie, 'Nuclear Energy' in Crawford *et al.*, *supra* n. 72, pp. 915–28.

[101] Convention on Civil Liability for Nuclear Damage, 21 May 1963, 1063 UNTS 265 ('Vienna Convention'). This treaty was amended by a Protocol to amend the Vienna Convention on Civil Liability for Nuclear Damage, 12 September 1997, 2241 UNTS 302, which leaves in place the two systems (initial system and amended system). The 1997 revision also resulted in the adoption of a Convention on Supplementary Compensation for Nuclear Damage, 12 September 1997, IAEA INFCIRC/567 ('Complementary Vienna Convention', not yet in force).

[102] Joint Protocol Relating to the Application of the Vienna Convention and the Paris Convention, 27 September 1988, 1672 UNTS 293.

[103] Protocol amending the International Convention on Civil Liability for Oil Pollution Damage, 27 November 1992, available at www.ecolex.org (TRE-001 177) ('CLC/92'). See J. L. Gabaldón García, *Curso de Derecho Marítimo Internacional* (Madrid: Marcial Pons, 2012), pp. 783–806.

[104] Protocol to Amend the International Convention on the Establishment of an International Fund for Compensation for Oil Pollution Damage, 27 November 1992, available at: www.ecolex.org (TRE-001 176) ('FUND/92').

[105] International Convention on Civil Liability for Oil Pollution Damage, 23 March 2001, available at: www.ecolex.org (TRE-001 377) ('BUNKERS 2001', not yet in force).

[106] Protocol to the International Convention on the Establishment of an International Fund for Compensation for Oil Pollution, 16 May 2003, available at: www.ecolex.org (TRE-001 401) ('FUND/2003').

[107] Protocol on Civil Liability and Compensation for Damage Caused by the Transboundary Effects of Industrial Accidents on Transboundary Waters, 21 May 2003, Doc. ECE/MP.WAT/11-ECE/CP.TEIA/9 ('Kiev Protocol', not yet in force).

[108] Convention Relating to Third Party Liability in the Field of Maritime Carriage of Nuclear Material, 17 December 1971, 944 UNTS 255; International Convention on Liability and Compensation for Damage in Connection with the Carriage of Hazardous and Noxious Substances, 3 May 1996 (amended by the Protocol of 30 April 2010), available at: www.ecolex.org (TRE-001 245) ('HNS Convention 2010', not yet in force); Basel Protocol on Liability and compensation for damage resulting from transboundary

organisms.[109] In addition, efforts to establish a more general system were under-taken through the ILC and the Council of Europe, which led to two texts, namely the ILC Principles mentioned earlier and the Lugano Convention.[110] Despite their limited practical influence (neither one became binding), these instruments nevertheless provide a synthesis of the general structure followed by the other instruments in the field of civil liability for environmental damage.

8.3.3.3.2 Main parameters of liability regimes

The liability regimes introduced in the previous section have four main parameters:[111] (i) the establishment of strict liability (without fault) of the economic operator; (ii) the requirement on economic operators to take out insurance; (iii) the creation of additional layers of compensation; (iv) the prohibition of discrimination regarding access to compensation procedures. In the following paragraphs, we will build on this general structure to present the main components of this approach. We illustrate these components by reference to the systems governing nuclear energy and oil pollution damage.

The first parameter is the most complex one and embodies the articulation of primary and secondary norms in a strict liability context. It involves specifying four elements, namely the *liable entity, the nature of the liability, the grounds for exemption and any applicable limitations to the extent of liability*. The identification of the liable entity must accommodate several considerations. It seems natural to require the entities benefiting from an activity to compensate for the damage that may result therefrom. Similarly, the entity that has *de facto* power over the dangerous activity, which is there-fore in the best position to ensure its success, may also be targeted. The difficulty is that these and other considerations[112] do not necessarily point to the same solutions. For example, in the nuclear energy regime the liable entity is the 'operator'[113] (which is both the beneficiary and the entity with *de facto* power over the activity), whereas in the oil pollution regime liability is

---

movements of hazardous wastes and their disposal, 10 December 1999, available on: www. ecolex.org (TRE-001341) ('Basel Protocol', not yet in force).

[109] Nagoya–Kuala Lumpur Supplementary Protocol on Liability and Redress to the Cartagena Protocol on Biosafety, 15 October 2010, UNEP/CBD/BS/COP-MOP/5/17 (not yet in force).

[110] Convention on Civil Liability for Damage Resulting from Activities Dangerous to the Environment, 21 June 1993, available at: www.ecolex.org (TRE-001 166) ('Lugano Convention', not yet in force).

[111] See ILC Principles, *supra* n. 76, Arts. 4, 6 and 7. See also Survey of Liability Regimes relevant to the Topic of International Liability for Injurious Consequences arising out of Acts not prohibited by International Law (International Liability in case of Loss from Transboundary Harm arising out of Hazardous Activities) 24 June 2004,UN Doc. A/CN.4/543 ('Study of the Secretariat').

[112] See G. Doeker and T. Gehring, 'Private or International Liability for Transnational Environmental Damage – The Precedent of Conventional Liability Regimes' (1990) 2 *Journal of Environmental Law* 7.

[113] Paris Convention, *supra* n. 100, Arts. 1(a)(vi) and 3; Vienna Convention, *supra* n. 101, Arts. I(a)(c) and IV(1).

channelled primarily to the owner of the ship[114] (*de facto* power over the activity) and not to the oil industry (beneficiary). Another difficulty arises when the damage is caused by the joint action of several contributing entities. We noted earlier that this is problematic in the context of the rules on State responsibility for internationally wrongful acts. In the context of civil liability regimes, this problem is solved through the establishment of joint liability:[115] each economic operator may have to respond for all the damage, but it has a right of action against the other liable entities. In all these contexts liability is *strict or objective in nature*, i.e. it is not necessary to establish fault (negligence or wilful misconduct). But such liability admits some degrees depending on the scope of the *grounds for exemption* (sometimes there may be a conceptual distinction between 'strict liability' and 'absolute liability', the latter allowing no ground for exemption). When the only advantage granted to injured persons is a reversal of the burden of proof, the economic entity could be exempted from liability by establishing diligence. This situation would be more appropriately characterised as a facilitated responsibility (fault-based) regime. When diligence is not allowed as a ground for exemption, the objective (strict or absolute) character of the liability regime will depend on the available grounds for exemption. An economic operator may be exempted from liability, for example, by proving that the damage was caused by circumstances such as armed conflict, a case of *force majeure* or the unlawful conduct of the victim or of a third person.[116] Strict liability systems normally entail *ceilings* limiting the amount that may be claimed from the liable entity.[117] Such ceilings pursue two competing objectives. On the one hand, ceilings are necessary to enable the pursuit of the regulated activity. Without these ceilings it would be very difficult to measure litigation risks and, as a result, economic operators would be reluctant to engage in such activities. On the other hand, ceilings must not be too low, as otherwise the economic operator would not have enough exposure to maintain the necessary level of care. One way to deal with this trade-off is to eliminate these ceilings where the economic operator is at serious fault.[118] This approach shows the establishment of a strict liability regime does not preclude a return to fault-based responsibility when relevant.

---

[114] CLC/92, *supra* n. 103, Arts. I(3), III(1) and (4).

[115] *Ibid.*, Art. IV; Vienna Convention, *supra* n. 101, Art. II(3)(a); Paris Convention, *supra* n. 100, Art. 5(b).

[116] CLC/92, *supra* n. 103, Art. III(2)–(3); Vienna Convention, *supra* n. 101, Art. IV(2)–(3); Paris Convention, *supra* n. 100, Art. 9.

[117] On the amounts that may be required in respect of a nuclear accident or pollution by hydrocarbons see ILC Principles, *supra* n. 76, Art. 4 comments, para. 23 and notes. CLC/92 conditions this limitation of liability by the responsible entity having to file with the court an action for damages for an amount equal to its limit of liability. See CLC/92, *supra* n.103, Art. V (3).

[118] See CLC/92, *supra* n. 103, Art. V(2); Kiev Protocol, *supra* n. 107, Art. 5; Basel Protocol, *supra* n. 108, Art. 5. See more generally the ILC Principles, *supra* n. 76, Art. 4, commentary, para. 24.

A practical difficulty that may arise is due to the possible insolvency of the economic operator. In general, strict liability regimes include the obligation for economic operators to *take out insurance*.[119] The insurance coverage normally extends to the ceiling applicable to the liable entity, whether the effects of the accident take place in the State of origin or abroad. The relationship between the insurer and the liable entity is contractual in nature and can change from one case to another, but they remain within the bounds set by the applicable treaty and domestic law. Normally, the injured party is entitled to bring an action directly against the insurer, which can avail itself of the same defences (particularly the grounds for exemption) as the liable entity.[120] Like the ceilings, insurance is an important component of strict liability regimes because it allows the commercial development of activities, which, despite their risks, are beneficial from a societal standpoint.

The recovery of capped amounts, even when facilitated by the compulsory insurance and the possibility of a direct action against the insurer, may not be sufficient to cover all damages. Nuclear accidents and oil spills may indeed cause large-scale environmental damage amounting to hundreds of millions or even billions of Euros. This is why strict liability regimes provide different *'layers' of compensation* borne by a beneficiary industry (in the oil pollution damage regime) or the State (nuclear energy accidents). Such additional layers have been introduced by instruments such as the Brussels Supplementary Convention,[121] the Supplementary Convention to the Vienna Convention,[122] FUND/71 (now FUND/92)[123] and FUND/2003.[124] They come into play when the economic operator and/or the insurer is/are insolvent, when the damage exceeds the maximum insured amount and/or when damage cannot be channelled to the economic operator.[125] Given the purpose of these supplementary layers, which is to ensure appropriate compensation, the injured persons can bring a claim directly against the relevant Fund, which cannot avail itself of all the defences available to the economic operator.[126] The situation of these Funds can be understood as one of absolute liability (triggered by damage alone) although, strictly speaking, they cannot be considered as entities liable for the damage caused.

Finally, strict liability regimes seek to *harmonise the situation of those affected by the occurrence of damage*. In order to do so, one possibility is to set up an international redress mechanism, such as the United Nations Compensation Commission established after the Gulf War or the Iran–United States Claims

---

[119] See CLC/92, *supra* n. 103, Art. VII(1); Vienna Convention, *supra* n. 101, Art. VII; Paris Convention, *supra* n. 100, Art. 10.

[120] CLC/92, *supra* n. 103, Art. VII(8); Kiev Protocol, *supra* n. 107, Art. 11(3); Basel Protocol, *supra* n. 108, Art. 14(4). See more generally the ILC Principles, *supra* n. 76, Art. 4, commentary, para. 34.

[121] Brussels Supplementary Convention, *supra* n. 100.

[122] Complementary Vienna Convention, *supra* n. 101.   [123] FUND/92, *supra* n. 104.

[124] FUND/2003, *supra* n. 106.   [125] FUND/92, *supra* n.104, Art. 4.   [126] *Ibid.*, Art. 4(2).

Tribunal established after the Iranian revolution of 1979.[127] When redress procedures take place at the domestic level, which is more common, it is important to avoid any discrimination by the State of origin of the damage (or its courts) between 'local' victims and foreign victims.[128] Non-discrimination is a key parameter of transnational redress and it illustrates the 'amphibious' nature of such mechanisms, which rely heavily on domestic law and State courts operating under certain broad parameters set by treaty.[129] Note also that this requirement encompasses an obligation to grant potentially affected persons (including foreigners) access to information about the risks or, as the case may be, the damage,[130] which highlights the relevance of the participation principle discussed in Chapter 3 for the conduct of industrial activities.

The foregoing observations summarise the general approach underpinning the civil liability regimes applicable to economic operators. However, an important question remains to be addressed, which will bring us back to the starting point of our analysis, namely the approaches followed to assess and repair environmental damage.

8.3.3.4 Assessment and reparation of environmental damage

The responsibility and liability regimes analysed in the foregoing sections organise the reparation of environmental damage.[131] We must now ask what the term 'environmental damage' covers and what specific modalities can follow its reparation. These two questions are related because certain types of damage 'must' be repaired only to the extent they 'can' be repaired.

To facilitate the presentation, we first introduce the basic principles governing this matter. There is no doubt that damage to people (loss of life or bodily injury) or to property (loss or damage) and *lucrum cessans* (loss of income from an activity affected by environmental damage) must be repaired.[132] However, these hypotheses do not cover damage to the environment *as such*, but rather bodily and economic injury resulting from environmental damage. Environmental damage as such is repaired by reference to the costs involved (or reasonably likely to be involved) in the adoption of certain measures. This is precisely where the modalities of reparation become important to identify those forms of damage that must be repaired. In this context, an initial distinction can be made between measures taken before an incident occurs and those taken in response to it. The first category

---

[127] ILC Principles, *supra* n. 76, Art. 6(4), commentary, para. 11.
[128] Paris Convention, *supra* n. 100, Art. 14(a); Vienna Convention, *supra* n. 101, Art. XIII.
[129] See CLC/92, *supra* n. 103, Art. X(2).
[130] ILC Principles, *supra* n. 76, Art. 6(5), commentary, paras. 13–15.
[131] See M. Bowman and A. Boyle (eds.), *Environmental Damage in International and Comparative Law: Problems of Definition and Evaluation* (Oxford University Press, 2002); SFDI, *Le dommage écologique en droit interne, communautaire et comparé* (Paris: Economica, 1992).
[132] See, e.g., Paris Convention, *supra* n. 100, Art. 3; Vienna Convention, *supra* n. 101, Art. I(k); CLC/92, *supra* n. 103, Art. I(6); Basel Protocol, *supra* n. 108, Art. 2.

is part of the prevention obligation and the associated cost is not part of the damage for compensation purposes. Response measures are generally compensable.[133] Within this category, one may further distinguish between clean-up and preventive (mitigation) measures. Measures to restore, reinstate or clean up the environment are generally compensated for,[134] subject to certain conditions of reasonableness and to the proof that they were indeed taken. As regards preventive (mitigation) measures, compensation depends on the treaty context. When such measures seek to mitigate the extent of damage that has already occurred, they are compensated according to the same logic as restoration measures. However, when the damage has not materialised, the cost of these measures may only be recovered if there was a 'grave and imminent threat of pollution damage'.[135]

A more difficult question is whether the environmental damage going beyond that considered heretofore, i.e. *pure ecological damage*, must be repaired. The main difficulty is that such damage is often irreversible and that, even when a loss in terms of environmental quality can be established, this loss cannot be easily assigned to an identifiable right-holder (other than the environment as such). A few examples will help grasp this concept. Should the depletion of the ozone layer or changes in the climate system, or the extinction of a species or ecosystem in an area beyond national jurisdiction be repaired? One solution to this problem is to quantify this loss by reference to measures that could be taken to address them. This is the approach underpinning the reimbursement of restoration or reinstatement measures (when at all possible), and it is also being explored in climate negotiations.[136] A variation of this approach consists of restoring or protecting a similar ecosystem in an area other than the damaged area. This approach underpins the various schemes of pollution credits trading (e.g. greenhouse gas emissions trading or trading of production/consumption capacity of ozone depleting or acidifying substances, or compensation quotas for the destruction of wetlands).[137] Another approach is to quantify (if at all possible) the value represented by the loss of a species or ecosystem for present and future generations and allocate the relevant sums to

---

[133] See CLC/92, *supra* n. 103, Art. I(6); Basel Protocol, *supra* n. 108, Art. 2.

[134] See CLC/92, *supra* n. 103, Art. I(6); Basel Protocol, *supra* n. 108, Art. 2.

[135] CLC/92, *supra* n. 103, Art. I(6)–(7)· FUND/92, *supra* n. 104, Art. 3(b) and 4(1)(c); IMO, *Claims Manual* (London, 2008), para 1.4.5., 1.4.6., 1.4.11.

[136] Decision – loss and damages, *supra* n. 91.

[137] See Chapter 5. See also the techniques of compensation for the loss of wetlands in the context of the Clean Water Act of the United States (Compensatory Mitigation for Losses of Aquatic Resources, 40 CFR Part 230 Subpart J and 33 CFR 332) or, more generally, the techniques of compensation under Directive 2004/35/CE of the European Parliament and Council of 21 April 2004 on environmental liability with regard to the prevention and remedying of environmental damage, OJ L143/56, 30 April 2004, para. 1.1.3: 'Compensatory remediation shall be undertaken to compensate for the interim loss of natural resources and services pending recovery. This compensation consists of additional improvements to protected natural habitats and species or water at either the damaged site or at an alternative site. It does not consist of financial compensation to members of the public'.

an entity established to represent this particular interest (e.g. a non-governmental organisation,[138] a local authority,[139] a 'Commissioner for the Environment'). This is the solution recommended by the IDI.[140] Overall, one may conclude that at present, international law addresses the compensation of pure ecological damage mostly through the lenses of restoration or reinstatement measures.[141]

Select bibliography

Anton, D. K. and D. Shelton, *Environmental Protection and Human Rights* (Cambridge University Press, 2011).

Barboza, J. A., 'International Liability for the Injurious Consequences of Acts Not Prohibited by International Law and Protection of the Environment' (1994) 247 *Recueil des cours de l'Académie de droit international* 293–405.

  The Environment, Risk and Liability in International Law (Leiden: Martinus Nijhoff, 2011).

Bergkamp, L., *Liability and Environment: Private and Public Law Aspects of Civil Liability for Environmental Harm in an International Context* (The Hague: Kluwer, 2001).

Betlem, G. and E. Brans (eds.), *Environmental Liability in the EU: The 2004 Directive Compared with US and Member State Law* (London: Cameron May, 2006).

Bianchi, A., 'Harmonisation of Laws on Liability for Environmental Damage in Europe' (1994) 6 *Journal of Environmental Law* 21.

Bowman, M. and A. Boyle (eds.), *Environmental Damage in International and Comparative Law: Problems of Definition and Evaluation* (Oxford University Press, 2002).

Boyle, A., 'State Responsibility and International Liability for Injurious Consequences of Acts not Prohibited by International Law: A Necessary Distinction?' (1990) 39 *International and Comparative Law Quarterly* 1.

Boyle, A. and M. R. Anderson (eds.), *Human Rights Approaches to Environmental Protection* (Oxford: Clarendon Press, 1998).

Brans, E. H. P., *Liability for Damage to Public Natural Resources: Standing, Damage and Damage Assessment* (The Hague: Kluwer, 2001).

Brunnée, J., 'Of Sense and Sensibility: Reflections on International Liability Regimes as Tools for Environmental Protection' (2004) 53 *International and Comparative Law Quarterly* 351.

Burns, W. C. G. and H. Osofsky (eds.), *Adjudicating Climate Change. State, National and International Approaches* (Cambridge University Press, 2009).

---

[138] See L. Neyret, *Atteintes au vivant et responsabilité civile* (Paris: LGDJ, 2006), pp. 577ff.

[139] See Tribunal correctionnel de Paris, 11th ch., 16 January 2008, No. 9934895010, cited in Y. Kerbrat, 'Le droit international face au défi de la réparation des dommages à l'environnement', in SFDI, *Le droit international face aux enjeux environnementaux* (Paris: Pedone, 2010), pp. 125–44, at 141.

[140] See IDI – Responsibility, *supra* n. 81, Art. 28.

[141] See Manual, *supra* n. 135, para. 3.6.1. to 3.6.4; Lugano Convention, *supra* n. 110, Art. 2(9)–(11).

Churchill, R. R., 'Facilitating (Transnational) Civil Liability Litigation for Environmental Damage by Means of Treaties: Progress, Problems, and Prospects' (2001) 12 *Yearbook of International Environmental Law* 3.

Doeker, G. and T. Gehring, 'Private or International Liability for Transnational Environmental Damage – The Precedent of Conventional Liability Regimes' (1990) 2 *Journal of Environmental Law* 7.

Dupuy, P.-M., 'A propos des mésaventures de la responsabilité internationale des Etats dans ses rapports avec la protection internationale de l'environnement', in M. Prieur (ed.), *Les hommes et l'environnement: quels droits pour le vingt-et-unième siècle? Etudes en hommage à Alexandre Kiss* (Paris: Frisson-Roche, 1998), pp. 269–82.

La responsabilité internationale des Etats pour les dommages d'origine technologique et industrielle (Paris: Pédone, 1976).

'La diligence due dans le droit international de la responsabilité', *Aspects juridiques de la pollution transfrontière* (Paris: OCDE, 1977), pp. 396–407.

'Où en est le droit international de l'environnement à la fin du siècle?' (1997) *Revue générale de droit international public* 873.

Francioni, F., 'International Human Rights in an Environmental Horizon' (2010) 21 *European Journal of International Law* 41.

Francioni, F. and T. Scovazzi (eds.), *International Responsibility for Environmental Harm* (London: Graham & Trotman, 1991).

French, D., 'Environmental Dispute Settlement: The First (Hesistant) Signs of Spring?' (2007) 19 *Hague Yearbook of International Law* 3.

Gabaldón García, J. L., *Curso de Derecho Marítimo Internacional* (Madrid: Marcial Pons, 2012).

Goldie, L. F. E., 'Concepts of Strict and Absolute Liability and the Ranking of Liability in Terms of Relative Exposure to Risk' (1985) 16 *Netherlands Yearbook of International Law* 175

'Liability for Damage and the Progressive Development of International Law' (1965) 14 *International and Comparative Law Quarterly* 1189.

Handl, G., 'Liability as an Obligation Established by a Primary Rule of International Law' (1985) 16 *Netherlands Yearbook of International Law* 49.

Jenks, W., 'Liability for Hazardous Activities', (1966) 117 *Recueil des cours de l'Académie de droit international* 102–200.

Jennings, R., 'Need for an Environmental Court' (1992) 20 *Environmental Policy and Law* 312

'The Role of the International Court of Justice in the Development of International Environment Protection Law' (1992) 1 *Review of European Community and International Environmental Law* 240.

Kerbrat, Y., 'Le droit international face au défi de la réparation des dommages à l'environnement', in SFDI, *Le droit international face aux enjeux environnementaux* (Paris: Pedone, 2010), pp. 125–44.

Larsson, M.-L., *The Law of Environmental Damage: Liability and Reparation* (The Hague: Kluwer, 1999).

Lecucq, O. and S. Maljean-Dubois (eds.), *Le rôle du juge dans le développement du droit de l'environnement* (Brussels: Bruylant, 2008).

Lefeber, R., *Transboundary Environmental Interference and the Origin of State Liability* (The Hague: Kluwer, 1996).

Lord, R., S. Goldberg, L. Rajamani and J. Brunnée (eds.), *Climate Change Liability: Transnational Law and Practice* (Cambridge University Press, 2011).

Lozano Contreras, J. F., *La noción de debida diligencia en derecho internacional público* (Barcelona: Atelier Libros Jurídicos, 2007).

Magraw, D. B., 'Transboundary Harm: The International Law Commission's Study of International Liability' (1986) 80 *American Journal of International Law* 305.

Maljean-Dubois, S., *La mise en œuvre du droit international de l'environnement* (Paris: Iddri, 2003).

Nègre, C., 'Responsibility and International Environmental Law', in J. Crawford, A. Pellet, S. Olleson and K. Parlett (eds.), *The Law of International Responsibility* (Oxford University Press, 2010), pp. 803–13.

Neyret, L., *Atteintes au vivant et responsabilité civile* (Paris: LGDJ, 2006).

Ouedraogo, A., *La diligence en droit international. Contribution à l'étude d'une notion aux contours imprécis* (Thesis of the Graduate Institute of International and Development Studies, Geneva, 2011).

Pisillo Mazzeschi, R., *Due diligence e responsabilità internazionale degli Stati* (Milan: Giuffrè, 1989).

'The Due Diligence Rule and the Nature of the International Responsibility of States' (1992) 35 *German Yearbook of International Law* 9.

Postiglione, A., 'A More Efficient International Law on the Environment and Setting up an International Court for the Environment within the United Nations' (1990) 20 *Environmental Law* 321.

Ranjeva, R., 'L'environnement, la Cour internationale de justice et sa chambre spéciale pour les questions d'environnement' (1994) 40 *Annuaire français de droit international* 433.

Ratliff, D. P., 'The PCA Optional Rules for Arbitration of Disputes Relating to Natural Resources and/or the Environment' (2001) 14 *Leiden Journal of International Law* 887.

Romano, C., *The Peaceful Settlement of International Environmental Disputes: A Pragmatic Approach* (The Hague: Kluwer, 2000).

Sachariew, K., 'Promoting Compliance with International Environmental Legal Standards: Reflections on Monitoring and Reporting Mechanisms' (1991) 2 *Yearbook of International Environmental Law* 31.

Sands, P., 'Existing Arrangements for the Settlement of International Environmental Disputes: a Background Paper', in *Towards the World Governing of the Environment: IV International Conference International Court of the Environment Foundation (ICEF), 2–5 June 1994* (Pavia: Iuculano, 1996), pp. 628–47.

Scovazzi, T., 'State Responsibility for Environmental Harm' (2001) 12 *Yearbook of International Environmental Law* 43.

Société française pour le droit international, *Le dommage écologique en droit interne, communautaire et compare* (Paris: Economica, 1992).

Stephens, T., *International Courts and Environmental Protection* (Cambridge University Press, 2009).

Viñuales, J. E., 'Managing Abidance by Standards for the Protection of the Environment', in A. Cassese (ed.), *Realizing Utopia* (Oxford University Press, 2012), pp. 326–39.

'The Contribution of the International Court of Justice to the Development of International Environmental Law' (2008) 32 *Fordham International Law Journal* 232.

'The Environmental Regulation of Foreign Investment Schemes under International Law', in P.-M. Dupuy and J. E. Viñuales (eds.), *Harnessing Foreign Investment to Promote Environmental Protection: Incentives and Safeguards* (Cambridge University Press, 2013), pp. 273–320.

Wetterstein, P. (ed.), *Harm to the Environment: The Right to Compensation and Assessment of Damage* (Oxford: Clarendon Press, 1997).

Wolfrum, R., 'Means of Ensuring Compliance with and Enforcement of International Environmental Law', (1998) 272 *Recueil des cours de l'Académie de droit international* 9–154.

9

Implementation: new approaches

9.1 Introduction

In the preceding chapter, we identified four stages in the process of compliance with a primary environmental norm. We saw that the traditional approaches used in international law to implement international obligations focus on the first (information) and the fourth stages (reparation). The techniques dealing with information gathering/reporting as well as with the characterisation of a breach (through adjudication) and the determination of the ensuing legal consequences (responsibility/liability) play a significant role in environmental protection, but they also raise significant challenges. We identified in the process going from compliance to non-compliance, a grey area characterised by uncertainty as to the level of compliance (information without breach characterisation). This area, which one might call the 'soft belly' of the compliance process, is important for our discussion because it is the main target of the implementation system of many environmental treaties.

This strategic choice is based on two main considerations. On the one hand, in an environmental protection context, prevention is much more important than the reparation of environmental damage, which is often very difficult.[1] On the other hand, the techniques relevant for the first and fourth stages assume that non-compliance with an obligation is a matter of willingness rather than one of financial and technological capacity.[2] This assumption is not necessarily accurate for all States. The costs and technical expertise involved in complying with environmental treaties sometimes make their implementation difficult for States that do not have the necessary resources. Moreover, even when a State has the resources, minimising the costs associated with the implementation of measures remains important to make compliance more efficient. These two factors have led to the development of new approaches to implementation. Figure 9.1[3] identifies the stages where these approaches intervene.

---

[1] See Section 8.3.3.4 of Chapter 8.
[2] See A. Chayes and A. Handler Chayes, *The New Sovereignty, Compliance with International Regulatory Agreements* (Cambridge MA: Harvard University Press, 1998).
[3] See P.-M. Dupuy, 'Où en est le droit international de l'environnement à la fin du siècle?' (1997) *Revue generale de droit international public* 873, in particular 893–5; J. E. Viñuales, 'Managing

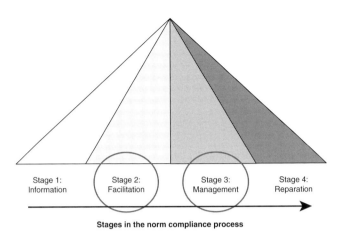

Stages in the norm compliance process

Figure 9.1: The 'soft belly' of the compliance process

The main techniques to facilitate compliance with environmental obliga-tions (Stage 2) seek to provide 'assistance' and 'efficiency' gains (9.2). Technical and financial assistance are intended to give developing States the means to create the necessary infrastructure for the implementation of their environ-mental obligations. Other techniques aim to increase efficiency so as to reduce the cost of compliance with environmental obligations. The latter are relevant for both developed and developing countries and they are usually structured as market mechanisms. Regarding techniques to manage cases of non-compliance (Stage 3), their purpose is to maintain the effectiveness of the regime within reasonable bounds through a combination of renewed assistance, diplomatic pressure and sanctions (9.3).

9.2 Techniques to facilitate compliance

9.2.1 Types of techniques

The analysis of techniques to facilitate compliance with environmental standards presents several difficulties. The diversity of these techniques and the specificities of each mechanism make them difficult to understand. Moreover, their operation is as much about political and economic factors as it is about law. It is therefore necessary to clarify the angle from which these techniques will be discussed here.

Often, international environmental law textbooks provide a description of various mechanisms such as development aid, environmental funds, technol-ogy transfer, capacity building and others. In this way, the constitutive rules of several instruments are presented succinctly without going into the details of

Abidance by Standards for the Protection of the Environment', in A. Cassese (ed.), *Realizing Utopia* (Oxford University Press, 2012), pp. 326–39.

their operation. This approach is understandable because, as noted earlier, the techniques differ and each mechanism has features that cannot be analysed in the limited context of a textbook, even a voluminous one. Our discussion adopts a slightly different yet complementary approach. Instead of providing a survey with a brief introduction to each mechanism, we focus on three aspects.

First, a key consideration in the context of this book is to clarify the nature of the innovative implementation approaches adopted by environmental treaties. This is why we emphasise the two goals pursued by the diverse range of facilitation techniques, namely the provision of assistance and the generation of efficiency gains. Second, given the significant number of potentially relevant instruments, it is not possible to cover every eventuality succinctly. To overcome this difficulty, we will select major illustrations of each technique, on the basis of both their emblematic character and their practical importance. A third aspect that we must consider is the particular angle adopted in the analysis. After introducing the basic features of each mechanism, we will pay particular attention to the legal issues that arise in their operation.

9.2.2 Techniques oriented towards assistance

9.2.2.1 Financial assistance
9.2.2.1.1 Overview
An important technique in the implementation of environmental agreements is the provision of financial assistance. The term 'financial assistance' includes a variety of public, private or even mixed mechanisms. These mechanisms are often established to bridge the positions of developed and developing countries in treaty negotiations. This was the case, for example, of the Multilateral Fund of the 1987 Montreal Protocol.[4] Indeed, the Fund was introduced in 1990 by an amendment to the Protocol designed to bring certain developing countries, in particular China and India, into the system. This mechanism, as several other innovations introduced by the Montreal Protocol, profoundly influenced the way differences between developed and developing countries came to be managed in subsequent environmental negotiations. We will discuss this mechanism in more detail later, but first it is useful to place it in the broader context of financial assistance techniques. Figure 9.2 gives an overview of these techniques.

More generally, in international negotiations the source of funding plays an important role. *Public finance* is often preferred by developing countries because it is, in theory, more predictable,[5] although the commitments of developed countries in this area are not always respected and often have

---

[4] Montreal Protocol on Substances that Deplete the Ozone Layer, 16 September 1987, 1522 UNTS 3 ('Montreal Protocol'). See also the Terms of Reference for the Multilateral Fund, 25 November 1992, UNEP/OzL.Pro.4/15, Annex IX ('Terms of Reference for the Multilateral Fund').
[5] Report of the United Nations Conference on Environment and Development, A/CONF.151/26/ Rev.l (Vol. l), Resolution 1, Annex 2: Action 21 ('Action 21'), para. 33.11(b).

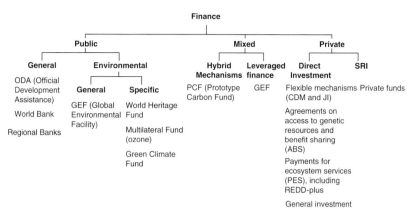

Figure 9.2: Techniques of financial assistance

strings attached. In contrast, developed countries often argue the need for a greater role of *private finance*, including through the liberalisation of capital movements and easier access for foreign direct investment. Within *public finance*, two distinct strands can be identified depending on whether financial resources are generally allocated to *development* or more specifically to *environmental protection*. We cannot dwell here on the broader issue of official development assistance ('ODA').[6] Suffice it to note that the emphasis on the provision of 'new and additional'[7] resources is intended to ensure that financial assistance goes beyond the mere reallocation of ODA to environmental projects. As for mechanisms focusing on environmental protection, a further distinction can be made between *general environmental funds* (e.g. the Global Environmental Facility or 'GEF') and *treaty-specific ones* (e.g. the World Heritage Fund, the Multilateral Fund or the Green Climate Fund). Regarding *private finance*, whether it is foreign direct investment, portfolio investment,[8] or simply commercial lending, its importance has been increasingly recognised since the 1992 Earth Summit. The legal questions raised by this source of finance will be discussed in Chapter 12. Another technique of growing importance is *mixed financing*, often under the aegis of a development bank or the GEF, which has mobilised substantial amounts of private capital as part of its leveraged finance activities. Another example is the Prototype Carbon Fund ('PCF') set up by the World Bank, which provides a template for the creation of other *hybrid funds* at the domestic level.

These general observations about the types of financing set the background for a more detailed analysis of three examples, namely treaty-specific

[6] See P. Kohona, 'UNCED – The Transfer of Financial Resources to Developing Countries' (1992) 1 *Review of European Community and International Environmental Law* 307.

[7] Action 21, *supra* n. 5, Chapter 33, particularly para. 33.1.

[8] See B. J. Richardson, *Socially Responsible Investment Law: Regulating the Unseen Polluters* (Oxford University Press, 2008).

environmental funds, the GEF and the PCF. The analysis of these mechanisms will emphasise their function as well as some selected legal questions.

9.2.2.1.2 Treaty-specific environmental funds

The first treaty-specific environmental fund was created in 1972 under Article 15 of the World Heritage Convention.[9] Despite the modest amounts (approximately $4 million dollars annually) managed by the *World Heritage Fund*, this mechanism is representative of a type of fund that we also find in other environmental treaties, including the Ramsar Convention[10] and the Basel Convention.[11] The World Heritage Fund is based on contributions from States, partly compulsory and partly voluntary, as well as donations from other entities, such as international organisations or private entities.[12] The amounts of the Fund are allocated to activities defined by the World Heritage Committee established by the Convention and only to the extent of amounts actually available.[13] These activities primarily involve capacity-building of States parties (provision of experts and training) and other forms of technical assistance (studies and the supply of equipment). Certain amounts of the Fund are allocated to maintain a reserve fund (referred to in Article 21(2) of the Convention) whose purpose is to lend prompt assistance in emergencies, such as the occurrence of natural disasters. The Committee has organised the target activities into three categories according to their priority in fund allocation:[14] emergency assistance (particularly regarding the sites included on the List of World Heritage in Danger[15]); support in the area of conservation and management; and preparatory assistance. The current strategy of the Fund is consistent with the broader trend of environmental funds to leverage additional capital through co-finance of projects.[16] Despite its iconic character, the World Heritage Fund is only representative of a first – and rather modest – generation

---

[9] Convention Concerning the Protection of the World Cultural and Natural Heritage, 16 November 1972, 1037 UNTS 151 ('WHC').

[10] Ramsar Convention on Wetlands of International Importance, especially as Waterfowl Habitat, 2 February 1971, 996 UNTS 245 ('Ramsar Convention'). The fund was established by the 'Resolution on a Wetland Conservation Fund', Resolution 4.3 (1990). In fact, this mechanism is known as the 'Ramsar Small Grants Fund'.

[11] Basel Convention on the Control of Transboundary Movements of Hazardous Wastes and Their Disposal, 22 March 1989, 1673 UNTS 57 ('Basel Convention'), Art. 14. The COP established a 'General Trust Fund' and a 'Trust Fund for Technical Cooperation'. See 'Financial Rules of the Conference of the Parties, its subsidiary bodies and the Secretariat of the Basel Convention on the Control of Transboundary Movements of Hazardous Wastes and their Disposal', Decision BC-10/28 (2011).

[12] Financial Regulations of the World Heritage Fund, available at www.whc.unesco.org (last visited on 15 March 2013) ('Financial Regulations'), Art. 3.1.

[13] *Ibid.*, Art. 4.

[14] Guidelines for the Implementation of the World Heritage Convention, July 2012, WHC 12/01 ('Guidelines'), para. 235.

[15] *Ibid.*, para. 236.

[16] *Ibid.*, para. 225. See M. Bowman, P. Davies and C. Redgwell, *Lyster's International Wildlife Law* (Cambridge University Press, 2nd edn, 2010), pp. 475–7 for concrete examples.

of treaty-specific environmental funds.[17] A second generation, capable of mobilising far more resources, was introduced with the establishment of the Multilateral Fund within the Montreal Protocol.

The *Multilateral Fund* is emblematic in two respects.[18] On the one hand, it is the first fund of the second generation, i.e. a fund large enough (more than US$ 400 million for each period[19]) to finance 'agreed incremental costs' incurred by developing countries as a result of the conversion of their infrastructure to comply with an environmental treaty. On the other hand, the composition of its governing body, the Executive Committee, which consists of seven developing countries and seven developed countries (despite the fact that only the developed countries contribute funds[20]), is an expression of the principle of common but differentiated responsibilities.[21] Created by an amendment to the Montreal Protocol in June 1990, the Fund was established in 1991 and made permanent in 1992 in order to cover the 'agreed incremental costs' (as designated under Article 10(1) of the Protocol).[22] These include costs arising from the conversion or the premature decommissioning of facilities producing controlled substances, the establishment of new facilities producing substitutes, the import of such substitutes, or the use of relevant patents and designs, to name a few categories.[23] Decisions about funding are taken by the Committee by consensus or, failing that, by two thirds of the members present and voting, provided that a double majority of both developing and developed countries is respected.[24] In practice, the Committee has always acted by consensus. The implementation of this system of financial assistance is managed by 'implementing agencies', in particular the United Nations Environment Programme ('UNEP'), the United Nations Development Programme ('UNDP'), the World Bank[25] and the United Nations Industrial Development Organisation ('UNIDO'). An example may be useful to understand how this mechanism operates. In 2011, the Executive Committee approved an amount of US$ 265 million to reduce the use of hydrochlorofluorocarbons ('HCFCs') pursuant to Article 2E of the Montreal Protocol.[26] These substances are also potent greenhouse gases. The

---

[17] On 'generations' of financial mechanisms, see L. Boisson de Chazournes, 'Technical and Financial Assistance', in D. Bodansky, J. Brunnée and E. Hey (eds.), *The Oxford Handbook of International Environmental Law* (Oxford University Press, 2007), pp. 948–72.

[18] On this mechanism, see P. Lawrence, 'Technology Transfer Funds and the Law: Recent Amendments to the Montreal Protocol on Substances that Deplete the Ozone Layer' (1992) 4 *Journal of Environmental Law* 15.

[19] The periods were as follows: 1991–3, 1994–6, 1997–9, 2000–2, 2003–5, 2006–8, 2009–11, 2012–14.

[20] Montreal Protocol, *supra* n. 4, Art. 10(5)–(6); Terms of Reference of the Executive Committee as Modified by the Ninth Meeting of the Parties in its Decision IX/16, 25 September 1997, UNEP/OzL.Pro.9/12, Annex V ('Terms of Reference of the Executive Committee'), para. 2. The Terms of Reference have been revised several times.

[21] See Chapter 3.   [22] Montreal Protocol, *supra* n. 4, Art. 10(1).

[23] Indicative List of Agreed Incremental Costs, 25 November 1992, UNEP/OzL.Pro.4/15, Annex VIII.

[24] Montreal Protocol, *supra* n. 4, Art. 10(9).

[25] Terms of Reference for the Multilateral Fund, *supra* n. 4, para. 2–7.

[26] Montreal Protocol, *supra* n. 4, Art. 2F and Annex C (Group I).

financial assistance is to be used for the conversion of hundreds of assembly lines that currently use HCFCs. As part of this project, which should first freeze and then reduce the consumption of HCFCs, China will be assisted by UNDP, UNEP, UNIDO, the World Bank and the German and Japanese governments.[27] All in all, the Multilateral Fund can be characterised by reference to three key features: coverage of 'agreed incremental costs' incurred by developing countries to comply with the treaty; decision-making by a Committee with equal membership of developed and developing countries; the implementation of assistance by 'implementing agencies'. As discussed next, negotiations on climate finance have deviated from this template on some significant points.

The third illustration of a treaty-specific environmental fund is the recent creation of the Green Climate Fund ('GCF').[28] This Fund was established by a decision of the Conference of the Parties ('COP') of the UN Framework Convention on Climate Change ('UNFCCC')[29] in December 2011, but it is the result of a process that had already begun in 2006 and that was strengthened at the Copenhagen Conference in December 2009. The controversial 'Copenhagen Accord' focused on the creation of a fund to mobilise considerable resources (US$ 100 billion per year in 2020), an idea that was taken up by the 'Cancun Agreements' in December 2010 and crystallised at the Durban Conference in 2011.[30] Despite the fact that at the time of writing, the GCF was only starting its financing operations, its institutional architecture merits attention because it largely reflects the lessons accumulated over decades of experience in the development of environmental funds. From this standpoint, five main features must be highlighted.

First, regarding the decision-making power in respect of the allocation of the funds, it is in the hands of a 'Board' with equal membership (twelve members representing developed countries and twelve members representing developing countries).[31] Decisions are taken by consensus and the Board has to adopt regulations governing cases where consensus cannot be reached.[32] Significantly, the Board felt the need to define the term 'consensus',[33] perhaps because of the controversy over the scope of this principle raised by the decision-making procedure of the UNFCCC COP in Cancun and Doha.

---

[27] See 'China Commits to Landmark Agreement on Dual Ozone and Climate Benefits', 29 July 2011, available at: www.multilateralfund.org (last visited on 15 March 2013).

[28] Implementation of the Green Climate Fund, Decision 3/CP.17, 15 March 2012, FCCC/CP/ 2011/9/Add.1, Annex: Governing Instrument for the Green Climate Fund ('GCF Instrument'). On this instrument, see L. Schalatek and S. Nakhooda, 'The Green Climate Fund', (November 2012) 11 *Climate Finance Fundamentals*.

[29] UN Framework Convention on Climate Change, 9 May 1992, 1771 UNTS 107 ('UNFCCC').

[30] On climate negotiations, see *supra* Chapter 5.   [31] GCF Instrument, *supra* n. 28, para. 9.

[32] *Ibid.*, para. 14.

[33] Revised Draft Additional Rules of Procedure of the Board, 12 March 2013, GCF/B.01–13/02/ Rev.01, Annex IX: Additional Rules of Procedure relating to Decision-making and Voting ('Additional Rules of Procedure'), para. 1 ('Decisions of the Board will be taken by consensus. Consensus exists when no objection is stated by any Board member or alternate member acting on behalf of a Board').

The second point concerns the Board's relations with, on the one hand, the COP and, on the other, the fund 'Trustee' (provisionally the World Bank). The GCF is an independent entity, but it serves as a financial mechanism of the UNFCCC under Article 11 of the convention. This places the GCF in a subordinate position as regards the COP. The instrument establishing the GCF only states that 'arrangements will be concluded' to this effect and sets some general parameters, including the need to comply with the general guidelines of, and submit annual reports to, the COP.[34] In practice, this formula conceals the divergent views between developing States (funding recipients) who want more control of the GCF by the COP, and developed countries that favour greater freedom. The divergence of views has also played out in the election of the administrator ('Trustee') who actually receives and holds the funds, even though it is managed in accordance with the decisions of the Board. At the request of the COP (on the initiative of donor countries), the World Bank acts as an interim Trustee for a period of three years.[35]

The third element is the source of the funds. The GCF is expected to become the most important mechanism in terms of the funds mobilised. The objective is to mobilise US$ 100 billion per year by 2020, although this target is probably too ambitious. One way to come closer to this target would be to use available public funds as the basis to raise much greater private funds. This is expressly provided for in the GCF Instrument. In fact, paragraph 30 provides '[t]he Fund may also receive financial inputs from a variety of other sources, public and private, including alternative sources'.

A fourth important aspect of the architecture of the GCF is how it will organise the distribution of the funds. This may include providing funds to implementing entities or organisations in charge of funding specific projects or, conversely, the GCF could directly undertake such funding activities, which would require a more sophisticated administrative structure.[36] The instrument suggests that the first model will be followed, with the GCF channelling its resources through international, regional but also national implementing entities accredited by the Board.[37] The role of domestic authorities is specifically addressed to ensure co-ordination among the proposals submitted for funding in a given country and consistency with the national mitigation and adaptation plans.

Finally, a fifth element characterising the GCF is that, unlike other funds, it can cover not only 'agreed incremental costs' incurred by developing countries but also 'agreed full costs' of projects related to adaptation, mitigation, technology transfer and capacity building.[38] These are the basic features of the GCF's architecture. They owe much to a financial mechanism that we will study next, namely the GEF.

---

[34] GCF Instrument, *supra* n. 28, para. 6.   [35] *Ibid.*, para. 26.
[36] Schalatek and Nakhooda, *supra* n. 28, p. 2.   [37] GCF Instrument, *supra* n. 28, para. 45.
[38] *Ibid.*, para. 35.

9.2.2.1.3 General environmental funds: the GEF

The *Global Environmental Fund* ('GEF')[39] is the main example of a general environmental fund that is not treaty-specific. Initially set up as a prototype (1991–4), the GEF was established as an independent entity in 1994.[40] As for the GCF, we will focus on five main architectural features of the GEF, namely (i) the decision-making power, (ii) relations with the COP, (iii) the source of funds, (iv) the implementation of assistance, and (v) the type of costs covered. However, the main feature of the GEF, when compared to other financial mechanisms, is its general purpose or, in other words, its coverage of several areas, whether addressed by specific treaty regimes (biodiversity, climate change, desertification, depletion of the ozone layer and persistent organic pollutants) or not (international waters).[41] The GEF serves as the financial mechanism of several environmental treaties, but it has a broader scope. This has often caused frictions with the respective COPs, as discussed in this section.

Regarding, first, the decision-making power, it rests on a 'Council' composed of thirty-two members (sixteen developing countries, fourteen developed countries and two transition States)[42] that normally acts by consensus but, when consensus is not possible, decisions are taken by a 'double weighted majority' (an affirmative vote representing both a 60 per cent majority of the total number of participants and a 60 per cent majority of the total contributions).[43] This system is a compromise between the interests of donor States (who favoured the weighted system of the World Bank) and developing countries that supported an equal-weight approach.

Relations between the GEF and COPs have raised a number of difficulties. The origin of these is the tension between developing countries, which seek to have greater control over the allocation of funds (via the COP), and developed countries, in particular donors, which favour a more autonomous model. The GEF has concluded agreements ('memoranda of understanding') with the secretariats of the respective treaties, subsequently approved by the COPs and annexed to a decision. However, as a general matter, relationships are organised in a rather broad fashion, with the COPs having the power to establish general policies for the allocation of funds and the GEF Council keeping responsibility for making decisions on specific projects.[44]

Regarding the origin of the funds, they take the form of contributions by the participant States to the 'Trustee', namely the World Bank, during four-year periods of 'replenishment',[45] which start with participants' pledges to contribute

---

[39] See A. S. Miller, 'The Global Environmental Facility and the Search for Financial Strategies to Foster Sustainable Development' (1999–2000) 24 *Vermont Law Review* 1229.

[40] The instrument establishing the GEF was revised several times thereafter. For the current version, see 'Instrument for the Establishment of the Restructured Global Environment Facility' (October 2011) ('GEF Instrument').

[41] *Ibid.*, para. 2.   [42] *Ibid.*, para. 16.   [43] *Ibid.*, para. 25(b) and (c)(i).

[44] *Ibid.*, para. 6(a). See 'Strengthening Relations with the Conventions in the GEF Network', 21 April 2011, GEF/C.40/15.

[45] GEF Instrument, *supra* n. 40, para. 10.

certain amounts. From this perspective, the GEF is a form of public finance. So far, the GEF has undergone five replenishment periods and a sixth one was initiated in 2013. Since its inception until 2013, the GEF had invested approximately US$ 11.5 billion in about 3,200 projects related to its areas of intervention. More important are the amounts from other sources, including private sources, which have been leveraged through GEF activities (US$ 57 billion). These 'hybrid' activities are undoubtedly one of the most realistic ways to mobilise the amounts required to meet large-scale environmental challenges. As already noted, the GEF is not the only mechanism that has leveraged its impact through a resort to private funds. The growing role of private finance and the market logic that drives its operations have been met with some reluctance from developing countries, which see this source of financing as insufficiently predictable and more difficult to manage. This is yet another manifestation of a common tension between pragmatism and equity, which underpins many areas of global environmental governance.

The financial assistance provided by the GEF is channelled through 'implementing agencies'. These include, mainly, UNDP, UNEP, and the World Bank,[46] although the GEF currently operates through ten implementing agencies, including the regional development and co-operation banks (African, Asian, European, and Inter-American).

Finally, as regards the type of expenditure covered by the GEF, in principle it only covers 'agreed incremental costs' of measures taken within its areas of intervention.[47] We have characterised this notion in our analysis of the Multilateral Fund of the Montreal Protocol, where this concept made its first appearance. An exception to this principle concerns the 'agreed full costs' involved in performing the procedural obligations set out in Article 12(1) of the UNFCCC, which may also be covered by the GEF.[48]

As suggested by the foregoing discussion, there are many common features between the GEF and the more recent GCF. The architecture of the latter is, indeed, based on the experience of the former. However, the GCF is expected to go beyond the GEF in terms of resource mobilisation, interaction with the private sector and the nature of covered costs. Conversely, the GCF's mandate is limited to climate change, even though the GCF Instrument defines this area broadly encompassing its interactions with other areas, such as the protection of biodiversity, particularly in respect of projects to reduce deforestation (known as 'REDD-plus').[49] More fundamentally, the GCF is a brand new instrument, and it has everything to prove, whereas the GEF has already more than twenty years of operation and has channelled dozens of billions of dollars towards environmental protection projects.

---

[46] *Ibid.*, para. 22.   [47] *Ibid.*, para. 2.   [48] *Ibid.*, para. 6(a) *in fine.*
[49] GCF Instrument, *supra* n. 28, para. 35.

9.2.2.1.4 Hybrid mechanisms: the PCF

A hybrid financial mechanism that merits some attention is the Prototype Carbon Fund ('PCF') established in 1999 under the aegis of the World Bank.[50] Despite the relatively modest amounts mobilised by the PCF (less than US$ 200 million), this mechanism is interesting as an institutional experiment. Its purpose is to facilitate the channelling of both public and private funds (offered by companies such as Electrabel or Mitsubishi Corporation) towards emissions reduction projects structured according to the rules of the Clean Development ('CDM') and Joint Implementation ('JI') mechanisms set up by the Kyoto Protocol.[51]

This is useful not only as a source of environmental finance but also as a testing ground to further develop this type of mechanism. In addition to the project management expertise accumulated by the PCF, the investor, whether public or private, obtains emission reduction units, which it can use later to fulfil its obligations in this area or to sell in the market for emission rights.

Despite the serious difficulties encountered in recent years by carbon trading, especially due to the global economic crisis (with the ensuing excess in the supply of emission rights) and the uncertain future of the Kyoto Protocol (which, despite the adoption of a second commitment period, will probably cease to impose quantifiable emissions targets in 2020), the contribution of the PCF must not be underestimated. It has, among others, prompted the development of similar mechanisms at the domestic level,[52] and it could serve as a model for other international initiatives of mixed funding.

9.2.2.2 Technical assistance

Technical assistance is closely related to financial assistance. Often, the latter aims to finance former, whether in the form of *capacity building* (personnel training, provision of experts or equipment, development of infrastructure and administrative capacities)[53] or the *transfer of technology* to developing countries (transfer of intellectual property rights or technical know-how to the public or private sectors of the recipient country).[54] There is some overlap in the definition of these two types of technical assistance. By way of illustration,

---

[50] IBRD, 'Amended and Restated Instrument Establishing the Prototype Carbon Fund', Resolution No. 99–1 ('PCF Instrument'). See D. Freestone, 'The World Bank's Prototype Carbon Fund: Mobilising new Resources for Sustainable Development', in S. Schemmer-Schulte and K. Y. Tung (eds.) *Liber Amicorum Ibrahim S. I. Shihata* (The Hague: Kluwer, 2001), pp. 265–341.

[51] Kyoto Protocol to the UN Framework Convention on Climate Change, 11 December 1997, 2302 UNTS 148 ('Kyoto Protocol'). See Chapter 5.

[52] World Bank, *Annual Report. Carbon Finance for Sustainable Development* (2010), pp. 23–77.

[53] See Action 21, *supra* n. 5, Chapter 37. More generally, see D. Ponce-Nava, 'Capacity-Building in Environmental Law and Sustainable Development', in W. Lang (ed.), *Sustainable Development and International Law* (London: Springer, 1995), pp. 131–6.

[54] See Action 21, *supra* n. 5, Chapter 34. See also L. Gündling, 'Compliance Assistance in International Environmental Law: Capacity-Building, Transfer of Finance and Technology' (1996) 56 *Zeitschrift für ausländisches öffentliches Recht und Völkerrecht* 796.

chapter 37 of Agenda 21 states that '(t)echnical cooperation, including that related to technology transfer and know-how, encompasses the whole range of activities to develop or strengthen individual and group capacities and capabilities'.[55] Similarly, chapter 34 of Agenda 21, on the transfer of 'environmentally sound technologies' refers repeatedly to the need to strengthen the technical and institutional capacity in developing countries.[56]

However, in practice, the two forms of technical assistance have their own distinctive features, and these specificities are important to understand the place of technical assistance in the architecture of environmental treaties. Capacity building is the type of technical assistance initially envisaged by environmental treaties. The World Heritage Fund provides a good illustration of this point.[57] We saw that this Fund was established to assist States parties in identifying sites of outstanding value, preparing the application to include them in the World Heritage List as well as taking measures for their protection, especially when they are threatened by circumstances such as natural disasters or armed conflicts. This type of technical assistance can be distinguished from certain forms of assistance envisaged by the Montreal Protocol and funded by its Multilateral Fund. As noted earlier,[58] the Montreal Protocol was amended in 1990 to attract some developing States. The 'London Amendment' created the Multilateral Fund, but it also introduced a provision (Article 10A) on the 'transfer of technology'. To understand the scope of the Amendment, not only as regards the ozone regime but, more generally, in relation to the issue of technology transfer in international environmental law, it is useful to recall some aspects of the negotiations of the Montreal Protocol.

The London Amendment helped to bring certain countries, such as China or India, into the system of the Montreal Protocol. These countries (operating under Article 5(1)) have undertaken obligations to eliminate the production and consumption of controlled substances, which are broadly similar to the obligations of developed countries (the main difference is the time-scale applicable to each group). In exchange for this commitment, developed countries agreed to cover the 'agreed incremental costs' incurred by developing countries in complying with their obligations.[59] But the deal was not a mere question of finance. We have studied in Chapter 5 the context in which the Montreal Protocol was negotiated and, in particular, the considerations of international competitiveness raised by the search for substitutes to controlled substances. In such a context, the commitment to no longer produce/use certain substances, important from an industrial standpoint, was not a realistic option for States that did not have substitutes, unless (i) sufficient time was granted to gradually convert their industrial infrastructure, (ii) financial assistance was given to them, and (iii) intellectual property

---

[55] Action 21, *supra* n. 5, para. 37.2.   [56] *Ibid.*, paras. 34.8, 34.14(d), 34.20, 34.22 and 34.26(b).
[57] See *supra* Section 9.1.2.2.   [58] See *supra* Section 9.1.2.2.
[59] Indicative list of agreed incremental costs, *supra* n. 23.

rights ('IPRs') and know-how relating to substitutes was transferred under reasonable conditions. These three considerations are important to understand the contents of the technology transfer provision (Article 10A) introduced by the London Amendment:

> Each Party shall take every practicable step, consistent with the programmes supported by the financial mechanism to ensure:
>
> (a) That the best available, environmentally safe substitutes and related technologies are expeditiously transferred to Parties operating under paragraph 1 of Article 5; and
>
> (b) That the transfers referred to in subparagraph (a) occur under fair and most favourable conditions.

In other words, unlike capacity building, the transfer of technology poses, in practice, important issues of IPRs and know-how protection and, thereby, of international competitiveness. These questions concern not only the financing of transfers but, more fundamentally, the provision of technologies. The holders of IPRs may restrict access to certain technologies (refusing to grant a licence) to prevent other companies (actual or potential) from developing competing products. This question effectively arose in connection with industries in India and Korea, which were denied licences (even against payment) to produce substitutes for substances regulated by the Montreal Protocol.[60] Such refusal meant that substitute products had to be purchased from the holder of the patent. The Multilateral Fund can cover the costs of importing substitutes but this is not a satisfactory solution to the problem because such assistance depends on the availability of sufficient funds. Moreover, there is a question of circularity to the extent that financial 'assistance' is being used to pay for the products of companies based in donor countries. This case illustrates some of the specific problems raised by technology transfer.

The interactions between IPRs and international environmental law will be discussed in more detail in Chapter 12. For present purposes, suffice to draw some general conclusions regarding technical assistance. A distinction can be made between capacity building and technology transfer (as characterised in this section). The second type of assistance raises specific problems of competitiveness and IPRs protection. We illustrated this difference in the context of the Montreal Protocol, but similar problems arise in other contexts, such as the fight against climate change[61] and the control of persistent organic pollutants.[62] The reference to India and China also highlighted the

---

[60] See UNDP, *Rapport sur le développement humain* 2001 (Brussels: DeBoeck Université, 2001), p. 109.
[61] See K. E. Maskus, 'Differentiated Intellectual Property Regimes for Environmental and Climate Technologies', (2010) No. 17 *OECD Environment Working Papers*.
[62] See 'Endosulfan ban call inspired by European interests', 29 April 2011, available at www.news. agropages.com (last visited on 10 April 2013).

tension between developed countries (which, as a rule, support the IPRs holders) and developing countries (technology recipients). This tension is reflected in legal terms by the 'form' in which technology transfer is envisaged.[63] While developed countries tend to favour lower tariffs applicable to such environmental products[64] (i.e. the export of substitution products), developing countries emphasise the need for genuine technology transfer, including the associated know-how, in favourable terms. Between these two extremes, the lawyer must find intermediate solutions to preserve the essential requirements of both sides. This research, which is strictly legal, is of considerable importance for the effectiveness of international environmental law.

One might ask, in this context, what are the instruments that can be used to address this trade-off? There are several possibilities, ranging from the issuing of compulsory licences to use IPRs[65] to the implementation of specific mechanisms for the development[66] or sharing of technologies,[67] in particular through the creation of 'markets' of IPRs.[68] A recent attempt to establish an innovative instrument was made at the 2010 COP of the UNFCCC held in Cancun. On this occasion, a 'Technology Mechanism' was created based on two institutional pillars, namely a 'Technology Executive Committee' and a 'Climate Technology Centre and Network'.[69] The Committee's function is essentially to provide guidance for technology transfer policies, while the Centre focuses on implementation. The Centre is currently managed by a consortium of intergovernmental (including UNEP and UNIDO), non-governmental and private organisations. The Centre is primarily intended to share information and expertise but, for the time being, specific references to the management of IPRs have been avoided. Of note is the emphasis on encouraging entrepreneurship, partnerships between organisations of the 'North' and 'South' and foreign direct investment. This form of

[63] The three 'forms' traditionally identified in economics, namely trade, licensing and foreign direct investment, have very different political and legal implications. On the economic approach, see W. Keller, 'International Technology Diffusion' (2004) 42 *Journal of Economic Literature* 752.

[64] See OECD, *Policy Brief: Opening Markets for Environmental Goods and Services* (Paris: OECD, 2005); R. Steenblink and J. A. Kim, 'Facilitating Trade in Selected Climate Change Mitigation Technologies in the Energy Supply, Buildings, and Industry Sectors', *OECD Trade and Environment Working Paper*, No. 2009–02 (4 May 2009).

[65] See C. Correa, 'Innovation and Technology Transfer of Environmentally Sound Technologies: The Need to Engage in a Substantive Debate' (2013) 22 *Review of European, Comparative and International Environmental Law* 54, at 60.

[66] See L. Diaz Anadon, 'Missions-oriented RD&D Institutions in Energy Between 2000 and 2010: A Comparative Analysis of China, the United Kingdom, and the United States' (2012) 41 *Research Policy* 1742.

[67] See Correa, *supra* n. 65.

[68] A. H. B. Monk, 'The Emerging Market for Intellectual Property: Drivers, Restrainers, and Implications' (2009) 9 *Journal of Economic Geography* 469.

[69] 'The Cancun Agreements: Outcome of the work of the Ad Hoc Working Group on Long-term Cooperative Action under the Convention', Decision 1/CP.16, 15 March 2011, Doc. FCCC/CP/2010/7/Add.1, paras. 117–27.

investment could be a good compromise between the protection of IPRs (which remain in the hands of the investor) and the development of national infrastructure sought by developing countries, but it does have a number of problems, which are discussed in Chapter 12.

9.2.3 Techniques oriented towards efficiency (*renvoi*)

Techniques seeking efficiency gains, such as the market mechanisms introduced by the Kyoto Protocol, have been studied in Chapter 5. Here, it will suffice to recall why they reduce the costs of compliance with international environmental obligations.

We saw in Chapter 5 that the Kyoto Protocol established a number of 'flexible mechanisms' in the form of emissions trading (Article 17) and project-based mechanisms (the JI (Article 6) and the CDM (Article 12)). These mechanisms have several advantages. From the perspective of assistance, they help channel funds to environmental projects and, as the case may be, also to transfer certain technologies that help reduce emissions as compared to a 'business as usual' ('BAU') scenario. Importantly, they can also generate efficiency gains in developed countries. The costs of achieving additional emissions reduction in countries like Switzerland or Germany, whose production processes already employ modern technology, may be much higher than achieving such reductions in countries where 'dirtier' technologies are still widespread. Thus, from a cost/benefit perspective, seeking to reduce emissions in countries such as Switzerland or Germany is likely to be less efficient than doing so in countries, such as China or Mexico, where the margin of improvement is wider. This is important because the emissions of carbon dioxide have the same impact on the global climate system regardless of whether they stem from Switzerland or China. In this context, mechanisms that allow countries like Switzerland to comply with their obligations by achieving (directly or indirectly) emissions reductions in countries (e.g. China) where this is cheaper clearly generate efficiency gains. This is the reasoning underpinning the search for efficiency through market mechanisms.[70]

Such an approach, however, also has its disadvantages. The main problem relates to the wrong message that it may send to economic operators based in developed countries, namely that there is no need to generate additional emissions reductions in their own production processes because they can offset any emissions at a lower cost in developing countries. It is for this reason that the use of such 'international measures' was limited under the Kyoto Protocol to a certain percentage of the reductions required by the quantified

---

[70] For a more general discussion of the use of market mechanisms in environmental law, see J. Freeman and C. Kolstad (eds.), *Moving to Markets in Environmental Regulation. Lessons from Thirty Years of Experience* (Oxford University Press, 2006).

commitments. A similar, albeit much more generous, approach has been followed at the EU and domestic levels (e.g. in a non-member country such as Switzerland). Thus, efficiency techniques must be used within reasonable bounds so as to avoid undermining the core message of most environmental protection instruments: reduce the level of pollution.

9.3 Techniques to manage non-compliance

9.3.1 Non-compliance procedures

Non-compliance procedures ('NCPs') play a very important role in the implementation of environmental treaties.[71] Their main objective is to ensure a satisfactory level of compliance with treaty obligations through the provision of financial or technical assistance or the adoption of a series of sanctions. The main components of NCPs will be analysed in the following sections. Here, we provide some background with respect to their historical origin, their approach to compliance and their main legal features.

Regarding the first element, like many other legal innovations, the origin of NCPs can be found in the Montreal Protocol and, more specifically in its Article 8, according to which: '[t]he Parties, at their first meeting, shall consider and approve procedures and institutional mechanisms for determining non-compliance with the provisions of this Protocol and for treatment of Parties found to be in non-compliance'. This provision was the basis for the establishment of the first modern NCP, and the model greatly influenced the treaties adopted after the Montreal Protocol as well as some older instruments that subsequently established NCPs.

It is this model that has defined the general approach of compliance underlying NCPs. We have already referred to this approach in Chapter 2. Its two main features are the non-confrontational character of the procedure and the emphasis on the prevention of environmental damage. These two features are closely related. Failure by a State to comply with an international obligation may not be due to a lack of willingness to comply, but rather down to certain technical or financial difficulties. In this context, NCPs are intended to help the State concerned to return to a situation of compliance or, at least, to keep non-compliance within reasonable bounds. In doing so, NCPs seek to prevent or mitigate environmental damage resulting from non-compliance without stigmatising the State concerned.[72] In those cases where the breach results

---

[71] On these procedures, see T. Treves *et al.* (eds.), *Non-Compliance Procedures and Mechanisms and the Effectiveness of International Environmental Agreements* (The Hague: TMC Asser Press, 2009); S. Urbinati, *Les mécanismes de contrôle et de suivi des conventions internationales de protection de l'environnement* (Milan: Giuffrè, 2009).

[72] See M. Koskenniemi, 'Breach of Treaty or Non-Compliance? Reflections on the Enforcement of the Montreal Protocol' (1992) 3 *Yearbook of International Environmental Law* 123.

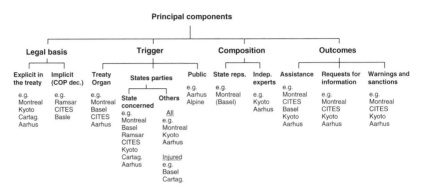

Figure 9.3: Overview of some NCPs

from State unwillingness to comply, some NCPs can be transmuted into something close to a judicial proceeding leading to a finding of non-compliance and even the adoption of sanctions. But, overall, the approach to compliance underpinning NCPs is clearly focused on prevention and assistance.

As for the main legal features of NCPs, they can be organised under four headings, namely (i) their legal basis, (ii) the parties authorised to trigger them, (iii) the composition of the compliance committees and (iv) the measures that they can adopt.[73]

Figure 9.3 provides an overview of these features referring to some examples drawn from specific NCPs (Montreal,[74] Kyoto,[75] Cartagena,[76] Aarhus,[77] Ramsar,[78] Basel,[79] CITES,[80] Alpine[81]). In what follows, we analyse each one of these features in turn.

[73] See Viñuales, *supra* n. 3, pp. 335–8.
[74] 'Non-compliance Procedure', Decision IV/5, 25 November 1992, UNEP/OzL.Pro4/15, Annex IV (Report of the Parties) as subsequently amended ('Montreal NCP').
[75] 'Procedure and Mechanisms relating to Compliance under the Kyoto Protocol', Decision 27/CMP.I, 30 March 2006, FCCC/KP/CMP/2005/8/Add.3, Annex ('Kyoto NCP').
[76] 'Establishment of Procedures and Mechanisms on Compliance under the Cartagena Protocol on Biosafety', Decision BS-I/7, 27 February 2004, UNEP/CBD/BS/COP-MOP/1/15, Annex I ('Cartagena NCP').
[77] 'Review of Compliance', Decision I/7, 2 April 2004, ECE/MP.PP/2/Add.8, Annex, ('Aarhus NCP').
[78] 'Mechanisms for Improved Application of the Ramsar Convention', Recommendation REC.C.4.7 (Rev) ('Ramsar NCP') Annex I.
[79] 'Establishment of a Mechanism for Promoting Implementation and Compliance', Decision VI/12, 10 February 2003, UNEP/CHW.6/40 (2003), Annex, as amended by COP.10 ('Basel NCP').
[80] 'CITES Compliance Procedures', Resolution Conf. 14.3, June 2007, Annex ('CITES NCP').
[81] 'Mechanism for the Verification of the Compliance with the Alpine Convention and its Implementation Protocols (Compliance Procedure)', Decision XII/I, 7 September 2012, ACXII/A1/1, Annex ('Alpine NCP').

9.3.2 The legal basis of NCPs and its implications

As a general matter, NCPs are based on a specific treaty provision. This is true of many treaties concluded after the adoption of the Montreal Protocol. In addition to Article 8 of this Protocol, examples include Article 18 of the Kyoto Protocol, Article 34 of the Biosafety Protocol[82] or Article 15 of the Aarhus Convention,[83] to name but a few. These provisions are then specified by a stream of decisions adopted by treaty bodies (most often the COPs or, for Protocols, the Meetings of the Parties or 'CMPs'). Some other treaties have established NCPs without an explicit legal basis. Examples include the procedures established under the Ramsar Convention, the CITES[84] and the Basel Convention. This difference is mostly explained by the time at which each treaty was adopted. Treaties adopted after the Montreal Protocol generally (albeit not always, e.g. the Basel Convention) include a specific provision regarding the establishment of an NCP, whereas previous instruments have been updated through COP decisions.

This difference is not without legal significance since the existence of a legal basis in the treaty may be important in determining the nature of the proceedings and, in particular, whether the decision resulting from the NCP is binding or not. It is a complex question that has not yet been settled, despite its practical significance. To address this question it is necessary to distinguish three levels.

First, the binding character must be analysed in light of the specific context of the treaty. It is at this level that the existence of a provision in the treaty is of particular importance. For example, Article 18 of the Kyoto Protocol recognises that decisions regarding compliance may be binding, but only if the NCP was established by amendment (i.e. it has been ratified by the States concerned). *A contrario* in the absence of such an amendment, the decisions are technically not binding. Conversely, the underlying treaty may also expressly provide for the optional and consultative nature of the NCP and thereby of the decisions adopted by the NCP. Such is the case of Article 15 of the Aarhus Convention. In other cases still, such as Article 8 of the Montreal Protocol or Article 34 of the Biosafety Protocol, the treaty is silent as to the binding character of decisions on compliance, which leads to the second level.

In such cases, the legal nature of these decisions must be analysed in the light of the general powers of the treaty bodies and, in particular, the COP (or the CMP). Some treaties authorise the CMP to adopt binding decisions. This is the case of Article 2(9) of the Montreal Protocol or Article 7(4) of the Biosafety

---

[82] Cartagena Protocol on Biosafety to the Convention on Biological Diversity, 29 January 2000, 2226 UNTS 208 ('Biosafety Protocol').

[83] Convention on Access to Information, Public Participation in Decision-making and Access to Justice in Environmental Matters, 25 June 1998, 2161 UNTS 447 ('Aarhus Convention').

[84] Washington Convention on International Trade in Endangered Species of Wild Fauna and Flora, 3 March 1973, United Nations, 993 UNTS 243 ('CITES').

Protocol.[85] The existence of such provisions suggests that the CMP, in fact, has the power to issue binding decisions in some cases (and therefore that it may delegate this power). But these provisions are normally formulated so as to restrict this power to specific types of decisions that do not necessarily encompass decisions on non-compliance. In any event, where the treaty does not give the possibility for the COP or CMP to adopt binding decisions, it seems clear *a fortiori* that the NCP will not be entitled to do so. This conclusion does not imply, however, that such decisions do not, in practice, have normative effects.

At the third level, it is important to determine whether the decisions arising from the NCP are respected or not, or at least whether they carry some authority.[86] The question arose with respect to certain countries, notably Greece, under the Kyoto Protocol.[87] The Compliance Committee considered that Greece had not complied with its obligations under Article 5(1) and 7 of the Kyoto Protocol and found 'Greece (to be) in non-compliance'. On this basis, it directed Greece to 'develop a plan referred to in paragraph 1 of section XV and submit it within three months' and, significantly, decided that in the meantime Greece was 'not eligible to participate in the mechanisms under Articles 6, 12 and 17 of the Protocol pending the resolution of the question of implementation'.[88] This suspension of Greece was later lifted without any explicit determination as to the binding nature of the Committee's decision.[89] This case is often cited to emphasise the authority of NCP decisions in practice. Among the numerous examples that could be mentioned to illustrate this point,[90] the decisions adopted by the Compliance Committee of the Aarhus Convention are particularly apposite. Although Article 15 of the Convention makes clear that decisions on compliance are not binding, the normative power they display in practice can hardly be questioned. The recommendations made by the COP to States parties on the basis of the Committee's decisions have indeed been largely followed in practice.[91]

---

[85] J. Brunnée, 'COPing with Consent: Law-making under Multilateral Environmental Agreements' (2002) 15 *Leiden Journal of International Law* 1, 21–3.

[86] *Ibid.*, 23ff.

[87] Compliance Committee, Final Decision: Greece, 17 April 2008, CC-2007–1-8/Greece/EB ('Decision – Greece'). See also Compliance Committee, *Final Decision: Croatia*, 19 February 2010, CC-2009–1-8/Croatia/EB.

[88] *Ibid.*, Annex, para. 18.

[89] Compliance Committee, Final Decision: Greece, 13 November 2008, CC-2007–1-13/Greece/EB.

[90] See M. Fitzmaurice, 'Non-Compliance Procedures and the Law of Treaties', in Treves *et al*, *supra* n. 71, pp. 453–81.

[91] See A. Andrusevich, T. Alge and C. Konrad (eds.), *Case Law of the Aarhus Convention Compliance Committee (2004–2011)* (Lviv: RACSE, 2nd edn, 2011), in particular Part III synthesising the 'outcomes' of the actions taken by States to respond to the recommendations of the COP (made on the basis of those of the Committee).

9.3.3 Triggering NCPs

A feature of NCPs that emphasises their fundamentally non-confrontational nature concerns the ways they may be triggered. Unlike judicial proceedings, NCPs can be triggered by the State that is in non-compliance.[92] As discussed later, self-triggering is linked to the possibility of applying for financial and/or technical assistance. In addition to the State in non-compliance, NCPs may also be triggered, depending on the cases, by (i) other States parties, (ii) some treaty bodies or (iii) the public.

Some NCPs can be triggered by other States parties without the need for them to prove that they have been particularly affected.[93] Here we approach the concept of *actio popularis inter omnes partes* (as opposed to the *actio popularis*, which does not exist – yet – in general international law[94]). This possibility is based on the nature of the object protected by the treaty (e.g. the ozone layer, climate system, endangered species, a certain level of transparency in environmental matters). Non-compliance by a State party is likely to affect the common good protected by the treaty and, thereby, the interests of all other States parties. When the treaty does not aim to protect a common resource (e.g. environmental protection in a transboundary context), NCPs normally give the right to initiate the procedure only to States specifically affected.[95]

As for the possibility given to some treaty bodies, e.g. the Secretariat, to initiate the procedure, it may either apply to non-compliance with specific obligations (e.g. procedural obligations[96]) or more generally to all treaty obligations without distinction.[97] This form of triggering has several advantages. First, the treaty bodies centralise information on the implementation of the treaty and are therefore in an ideal position to detect cases of non-compliance. In addition, triggering by treaty bodies avoids confrontation between States parties while producing similar results in the management of non-compliance. Finally, treaty bodies may informally relay the concerns of groups of civil society that are not usually allowed to initiate NCPs.

The latter point leads us to the third form of triggering, namely referral by the public. This possibility has only been provided for in environmental treaties of regional scope, such as the Alpine Convention[98] or the Aarhus Convention.[99] It is thanks to this type of triggering that the Compliance Committee of the Aarhus Convention has been able to develop an important

---

[92] See, e.g., Montreal NCP, *supra* n. 74, para. 44; Basel NCP, *supra* n. 79, para. 9(a); Ramsar NCP, *supra* n. 78, para. 1; CITES NCP, *supra* n. 80, para. 19; Kyoto NCP, *supra* n. 75, para. VI.1(a); Cartagena NCP, *supra* n. 76, para. IV.1(a); Aarhus NCP, *supra* n. 77, para. 16.

[93] See, e.g., Montreal NCP, *supra* n. 74, para. 1; NCP Kyoto, *supra* n. 75, para. VI.1(b); CITES NCP, *supra* n. 80, para. 18; Aarhus NCP, *supra* n. 77, para. 15.

[94] See F. Voeffray, *L'actio popularis ou la défense de l'intérêt collectif devant les juridictions internationales* (Paris: Presse Universitaires de France, 2004).

[95] See, e.g., Basel NCP, *supra* n. 79, para. 9(b); Cartagena NCP, *supra* n. 76, para. IV.1(b).

[96] See, e.g., Basel NCP, *supra* n. 79, para. 9(c).   [97] See, e.g., Montreal NCP, *supra* n. 74, para. 3.

[98] Alpine NCP, *supra* n. 81, para. 2.   [99] Aarhus NCP, *supra* n. 77, para. 18.

body of 'jurisprudence' on 'environmental democracy'. Indeed, the vast majority of communications brought before the Committee come from civil society groups. Note that it is not necessary to show a specific interest to use this avenue. The rules on *locus standi* and admissibility make way for communications by non-governmental organisations with an interest of a general nature, which allows them to contribute to compliance with the standards of environmental transparency introduced by the Convention.[100]

9.3.4 Composition of NCP organs

The composition of NCP organs has some practical importance. The question can be considered from several standpoints, depending on whether one is interested in the geographical distribution of the members (as in the case of environmental funds), the processes of nomination, or the capacity in which members act. Generally, we distinguish between organs composed of representatives of States and organs consisting of independent experts. The nomination procedure can, however, blur these two categories to some extent as 'independent' experts can be selected by States. In addition, representatives of States can sometimes show some independence. But the distinction remains useful to understand how NCPs function.

The NCP of the Montreal Protocol is governed by a body (the 'Compliance Committee') consisting of ten State representatives elected by the COP for a period of two years in accordance with an equitable geographical distribution.[101] The same applies to other compliance committees, such as those established under the LRTAP Convention[102] and the Espoo Convention.[103] At the other extreme, the NCP of the Kyoto Protocol is governed by a complex organ (also a 'Compliance Committee') consisting of twenty experts elected by the COP and acting in their independent capacity.[104] The Committee holds plenary sessions (twenty members), but also has two branches (each with ten members) known as a 'facilitative branch' (whose purpose is to provide assistance) and an 'enforcement branch' (which may characterise situations of non-compliance and impose sanctions). The selection of members must also take into account geographic representation as well as technical expertise.[105] The Aarhus Compliance Committee is composed of independent experts. It has eight members serving in a personal capacity (and *pro bono*) who are recognised experts, including in the legal matters.[106] Between these two extremes, one finds other bodies, such as the committee

---

[100] See Andrusevich *et al., supra* n. 91, pp. 102ff.   [101] Montreal NCP, *supra* n. 74, para. 5.

[102] Convention on Long-range Transboundary Air Pollution, 13 November 1979, 1302 UNTS 217 ('LRTAP Convention').

[103] Convention on Environmental Impact Assessment in a Transboundary Context, 25 February 1991, 1989 UNTS 309 ('Espoo Convention').

[104] Kyoto NCP, *supra* n. 75, para. II(3) and (6).   [105] *Ibid.*, para. II(6), IV(1) and V(1).

[106] Aarhus NCP, *supra* n. 77, para. I(1)–(2).

established under the Basel Convention, whose members are in fact representatives of States, although this may not be made explicit in the instrument establishing the NCP.[107]

The composition of the organs in charge of administering the NCPs can explain how these procedures function. Aside from questions of independence, which may be driven by personal considerations as much as by the institutional structure of an organ, the composition helps to understand the different approaches (whether technical or more political) favoured by each organ. Commentators have observed that adopting a more political approach runs the risk of making compliance 'negotiable'.[108] Yet, the political dimension of NCPs may also be seen as a necessary feature of their operation to the extent that they are mostly intended to manage non-compliance and not to characterise a breach and determine the ensuing legal consequences.

9.3.5 Measures adopted by NCPs

We saw in Section 9.2.2 that the legal nature of the decisions adopted by NCPs remains unsettled. However, we also noted that they have a significant normative influence in practice. We must now complete the analysis through a survey of different types of measures that can be adopted by compliance committees.

The primary objective of NCPs is to determine the reasons for non-compliance and to provide financial and technical assistance. This is reflected in the measures they are entitled to adopt. For example, the Facilitation Branch of the Committee established under the Kyoto Protocol can conclude to the '(p)rovision of advice and facilitation of assistance' or the '(f)acilitation of financial and technical assistance, including technology transfer and capacity building'.[109] The same applies to all other committees that administer NCPs. But the analysis of the causes of non-compliance in a given case may also lead to a stronger stance, including the adoption of sanctions. These can range from simple requests for additional information[110] to the issuance of warnings[111] or findings of non-compliance,[112] or even the adoption of real sanctions such as the suspension of certain benefits under the respective treaty or the application of penalties.[113]

---

[107] See Urbinati, *supra* n. 71, pp. 58–9.
[108] See G. Handl, 'Compliance Control Mechanisms and International Environmental Obligations' (1997) 9 *Tulane Journal of International and Comparative Law* 29, 37.
[109] Kyoto NCP, *supra* n. 75, para. XIV.
[110] See, e.g., Montreal NCP, *supra* n. 74, paras. 3 and 5(c); Basel NCP, *supra* n. 79, para. 22(a); CITES NCP, *supra* n. 80, para. 29(b); Cartagena NCP, *supra* n. 76, para. VI.1(d); Kyoto NCP, *supra* n. 75, para. IX(3).
[111] See, e.g., Basel NCP, *supra* n. 79, para. 20(b); CITES NCP, *supra* n. 80, para. 29(c) and (g); Cartagena NCP, *supra* n. 76, para. VI.2(b); Aarhus NCP, *supra* n. 77, para. XII.37(f).
[112] See, e.g., Montreal NCP, *supra* n. 74, para. 9; Kyoto NCP, *supra* n. 75, paras. IX(4)(a) and (7) and XV(1)(a); CITES NCP, *supra* n. 80, para. 29(g); Aarhus NCP, *supra* n. 77, para. XII.37(e).
[113] See, e.g., Aarhus NCP, *supra* n. 77, para. XII.37(g); CITES NCP, *supra* n. 80, paras. 30 and 34; Kyoto NCP, *supra* n. 75, para. XV(5).

The transition from facilitative measures to firmer measures is also characterised by the passage from a non-confrontational approach to a logic that is closer to the traditional methods of implementation in international environmental law studied in Chapter 8.

Select bibliography

Andrusevich, A., T. Alge and C. Konrad (eds.), *Case Law of the Aarhus Convention Compliance Committee (2004–2011)* (Lviv: RACSE, 2nd edn, 2011).

Biermann, F., 'Financing Environmental Policies in the South: Experiences from the Multilateral Ozone Fund' (1997) 9 *International Environmental Affairs* 179.

Boisson de Chazournes, L., 'La mise en œuvre du droit international dans le domaine de la protection de l'environnement: Enjeux et défis' (1995) *Revue générale de droit international public* 37.

'Le Fonds pour l'environnement mondial: Recherche et conquête de son identité' (1995) 41 *Annuaire français de droit international* 612.

'Technical and Financial Assistance', in D. Bodansky, J. Brunnée and E. Hey (eds.), *The Oxford Handbook of International Environmental Law* (Oxford University Press, 2007), pp. 948–72.

Brown Weiss, E. and H. K. Jacobson (eds.), *Engaging Countries: Strengthening Compliance with International Environmental Accords* (Cambridge MA: MIT Press, 1998).

Brunnée, J., 'COPing with Consent: Law-making under Multilateral Environmental Agreements' (2002) 15 *Leiden Journal of International Law* 1.

Chayes, A. and A. Handler Chayes, *The New Sovereignty, Compliance with International Regulatory Agreements* (Cambridge MA: Harvard University Press, 1998).

Correa, C., 'Innovation and Technology Transfer of Environmentally Sound Technologies: The Need to Engage in a Substantive Debate' (2013) 22 *Review of European, Comparative and International Law* 54.

Diaz Anadon, L., 'Missions-oriented RD&D Institutions in Energy Between 2000 and 2010: A Comparative Analysis of China, the United Kingdom, and the United States' (2012) 41 *Research Policy* 1742.

Fitzmaurice, M. and C. Redgwell, 'Environmental Non-Compliance Procedures and International Law' (2000) 31 *Netherlands Yearbook of International Law* 35.

Freeman, J. and C. Kolstad (eds.), *Moving to Markets in Environmental Regulation. Lessons from Thirty Years of Experience* (Oxford University Press, 2006).

Freestone, D., 'The World Bank's Prototype Carbon Fund: Mobilising new Resources for Sustainable Development', in S. Schemmer-Schulte and K.-Y. Tung (eds.), *Liber Amicorum Ibrahim S. I. Shihata* (The Hague: Kluwer, 2001), pp. 265–341.

'The World Bank and Sustainable Development', in M. Fitzmaurice, D. Ong and P. Merkouris (eds.), *Research Handbook on International Environmental Law* (Cheltenham: Edward Elgar, 2010), pp. 138–60.

Gündling, L., 'Compliance Assistance in International Environmental Law: Capacity-Building, Transfer of Finance and Technology' (1996) 56 *Zeitschrift für ausländisches öffentliches Recht und Völkerrecht* 796.

Handl, G., 'Compliance Control Mechanisms and International Environmental Obligations' (1997) 9 *Tulane Journal of International and Comparative Law* 29.

Impériali, C. (ed.), *L'effectivité du droit international de l'environnement. Contrôle de la mise en œuvre des conventions internationales* (Paris: Economica, 1998).

Keller, W., 'International Technology Diffusion' (2004) 42 *Journal of Economic Literature* 752.

Kiss, A., D. Shelton and K. Ishibashi (eds.), *Economic Globalization and Compliance with International Environmental Agreements* (The Hague: Kluwer, 2003).

Kohona, P., 'UNCED – The Transfer of Financial Resources to Developing Countries' (1992) 1 *Review of European Community and International Environmental Law* 307.

Koskenniemi, M., 'Breach of Treaty or Non-Compliance? Reflections on the Enforcement of the Montreal Protocol' (1992) 3 *Yearbook of International Environmental Law* 123.

Langer, M.-J., 'Key Instruments of Private Environmental Finance: Funds, Project Finance and Market Mechanisms', in P.-M. Dupuy and J. E. Viñuales (eds.), *Harnessing Foreign Investment to Promote Environmental Protection: Incentives and Safeguards* (Cambridge University Press, 2013), pp. 131–75.

Lawrence, P., 'Technology Transfer Funds and the Law: Recent Amendments to the Montreal Protocol on Substances that Deplete the Ozone Layer' (1992) 4 *Journal of Environmental Law* 15.

Maljean-Dubois, S., 'Mécanismes internationaux de suivi et mise en œuvre des conventions internationales de protection de l'environnement' (2004) 9 *Analyses* 1.

Maskus, K. E., 'Differentiated Intellectual Property Regimes for Environmental and Climate Technologies', *OECD Environment Working Papers*, No. 17 (2010).

Miller, A. S., 'The Global Environmental Facility and the Search for Financial Strategies to Foster Sustainable Development' (1999–2000) 24 *Vermont Law Review* 1229.

Monk, A. H. B., 'The Emerging Market for Intellectual Property: Drivers, Restrainers, and Implications' (2009) 9 *Journal of Economic Geography* 469.

Nanda, N., 'Diffusion of Climate Friendly Technologies: Can Compulsory Licensing Help?' (2009) 14 *Journal of Intellectual Property Rights* 241.

Nollkaemper, A., 'Compliance Control in International Environmental Law: Traversing the Limits of the National Legal Order' (2002) 13 *Yearbook of International Environmental Law* 165.

Ponce-Nava, D., 'Capacity-Building in Environmental Law and Sustainable Development', in W. Lang (ed.), *Sustainable Development and International Law* (London: Springer, 1995), pp. 131–6.

Richardson, B. J., *Socially Responsible Investment Law: Regulating the Unseen Polluters* (Oxford University Press, 2008).

Romanin Jacur, F., *The Dynamics of Multilateral Environmental Agreements. Institutional Architectures and Law-Making Processes* (Naples: Editoriale Scientifica, 2013).

Schalatek, L. and S. Nakhooda, 'The Green Climate Fund', in *Climate Finance Fundamentals*, No. 11, November 2012.

Steenblink, R. and J. A. Kim, 'Facilitating Trade in Selected Climate Change Mitigation Technologies in the Energy Supply, Buildings, and Industry Sectors', *OECD Trade and Environment Working Paper*, No. 2009–02 (4 May 2009).

Streck, C., 'The Global Environmental Facility – A Role Model for International Environmental Governance?' (2001) 1 *Global Environmental Politics* 71.

Treves, T., L. Pineschi, A. Tanzi, C. Pitea, C. Ragni and F. Romanin Jacur (eds.), *Non-Compliance Procedures and Mechanisms and the Effectiveness of International Environmental Agreements* (The Hague: TMC Asser Press, 2009).

Ulfstein, G. and T. Marauhn (eds.), *Making Treaties Work: Human Rights, Environment and Arms Control* (Cambridge University Press, 2007).

United Nations Environment Programme, *Manual on Compliance with and Enforcement of Multilateral Environmental Agreements* (Nairobi: UNEP, 2006).

Urbinati, S., *Les mécanismes de contrôle et de suivi des conventions internationales de protection de l'environnement* (Milan: Giuffrè, 2009).

Viñuales, J. E., 'Managing Abidance by Standards for the Protection of the Environment', in A. Cassese (ed.), *Realizing Utopia* (Oxford University Press, 2012), pp. 326–39.

Wolfrum, R., P. T. Stoll and U. Beyerlin (eds.), *Ensuring Compliance with Multilateral Environmental Agreements. A Dialogue between Practitioners and Academia* (The Hague: Martinus Nijhoff, 2006).

Part IV

International environmental law as a perspective

10

Human rights and the environment

10.1 Introduction

Environmental protection and human rights law have influenced each other in many ways. The main prism through which this complex relationship has been analysed and understood is that of 'synergies'. One underlying condition for the full respect of at least some human rights is an environment of sufficient quality to avoid significant impacts on human health and living standards. One obvious illustration of this point concerns the devastating impact that water or air pollution can have on health or even on the lifespan of humans in many regions of the world.[1] From a legal standpoint, this has resulted in an expansion of human rights provisions to account for some measure of environmental protection, thus bringing human rights (provided in treaties but also in domestic constitutions) and their institutional arsenal (regional courts, committees, domestic adjudication) to bear on questions of environmental regulation.

This basic observation suffices to introduce the two main questions that will be analysed in this chapter, namely (i) which human rights can be mobilised as a tool for environmental protection, and (ii) to what extent. The answer to these questions has kept commentators, advocacy groups and policy-makers busy for several decades, and it has raised many other questions relating to 'human rights approaches to environmental protection', such as the formulation of a right to an environment of a certain quality or the connection between human rights and climate change. It is noteworthy, however, that in more than twenty years of debates, little attention has been paid to a third question discussed in this chapter, i.e. (iii) the potential conflicts between human rights and environmental protection. One conspicuous illustration of this omission is provided by the absence of any clear reference to such conflicts in the *Analytical Study on the Relationship between Human Rights and the Environment* commissioned by the Office of the High Commissioner for

---

[1] Pollution in China has been estimated to reduce life expectancy by an average of 5.5 years. See Yuyu Chen, A. Ebenstein, M. Greenstone and Hongbin Li, 'Evidence on the Impact of Sustained Exposure to Air Pollution on Life Expectancy from China's Huai River Policy' (2009) 110 *Proceedings of the National Academy of Sciences* 12936.

Human Rights, following the initiative of the UN Human Rights Council.[2] Such omission may be the result of simple inadvertence or of a policy stance, but it must be highlighted because such conflicts do exist[3] and they may further develop as environmental policies become increasingly demanding.[4]

The first section of the chapter explores the conceptual relationship between human rights and environmental protection (10.2). The observations made in this section provide some analytical distance to undertake the analysis of synergies (10.3) and conflicts (10.4) between values as well as norms formulated to protect them.

10.2 The relationship between human rights and environmental protection

The roots of the modern understanding of the relationship between human rights and environmental protection as purely synergistic can be found in the 1972 Stockholm Conference on the Human Environment.[5] The Stockholm Declaration emphasised the deep synergies between these two bodies of international law. Principle 1 provides indeed that '[m]an has the fundamental right to freedom, equality and adequate conditions of life, in an environment of a quality that permits a life of dignity and well-being'.[6] This synergistic conception has deeply influenced international practice ever since, not only in the adoption of new international instruments but also in the context of adjudicatory and quasi-adjudicatory proceedings. This is understandable given that the values protected by these bodies of international law are closely interconnected. But this is not a reason to disregard the possibility of conflicts, particularly if one takes into account that, before Stockholm, the 'conservation

---

[2] Office of the High Commissioner for Human Rights (OHCHR), *Analytical Study on the Relationship between Human Rights and the Environment*, 16 December 2011, UN Doc. A//HRC/19/34 ('OHCHR Analytical Study').

[3] Such conflicts have received significant attention in other disciplines. See e.g. R. P. Neumann, *Imposing Wilderness: Struggles over Livelihood and Nature Preservation in Africa* (Berkeley: University of California Press, 1998); M. Dowie, *Conservation Refugees: The Hundred Years Conflict between Global Conservation and Native Peoples* (Cambridge MA: MIT Press, 2009); A. Agrawal and K. Redford, 'Conservation and Displacement: An Overview' (2009) 7 *Conservation & Society* 1. For a legal perspective, see D. Shelton, 'Resolving Conflicts between Human Rights and Environmental Protection: Is There a Hierarchy?', in E. de Wet and J. Vidmar (eds.), *Hierarchy in International Law: the Place of Human Rights* (Oxford University Press, 2012), pp. 206–35.

[4] An indication of the potential for conflicts is provided by the increasing clashes between investment disciplines (many of which – non-discrimination, due process, guarantee of private property – have a content similar to human rights) and environmental protection. On this point see J. E. Viñuales, *Foreign Investment and the Environment in International Law* (Cambridge University Press, 2012).

[5] See *supra* Chapter 1.

[6] 'Declaration of the United Nations Conference on the Human Environment', Stockholm, 16 June 1972, UN Doc. A/CONF 48/14/Rev.1, pp. 2ff ('Stockholm Declaration'). On this principle, see L. Sohn, 'The Stockholm Declaration on the Human Environment' (1972) 14 *Harvard International Law Journal* 423, 451–5.

of nature' sometimes ran foul of the use of spaces and resources to satisfy human needs. Tensions between the creation of natural preserves and the rights of indigenous or tribal peoples living in the protected area offer a clear illustration of this point.[7] We will come back to this issue in Section 10.3. Here, it will suffice to note that reference to conflicts was progressively excluded from diplomatic language from the Stockholm Conference onwards, which, by reorienting the terminology from 'nature' to the 'environment', highlighted the synergies between humans and their milieu.[8]

Nowadays, the synergistic view is deeply rooted in international practice. The OHCHR Analytical Study, published in 2011,[9] reflects this intellectual prism when it identifies the three 'major approaches' (all synergistic) to the relations between human rights and environmental protection.

First, and following the Stockholm Declaration, a satisfactory environment is seen as a necessary condition for the enjoyment of human rights.[10] This stance could imply that, from a human rights perspective, environmental protection has only an instrumental value in that it is but a contribution to the respect of such rights. Conversely, the protection of the environment *per se* (irrespective of whether this is useful or not for the protection of human rights) remains open.

This ambiguity has significant implications for the second approach identified by the Analytical Study, namely the instrumental use of human rights as a legal technique to ensure a certain level of environmental protection.[11] This approach is based upon three main considerations. One is that the holders of human rights are numerous and can be specifically identified (individuals) whereas the protection of the environment does not have a clear 'right-holder'.[12] The second is that such numerous and specifically identified right-holders can bring a claim before a growing number of adjudicatory and quasi-adjudicatory bodies (regional courts, committees, etc.) which are more sophisticated than those available in international environmental law.[13] Finally, human rights are perceived, at least for the time being, as a higher value and, as a result, they have a stronger social and political pull than pure environmental considerations.[14] But because of the nature of such drivers, the

---

[7] See *supra* n. 3.

[8] See P.-M. Dupuy, 'International Environmental Law: Looking at the Past to Shape the Future', in P.-M. Dupuy and J. E. Viñuales (eds.), *Harnessing Foreign Investment to Promote Environmental Protection: Incentives and Safeguards* (Cambridge University Press, 2013), p. 9.

[9] OHCHR Analytical Study, *supra* n. 2   [10] *Ibid.*, para. 7.   [11] *Ibid.*, para. 8.

[12] This is why the Institut de Droit International has proposed the creation of a 'High Commissioner for the Environment' that would act for the 'international community' in the context of responsibility and liability claims. See 'Responsibility and Liability under International Law for Environmental Damage' (1997) *Annuaire de l'IDI* (Session of Strasbourg), Art. 28.

[13] See A. Boyle and M. Anderson (eds.), *Human Rights Approaches to Environmental Protection* (Oxford University Press, 1996).

[14] See D. Shelton, 'Substantive Rights', in M. Fitzmaurice, D. Ong and P. Merkouris (eds.), *Research Handbook on International Environmental Law* (Cheltenham: Edward Elgar, 2010), pp. 265–83, particularly pp. 265–6.

level of environmental protection that can be achieved through human rights has significant limitations.[15] Specifically, environmental degradation is only a violation of human rights when a direct link between such degradation and a serious impairment of a protected human right can be established. In the absence of such a link, human rights instruments would have little to say about cases of environmental degradation.

The third approach identified by the Analytical Study is perhaps the most ambiguous of the three.[16] It states that human rights must be seen as an integral component of the concept of sustainable development. One could translate this statement into the terms in use in international environmental law and speak of the 'social pillar' of sustainable development (the other two pillars are 'environmental protection' and 'economic development').[17] This is, of course, uncontroversial. The real difficulty lies in going beyond the article of faith according to which the three pillars of sustainable development interact harmoniously and looking at the many situations, such as the extraction of mineral resources, where economic, social and environmental considerations are not necessarily aligned. Thus reformulated, the third approach is no longer purely synergistic (hence the ambiguity) and paves the way for a more nuanced understanding of the relationship between human rights and environmental protection, where conflicts are a possibility.[18]

These three approaches are useful to understand what is at stake in choosing one conceptual view rather than another. In this light, the questions identified in the introduction can be better spelled out. On the one hand, we will assess the extent to which environmental considerations can be brought within human rights provisions and the ensuing consequences for the use of human rights adjudicatory and quasi-adjudicatory bodies to protect the environment. The term 'extent' is important in this context. It largely summarises the core issue at stake in the debate over synergies. On the other hand, the possibility of conflicts must also be taken into account, sometimes lying beneath approaches or concepts, such as sustainable development, which apparently exclude any friction or collision. Figure 10.1 summarises the main conceptual issues arising from the relationship between human rights and environmental protection.

The field opened by these six issues is vast and complex both theoretically and policy-wise. Legal commentators and international instruments focus mostly on issue 1 and refer only marginally to the other issues.[19] Within this context, Section 10.3 of this chapter concentrates on the two main questions

---

[15] See F. Francioni, 'International Human Rights in the Environmental Horizon' (2010) 21 *European Journal of International Law* 41.

[16] OHCHR Analytical Study, *supra* n. 2, para. 9.   [17] See *supra* Chapter 1.

[18] See J. E. Viñuales, 'The Rise and Fall of Sustainable Development' (2013) 22 *Review of European Comparative and International Environmental Law* 3.

[19] On these other issues, see e.g. S. Chuffart and J. E. Viñuales, 'From the Other Shore: Economic, Social and Cultural Rights from an International Environmental Law Perspective', in E. Riedel, G. Giacca and C. Golay (eds.), *Economic, Social and Cultural Rights: Current Issues and Challenges* (Oxford University Press, 2014), pp. 286–307 (focusing on issue 2 and reviewing

Synergies			Conflicts		
Issue 1	**Issue 2**	**Issue 3**	**Issue 4**	**Issue 5**	**Issue 6**
Using human rights to protect the environment	Using environmental law to protect human rights	Doctrine of mutual supportiveness between the 'pillars' of sustainable development (environmental, economic, social)	Tensions between the 'pillars' of sustainable development	Tensions between conservation and the rights of indigenous and tribal peoples	Tensions between environmental interventionism and human rights

Figure 10.1: Relations between human rights and environmental protection

raised by issue 1 (which human rights provisions can contribute to environmental protection and to what extent) but, in doing so, our discussion touches upon issues 2 and 3. As for the remaining issues, they will be briefly discussed in Section 10.4.

10.3 Synergies

10.3.1 Two key questions

The importance of environmental parameters for human life and health has been acutely perceived since the beginning of Western medicine. Already in the fifth century BC, Hippocrates, the father of medical sciences, wrote that:

> [w]hoever wishes to investigate medicine properly, should proceed thus: . . . one ought to consider most attentively, and concerning the waters which the inhabitants use, whether they be marshy and soft, or hard, and running from elevated and rocky situations, and then if saltish and unfit for cooking; and the ground, whether it be naked and deficient in water, or wooded and well watered, and whether it lies in a hollow, confined situation, or is elevated and cold.[20]

Later came the first measures of public health and sanitation pursued in Roman times and the discoveries of Avicena and Maimonides, those of Lavoisier in the eighteenth century, and the attempts by Jeremy Bentham at having sanitation laws adopted by the English parliament. But it was not until

the relevant literature); K. Murphy, 'The Social Pillar of Sustainable Development: A Literature Review and Framework for Policy Analysis' (2012) 8 *Sustainability: Science, Practice, & Policy* 5 (analysing the body of literature on issues 3 and 4, within which specifically legal contributions are rare); the studies mentioned *supra* n. 3 (focusing on issue 5, although most of them come from disciplines other than law); T. Hayward, *Political Theory and Ecological Values* (London: Polity Press, 1998) (analysing issue 6 from the perspective of political theory) and Viñuales, *supra* n. 4 (analysing issue 6 from the perspective of how to structure environmental policies to minimise conflicts with investment disciplines).

[20] Hippocrates, 'On Airs, Waters and Places', in *The Genuine Works of Hippocrates*, translated by Francis Adams (Whitefish, MT: Kessinger Legacy Reprints, 2010), part I. See P.-M. Dupuy, 'Le droit à la santé et la protection de l'environnement', in R.-J. Dupuy (ed.), *Le droit à la santé en tant que droit de l'homme* (The Hague: Sijthoff, 1978), pp. 340–427.

the Industrial Revolution had left its scar, with its smokestacks, its miserable dwellings, the polluted air and rivers, and more recently the flood of chemical substances in all areas of human activity that the Western world started to take seriously into account the consequences of environmental degradation on human living conditions. In Africa or Asia, the impact of the Industrial Revolution was less visible than that of naturally occurring catastrophes or great epidemics, and it was not until the twentieth century that the consequences of pollution started to be felt in these regions. Yet, the belief in progress and the quest for profit delayed the adoption of measures until the second half of the twentieth century, when environmental degradation was identified as a major global concern. Even today, although the relations between the environment and human subsistence are far better understood, the relevant regulatory frameworks remain lacunary and often shy. An example is offered by China where coal-fired power plants are polluting the air and the water to such an extent that the government now sees environmental protection as a priority worth paying for.

If human life and health depend upon appropriate environmental conditions, it is then necessary to clarify the connection between environmental degradation and human rights. This connection has been recognised several times at the international level, particularly since the early 1990s.[21] The OHCHR Analytical Study surveys a number of environmental threats to human rights, including atmospheric pollution (e.g. air pollution, ozone depletion, climate change), land degradation (e.g. deforestation and desertification), pollution of water-bodies, pollution arising from the release of chemicals and hazardous waste into the environment, biodiversity loss or human-induced aggravation of natural catastrophes (e.g. through the human contribution to climate change).[22] Despite the essentially descriptive nature of this list, one can draw from it an important analytical conclusion: the impact of the environment on the realisation of human rights is predominantly (although not exclusively) understood in terms of actual or potential impairments to human health. Of course, environmental threats can also encroach on other human values, particularly cultural or aesthetic, but the main reason why an environment of a certain quality must be preserved from a human rights perspective is the protection of human health broadly defined.

The latter point has two additional analytical consequences. On the one hand, the types of human rights provisions that can be mobilised to protect the environment are essentially those relating to human health and integrity in general (e.g. the right to health, but also the rights to private and family life, life, water, food, a decent living standard or environmental information and

---

[21] See, in particular, Human Rights and the Environment. Final report presented by Mrs Fatma Zohra Ksentini, Special Rapporteur, 6 July 1994, UN Doc. E/CN.4/Sub.2/1994/9 ('Ksentini Report'), paras. 161–234 (discussing the impact of environmental degradation on the enjoyment of ten specific human rights).

[22] OHCHR Analytical Study, *supra* n. 2, para. 15–22.

participation) and, to some extent, also those relating to cultural considerations (cultural rights, the right to property and the rights to environmental information and participation). On the other hand, depending on the protected value (health, culture) and the tolerated level of impairment of such value, the required link between environmental degradation and the realisation of a human right will be more or less demanding. Such a link determines, in turn, the scope of protection that human rights provisions, as a legal tool, may provide for environmental considerations. These analytical consequences provide the conceptual basis of the following discussion.

10.3.2 Identifying human rights provisions with environmental content

10.3.2.1 Some analytical distinctions

Throughout the years, the progressive ('teleological') interpretation normally applied to human rights provisions has allowed for the recognition of some environmental contents within several rights. As already noted, it is mostly human health considerations that have become a bridge between environmental degradation and the realisation of human rights, although other considerations (mostly cultural) have also played a significant role. To find one's way within the dense forest of environment-related human rights a number of classifications have been suggested. We will introduce here some of them, which are useful for subsequent discussions.

The first classification concerns the elementary structure underpinning all human rights, irrespective of whether they are characterised as 'civil and political' or as 'economic, social and cultural rights'. Every human right imposes on its obligor or debtor (normally the State) three types of correlative obligations:[23] (i) an obligation to respect the content of the human right; (ii) an obligation to protect this right from encroachments by third parties (e.g. other individuals or non-State actors, including multinational corporations); and (iii) an obligation to progressively fulfil the necessary conditions for the full enjoyment of the right. The environmental content of a human right can be found within each obligation, and it is therefore not limited, as a superficial understanding of this distinction could suggest, to the third type of obligation.

The second classification relates to the 'substantive' or 'procedural' nature of a given right.[24] There is some overlap between these two types of rights to the

---

[23] On this influential conceptualisation, see H. Shue, *Basic Rights: Subsistence, Affluence and U.S. Foreign Policy* (Princeton NJ: Princeton University Press, 1980); *Report on the Right to Adequate Food as a Human Right. Final Report presented by the Special Rapporteur Asbjørn Eide*, 7 July 1987, UN Doc. E/CN.4/Sub.2/1987/23 (1987), paras. 66–9; Committee on Economic, Social and Cultural Rights, *General comment No. 12: The Right to Adequate Food (Art. 11)*, 12 May 1999, UN Doc. E/C.12/1999/5 (1999), para. 15; Human Rights Committee, *General Comment No. 6: Article 6 (Right to life)*, 30 April 1982, UN Doc. HRI/GEN/1/Rev.9 (Vol. I), paras. 3–5; I. E. Koch, 'Dichotomies, Trichotomies or Waves of Duties?' (2005) 5 *Human Rights Law Review* 81.

[24] See e.g. the distinction made in Fitzmaurice *et al., supra* n. 14, Chapters 13 and 14.

extent that a substantive right may carry some procedural obligations. But the distinction remains useful as a tool for the examination of the relevant literature and practice. Specifically, it helps capture the significant development of procedural environmental rights over the last twenty years and their regional epicentre, the Aarhus Convention concluded under the aegis of the UNECE.[25]

The third classification concerns the importance of the environmental dimension within a given human right. From this standpoint, a distinction can be made between 'general' rights, i.e. human rights that only have an indirect connection with environmental protection, and 'specifically environmental' rights, such as the right to a clean environment, the right to water or the rights to environmental information, participation and access to justice.

In what follows, the latter classification will be used to organise the overall discussion, whereas the two other classifications will help us analyse the particular features of different 'general' and 'specifically environmental' rights.

10.3.2.2 General rights
10.3.2.2.1 Overall context
The defining feature of 'general' rights is that they were not formulated with the specific purpose of protecting the environment. Their environmental dimension has been subsequently introduced by means of progressive interpretation, whether by a regional human rights court or commission or by a quasi-adjudicatory committee entitled to hear individual complaints. As a result, the list of the relevant 'general' rights with an environmental dimension, such as cultural rights or the rights to health, private and family life, life, property, food or an adequate living standard, is in constant evolution as it may incorporate new environmental components within one of the above-mentioned rights or even within other rights that had previously not been associated with the environment.

There is a wealth of legal commentary on most of these rights.[26] Our intention here is not to summarise this literature but, more generally, to

---

[25] Aarhus Convention on Access to Information, Public Participation in Decision-making and Access to Justice in Environmental Matters, 25 June 1998, 2161 UNTS 447 ('Aarhus Convention'). See also the policy basis of this instrument, namely principle 10 of the Rio Declaration on Environment and Development, 13 June 1992, UN Doc. A/CONF.151/26.Rev.1, ('Rio Declaration').

[26] See e.g. D. K. Anton and D. Shelton, *Environmental Protection and Human Rights* (Cambridge University Press, 2011); Francioni, *supra* n. 15; D. Shelton, 'Human Rights and the Environment: Jurisprudence of Human Rights Bodies' (2002) 32 *Environmental Policy and Law* 158; F. Francioni and M. Scheinin (eds.), *Cultural Human Rights* (Leiden: Martinus Nijhoff, 2008); S. Joseph, J. Schultz and M. Castan, *The International Covenant on Civil and Political Rights. Cases, Materials and Commentary* (Oxford University Press, 2nd edn, 2004); D. J. Harris, M. O'Boyle, E. P. Bates and C. M. Buckley, *Law of the European Convention on Human Rights* (Oxford University Press, 2nd edn, 2009); L. Burgorgue-Larsen and A. Ubeda de Torres, *The Inter-American Court of Human Rights. Case Law and Commentary* (Oxford University Press, 2011); M. Evans and R. Murray (eds.), *The African Charter on Human and Peoples' Rights. The System in Practice, 1986–2006* (Cambridge University Press, 2nd edn, 2008).

highlight the conditions under which a number of adjudicatory and quasi-adjudicatory bodies have been led to identify the environmental dimensions of certain rights and specify their contours. In this regard, a useful starting point is a brief reference to interpretation methods normally applied to human rights provisions and the institutional context where this interpretive exercise takes place. Such methods are themselves an application of the general rules on treaty interpretation emphasising a progressive and teleological reading of human rights norms in order to adapt to social change.[27] The impact of this method must be assessed in the light of the strong level of institutionalisation characterising human rights protection. Major institutions in this regard include the European Court of Human Rights ('ECtHR'), the Inter-American Commission and Court of Human Rights ('ICommHR' and 'ICtHR'), the African Commission and Court on Human and Peoples' Rights ('African Commission' and 'African Court')[28] as well as several bodies created under the aegis of the UN, such as the Human Rights Committee ('HRC') and the Committee on Economic, Social and Cultural Rights ('ESCR Committee').

It is also worth noting that several human rights treaties, such as the European Human Rights Convention (1950),[29] the International Covenants on Civil and Political Rights[30] and on Economic, Social and Cultural Rights (1966)[31] or the American Convention on Human Rights (1969),[32] were all concluded before the Stockholm Conference on the Human Environment in 1972. Thus, the integration of environmental considerations in these treaties could be expected to proceed through progressive interpretation, with the exception of the San Salvador Protocol to the American Convention (1988),[33] which explicitly takes into account environmental protection.

---

[27] See *Loizidou* v. *Turkey* (Preliminary objections), Judgment of 23 May 1995, ECtHR Application No. 15318/89, para. 72; *The Right to Information on Consular Assistance in the Framework of the Guarantees of the Due Process of Law*, ICtHR Advisory Opinion OC-16/99, 1 October 1, 1999, Ser. A, No. 16 (1999), paras. 114–15; Human Rights Committee, *General Comment 24: General Comment on Issues Relating to Reservations made upon Ratification or Accession to the Covenant or the Optional Protocols thereto, or in Relation to Declarations under Article 41 of the Covenant*, UN Doc. CCPR/C/21/Rev.1/Add.6 (1994) ('General Comment No. 24').

[28] So far, the African Court has only dealt with environmental considerations once, within the context of a pending case: *African Commission on Human and Peoples' Rights* v. *Kenya*, Order on Provisional Measures, 15 March 2013, African Court Application No. 006/2012 (regarding an eviction decree issued against the Ogiek indigenous community to force them to leave the Mau forest, a protected area).

[29] Convention for the Protection of Human Rights and Fundamental Freedoms, 4 November 1950, 213 UNTS 221.

[30] International Covenant on Civil and Political Rights, 16 December 1966, 999 UNTS 171 ('ICCPR').

[31] International Covenant on Economic, Social and Cultural Rights, 16 December 1966, 993 UNTS 3 ('ICESCR').

[32] American Convention on Human Rights, 22 November 1969, 1144 UNTS 123 ('ACHR' or 'American Convention').

[33] Additional Protocol to the American Convention on Human Rights in the Area of Economic, Social and Cultural Rights, 16 November 1988, OAS Treaty Series No. 69, Art. 11.

10.3.2.2.2 A possible starting-point: the Human Rights Committee

The first interpretive openings in this regard took place during the 1980s, particularly in the jurisprudence of the HRC. The environmental dimension of the ICCPR was first tested by reference to the right to life and the risks presented by nuclear tests or waste.[34] But such complaints were rejected by the Committee at the admissibility stage.

It was not until the early 1990s that the environmental dimension of human rights found a way of expression within the ICCPR. Quite unexpectedly, the entry point was mainly Article 27 of the Covenant, i.e. the right to the enjoyment of one's culture. The cultural ties linking certain groups to their traditional land, resources and activities (and thereby to their natural environment) was recognised by the HRC as an object capable of protection,[35] although in most cases the complaint was eventually considered inadmissible or rejected on the merits.[36] In spite of its limitations, the jurisprudence of the HRC is useful to identify the two main access points for environmental considerations that have been explored in other institutional settings, namely the impact of environmental degradation on human health broadly defined and this same impact from the perspective of cultural rights.

As discussed next, the jurisprudence of the ECtHR has predominantly (but not exclusively[37]) followed the first access point, whereas those of the ICommHR and the ICtHR have emphasised the second one. As for the African Commission, its jurisprudence has explored both entry points probably because of its focus not only on individual but also on peoples' rights. These broad observations must of course be nuanced, as no adjudicatory body has focused exclusively on one single issue. Yet, schematically, it is useful to identify the issues that each body has emphasised in its jurisprudential practice. Figure 10.2 introduces this point graphically.

---

[34] See *E.H.P.* v. *Canada*, HRC Communication no. 67/1980 (27 October 1982); *Bordes et Temeharo* v. *France*, HRC Communication No. 645/1995 (22 July 1996). See also *Brun* v. *France*, HRC Communication No. 1453/2006 (18 October 2006) (relating to GMOs).

[35] See HRC, *General Comment No. 23: Protection of Minorities (Art. 27)*, 4 August 1994, CCPR/C/21/Rev.1/Add.5, para. 3.2. By way of illustration, see *Kitok* v. *Sweden*, HRC Communication 197/1985 (27 July 1988); *Bernard Ominayak and the Lubicon Lake Band* v. *Canada*, HRC Communication No. 167/1984 (26 March 1990); *Ilmari Länsman and others* v. *Finland*, HRC Communication No. 511/1992 (8 November 1995); *Jouni E. Länsman and others* v. *Finland*, HRC Communication No. 671/1995 (30 October 1996); *Apirana Mahuika and others* v. *New Zealand*, HRC Communication No. 547/93 (27 October 2000); *Diergaardt* v. *Namibia*, HRC Communication No. 760/1997 (6 September 2000); *Poma Poma* v. *Peru*, HRC Communication No. 1457/2006 (27 March 2009) (concluding to a violation of Art. 27).

[36] See D. Shelton, 'The Human Rights Committee's Decisions', *Carnegie Council for Ethics in International Affairs*, 22 April 2005, available at: www.carnegiecouncil.org (last visited on 15 January 2014).

[37] See e.g. T. Koivurova, 'Jurisprudence of the European Court of Human Rights Regarding Indigenous Peoples: Retrospect and Prospects' (2011) 18 *International Journal on Minority and Group Rights* 1.

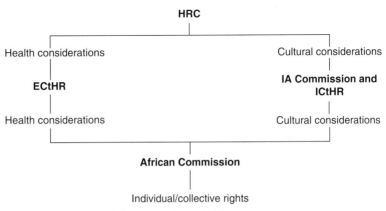

Figure 10.2: Environmental dimensions of general rights

10.3.2.2.3 The European Court of Human Rights

The environmental jurisprudence of the ECtHR has mainly been concerned with human rights relating to various aspects of human health and integrity broadly understood, particularly the right to private and family life provided in Article 8 of the European Convention.

The leading case, *Lopez Ostra* v. *Spain*,[38] was decided in the early 1990s. The Court had already considered, in earlier cases, encroachments of an environmental nature (e.g. nuisances caused by the operation of an airport) but it had concluded that the social usefulness of the activities concerned prevailed over the private interests of the applicants.[39] In *Lopez Ostra*, the Court reached the opposite conclusion, finding that the nuisance caused to the Lopez Ostra family by a facility built to treat the waste of a number of local tanneries amounted to a violation of the right to private and family life (Article 8). It noted, specifically, that:

> [n]aturally, severe environmental pollution may affect individuals' well-being and prevent them from enjoying their homes in such a way as to affect their private and family life adversely, without, however, seriously endangering their health.[40]

It thus distinguished the right to health narrowly defined from other impairments to human integrity broadly conceived, such as the right to private and family life. In addition, the Court laid the foundations for the understanding of States' obligations in this context:

---

[38] *Lopez Ostra* v. *Spain*, ECtHR Application No. 16798/90, Judgment (9 December 1994).
[39] See e.g. *Powell and Rayner* v. *United Kingdom*, ECtHR Application No. 9310/81, Judgment (21 February 1990). Later, in *Hatton and others* v. *United Kingdom*, ECtHR Application No. 36022/97, Judgment (8 July 2003), the Court had rejected the claim for breach of Article 8.
[40] *Lopez Ostra, supra* n. 38, para. 51.

Whether the question is analysed in terms of a positive duty on the State – to take reasonable and appropriate measures to secure the applicant's rights under paragraph 1 of Article 8 (art. 8–1) –, as the applicant wishes in her case, or in terms of an 'interference by a public authority' to be justified in accordance with paragraph 2 (art. 8–2), the applicable principles are broadly similar. In both contexts regard must be had to the fair balance that has to be struck between the competing interests of the individual and of the community as a whole, and in any case the State enjoys a certain margin of appreciation. Furthermore, even in relation to the positive obligations flowing from the first paragraph of Article 8 (art. 8–1), in striking the required balance the aims mentioned in the second paragraph (art. 8–2) may be of a certain relevance.[41]

The Court has further specified this approach in three main respects. First, the environmental content of general rights has been expanded, most notably through (i) the recognition of supplementary procedural obligations,[42] (ii) the use of the right to a fair process (Article 6)[43] and the right to life (Article 2) as entry points of environmental considerations,[44] and (iii) the spelling out of the 'positive' obligation of States to protect individuals from deprivation of their human rights by third parties[45] or natural catastrophes.[46] Second, the Court has further expanded environmental protection by recognising it as an objective that can justify restrictions to certain human rights, particularly the right to property.[47] Third, the scope of the environmental protection afforded by the European Convention has been conditioned on the existence of a direct link between environmental degradation and an impairment of an individual right.[48]

All in all, the European Convention has provided the basis for the development of an environmental jurisprudence focusing not only on State discipline but also (indirectly) on the conduct of third (non-State) parties. This said, the emphasis on human health and integrity broadly understood entails significant limitations in the scope for environmental protection afforded by the Convention. Indeed, the Convention remains a personal-injury-based legal

---

[41] *Ibid.*, para. 51.

[42] See *Guerra and others* v. *Italy*, ECtHR Application No. 116/1996/735/932, Judgment (19 February 1998), para. 60; *Oneryildiz* v. *Turkey*, ECtHR Application No. 48939/99, Judgment (30 November 2004), paras. 91–96; *Taskin and others* v. *Turkey*, ECtHR Application No. 46117/99, Judgment (30 March 2005), paras. 118–25; *Tatar* v. *Romania*, ECtHR Application No. 67021/01, Judgment (6 July 2009), paras. 96–7 and 116–25; *Ivan Atanasov* v. *Bulgaria*, ECtHR Application No. 12853/03, Judgment (11 April 2011), para. 78 (concluding there was an absence of breach).

[43] *Okyay and others* v. *Turkey*, ECtHR Application No. 36220/97, Judgment (12 October 2005), paras. 61–9 (on the applicability *in casu* of Art. 6.1).

[44] *Oneryildiz, supra* n. 42, paras. 89–90.   [45] *Tatar* v. *Romania, supra* n. 42, paras. 85–8.

[46] *Budayeva and others* v. *Russia*, ECtHR Applications No. 15339/02, 21166/02, 20058/02, 11673/02 and 15343/02, Judgment (29 September 2008), paras. 128–37.

[47] *Turgut* v. *Turkey*, ECtHR Application No. 1411/03, Judgment (merits) (8 July 2008), para. 90.

[48] *Fadeyeva* v. *Russia*, ECtHR Application No. 55723/00, Judgment (30 November 2005), paras. 68–70.

system and, as a result, instances of environmental degradation that are only indirectly linked to a personal injury or impairment are, at least for the time being, beyond its scope.

10.3.2.2.4 The Inter-American Court of Human Rights

The environmental jurisprudence of the ICtHR as well as some reports adopted by the ICommHR have followed a quite different path. The focus of this body of decisions is on cultural considerations, and the legal vehicle used for their protection is the right to property enshrined in Article 21 of the American Convention. Conceptually, the link between environmental degradation and this right lies in the integrity of the ancestral land which indigenous and tribal groups have traditionally inhabited, which has therefore become an indispensable part of their way of life.

The leading case in this connection, *Awas Tingni* v. *Nicaragua*, was decided by the ICtHR in 2001,[49] although a similar approach can be found in some previous decisions rendered by the ICommHR.[50] In this case, the Nicaraguan government had granted a logging concession to a Korean investor, which included the possibility of extracting wood from a forest located in the traditional land of the Awas Tingni community. Through an 'evolutionary interpretation' of Article 21 of the American Convention, the Court reasoned that:

> the close ties of indigenous people with the land must be recognized and understood as the fundamental basis of their cultures, their spiritual life, their integrity, and their economic survival. For indigenous communities, relations to the land are not merely a matter of possession and production but a material and spiritual element which they must fully enjoy, even to preserve their cultural legacy and transmit it to future generations.[51]

On this basis, it concluded that, by not recognising such entitlement, Nicaragua had breached Article 21 of the Convention.[52] The stance taken by the ICtHR in the *Awas Tingni* case was subsequently confirmed and further refined. The entire trajectory followed by this body of decisions is summarised in the *Sarayaku* v. *Ecuador* case.[53]

Here, our discussion will be limited to four main observations useful for the assessment of the scope for environmental protection allowed by the ICtHR case law. First, the Court has extended the protection afforded under Article 21 also to 'tribal' peoples (even if they cannot be considered

---

[49] *Mayagna (Sumo) Awas Tingni Community* v. *Nicaragua*, ICtHR Series C No. 79, Judgment (31 August 2001) ('*Awas Tingni* v. *Nicaragua*'), paras. 145–55.

[50] See *Yanomani Indians* v. *Brazil*, ICommHR case 7615 (decision of 5 March 1985), subsequently confirmed most notably in *Maya Indigenous Community of the Toledo District* v. *Belize*, ICommHR case 12.053 (report of 12 October 2004).

[51] *Awas Tingni* v. *Nicaragua*, *supra* n. 49, para. 149.　[52] *Ibid.*, para. 155.

[53] See *Indigenous People Kichwa of Sarayaku* v. *Ecuador*, ICtHR Series C No. 245, Judgment (merits and compensation) (27 June 2012), paras. 145–7 (right to property) and 159–68 (participatory rights).

'indigenous').[54] Second, it has specified that the protection granted in this context also covers the natural resources located in these lands that have been traditionally used by indigenous and tribal peoples.[55] Third, the Court has also specified that the right to property (even that recognised to indigenous and tribal peoples) is not absolute and can be restricted under certain conditions, namely (i) a sufficient degree of participation from the community concerned, (ii) the sharing of the benefits of the activity in question with the relevant community and (iii) the prior conduct of an environmental and social assessment.[56] Fourth, in case of conflict between the protection of the right to property of an indigenous or tribal people and that of a private owner, the Court has suggested (implicitly[57]) that the former would prevail, at least to the extent that the State could be required to expropriate the land (paying compensation to the owner) in order to give it to the relevant people.[58]

10.3.2.2.5 The African Commission

As for the jurisprudence of the African Commission, it has focused on both health and cultural considerations. Despite some formulation problems that have been singled out in the text of the African Charter,[59] the approach conveyed by this instrument combines an individual dimension (which, in the context of this chapter, one could link to health considerations broadly understood) with a group dimension (peoples' rights) based on cultural considerations. Generally speaking, these two dimensions can be illustrated by reference to two main cases.

The first, *SERAC* v. *Nigeria*,[60] concerns the effects on the Ogoni people of the severe environmental degradation caused by oil exploration and extraction activities undertaken by the Nigerian national oil company and a foreign investor. Such encroachments on the rights of the Ogoni people were further compounded by the brutal repression unleashed by the Nigerian authorities against the attempts by the Ogoni people to oppose the oil extraction activities. The case was brought before the African Commission by a Spanish NGO, SERAC, claiming the

---

[54] See *Saramaka People* v. *Suriname*, ICtHR Series C No. 172, Judgment (28 November 2007), paras. 80–6 (regarding black communities descending from the slave trade of the seventeenth century).

[55] See *Indigenous community Yakye Axa* v. *Paraguay*, ICtHR Series C No. 125 (17 June 2005), para. 137; *Sawhoyamaxa Indigenous Community* v. *Paraguay*, ICtHR Series C No. 146 (29 March 2006), para. 118.

[56] See *Saramaka* v. *Suriname, supra* n. 54, paras. 125–30.

[57] See *Sawhoyamaxa* v. *Paraguay, supra* n. 55, para. 136 (the Court noted that it did not intend to settle the question of hierarchy between the two forms of protected property, although it thereafter gave some indications on how to address it).

[58] *Ibid.*, para. 210; *Yakye Axa* v. *Paraguay, supra* n. 55, para. 148.

[59] African Charter on Human and Peoples' Rights, 27 June 1981, 21 ILM 58 (1982) ('African Charter'). See F. Ouguergouz, *La Charte africaine des droits de l'homme et des peuples* (Paris: Presses Universitaire de France, 1995); Evans and Murray, *supra* n. 26.

[60] *Social and Economic Rights Action Center (SERAC) and others* v. *Nigeria*, African Commission Application no. 155/96 (2001–2002) ('*Ogoni*').

violation of several provisions of the African Charter. The Commission considered, among others, the impact of the environmental degradation generated by the companies on the individual right to health (Article 16) and the collective right to a generally satisfactory environment (Article 24) and concluded that Nigeria had failed to respect the human rights of the Ogoni people as well as to protect them from deprivation by the action of third parties.[61] In addition, it identified some procedural obligations stemming from these rights, particularly in connection with environmental impact assessment and participation.[62]

The *Ogoni* case also has a cultural dimension, but this point is better illustrated by reference to the *Endorois* case, which involved measures taken by Kenya to the detriment of a tribal minority.[63] The Kenyan authorities had forcefully evicted the Endorois minority from their traditional land in order to create a protected area. The *Endorois* case is interesting among others because it relies on the jurisprudence of the ICtHR on indigenous and tribal property[64] in order to assert the existence of a cultural link between such a minority and its natural environment (a link protected by Articles 14 – individual right to property – and 21 – collective right to free disposal of wealth and natural resources)[65] as well as to derive specific obligations of consultation, impact evaluation and reparation.[66] Moreover, the Commission also referred to the HRC's General Comment on Article 27 of the ICCPR to conclude that Kenya had violated the cultural rights (Article 17) of the Endorois people.[67]

Thus, the jurisprudence of the African Commission not only brings together the two main avenues through which regional human rights courts have made some room for environmental protection but it also illustrates the operation of specifically environmental rights, discussed next.

10.3.2.3 Specifically environmental rights

In addition to the general human rights with environmental components discussed in the foregoing section, some specifically environmental rights, both substantive and procedural, have been recognised at the international level. Figure 10.3 gives an overview of the main legal sources.

10.3.2.3.1 A right to an environment of a certain quality

From a substantive perspective, the main development has been the increasing recognition of a right to an environment of a certain quality.[68] The adjective

---

[61] *Ibid.*, para. 52. [62] *Ibid.*, para. 53.

[63] *Centre for Minority Rights Development (Kenya) and Minority Rights Group International on behalf of Endorois Welfare Council* v. *Kenya*, African Commission Application no. 276/2003 ('*Endorois*').

[64] *Ibid.*, paras. 190–8, 205–8, 257–66. [65] *Ibid.*, para. 209. [66] *Ibid.*, paras. 225–38, 266–8.

[67] *Ibid.*, paras. 250–1.

[68] See P. Kromarek, *Le droit à un environnement équilibré et sain, considéré comme un droit de l'homme: sa mise en oeuvre nationale, européenne et internationale*, Introductory report, European Conference on the Environment and Human Rights, Strasbourg, 19–20 January 1979; P. Cullet, 'Definition of an Environmental Right in a Human Rights Context' (1995) 13 *Netherlands Quarterly of Human Rights* 25; M. Paellemarts, 'The Human Right to a Healthy

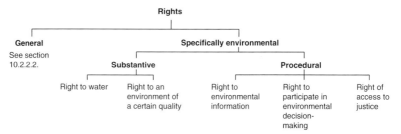

Figure 10.3: Overview of specifically environmental rights

used to characterise this quality (e.g. 'healthy' or 'satisfactory') has been often neglected by commentators. Yet, as we will see in Section 10.2.3, such characterisation can be important from a strategic point of view. Here, we will limit our discussion to some of the main milestones in the recognition of such a right domestically and internationally.

At the domestic level, the Stockholm (1972) and Rio (1992) Conferences had a significant impact on the adoption on domestic constitutional provisions recognising this right. According to the OHCHR Analytical Study:

> In 2010, the number of constitutions including explicit references to environmental rights and/or responsibilities had increased to 140, meaning that more than 70 per cent of the world's national constitutions include such provisions.[69]

According to another estimate, the overwhelming majority of constitutions adopted after 1992 recognise the right to a healthy environment.[70] This study also refers to a number of domestic judicial decisions considering this right as justiciable.[71] At the international level, the connection between the enjoyment of human rights and an environment of a certain quality had already been recognised by Principle 1 of the Stockholm Declaration.

Such connection was subsequently confirmed and developed by a number of international instruments. A first illustration is the African Charter, which provides in Article 24 that '[a]ll peoples shall have the right to a general satisfactory environment favourable to their development'. This provision was discussed and applied in the aforementioned *Ogoni* case, where the Commission noted that this right:

> imposes clear obligations upon a government. It requires the State to take reasonable and other measures to prevent pollution and ecological degradation, to promote conservation, and to secure an ecologically sustainable development and use of natural resources.[72]

Environment as a Substantive Right', in M. Dejeant-Pons and M. Paellemarts (eds.), *Human Rights and the Environment* (Strasbourg: Council of Europe, 2002), pp. 11ff.

[69] OHCHR Analytical Study, *supra* n. 2, para. 30.   [70] Shelton, *supra* n. 14, p. 267.
[71] *Ibid.*, pp. 267–8.   [72] *Ogoni, supra* n. 60, para. 52.

Moreover, the Commission highlighted the close ties between this collective right and some individual rights recognised by the ICESCR, particularly the right to health (Article 12 of the Covenant and Article 16 of the African Charter).[73] It is also noteworthy that the Commission derived procedural obligations from this right, namely the obligation to conduct an environmental and social impact assessment of industrial projects, monitor such impact and provide access to environmental information and meaningful opportunities for participation in the relevant decision-making process.[74] In the Inter-American context, Article 11(1) of the San Salvador Protocol provides that '[e]veryone shall have the right to live in a healthy environment and to have access to basic public services'.[75] The possibility of bringing an individual claim for breach of this provision seems excluded by the terms of Article 19(6) of the Protocol but this right has been used to interpret other provisions of the American Convention.[76] Another illustration is provided by Article 24(2)(c) of the Convention on the Rights of the Child (1989), which expressly refers to 'the dangers and risks of environmental pollution' in connection with the implementation of the right to the highest attainable standard of health recognised by this instrument.[77] Finally, the 2012 ASEAN Human Rights Declaration provides in Article 28(f) the right of 'every person ... to an adequate standard of living ... including ... (e) The right to a safe, clean and sustainable environment'.[78]

The reception of this right within international human rights law has been supported by a number of codification efforts undertaken by different UN bodies, particularly the Human Rights Council and its predecessor the Human Rights Commission. The latter commissioned a study on the link between environmental degradation and human rights as early as August 1989. This study, often called the 'Ksentini Report' (after the Special Rapporteur, Mrs Fatma Zohra Ksentini), was presented in 1994.[79] It appended, in an Annex, an ambitious project of principles on human rights and the environment where environmental protection is spelled out as a series of rights (and duties) both individual and collective. Unfortunately, this project had limited practical impact at the time. A similar initiative has been recently undertaken under the aegis of the Human Rights Council in order to have 'the issue of human rights obligations relating to the enjoyment of a safe, clean, healthy and sustainable environment' examined by 'an independent expert'.[80] It must be

---

[73] *Ogoni, supra* n. 60, para. 52.   [74] *Ibid.*, para. 53.

[75] Protocol of San Salvador, *supra* n. 33, Art. 11(1).

[76] See *Kawas-Fernandez* v. *Honduras*, ICtHR Series C No. 196, Judgment (merits, reparation and costs) (3 April 2009), para. 148.

[77] Convention on the Rights of the Child, 20 November 1989, 1577 UNTS 3 ('CRC').

[78] ASEAN Human Rights Declaration, 19 November 2012, available at: www.asean.org (last visited on 3 February 2014).

[79] Ksentini Report, *supra* n. 21.

[80] Human Rights Council, Resolution 19/10: 'Human Rights and the Environment', 19 April 2012, A/HRC/RES/19/10, para. 2.

noted that the terms of the mandate entrusted to the expert, Professor John Knox, are sufficiently pragmatic to avoid reaching conclusions which would be unpracticable. Indeed, the mandate focuses on the assessment of the environmental dimension of existing human rights rather than on the analysis of the contours of a human right to an environment of a certain quality.

10.3.2.3.2 The right to water and sanitation

Another right that is often considered as having a specifically environmental nature is the right to water and sanitation.[81] This right has been recognised to a varying degree in domestic and international instruments, although most often as a derivative of other general human rights.[82]

The main example is provided by Articles 11 (right to an adequate standard of living as well as adequate food and housing) and 12 (right to health) of the ICESCR, which have been considered as the basis for the recognition of a right to water by the Committee on Economic, Social and Cultural Rights in its General Comment 15 ('GC 15').[83] In GC 15, the Committee defines the right to water as follows: 'The human right to water entitles everyone to sufficient, safe, acceptable, physically accessible and affordable water for personal and domestic uses'.[84] In some other instruments, a right to water is explicitly recognised, although in respect of a narrow category of right-holders, such as children,[85] women,[86] war prisoners or civilian populations during armed conflict.[87] By way of illustration, the CEDAW provides in Article 14(2)(h) that:

> States Parties shall take all appropriate measures to eliminate discrimination against women in rural areas in order to ensure, on a basis of equality of men and women, that they participate in and benefit from rural development and, in particular, shall ensure to such women the right: . . . (h) To enjoy adequate living

---

[81] See P. Thielboerger, *The Human Right(s) to Water* (Ph.D. dissertation, European University Institute, 2011); I. T. Winkler, *The Human Right to Water* (Oxford: Hart, 2012); M.-C. Petersmann, *Les sources du droit à l'eau en droit international* (Paris: Johanet, 2013).

[82] On the extent of this recognition, see Petersmann, *supra* n. 81.

[83] Committee on Economic, Social and Cultural Rights, *General Comment No. 15 (2002), The Right to Water (Arts. 11 and 12 of the International Covenant on Economic, Social and Cultural Rights)*, 26 November 2002, UN ESCOR Doc. E/C.12/2002/11 ('GC 15').

[84] *Ibid.*, para. 2.   [85] CRC, *supra* n. 77.

[86] Convention on the Elimination of All Forms of Discriminationa Against Women, 18 December 1979, 1249 UNTS 13 ('CEDAW').

[87] See e.g. Convention (III) relative to the Treatment of Prisoners of War, 12 August 1949, 75 UNTS 31, Arts. 20, 26, 29 and 46; Convention (IV) relative to the Protection of Civilian Persons in Time of War, 12 August 1949, 75 UNTS 287, Arts. 85, 89 and 127; Protocol Additional to the Geneva Conventions of 12 August 1949, and relating to the Protection of Victims of International Armed Conflicts (Additional Protocol I), 8 June 1977, 1125 UNTS 3, Arts. 54 and 55; Protocol Additional to the Geneva Conventions of 12 August 1949, and relating to the Protection of Victims of Non-International Armed Conflicts (Protocol II), 8 June 1977, 1125 UNTS 609, Arts. 5 and 14.

conditions, particularly in relation to housing, sanitation, electricity and water supply, transport and communications.[88]

In a similar vein, Article 24(2)(c) of the CRC requires States to take measures in order to:

combat disease and malnutrition, including within the framework of primary health care, through, inter alia, the application of readily available technology and through the provision of adequate nutritious foods and clean drinking-water.[89]

More recently, the UN General Assembly and the Human Rights Council explicitly recognised (albeit in non-binding resolutions) the right to water and sanitation as a human right.[90] The Special Rapporteur appointed by the Human Rights Council on this right, Catarina de Albuquerque, has elaborated on the sanitation dimension, which is increasingly recognised as either a component of the right to water or as a distinct, albeit related, right.[91]

Properly understood, this right is half way between human rights law and environmental law, particularly if considered from the perspective of instruments such as the Protocol on Water and Health to the Helsinki Convention,[92] where the fulfilment of this right is structured in terms of States' obligations to ensure 'access' to water. This point is also useful to highlight the conceptual relationship between provisions formulated in terms of 'individual rights' (whether negative or positive liberties) and those formulated in terms of 'obligations' pertaining essentially to States.[93] As already noted, each individual right carries three types of correlative State obligations, namely to respect the right (negative obligation of non-interference), to protect the enjoyment of a right from deprivation by third parties (positive obligation to prevent encroachments by other entities) and to progressively fulfil the necessary conditions for the full enjoyment of the right (positive obligation). The content of these obligations must be specified not only by looking at the components of human rights provisions (the GC 15 takes this approach) but also by reference to instruments that clarify correlative State obligations without specifically providing for an individual right (e.g. the Protocol on Water and Health as well as most other environmental treaties). In other words, to understand the legal framework governing access to water as a human need one must look

---

[88] CEDAW, *supra* n. 86, Art. 14(2)(h).   [89] CRC, *supra* n. 77, Art. 24(2)(c).

[90] Resolution A/64/292, 'The Human Right to Water and Sanitation', 28 July 2010, UN Doc. A/64/L.63/Rev.1; Resolution 15/9: 'Human Rights and Access to Safe Drinking Water and Sanitation', 24 September 2010, A/HRC/15/L.14.

[91] See 'Human Rights Obligations related to Access to Sanitation', 1 July 2009, UN Doc. A/HRC/12/24.

[92] Protocol on Water and Health to the 1992 Convention on the Protection and Use of Transboundary Watercourses and International Lakes, 17 June 1999, 2331 UNTS 202 ('Protocol on Water and Health').

[93] See e.g. the international humanitarian law instruments mentioned *supra* n. 87.

both at human rights provisions and at norms formulated in terms of State obligations or duties.[94]

10.3.2.3.3 Procedural environmental rights

Moving on now to procedural rights, we have seen that some international adjudicatory bodies have identified procedural components (evaluation, monitoring, participation, etc.) within a number of substantive general rights. But there are also some procedural rights that are specifically environmental. Such rights, initially outlined in Principle 10 of the Rio Declaration,[95] have been spelled out in detail in the Aarhus Convention.[96] Although this Convention is a regional instrument (adopted under the aegis of the UNECE), it is open to accession by other countries,[97] a feature that in practice has extended its geographical scope far beyond Europe. The main purpose of the Aarhus Convention is 'to contribute to the protection of the right of every person of present and future generations to live in an environment adequate to his or her health and wellbeing'.[98] With this aim, the Convention requires States parties to implement three clusters of environmental procedural rights.

The first cluster concerns the right to access environmental information (Articles 4 and 5). The term 'environmental information' is broadly defined in Article 2(3) by reference to three categories of what that information could concern, namely '[t]he state of elements of the environment' (letter (a)), '[f]actors, such as substances, energy, noise and radiation, and activities or measures' (letter (b)) and:

> [t]he state of human health and safety, conditions of human life, cultural sites and built structures, inasmuch as they are or may be affected by the state of the elements of the environment or, through these elements, by the factors, activities or measures referred to in subparagraph (b) above [letter (c)].

The link formulated in the latter paragraph between, on one hand, 'human health and safety' or 'conditions of human life' and, on the other hand, the environment highlights the interest in broadening the scope of human rights to include environmental components. Through such broadening, this link could become increasingly explicit, extending the right to have access to environmental information to measures and policies relating to economic, social and cultural rights (e.g. measures and policies concerning standards of water quality, the use of communal lands by third parties, health-related zoning requirements). This link is further clarified by the Implementation Guide of the Aarhus Convention, which refers, for instance, to the fact that:

---

[94] See Chuffart and Viñuales, *supra* n. 19.   [95] See *supra* Chapter 3.
[96] Aarhus Convention, *supra* n. 25. The following presentation draws upon Chuffart and Viñuales, *supra* n. 19.
[97] Aarhus Convention, *supra* n. 25, Art. 19(2)–(3).   [98] *Ibid.*, Art. 1.

human health may include a wide range of diseases and health conditions that are directly or indirectly attributable to or affected by changes in environmental conditions.[99]

For present purposes, the link between environmental information and human rights conditions provides an illustration of what has been referred to above as 'issue 2', namely how the implementation of human rights could be fostered by the use of environmental instruments. However, the broadening of the concept of 'environmental information' has limits. Although the Implementation Guide states that the three categories of 'environmental information' identified are non-exhaustive,[100] it would be difficult to argue that measures presenting no discernible link to the environment are encompassed. Thus, information relating to measures concerning the right to education or the right to work would not be covered by the term 'environmental information' unless a sufficient link with the 'state of elements of the environment' or with '[f]actors, such as substances, energy, noise and radiation, and activities or measures' can be established.

The second cluster of environmental procedural rights concerns public participation in decisions regarding specific activities (Article 6), plans, programmes and policies relating to the environment (Article 7), as well as public participation during the preparation of executive regulations and/or legally binding instruments of general application (Article 8). These rights can be seen as specific applications of a broader right to participate in public affairs provided, most notably, in Article 25(a) of the ICCPR,[101] which applies also to economic, social and cultural rights.[102] Among the many questions raised by this cluster,[103] a particularly relevant one is the identification of the types of activities that require public participation under the Aarhus Convention. Two basic standards are used in this regard. Articles 6(1) and 8 (chapeau) refer to those activities or generally binding rules that 'may have a significant effect on the environment'. This expression is not defined in the Convention, but the Implementation Guide[104] defines it by reference to paragraph I of Appendix III to the Espoo Convention on Environmental Impact Assessment in a

---

[99] The Aarhus Convention: An Implementation Guide, available at: www.unece.org/env/pp/imple mentation%20guide/english/part2.pdf (last visited 24 January 2014) ('Implementation Guide'), p. 38.

[100] *Ibid.*, p. 35. [101] ICCPR, *supra* n. 30, Art. 25(a).

[102] On the scope of Article 25 of the ICCPR, see HRC, *General Comment No. 25: The Right to Participate in Public Affairs, Voting Rights and the Right of Equal Access to Public Service (Art. 25)*, 12 July 1996, CCPR/C/21/Rev.1/Add.7, paras. 5–8 (referring to applications of the Art. 25(a)).

[103] One important question concerns the scope of public participation. This is discussed in detail in the Implementation Guide (Implementation Guide, *supra* n. 99, pp. 85–122). For our purpose, it will suffice to note that the requirement of public participation does not mean that the public has a veto on activities, measures or plans (See Aarhus Convention, *supra* n. 25, Arts. 6(8), 7, and 8 *in fine*; Implementation Guide, *supra* n. 99, pp. 109–10).

[104] Implementation Guide, *supra* n. 99, p. 94.

Transboundary Context.[105] The Espoo Convention refers to several criteria
that must be considered to assess 'significance'. Generally speaking, these
include size, location and effects. More specifically, the Convention mentions
'proposed activities in locations where the characteristics of proposed development would be likely to have significant effects on the population'[106] or
those 'giving rise to serious effects on humans'.[107] Article 7 uses a somewhat
lower standard by referring to plans and programmes 'relating to the environment'. According to the Implementation Guide such connection must be
'determined with reference to the implied definition of "environment" found
in the definition of "environmental information" (Article 2, paragraph 3)'.[108]
Thus, in both cases, there is some room for activities, measures and regulations
affecting the situation of human beings and their human rights to be included
among those requiring public participation. Indeed, the activities and measures targeted are those with potentially serious consequences for the environment, a category that overlaps, to a significant degree, with those affecting
human health and culture broadly understood (e.g. through the safety and
quality of water, food production, the safety of the working environment, etc.).
Thus, the public participation requirements laid out in the Aarhus Convention
could operate as an additional layer of protection based on which measures
relating to the implementation of human rights could be further scrutinised by
the public.

The third cluster of environmental procedural rights concerns access to
justice in connection with access to environmental information and public
participation in environmental decision-making (Article 9). Interestingly, this
right is further extended by Article 9, paragraph 3, to empower members of the
public 'to challenge acts and omissions by private persons and public authorities which contravene provisions of its national law relating to the environment'. In the language of human rights, this extension can be seen as an
expression of States' obligations 'to protect from deprivation' by third parties.

For all three clusters of rights, the public concerned encompasses 'the public
affected or likely to be affected by, or having an interest in, the environmental
decision-making ... and meeting any requirements under national law'.[109]
Moreover, Article 9(b) expressly states that:

> the interest of any non-governmental organization meeting the requirements
> referred to in article 2, paragraph 5, shall be deemed sufficient for the purpose of
> subparagraph (a) above [sufficient interest by members of the public]. Such

---

[105] Convention on Environmental Impact Assessment in a Transboundary Context, 25 February
1991, 1989 UNTS 309 ('Espoo Convention').
[106] *Ibid.*, Appendix III, para. 1(b) *in fine.*   [107] *Ibid.*, Appendix III, para. 1(c).
[108] Implementation Guide, *supra* n. 99, p. 115. According to the guide, this would include 'land-
use and regional development strategies, and sectoral planning in transport, tourism, energy,
heavy and light industry, water resources, health and sanitation, etc., at all levels of
government'.
[109] Aarhus Convention, *supra* n. 25, Art. 2(5).

organizations shall also be deemed to have rights capable of being impaired for the purpose of subparagraph (b) above [maintaining impairment of its own right].

The application of the Aarhus framework is thus facilitated, making the Convention a powerful tool for the enforcement of States' obligations. In addition, as discussed in Chapter 9, when a State Party fails to implement the obligations arising from the Convention within its domestic system, the affected individuals or groups may resort to the non-compliance procedure established by the Convention. Thus, overall, the Convention epitomises the close ties between the objectives pursued by human rights and environmental law instruments.

10.3.3 The 'extent' of environmental protection afforded by human rights instruments

10.3.3.1 Overview

As discussed earlier in this chapter, the protection afforded by human rights instruments to the environment is conditioned on the existence of a link between environmental degradation and an impairment of a protected human value (typically health and integrity broadly understood or cultural considerations). This is because human rights law – much as tort law – is based on a personal-injury-based approach to legal protection. Within such an approach there is little room, if any, for pure – 'ecocentric'[110] – environmental protection or perhaps even for integrating the rights of unborn generations.[111] Thus, the overlap in the scope of protection of human rights norms and environmental norms is not total.

Human rights approaches to environmental protection, albeit very useful, have some important limitations. This difficulty is aptly summarised by Professor Francesco Francioni when he notes that:

> In our search for progress in this field [environmental justice], we ought to ask whether we need to fashion new rights – I will avoid the pedantic and useless schematization of 'generation rights' – inherently related to the environment and new technology related risks, or alternatively whether we can 'adapt' the conceptual and normative framework of international human rights to new situations so as to extend the scope of protection to novel risks and to the impact of environmental degradation on human rights.[112]

---

[110] On the distinction between 'anthropocentric' and 'ecocentric' approaches, see C. Stone, 'Ethics and International Environmental Law', in D. Bodansky, J. Brunnée and E. Hey (eds.), *The Oxford Handbook of International Environmental Law* (Oxford University Press, 2007), pp. 291–312.

[111] See *E.H.P. v. Canada*, *supra* n. 34, para. 8(a), where the reference to future generations was seen as a mere 'expression of concern'.

[112] Francioni, *supra* n. 15, p. 42.

The discussion in the following paragraphs focuses on the second approach identified by Francioni, namely the adaptation of the existing conceptual and normative framework to adjust – without distorting – the logic underpinning human rights. We will do so by discussing the limitations and turning then to some possible solutions and their implications for two issues, i.e. collective claims and the connection between human rights and climate change.

10.3.3.2 The 'link' requirement

The scope for environmental protection in all existing human rights, as interpreted by their respective adjudicatory bodies, is conditioned upon the establishment of a 'link' between environmental degradation and the impairment of a protected right. Depending on the legal context, this link is narrowly or more broadly understood. Although the expression 'legal context' should normally refer here to the treaty in question (e.g. the European, American or African Conventions), a more detailed analytical grid is required to capture the limitations arising from the 'link' requirement. Indeed, the adjudicatory bodies of each 'treaty context' have taken different stances depending not only on the particular 'human right' at stake (e.g. Articles 6 or 8 of the European Convention) but also on the 'circumstances' of the case. Thus, it is difficult to set a level sufficiently detailed to capture the nuances of the case law while at the same time broad enough to draw general conclusions. In what follows, we set a rather broad level in order to highlight the pervasive need for a 'link'. More detail can be found in the specialised literature.[113]

The most developed regional human rights adjudication systems have recognised the need for a link with more or less precision depending on the context. By way of illustration, the ECtHR noted, in *Kyrtatos* v. *Greece* (in the context of Article 8 of the ECHR) that:

> [n]either Article 8 nor any of the other Articles of the Convention are specifically designed to provide general protection of the environment as such; to that effect, other international instruments and domestic legislation are more pertinent.[114]

The same point was made in the context of Article 6 of the ECHR in *Athanassoglou* v. *Switzerland*:

> [t]he applicants in their pleadings . . . were alleging not so much a specific and imminent danger in their personal regard as a general danger in relation to all

---

[113] See Francioni, *supra* n. 15; C. Schall, 'Public Interest Litigation Concerning Environmental Matters before the Human Rights Courts: A Promising Future Concept?' (2008) 20 *Journal of Environmental Law* 417; ICommHR, *Indigenous and Tribal Peoples' Rights over their Ancestral Lands and Natural Resources: Norms and Jurisprudence of the Inter-American Human Rights System*, 30 December 2009, Doc OEA/Ser.L/V/II, Doc. 56/09,; R. Pavoni, *Interesse pubblico e diritti individuali nella giurisprudenza ambientale della Corte europea dei diritti umani* (Naples: Editoriale scientifica, 2013).

[114] *Kyrtatos* v. *Greece*, ECtHR Application No. 41666/98, Judgment (22 May 2003), para. 52.

nuclear power plants; and many of the grounds they relied on related to safety, environmental and technical features inherent in the use of nuclear energy.[115]

In the American context, the ICommHR made a similar point in connection with a petition against the construction of a road running through a natural reserve in Panama:

> The Commission ... holds the present complaint to be inadmissible since it concerns abstract victims represented in an actio popularis rather than specifically identified and defined individuals. The Commission does recognize that given the nature of the complaint, the petition could hardly pinpoint a group of victims with particularity since all the citizens of Panama are described as property owners of the Metropolitan Nature Reserve. The petition is inadmissible, further, because the environmental, civic, and scientific groups considered most harmed by the alleged violations are legal entities and not natural persons, as the Convention stipulates. The Commission therefore rules that it has not the requisite competence ratione personae to adjudicate the present matter in accordance with jurisprudence establishing the standard of interpretation for Article 44 of the Convention as applied in the aforementioned cases.[116]

Even the more generous jurisprudence of the ICtHR with respect to the rights of indigenous and tribal peoples maintains the need for a link without which environmental protection would not be required. In *Saramaka People* v. *Suriname*, the Court spelled out the reason why the environment is to be protected under Article 21 of the Convention (right to property):

> [t]he aim and purpose of the special measures required on behalf of the members of indigenous and tribal communities is to guarantee that they may continue living their traditional way of life, and that their distinct cultural identity, social structure, economic system, customs, beliefs and traditions are respected, guaranteed and protected by States.[117]

As for the African Commission, despite the explicit recognition of a peoples' right to a generally satisfactory environment in Article 24 of the African Charter, pure environmental degradation does not (so far) appear sufficient to conclude to an impairment of a human or a people's right. Indeed, in the *Ogoni* case,[118] the African Commission interpreted Article 24 in the light of Article 16 (right to health) and spoke of a 'right to a healthy environment'. Although it characterised the obligations arising from Article 24 in a general manner,[119] it grounded its conclusion that the Charter had been violated on

---

[115] *Athanassoglou and others* v. *Switzerland*, ECtHR Application No. 27644/95, Judgment (6 April 2000), para. 52.
[116] *Metropolitan Nature Reserve* v. *Panama*, Case 11.533, Report No. 88/03, ICommHR, OEA/Ser. L/V/II.118 Doc. 70 rev. 2 at 524 (2003), para. 34.
[117] *Saramaka* v. *Suriname, supra* n. 54, para. 121.   [118] *Ogoni, supra* n. 60.
[119] According to the Commission, this right requires the State 'to take reasonable and other measures to prevent pollution and ecological degradation, to promote conservation, and to secure an ecologically sustainable development and use of natural resources', *Ibid.*, para. 52.

the effects of the activities in question on the Ogoni community and its members:

> Undoubtedly and admittedly, the Government of Nigeria, through NNPC has the right to produce oil, the income from which will be used to fulfil the economic and social rights of Nigerians. But the care that should have been taken as outlined in the preceding paragraph and which would have protected the rights of the victims of the violations complained of was not taken. To exacerbate the situation, the security forces of the government engaged in conduct in violation of the rights of the Ogonis by attacking, burning and destroying several Ogoni villages and homes.[120]

The 'link' requirement has been characterised in different ways depending on the legal context. The ECtHR refers, in the context of Article 8, to a 'direct' link between environmental degradation and an encroachment on a human right of a 'certain minimum level of severity'.[121] The degree of the interference must be assessed in the light of a variety of factors:

> The assessment of that minimum is relative and depends on all the circumstances of the case, such as the intensity and duration of the nuisance, and its physical or mental effects. The general context of the environment should also be taken into account. There would be no arguable claim under Article 8 if the detriment complained of was negligible in comparison to the environmental hazards inherent to life in every modern city.[122]

In *Fägerskiöld* v. *Sweden*, the ECtHR rejected the claim that the nuisance caused by noise and light reflections arising from wind turbines located near the applicant's home were serious enough to constitute a breach of Article 8. The Court noted in this context that such nuisance was not 'so serious as to reach the high threshold established in cases dealing with environmental issues'.[123] As for the 'directness' of the link, the ECtHR follows a rather ambiguous test, as suggested by a much – commented – on paragraph in *Kyrtatos* v. *Greece*:

> [E]ven assuming that the environment has been severely damaged by the urban development of the area, the applicants have not brought forward any convincing arguments showing that the alleged damage to the birds and other protected species living in the swamp was of such a nature as to directly affect their own rights under Article 8 § 1 of the Convention. It might have been otherwise if, for instance, the environmental deterioration complained of had consisted in the destruction of a forest area in the vicinity of the applicants' house, a situation which could have affected more directly the applicants' own well-being.[124]

---

[120] *Ibid.*, para. 54. [121] *Fadeyeva* v. *Russia, supra* n. 48, paras. 68–70. [122] *Ibid.*, para. 69.
[123] *Fägerskiöld* v. *Sweden*, ECtHR Application No. 37664/04, Decision as to admissibility (26 February 2008).
[124] *Kyrtatos* v. *Greece, supra* n. 114, para. 53.

Still in the European context, the 'link' requirement seems even more demanding in connection with claims under Article 6 of the Convention. In *Balmer-Schafroth* v. *Switzerland*, the ECtHR characterised this requirement as entailing both the existence of a 'dispute' over a 'civil right' recognised domestically and that the outcome of the allegedly flawed proceedings be 'directly decisive for the right in question'.[125] *In casu*, the applicants had opposed the extension of the operation permit of a nuclear power plant arguing that such operation threatened their life and health. The domestic authorities (the Swiss Federal Council) rejected their claim and the applicants challenged this proceeding before the ECtHR. The Court declared the application inadmissible. After noting that 'mere tenuous connections or remote consequences are not sufficient to bring Article 6 §1 into play',[126] it concluded indeed that the applicants had failed:

> to show that the operation of Mühleberg power station exposed them personally to a danger that was not only serious but also specific and, above all, imminent. In the absence of such a finding, the effects on the population of the measures which the Federal Council could have ordered to be taken in the instant case therefore remained hypothetical.[127]

In the American and African contexts, the 'link' requirement has been characterised more loosely. This is largely a consequence of the more progressive approach adopted by the case law of the ICtHR in connection with indigenous and tribal peoples and the explicit formulation of peoples' rights in the African Charter. However, the understanding of the 'link' requirement remains demanding when no such collective rights are at stake. The ICommHR made this distinction in the abovementioned *Metropolitan Nature Reserve*, where it noted that:

> petitions filed as actions for the common good are deemed inadmissible [but that] does not imply that the petitioner must always be able to identify with particularity each and every victim on whose behalf the petition is brought ... the Commission has considered admissible certain petitions submitted on behalf of groups of victims when the group itself was specifically defined, and when the respective rights of identifiable individual members were directly impaired by the situation giving rise to a stated complaint. Such is the case of members of a specific community.[128]

The Commission referred to two examples of 'specific communities'. One reference is to indigenous groups, which have increasingly been treated as a collective human rights subject[129] and for which the 'link' requirement is more lenient. The other reference is to a group of victims of a Colombian

---

[125] *Balmer-Schafroth and others* v. *Switzerland*, ECtHR Application No. 22110/93, Judgment (26 August 1997), para. 32.
[126] *Ibid.*   [127] *Ibid.*, para. 40.   [128] *Metropolitan Nature Reserve*, *supra* n. 116, para. 32.
[129] See *Sarayaku* v. *Ecuador, supra* n. 53, para. 231.

paramilitary group that share no indigenous or tribal identity. Yet, the circumstances of the case (particularly the fact that the corpses of most of the victims had been thrown into the river and lost) justified their treatment as a group of petitioners despite the lack of individual identification. Thus, it would be difficult (albeit not impossible) to make an analogy between this (non-indigenous and non-tribal) group and a 'class' of people affected by some form of environmental degradation.

The latter point raises the question of what has been referred to in the literature as 'mass claims' brought before human rights bodies[130] and their potential use in the context of environmental protection.

10.3.3.3 Mass human rights claims: who speaks for the environment?

One significant development that has carved out some additional room for environmental protection within human rights has been the loosening of the link requirement in two main respects, namely the determination of those whose rights have been violated and of the entity that may bring the claim. These two issues are important to assess the room for bringing mass or collective claims, which require the identification of a class (by contrast to that of specific individuals) as well as of an entity representing such class (by contrast to a multitude of individual claims).

In turn, mass or collective claims may be a key instrument of environmental protection because: (i) environmental degradation tends to affect many people; (ii) the individuals within such a group differ as to their position (whether with respect to location, vulnerability or impact) and their ability to bring a claim (including in their available resources); and (iii) granting individual relief (even to a number of different people) is a very reductive way of redressing widespread environmental harm. Thus, loosening the 'link' requirement to facilitate collective claims may help expand the room for environmental protection within human rights.

In this regard, there is a noticeable difference between, on the one hand, the European context and, on the other hand, the American and African contexts. Whereas in the former significant restrictions have been placed on the ability to bring a mass claim, in the latter such claims are made admissible either as a result of an explicit legal basis (in the African Charter) or of jurisprudential developments (in the American context). This broad picture must, however, be nuanced, as even in the European context there is some room for collective claims and, conversely, it remains unclear to what extent such claims could be brought in the American context when indigenous and tribal peoples are not concerned. Let us look at this question in some more detail.

The ECtHR's overall position regarding environment-related mass claims is restrictive. A useful starting point to analyse this question is the ECtHR's decision in *Atanasov* v. *Bulgaria*.[131] This case is interesting not only for the

---

[130] Pavoni, *supra* n. 113, pp. 37–47. [131] *Atanasov* v. *Bulgaria, supra* n. 42.

overview of the relevant ECtHR's environmental jurisprudence that it provides[132] but also because the deficient environmental reclamation scheme at stake in the case threatened both the applicant and a class (i.e. the local community living in the surroundings of the reclaimed mining pond). Indeed, the Bulgarian courts had found that the applicant and other people living in the area had a sufficient interest to bring proceedings under domestic law. Yet, the Court distanced itself from this finding and simply applied the basic test under Article 8 of the Convention requiring a direct link between environmental degradation and a serious individual impairment of a human right.[133] On this basis, it rejected the claim for breach of Article 8. Another – perhaps clearer – example is the decision of the Court in *Aydin* v. *Turkey*,[134] where a group of owners challenged a dam and hydroelectricity development project affecting a natural park. The applicants invoked Articles 6 and 8 of the ECHR and claimed also a right to a healthy environment. The Court rejected both grounds and noted, in connection with Article 8, that, in truth, the applicants were trying to protect the environment rather than their rights:

> The applicants complain about the impact of the project on the ecosystem of the Munzur valley; they do not establish the repercussions of the construction of the dam on their way of life or their property or the existence of a precise and direct threat against one of them.[135]

In a subsequent case, *Di Sarno* v. *Italy*,[136] the Court slightly softened its approach. The applicants argued that the Italian authorities had failed to establish a satisfactory waste collection and management system thus encroaching on the rights of the entire population of the Campania region. The Court did not accept this argument as such but, instead, it implicitly lowered the requirement for the establishment of a direct and serious impact by admitting that the population of a specific municipality (Soma Vesuviana), including the applicants, had been affected by the 'waste crisis'.[137] However, all in all, the ECtHR has yet to admit collective environmental claims as such, and it conditions their admissibility upon their conversion into an individual claim subject to a demanding 'link' requirement. In other words, while individuals affected by environmental degradation may bring a claim and seek specific relief, the environment as such still has no voice in this legal context.

The ICtHR has followed a different approach, although so far only in connection with indigenous and tribal peoples. As discussed earlier in this chapter, the ICtHR has expanded the scope of Article 21 (the right to property) to protect the relationship between such peoples or communities and their traditional lands. This amounts not only to giving a voice to such entities as a

---

[132] *Ibid.*, paras. 66–75.   [133] *Ibid.*, paras. 76–9.
[134] *Aydin and others* v. *Turkey*, ECtHR Application No. 40806/07), Decision (15 May 2012).
[135] *Ibid.*, para. 28 (our translation from the French text).
[136] *Di Sarno and others* v. *Italy*, ECtHR Application No. 30765/08, Judgment (10 January 2012).
[137] *Ibid.*, para. 81.

distinct subject of human rights but also to extending the scope of environmental protection to the entire area potentially affecting such peoples, which is of course far broader than the one affecting a specific individual. In addition, the centre of gravity of the protection thus offered is not human health and integrity broadly conceived but the general state of the environment, at least to the extent that such environment must be preserved to ensure the traditional way of life of indigenous and tribal peoples. Environment-related collective claims thus become possible because there are criteria to identify a class (cultural criteria defining indigenous and tribal peoples) and there is a class representative (the authorities of the indigenous or tribal people). The rights protected are not merely those of a particular individual but those of a collective subject. As noted by the ICtHR in *Sarayaku* v. *Ecuador*:

> On previous occasions, in cases concerning indigenous and tribal communities or peoples, the Court has declared violations to the detriment of members of indigenous or tribal communities and peoples. However, international legislation concerning indigenous or tribal communities and peoples recognizes their rights as collective subjects of International Law and not only as individuals [reference to the UN Declaration on the Rights of Indigenous Peoples, ILO Convention 169 and the African Charter]. Given that indigenous or tribal communities and peoples, united by their particular ways of life and identity, exercise certain rights recognized by the Convention on a collective basis, the Court points out that the legal considerations expressed or issued in this Judgment should be understood from that collective perspective.[138]

And these collective subjects are in a better position than any individual member to speak for the environment and to claim general environmental redress because they are more broadly concerned with the state of the environment than any particular person or family living in a specific location. As noted in the United Nations Declaration on the Rights of Indigenous Peoples: '[i]ndigenous peoples have the right to the conservation and protection of the environment and the productive capacity of their lands or territories and resources'.[139] Moreover, the ability to bring environment-related collective claims is further strengthened by the existence of a procedural basis in Article 44 of the American Convention, according to which any:

> group of persons, or any non governmental entity legally recognized in one or more member states of the Organization [the OAS], may lodge petitions with the Commission [ICommHR] containing denunciations or complaints of violation of this Convention by a State Party.

Thus, in the American context, the environment benefits from a collective voice both at the substantive and the procedural level.

---

[138] *Sarayaku* v. *Ecuador, supra* n. 53, para. 231.
[139] United Nations Declaration on the Rights of Indigenous Peoples, 13 September 2007, UN Doc. A/RES/61/295, para. 29(1).

As for the African context, the need for jurisprudential elaboration of collective claims is less acute because the African Charter explicitly provides for collective rights and representation. This can be illustrated by the already mentioned *Ogoni* case,[140] which was brought before the African Commission by two European NGOs and concerned both individual (e.g. Article 16) and collective (e.g. Articles 21 and 24) rights.

Despite the potential of collective claims for environmental protection, the recognition of collective rights and *jus standi* is still limited by the application of the link requirement to such rights. For environmental degradation to be brought under human rights instruments, a link must be established between acts or omissions of a State, environmental degradation and an impairment of a collective right. This may be particularly challenging in some contexts, such as climate change, where the obstacles to prove such a link are formidable.

10.3.3.4 Human rights and climate change[141]

In the previous sections we have seen that human rights approaches to environmental protection require a link between environmental degradation and an impairment of a human right. Such link can be understood at different levels. One is the type of considerations (health or culture related) that have been used so far to argue that environmental degradation violates human rights. The other is the legal characterisation of the link (severity and directness). Both vary according to the legal context (treaty, specific provision, circumstances) but, generally speaking, the ECtHR has emphasised health considerations broadly understood whereas the ICtHR has concentrated on cultural considerations. The African Commission, because of the particular contents of the African Charter, has focused on both.

This overall picture is useful to understand the issue we now turn to, namely the 'adjective' used to characterise the right to an environment of a certain quality. Commentators and adjudicatory bodies seem to pay little attention to this adjective assuming, perhaps justifiably, that using one or the other adjective will not change the content and operation of such a right. Yet, wording is often important in facilitating legal breakthroughs. Speaking of a right to a 'healthy' environment may capture questions that go beyond health and into human integrity more broadly understood but it may not easily encompass the protection of a traditional economic activity (e.g. tobacco production, fishing or animal husbandry[142]) or of aesthetic considerations. Similar limitations

---

[140] *Ogoni, supra* n. 60.

[141] This section draws partly upon J. E. Viñuales, 'A Human Rights Approach to Extraterritorial Environmental Protection? An Assessment', in N. Bhuta (ed.), *Human Rights as Cosmopolitan Law? Extraterritorial Human Rights Obligations in International Law* (Oxford University Press, forthcoming 2015).

[142] Tobacco production was claimed to be protected investments by reference to chapter eleven of the NAFTA interpreted in the light of certain instruments on indigenous peoples' rights. See *Grand River Enterprises Six Nations, Ltd, and others* v. *United States of America*, NAFTA Arbitration (UNCITRAL Rules), Award (12 January 2011), paras. 66–7, 190. More generally, activities such as fishing or animal husbandry are protected as part of the traditional livelihood

may apply to a right to a 'safe' (and perhaps also to a 'sound') environment, although this characterisation may be easier to use for a 'collective' subject, to the extent that 'health' is an individual interest and can only be used for groups by analogy. Conversely, a right to a 'decent' or 'generally satisfactory' environment does not place the centre of gravity of the right on health and integrity considerations and it may more easily encompass cultural and even aesthetic considerations. Similarly, such right is better suited for a collective subject.

These observations about wording may appear purely academic at first sight, but they are not. At present, human rights approaches are being explored to tackle environmental questions, including climate change and its effects (particularly through the so-called 'slow onset events') that are very difficult to capture.[143] In order to use a personal-injury based system such as human rights law to prompt States to take mitigation and adaptation measures the wording of a potential right to an environment of a certain quality must be carefully set. It is particularly challenging to bring climate change under the 'link' requirement discussed in the previous section because the applicant must establish that acts or omissions of the State have resulted in interference with the climatic system that has triggered a specific extreme (or slow onset) weather event, which, in turn, has affected his/her rights. This complex configuration normally takes place in a global context, which human rights law can only address through the assertion of extraterritorial human rights obligations.[144] Conceptually, establishing causality in such circumstances requires three steps: (i) the State (through acts or omissions) interferes with the climatic system; (ii) such interference causes an extreme weather event (e.g. a drought, a heat wave, a hurricane, etc.) or a slow onset event (e.g. melting of polar icecaps or rise of the sea level); and (iii) such extreme or slow onset event results in a specific and sufficiently severe impairment of a human right.

The practice of human rights courts has only addressed some portions of this complex configuration. Instead of extreme or slow onset environmental phenomena, the practice so far looks at more localised environmental threats or degradation. There are two causality inquiries to be conducted in this context: one between State action or inaction and such threats or degradation and the other between the latter and an individual impairment of a human right. Figure 10.4 summarises this point.

Although the proof of these connections may be challenging, it is far from impossible in the usual context where environmental cases have arisen, as suggested by the many decisions where human rights courts have found a violation of the relevant treaties. In the context of climate change, these two

---

of some minorities for cultural reasons. See *Ominayak* v. *Canada, supra* n. 35; *Ilmari Länsman* v. *Finland, supra* n. 35.

[143] See OHCHR, *Report of the Office of the United Nations High Commissioner for Human Rights on the Relationship between Climate Change and Human Rights*, 15 January 2009, UN Doc. A/HRC/10/61.

[144] See A. Boyle, 'Human Rights and the Environment: Where Next?' (2012) 23 *European Journal of International Law* 613, 636–41.

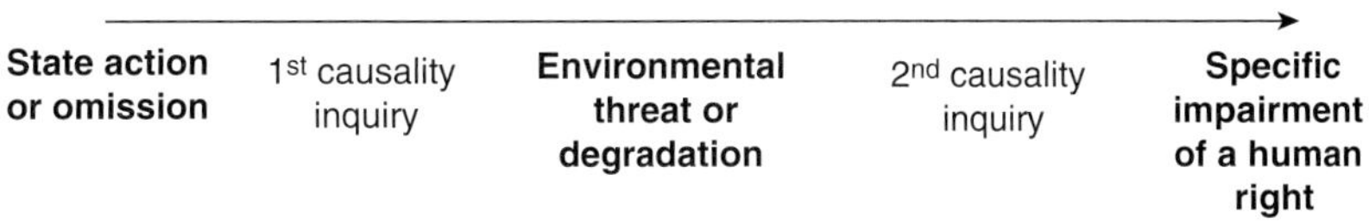

Figure 10.4: Basic causality inquiries

inquiries are far more complex. Whereas it is now well established that emissions of greenhouse gases are the main driver of climate change in the twentieth century (first causal inquiry),[145] the attribution of a specific weather event to climatic change is still too difficult to establish. This difficulty interrupts the causality flow. It is well known that climatic change causes an increase in the frequency of extreme weather events and drives slow onset events. It is even possible to identify which types of events (e.g. heat waves, droughts, hurricanes, ice-melting, sea level rise, redistribution of some diseases, etc.) can be triggered by climate change. What is missing is the link with a specific event affecting a specific area on a specific date. That is precisely what the second causality inquiry seeks to establish.

Such difficulties can be illustrated by reference to the Inuit petition before the Inter-American Commission on Human Rights.[146] The petition was brought by the Inuit Circumpolar Conference on behalf of sixty-three named individuals and the Inuit people against the United States for breach of the American Declaration on Human Rights. According to the petition, through its acts and omissions, the United States, as the (then) world's major emitter of greenhouse gases, had contributed to climate change leading to a severe modification of the Arctic environment where the Inuit live and, thereby, to a violation of the human rights of the petitioners. The petition faced major obstacles in connection with both causality inquiries. With respect to the first inquiry, the petition referred to the correlation between the United States, estimated historical emissions (Section IV.D), resulting from its lack of regulatory action (Section V.D), and 30 per cent of the observed increase in temperature of approximately 0.6° Celsius in the period from 1850 and

---

[145] See Intergovernmental Panel for Climate Change (IPCC), *Climate Change 2013: The Physical Science Basis, Summary for Policymakers*, section B, p. 2, and section D.3, p. 15 stating that 'Warming of the climate system is unequivocal, and since the 1950s, many of the observed changes are unprecedented over decades to millennia ... It is extremely likely that human influence has been the dominant cause of the observed warming since the mid-20th century' (the term 'extremely likely' indicates, in the language of the IPCC, a probability of no less than 95 per cent).

[146] See Inuit Circumpolar Conference, *Petition to the Inter American Commission on Human Rights Seeking Relief from Violations Resulting from Global Warming Caused by Acts and Omissions of the United States* (2005), available at: www.inuitcircumpolar.com/files/uploads/icc-files/FINALPetitionICC.pdf (last visited in January 2014). On this case see D. Shelton, 'Human Rights Violations and Climate Change: The Last Days of the Inuit People' (2010) 37 *Rutgers Law Record* 182.

2000.[147] The petitioners acknowledged, however, that 'the actual correlation between cumulated emissions and temperature increase is subject to some uncertainty'.[148] And even if it were not, the causation theories used in general international law are not well adapted to substitute correlation for causation. Regarding the second causality inquiry, the petition identified in its Section IV.C several effects on the Arctic environment attributable to climate change, including changes in ice and snow conditions, thawing permafrost, species redistribution and increasingly unpredictable weather conditions. But no specific link between climate change, a specific weather event and a specific impairment of a human right could be established (or between an instance of regulatory deficiency and these other steps). The Inter-American Commission did not take position on the merits of the Inuit Petition.[149] It is therefore unclear whether the scientific evidence currently available on the impact of climate change on the Arctic environment would be sufficient for litigation purposes before an international human rights body. This said, the approach followed by the petition to formulate its claim provides a good illustration of the types of challenges faced by international human rights litigation in connection with climate change. Of note is the fact that whereas the first causality inquiry could be addressed scientifically (albeit through 'correlation'), the second one seemed far more difficult to bridge explicitly.

There are different ways to overcome this important obstacle. The first way is of a scientific nature. Instead of changing the legal requirements, one would have to wait until it is scientifically possible to attribute a specific weather event to climatic change. The Inter-Governmental Panel on Climate Change ('IPCC') has tried to gather scientific evidence in the last several years to do precisely this type of specific attribution[150] but, whereas this link may eventually become well established for some high profile weather events, it is unlikely that such will be the case for any extreme weather event that may arise in litigation.

The second way would be to establish a compensation fund based on the contributions of States and companies that emit large amounts of greenhouse gases. This solution consists, in fact, in overcoming the aforementioned obstacle in a legal manner by setting up a system that treats the emission of greenhouse gases on the same footing with some hazardous but tolerated activities, as is the case with nuclear energy production or the transportation of oil.[151] Such a question could potentially fall under the remit of the 'loss and damage'

---

[147] Inuit petition, *supra* n. 146, pp. 68–9.   [148] *Ibid.*, p. 69.

[149] A. C. Revkin, 'Inuit Climate Change Petition Rejected', *New York Times*, 16 December 2006, www.nytimes.com/2006/12/16/world/americas/16briefs-inuitcomplaint.html. But see HRC Res. 10/4, UN Doc. A/HRC/RES/10/4 (31 March 2009) (adopting a position on the issue); HRC Res. 7/23, UN Doc. A/HRC/RES/7/23 (28 March 2008) (deciding to study the issue).

[150] IPCC, *Managing the Risks of Extreme Weather Events and Disasters to Advance Climate Change Adaptation* (2011) (so-called 'SREX').

[151] See Chapter 8.

negotiations conducted under the UNFCCC, although developed countries have strongly opposed attempts at framing this negotiation agenda from a 'compensation' perspective.[152]

A third possibility would be to overcome this obstacle legally by recognising a right to an 'ecologically balanced' or 'generally satisfactory' environment with the understanding that significant interference with the climatic system (first causality inquiry) may as such amount to a breach of such a right. This possibility has not been explored yet, and it may well remain unexplored until the implications of choosing the appropriate 'adjective' to characterise the right to an environment of a certain quality are well understood. Whereas such an approach would still pose several causality difficulties (e.g. what would amount to 'significant' interference with the climate? What is the meaning of 'ecologically balanced' or 'generally satisfactory' as an adjective?), they would arise at the level of the first causality inquiry, which is currently more manageable than the second one. Moreover, granting such a right to a collective human rights subject, such as an indigenous or tribal people, another minority or perhaps even an entire population, would facilitate the proof that the environment is not 'ecologically balanced' or 'generally satisfactory' for a group that has traditionally lived in a now melting area (such as the Inuit[153]) or in a low-lying island that may disappear as a result of sea level rise.[154] In the context of this book, this question can only be asked in the hope that it will nurture careful reflection as to the potential of adjusting such a right.

10.4 Conflicts

As noted in the introduction to this chapter, the conflicting dimension between human rights law and environmental law has been largely neglected by legal commentators and in international debates. The focus on synergies contrasts with the way the interactions between environmental norms and other bodies of law (e.g. trade law or investment law) have been studied, paying attention both to synergies and conflicts.[155] There is perhaps a larger scope for synergies between human rights and environmental protection than between

---

[152] See Warsaw international mechanism for loss and damage associated with climate change (Decision –/CP.19), which carefully avoids framing this issue from a compensation perspective.

[153] Inuit petition, *supra* n. 146, p. 70.

[154] See e.g. Kalinga Seneviratne, *Tuvalu Steps up Threat to Sue Australia, US*, 8 September 2002, available at: www.tuvaluislands.com/news/archived/2002/2002–09-10.htm (describing the efforts of Tuvalu to initiate a lawsuit against the United States and Australia. In this case, the lawsuit envisioned was of an inter-State nature, but the population of Tuvalu could be considered as a collective subject in a human rights context). The Maldives has also been very active in linking climate change to human rights. See J. Knox, 'Linking Human Rights and Climate Change at the United Nations' (2009) 33 *Harvard Environmental Law Review* 477.

[155] See e.g. J. Pauwelyn, *Conflict of Norms in Public International Law* (Cambridge University Press, 2003); Viñuales, *supra* n. 4.

such other bodies of law, but it is important not to take such synergies for granted. Our purpose here is to illustrate the types of conflicts that may arise and the analytical level at which they should be addressed to strike an appropriate balance between different interests.

In Chapters 1 and 3 of this book, we studied the historical emergence and evolution of international environmental law and the limited legal content of the concept of sustainable development. Sustainable development is said to consist of three mutually reinforcing pillars, namely environmental protection, economic development and social development. Yet, there is ample evidence that such pillars do not necessarily interact harmoniously. The tension between, on the one hand, economic growth and development (which has so far been largely driven by fossil fuels-based energy) and, on the other hand, environmental protection is a prominent feature of many environmental negotiations. The environment-development equation is perhaps the main source of tension underpinning the climate negotiations, to mention one example. There is, however, much more to development than mere economic considerations. The outcome document of the 2012 Rio Summit stressed indeed that 'poverty eradication is the greatest global challenge facing the world today and an indispensable requirement for sustainable development'.[156] It is difficult to disagree with this statement. One may at best note that environmental protection is also a need and, particularly, that protecting the environment is important among others to foster social inclusion and combat poverty. But the question of what to do when a policy to combat poverty (e.g. increasing access to energy in poor regions) has adverse environmental repercussions (e.g. emissions of greenhouse gases) is unlikely to vanish away. Our own view on this issue is that such questions cannot be answered in the abstract, i.e. at the level of the sustainable development concept, but only *in concreto*, whether for a specific policy or in a specific case. In what follows, we provide a few illustrations of this point.

In many cases, tensions between an environmental policy and social development considerations have been solved specifically through narrow and manageable exceptions. One illustration is provided by Annex B of the Stockholm Convention on Persistent Organic Pollutants[157] discussed in Chapter 7. The POP Convention banned the production and use of several substances, including the so-called 'dirty dozen', including the pesticide DDT the environmental effects of which had been targeted by Rachel Carson in her 1962 book *Silent Spring*.[158] However, DDT is not entirely banned. It is only restricted, which means that it can still be produced and used for one specific

---

[156] See 'The Future We Want', 11 September 2012, UN Doc. A/Res/66/288, para. 2. The eradication of poverty has been singled out as the first sustainable development goal ('SDG') of the post-2015 agenda.

[157] Stockholm Convention on Persistent Organic Pollutants, 22 May 2001, 2256 UNTS 119 ('Stockholm Convention' or 'POP Convention').

[158] R. Carson, *Silent Spring* (Boston: Houghton Mifflin, 1962).

purpose, namely to combat the vectors of malaria in accordance with the recommendations of the World Health Organisation. Indeed, Annex B Part I identifies as an 'acceptable purpose' for the production and use of DDT '[d]isease vector control in accordance with Part II of this Annex'. Annex B, Part II, states in turn that:

> Each Party that produces and/or uses DDT shall restrict such production and/or use for disease vector control in accordance with the World Health Organization recommendations and guidelines on the use of DDT and when locally safe, effective and affordable alternatives are not available to the Party in question.[159]

The WHO recommends such use only for 'indoor residual spraying' and 'until locally appropriate and cost-effective alternatives are available for a sustainable transition from DDT'.[160] Thus circumscribed, the negative environmental impact of DDT is tolerated in some areas for pragmatic human health reasons. A similar approach has been followed in the context of the Minamata Convention on Mercury[161] in connection with the use of thiomersal, a mercury-containing substance that is used to extend the lifespan of certain vaccines without the need for refrigeration, which facilitates their use in remote areas. During the negotiation of the Minamata Convention, the WHO supported such exclusion in accordance with its recommendations on the use of thiomersal, whereas the Coalition for Mercury-Free Drugs advocated for a phase-out.[162] Eventually, the delegates aligned with the WHO position. Thus, Annex A of the Convention explicitly excludes from control measures 'vaccines containing thiomersal as preservatives'.[163]

In other cases, potential tensions are not addressed in the text of the treaty and, as with other areas of international law, the adjudicatory bodies seized of the matter must balance different considerations and take a case-specific stance. There are several examples of this approach. In a case before the African Court of Human and Peoples' Rights, the Court granted provisional measures against the eviction decree issued by Kenyan authorities to force the Ogiek indigenous community to leave the Mau forest for environmental protection reasons.[164] A similar case arose before the African Commission in connection with an eviction order adopted by Kenya against the Endorois people to create a natural preserve. The Commission concluded that Kenya's actions amounted to a breach of the African Charter.[165] In an earlier case against Sweden, an individual excluded from the Sami community claimed

---

[159] POP Convention, *supra* n. 157, Annex B, Part II, para. 2.

[160] World Health Organization, *The Use of DDT in Malaria Vector Control. WHO Position Statement* (Geneva: WHO, 2011).

[161] Minamata Convention on Mercury, 10 October 2013, available at: www.mercuryconvention.org (last visited on 10 March 2014).

[162] See H. Selin, 'Global Environmental Law and Treaty-Making on Hazardous Substances: The Minamata Convention and Mercury Abatement' (2014) 14 *Global Environmental Politics* 1, 10.

[163] Minamata Convention, *supra* n. 161, Annex A, chapeau, letter (e).

[164] *African Commission* v. *Kenya*, *supra* n. 28.   [165] *Endorois*, *supra* n. 63.

that the State had violated his right to enjoy aspects of his culture (Article 27 of the ICCPR) by reason of a statute that deprived him from the right to conduct reindeer husbandry.[166] Sweden argued that the regulation of this activity was based, among other things, on ecological reasons.[167] The HRC sided with Sweden finding that the requirements imposed by the statute were overall reasonable and consistent with Article 27. Conflicts between conservation measures and the rights of indigenous and tribal peoples are a frequent occurrence in practice, although they seldom reach international courts and tribunals.[168]

Other courts have also addressed conflicts between human rights and environmental policy. In fact, part of our discussion of synergies also addressed tensions, particularly as regards the margin of appreciation left to States to restrict human rights for environmental policy purposes or to favour certain dimensions of a right (the right of indigenous or tribal peoples to their traditional land) over others (the private property right of the owner) in connection with the appropriate remedy (expropriation of the latter to restitute the land to the former). By way of illustration, in *Turgut* v. *Turkey*, the ECtHR recognised that 'economic imperatives and even some fundamental rights, such as the right to property, should not be accorded primacy against considerations of environmental protection'.[169] The Court concluded that when such is the case fair compensation must be paid but, in practice, this has meant less than the full value of the property.[170] Similarly, the ICtHR reasoned in *Sawhoyamaxa* v. *Paraguay* that '[t]he restitution of traditional lands ... is the reparation measure that best complies with the *restitutio in integrum* principle'.[171] The stances taken by permanent human rights courts with respect to conflicts between environmental protection and human rights are also important for the growing body of investment cases where frictions between environmental policies and investment disciplines arise.[172] Indeed, investment disciplines and human rights have a common origin and share some of their content.[173] As a result, tensions between environmental protection and foreign investment protection can also be seen as a manifestation of the conflicting dimension between human rights and environmental law.

These examples suggest that there is a significant amount of material falling under what we referred to, in Section 10.3 above, as issues 4 to 6, relating to

[166] *Kitok* v. *Sweden, supra* n. 35.   [167] *Ibid.,* para. 9.5.   [168] See *supra* n. 3.

[169] *Turgut* v. *Turkey, supra* n. 47, para. 90 (unofficial translation of the French text).

[170] *Ibid.,* Judgment – Just Satisfaction (13 October 2009), para 14. On the wider implications of this case, see Viñuales, *supra* n. 4, p. 297.

[171] *Sawhoyamaxa* v. *Paraguay, supra* n. 55, para 210; *Yakye Axa* v. *Paraguay, supra* n. 55, para. 148.

[172] See *infra* Chapter 12.

[173] See P.-M. Dupuy and J. E. Viñuales, 'Human Rights and Investment Disciplines: Integration in Progress', in M. Bungenberg, J. Griebel, S. Hobe and A. Reinisch (eds.), *International Investment Law* (Munich/London: C.H. Beck/Hart/Nomos, forthcoming 2015), Chapter 77.

tensions between human rights and environmental protection. This topic would call for sustained analysis not only to assess its overall importance but also to understand how such tensions can be addressed. In the context of this book, we can only flag this need in the hope it will steer further research.

Select bibliography

Agrawal, A. and K. Redford, 'Conservation and Displacement: An Overview' (2009) 7 *Conservation & Society* 1.

Anaya, J., 'Environmentalism, Human Rights and Indigenous Peoples: A Tale of Converging and Diverging Interests' (1999/2000) 7 *Buffalo Environmental Law Journal* 1.

Andrusevych, A., T. Alge and C. Konrad (eds.), *Case Law of the Aarhus Convention Compliance Committee (2004–2011)* (Lviv: RACSE, 2nd edn, 2011).

Anton, D. K. and D. Shelton, *Environmental Protection and Human Rights* (Cambridge University Press, 2011).

Boisson de Chazournes, L., 'Le droit à l'eau et la satisfaction des besoins humains: Notions de justice', in D. Alland, V. Chetail, O. de Frouville and J. E. Viñuales (eds.), *Unity and Diversity of International Law: Essays in Honour of Professor Pierre-Marie Dupuy / Unité et diversité du droit international: Ecrits en l'honneur du Professeur Pierre-Marie Dupuy* (Leiden: Martinus Nijhoff, 2014), pp. 967–81.

Boyle, A., 'Human Rights and the Environment: Where Next?' (2012) 23 *European Journal of International Law* 613.

Boyle, A. and M. Anderson (eds.), *Human Rights Approaches to Environmental Protection* (Oxford University Press, 1996).

Cançado Trindade, A. A. (ed.), *Human Rights, Sustainable Development and the Environment* (San José: Instituto Interamericano de Derechos Humanos, 1992).

Chuffart, S. L. and J. E. Viñuales, 'From the Other Shore: Economic, Social and Cultural Rights from an International Environmental Law Perspective', in E. Reidel, G. Giacca and C. Golay (eds.), *Economic, Social and Cultural Rights: Current Issues and Challenges* (Oxford University Press, 2014).

Cullet, P., 'Definition of an Environmental Right in a Human Rights Context' (1995) 13 *Netherlands Quarterly of Human Rights* 25.

Dejeant-Pons, M. and M. Pallemaerts, *Droits de l'homme et environnement* (Strasbourg: Conseil de l'Europe, 2002).

Desgagne, R., 'Integrating Environmental Values into the European Convention on Human Rights' (1995) 89 *American Journal of International Law* 263.

Dowie, M., *Conservation Refugees: The Hundred Years Conflict between Global Conservation and Native Peoples* (Cambridge MA: MIT Press, 2009).

Dupuy, P.-M., 'Le droit à la santé et la protection de l'environnement', in R.-J. Dupuy (ed.), *Le droit à la santé en tant que droit de l'homme* (The Hague: Sijthoff, 1978), pp. 340–427.

'Le droit à l'eau: droit de l'homme ou droit des Etats?', in M. G. Kohen (ed.), *Promoting Justice, Human Rights and Conflict Resolution Through International Law / La promotion de la justice, des droits de l'homme et du règlement des conflits par le droit international: Liber Amicorum Lucius Caflisch* (The Hague: Martinus Nijhoff, 2007), pp. 701–15.

Dupuy, P.-M. and J. E. Viñuales, 'Human Rights and Investment Disciplines: Integration in Progress', in M. Bungenberg, J. Griebel, S. Hobe and A. Reinisch (eds.), *International Investment Law* (Munich/London: C.H. Beck/Hart/Nomos, forthcoming 2015), Chapter 77.

Ebeku, K. S. A., 'The Right to a Satisfactory Environment and the African Commission' (2003) 3 *African Human Rights Journal* 149.

Fitzmaurice, M., 'The Human Right to Water' (2007) 18 *Fordham Environmental Law Review* 537.

Fitzmaurice, M. and J. Marshall, 'The Human Right to a Clean Environment – Phantom or Reality? The European Court of Human Rights and English Courts' Perspective on Balancing Rights in Environmental Cases' (2007) 76 *Nordic Journal of International Law* 103.

Francioni, F., 'International Human Rights in the Environmental Horizon' (2010) 21 *European Journal of International Law* 41.

Francioni, F. and M. Scheinin (eds.), *Cultural Human Rights* (Leiden: Martinus Nijhoff, 2008).

Gattini, A., 'Mass Claims at the European Court of Human Rights', in S. Breitenmoser, B. Ehrenzeller and M. Sassoli (eds.), *Human Rights, Democracy and the Rule of Law. Liber amicorum Luzius Wildhaber* (Zurich: Dike, 2007), pp. 271–94.

Golay, C., *Droit à l'alimentation et accès à la justice* (Bruxelles: Bruylant, 2011).

Hayward, T., *Political Theory and Ecological Values* (London: Polity Press, 1998).

Hodkova, I., 'Is There a Right to a Healthy Environment in the International Legal Order?' (1991) 7 *Connecticut Journal of International Law* 65.

Humphreys, S. (ed.), *Human Rights and Climate Change* (Cambridge University Press, 2009).

Inter-American Commission on Human Rights, *Indigenous and Tribal Peoples' Rights over their Ancestral Lands and Natural Resources: Norms and Jurisprudence of the Inter-American Human Rights System*, doc OEA/Ser.L/V/II, doc. 56/09, 30 December 2009.

Kiss, A.-C., 'Le droit à la conservation de l'environnement' (1990) 2 *Revue universelle des droits de l'homme* 445.

   'Peut-on définir le droit de l'homme à l'environnement?' (1976) *Revue juridique de l'environnement* 15.

Knox, J., 'Linking Human Rights and Climate Change at the United Nations' (2009) 33 *Harvard Environmental Law Review* 477.

Koch, I. E., 'Dichotomies, Trichotomies or Waves of Duties?' (2005) 5 *Human Rights Law Review* 81.

Koivurova, T., 'Jurisprudence of the European Court of Human Rights Regarding Indigenous Peoples: Retrospect and Prospects' (2011) 18 *International Journal on Minority and Group Rights* 1.

Kromarek, P., *Le droit à un environnement équilibré et sain, considéré comme un droit de l'homme: sa mise en oeuvre nationale, européenne et internationale*, Introductory report, European Conference on the Environment and Human Rights, Strasbourg 19–20 January 1979.

Limon, M., 'Human Rights Obligations and Accountability in the Face of Climate Change' (2010) 38 *Georgia Journal of International and Comparative Law* 543.

Loucaides, L., 'Environmental Protection through the Jurisprudence of the European Convention on Human Rights' (2004) 75 *British Yearbook of International Law* 249.

Murphy, K., 'The Social Pillar of Sustainable Development: A Literature Review and Framework for Policy Analysis' (2012) 8 *Sustainability: Science, Practice, & Policy* 5.

Neumann, R. P., *Imposing Wilderness: Struggles over Livelihood and Nature Preservation in Africa* (Berkeley: University of California Press, 1998).

Office of the High Commissioner for Human Rights, Analytical Study on the Relationship between Human Rights and the Environment, 16 December 2011, UN Doc. A//HRC/19/34.

Paellemarts, M., 'The Human Right to a Healthy Environment as a Substantive Right', in M. Dejeant-Pons and M. Paellemarts (eds.), *Human Rights and the Environment* (Strasbourg: Council of Europe, 2002), pp. 11ff.

Pasqualucci, J., 'The Inter-American Human Rights System: Progress Made and Still to be Made' (2009) 52 *German Yearbook of International Law* 181.

Pavoni, R., *Interesse pubblico e diritti individuali nella giurisprudenza ambientale della Corte europea dei diritti umani* (Naples: Editoriale scientifica, 2013).

Petersmann, M.-C., *Les sources du droit à l'eau en droit international* (Paris: Johanet, 2013).

Report of the Office of the United Nations High Commissioner for Human Rights on the Relationship between Climate Change and Human Rights, 15 January 2009, UN Doc. A/HRC/10/61.

Schall, C., 'Public Interest Litigation Concerning Environmental Matters before the Human Rights Courts: A Promising Future Concept?' (2008) 20 *Journal of Environmental Law* 417.

Shelton, D., 'Human Rights and the Environment: Jurisprudence of Human Rights Bodies' (2002) 32 *Environmental Policy and Law* 158.

   'Human Rights, Environmental Rights, and the Right to the Environment' (1991) 28 *Stanford Journal of International Law* 103.

   'Human Rights, Health and Environmental Protection: Linkages in Law and Practice' (2007) 1 *Human Rights and International Legal Discourse* 9.

   'Human Rights Violations and Climate Change: The Last Days of the Inuit People' (2010) 37 *Rutgers Law Record* 182.

   'Resolving Conflicts between Human Rights and Environmental Protection: Is There a Hierarchy?', in E. de Wet and J. Vidmar (eds.), *Hierarchy in International Law: The Place of Human Rights* (Oxford University Press, 2012), pp. 206–35

   'Substantive Rights', in M. Fitzmaurice, D. Ong and P. Merkouris (eds.), *Research Handbook on International Environmental Law* (Cheltenham: Edward Elgar, 2010), pp. 265–83.

Sironi, A., 'La tutela della persona in conseguenza di danni all'ambiente nella giurisprudenza della Corte europea dei diritti umani' (2011) 5 *Diritti umani e diritto internazionale* 5.

Sohn, L., 'The Stockholm Declaration on the Human Environment' (1972) 14 *Harvard International Law Journal* 423.

Stone, C., 'Ethics and International Environmental Law', in D. Bodansky, J. Brunnée and E. Hey (eds.), *The Oxford Handbook of International Environmental Law* (Oxford University Press, 2007), pp. 291–312.

Thielboerger, P., *The Human Right(s) to Water* (European University Institute, Ph.D. dissertation, 2011).

Viñuales, J. E., *Foreign Investment and the Environment in International Law* (Cambridge University Press, 2012).

'The Rise and Fall of Sustainable Development' (2013) 22 *Review of European, Comparative and International Environmental Law* 5.

Weston, B. H. and D. Bollier, 'Toward a Recalibrated Human Right to a Clean and Healthy Environment: Making the Conceptual Transition' (2013) 4 *Journal of Human Rights and the Environment* 116.

Winkler, I. T., *The Human Right to Water* (Oxford: Hart, 2012).

11

Environmental dimensions of international security

11.1 Introduction

As early as 1987, the World Commission on Environment and Development called, in its report *Our Common Future*, for States to expand their understanding of the concept of security to incorporate environmental considerations:

> The first step in creating a more satisfactory basis for managing the interrelationships between security and sustainable development is to broaden our vision. Conflicts may arise not only because of political and military threats to national sovereignty; they may derive also from environmental degradation and the pre-emption of development options.[1]

Starting in the 1990s[2] and particularly in the last decade, this core message has increasingly found expression in a number of concrete initiatives undertaken not only by environmental organisations but also, and remarkably, by organisations focusing on international security.

An apposite example is provided by the joint initiative launched in 2002 by the UNEP, the UNDP and the Organisation for Security and Cooperation in Europe ('OSCE') called 'An Environment Agenda for Security and Cooperation in South Eastern Europe and Central Asia' or 'ENVSEC Initiative'.[3] This initiative aims to incorporate the environmental dimension into the security policies relating to countries and regions with significant exposure to conflict, such as the Balkans, the Caucasus or Central Asia. The initiative was subsequently enlarged to three other organisations, namely the North Atlantic Treaty Organisation ('NATO'), the United Nations Economic Commission for Europe ('UNECE') and the Regional Environmental Centre for Central and Eastern Europe ('REC'). The main idea underpinning this and other efforts to redefine the concept of security is the need to understand the impact of problems such as environmental degradation, asymmetric access to

---

[1] Report of the World Commission on Environment and Development, *Our Common Future*, 10 March 1987 ('Our Common Future' or 'Brundtland Report'), Chapter 11, para. 37.

[2] On previous efforts to recharacterise the concept of security, see J. Mathews, 'Redefining Security' (1989) *Foreign Affairs* 162.

[3] See www.envsec.org (last visited on 20 April 2014).

natural resources or the transboundary movement of dangerous substances on the triggering, amplification or duration of conflicts or their resumption. More generally, these efforts highlight the active rather than merely passive role played by environmental change in connection with conflict.

The purpose of this chapter is to analyse how the environmental dimension of international security has been increasingly reflected in international law, whether to protect the environment from armed conflict or, conversely, to address environmental threats as conflict drivers. The first substantive section focuses on the protection of the environment in what has traditionally been called the law of war (11.2), which encompasses both the laws applicable to the conduct of hostilities and the law governing recourse to force. The following section analyses the link between environmental degradation and security (11.3), with particular reference to two environment-driven phenomena that pose significant security threats, namely environmentally-induced displacement and environmental security in post-conflict reconstruction.

11.2 The environment and the law of war

11.2.1 The environment and armed conflict

11.2.1.1 Overview

The protection of the natural environment in armed conflict became a major subject of legal discussion following the environmental damage caused by the United States during the Vietnam War through the use of agent orange, a chemical defoliant.[4] The debate reignited at the time of the 1990–1 Gulf War[5] and, some years later, as a result of the International Court of Justice's *Advisory Opinion on the Legality of Nuclear Weapons*.[6] Over time, the question has been addressed from three main angles.

Most often, the scholarship on international humanitarian law has provided detailed assessments of the environmental coverage of some *jus in bello* instruments and rules ('first approach'). The epicentre of this approach is provided by Articles 35(3) and 55 of the First Additional Protocol to the Geneva Conventions,[7] with seismic waves covering several instruments on

---

[4] For a concise overview of these developments, see M. N. Schmitt, 'War and the Environment: Fault Lines in the Prescriptive Landscape', in J. E. Austin and C. E. Bruch (eds.), *The Environmental Consequences of War: Legal, Economic and Scientific Perspectives* (Cambridge University Press, 2000), pp. 87–136, at 87–92.

[5] See K. Hulme, 'Armed Conflict, Wanton Ecological Devastation and Scorched Earth Policies: How the 1990–91 Gulf Conflict Revealed the Inadequacies of the Current Laws to Ensure Effective Protection and Preservation of the Natural Environment' (1997) 2 *Journal of Armed Conflict Law* 55.

[6] *Legality of the Threat or Use of Nuclear Weapons*, ICJ Reports 1996, p. 226 ('*Legality of Nuclear Weapons*'), paras. 27–33.

[7] Protocol Additional to the Geneva Conventions of 12 August 1949, and Relating to the Protection of Victims of International Armed Conflicts, 6 August 1977, 1125 UNTS 3 ('Additional Protocol I').

Approach 1	Approach 2	Approach 3
Environmental coverage of *jus in bello* norms	Whether and how environmental norms apply during armed conflict	Life cycle regulation of weapons as pollutants

Figure 11.1: Legal approaches to environmental protection in armed conflict

the means of warfare, such as the ENMOD Convention,[8] and reaching as far as the potential existence of an 'Environmental Martens Clause',[9] the definition of international crimes arising from harm to the environment during hostilities,[10] or even the opportunity of a 'Fifth Geneva Convention' focusing on environmental protection.[11]

In addition to this approach, since the 1992 Earth Summit much has been written on 'whether' international environmental law remains applicable in times of armed conflict, with particular emphasis on customary principles (e.g. prevention) and the wording of certain multilateral environmental agreements ('MEAs') ('second approach').[12] Aside from the question of 'whether', the second approach must also clarify 'how' international environmental law applies or, in other words, what is the specific impact of environmental norms in this context.

The 'third approach' focuses on the regulation of certain types of weapons (biological, chemical and nuclear weapons) but, unlike the first approach, it looks beyond their mere use and encompasses a larger portion of the life cycle of such weapons. From an environmental perspective, the third approach sees weapons as 'pollutants', the production, stockpiling, transportation, use and disposal of which must be regulated for their effects to be effectively neutralised. The scope and stringency of the regulatory framework varies from one type of weapon to the other, an issue that has raised vivid controversies in connection with nuclear weapons. Figure 11.1 summarises these three approaches.

In the following sections, we briefly discuss each approach highlighting the most relevant legal instruments and provisions as well as their main limitations.

---

[8] Convention for the Prohibition of Military or other Hostile Use of Environmental Modification Techniques, 10 December 1976, 1108 UNTS 151 ('ENMOD Convention').

[9] See Report of the Second IUCN World Conservation Congress, 4–11 October 2000, Resolution CGR2.CNV019 'Martens Clause for Environmental Protection'.

[10] See M. Bothe, 'Criminal Responsibility for Environmental Damage in Times of Armed Conflict', in R. J. Grunawalt, J. E. King and R. S. McClain (eds.), *Protection of the Environment during Armed Conflict* (Newport RI: Naval War College, 1996), pp. 473–8. The 1998 Statute of the International Criminal Court ('ICC') contains a specific provision (Art. 8(a) (b)(iv)) establishing criminal responsibility for environmental damage.

[11] See G. Plant (ed.), *Environmental Protection and the Law of War: A 'Fifth Geneva' Convention on the Environment in Times of Armed Conflict?* (London: Belhaven Press, 1992).

[12] See e.g. S. Vöneky, 'Peacetime Environmental Law as a Basis of State Responsibility for Environmental Damage Caused by War' in Austin and Bruch, *supra* n. 4; K. Mollard-Bannelier, *La protection de l'environnement en temps de conflit armé* (Paris: Pédone, 2001).

11.2.1.2 The environment and *jus in bello*
11.2.1.2.1 'Specific' and 'general' regulation
International humanitarian law captures environmental considerations in two main forms. First, the Vietnam War led to the adoption of a treaty, the ENMOD Convention, prohibiting environmental modification techniques as a way of waging war as well as to the inclusion of two specific provisions in the 1977 Protocol I to the Geneva Conventions, Articles 35(3) and 55, relating to the protection of the natural environment. In addition, there is substantial evidence of the existence of some customary norms of *jus in bello* with specific environmental content.[13]

Commentators refer to this body of norms as 'specific', 'express' or 'special' regulation of environmental protection in armed conflict in order to contrast it with the much larger body of international humanitarian law which, despite the absence of any specific wording, protects the natural environment either through the regulation of means and methods of warfare or through the protection granted to specific objects (e.g. installations containing dangerous forces).

11.2.1.2.2 Specifically environmental norms
The two key instruments of *jus in bello* providing specific protection to the environment during armed conflict use similar language but, on close examination, they set clearly different thresholds. Article 35(3) of Additional Protocol I provides that '[i]t is prohibited to employ methods or means of warfare which are intended, or may be expected, to cause widespread, long-term *and* severe damage to the natural environment' (italics added). The same qualification is used by Article 55(1) of Additional Protocol I, with the additional requirement that the damage must affect human health:

> Care shall be taken in warfare to protect the natural environment against widespread, long-term *and* severe damage. This protection includes a prohibition of the use of methods or means of warfare which are intended or may be expected to cause such damage to the natural environment and *thereby to prejudice the health or survival of the population*. (italics added)

Despite the similarity of these two provisions, their target is not the same. The question of redundancy arose during the negotiations of the Additional Protocol and it was eventually discarded on the grounds that, whereas Article 35(3) places a general limitation on the means of waging war, Article 55 seeks to protect the civilian population that may be harmed by environmental degradation.[14]

Duplication was also an issue with respect to the ENMOD Convention, which was also being negotiated in Geneva in the mid 1970s. It was, however,

---

[13] See J.-M. Henckaerts. and L. Doswald-Beck, *Customary International Humanitarian Law* (Cambridge University Press, 2009), Rules 43, 44 and 45.

[14] Y. Sandoz, C. Swinarsky and B. Zimmermann, *Commentary on the Additional Protocols of 8 June 1977 to the Geneva Convention of 12 August 1949* (Leiden/Geneva: Martinus Nijhoff/International Committee of the Red Cross, 1987) ('ICRC Commentary'), ad Art. 35(3), para. 1449.

discarded because, as noted by the United States delegation, the provisions in Additional Protocol I covered any weapon, whilst the ENMOD Convention only concerned environmental modification techniques as a weapon.[15] Moreover, Article 1(1) of the ENMOD Convention uses the conjunction 'or' instead of 'and' and, as a result, the three adjectives used to qualify the level of environmental damage are not envisioned as cumulative requirements:[16]

> Each State Party to this Convention undertakes not to engage in military or any other hostile use of environmental modification techniques having widespread, longlasting *or* severe effects as the means of destruction, damage or injury to any other State Party. (italics added)

In addition, the interpretation of each of the adjectives used in Article 1(1) differs in important ways from the understanding of those used in Articles 35(3) and 55(1) of Additional Protocol I. The latter were understood as being much more demanding than the former (e.g. 'long-term' would refer to decades[17] whereas 'longlasting' would only require 'a period of months, approximately a season'[18]) and some delegations expressly stated that Additional Protocol I had to be interpreted in this regard without reference to other international instruments, such as the ENMOD Convention.[19]

From a practical perspective, these differences can have significant consequences. Specifically, it is widely considered that the threshold for the operation of Articles 35(3) and 55 is so high that it provides little or no protection to the natural environment.[20] One illustration is provided by the Report of the Committee set up by the Prosecutor of the International Criminal Tribunal for the Former Yugoslavia ('ICTY') to advise her on the grounds to develop a case against NATO forces in connection, *inter alia*, with the use of depleted uranium projectiles and the resulting environmental damage during the 1999 Kosovo conflict.[21] In its assessment, the Committee considered whether Articles 35(3) and 55 of Additional Protocol I could provide legal grounds for prosecution. At the outset, the Report acknowledges that:

> Articles 35(3) and 55 have a very high threshold of application. Their conditions for application are extremely stringent and their scope and contents

---

[15] *Ibid.*, para. 1450.   [16] *Ibid.*, para. 1457.   [17] *Ibid.*, para. 1454.

[18] ENMOD Convention, *supra* n. 8, understandings relating to Art. 1 (the other adjectives are characterised as follows: '"widespread": encompassing an area on the scale of several hundred square kilometres' and '"severe": involving serious or significant disruption or harm to human life, natural and economic resources or other assets.').

[19] See ICRC Commentary, *supra* n. 14, ad Art. 35(3), para. 1459.

[20] United Nations Environment Programme, *Protecting the Environment During Armed Conflict. An Inventory and Analysis of International Law* (Nairobi: UNEP, 2009) ('UNEP Report'), p. 11 (and authorities referred to therein).

[21] Final Report to the Prosecutor by the Committee Established to Review the NATO Bombing Campaign against the Federal Republic of Yugoslavia, 13 June 2000 ('Report to the Prosecutor').

imprecise . . . For instance, it is thought that the notion of 'long-term' damage in Additional Protocol I would need to be measured in years rather than months, and that as such, ordinary battlefield damage of the kind caused to France in World War I would not be covered.[22]

It then reached the conclusion that 'on the basis of information currently in its possession . . . the environmental damage caused during the NATO bombing campaign does not reach the Additional Protocol I threshold'.[23] The Committee noted in passing the disagreement regarding the application of these provisions to the vast environmental damage caused by Iraq during the Gulf War 1990–1,[24] which is further evidence of the inadequacy of the threshold set in Additional Protocol I to protect the natural environment. The main hypothesis where environmental damage is likely to be 'widespread, long-term and severe' is the detonation of nuclear weapons and, yet, in its 1996 Advisory Opinion the ICJ was not able to rule out their legality 'in an extreme circumstance of self-defence, in which the very survival of a State would be at stake'.[25] Another aspect of the Committee's Report that deserves attention is the reference to customary rules of *jus in bello* of both specific and general nature.[26] This reference is noteworthy because customary law applies to all States, even those such as the United States or Israel, that have not ratified Additional Protocol I.

An important study undertaken under the aegis of the ICRC has indeed concluded that customary international humanitarian law specifically protects the natural environment in at least three ways.[27] First, the general principles applicable to the protection of objects (distinction between military and non-military targets, military necessity and proportionality) specifically protect the natural environment:

> Rule 43. The general principles on the conduct of hostilities apply to the natural environment:
>
> A. No part of the natural environment may be attacked, unless it is a military objective.
> B. Destruction of any part of the natural environment is prohibited, unless required by imperative military necessity.
> C. Launching an attack against a military objective which may be expected to cause incidental damage to the environment which would be excessive in relation to the concrete and direct military advantage anticipated is prohibited.[28]

Second, the selection and use of methods and means of warfare is also limited by the need to protect the natural environment:

---

[22] *Ibid.*, para. 15. [23] *Ibid.*, para. 17. [24] *Ibid.*, para. 15.
[25] *Legality of Nuclear Weapons, supra* n. 6, operative part, para. 2)E.
[26] *Report to the Prosecutor, supra* n. 21, para. 15.
[27] See Henckaerts and Doswald-Beck, *supra* n. 13.
[28] *Ibid.*, p. 143 (and authorities referred to therein)

Rule 44. Methods and means of warfare must be employed with due regard to the protection and preservation of the natural environment. In the conduct of military operations, all feasible precautions must be taken to avoid, and in any event to minimise, incidental damage to the environment. Lack of scientific certainty as to the effects on the environment of certain military operations does not absolve a party to the conflict from taking such precautions.[29]

The term 'precaution' used in this rule is best understood as encompassing references to both the prevention principle and the precautionary principle/ approach.[30] Indeed, there is no doubt that military operations create a 'risk' for the environment (i.e. a non-negligible probability of an adverse outcome) which requires careful prior assessment. The scientific uncertainty mentioned in the rule differs conceptually, at least in most cases, from the uncertainty faced by peacetime regulation to the extent that, in the latter case, there is doubt as to the adverse nature of the effects whereas in the former case the effects on the environment are undoubtedly negative. Thus, 'precaution' understood as something more than 'prevention' would only come into play under very specific circumstances, such as the use of particular weapons whose effects on the environment are truly unknown.

Third, according to the ICRC study, the rules stated in Articles 35(3) and 55(1) of Additional Protocol I and Article 1(1) of the ENMOD Convention have crystallised into a customary rule with the following content:

Rule 45. The use of methods or means of warfare that are intended, or may be expected, to cause widespread, long-term and severe damage to the natural environment is prohibited. Destruction of the natural environment may not be used as a weapon.[31]

According to the study, the persistent objection to this rule by the United States, France or the United Kingdom can, at best, exclude its application to them in connection with the use of nuclear weapons but not as a general matter. This is because their contrary practice beyond the specific case of nuclear weapons is not consistent and, more generally, because they can only claim to be 'specially affected' with respect to nuclear weapons and not for any type of weapons.[32] Whether or not this specific customary rule is applicable to these countries 'it does not prevent any use of nuclear weapons being found unlawful on the basis of other rules, for example the prohibition of indiscriminate attacks ... and the principle of proportionality.'[33] This conclusion follows from the proper understanding of the relations between Rule 45 and other more general rules. As explained in the study, Rule 45 is absolute. If its stringent threshold is reached, then military necessity or proportionality cannot offer any form of justification. Conversely, whilst Rules 43 and 44 do

---

[29] Ibid., p. 147 (and authorities referred to therein).   [30] On these principles see Chapter 3.
[31] Henckaerts and Doswald-Beck, supra n. 13, p. 151 (and the authorities referred to therein).
[32] Ibid., p. 154.   [33] Ibid., p. 155.

not set such a stringent threshold, the resulting damage to the environment can be justified (and therefore a violation of the rule avoided) by military necessity or on the grounds that all due caution was taken. This is also why it is important to consider not only the protection afforded to the natural environment by 'specific' provisions of *jus in bello* but also the more 'general' rules and principles that may potentially apply in this context.

11.2.1.2.3 General norms of *jus in bello*

There are many norms of *jus in bello*, whether treaty-based or of customary nature, that can be mobilised to provide protection to the natural environment. These norms are generally concerned either with the protection of certain 'objects', understood as encompassing the civilian population, civilian property and some specific resources/installations, or with the regulation of the 'methods and means' of warfare, typically excluding the use of certain weapons deemed to cause more damage than what is militarily required.[34] This is not the place to review the entire range of relevant norms,[35] but a brief reference to some of them seems warranted to understand the broader principles and rules from which the specific norms discussed in the preceding section are derived.

The principles of distinction, military necessity and proportionality are relevant for environmental protection purposes to the extent that the natural environment can be considered as civilian property or is important for the subsistence of the civilian population. The principle of distinction is stated in Articles 48 and 52 of Additional Protocol I. According to the latter:

> Article 52 – General protection of civilian objects
>
> 1. Civilian objects shall not be the object of attack or of reprisals. Civilian objects are all objects which are not military objectives as defined in paragraph 2.
> 2. Attacks shall be limited strictly to military objectives. In so far as objects are concerned, military objectives are limited to those objects which by their nature, location, purpose or use make an effective contribution to military action and whose total or partial destruction, capture or neutralization, in the circumstances ruling at the time, offers a definite military advantage.

The principle of military necessity was stated as early as 1907 in Article 23(g) of the Hague Regulations annexed to the IV Hague Convention on the Laws and Customs of War on Land:

> In addition to the prohibitions provided by special Conventions, it is especially forbidden: . . .

---

[34] See *infra* Section 11.2.1.4.

[35] See Mollard-Bannelier, *supra* n. 12. For shorter inventories see: UNEP Report, *supra* n. 20, pp. 12–21; Schmitt, *supra* n. 4, pp. 94–104. The following overview is based on the study by Schmitt, updated when necessary to integrate subsequent developments.

(g) To destroy or seize the enemy's property, unless such destruction or seizure be imperatively demanded by the necessities of war.[36]

As for proportionality, Articles 51(5)(b) and 57(2)(a)(iii) of Additional Protocol I state the principle in connection with any damage that appears excessive as compared to the military advantage sought:

Article 51 – Protection of the civilian population . . .

5. Among others, the following types of attacks are to be considered as indiscriminate: . . .

(b) an attack which may be expected to cause incidental loss of civilian life, injury to civilians, damage to civilian objects, or a combination thereof, which would be excessive in relation to the concrete and direct military advantage anticipated.

Article 57 – Precautions in attack . . .

2. With respect to attacks, the following precautions shall be taken:

(a) those who plan or decide upon an attack shall: . . .

(iii) refrain from deciding to launch any attack which may be expected to cause incidental loss of civilian life, injury to civilians, damage to civilian objects, or a combination thereof, which would be excessive in relation to the concrete and direct military advantage anticipated.

Significantly, the violation of some norms relevant for the protection of the environment may entail heightened consequences in terms of enforcement, including a duty of the State where the alleged perpetrator is found to prosecute or extradite.[37] By way of illustration, violation of Article 53 of the IV Geneva Convention (destruction by the occupying power of certain civilian property[38]) may, under certain circumstances defined in Article 147, amount to a 'grave breach' of the Convention. Similarly, violation of Article 56 of Additional Protocol I (which prohibits attacks on installations, such as dykes, dams or nuclear electricity facilities, when that may unleash dangerous forces) can amount to a 'grave breach' of the Protocol if launched with a certain intent or *mens rea*.[39]

The environmental relevance of the general principles and rules of *jus in bello* discussed so far has seldom been addressed by international(ised) courts either from an individual (criminal responsibility) or an inter-State

---

[36] Convention (No. IV) respecting the Laws and Customs of War on Land and its Annex: Regulations concerning the Laws and Customs of War on Land, 18 October 1907, 205 CTS 277 ('Hague Convention IV').

[37] See Geneva Convention (IV) Relative to the Protection of Civilian Persons in Time of War, 12 August 1949, 75 UNTS 287 ('IV Geneva Convention'), Art. 146; Additional Protocol I, *supra* n. 7, Art. 85(1). The literature on the duty to prosecute or extradite (*aut dedere aut judicare*) is extensive. See among others L. Reydams, *Universal Jurisdiction. International and Municipal Legal Perspectives* (Oxford University Press, 2003); R. O'Keefe, 'The Grave Breaches Regime and Universal Jurisdiction' (2009) 7 *Journal of International Criminal Justice* 811.

[38] Article 55 of the Hague Regulations, *supra* n. 36, assimilated the duties of the occupying power with respect to the property and resources of the occupied party as those of an usufructuary.

[39] Additional Protocol I, *supra* n. 7, Art. 85(3)(c).

(international responsibility) perspective. From a criminal responsibility perspective, an interesting illustration is provided by the so-called *Hostage Case*.[40] One of the defendants in this case was Lothar Rendulic, the commander-in-chief of the German troops in Norway, who ordered the destruction of all shelter and means of subsistence as part of his military retreat from Norwegian territory. This order, prompted by Rendulic's (mistaken) understanding that he was being chased by Russian troops, was effectively carried out between October and November 1944. Yet, Rendulic was acquitted on the grounds that he reasonably believed his action to be required by military necessity. According to the tribunal:

> The evidence shows that the Russians had very excellent troops in pursuit of the Germans. Two or three land routes were open to them as well as landings by sea behind the German lines ... The information obtained concerning the intentions of the Russians was limited ... It was with this situation confronting him that he carried out the 'scorched earth' policy in the Norwegian province of Finmark ... The destruction was as complete as an efficient army could do it ... There is evidence in the record that there was no military necessity for this destruction and devastation. An examination of the facts in retrospect can well sustain this conclusion. But we are obliged to judge the situation as it appeared to the defendant at the time. If the facts were such as would justify the action by the exercise of judgment, after giving consideration to all the factors and existing possibilities, even though the conclusion reached may have been faulty, it cannot be said to be criminal.[41]

This case shows the limitations of resorting to general principles of *jus in bello*, under which environmental devastation may be justified by military necessity. However, the laws of war have made some progress since the times of the *Hostage Case*. In the aforementioned NATO case, the Committee noted indeed, by reference to Article 52 of Additional Protocol I, that:

> Even when targeting admittedly legitimate military objectives, there is a need to avoid excessive long-term damage to the economic infrastructure and natural environment with a consequential adverse effect on the civilian population.[42]

Moving to the inter-State level, the ICJ has analysed the relevance of the principles of military necessity, proportionality and the duties of the occupying powers in an environmental light in two main cases. In the aforementioned Advisory Opinion on the *Legality of Nuclear Weapons*, the Court highlighted the implications of environmental protection for the proper interpretation of necessity and proportionality:

---

[40] *Hostage Case (US v. List)*, 11 TWC 759 (1950). See also *High Command Case (US v. Von Leeb)*, 11 TWC 462 (1950). The cases were brought before the US authorities in their German occupation zone. Both cases are referred to in Schmitt, *supra* n. 4, p. 99.

[41] Excerpt reproduced in G. D. Solis, *The Law of Armed Conflict: International Humanitarian Law in War* (Cambridge University Press, 2010), p. 289.

[42] *Report to the Prosecutor, supra* n. 21, para. 18.

States must take environmental considerations into account when assessing what is necessary and proportionate in the pursuit of legitimate military objectives. Respect for the environment is one of the elements that go to assessing whether an action is in conformity with the principles of necessity and proportionality.[43]

In a subsequent case, the Court concluded that Uganda, as the occupying power of the Ituri district in the Democratic Republic of the Congo ('DRC'), had violated its obligation of vigilance 'by not taking adequate measures to ensure that its military forces did not engage in the looting, plundering and exploitation of the DRC's natural resources'.[44] As the basis for this obligation, the Court referred *inter alia* to Articles 43 and 47 of the Hague Regulations and Article 33 of the IV Geneva Convention.[45] Interestingly, the Court also referred to a peacetime treaty, i.e. Article 21 of the African Charter on Human and Peoples' Rights (collective right to natural resources), as a further legal ground supporting its conclusion.[46] This is consistent with the prior practice of the Court, which considers that human rights treaties remain applicable despite the outbreak of armed conflict.[47] As discussed next, the same question has been asked with respect to the application of peacetime environmental treaties during armed conflict.

11.2.1.3 Armed conflict and environmental law[48]
11.2.1.3.1 Overview

In its Advisory Opinion on the *Legality of Nuclear Weapons*, issued only a few years after the 1992 Earth Summit, the ICJ refrained from giving a clear answer to the question of 'whether' environmental treaties remain applicable during armed conflict. Instead, the Court reformulated the question to ask 'whether the obligations stemming from these treaties were intended to be obligations of total restraint during military conflict'.[49] It then concluded that such was not the case, while stressing at the same time that States had to interpret their right to self-defence and their *jus in bello* obligations in the light of environmental considerations.[50] The 'whether' question thus left open has largely occupied commentators ever since.[51]

---

[43] *Legality of Nuclear Weapons, supra* n. 6, para. 30.
[44] *Armed Activities on the Territory of the Congo (Democratic Republic of the Congo v. Uganda)*, Judgment, ICJ Reports 2005, p. 168 ('*DRC* v. *Uganda*'), para. 246.
[45] *Ibid.*, paras. 245 and 250.   [46] *Ibid.*, para. 245.
[47] *Legality of Nuclear Weapons, supra* n. 6, para. 25; *Legal Consequences of the Construction of a Wall in the Occupied Palestinian Territory*, Advisory Opinion, ICJ Reports 2004, p. 136 ('*Wall Advisory Opinion*'), para. 106.
[48] This section draws upon M. Kunz and J. E. Viñuales, 'Environmental Approaches to Nuclear Weapons', in G. Nystuen, S. Casey-Maslen and A. Golden Bersagel (eds.), *Nuclear Weapons under International Law* (Cambridge University Press, 2014), pp. 269–91.
[49] *Legality of Nuclear Weapons, supra* n. 6, para. 30.   [50] *Ibid.*, paras. 30–3.
[51] See references mentioned *supra* n. 12.

In assessing the extent to which environmental treaties may apply in armed conflict, in addition to the usual criteria defining the scope of application of a treaty (scope *ratione materiae, personae, loci, temporis*), one needs to consider a number of challenges that have traditionally been raised by scholars and practitioners to the application of peacetime treaties in times of armed conflict. There are three types of effects that the outbreak of hostilities may directly or indirectly have on peacetime treaties, namely it may (i) affect the continuance in force or in operation of such treaties for belligerent States (suspension, withdrawal, termination), (ii) trigger a treaty-specific response (derogations, flexibilities, enhanced protection), and/or (iii) give rise to complex interactions with other norms, particularly of *jus in bello*. In the next sections, these three effects are discussed in turn.

Before undertaking the analysis, two observations are in order. First, each one of these potential effects must be considered before moving to the next effect, and the above is the logical order in which to proceed. Indeed, if environmental treaties are terminated or suspended in armed conflict, there would be little interest in considering the second and third potential effects. Likewise, if a given treaty continues in operation but States are allowed under the treaty to derogate from its core provisions in situations of national emergency, there is no need to clarify the interaction between such norms and *jus in bello* obligations. Only if a relevant environmental treaty obligation survives these preliminary tests, its concurring application with *jus in bello* obligations will require further clarification. The latter caveat leads to the second observation, namely that, as we move up the analytical ladder just described, the question of 'whether' environmental norms apply in armed conflict subtly becomes one of 'how' they do so.

11.2.1.3.2 Continued operation

Termination of a treaty, its denunciation or the withdrawal of a party, as well as suspension of the operation of a treaty for some or all of its parties, may take place only in accordance with the provisions of the given treaty or under the default rules codified by the Vienna Convention on the Law of Treaties ('VCLT').[52] However, the latter contains a general reservation in its Article 73 pursuant to which the Convention 'shall not prejudge any question that may arise in regard to a treaty from … the outbreak of hostilities between States'. The International Law Commission ('ILC') decided to address this point in 2004 and, in 2011, adopted a set of *Draft Articles on the Effects of Armed Conflict on Treaties*.[53]

The 2011 Draft Articles deal specifically with the first type of effect, continuance in operation. The system proposed by the ILC is built in four stages.

---

[52] Vienna Convention on the Law of Treaties, Vienna, 23 May 1969, 1155 UNTS 331 ('VCLT'), Art. 42(2).

[53] ILC, Draft Articles on the Effects of Armed Conflict on Treaties, 9 December 2011, GA Res. 66/99, UN Doc. A/RES/66/99 ('2011 ILC Draft Articles').

First and most importantly, the Draft Articles state that armed conflict does not *ipso facto* terminate or suspend the operation of treaties between belligerents or with third States (Article 3). Second, and unsurprisingly, if a given treaty contains provisions regulating its operation in the event of an armed conflict, those provisions govern the situation (Article 4). Third, when no such provisions exist, as is the case for the vast majority of environmental treaties,[54] the international rules on treaty interpretation apply in order to determine whether a given treaty may be (unilaterally) suspended, terminated or denounced as a result of an armed conflict (Article 5). This determination must not only be based on the interpretation of relevant treaty provisions, but also take into account a variety of broader factors linked to the characteristics of the armed conflict and treaty considered, in particular the subject-matter of the latter, with treaties on certain subjects – including those on environmental protection and waterbodies – being presumed to continue in operation, in whole or in part, during armed conflict (Article 6, Article 7 and Annex). Fourth and finally, the suspension, denunciation or termination of a treaty 'as a consequence of an armed conflict' are characterised in the remainder of the Draft Articles, adapting the provisions of the VCLT to the context of armed conflict while referring to the rules of general international law for questions not treated in the Draft Articles.[55] These contours specify, in short, that the right to suspend or withdraw from certain treaties in the event of an armed conflict, which is complementary to the customary grounds embodied in the VCLT,[56] may not benefit the aggressor State,[57] and is forfeited if the State expressly or by its conduct acquiesces in the treaty's continued operation.[58] It is important to note in this context that prior notification of the intention to

---

[54] Most major multilateral environmental treaties make no explicit reference to their continued operation during hostilities. Examples include: Convention on International Trade in Endangered Species of Wild Fauna and Flora, Washington, 3 March 1973, 993 UNTS 243 ('CITES'); Convention on the Conservation of Migratory Species of Wild Animals, Bonn, 23 June 1979, 1651 UNTS 333 ('CMS'); Montreal Protocol on Substances that Deplete the Ozone Layer, 16 September 1987, 1522 UNTS 3 ('Montreal Protocol'); Basel Convention on the Control of Transboundary Movements of Hazardous Wastes and their Disposal, 22 March 1989, 1673 UNTS 57 ('Basel Convention'); Convention on Biological Diversity, 5 June 1992, 1760 UNTS 79 ('CBD'); United Nations Framework Convention on Climate Change, Rio de Janeiro, 9 May 1992, 1771 UNTS 107 ('UNFCCC'); Rotterdam Convention on the Prior Informed Consent Procedure for Certain Hazardous Chemicals and Pesticides in International Trade, 10 September 1998, 2244 UNTS 337 ('PIC Convention'); Stockholm Convention on Persistent Organic Pollutants, Stockholm, 22 May 2001, 2256 UNTS 119 ('POP Convention'). See UNEP Report, *supra* n. 20, pp. 39–40.

[55] 2011 ILC Draft Articles, *supra* n. 53, Arts. 8–18. The commentary ad Art. 8 explains that the ILC intentionally omitted to treat matters of lawfulness of agreements on modification or suspension, such as the conditions for modification or suspension of a multilateral treaty by certain of the parties only, contained in Arts. 41 and 58 VCLT, 'preferring to leave such matters to the operation of general rules of international law, including those reflected in the 1969 Vienna Convention' (para. 5).

[56] *Ibid.*, Art. 18.   [57] *Ibid.*, Art. 15.   [58] *Ibid.*, Art. 12.

suspend or withdraw from a treaty is a formal requirement and may encounter objections, in which case States must pursue peaceful means of dispute resolution.[59] Thus, as a general matter, under the 2011 ILC Draft Articles, environmental treaties are presumed to continue in operation during armed conflict, unless the treaty provides otherwise.

One important question in this regard concerns the customary status of the rules formulated in the 2011 ILC Draft Articles. The fundamental principle rejecting automatic suspension of treaties is clearly consistent with the jurisprudence of the ICJ. The Court dealt with this question recently in connection with human rights treaties in two advisory opinions[60] and one contentious case.[61] In these cases, the Court made no reference to the old doctrine of automatic suspension of the operation of peacetime treaties in the event of an armed conflict, focusing instead on the second and third types of effect, discussed below. Whereas the ICJ seems to reject the classical theory of *ipso facto* suspension or termination of peacetime treaties during hostilities, this theory featured in a recent award of the Eritrea Ethiopia Claims Commission.[62] The Commission reasoned that in cases:

> where the intention to maintain a treaty in operation during hostilities is not plainly apparent from the text or the surrounding circumstances ... [w]riters generally maintain that parties should be presumed to intend that such treaties be at least suspended during the hostilities. The Commission concludes that this principle applies here.[63]

The conclusion of the Commission on this point did not seem to take into account the relevant ICJ jurisprudence or the work of the International Law Commission on the topic ongoing at the time. For this and other case-specific reasons,[64] the award is unlikely to inform the contemporary approach adopted in the ICJ practice. This is all the more important if one considers that, as noted earlier, most environmental treaties do not explicitly address their operation during hostilities.

---

[59] *Ibid.*, Art. 9.
[60] See *Legality of Nuclear Weapons, supra* n. 6, para. 25; *Wall Advisory Opinion, supra* n. 47, para. 106.
[61] *DRC v. Uganda, supra* n. 44, paras. 216, 219–20.
[62] Eritrea Ethiopia Claims Commission, *Final Award – Pensions: Eritrea's Claims 15, 19 & 23* (19 December 2005), RIAA, vol. XXVI, p. 471.
[63] *Ibid.*, para. 30.
[64] The treaty at stake was a bilateral treaty which obliged Ethiopia to pay pensions to former Ethiopians living in Eritrea after it formally gained independence in 1993, but it was only an interim arrangement while the negotiations on a permanent solution continued (which were interrupted by the armed conflict) and in any event the treaty could be terminated by either of the parties upon twelve months' notice. Ethiopia argued that the treaty ended because of one of these two reasons, not *ipso facto* suspension under the law of treaties as the Commission itself acknowledged in para. 31.

11.2.1.3.3 Treaty-specific response

There are a number of environmental treaties that do contain provisions allowing for derogations in exceptional circumstances such as armed conflicts, or which give some leeway to States in the implementation of their substantive obligations by way of flexible formulations. Conversely, some treaties provide for unaltered or even enhanced environmental protection during armed conflicts. It is this treaty-specific response to such situations that we now turn to.[65]

Regarding, first, the most protective category, some environmental treaties make it clear that they seek to prevent further deterioration of their environmental object of protection even in the event of an armed conflict. The main illustration is Article 11(4) of the World Heritage Convention,[66] which provides that the World Heritage Committee shall keep a 'List of World Heritage in Danger' in addition to the normal 'World Heritage List', including 'only such property forming part of the cultural and natural heritage as is threatened by serious and specific dangers, such as . . . the outbreak or the threat of an armed conflict'. The Operational Guidelines further specify the criteria for the inclusion of a site in this list.[67] Here the occurrence of an armed conflict is a trigger for strengthening the protective regime of the affected World Heritage site that may go from a mere 'message of concern' sent by the Committee, to a system of international assistance to preserve the site as much as possible.[68] In this context it is also worth pointing to Article 6(3) of the WHC, according to which States parties undertake 'not to take any deliberate measures which might damage directly or indirectly the cultural and natural heritage referred to in Articles 1 and 2 situated on the territory of other States Parties to this Convention'.

Some other treaties take a reverse stance and, instead of heightening the protection of the environment, they grant more flexibility in exceptional circumstances threatening 'urgent national interest'[69] or 'the paramount interest of the State',[70] either contemplating the possibility to derogate from certain treaty obligations or specifying less stringent protection obligations in such cases. By way of illustration, Article 4(2) of the Ramsar Convention describes

---

[65] For an inventory, see UNEP Report, *supra* n. 20, pp. 35–9.

[66] Convention Concerning the Protection of the World Cultural and Natural Heritage, 16 November 1972, 1037 UNTS 151 ('WHC').

[67] UNESCO World Heritage Committee, 'Operational Guidelines for the Implementation of the World Heritage Convention', UN Doc. WHC.13/01, July 2013, paras. 177–82, available at: http://whc.unesco.org/en/guidelines (last visited on 20 April 2014).

[68] *Ibid.*, paras. 183–9.

[69] Convention on Wetlands of International Importance especially as Waterfowl Habitat, 2 February 1971, 996 UNTS 245 ('Ramsar Convention'), Art. 4(2).

[70] African Convention on the Conservation of Nature and Natural Resources, Algiers, 15 September 1968, 1001 UNTS 3, Art. XVII(1)(i). An important amendment to this Convention was adopted on 11 July 2003 deleting the exception for paramount interest of the State and replacing it with detailed environmental protection obligations for armed conflicts based on principles of international humanitarian law, but this amendment is not yet in force. See au.int/en/treaties (last visited on 10 September 2013).

the alternative protective regime that comes into play under such exceptional circumstances:

> Where a Contracting Party in its urgent national interest, deletes or restricts the boundaries of a wetland included in the List, it should as far as possible compensate for any loss of wetland resources, and in particular it should create additional nature reserves for waterfowl and for the protection, either in the same area or elsewhere, of an adequate portion of the original habitat.

The rationale of this provision differs from the one underlying Article 11(4) of the WHC. Whereas the latter seeks to preserve, as much as possible, the endangered site, Article 4(2) of Ramsar admits the loss and simply calls for compensating measures. Thus, the 'urgent national interest' is seen as an overriding consideration. In practice, however, the Secretariat keeps a list (the 'Montreux Record') similar to the List of World Heritage in Danger, and it has intervened in some cases to preserve existing sites as much as possible.[71]

11.2.1.3.4 Norm articulation

Even when a treaty continues in operation and the relevant provisions are not subject to derogations, the application of environmental norms during armed conflict must be articulated with that of other norms, particularly those of *jus in bello*. The resulting interactions are potentially complex, but for present purposes they can be analysed from two main perspectives, namely conflicting (i.e. when respecting one applicable norm entails violating another applicable norm) and synergistic (i.e. when both norms can be applied together, one serving to interpret or complete the other).

The ILC addressed the question of norm conflicts in its work on the fragmentation of international law,[72] providing a useful summary of the relevant practice and the different legal techniques to deal with such conflicts. Strictly speaking, a conflict of norms arises only when two mutually exclusive norms govern the same situation and thus preclude State compliance with both norms. Another type of conflict can arise between authorisations and obligations to the extent that an authorisation entails a permission to do or not to do something, which would conflict with an obligation not to do or to do

---

[71] In the pending border dispute between Costa Rica and Nicaragua, where Costa Rica argued that Nicaragua was destroying a Ramsar-protected wetland as part of the construction works of a canal, the Ramsar Secretariat sent a mission to evaluate the impact of Nicaragua's actions on the relevant wetland. The ICJ encouraged this intervention by noting, in an order for provisional measures, that the Ramsar Secretariat was to be consulted by Costa Rica in connection with the protection of a wetland located in disputed territory. See ICJ, *Certain Activities carried out by Nicaragua in the Border Area (Costa Rica v. Nicaragua)*, Request for the indication of provisional measures, Order of 8 March 2011, para. 86(2).

[72] ILC, *Conclusions of the work of the Study Group on the Fragmentation of International Law: Difficulties arising from the Diversification and Expansion of International Law* (2006) ('Conclusions'). See also the Report of 13 April 2006 (Doc. A/CN.4/L.682) on which the Conclusions are based ('Report').

something. More generally, one may speak of conflict of norms (*conflit de lois*) in connection with the determination of the law applicable to a situation that may be governed by more than one norm, even if the conduct required by the different norms involved are potentially similar. Among the general conflict norms (*lex superior, lex specialis* and *lex posterior*) widely recognised in international law, the most relevant for the relations between environmental norms and norms of *jus in bello* is the *lex specialis* principle. In its Advisory Opinions on the *Legality of Nuclear Weapons* and on the *Construction of a Wall in Occupied Palestinian Territory*, the ICJ referred to this principle to assert the priority of application of *jus in bello* norms with respect to human rights norms.[73] However, in the *DRC* v. *Uganda* case, the ICJ did not exclude the concurring application of Article 21 of the African Charter (a human rights provision) together with *jus in bello*.[74] The latter approach suggests that the *lex specialis* principle may not necessarily exclude the concurrent application of other norms. The question then becomes how precisely the different applicable norms are to be articulated.

The articulation of two or more norms applicable to the same situation may take different forms. If *jus in bello* is deemed to be the governing *lex specialis*, then environmental norms may apply for interpretation purposes or to complement the governing norm addressing aspects not covered by the latter. The first hypothesis is hardly controversial. The need to take into account the prevention principle in assessing the overall legality of the threat or the use of nuclear weapons and, more specifically, the norms regulating the exercise of self-defence or the conduct of hostilities was recognised by the ICJ in its aforementioned Advisory Opinion on the *Legality of Nuclear Weapons*.[75] Such stance can be seen as an application of the broader rule of systemic integration codified in Article 31(3)(c) of the VCLT according to which the interpreter of a treaty must take into account, together with the context, '[a]ny relevant rules of international law applicable in the relations between the parties'.[76] The second hypothesis is more difficult. The extent to which environmental norms may be brought in to cover aspects not clearly addressed by a *lex specialis* may be understood as mere interpretation or, alternatively, as a direct application of a norm to a situation for which there is, in point of fact, no *lex specialis*. By way of illustration, even when an action has destroyed a legitimate military target without excessive environmental damage, as permitted by Article 52 of Additional Protocol I, an environmental norm may come into play to distribute the financial burden of rehabilitating the damaged environment. Similarly, the requirement in Article 57(2)(a)(iii) of Additional Protocol I to refrain from launching an attack with excessive collateral damage

---

[73] *Legality of Nuclear Weapons, supra* n. 6, para. 25; *Wall Advisory Opinion, supra* n. 47, para. 106.
[74] *DRC* v. *Uganda, supra* n. 44, para. 245.
[75] *Legality of Nuclear Weapons, supra* n. 6, para. 30 read in the context of para. 29.
[76] This interpretation rule was discussed by the ICJ in *Oil Platforms Case (Islamic Republic of Iran* v. *United States of America)*, ICJ Reports 2003, p. 161, para. 41.

on civilians or civilian property may entail, if read in the light of the customary environmental obligation to conduct an environmental impact assessment, some formal procedural steps in the planning of military operations. Such articulation is difficult to achieve in the abstract but, as environmental protection becomes more present in other areas of international law, one may expect its impact on general norms of *jus in bello* to increase.

11.2.1.4 Weapons as pollutants
11.2.1.4.1 Overview
When it comes to the methods and means of warfare, the norms and instruments of *jus in bello* target the 'use' of certain weapons that may cause unnecessary suffering or have indiscriminate or excessive effects on civilians, civilian property or the environment. By contrast, the international law of arms control (or 'disarmament') adopts a wider perspective and regulates, for some types of weapons considered as weapons of 'mass destruction',[77] their entire life cycle, from development to destruction or conversion. The difference in terms of regulatory focus can be illustrated by reference to the two key instruments regulating biological weapons, namely the 1925 Geneva Protocol,[78] which bans their use, and the 1972 Convention on Biological Weapons,[79] which bans the remaining aspects of the life-cycle of such weapons (and implicitly also their use).

For present purposes, the main feature to be highlighted is the similarity between this more comprehensive regulatory approach and the approach followed in environmental treaties, such as the Montreal Protocol,[80] the POP Convention[81] or the Minamata Convention,[82] which regulate the entire life cycle of certain pollutants (or a significant portion of it). In the following paragraphs, the regimes applicable to the three main weapons of mass destruction (nuclear, biological and chemical weapons) are briefly discussed in order to show the extent to which the third regulatory approach identified earlier in this chapter has found concrete legal expression.

---

[77] Although the term 'weapons of mass destruction' was defined in the late 1940s by a United Nations Committee (on the basis of their destructive and indiscriminate effect), in contemporary international law it is used to refer to nuclear, biological and chemical weapons and to contrast these three types of weapons to 'conventional' weapons. See H. A. Strydom, 'Weapons of Mass Destruction', in *Max Planck Encyclopedia of Public International Law*, available at: www.opil.ouplaw.com (last visited on 20 April 2014).

[78] Protocol for the Prohibition of the Use in War of Asphyxiating, Poisonous or Other Gases, and of Bacteriological Methods of Warfare, 17 June 1925, 94 LNTS 65 ('1925 Geneva Protocol').

[79] Convention on the Prohibition of the Development, Production and Stockpiling of Bacteriological (Biological) and Toxin Weapons and on their Destruction, 10 April 1972, 1015 UNTS 163 ('BWC').

[80] Montreal Protocol, *supra* n. 54. On the scope of this treaty, see Chapter 5.

[81] POP Convention, *supra* n. 54. On the scope of this treaty see Chapter 7.

[82] Minamata Convention on Mercury, 10 October 2013, available at: www.mercuryconvention. org (last visited on 20 April 2014) ('Minamata Convention'). On the scope of this treaty, see Chapter 7.

As we shall see, whereas the first set of instruments to follow this approach concerned biological weapons, the most comprehensive and far-reaching one came twenty years later and targeted chemical weapons. As for nuclear weapons, the deep political opposition of several nuclear States has so far prevented the emergence of a clear ban with respect to their threat or use, although the other phases of their life cycle are highly regulated.

11.2.1.4.2 Biological weapons

Biological (including bacteriological) weapons are devices intended to disperse disease-causing agents (bacteria, viruses or fungi) or toxins to kill or harm humans or the environment.[83] Their effect is seldom immediate and, as a result, the military advantage they may provide in the battlefield is less important than the strategic advantage they may give in the longer term as a means to weaken the adversary.[84] Their environmental effect is potentially very significant because, by their very nature, they entail the release of a virulent pathogen into the environment.

Efforts to control the use of biological weapons can be traced back to at least the 1899 and 1907 Hague Conferences.[85] The current legal system is based on an old and very concise instrument, the aforementioned 1925 Geneva Protocol, which bans the 'use' in war of 'asphyxiating, poisonous or other gases, and of all analogous liquids materials or devices' and extends this prohibition to 'bacteriological methods of warfare'.[86] However, the main instrument banning biological weapons is the BWC negotiated under the aegis of the then UN Conference on Disarmament between 1969 and 1972. Pursuant to Article I of the BWC:

> Each State Party to this Convention undertakes never in any circumstances to develop, produce, stockpile or otherwise acquire or retain:
>
> 1. microbial or other biological agents, or toxins whatever their origin or method of production, of types and in quantities that have no justification for prophylactic, protective or other peaceful purposes;
> 2. weapons, equipment or means of delivery designed to use such agents or toxins for hostile purposes or in armed conflict.

The ban is comprehensive and concerns the full life cycle of biological weapons, including (implicitly) their use. Indeed, at the Fourth Review Conference

---

[83] See D. Svarc, 'Biological Weapons and Warfare', in *Max Planck Encyclopedia of Public International Law* (2011), available at: www.opil.ouplaw.com (last visited on 20 April 2014), para. 1; D. H. Joyner, *International Law and the Proliferation of Weapons of Mass Destruction* (Oxford University Press, 2009), Chapter 2.

[84] Svarc, *supra* n. 83, para. 3.

[85] See Hague Declaration (IV, 2) concerning Asphyxiating Gases, 29 July 1899, 187 CTS 453; Hague Convention IV, *supra* n. 36, Regulations, Art. 23(a).

[86] 1925 Geneva Protocol, *supra* n. 78, preamble, para. 1 and declaration, para. 1.

of the BWC, held in Geneva in 1996, States parties reaffirmed 'that under any circumstances the use, development, production and stockpiling of bacteriological (biological) and toxin weapons is effectively prohibited under Article I of the Convention'.[87] As for existing stocks of agents or equipment, States parties are required to destroy them or divert them to peaceful purposes[88] and they are also under the obligation not to transfer to any recipient or give other States or organisations assistance or encouragement for the development of such agents or equipment.[89] The BWC also contains specific provisions to prevent biological weapons from being acquired by terrorist groups.[90]

The Achilles heel of the regime is the lack of an adequate system of verification and implementation. Although a complaint may be lodged with the UN Security Council (a possibility that has so far not been used),[91] the verification system and, more generally, the institutional dimension of the regime are particularly weak. Although a number of 'confidence building measures' were introduced in 1986 and a small 'Implementation Support Unit' was set up in 2006, other meaningful steps, including a verification protocol, have encountered much resistance mostly from the United States and Russia.[92] Another problem, which may appear as quite puzzling from a disarmament standpoint but must nevertheless be noted from an environmental perspective, is the impact of destruction or disposal of agents or the decommissioning of equipment and facilities. As noted by a former UN Under-Secretary General for Disarmament Affairs '[t]he supreme irony is that in getting rid of such weapons in the interests of peace and security, we have arguments brought out in the name of environmental protection from the very quarters that created the arms'.[93] Article II of the BWC expressly referred to this concern, noting that '[i]n implementing the provisions of this Article all necessary safety precautions shall be observed to protect populations and the environment'. This challenge is also relevant for the other two weapons of mass destruction.

11.2.1.4.3 Chemical weapons

The 1925 Geneva Protocol and the BWC are also relevant for the regulation of chemical weapons but the centre of gravity in this area is provided by the Chemical Weapons Convention ('CWC'), also negotiated under the aegis of the UN Conference on Disarmament and opened for signature in

---

[87] Fourth Review Conference, Geneva, 25 November–6 December 1996, Final Declaration, para. 3.
[88] BWC, *supra* n. *79*, Art. II.   [89] *Ibid.*, Art. III.   [90] *Ibid.*, Art. IV.   [91] *Ibid.*, Art. VI.
[92] On this issue see J. Littlewood, 'The Verification Debate in the Biological and Toxin Weapons Convention in 2011' (2010) 3 *Disarmament Forum* 15.
[93] J. Dhanapala, 'The Environmental Impacts of Manufacturing, Storing, Deploying and Retiring Weapons', in *Symposium: Arms and the Environment: Preventing the Perils of Disarmament*, National Energy-Environment Law and Energy Policy Institute, The University of Tulsa College of Law Tulsa, Oklahoma, 9 December 1999, available at: www.un.org/disarmament/ (last visited on 20 April 2014).

1993.[94] Although there is some overlap between the concepts of biological and chemical weapons (as regards toxins produced by living organisms), the latter are characterised as non-living toxic substances. Due to their indiscriminate and potentially large-scale effects, chemical weapons are considered as weapons of mass destruction.

The CWC is both a *jus in bello* and a disarmament/non-proliferation treaty. The fundamental obligation stated in Article 1 is wide-ranging and encompasses (i) use, (ii) development, production, acquisition, stockpiling, retention and transfer, (iii) assistance or encouragement in this regard, and (iv) destruction of existing weapons and facilities, including those abandoned in the territory of another State party. 'Chemical Weapons' and 'Chemical Weapons Production Facilities' are characterised in detail by reference to their purpose (civilian, protective and domestic riot control uses are allowed[95]) and quantities in Article 2. From an environmental perspective, it is noteworthy that the 'Toxic Chemicals' that may qualify as a 'Chemical Weapon' are defined by reference to their 'chemical action on life processes [that] can cause death, temporary incapacitation or permanent harm to humans or animals'. The question of chemicals causing harm to the non-human and non-animal environment is partly dealt with in the preamble to the CWC, which recognises: 'the prohibition, embodied in the pertinent agreements and relevant principles of international law, of the use of herbicides as a method of warfare'. The reference is, among others, to the 1925 Geneva Protocol and the ENMOD Convention, discussed earlier in this chapter, which sets a significant threshold (albeit lower than Additional Protocol I) for its prohibition to apply.

Unlike the BWC, the CWC has a much stronger institutional component, in the form of an Organisation for the Prohibition of Chemical Weapons ('OPCW'),[96] which is based in The Hague, as well as a sophisticated verification and implementation system. The latter consists mainly of initial and annual declarations by the States parties followed by verification by the OPCW Secretariat,[97] but also of *ad hoc* inspections in case of suspicion of non-compliance.[98] Also of note is the sophisticated framework for the destruction of existing chemical weapons.[99] Much like phase outs in environmental treaties, the CWC contains an 'Annex on Chemicals' with three 'Schedules'

---

[94] Convention on the Prohibition of the Development, Production, Stockpiling and Use of Chemical Weapons and on their Destruction, 13 January 1993, 1974 UNTS 45 ('CWC'). See T. Marauhn, 'Chemical Weapons and Warfare', in *Max Planck Encyclopedia of Public International Law* (2010), available at: www.opil.ouplaw.com (last visited on 20 April 2014); W. Krutzsch, E. Meijer and R. Trapp (eds.), *The Chemical Weapons Convention. A Commentary* (Oxford University Press, 2014).

[95] CWC, *supra* n. 94, Art. II(9).

[96] *Ibid.*, Art. VIII. See http://www.opcw.org (last visited on 20 April 2014). On the OPCW see R. Trapp, 'The OPCW in Transition: From Stockpile Elimination to Maintaining a World Free of Chemical Weapons' (2012) 1 *Disarmament Forum* 41.

[97] CWC, *supra* n. 94, Arts. III and VI. [98] *Ibid.*, Art. IX(8)–(25).

[99] *Ibid.*, Art. IV, Annex on Chemicals and Verification Annex.

distinguishing regulated chemicals depending on the extent they can or cannot be used for purposes other than military.[100] Destruction of these chemicals must follow an 'order of destruction', and it had to be completed within ten years from the entry into force of the CWC.[101] Extensions were possible but only up to an absolute deadline set for end April 2012.[102] Although much progress has been made in the elimination of stockpiles (as of April 2012, 78 per cent of declared stockpiles had been destroyed), some countries, including the United States and Russia are still in the process of destroying their holdings.[103] As with the BWC, the CWC expressly required States, when destroying their holdings of regulated weapons, to 'assign the highest priority to ensuring the safety of people and to protecting the environment'.[104]

11.2.1.4.4 Nuclear weapons

The body of international norms regulating nuclear materials intended for military purposes is vast and complex, but it is not comprehensive. Despite considerable debate, particularly after the ICJ's Advisory Opinion on the *Legality of Nuclear Weapons* in the 1990s, there is, to date, no global ban on either their use or the other phases of their life cycle (development, production, acquisition, stockpiling, etc.).[105] Thus, whereas one can confidently assert that biological and chemical weapons are banned, such an assertion would be legally inaccurate, or at least very controversial, if made in connection with nuclear weapons. As noted by ICJ:

> The pattern until now has been for weapons of mass destruction to be declared illegal by specific instruments . . . In the last two decades, a great many negotiations have been conducted regarding nuclear weapons; they have not resulted in a treaty of general prohibition of the same kind as for bacteriological and chemical weapons.[106]

---

[100] Schedule I includes chemicals such as sarin or sulphur and nitrogen mustards, which have little or no use other than military. Schedule II includes chemicals such as amiton, a nerve agent, which is not produced in large commercial quantities for purposes permitted under the convention. Schedule III includes chemicals such as hydrogen cyanide, which is produced in large commercial quantities as a precursor to obtain other substances used in gold and silver mining.

[101] *Ibid.*, Art. IV(6) and Verification Annex, part IV(A), C.15–19.

[102] CWC, *supra* n. 94, Verification Annex, part IV(A), C.24–28 (the absolute limit is set in paragraph 25 by reference to 15 years since entry into force of the CWC, which did so on 29 April 1997).

[103] See Report of the OPCW on the Implementation of the Convention on the Prohibition of the Development, Production, Stockpiling and Use of Chemical Weapons and on their Destruction, 4 December 2013, C-18/4, paras. 2–3.

[104] CWC, *supra* n. 94, Art. IV(10).

[105] *Legality of Nuclear Weapons, supra* n. 6, para. 53–74 (concluding to the absence of a specific treaty or customary 'norm' generally banning the use of nuclear weapons). See S. Kadelbach, 'Nuclear Weapons and Warfare', in *Max Planck Encyclopedia of Public International Law* (2009), available at: www.opil.ouplaw.com (visited on 20 April 2014); Nystuen, *et al.*, *supra* n. 48.

[106] *Legality of Nuclear Weapons, supra* n. 6, paras. 57–8.

This is of course unintuitive, as nuclear weapons are by far the most dangerous weapons of mass destruction and certainly those with the highest impact on the natural environment. Yet, international law is not always reasonable or, more precisely, it sometimes follows peculiar but politically powerful reasons. The purpose of this section is not to re-open the debate on the legality of nuclear weapons but only to illustrate how significant aspects of the life cycle of nuclear weapons are indeed regulated which, in turn, provides some measure of protection to the environment.

Aside from the regulation of nuclear energy, discussed in Chapter 7, several international instruments specifically address portions of the life cycle of nuclear weapons. In its aforementioned Advisory Opinion, the ICJ provided an overview of treaties regulating (i) the acquisition, manufacturing or possession of nuclear weapons, (ii) their deployment, (iii) the testing of such weapons, and (iv) their use.[107] None of these treaties is geographically or substantively comprehensive. Thus, the specific commitments regarding the prohibition of use apply in some specific regions (Latin America; the South Pacific)[108] or under some circumstances (e.g. between nuclear-weapons and non-nuclear-weapons States parties to the NPT and subject to exceptions).[109] Similarly, the ban on the acquisition, manufacturing or possession of nuclear weapons only applies to certain countries (e.g. Germany[110]) or categories of countries (e.g. non-nuclear-weapons States under the NPT[111]). As for the regulation of deployment and testing, it has a more explicit environmental protection impact, for example, through the denuclearisation of common areas such as Antarctica[112] or the

---

[107] *Ibid.*, paras. 58–63.

[108] See for Latin America: Treaty for the Prohibition of Nuclear Weapons in Latin America, 14 February 1967, 634 UNTS 281 ('Treaty of Tlatelcoco'), Art. 1; Additional Protocol I to the Treaty for the Prohibition of Nuclear Weapons in Latin America, 14 February 1967, 634 UNTS 360 (opening the treaty to non Latin-American countries with territories in the covered area); Additional Protocol II to the Treaty for the Prohibition of Nuclear Weapons in Latin America, 14 February 1967, 634 UNTS 364 (under which the five NPT nuclear-weapons States commit to respect the denuclearisation of the covered area). For the South Pacific: South Pacific Nuclear Free Zone Treaty, 6 August 1985, 1445 UNTS 177 ('Treaty of Rarotonga'), Art. 3; Protocol 2 to the South Pacific Nuclear Free Zone Treaty, 1 December 1986, 1971 UNTS 475, Art. 1 (ratified by four of the five NPT nuclear-weapons States). For an overview of these and other areas see S. Szurek, 'De Rarotonga à Bangkok et Pelindaba: Note sur les traités constitutifs de nouvelles zones exemptes d'armes nucléaires' (1996) 42 *Annuaire français de droit international* 164.

[109] See Treaty on the Non-Proliferation of Nuclear Weapons, 1 July 1968, 729 UNTS 161 ('NPT'). In 1995, the NPT was extended and the five NPT nuclear-weapons States made unilateral declarations undertaking not to use nuclear weapons against non-nuclear States parties to the NPT, with some narrow exceptions.

[110] See Treaty on the Final Settlement with Respect to Germany, 12 September 1990, 1696 UNTS 115, Art. 3(1).

[111] NPT, *supra* n. 109, Art. 2.

[112] See Antarctic Treaty, 1 December 1959, 402 UNTS 71, Arts. I and V; Treaty on the Prohibition of the Emplacement of Nuclear Weapons and Other Weapons of Mass Destruction on the Sea-Bed and the Ocean Floor and in the Subsoil Thereof, 11 February 1971, 955 UNTS 115, Art. I.

seabed,[113] or the prohibition of atmospheric and under water testing.[114] Overall, as the Court noted in 1996 'these treaties could therefore be seen as foreshadowing a future general prohibition of the use of such weapons'. Yet, it immediately added that 'they do not constitute such a prohibition by themselves'.[115]

In the period since 1996, other relevant treaties have been concluded, including one setting a 'nuclear weapon free' zone in Central Asia.[116] Although such zones may be expanding geographically, nuclear powers staunchly oppose the principle of a comprehensive ban and this is not likely to change in the near future. As a result, environmental protection may be best served by focusing on the regulation of deployment, testing and non-proliferation broadly understood, encompassing (i) not only the prohibition of extension of the nuclear States 'club' but also (ii) the reduction, within the latter, of the stocks of nuclear weapons[117] as well as, potentially, (iii) a ban on the production of the basic pollutant, i.e. fissile materials for nuclear weapons or other military devices.[118]

11.2.1.5 Current codification efforts

As suggested by the foregoing sections on the relevance of peacetime environmental treaties and the regulation of weapons of mass destruction, there is a clear case for approaching the protection of the environment in armed conflict not only through the lens of norms of *jus in bello* but also by taking into account a broader set of norms that intervene before, during and after the hostilities. Over time, several codification efforts have been undertaken to address the impact of armed conflict on the environment[119] or on related topics, such as the effect of armed conflict on treaties.[120]

---

[113] Treaty on Principles Governing the Activities of States in the Exploration and Use of Outer Space, including the Moon and other Celestial Bodies, 27 January 1967, 610 UNTS 205 ('Outer Space Treaty'), preamble and Art. IV.

[114] See among others the Treaty Banning Nuclear Weapons Tests in the Atmosphere, in Outer Space and under Water, 5 August 1963, 480 UNTS 43 ('PNTB').

[115] *Legality of Nuclear Weapons, supra* n. 6, para. 62.

[116] Treaty on a Nuclear-Weapon-Free Zone in Central Asia, 8 September 2006, 2212 UNTS 257 ('Treaty of Semipalatinsk'), followed by a Protocol signed by the five NPT nuclear-weapons States on 6 May 2014.

[117] There have been significant efforts to accomplish such reduction, particularly between the United States and the USSR (now Russia). For a concise overview see Kadelbach, *supra* n. 105, paras. 23–7.

[118] On the efforts and implications of developing a 'Fissile Material Cut-off Treaty' see United Nations Institute for Disarmament Research, *A Fissile Material Cut-off Treaty. Understanding the Critical Issues* (Geneva: UNIDIR, 2010).

[119] International Committee of the Red Cross ('ICRC'), *Guidelines for Military Manuals and Instructions on the Protection of the Environment in Times of Armed Conflict*, 1993, available at: www.icrc.org (last visited on 20 April 2014). The UN General Assembly encouraged States to incorporate these guidelines into their military manuals. See UN Doc. A/RES/49/50, 17 February 1995, para. 11.

[120] 2011 ILC Draft, *supra* n. 53.

In 2013, the ILC undertook work on the topic 'Protection of the Environment in Relation to Armed Conflict'. The expression 'in relation to' was specifically chosen in order to broaden the spectrum of norms to be considered. The Special Rapporteur, Marie Jacobsson from Sweden, has framed the work in temporal terms distinguishing 'three temporal phases: before, during and after an armed conflict (phase I, phase II and phase III, respectively)'.[121] Interestingly, the Rapporteur intends to focus on phases I and III, which have received less attention in codification efforts, and to target non-international armed conflicts in her work on phase II. At the same time, the Rapporteur has expressed its intention not to address questions such as environment-driven conflict, the protection of cultural property, the regulation of weapons and environment-driven displacement.[122]

The work on this topic is expected to result in 'conclusions' or 'guidelines' rather than on a draft leading to a treaty. Such conclusions will be most useful to clarify the operation of a wide corpus of norms addressing the impact of conflict on environmental protection.

11.2.2 Environmental dimensions of recourse to war

11.2.2.1 Overview

The body of norms regulating the recourse to force in international law may also be relevant for the protection of the natural environment. This topic has been addressed from three main angles.

One angle concerns the impact of environmental protection on the rules circumscribing the two exceptions to the prohibition of the use of force, i.e. self-defence and enforcement action under Chapter VII of the United Nations Charter. From a legal standpoint, this amounts to assessing the extent to which environmental protection is taken into account by these norms.

The second angle relates to the legal consequences of violating *jus ad bellum* with respect to the environmental damage caused during armed conflict. This question arose in connection with the UN Security Council's Resolution 687 (1991) condemning the environmental damage caused by Iraq on the territory of Kuwait.[123]

The third angle is broader, encompassing the new types of security threats that may arise as a result of environmental degradation. Properly understood, the questions raised go well beyond the norms of *jus ad bellum* and call for more general discussion. For this reason, only the first two angles are discussed in this section. The latter is discussed in some more detail in Section 11.3 of this chapter.

---

[121] Preliminary Report on the Protection of the Environment in Relation to Armed Conflicts. Submitted by Marie G. Jacobsson, Special Rapporteur, 30 May 2014, UN Doc. A/CN.4/674 ('2014 Preliminary Report'), para. 58.

[122] *Ibid.*, paras. 64–7.

[123] UN Security Council Resolution 687 (1991), 8 April 1991, UN Doc. S/RES/687 (1991).

11.2.2.2 *Jus ad bellum* and environmental protection

In its Advisory Opinion on the *Legality of Nuclear Weapons*, the ICJ briefly addressed the implications of environmental protection for the rules of *jus ad bellum* and, more specifically, for the customary and treaty rule on the right to self-defence. After concluding that environmental treaties could not be construed as entailing obligations of 'total restraint during military conflict', the Court concluded that environmental protection had to be taken into account in assessing whether an action is necessary and proportionate:

> The Court does not consider that the treaties in question could have intended to deprive a State of the exercise of its right of self-defence under international law because of its obligations to protect the environment. Nonetheless, *States must take environmental considerations into account when assessing what is necessary and proportionate in the pursuit of legitimate military objectives*. Respect for the environment is one of the elements that go to assessing whether an action is in conformity with the principles of necessity and proportionality.[124]

Necessity and proportionality are both requirements of resort to self-defence and general principles governing the conduct of hostilities. Although distinct (because such general principles apply irrespective of whether the resort to force has been lawful), the two obligations are connected to the extent that, as noted by the Court:

> a use of force that is proportionate under the law of self-defence, must, in order to be lawful, also meet the requirements of the law applicable in armed conflict which comprise in particular the principles and rules of humanitarian law.

Thus, environmental considerations intervene already in the assessment of the legality of the use of force, which is distinct from the assessment of whether the hostilities have been lawfully conducted. One implication of this distinction, discussed in Section 11.2.2.3 *infra*, is that the mere breach of *jus ad bellum* may entail liability for environmental damage irrespective of an assessment of breach of *jus in bello*.

Environmental considerations are also relevant in connection with enforcement action under Chapter VII of the UN Charter.[125] One question is whether environment-driven conflict or, more broadly, environmental threats such as natural disasters and the like, may trigger the system of collective security. Legally, the UN Security Council could characterise such events as 'threats to international peace and security' and therefore adopt binding decisions under Chapter VII, whether they entail the use of force or softer forms of intervention, such as the provision of assistance to distressed populations despite the lack of authorisation of the territorial State or the adoption of economic

---

[124] *Legality of Nuclear Weapons, supra* n. 6, para. 30 (italics added).
[125] See C. Gray, 'Climate Change and the Law on the Use of Force', in R. Rayfuse and S. V. Scott (eds.), *International Law in the Era of Climate Change* (Cheltenham: Edward Elgar, 2011), pp. 219–40.

sanctions. In the past, the Security Council has considered human rights violations, flows of refugees and humanitarian disasters as threats to peace under Article 39 of the Charter, enabling the use of Chapter VII.[126] However, the involvement of the Security Council in environment-driven situations that are only loosely connected to the maintenance of international peace and security remains controversial. This is suggested by the different positions taken by States in two debates held by the Security Council in 2007 and, again, in 2011, on the issue of climate change.[127] The main opposition stems from the G-77 and China, which are reluctant to give a forum such as the Security Council, where their interests are less represented than in the UN General Assembly or ECOSOC, an additional opportunity to expand its remit.

11.2.2.3 Violations of *jus ad bellum* and environmental damage

An important, albeit controversial, environmental implication of violating the rules of *jus ad bellum* can be illustrated by reference to the 1990–1 Gulf War. After the invasion of Kuwait by Iraq, the UN Security Council adopted a stream of resolutions, including Resolution 687 (1991).[128] Paragraph 16 of this resolution reaffirmed that Iraq was to be considered:

> liable under international law for any direct loss, damage, including environmental damage and the depletion of natural resources, or injury to foreign Governments, nationals and corporations, as a result of Iraq's unlawful invasion and occupation of Kuwait.

The body set up to manage the claims, the United Nations Compensation Commission ('UNCC'), acted on the premise that Iraq was liable for all the environmental damage in a relation of causality with its invasion of Kuwait. No legal assessment of the principle of liability (which would have included consideration of *jus in bello* and environmental norms) was conducted by the UNCC. In fact, the panels established to hear the different claims[129] regularly reiterated this premise. By way of illustration, in the *Well Blowout Control Claim* ('*WBC Claim*'),[130] which related to the extinction of the oil wells set on fire by Iraqi troops in their retreat from Kuwait, the panel recalled that:

---

[126] *Ibid.*, p. 230.   [127] On these debates, see *ibid.*, pp. 231–3.   [128] See *supra* n. 123.

[129] The structure of the claims is rather complex. Six broad categories of claims were established (A, B, C, D, E and F). The F category, which concerned claims brought by other States (e.g. Kuwait, Saudi Arabia, Iran, etc.) and international organisations, was further subdivided into four sub-categories. Sub-category 4 covered claims for environmental damage and natural resource depletion. The panel established to hear F4 claims organised its work in five instalments of claims. By 2005 all claims (including F claims) had been processed.

[130] This claim was brought by the Kuwait Oil Company, under category E (claims from corporations). It provides, however, an apposite illustration of the constant position adopted by the UNCC panels regarding the premise of Iraq's liability. See *Report and Recommendation made by the Panel of Commissioners Appointed to Review the Well Blowout Control Claim ('WBC Claim')*, S/AC.26/1996/5/Annex, 18 December 1996.

The Security Council having determined, under Chapter VII of the Charter, that compensation in accordance with international law should be provided to foreign Governments, nationals and corporations for any direct loss, damage or injury sustained by them as a result of Iraq's unlawful invasion and occupation of Kuwait, in order to restore international peace and security, *the issue of Iraq's liability has been resolved by the Security Council and constitutes part of the law applicable before the Commission.*[131]

Thus, the UNCC panels could not – and did not – assess whether the damage caused by Iraq in some cases was not excessive or was commensurate with the military advantage pursued, as potentially allowed by the rules of *jus in bello* normally applicable as a *lex specialis.*[132] The approach followed by the Security Council and the UNCC came under much criticism from legal commentators, who viewed it as a victor's justice.[133] Eventually, out of the US$ 85 billion claimed for environmental damage and resource depletion (F4), the UNCC awarded compensation for US$ 5.3 billion.[134]

For present purposes, the case of the UNCC is illustrative of the connection between *jus ad bellum* and environmental protection, but it also highlights the practical implications of what may otherwise appear as a purely theoretical distinction between breaches of *jus ad bellum* and *jus in bello* (or, by analogy, of environmental norms).

11.3 Environmental security in international law

11.3.1 Preventing environment-driven conflict

The connection between environmental protection and conflict is bi-directional. In the previous sections, we discussed the extent to which international law protects the environment from the consequences of armed conflict. This section takes the reverse approach and looks at how peace can be 'protected' (and conflicts be prevented) from environmental threats.

The importance of this connection must not be underestimated. According to a 2009 UNEP Report, no less than eighteen violent conflicts have been 'fuelled' by the exploitation of natural resources and at least 40 per cent of intra-State conflicts in the last sixty years can be 'associated' with natural

---

[131] *Ibid.*, para. 68 (italics added).

[132] See the discussion in Section 11.2.1.2.3 in connection with the *Hostages Case* and, more generally, the difference between, on the one hand, the general principles of military necessity and proportionality and, on the other hand, Arts. 35(3) and 55(1) of the Additional Protocol I.

[133] See Mollard-Bannelier, *supra* n. 12, pp. 417–19; C. Greenwood, 'State Responsibility and Civil Liability for Environmental Damage caused by Military Operations', in Grunawalt, *supra* n. 10, pp. 397–415, at p. 407.

[134] On the valuation methods used by the F4 panel, see O. Das, *Environmental Protection, Security and Armed Conflict: A Sustainable Development Perspective* (Cheltenham: Edward Elgar, 2013), pp. 200–5.

resources.[135] From this perspective, environmental and natural resource variables are seen (i) to contribute to the outbreak of conflict (e.g. Darfur; Sierra Leone and Liberia), (ii) to finance or sustain conflict (e.g. Sierra Leone and Liberia; Angola; Cambodia), or (iii) undermining peace (e.g. Ivory Coast).[136]

The bi-directional character of the environment-conflict link has been increasingly recognised in policy instruments.[137] One example is Principle 25 of the Rio Declaration, according to which '[p]eace, development and environmental protection are interdependent and indivisible'.[138] More recently, the UN has undertaken some initiatives, including the establishment of an International Resource Panel,[139] a UN–EU Partnership on Natural Resources and Conflict Prevention,[140] and a Division of Early Warning and Assessment ('DEWA') within the UNEP.[141]

Yet, concrete legal initiatives in this regard have so far remained elusive. As noted earlier in this chapter, the UN Security Council has discussed the implications of climate change on two occasions but it has not addressed specifically any environment-driven situation as a 'threat to peace' under Article 39 of the Charter. Similarly, the ILC Special Rapporteur on the 'Protection of the Environment in Relation to Armed Conflict' has explicitly excluded the question of environment-driven conflict from the scope of her work.[142] As for treaties, although several environmental treaties can be relevant to address the root environmental causes that may fuel conflict (e.g. the UN Convention to Combat Desertification[143]), there is to date no treaty framework specifically addressing the prevention of environment-driven conflict. As discussed next, for some questions such as environmentally-induced displacement, international law offers in fact very little to accommodate problems that may become increasingly pressing in the near future.

---

[135] See UNEP, *From Conflict to Peacebuilding: The Role of Natural Resources and the Environment* (Geneva: UNEP, 2009) ('UNEP Environmental Conflict Report'), p. 8.

[136] *Ibid.*, pp. 8–14.   [137] For a concise overview, see Das, *supra* n. 134, pp. 66–119.

[138] Rio Declaration on Environment and Development, 13 June 1992, UN Doc. A/CONF.151/26 ('Rio Declaration').

[139] See www.unep.org/resourcepanel/ (last visited on 20 April 2014). The objective of this panel is to provide reliable policy-relevant information on the use and state of the world's natural resources.

[140] The partnership brings together the UNEP, the UN Development Programme, UN Habitat, the UN Department of Political Affairs, the UN Department of Economic and Social Affairs, the UN Peacebuilding Support Office, and the EU. The key project is to develop a 'Tool-kit and Guidance for Preventing and Managing Land and Natural Resource Conflict'. See www.un.org/en/land-natural-resources-conflict/ (last visited on 20 April 2014).

[141] See www.unep.org/dewa/ (last visited on 20 April 2014). DEWA develops and provides policy-relevant information and capacity building regarding environmental threats.

[142] See 2014 Preliminary Report, *supra* n. 121, para. 64.

[143] United Nations Convention to Combat Desertification in those Countries Experiencing Serious Drought and/or Desertification, Particularly in Africa, UN Doc. A/AC.241/15/Rev. 7 (1994), 17 June 1994, 33 ILM 1328 ('UNCCD'). This example is referred to in Das, *supra* n. 134, p. 112. On this treaty, see Chapter 6.

11.3.2 Environmentally-induced displacement

11.3.2.1 Circumscribing the problem

In the last two decades, growing concern has been expressed as to the impact of environmentally-induced migrations, particularly in connection with the effects (sudden, such as a hurricane, or slow-onset, such as sea-level rise or desertification) of climate change.[144] From a legal perspective, the question is extremely challenging both because of the potential magnitude of the phenomenon (some estimates go as far as to predict movements of many millions of people[145]) and because of the perceived inadequacy of existing international instruments. Perhaps more fundamentally, it is not even clear how to legally frame the phenomenon given that environmental displacement is but a general term encompassing a diverse array of more specific types of population movements (temporary or permanent; forced or voluntary; environment-driven or environmentally-induced; internal or international; etc.).[146]

A useful characterisation of five scenarios encompassed by the notion of environmentally-induced displacement has been provided by Walter Kälin, the former UN Secretary-General's Representative on the Human Rights of Internally Displaced Persons.[147] These scenarios are intended as a taxonomy of 'causes of movement': (i) sudden onset disasters (e.g. hurricanes, typhoons, cyclones, floods, mudslides); (ii) slow onset environmental

---

[144] Aside from some previous occasional uses, the term environmental refugee was introduced in a 1985 UNEP report: E. El-Hinnawi, *Environmental Refugees* (United Nations Environment Programme, 1985). The current debate is however more recent and it was not until the mid-2000s that major international organisations took full notice of its importance. See e.g. Council of Europe Parliamentary Assembly, Committee on Migration, Refugees and Population, *Environmentally Induced Migration and Displacement: A 21st Century Challenge*, COE Doc 11785 (23 December 2008); *Report of the Office of the United Nations High Commissioner for Human Rights on the Relationship between Climate Change and Human Rights*, UN Doc. A/HRC/10/61, 15 January 2009, paras. 55–60; *Climate Change and Its Possible Security Implications: Report of the Secretary-General*, UN Doc. A/64/350, 11 September 2009, paras. 54–63; United Nations High Commissioner for Refugees, *Climate Change, Natural Disasters and Human Displacement: A UNHCR Perspective* (14 August 2009) ('UNHCR Report'). For a concise overview of the literature see J. Morrissey, 'Rethinking the "Debate on Environmental Refugees": from "Maximilists and Minimalists" to "Proponents and Critics"' (2012) 19 *Journal of Political Ecology* 36.

[145] On the limitations of these estimates see D. Kniveton, K. Schmidt-Verkerk and C. Smith, 'Climate Change and Migration: Improving Methodologies to Estimate Flows' (2008) *IOM Migration Research Series* No. 33.

[146] See J. McAdam, 'Climate Change, Displacement and the Role of International Law and Policy', paper presented at International Dialogue on Migration 2011, Intersessional Workshop on Climate Change, Environmental Degradation and Migration, 29–30 March 2011, p. 1.

[147] 'Displacement and Climate Change: Towards Defining Categories of Affected Persons', *Working paper submitted by the Representative of the UN Secretary-General on the Human Rights of Internally Displaced Persons* (25 August 2008). The initial typology (hydrometeorological disasters, areas designated as high risk zones, environmental degradation and slow onset disasters, sinking islands, armed conflict and violence driven by resource depletion) was subsequently revised in W. Kälin and N. Schrepfer, *Protecting People Crossing Borders in the Context of Climate Change Normative Gaps and Possible Approaches*, UNHCR (PPLA/2012/01), February 2012. We follow the latter.

degradation (e.g. sea-level rise, salinization of groundwater, drought, desertification); (iii) slow onset events for low lying small island States (resulting in the loss of their territory); (iv) designation of areas prohibited for human habitation (either because they present risks or because they are allocated to mitigation/adaptation purposes); (v) resource stress triggering disturbances, violence and armed conflict.[148]

This characterisation is very helpful because the law applicable or at least relevant for different scenarios is not the same. It thus advances our understanding of how international law may capture an object as multifaceted as environmentally-induced displacement.

11.3.2.2 Legal response

With respect to the legal response given to this problem at the international level, there are two main lines in the debate. The first concerns the extent to which it is legally possible or wise to address environmentally-induced displacement through international refugee law. If it is not, as argued among others by the UNHCR itself, the second debate focuses on what would be the most promising alternative frameworks of protection.

Regarding the first debate, one question is whether the 1951 Refugees Convention[149] could potentially be used to provide protection to 'environmental refugees'. In most cases, it cannot, because the Convention requires the crossing of an international border (thus excluding people displaced within the territory of their own State, which makes for a large proportion of environmental refugees) and, most importantly, it seems extremely difficult to characterise the environmental driver of displacement as 'persecution' and, even more so, as persecution 'for reasons of race, religion, nationality, membership of a particular social group or political opinion'.[150] Although the African and Latin American regional instruments on refugee law[151] contain somewhat broader definitions of refugees, potentially covering people fleeing natural disasters,[152] their expansion could at best cover movements caused by sudden onset disasters. More generally, there is a general policy reluctance to bring environmentally-induced displacement under the framework protecting refugees to avoid blurring a line that it took so much effort to clarify. In its 2009

---

[148] Kälin and Schrepfer, *supra* n. 147, pp. 13–17.

[149] Convention relating to the Status of Refugees, 28 July 1951, 189 UNTS 137 ('1951 Refugees Convention'), and Protocol Relating to the Status of Refugees, 31 January 1967, 606 UNTS 267 (removing the geographical and time limitations included in the text of the Convention).

[150] 1951 Refugees Convention, *supra* n. 149, Art. 1A(2).

[151] Convention Governing the Specific Aspects of Refugee Problems in Africa, 10 September 1969, 1001 UNTS 45, and the Cartagena Declaration on Refugees, 22 November 1984, Annual Report of the Inter-American Commission on Human Rights, OAS Doc. OEA/Ser.L/V/II.66/doc.10, rev. 1, pp. 190–3 (1984–5).

[152] See W. Kälin, 'Conceptualising Climate-Induced Displacement' in J. McAdam (ed.), *Climate Change and Displacement: Multidisciplinary Perspectives* (Oxford: Hart Publishing, 2010), pp. 81–103, at pp. 88–9.

initial report on the question, the UNHCR expressed 'serious reservations with respect to the terminology and notion of environmental refugees or climate refugees' and took the stance that:

> the use of such terminology could potentially undermine the international legal regime for the protection of refugees whose rights and obligations are quite clearly defined and understood. It would also not be helpful to appear to imply a link and thus create confusion regarding the impact of climate change, environmental degradation and migration and persecution that is at the root of a refugee fleeing a country of origin and seeking international protection.[153]

Given the challenges of addressing the problem through international refugee law, the attention has moved towards alternative legal frameworks, including the instruments on international humanitarian law, international human rights law (most notably under the so-called 'complementary protection'), the law governing internally displaced persons ('IDPs') and international environmental law.

In the latter context, the question has received some attention in climate negotiations, particularly after the 2010 Cancun Agreements, which set up a 'Cancun Adaptation Framework' encompassing matters of 'climate change induced displacement, migration and planned relocation … at national, regional and international levels'.[154]

Yet, from a practical perspective, the most important instruments regarding this problem are those relating to IDPs. An influential soft-law instrument, the 1998 Guiding Principles on Internal Displacement, provide a sufficiently broad definition of covered persons, namely:

> persons or groups of persons who have been forced or obliged to flee or leave their homes or habitual places of residence, *in particular as a result of or in order to avoid the effects of … natural or human-made disaster*, and who have not crossed an internationally recognized State border.[155]

These principles operate in addition to human rights and international humanitarian law[156] and stress the obligation of States to grant covered persons protection against displacement, participatory rights in the decision-making process relating to displacement, return or relocation, the right to remain together as a family or be reunited, or the right to seek safety in other parts of the country or leave the country, among others. Although the Guiding Principles are a soft-law instrument, a significant part of its content reflects basic human rights and humanitarian law obligations with customary

---

[153] UNHCR Report, *supra* n. 144, pp. 8–9.
[154] 'The Cancun Agreements: Outcome of the Work of the Ad Hoc Working Group on Long-term Cooperative Action under the Convention', Decision 1/CP.16, 15 March 2011, Doc. FCCC/CP/2010/7/Add.1, paras. 13, 14(f).
[155] 'Guiding Principles on Internal Displacement', 11 February 1998, UN Doc. E/CN.4/1998/53/Add.2 (1998), Annex, para. 2 (italics added).
[156] *Ibid.*, Principle 2(2).

grounding. In addition, an important treaty was concluded in 2009 in Kampala (Uganda) addressing the situation of IDPs in Africa.[157] The Kampala Convention largely incorporates the wording used in the 1998 Guiding Principles, but it provides further elaboration in areas such as the right to be protected from arbitrary displacement[158] or accountability.[159]

Basic human rights provisions are also relevant in connection with 'complementary protection'.[160] This is the human rights-based protection owed to persons who are not entitled to protection under the 1951 Refugees Convention but, at the same time, cannot be returned to their countries because of serious risks that they may be tortured or subject to cruel, inhuman and degrading treatment. However, the risks justifying complementary protection have been judicially construed in a manner that leaves limited room for accommodating environmental threats.[161]

Still another option would be to adopt a new treaty or amend an existing one. There have been proposals to amend the 1951 Refugees Convention to accommodate environmental refugees,[162] but they have met with much scepticism, including from the UNHCR itself.[163] Some commentators go further and propose an entire new instrument.[164] Among these efforts the 2005 *Appel de Limoges* deserves to be singled out,[165] as it has been followed by a detailed and regularly updated Draft Convention on the International Status of Environmentally-Displaced Persons.[166] Article 2(2) of the Draft defines 'environmentally-displaced persons' as:

> individuals, families, groups and populations confronted with a sudden or gradual environmental disaster that inexorably impacts their living conditions, resulting in their forced displacement, at the outset or throughout, from their habitual residence.

---

[157] African Union Convention for the Protection and Assistance of Internally Displaced Persons in Africa, 23 October 2009, 49 ILM 86 ('Kampala Convention').

[158] *Ibid.*, Art. 4.

[159] Significantly, Art. 12(3) of the Convention provides that a 'State Party shall be liable to make reparation to internally displaced persons for damage when such a State Party refrains from protecting and assisting internally displaced persons in the event of natural disasters'.

[160] See J. McAdam, *Complementary Protection in International Refugee Law* (Oxford University Press, 2007).

[161] For a detailed discussion of the different legal bases that could be used, see J. McAdam, *Climate Change Displacement and International Law: Complementary Protection Standards*, UNHCR (PPLA/2011/03), May 2011, pp. 15–36.

[162] See the proposals of the Maldives and Bangladesh, reported in E. Piguet *et al.* (eds.), *Migration and Climate Change* (Cambridge University Press, 2011), p. 103.

[163] UNHCR Report, *supra* n. 144, p. 9.

[164] See e.g. B. Docherty and T. Giannini, 'Confronting a Rising Tide: A Proposal for a Convention on Climate Change Refugees' (2009) 33 *Harvard Environmental Law Review* 349.

[165] 'Appel de Limoges sur les refugiés écologiques et environnementaux', 23 June 2005, available at: www.cidce.org (last visited on 20 April 2014).

[166] The third version of this text was elaborated in May 2013. See www.cidce.org (last visited on 20 April 2014).

The Draft makes a distinction between persons threatened with displacement, whose rights are addressed in Chapter 3, and environmentally-displaced persons, whose rights are defined in Chapters 4 and 5, including a right to the recognition of their status. Despite the considerable political obstacles that would have to be overcome for an amendment or a new instrument to be adopted on this topic, the Limoges project provides a useful outline of how the many difficult questions raised by commentators could be addressed in the actual drafting of a text.

11.3.3 Environmental security in post-conflict settings

11.3.3.1 The rise of environmental peacebuilding

Together with the role of environmental variables in igniting conflict, increasing attention has been paid in the last years to their role in a post-conflict setting and, more precisely, in reigniting conflict or, conversely, in helping build trust.[167]

The focus of this work is on the economic and political dimensions of peacebuilding processes and how they are affected (positively or negatively) by environmental variables such as natural resource exploitation, the availability of basic resources and services (food and water), and the broader impact of massive pollution. Environmental variables are seen as both threats and opportunities and the bulk of the work is, understandably, on the analysis of case-studies as a basis for deriving policy lessons.

Somewhat less clear is the role of law in this context. Of course, the importance of legal and institutional frameworks cannot be questioned as they are a necessary part of establishing agreed solutions, from the negotiation of a peace agreement,[168] to the arbitral settlement of a dispute,[169] to the implementation of a land-tenure regime.[170] But the role of international law and, specifically, of international environmental obligations in this context needs further clarification.

---

[167] For overviews of this work, see UNEP Environmental Conflict Report, *supra* n. 135; Das, *supra* n. 134; C. Bruch, D. Jensen, M. Nakayama and J. Unruh, 'Post-Conflict Peace Building and Natural Resources' (2008) 19 *Yearbook of International Environmental Law* 58.

[168] See e.g. section 3.7 of the Comprehensive Peace Agreement between the Government of Nepal and the Communist Party of Nepal (Maoist), which requires the implementation of a land reform programme, referred to in Bruch *et al., supra* n. 167, pp. 63–4.

[169] See e.g. the allocation of oil resources resulting from the arbitral award in the *Abyei* case: *In the Matter of an Arbitration before a Tribunal Constituted in Accordance with Article 5 of the Arbitration Agreement between the Government of Sudan and the Sudan People's Liberation Movement/Army on Delimiting Abyei Area*, Final Award, 22 July 2009, available at: www.pca-cpa.org (last visited on 20 April 2014).

[170] See J. Unruh and R. C. Williams, 'Land: A Foundation for Peacebuilding', in J. Unruh and R. C. Williams (eds.), *Land and Post-Conflict Peacebuilding* (London: Earthscan, 2013), pp. 1–20.

11.3.3.2 Environmental peacebuilding and environmental obligations

International environmental obligations will likely require the proper consideration of international environmental and human rights' principles (e.g. prevention, environmental impact assessment, participation, the rights to health, natural resources and a generally satisfactory environment, indigenous peoples' rights) in developing the domestic legal frameworks applicable to the management of high-value (e.g. timber, diamonds, gold or oil) and other resources (e.g. land and water), to prevent situations such as the conflict in the Niger Delta[171] or in many other regions of the world where the interests of States, extractive industries and local communities conflict with each other.[172]

International environmental law may also help to mainstream environmental considerations into the post-conflict activities of international organisations, either through the setting up of a 'fund'[173] or a dedicated 'branch'[174] or, still, through the development of guidelines to reduce the environmental impact of the organisation's activities.[175] This type of impact is perhaps less legal but not less important, as it provides organisations with the legal mandate to integrate environmental considerations in to their work. Since 1999, UNEP's Post Conflict and Disaster Management Branch has conducted several post-crisis environmental assessments in regions such as the Balkans, Afghanistan, the occupied Palestinian territories, Nigeria or the Democratic Republic of the Congo.[176] This type of assessments may feature in international litigation, as illustrated by the Report of the Committee established by

---

[171] On the legal dimensions of this conflict from a human rights perspective, see *Social and Economic Rights Action Center (SERAC) and others* v. *Nigeria*, African Commission Application no. 155/96 (2001–2002) ('*Ogoni*').

[172] For a map of environmental conflicts (including this form of tripartite conflicts) in the world see: www.ejolt.org (last visited on 20 July 2014).

[173] In 1997, the World Bank created a Post-Conflict Fund that has financed programmes with environmental sustainability components. An example is the participation of the PCF in the recovery plan of the Mindanao area, in the Philippines. See World Bank, *Post-Conflict Fund and Licus Trust Fund. Annual Report (fiscal year 2006)*, p. 5, available at: http://www.world bank.org (last visited on 20 April 2014).

[174] UNEP started its dedicated programme in 1999 leading to the Post-Conflict and Disaster Management Branch, based in Geneva. See www.unep.org/disastersandconflicts/ (last visited on 20 April 2014). Similarly, the International Union for the Conservation of Nature ('IUCN') has established an Armed Conflict and the Environment Specialist Group, active mostly in research and advocacy. See www.iucn.org/about/union/commissions/cel/cel_working/cel_w t_sg/cel_sg_armed/ (last visited on 20 April 2014).

[175] In June 2009, the UN Departments of Peacekeeping Operations and of Field Support, with input from UNEP, adopted an 'Environmental Policy for UN Field Missions' aimed at reducing the environmental footprint of peacekeeping operations. Environmental considerations have also been integrated into the Global field support strategy. Report of the Secretary General, 26 January 2010, UN Doc. A/64/633. Similar steps had previously been taken by the UNHCR. See the UNHCR's 2005 Environmental Guidelines, available at: www.unhcr.org/3b 03b2a04.html (last visited on 20 April 2014).

[176] For a concise overview, see K. Conca and J. Wallace, 'Environment and Peacebuilding in War-torn Societies: Lessons from the UN Environment Programme's Experience with Post-conflict Assessment', in D. Jensen and S. Lonergan (eds.), *Assessing and Restoring Natural Resources in Post-Conflict Peacebuilding* (London: Earthscan, 2012), pp. 63–84.

the ICTY Prosecutor in connection with the NATO bombing mentioned earlier in this chapter.[177]

More specifically, the international or internationalised management of natural resources may provide a useful opportunity to build confidence between the parties to a conflict. Examples referred to in the literature include the 'peace parks' (i.e. cross-border ecological preserves) jointly managed by Ecuador and Peru as part of peacebuilding efforts ending a long-lasting border dispute[178] or cooperation on water resources between Israel and Jordan following the October 1994 peace agreement.[179]

Overall, these efforts suggest that although the explicit presence of international environmental law may still be limited, environmental protection considerations are increasingly influencing peacemaking activities at the international level.

Select bibliography

Austin, J. E. and C. E. Bruch (eds.), *The Environmental Consequences of War: Legal, Economic and Scientific Perspectives* (Cambridge University Press, 2000).

Bardonnet, D., *La convention sur l'interdiction et l'élimination des armes chimiques* (Dordrecht: Martinus Nijhoff, 1995).

Boelaert-Suominen, S. A. J., *International Environmental Law and Naval War: The Effect of Marine Safety and Pollution Conventions During International Armed Conflict* (Newport RI: Naval War College, 2000).

Boisson de Chazournes, L. and P. Sands (eds.), *International Law, the International Court of Justice and Nuclear Weapons* (Cambridge University Press, 1999).

Bothe, M., 'Criminal Responsibility for Environmental Damage in Times of Armed Conflict', in R. J. Grunawalt, J. E. King and R. S. McClain (eds.), *Protection of the Environment during Armed Conflict* (Newport RI: Naval War College, 1996), pp. 473–8.

Bothe, M., C. Bruch, J. Diamond and D. Jensen, 'International Law Protecting the Environment during Armed Conflict: Gaps and Opportunities' (2010) 92 *International Review of the Red Cross* 569.

Bruch, C., D. Jensen, M. Nakayama, J. Unruh, R. Gruby and R. Wolfarth, 'Post-Conflict Peace Building and Natural Resources' (2008) 19 *Yearbook of International Environmental Law* 58.

Chevrier, M. I., K. Chomiczewski, H. Garrigue, G. Granasztói, M. R. Dando and G. S. Pearson (eds.), *The Implementation of Legally Binding Measures to Strengthen the Biological and Toxin Weapons Convention* (Dordrecht: Kluwer, 2004).

---

[177] See *supra* n. 21.

[178] The Acta de Brasilia, signed on 26 October 1998, mentions in Art 3 a number of bilateral co-operation agreements, which among others led to the creation of adjacent natural preserves. The treaty is available at: www.afese.com/img/revistas/revista44/tratadopaz.pdf (last visited on 20 April 2014).

[179] Environmental co-operation is specifically addressed in Annex IV (Environment) of the Treaty of Peace between the State of Israel and the Hashemite Kingdom of Jordan, 26 October 1994, referred to in Bruch *et al.*, *supra* n. 167, pp. 65–6.

Conca, K. and G. Dabelko (eds.), *Environmental Peacemaking* (Princeton NJ: Woodrow Wilson Center Press, 2002).

Council of Europe Parliamentary Assembly, Committee on Migration, Refugees and Population, *Environmentally Induced Migration and Displacement: A 21st Century Challenge*, COE Doc 11785 (23 December 2008).

Cournil, C. and B. Mayer, *Les migrations environnementales. Enjeux et gouvernance* (Paris: Presses de Sciences Po, 2014).

Das, O., *Environmental Protection, Security and Armed Conflict: A Sustainable Development Perspective* (Cheltenham: Edward Elgar, 2013).

Gray, C., 'Climate Change and the Law on the Use of Force', in R. Rayfuse and S. V. Scott (eds.), *International Law in the Era of Climate Change* (Cheltenham: Edward Elgar, 2011), pp. 219–40.

Greenwood, C., 'State Responsibility and Civil Liability for Environmental Damage caused by Military Operations', in R. J. Grunawalt, J. E. King and R. S. McClain (eds.), *Protection of the Environment during Armed Conflict* (Newport RI: Naval War College, 1996), pp. 397–415.

Grunawalt, R. J., J. E. King and R. S. McClain (eds.), *Protection of the Environment during Armed Conflict* (Newport RI: Naval War College, 1996).

Henckaerts, J.-M. and L. Doswald-Beck, *Customary International Humanitarian Law* (Cambridge University Press, 2009).

Hulme, K., 'Armed Conflict, Wanton Ecological Devastation and Scorched Earth Policies: How the 1990–91 Gulf Conflict Revealed the Inadequacies of the Current Laws to Ensure Effective Protection and Preservation of the Natural Environment' (1997) 2 *Journal of Armed Conflict Law* 55.

Jensen, D. and S. Lonergan (eds.), *Assessing and Restoring Natural Resources in Post-Conflict Peacebuilding* (London: Earthscan, 2012).

Joyner, D. H., *International Law and the Proliferation of Weapons of Mass Destruction* (Oxford University Press, 2009).

Kadelbach, S., 'Nuclear Weapons and Warfare', in *Max Planck Encyclopedia of Public International Law* (2009).

Kälin, W., 'Conceptualising Climate-Induced Displacement' in J. McAdam (ed.), *Climate Change and Displacement: Multidisciplinary Perspectives* (Oxford: Hart Publishing, 2010), pp. 81–103.

Kälin, W. and N. Schrepfer, *Protecting People Crossing Borders in the Context of Climate Change Normative Gaps and Possible Approaches*, UNHCR (PPLA/2012/01), February 2012.

Kazazi, M., 'Environmental Damage in the Practice of the UN Compensation Commission' in M. Bowman and A. Boyle (eds.), *Environmental Damage in International and Comparative Law* (Oxford University Press, 2002), pp. 111–31.

'The UNCC Follow-up Programme for Environmental Awards', in *Law of the Sea, Environmental Law and Settlement of Disputes: Liber Amicorum Judge Thomas A. Mensah* (Leiden: Martinus Nijhoff, 2007), pp. 1109–29.

Koppe, E., *The Use of Nuclear Weapons and the Protection of the Environment during International Armed Conflict* (Oxford: Hart, 2008).

Krutzsch, W., E. Myjer and R. Trapp (eds.), *The Chemical Weapons Convention. A Commentary* (Oxford University Press, 2014).

Kunz, M. and J. E. Viñuales, 'Environmental Approaches to Nuclear Weapons', in G. Nystuen, S. Casey-Maslen and A. Golden Bersagel (eds.), *Nuclear Weapons under International Law* (Cambridge University Press, 2014), pp. 269–91.

Lujala, P. and S. A. Rustad (eds.), *High-Value Natural Resources and Post-Conflict Peacebuilding* (London: Earthscan, 2011).

Marauhn, T., 'Chemical Weapons and Warfare', in *Max Planck Encyclopedia of Public International Law* (2010).

McAdam, J., *Climate Change Displacement and International Law: Complementary Protection Standards*, UNHCR (PPLA/2011/03), May 2011.

 Complementary Protection in International Refugee Law (Oxford University Press, 2007).

Mollard-Bannelier, K., *La protection de l'environnement en temps de conflit armé* (Paris: Pédone, 2001).

Morrissey, J., 'Rethinking the "Debate on Environmental Refugees": from "Maximilists and Minimalists" to "Proponents and Critics"' (2012) 19 *Journal of Political Ecology* 36.

Nystuen, G., S. Casey-Maslen and A. Golden Bersagel (eds.), *Nuclear Weapons under International Law* (Cambridge University Press, 2014).

Penny, C., 'Greening the Security Council: Climate Change as an Emerging "Threat to International Peace and Security"' (2007) 7 *International Environmental Agreements: Politics, Law, Economics* 35.

Piguet, E. *et al.* (eds.), *Migration and Climate Change* (Cambridge University Press, 2011).

Sandoz, Y., C. Swinarsky and B. Zimmermann, *Commentary on the Additional Protocols of 8 June 1977 to the Geneva Convention of 12 August 1949* (Leiden/ Geneva: Martinus Nijhoff/International Committee of the Red Cross, 1987).

Schmitt, M. N., 'Green War: An Assessment of the Environmental Law of International Armed Conflict' (1997) 22 *Yale Journal of International Law* 1.

 'War and the Environment: Fault Lines in the Prescriptive Landscape', in J. E. Austin and C. E. Bruch (eds.), *The Environmental Consequences of War: Legal, Economic and Scientific Perspectives* (Cambridge University Press, 2000), pp. 87–136.

Shelton, D. and A. Kiss, 'Martens Clause for Environmental Protection' (2000) 30 *Environmental Policy and Law* 285.

Sindico, F., 'Climate Change: A Security (Council) Issue?' (2007) 1 *Carbon and Climate Law Review* 26.

Sur, S. (ed.), *Le droit international des armes nucléaires* (Paris: Pedone, 1998).

Svarc, D., 'Biological Weapons and Warfare', in *Max Planck Encyclopedia of Public International Law* (2011).

Szurek, S., 'De Rarotonga à Bangkok et Pelindaba: Note sur les traités constitutifs de nouvelles zones exemptes d'armes nucléaires' (1996) 42 *Annuaire français de droit international* 164.

Tignino, M., L'eau et la guerre : éléments pour un régime juridique (Brussels: Bruylant, 2011).

United Nations Environment Programme, *From Conflict to Peacebuilding: The Role of Natural Resources and the Environment* (Geneva: UNEP, 2009).

 Protecting the Environment During Armed Conflict. An Inventory and Analysis of International Law (Nairobi: UNEP, 2009).

United Nations High Commissioner for Refugees, *Climate Change, Natural Disasters and Human Displacement: A UNHCR Perspective* (14 August 2009).

United Nations Institute for Disarmament Research, *A Fissile Material Cut-off Treaty. Understanding the Critical Issues* (Geneva: UNIDIR, 2010).

United Nations Secretary-General, *Climate Change and Its Possible Security Implications: Report of the Secretary-General*, UN Doc. A/64/350, 11 September 2009.

Unruh, J. and R. C. Williams (eds.), *Land and Post-Conflict Peacebuilding* (London: Earthscan, 2013).

Vöneky, S., 'A New Shield for the Environment: Peacetime Treaties as Legal Restraints of Wartime Damage' (2000) 9 *Review of Community and International Environmental Law* 20.

  'Peacetime Environmental Law as a Basis of State Responsibility for Environmental Damage Caused by War' in J. E. Austin and C. E. Bruch (eds.), *The Environmental Consequences of War: Legal, Economic and Scientific Perspectives* (Cambridge University Press, 2000), pp. 190–225.

Weinthal, E., J. Troel and M. Nakayama (eds.), *Water and Post-Conflict Peacebuilding* (London: Earthscan, 2014).

Yee Woon Chin, L., 'Nuclear Weapon-Free Zones – A Comparative Analysis of the Basic Undertakings in the SEANWFZ Treaty and their Geographical Scope of Application' (1998) 2 *Singapore Journal of International and Comparative Law* 275.

12

Environmental protection and international economic law

12.1 Introduction

In Chapter 10, we analysed the relationship between human rights and environmental protection, as an expression of the interactions between the social and environmental pillars of sustainable development. This chapter follows a similar approach with respect to the connection between environmental protection and economic development. The latter finds expression in an increasingly important body of norms regulating investment, trade and technology at the international level.

Unlike the link between human rights and the environment, which has been approached mostly from a synergistic perspective, the connection between environmental protection and international economic law has been largely understood as conflicting. Environmental protection measures have been considered as covert protectionism or, alternatively, as a luxury of industrialised countries that no longer have serious development concerns. Conversely, the international protection of foreign investment, trade transactions and intellectual property rights ('IPRs') has come under criticism as a result of the constraints it places on States' regulatory powers, including for environmental protection.

In reality, environmental protection and international economic law may entertain both synergistic and conflicting relations, depending on the specific issue at stake and the context where it arises. This chapter discusses these two dimensions focusing *tour-à-tour* on investment, trade and intellectual property regulation. This presentation order is suggested by the production cycle, which begins with investment to develop certain products (12.2), then involves (in addition to domestic sales) the export of the products to foreign markets (12.3) and, for technology-intensive goods, it seeks to ensure a certain level of protection of IPRs abroad, through the regulation of trade-related aspects of IPRs (12.4). A different presentation order could, of course, be followed, taking into account the fact that a significant proportion of production processes use goods imported from abroad, including from other companies within the same multinational group (intra-firm trade)[1] or that, as driver of innovation, IPRs intervene at the earlier stage of research and development, which entails investment.[2] These are important issues, and they will be integrated in the presentation order of investment, trade and IPRs regulation followed in this chapter.

12.2 Foreign investment and the environment in international law

12.2.1 Overview

Foreign investment is much needed for the 'development' (economic and social) component of 'sustainable development' but it entertains an ambiguous relationship with the other component of this concept, i.e. 'environmental protection'. On the one hand, foreign investment can harness the resources (financial and technological) to promote environmental protection through a variety of channels (e.g. energy efficiency, reduction of greenhouse gas (GHG) emissions, waste treatment and other 'clean' technologies). On the other hand, foreign investment may adversely affect the environment of the host State (e.g. destruction of biodiversity, pollution of water resources, improper disposal of hazardous waste, commercialisation of dangerous chemicals banned/restricted in developed countries).

This ambiguity also arises in the relationship between the bodies of international law primarily regulating foreign investment schemes and environmental protection.[3] International investment law may contribute to environmental goals through the protection afforded to foreign investment schemes under international investment agreements ('IIAs'). Aside from the contractual relationships that a foreign investor may entertain with a host State, two main types of treaties have been developed to promote and protect foreign investment, namely 'bilateral investment treaties' ('BITs') and investment chapters in bilateral or multilateral free trade agreements ('FTAs'). In both cases, the basic components are fundamentally similar: (i) provisions defining protected investments and investors; (ii) provisions defining the type

---

[1] For a concise overview see R. Lanz and S. Miroudot, 'Intra-Firm Trade: Patterns, Determinants and Policy Implications' (2011) *OECD Trade Policy Papers*, No. 114, OECD Publishing, available at: last dx.doi.org/10.1787/5kg9p39lrwnn-en (visited on 20 April 2014).

[2] For an early statement of the link IPRs-innovation, see E. Penrose, *The Economics of the International Patent System* (Baltimore MD: Johns Hopkins Press, 1951). For a contemporary statement, see World Intellectual Property Organisation, *The Changing Face of Innovation* (Geneva: WIPO, 2011). Some recent research suggests, however, that this link may not be as robust as initially thought. See C. Correa, 'Innovation and Technology Transfer of Environmentally Sound Technologies: The Need to Engage in a Substantive Debate' (2013) 22 *Review of European, Comparative and International Environmental Law* 54, 55–7.

[3] This section is based on J. E. Viñuales, *Foreign Investment and the Environment in International Law* (Cambridge University Press, 2012); P.-M. Dupuy and J. E. Viñuales (eds.), *Harnessing Foreign Investment to Promote Environmental Protection: Incentives and Safeguards* (Cambridge University Press, 2013).

of treatment that must be granted to the latter (e.g. provisions on takings, fair and equitable treatment and non-discrimination); (iii) an arbitration clause entitling covered investors to bring a claim against the host State before *ad hoc* arbitration tribunals.[4] Although environmental protection is not an explicit target of such instruments, reducing the risk of investing abroad may be useful to foster sustainable development through the transfer of capital and technology that investment often entails. Yet, the obligations of the host State under IIAs may sometimes conflict – at least to some extent – with its international environmental obligations. Investment protection may, more generally, collide with purely domestic environmental measures, as evidenced by an increasing number of investment disputes.[5]

In the following sections, we analyse the synergistic and conflicting aspects of environmental and investment protection. Synergies (12.2.2) are mapped by reference to some international policy instruments capable of channelling foreign investment towards pro-environment projects and, more generally, by reference to ongoing policy processes aimed at a broader harmonisation of these two areas of regulation. As for conflicts (12.2.3), we pay particular attention to the practice of investment arbitration tribunals and the current trend in investment treaty-making.

12.2.2 Synergies

12.2.2.1 Instruments
In Chapter 9, we discussed a number of policy instruments, including funds and the so-called market mechanisms, which are used to facilitate compliance with international environmental law. This section looks at some of these instruments from a particular angle, namely the role that the private sector as a proxy for foreign investors, can play within them. The discussion is limited to three examples, which are illustrative of different types of instruments: environmental funds, public-private partnerships ('PPPs'), and market mechanisms.

Regarding the first instrument, the most important example so far is the Global Environmental Facility ('GEF'), discussed in Chapter 9. The GEF recognised the importance of engaging the private sector in its activities since its inception. In an information document prepared by the Secretariat in October 1995 and entitled 'Engaging the Private Sector' it was noted that 'the challenge for the GEF [was] to find effective modalities to influence ("leverage") ... private ... investment flows in ways that are beneficial to

---

[4] For a concise introduction to international investment law, see R. Dolzer and C. Schreuer, *Principles of International Investment Law* (Oxford University Press, 2013). For an analysis of the most salient contemporary issues in this field, see Z. Douglas, J. Pauwelyn and J. E. Viñuales (eds.), *The Foundations of International Investment Law* (Oxford University Press, 2014).

[5] See *infra* Section 12.2.3.2.

the global environment'.[6] Over the years, the GEF developed a 'Strategy to Engage with the Private Sector' embodied in a number of documents, including a set of 'Principles for Engaging the Private Sector'[7] and additional action to 'enhance' the initial strategy.[8] The approach described by these documents and followed by the GEF involved different types of engagement, including 'indirect' (i.e. creating market conditions in countries receiving GEF funds conducive to pro-environment firms) or 'direct' engagement by the GEF (i.e. providing funds to a private company to cover the incremental costs of a project), the 'co-financing' of GEF-leveraged projects by the private sector (i.e. the role of the GEF is to lower the risks of private sector participation) or, still, the facilitation of private sector participation in the public procurement process of GEF-financed governmental projects. After the adoption of the GEF's Resource Allocation Framework in 2006, 'direct' engagement has become more difficult, because the needs of the private sector have not always been sufficiently taken into account in country allocations.[9] Currently, the GEF envisages private sector involvement mostly through the first (indirect) and the third (co-financing) types of engagement. In particular, implementing agencies are being encouraged to identify certain PPPs that could receive funding and attract co-financing by other lenders.[10]

The second instrument, PPPs, has received increasing attention as a tool for environmental protection since the 2002 World Summit on Sustainable Development, in Johannesburg.[11] PPPs can be used as project finance vehicles, as is currently the case of the GEF.[12] So far, tapping into the financial resources of the private sector has been perhaps the most important use of PPPs. Yet, PPPs can also provide a vehicle for projects jointly undertaken in the field. The so-called 'Type II outcomes' of the WSSD covered indeed 'commitments to specific targets and objectives for the implementation of sustainable

---

[6] GEF, 'Engaging the Private Sector', 5 October 1995, GEF/C.6/Inf.4, para. 7 ('Engaging the Private Sector').

[7] GEF, 'Principles for Engaging the Private Sector', 16 April 2004, GEF/C.23/11 ('GEF Principles').

[8] GEF, 'Revised Strategy for Enhancing Engagement with the Private Sector', 7 October 2011, GEF/C.41/09 ('GEF Revised Strategy'), Annex 1

[9] *Ibid.*, para. 35. [10] *Ibid.*, para. 32.

[11] Report of the World Summit on Sustainable Development, A/CONF.199/20, Part I, item 2: Plan of Implementation of the World Summit on Sustainable Development ('Plan of Implementation'), paras. 7(j), 9(g), 20(t), 25(g), 43(a) or 49. Calls for more private sector involvement in environmental protection can be traced back to at least the 1992 Agenda 21: Report of the United Nations Conference on Environment and Development, A/CONF.151/26/Rev.l (Vol. l), Resolution 1, Annex 2: Agenda 21, 13 June 1992 ('Agenda 21'), Chapter 30. See also Report of the Secretary-General: Renewing the United Nations: A Programme for Reform, 14 July 1997, UN Doc. A/51/1950, paras. 59–60; Report of the Secretary General: Enhanced Cooperation between the UN and All Relevant Partners, in particular the Private Sector, 10 August 2005, UN Doc. A/60/214; United Nations Millennium Declaration, UNGA Res 55/2, 8 September 2000, para. 20.

[12] GEF Revised Strategy, *supra* n. 8, paras. 28–34, 39.

development made by a coalition of actors',[13] including the private sector. Over the years, more than 300 partnerships were registered with the now discontinued UN Commission on Sustainable Development, mainly in the areas of water, energy and education[14] and with global (180), regional (69) or subregional (79) geographic scopes.[15] In addition to these PPPs, a number of initiatives have been jointly undertaken by the bodies of some environmental treaties and some private companies.[16] Examples include the 'Danone-Evian Fund for Water Resources' established in 2002 following an agreement between the Secretariat of the Ramsar Convention[17] and the Danone Group,[18] the collaboration between the Convention on Migratory Species ('CMS')[19] and the German air carrier Lufthansa to show a documentary on the activities of the CMS in certain Lufthansa flights[20] or, still, the 'Mobile Phone Partnership Initiative'[21] jointly undertaken by the Basel Convention and a number of private companies for the 'environmentally sound management of used and end-of-life mobile phones' not covered by the Convention's definition of waste.[22]

The third instrument, market mechanisms, has already been discussed in connection with the Kyoto Protocol (see Chapter 5). Yet, it seems useful to characterise here the type of 'synergy' between foreign investment and environmental protection that they are intended to provide. Unlike environmental funds, market mechanisms do not disburse funds or provide guarantees to either States or private companies. Their purpose is to create an incentive for States or private companies to conduct certain types of pro-environment transactions. They do so by creating an environmental market. From the perspective of a foreign investor, the type of incentive could be characterised as a variant of 'indirect engagement' in the meaning ascribed to this term by

---

[13] C. Streck, 'The World Summit on Sustainable Development: Partnerships as New Tools in Environmental Governance' (2002) 13 *Yearbook of International Environmental Law* 63, 67.

[14] See webapps01.un.org/dsd/partnerships/public/partnerships/stats/primary_theme.jpg (last visited on 20 April 2014).

[15] See webapps01.un.org/dsd/partnerships/public/partnerships/stats/geographic_scope.jpg (last visited on 20 April 2014).

[16] E. Morgera, *Corporate Accountability in International Environmental Law* (Oxford University Press, 2009), pp. 251–4.

[17] Convention on Wetlands of International Importance especially as Waterfowl Habitat, 2 February 1971, 996 UNTS 245 ('Ramsar Convention').

[18] Action Programme for Water Resource and Water Quality Protection in Wetlands of International Importance, Memorandum of Understanding, 27 January 1998. The initial instrument has been subsequently completed and amended by a number of other instruments. See www.ramsar.org (last visited on 20 April 2014).

[19] Convention on the Conservation of Migratory Species of Wild Animals, 23 June 1979, 1651 UNTS 356 ('CMS Convention').

[20] Morgera, above n. 16, p. 253.

[21] 'Sustainable Partnership for the Environmentally Sound Management of End-of-life Mobile Telephones', Decision VI/31, 10 February 2003, UNEP/CHW.6/40.

[22] On this basis, the Basel Convention Secretariat has developed a 'Guidance Document on the Environmentally Sound Management of Used and End-of-life Mobile Phones', 14 July 2011, UNEP/CHW.10/INF/27.

the GEF. In the case of the flexible mechanisms of the Kyoto Protocol, the market is created by the existence of a cap on the emissions of certain greenhouse gases (Annex A) by certain countries (Annex B). The right to emit a ton of carbon dioxide equivalent thus acquires value for States subject to the cap, because these 'emission rights' can be used to comply with an international obligation. This, in turn, is implemented by domestic or regional legislation (e.g. the European ETS Directive[23]) extending the market of emission rights to the private sector. For a private company an emission right is valuable not only because it can be used to comply with a legal obligation but also for other purposes, such as branding, hedging or simply avoiding investment in a restructuring of its production methods. Similarly, certain 'ecosystem services' (e.g. carbon capture and storage by trees, water purification and replenishment or flood control by wetlands, biodiversity conservation by tropical forests) can be structured in a way that allows them to be marketed. Depending on the structure given to such services, the market will have different features. Some countries, such as Brazil and Ecuador, have set up funds where public and private investors can invest in preserving the tropical forests.[24]

12.2.2.2 Policy processes

In addition to the specific instruments discussed above, broader synergies are being explored by a number of international organisations, including the Organisation for Economic Co-operation and Development ('OECD') and the UN Commission on Trade and Development ('UNCTAD').

The OECD has conducted research on the economic dimensions of the connection between foreign investment and environmental protection since the 1990s.[25] More recently, it has turned its attention to the legal aspects of this link, with a particular interest in IIAs and investment arbitration. In addition to several useful studies published in this context, in 2011, the delegates of States parties to the organisation adopted a 'OECD Statement on Harnessing Freedom of Investment for Green Growth', identifying seven 'findings' and highlighting the importance of:

> (i) mutual supportiveness of international environmental and investment law; (ii) monitoring investment treaty practices regarding the environment; (iii) ensuring the integrity and competence, and improving the transparency of investor–state dispute settlement; (iv) strengthening compliance with international investment law through prior review of proposed environmental measures and through effective environmental law and regulatory practices;

---

[23] Directive 2003/87/EC of the European Parliament and of the Council of 13 October 2003 establishing a scheme for greenhouse gas emission allowance trading within the Community and amending Council Directive 96/61/E, OJ 2003 L 0087, 25 June 2009 (consolidated version) ('ETS Directive').

[24] See www.amazonfund.org and www.sosyasuni.org (last visited on 20 April 2014).

[25] For a useful survey, see OECD, *FDI and the environment – An Overview of the Literature* (Paris: OECD, 1997).

(v) vigilance against green protectionism; (vi) encouraging business' contribution to greening the economy; and (vii) spurring green growth through FDI.[26]

These findings are the result of substantial preparatory work, consultations and discussion among delegates during a round-table held in April 2011. They have no particular legal status, as they are not generalisations of the legal practice of States. They constitute a common policy statement approved by the delegates of OECD Member States[27] and providing an indication of how they see the interactions of these bodies of law in the future.

Similar efforts have also been conducted under the aegis of the UNCTAD, a forum that, due to its mandate, better reflects the interest of developing countries. In its 2012 World Investment Report, the UNCTAD introduced an 'Investment Policy Framework for Sustainable Development' ('IPFSD') calling for a new generation of investment policies, including investment treaties.[28] The IPFSD is more ambitious than the OECD Statement and includes (i) a set of 'Core Principles for Investment Policymaking', (ii) a set of 'National Investment Policy Guidelines', and (iii) a selection of 'Policy options' for investment treaty making. Regarding (i), the principles are presented as an integral part of the IPFSD and not as a separate instrument. There are eleven core principles, which can be classified under four categories: overall objectives of investment policymaking (Principle 1); general policymaking process (Principles 2, 3 and 4); specific investment policymaking process (Principles 5–10); international co-operation (Principle 11).[29] A noteworthy aspect of these principles is the focus on the 'promotion' of investment for 'inclusive growth and sustainable development', a feature that may have specific implications for the interpretation of investment protection standards and arbitration clauses.[30] Synergies are explicitly contemplated in Principle 2, which states that '[a]ll policies that impact on investment should be coherent and synergetic at both the national and international level'.[31] Also, the principles focus on

---

[26] OECD, *Harnessing Freedom of Investment for Green Growth*, Freedom of Investment Roundtable, 14 April 2011, available at: www.oecd.org (last visited on 20 April 2014).

[27] Australia, Austria, Belgium, Canada, Chile, the Czech Republic, Denmark, Estonia, Finland, France, Germany, Greece, Hungary, Iceland, Ireland, Israel, Italy, Japan, Korea, Luxembourg, Mexico, Morocco, the Netherlands, New Zealand, Norway, Peru, Poland, Portugal, the Slovak Republic, Slovenia, Spain, Sweden, Switzerland, Romania, Turkey, United Kingdom and the United States.

[28] UNCTAD, *World Investment Report. Towards a New Generation of Investment Policies* (2012), Chapter IV (Investment Policy Framework for Sustainable Development). See also the report specifically on the IPFSD available at: unctad.org/en/PublicationsLibrary/diaepcb2012d5_en.pdf ('IPFSD Report').

[29] *Ibid.*, pp. 10–14.

[30] The contribution of foreign investment to the development of the host country has been widely discussed in connection with the jurisdictional requirements for arbitration tribunals acting under the aegis of the International Centre for Settlement of Investment Disputes ('ICSID'). For an overview of the debate, see J. D. Mortenson, 'Meaning of "Investment": ICSID *Travaux* and the Domain of International Investment Law' (2010) 51 *Harvard International Law Journal* 257.

[31] IPFSD Report, *supra* n. 28, p. 11.

post-establishment treatment, unlike the OECD's statement, which also seeks to liberalise investment by granting or facilitating access to foreign markets. Moving to the 'Guidelines' and 'Policy options' included in the IPFSD, they are of course consistent and aligned with the Core Principles. Of note, however, is the call for 'negotiating sustainable development-friendly IIAs [international investment agreements]'[32] and the detailed discussion of common investment treaty terms and of how they could be adjusted to give appropriate room to sustainable development considerations.

Underpinning the latter point is the recognition that environmental regulatory change can indeed lead to conflicts, broadly understood, with existing IIAs, at least with the current interpretation of their broad language by investment tribunals.

12.2.3 Conflicts

12.2.3.1 Normative conflicts v. legitimacy conflicts

In the last decade, the number of investment disputes with environmental components has increased steeply. Whereas before 1990 only two such claims had been brought, the number increased between 1990 and 2000 (nine claims brought) and particularly between 2001 and 2013 (more than forty claims brought, many still pending). And these numbers are only a conservative estimation, as they do not take into account undisclosed disputes (believed to be numerous) or claims brought before other jurisdictions (e.g. domestic courts or human rights courts). The issues arising in these disputes include takings of investors' property for environmental reasons (e.g. protection of a natural or cultural site), delay/suspension/retreat of a permit to operate (e.g. waste treatment facilities, power generators, production and commercialization of certain chemical substances), imposition of liability for environmental damage (e.g. site decontamination), adoption of sanitary or health measures, design and administration of feed-in tariffs schemes (e.g. requirement of 'buy local' to participate in a renewable energy subsidy scheme) or tariff setting in some regulated industries (e.g. water or gas distribution). As to the amounts involved, they range from a few million dollars to some astronomical amounts (e.g. with $18 billion at stake in the case brought by Chevron Corporation against the Republic of Ecuador).

One important legal question that arises in this context is the extent to which international environmental law is relevant for solving these investment disputes. Even in those cases where the environmental measures challenged are domestic in nature, they may be induced – explicitly or implicitly – or justified by the obligations undertaken by the State hosting the investment under international environmental law. In practice, the treatment of purely domestic and internationally-induced measures has been amalgamated by investment

---

[32] *Ibid.*, p. 39.

tribunals. Conflicts between two norms of international law ('normative conflicts') have thus been conflated with conflicts between a domestic (environmental) measure and an international (investment) norm ('legitimacy conflicts').

The difference between framing the issue in one or the other way is legally significant, because the rules applicable to solve potential conflicts and the broader understanding of the dispute are not the same in the two scenarios. Specifically, the general rule of international law (followed by international tribunals) according to which international law prevails over domestic law[33] would place domestic environmental measures (even those that implement environmental treaties) in a subordinate position with respect to investment treaties. More generally, the perceived disconnection between domestic environmental measures and environmental treaties may undermine the legitimacy attached to such measures by investment tribunals.

As a result, the impact of environmental treaties on foreign investment disputes is difficult to determine. As a general matter, investment tribunals can follow three different approaches in this regard.

12.2.3.2 The practice of investment tribunals[34]

The 'traditional approach' was to consider all conflicts as legitimacy conflicts. The environmental measures adopted by host States were thus seen as 'suspicious' (unilateral protectionism in disguise) and in all events 'subordinated' to international (investment) law (as a result of the aforementioned rule that international law prevails over domestic law). This view, which may have reflected the specific factual configurations of some early cases (e.g. *S.D. Myers* v. *Canada*,[35] *Metalclad* v. *Mexico*,[36] *CDSE* v. *Costa Rica*,[37] *Tecmed* v. *Mexico*[38]), has sometimes been extrapolated to the assessment of genuinely

---

[33] See e.g. *Southern Pacific Properties (Middle East) Limited (SPP)* v. *Arab Republic of Egypt*, ICSID Case No. ARB/84/3, Award (20 May 1992) ('*SPP* v. *Egypt*'), paras. 75–6; *Compañía del Desarrollo de Santa Elena SA* v. *Republic of Costa Rica*, ICSID Case No. ARB/96/1, Award (17 February 2000) ('*CDSE* v. *Costa Rica*'), paras. 64–5.

[34] For a detailed analysis of the issues discussed in this section, see J. E. Viñuales, 'The Environmental Regulation of Foreign Investment Schemes under International Law', in Dupuy and Viñuales, *supra* n. 3, pp. 273–320.

[35] *S.D. Myers Inc.* v. *Canada*, NAFTA Arbitration (UNCITRAL Rules), Partial Award (13 November 2000) ('*S.D. Myers* v. *Canada*'). The evidence of the case led to the conclusion that the export ban of hazardous waste that was challenged by the US investor had indeed been adopted to favour Canadian competitors.

[36] *Metalclad Corp.* v. *United Mexican States*, ICSID Case No. ARB(AF)/97/1, Award (25 August 2000) ('*Metalclad* v. *Mexico*'). The decree creating a natural preserve for the protection of cacti came very late in the dispute, which concerned the refusal of a permit to build a landfill for non-genuinely environmental reasons.

[37] *CDSE* v. *Costa Rica*, *supra* n. 33. The decree formally expropriating the land owned by investor did not refer to any of the potentially applicable environmental treaties.

[38] *Técnicas Medioambientales Tecmed S.A.* v. *United Mexican States*, ICSID Case No. ARB(AF)/00/2, Award (29 May 2003) ('*Tecmed* v. *Mexico*'). Despite genuine environmental concerns, the refusal to renew the operation permit of the investor's waste treatment facility followed the growing public opposition regarding the scheme.

environmental and even internationally-induced measures, with the unfortunate result that environmental considerations remain legally subordinated to purely economic considerations.

At the opposite side of the spectrum, it would be possible to consider conflicts as 'normative conflicts'. Under this view, most domestic environmental measures would be seen as being internationally-induced (standing on an equal footing with other international norms, such as investment disciplines) and reflecting multilateral action (thus defeating the suspicion of unilateral protectionism). This view would, in fact, apply a different set of conflict rules to different types of conflicts ('legitimacy' and 'normative' conflicts)[39] and, more generally, defuse the suspicion and mistrust that some tribunals still see, despite the rise of environmental awareness at the global level, as the starting-point in the analysis of environmental regulation. While such an approach would be more accurate from a strictly legal perspective, it faces daunting practical challenges. First, as we saw in Chapters 4 to 7, international environmental norms tend to be couched in rather broad (even vague) terms, making it difficult – albeit not impossible – to establish a clear link between a domestic environmental measure and an international environmental obligation. Two contrasting examples are provided by the *Aviation* case before the CJEU, where Article 2 of the Kyoto Protocol was deemed to require action to curb emissions but not the adoption of any specific measure,[40] and the *Bonaire* case, where a Dutch court concluded that a norm as broadly stated as Article 3 of the Ramsar Convention was directly applicable and justified the refusal of an authorisation by Dutch authorities.[41] Second, this link would in all events have to be recognised by the arbitral tribunals specifically established to deal with investment (not environmental) disputes. Although the question whether such tribunals are biased in favour of investors'

---

[39] In *SD Myers* v. *Canada*, the tribunal considered the Canadian argument that the measure challenged had been adopted pursuant to the Basel Convention on Hazardous Waste, which prevailed over the obligations arising from the NAFTA as a result of the conflict norm in Art. 104 of NAFTA. This conflict norm was not technically applied because the US had not ratified the Basel Convention. See *SD Myers* v. *Canada, supra* n. 35, para. 150 (Canadian argument) and 213–15 (tribunal's rejection of the argument).

[40] The case concerned a challenge to the extension of the ETS Directive (*supra* n. 23) to the aviation sector. The Court reasoned that the Protocol allowed the parties to comply with the objectives in the manner and at the pace they deemed most appropriate and added that Article 2(2) was not sufficiently precise to be directly relied upon. *Air Transport Association of America and Others* v. *Secretary of State for Energy and Climate Change*, CJEU Case C-366/10 (21 December 2011), paras. 76–7.

[41] *Netherlands Crown Decision (in Dutch) in the case lodged by the Competent Authority for the Island of Bonaire on the annulment of two of its decisions on the Lac wetland by the Governor of the Netherlands Antilles*, 11 September 2007, Staatsblad 2007, 347 ('*Bonaire*'). Specifically, the Dutch Council of State judged that Article 3 was directly enforceable at the domestic level and upheld on this basis an administrative decision cancelling a permit to build a holiday resort in a buffer zone surrounding a Ramsar protected site. See M. Bowman, P. Davies and C. Redgwell, *Lyster's International Wildlife Law* (Cambridge University Press, 2nd edn., 2010), p. 419.

interests or not is highly controversial, it seems clear that, with (still) rare exceptions,[42] they are not yet ready to treat international environmental law on an equal footing with investment treaties. To use a metaphor, international environmental law would at best be an 'immigrant' in the land of international investment law, much in the same way as in the context of the WTO dispute settlement, discussed later in this chapter. In both cases, international environmental law is only granted the space specifically allocated to it by investment or trade law.

However, some recent developments suggest that there may be an alternative approach between the inadequate traditional view and the unrealistic progressive view. Indeed, environmental considerations are now finding increasing room in foreign investment disputes through the interpretation of some legal concepts such as the police powers doctrine, the definition of 'like circumstances', the level of reasonableness required from investors or the use of emergency and necessity clauses. Thus, in *Chemtura* v. *Canada*, the tribunal considered that a measure banning the production and commercialisation of an environmentally harmful pesticide was a valid exercise of the police powers of Canada and therefore rejected the investor's claim for compensation.[43] In *Parkerings* v. *Lithuania*, the tribunal rejected a claim for breach of the most-favoured-nation clause (a non-discrimination standard) on the grounds that the project of the claimant had an adverse impact on a UNESCO-protected site and, as a result, it was not in 'like circumstances' with the project of the other investor identified as the comparator.[44] In *Plama* v. *Bulgaria*, the tribunal considered that a change in the domestic environmental laws placing the financial burden of decontaminating a site on the investor was not in breach of the applicable investment agreement because the investor should have been aware, had it deployed all the due diligence expected from it, that such a regulatory change was being discussed in the Bulgarian parliament at the time it made the investment.[45] Finally, in some cases against Argentina, particularly in the one brought by *LG&E*, the tribunal considered that the violation of an investment treaty by Argentina was justified by the need to

---

[42] In *SPP* v. *Egypt*, an arbitral tribunal chaired by the former President of the International Court of Justice concluded that Egypt had breached its investment obligations (based on domestic law and a contract) but added that no compensation was due for the period after the inscription of the pyramids site in the World Heritage List, because from that moment onwards the investment would have become illegal under international law, namely the World Heritage Convention. See *SPP* v. *Egypt, supra* n. 33, para. 191.

[43] *Chemtura Corporation (formerly Crompton Corporation)* v. *Government of Canada*, UNCITRAL, Award (2 August 2010) ('*Chemtura* v. *Canada*'), para. 266. The tribunal referred to its analysis of the claim under Art. 1105, which explained that the measure adopted by Canada was consistent with its obligations under international environmental law (the POP Protocol to the LRTAP Convention and the POP Convention, discussed in Chapters 5 and 7).

[44] *Parkerings-Compagniet AS* v. *Republic of Lithuania*, ICSID Case No. ARB/05/8, Award (11 September 2007) ('*Parkerings* v. *Lithuania*'), para. 392.

[45] *Plama Consortium Ltd.* v. *Republic of Bulgaria*, ICSID Case No. ARB/03/24, Award (27 August 2008), para. 219–21.

	Whether environmental measures tend to be seen as:			
	Covert protectionism	Genuine regulation	Domestic in nature	Internationally-induced
Traditional approach	✓		✓	
Progressive approach		✓		✓
Upgraded approach		✓	✓	

Figure 12.1: Jurisprudential approaches to the investment/environment link

ensure the affordability of some basic public services during an economic and social crisis.[46] The three approaches discussed so far are summarised in Figure 12.1.

Of course, each measure and each case have their specific legal and political contexts, and tribunals must decide on that basis. The three approaches summarised in Figure 12.1 are only intended to depict trends or general 'mindsets' that may co-exist and the relative weight and influence of which varies over time to reflect the changing perception of environmental protection as an increasingly important regulatory object. The latter ('upgraded') approach is no doubt the most pragmatic one, and it is therefore unsurprising that contemporary practice in investment treaty making is consistent with the need to give more explicit policy space for environmental regulation.

12.2.3.3 Investment treaty practice

In the last two decades the space devoted to environmental considerations in both investment and free-trade agreements ('IIAs') has significantly expanded. According to a report published by the OECD in 2011 and covering 1623 IIAs (approximately 50 per cent of the then existing IIAs) only 8.2 per cent of IIAs analysed include express references to environmental concerns.[47] However, if a time dimension is added, the overall picture changes drastically. Indeed, the OECD Report shows that, since the mid 1990s:

---

[46] *LG&E* v. *Argentina*, ICSID Case No. ARB/02/1, Decision on Liability (13 October 2006) ('*LG&E* v. *Argentina*'), paras. 234–37, 245. In two other cases, the arbitral tribunals considered that the provision of water and sanitation services was an 'essential interest' of States in the meaning of the necessity rule codified in the 2001 ILC Articles on State Responsibility. See *Suez, Sociedad General de Aguas de Barcelona S.A. and InterAguas Servicios Integrales del Agua SA v. The Argentine Republic*, ICSID Case No. ARB/03/17, Decision on Liability (30 July 2010), para. 238; *Suez, Sociedad General de Aguas de Barcelona, SA and Vivendi Universal, SA v. The Argentine Republic*, ICSID Case No. ARB/03/19, Decision on Liability (30 July 2010), para. 260.

[47] K. Gordon and J. Pohl, 'Environmental Concerns in International Investment Agreements: A Survey' (2011) *OECD Working Papers on International Investment* No. 2011/1 ('OECD Report'), p. 8.

the proportion of newly concluded IIAs that contain environmental language began to increase moderately, and, from about 2002 onwards, steeply ... reaching a peak in 2008, when 89% of newly concluded treaties contain[ed] reference to environmental concerns.[48]

There are different types of references to environmental considerations. The Report identifies seven categories of recurring environmental provisions in IIAs:

[1] General language in preambles that mentions environmental concerns and establishes protection of the environment as a concern of the parties to the treaty ...

[2] Reserving policy space for environmental regulation ...

[3] Reserving policy space for environmental regulation for more specific, limited subject matters (performance requirements and national treatment) ...

[4] [P]rovisions that clarify the understanding of the parties that non-discriminatory environmental regulation does not constitute 'indirect expropriation' ...

[5] [P]rovisions that discourage the loosening of environmental regulation for the purpose of attracting investment ...

[6] [P]rovisions related to the recourse to environmental experts by arbitration tribunals ...

[7] [P]rovisions that encourage strengthening of environmental regulation and cooperation.[49]

The frequency of these provisions varies from one country to another and over time. The most common category (62 per cent of the 133 IIAs including environmental language) is the general reservation of policy space for environmental regulation (category 2), which has, indeed, a potentially permissive effect. More specific (categories 3 and 4) and more progressive (category 7) provisions are less frequent (14 per cent for category 3; 9 per cent for category 4; and 18 per cent for category 7).

Overall, these results suggest that IIAs are increasingly sensitive to environmental considerations, but that the current approach tends to favour broad and to some extent uncertain clauses. For present purposes, the main message is that the practice of investment treaty-making reflects the same trend as the jurisprudence of investment tribunals and the policy processes discussed earlier, namely the increasing interaction between the norms protecting the environment and those for the promotion and protection of foreign investment. As discussed next, the connection between trade and environmental regulation followed a similar path, although starting already in the 1990s, largely as a result of the parallel negotiation processes

---

[48] *Ibid.*, p. 8.   [49] *Ibid.*, p. 11 (the numbering has been added and italics omitted).

leading to the 1992 Earth Summit and to the conclusion of the Uruguay trade round in 1994.[50]

12.3 Environmental protection and international trade law

12.3.1 Overview

Much like the investment/environment connection, the impact of trade liberalisation on environmental protection is ambiguous, as it may lead to a more efficient use of natural resources, as a result of global competition among producers, or to a wider circulation of environment-friendly goods and technologies, but it may also place constraints on legitimate environmental restrictions or contribute to the wider circulation of polluting substances.[51] Unlike the investment/environment connection, however, the trade/environment link has occupied the attention of legal commentators for at least two decades.[52]

In point of fact, the importance of reconciling these two bodies of law was recognised very early in the history of trade regulation. The failed 1948 Havana Charter[53] and even its predecessor, the 1927 Convention for the Abolition of Import and Export Prohibitions and Restrictions,[54] both contained explicit exceptions to accommodate what today would be called environmental measures.[55] The question arose again in the run-up to the Stockholm

---

[50] On this connection, see K. von Moltke, 'The Last Round: The General Agreement on Tariffs and Trade in Light of the Earth Summit' (1993) 23 *Environmental Law* 519.

[51] On this debate see e.g. J. Frankel and A. Rose, 'Is Trade Good or Bad for the Environment? Sorting out the Causality' (2005) 87 *Review of Economics and Statistics* 85 (who find that trade tends to reduce air pollution and is not generally negative on other environmental indicators); J. Frankel, *Environmental Effects of International Trade*, Expert Report no. 301, commissioned by Sweden's Globalisation Council (2008), available at: www.hks.harvard.edu (last visited on 20 April 2014).

[52] Some of the seminal work on this connection includes D. Zaelke, R. Housman and P. Orbach (eds.), *Trade and the Environment: Law, Economics and Policy* (Washington DC: Island Press, 1993); D. Esty, *Greening the GATT: Trade, Environment, and the Future* (Washington DC: Institute for International Economics, 1994); E. U. Petersmann, *International and European Trade and Environmental Law after the Uruguay Round* (The Hague: Kluwer, 1995); E. Brown Weiss and J. Jackson (eds.), *Reconciling Environment and Trade* (Ardsley NY: Transnational Publishers, 2001). For two more recent studies, see E. Vranes, *Trade and the Environment. Fundamental Issues in International Law, WTO Law, and Legal Theory* (Oxford University Press, 2009); J. Watson, *The WTO and the Environment* (London: Routledge, 2013). For concise overviews, see S. Charnovitz, 'The WTO's Environmental Progress', in W. J. Davey and J. Jackson (eds.), *The Future of International Economic Law* (Oxford University Press, 2008), pp. 247–68; D. Bodansky and J. Lawrence, 'Trade and Environment', in D. Bethlehem, D. McRae, R. Neufeld and I. Van Damme (eds.), *The Oxford Handbook of International Trade Law* (Oxford University Press, 2009), pp. 505–38.

[53] Havana Charter for an International Trade Organisation, 24 March 1948, UN Doc. E/Conf. 2178, Art. 45(1)(a)(x).

[54] Convention for the Abolition of Import and Export Prohibitions and Restrictions, 8 November 1927, 97 LNTS 391, Art. 4.

[55] Both instruments are referred to in Charnovitz, *supra* n. 52, pp. 247–8.

Conference and, in 1971, it led to the creation by the States parties to the GATT of a 'Working Group on Environmental Measures and International Trade' ('EMIT Group'), which was to remain inactive until the 1992 Earth Summit.[56] Indeed, it was not until the early 1990s that the debate was reignited as a result of different interlinked processes including the dispute between Mexico and the United States over imports of tuna,[57] the negotiation of the North American Free Trade Agreement ('NAFTA'),[58] the process leading to the Earth Summit and, of course, the Uruguay trade round concluded in 1994.[59]

The establishment of the WTO brought a number of environmentally significant advances, including the introduction of a reference to sustainable development in the preamble of the Marrakesh Agreement[60] and the adoption of a Ministerial Decision on Trade and Environment, setting up the Committee on Trade and Environment ('CTE') in lieu of the dormant EMIT Group.[61] The CTE has contributed to the clarification of the trade/environment interface through discussions and studies, and it has fostered interactions between trade and environment officials at the national and international levels. Over time, environmental considerations have grown in importance within the WTO context, as acknowledged by the 'trade and environment' work programme envisioned in the 2001 Ministerial Declaration launching the Doha negotiation round.[62] The negotiations in this regard were entrusted to the CTE or to special sessions of it ('CTESS') focusing on the connection between trade law and environmental treaties as well as on the facilitation of trade in environmental goods and services ('EGS'). At the time of writing, however, very limited progress had been made on these items from a legal perspective.

The Doha Ministerial Declaration remains, nevertheless, a useful indication of the main areas where synergies are being explored (mostly through 'mutual supportiveness' and EGS) and potential tensions are being circumscribed in an attempt to avert or minimise them (conflicts between trade law and environmental treaties and environmental differentiation within trade law). Figure 12.2 summarises the areas discussed in the following sections.

---

[56] See Bodansky and Lawrence, *supra* n. 52, p. 514.
[57] *United States – Restrictions on Imports of Tuna*, Panel Report, DS21/R-39S/155 (3 September 1991) ('*Tuna-dolphin I*').
[58] North American Free Trade Agreement, 17 December 1992, 32 ILM 296 ('NAFTA'). Together with the NAFTA, the parties concluded a parallel North American Agreement on Environmental Cooperation, 17 September 1992, 32 ILM 1519 ('NAAEC').
[59] See von Moltke, *supra* n. 50.
[60] Agreement establishing the World Trade Organisation, 15 April 1994, 1867 UNTS 154.
[61] Marrakesh Ministerial Decision on Trade and Environment, 14 April 1994, MTN.TNC/45MIN.
[62] WTO Ministerial Conference Fourth Session, Ministerial Declaration, WT/MIN(01)/DEC/1 (20 November 2001) ('Doha Declaration'), para 28, 31–3, 51.

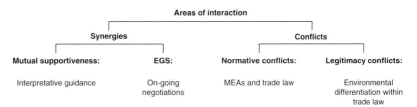

Figure 12.2: Legal aspects of the trade/environment link

There are significant connections and, sometimes, partial overlaps among these areas. Some of the solutions to potential conflicts (e.g. mutually supportive interpretation) can, in fact, be seen as synergistic approaches. Yet, the distinction between synergies and conflicts is helpful to bring trade under the same conceptual chart used to assess the connection between environmental protection and investment or human rights law.

12.3.2 Synergies

12.3.2.1 Mutual supportiveness

The environmental aspects of trade regulation received much attention in the negotiation process leading to the 1992 Earth Summit. The results of the Summit and, specifically, Principle 12 of the Rio Declaration[63] and Chapter 2 of Agenda 21[64] addressed the concern expressed by developing countries that environmental regulation may be used to curtail market access to their exports. Agenda 21 stressed the need to make trade and environment 'mutually supportive'.[65] Similar considerations underpin the reference to sustainable development in the first paragraph of the preamble of the WTO Agreement, although the emphasis is placed here on the efficient use of natural resources.

Over the following two decades, the concept of 'mutual supportiveness', much as that of 'sustainable development', was used in a number of international instruments to articulate the connection between environmental treaties and trade disciplines from a synergistic rather than a conflicting perspective.[66] Examples include the preambles of the 1998 PIC Convention,[67] the 2000

---

[63] 'Rio Declaration on Environment and Development', 13 June 1992, UN Doc. A/CONF.151/26. Rev.1 ('Rio Declaration').

[64] Agenda 21, *supra* n. 11.   [65] *Ibid.*, paras. 2.3(b) and 2.9(d).

[66] See R. Pavoni, 'Mutual Supportiveness as a Principle of Interpretation and Law-Making: A Watershed for the "WTO-and-Competing-Regimes" Debate?' (2010) 3 *European Journal of International Law* 649, 654–5 (referring to the 'conflict clause' in Art. 22(1) of the Convention on Biological Diversity. One may add Art. 104 of the NAFTA as an illustration of this approach).

[67] Rotterdam Convention on the Prior Informed Consent Procedure for Certain Hazardous Chemicals and Pesticides in International Trade, 10 September 1998, 2244 UNTS 337, preamble, paras. 8–10.

Biosafety Protocol,[68] the 2001 Treaty on Plant Genetic Resources,[69] the 2001 POP Convention[70] or, more recently, Articles 20 of the 2005 UNESCO Convention on Cultural Diversity[71] and 4 of the 2010 Nagoya Protocol.[72]

One important legal question that arises in this context concerns the implications of 'mutual supportiveness'. These may range from a mere policy statement, to an interpretative guideline (or according to some commentators 'principle'), to a conflict clause allocating hierarchy, to even a 'law-making' principle.[73] The question has not been explicitly addressed, let alone settled, in the case-law but there is some authority for the proposition that mutual supportiveness may at least play an interpretative role in trade disputes. The high water mark on this point remains the 1998 report of the WTO Appellate Body ('AB') in the *Shrimp-Turtle* case.[74] The case concerned a domestic environmental measure adopted by the United States and affecting the imports of shrimp harvested in a manner that did not afford sufficient protection to sea turtles. As part of its defence, the United States invoked the general exception in Article XX(g) of the GATT concerning the protection of exhaustible natural resources. Despite the fact that the AB eventually concluded that the measure was not justified under Article XX (as it violated its chapeau), it referred both to the preamble of the WTO Agreement and to two environmental treaties, the UNCLOS[75] and the CITES,[76] to interpret Article XX(g). According to the AB, the terms 'exhaustible natural resources' in Article XX(g) had to be interpreted 'in the light of contemporary concerns of the community of nations about the protection and conservation of the environment'.[77]

This approach to interpretation, which can be seen as a general application of the customary rule of systemic integration codified in Article 31(3)(c) of the Vienna Convention on the Law of Treaties,[78] has not been consistently

---

[68] Cartagena Protocol on Biosafety to the Convention on Biological Diversity, 29 January 2000, 39 ILM 1027, preamble, paras. 9–11.

[69] International Treaty on Plant Genetic Resources for Food and Agriculture, 3 November 2001, 2400 UNTS 379, preamble, paras. 9–11.

[70] Stockholm Convention on Persistent Organic Pollutants, 22 May 2001, 40 ILM 532 (2001), preamble, para. 9.

[71] Convention on the Protection and Promotion of the Diversity of Cultural Expressions, 20 October 2005, 2440 UNTS 311.

[72] Nagoya Protocol on Access to Genetic Resources and the Fair and Equitable Sharing of the Benefits Arising from their Utilization to the Convention on Biological Diversity, 29 October 2010, available at: www.cbd.int/abs/doc/protocol/nagoya-protocol-en.pdf (last visited on 20 April 2014).

[73] See Pavoni, *supra* n. 66, who argues that the principle requires good faith negotiations to amend, as necessary, the relevant treaties so as to achieve mutual supportiveness.

[74] *United States – Import Prohibition of Certain Shrimp and Shrimp Products*, Report of the Appellate Body, 12 October 1998, WT/DS58/AB/R ('*Shrimp-Turtle*').

[75] United Nations Convention on the Law of the Sea, 10 December 1982, 1833 UNTS 397.

[76] Convention on International Trade in Endangered Species of Wild Fauna and Flora, 3 March 1973, 983 UNTS 243.

[77] *Shrimp-Turtle, supra* n. 74, paras. 129–32.

[78] Vienna Convention on the Law of Treaties, 23 May 1969, 1155 UNTS 331 ('VCLT'). See *Oil Platforms case (Islamic Republic of Iran v. United States of America)*, ICJ Reports 2003, p. 161, para. 41.

followed by the WTO Dispute Settlement Body. In a 2006 panel report in the *EC – Biotech* case, a restrictive understanding of systemic integration was used to disregard the potential impact of the Convention on Biological Diversity and the Cartagena Protocol on Biosafety on the interpretation of the applicable trade disciplines.[79]

More recently, in *China – Raw Materials*, China referred to mutual supportiveness and to permanent sovereignty over natural resources to justify, under Article XX(g), the export restrictions it imposed on certain raw materials.[80] In a much debated ruling, the panel and later the AB considered that China could not rely on Article XX to justify a breach of its Protocol of Accession, but they nevertheless discussed the availability of Article XX both *arguendo* and in connection with breaches of the GATT. The panel mentioned among others the characterisation of the term 'conservation' in a number of environmental agreements, including the CBD, as guidance to clarify the ordinary meaning of Article XX(g).[81] It then referred to the report of the AB in *Shrimp-Turtle* and, specifically, to the preamble of the WTO Agreement and its reference to sustainable development.[82] Significantly, the panel expressly acknowledged the need to 'take into account in interpreting Article XX(g) principles of general international law applicable to WTO Members' but it quoted, as an authority for this assertion, the report of the panel in *EC – Biotech*.[83] It thereafter reasoned that the interpretation of Article XX(g) had to take into account the customary principle of sovereignty over natural resources. The customary nature of such principle excluded any difficulties arising from the narrower understanding of systemic integration expounded in *EC – Biotech*. For present purposes, the main point to be highlighted is the express recognition of mutual supportiveness by the panel: '[c]onservation and economic development are not necessarily mutually exclusive policy goals; they can operate in harmony'.[84]

12.3.2.2 Environmental goods and services

Paragraph 31 of the Doha Mandate entrusted the negotiations on EGS to a special session of the CTE. Facilitating trade on EGS could serve a number of purposes, including incentivising green industries worldwide, creating 'green jobs' and increasing the diffusion of green products. Portrayed as one of the areas where 'triple win' outcomes (i.e. good for trade, the environment and development) could be achieved, the negotiations on EGS have, however, stalled at the WTO level. The main reason is that there is no agreement as to

---

[79] *European Communities – Measures affecting the Approval and Marketing of Biotech Products*, WT/DS291/R, WT/DS292/R, WT/DS293/R (29 September 2006), paras. 7.74 and 7.75.
[80] *China – Measures related to the Exportation of Various Raw Materials*, Panel Reports, WT/DS394/R; WT/DS395/R; WT/DS398/R (5 July 2011) ('*China – Raw Materials (Panel)*'), para. 7.364.
[81] *Ibid.*, para. 7.372, footnote 594.   [82] *Ibid.*, para. 7.373.   [83] *Ibid.*, para. 7.377.
[84] *Ibid.*, para. 7.381.

what should be treated as an 'environmental good' or as a related environmental service. There are of course some guiding definitions, such as the one provided by the European Commission and taken up by the OECD:

> goods and services capable of measuring, preventing, limiting or correcting environmental damage such as the pollution of water, air, soil, as well as waste and noise-related problems. They include clean technologies where pollution and raw material use is being minimized.[85]

However, as noted in the 2015 UNEP's Handbook on *Trade and Green Economy*,[86] each of the categories potentially encompassed by this facilitated trade regime faces daunting definitional challenges.

The first category would cover goods that can be used for prevention, monitoring and remediation of environmental impacts. Yet, many of these goods have 'dual uses' (e.g. a thermostat) and, as a result, the link they entertain with such specifically environmental uses could be turned into an excuse for their facilitated trading for other uses. The second category concerns goods with an allegedly lower environmental footprint. This category faces a major issue of comparability and ranking. By way of illustration, how a gasoline-run but fuel-efficient car should be compared with a biofuel-run but fuel-less-efficient car, particularly if we take into account not only emissions but also impact on land-use change and water efficiency? The third category is, quite ironically, deemed to be more 'environmental' as a result of their processes and production methods ('PPMs'). This issue, as discussed later in this chapter, is very controversial in the trade context because it would entail differential treatment of two 'like' or even identical goods because of the way (more or less polluting) in which they have been produced. Thus, the EGS debate is potentially an environmental 'Trojan horse' within the WTO if not adequately circumscribed to maintain the focus on product characteristics rather than on production processes.

Despite these obstacles, significant progress has been made on this front at the regional level. In September 2012, the twenty-one countries of the Asia-Pacific Economic Cooperation group ('APEC') reached an agreement to reduce tariffs to a ceiling of 5 per cent on a list of fifty-four environmental goods[87] in which they already handled a large majority of world trade. The 'Declaration' embodying this agreement expressly notes that their reduction

---

[85] OECD, *The Global Environmental Goods and Services Industry* (Paris: OECD, 1994), p. 4. For more recent overviews of characterisations see: A. Viklhyaev, 'Environmental Goods and Services: Defining Negotiations or Negotiating Definitions?' (2004) *UNCTAD Trade and Environment Review*, available at: unctad.org/en/docs/ditcted20034a2_en.pdf (last visited on 20 April 2014); World Bank, *Inclusive Green Growth: The Pathway to Sustainable Development* (Washington DC: World Bank, 2012), pp. 92–3.

[86] UNEP, *Trade and Green Economy: A Handbook* (Geneva: UNEP, 3rd edn, forthcoming,) ('Handbook'), Section 4.10.

[87] See '20th APEC Economic Leaders' Declaration', Vladivostok, Russia, 9 September 2012, Annex C: APEC List of Environmental Goods, available at: www.apec.org (last visited on 20 April 2014).

commitment 'is without prejudice to [the APEC countries'] positions in the World Trade Organization (WTO)'. A similar initiative, focusing only on goods, is currently being negotiated on a plurilateral level, i.e. involving some members of the WTO from different regions, including Australia, Canada, China, the EU, Japan, Korea, New Zealand, Norway, Singapore, Switzerland and the United States, among others. The idea emerged on the side of the 2014 Davos forum and it was formally launched in July 2014.[88]

As suggested by these examples, there is significant room for specific synergies within the trade/environment link. Although so far synergies have mostly been of a general nature (resource efficiency gains through increased competition and technology transfer through trade), the regional APEC initiative and the potential plurilateral Agreement on Environmental Goods illustrate ways in which trade law can be specifically harnessed to promote environmental protection. However, the potential for synergies must not overshadow the need for prevention and minimisation of frictions between trade and environmental law.

12.3.3 Conflicts

12.3.3.1 Normative conflicts v. legitimacy conflicts

The distinction introduced earlier in this chapter between normative conflicts (conflicts involving two or more norms of international law) and legitimacy conflicts (conflicts involving one international obligation and one domestic measure) is useful to frame the interactions between trade and investment regulation. Much like in investment law, the impact of international environmental law on trade law remains unclear.

Although the potential frictions between them were recognised early in the history of trade regulation[89] and several initiatives have been taken to clarify it, including as part of the Doha mandate,[90] the attempts at developing some form of 'progressive' approach have been unsuccessful. However, as discussed next, over time trade panels have paid increasing attention to environmental protection moving from a 'traditional' approach (sometimes called 'inward looking'), which saw environmental measures as protectionist and subordinated to trade disciplines, to an 'upgraded' one (sometimes called 'outward looking'),[91] a sort of 'glasnost' where environmental considerations and international environmental law are taken into account to interpret trade law.

---

[88] See 'Group of WTO Members Launch Talks on "Green Goods"', available at: www.twnside.org. sg/title2/wto.info/2014/ti140706.htm (last visited on 20 April 2014).

[89] See *supra* n. 53.   [90] See *supra* n. 62, para. 31.

[91] A famous passage of the AB Report in *US – Reformulated Gasoline* is often referred to as the beginning of this openness process. The AB noted that the GATT was 'not to be read in clinical isolation from public international law', *United States – Standards for Reformulated and Conventional Gasoline*, AB Report (29 April 1996), WT/DS2/AB/R ('*US – Reformulated Gasoline*'), p. 17.

This is important in practice because many States are increasingly pursuing 'green industrial policies', namely policies aimed at developing strong and competitive industries in environment-related sectors (e.g. renewable energies), which, in turn, may fall foul of international trade and investment disciplines. Recent examples of frictions arising from such policies include the dispute between China and the EU over local content requirements in the renewable energy policy of some European States,[92] those between Japan and Canada[93] or the US and India relating to a similar issue[94] or, still, the suits filed by Argentina and Indonesia against the antidumping measures on biofuels imposed by the EU.[95]

12.3.3.2 Multilateral environmental treaties and trade regulation

The potential normative conflicts between trade and environmental treaties have been mostly analysed in connection with the so-called 'TREMs' or 'trade-related environmental measures'. Indeed, several important environmental treaties impose trade restrictions or even ban the trade in certain substances.

Broadly speaking, a distinction can be made between those treaties the main purpose of which is to impose trade restrictions and those in which trade restrictions are one implementation tool among others. The first category includes treaties spelling out the principle of prior informed consent ('PIC') analysed in Chapter 3, such as the Basel Convention,[96] the PIC Convention[97] or the Cartagena Protocol on Biosafety,[98] but also others such as the CITES, which seeks to protect endangered species (mostly located in developing countries) through the control of demand (from developed countries).[99] The

---

[92] See *European Union and certain Member States – Certain Measures Affecting the Renewable Energy Generation Sector – Request for Consultations by China* (7 November 2012), WT/DS452/1, G/L/1008, G/SCM/D95/1, G/TRIMS/D/34. The dispute was settled in late July 2013, although there have been several iterations on more specific components of solar panels.

[93] See *Canada – Certain Measures Affecting the Renewable Energy Generation Sector*, Panel Report (19 December 2012), WT/DS412/R and *Canada – Measures Relating to the Feed in Tariff Program*, WT/DS426/R, AB Report (6 May 2013), WT/DS412/AB/R and WT/DS426/AB/R ('*Canada – Renewables*'). At least two claims have been brought against Canada by foreign investors claiming that some aspects of the feed-in-tariff scheme introduced by Ontario are in breach of the investment chapter of the NAFTA. See *Mesa Power Group LLC v. Government of Canada*, NAFTA (UNCITRAL) Arbitration, Notice of Arbitration (4 October 2011); *Windstream Energy LLC v. Government of Canada*, NAFTA (UNCITRAL), Notice of Arbitration (28 January 2013).

[94] *India – Certain Measures Relating to Solar Cells and Solar Modules*, DS456. A panel was established on May 2014.

[95] See *European Union and certain Member States – Certain Measures on the Importation and Marketing of Biodiesel and Measures Supporting the Biodiesel Industry – Request for Consultations by Argentina* (23 May 2013), WT/DS459/1, G/L/1027, G/SCM/D97/1, G/TRIMS/D/36, G/TBT/D/44; *European Union – Anti-Dumping Measures on Biodiesel from Indonesia – Request for consultations by Indonesia* (17 June 2014), WT/DS480/1, G/L/1071, G/ADP/D104/1.

[96] Basel Convention on the Control of Transboundary Movements of Hazardous Wastes and their Disposal, 22 March 1989, 1673 UNTS 57 ('Basel Convention').

[97] See *supra* n. 67.   [98] See *supra* n. 68.   [99] See *supra* n. 76.

second category includes treaties such as the Montreal Protocol[100] or the POP Convention,[101] where trade measures (typically a ban of transfers to non-parties) are useful to avoid shifting the production and/or the consumption of regulated substances to States that are not parties to the treaty. Of course, as most treaties use different regulatory techniques, such trade bans are also found in treaties of the first category, such as the Basel Convention, which bans trade with non-parties unless they have a similarly protective system regulating hazardous waste.[102]

Such TREMs have been analysed in some detail in trade circles. By way of illustration, the WTO Secretariat has compiled a 'matrix' of environmental treaties containing TREMs[103] and the Doha mandate entrusted to a special session of the CTE the task of clarifying the relations between such TREMs and the WTO Agreements.[104] Despite their limited success, the value of these efforts to broaden the trade 'mindset' must not be underestimated. This said, it is important not to confine this analysis within a broader but still narrow understanding of conflicts or frictions as essentially limited to TREMs.

Indeed, TREMs are not the only measures required or authorised by environmental treaties that may conflict with trade disciplines. A treaty that does not explicitly require the adoption of a TREM, such as the UNFCCC or the Kyoto Protocol, may be interpreted as authorising the adoption of TREMs or other (non-TREM) trade relevant measure (e.g. a measure of green industrial policy hitting production of a certain good and thereby lowering the demand of that industry for certain other goods produced both locally and abroad). The debate on the so-called 'border carbon adjustments', i.e. the duties imposed by the importing country on imports that have been produced abroad with a higher level of emissions or, alternatively, the subsidies given to its local producers to compete with foreign products, has overlooked this dimension. The question asked is whether such adjustments would be justified under the general exception (Article XX) of the GATT or consistent with the SCM Agreement,[105] i.e. with trade law, rather than whether such measures are required or justified by environmental treaties. Both questions are important, but a focus on the first must not overshadow the relevance of the second. The misguided understanding that a broadly stated environmental norm is not 'binding' or is 'soft-law' is simply legally incorrect. Broad norms such as 'States shall accord fair and equitable treatment' (in international investment law) or '[c]ongress shall have power to regulate commerce with foreign nations, and

---

[100] Montreal Protocol on Substances that Deplete the Ozone Layer, 16 September 1987, 1522 UNTS 28 ('Montreal Protocol'), Arts. 4 and 4A.

[101] POP Convention, *supra* n. 70, Art. 3(1)(a)(ii) and 3(2).

[102] Basel Convention, *supra* n. 96, Arts. 4(5) and 11(1).

[103] WTO/CTE, Matrix on Trade Measures pursuant to Selected Multilateral Environmental Agreements, 14 March 2007, WT/CTE/W/160/Rev.4, TN/TE/S/5/Rev.2.

[104] Doha Declaration, *supra* n. 62, para. 31.

[105] Agreement on Subsidies and Countervailing Measures, 15 April 1994, 1867 UNTS 14 ('SCM Agreement').

among the several states' (the commerce clause in the United States Constitution) have been interpreted and applied in great detail. The same logic governs the application of broad environmental norms by an appropriately empowered court. Whether a measure is authorised or prohibited under such broad norms is indeed relevant as the applicable conflict rules or, at the very least, the interpretative approach (Article 31(3)(c) of the VCLT) would be different from that used in a pure trade dispute.

12.3.3.3 Environmental protection in practice
12.3.3.3.1 Processes and production methods ('PPMs')

In international trade adjudication, environmental protection measures remain so far confined to the modest role of a legal possibility 'exceptionally' allowed by trade law. Even if, as discussed in the previous section, it seems unrealistic to expect that trade panels or the AB will treat environmental law on the same footing as trade law (a 'progressive' approach), handling it through 'exceptions' rather than through 'carve-outs' entails significant legal consequences, not the least for the key debate over PPMs. From this perspective, the current approach pursued in trade adjudication can be seen as a shy variation of the 'upgraded approach' referred to earlier.

Indeed, trade law prohibits differentiation between two 'like' products on the basis of the environmental impact of their PPMs. In order to understand this point, it is useful to recall the characterisation of 'likeness' given by the AB in the *EC – Asbestos* case. According to the AB, four sets of characteristics must be taken into account:

> (i) the physical properties of products; (ii) the extent to which the products are capable of serving the same or similar end-uses; (iii) the extent to which consumers perceive and treat the products as alternative means of performing particular functions in order to satisfy a particular want or demand; and (iv) the international classification of the products for tariff purposes.[106]

In casu, Canada had challenged a French measure banning the imports of products containing asbestos. One key issue was whether chrysotile asbestos fibres and fibres that can be substituted for them were 'like' products under Article III(4) of the GATT. The panel concluded that they were, but that the measure was justified under Article XX(b) of the GATT ('necessary to protect human, animal or plant life or health'). On appeal, the AB reversed the panel's conclusion stating that the two products were not alike because the different composition of the two products had important health implications. The AB confirmed that in all events the measure was justified under Article XX(b). This case thus stands for the proposition that the different composition of two products may not only give access to an 'exception' (which presupposes a

---

[106] *European Communities – Measures Affecting Asbestos and Products Containing Asbestos*, AB Report (12 March 2001), WT/DS135/AB/R, para. 101.

breach) but also require an adjustment of the meaning of 'likeness' excluding a breach in the first place. A different matter is whether two products which do not differ in their composition but only in the way they have been produced (non-product-related PPMs) can be lawfully treated differently under one of the above two arguments. This is important from an environmental perspective because the environmental footprint of different PPMs is seldom reflected in the composition of a product.

The 'traditional' or 'inward looking' approach to this question held such differentiation to be discriminatory, excluding even their justification under the general exception clause of Article XX. In the well-known *Tuna-dolphin* cases, the panels concluded that the restriction imposed by the US on imports of tuna harvested with high levels of incidental killing of dolphins were in violation of Article XI of the GATT (which prohibits quantitative restrictions to trade) and could not be justified under the general exception clause in Article XX of the GATT, letters (b) and (g) ('relating to the conservation of exhaustible natural resources').[107] With the advent of the WTO system, a shy 'upgraded' approach, sometimes called 'outward looking', was first introduced by the AB Report in *US – Reformulated Gasoline*[108] and subsequently confirmed in the *Shrimp-turtle* case.[109] Under this approach, PPM-based differentiation is discriminatory (so the two products are deemed 'alike' despite the different environmental impact of their PPMs) but it can be potentially justified if the requirements of Article XX, including its chapeau, are met. Compared to the 'upgraded' approach followed in investment law, this approach is 'shy' in two main respects. First, PPMs are not understood as changing the interpretation of a trade discipline (e.g. the term 'like').[110] Second, although such PPMs can be taken into account to justify a measure under an exception clause, so far this possibility has never been admitted in practice.

12.3.3.3.2 The use of general exceptions

Beyond the question of PPMs, the use of exceptions is at present the main avenue through which environmental protection is being brought under trade law. Article XX, sub-paragraphs (a), (b) or (g) of the GATT have been invoked to justify measures such as import bans of retreaded tyres[111] or seal products[112]

---

[107] See *Tuna-dolphin I*, *supra* n. 57, and *United States – Measures Concerning the Importation, Marketing and Sale of Tuna and Tuna Products*, Panel report (16 June 1994), DS29/R ('*Tuna-dolphin II*').

[108] *US – Reformulated Gasoline*, *supra* n. 91, p. 17.

[109] *Shrimp-Turtle*, *supra* n. 74, paras. 129–32.

[110] See by contrast the analysis of likeness in *Parkerings* v. *Lithuania*, *supra* n. 44.

[111] *Brazil – Measures Affecting Imports of Retreaded Tyres*, AB Report (3 December 2007), WT/DS332/AB/R ('*Brazil – Retreaded Tyres*').

[112] *European Communities – Measures Prohibiting the Importation and Marketing of Seal Products*, AB Report (22 May 2014), WT/DS400/AB/R, WT/DS401/AB/R ('*EC – Seal Products*').

or export restrictions of certain raw materials[113] for environmental reasons. In all these cases, the defence based on Article XX failed, mainly because the measures challenged did not meet the exacting requirements of the chapeau, namely that:

> measures are not applied in a manner which would constitute a means of arbitrary or unjustifiable discrimination between countries where the same conditions prevail, or a disguised restriction on international trade.[114]

Yet, these cases have greatly contributed to the understanding of Article XX and its potential for environmental protection.

By way of illustration, in *Brazil – Retreaded Tyres*, the AB discussed *inter alia* what it means for a measure to be 'necessary' to protect human, animal or plant health. It concluded that the measure must be both 'apt to make a material contribution to the achievement of its objective'[115] and proportionate, in that it must be less trade restrictive than other realistically available measures pursuing the same objective.[116] Significantly, the AB recognised that:

> [C]ertain complex public health or environmental problems may be tackled only with a comprehensive policy comprising a multiplicity of interacting measures. In the short-term, it may prove difficult to isolate the contribution to public health or environmental objectives of one specific measure from those attributable to the other measures that are part of the same comprehensive policy. Moreover, the results obtained from certain actions – for instance, measures adopted in order to attenuate global warming and climate change, or certain preventive actions to reduce the incidence of diseases that may manifest themselves only after a certain period of time – can only be evaluated with the benefit of time.[117]

This understanding was subsequently confirmed in *China – Raw Materials*.[118]

In the more recent *EC – Seal Products* case, a ban on the import of seal products was considered 'necessary to protect public morals' under Article XX(a), although the challenged measures failed to meet the requirements of the chapeau. This is the first case where an environmental concern such as animal welfare is brought under the protection of public morals in Article XX(a). The content of 'public morals' may change over time reflecting the increasing environmental awareness of a State's population. In this context, the panel and the AB confirmed an earlier finding in a non-environmental case according to which:

---

[113] *China – Raw Materials (Panel), supra* n 80.
[114] For a recent overview of the WTO jurisprudence on the chapeau, see *EC – Seal Products, supra* n. 112, paras. 5.296–5.306.
[115] *Brazil – Retreaded Tyres, supra* n. 111, para.150.   [116] *Ibid.*, para. 156.   [117] *Ibid.*, para. 151.
[118] *China – Raw Materials (Panel), supra* n 80, para. 7.481, 7.485.

the content of public morals can be characterized by a degree of variation, and that, for this reason, Members should be given some scope to define and apply for themselves the concept of public morals according to their own systems and scales of values.[119]

Despite these encouraging developments, one may question whether the use of general exceptions is a suitable approach, let alone the most suitable one, to accommodate environmental protection within trade law. If environmental law is appropriately construed and applied, there is no reason to confine its operation to the availability of an exception. The interpretation of trade disciplines such as Articles I, III or XI of the GATT in the light of other relevant rules of international law applicable between the parties (Article 31(3)(c) of the VCLT) may require an adjustment in the meaning of a term such as 'like' products or other relevant expressions. Establishing the appropriate meaning of a term is not equivalent to proving the availability of a narrow exception. In the latter case, the respondent State has already been found in breach of the treaty and it will have the burden of proving that the measure is justified under an available exception.[120] So far, the requirements of the chapeau of Article XX have proved to be a formidable obstacle to the justification of environmental measures.

12.3.3.3.3 Specific trade agreements: SPS and TBT

The power of States to adopt trade-restrictive measures necessary to protect human, animal or plant health is not only covered by an exception in Article XX (which can only come into play once a breach of a trade discipline has been established) but it is also regulated at the level of trade disciplines (primary norms). Indeed, in addition to the general disciplines contained in Articles I, III and XI of the GATT, the SPS Agreement[121] subjects the adoption of such measures to specific requirements aimed at ensuring transparency (through a notification requirement),[122] administrative due process (through expediency and reasonableness requirements in inspection procedures),[123] and some measure of international harmonisation (through references to equivalence and to international standards).[124] Importantly, the relevant measures must be based on scientific evidence and a risk assessment.[125]

From an environmental perspective, this treaty can be seen as an attempt to circumscribe the scope of prevention within trade law. Beyond prevention (i.e. beyond risk) the scope for the adoption of measures on the basis of

---

[119] *EC – Seal Products, supra* n. 112, para. 5.199.
[120] The burden of proving that the requirements of the chapeau are met comes in addition to that of proving the availability of an exception. See *ibid.*, para. 5.297.
[121] Agreement on the Application of Sanitary and Phytosanitary Measures, 15 April 1994, 1867 UNTS 493 ('SPS Agreement').
[122] *Ibid.*, Art. 7 and Annex B.   [123] *Ibid.*, Art. 8 and Annex C.
[124] *Ibid.*, Art. 3 and 4 and Annex A.   [125] *Ibid.*, Art. 2(2) and 5.

precaution (i.e. when there is uncertainty) is tightly defined. Article 5.7 of SPS provides in this regard:

> In cases where relevant scientific evidence is insufficient, a Member may provisionally adopt sanitary or phytosanitary measures on the basis of available pertinent information, including that from the relevant international organizations as well as from sanitary or phytosanitary measures applied by other Members. In such circumstances, Members shall seek to obtain the additional information necessary for a more objective assessment of risk and review the sanitary or phytosanitary measure accordingly within a reasonable period of time.

The room left by the SPS Agreement for the adoption of environmental measures on a precautionary basis has been widely discussed, particularly in connection with two cases, *EC – Hormones*[126] and *EC – Biotech*.[127] In both cases, the EC sought to justify trade restrictive measures by reference to the precautionary principle discussed in Chapter 3. The argument was unsuccessful. In *EC – Hormones*, the AB declined to take a general stance on the customary basis of the precautionary principle[128] and noted that, in all events, 'the precautionary principle ha[d] been incorporated and given a specific meaning in Article 5.7 of the SPS Agreement'.[129] Similarly, in *EC – Biotech*, the panel reasoned that the legal status of the precautionary principle was still unsettled in general international law[130] and, as a result, the principle was not relevant for the interpretation of the SPS Agreement.[131]

Another important question is that of international standards. This question arises in the context of both the SPS Agreement and the TBT Agreement,[132] which defines the trade disciplines governing the enactment of technical barriers to trade, such as a variety of environmental and efficiency standards. Both agreements seek to harmonise the basis for the adoption of the relevant measures through the introduction of a rebuttable presumption. Measures based on recognised international standards are deemed to be proportionate (no more trade restrictive than necessary to achieve the goal pursued) under the TBT Agreement[133] as well as scientifically sound and necessary under the SPS Agreement.[134] The availability of this presumption is conditioned on the definition of 'international standard'. Both the SPS and the TBT Agreements provide some guidance on the identification of appropriate standards. Annex

---

[126] *European Communities – Measures concerning Meat and Meat Products (Hormones)*, AB Report (16 January 1998), WT/DS26/AB/R, WT/DS48/AB/R ('*EC– Hormones*').

[127] *EC – Biotech, supra* n. 79.

[128] It noted that 'it is unnecessary, and probably imprudent, for the Appellate Body in this appeal to take a position on this important, but abstract, question', *EC – Hormones, supra* n. 126, para. 123.

[129] *Ibid.*, para. 120.   [130] *EC – Biotech, supra* n. 79, para. 7.88.   [131] *Ibid.*, paras. 7.89 and 7.90.

[132] Agreement on Technical Barriers to Trade, 15 April 1994, 1868 UNTS 120 ('TBT Agreement').

[133] *Ibid.*, Art. 2(5).

[134] See SPS Agreement, *supra* n. 121, Arts. 2(2) (for the requirement) and 3(2) (for the presumption).

A, Section 3 of the SPS Agreement refers to the standards, guidelines and recommendations of the Codex Alimentarius Commission (for food safety), those of the International Office for Epizootics (for animal health) or to those of the International Plant Convention's Secretariat (for plant health). For questions not covered, Section 3(d) refers to 'other relevant international organizations open for membership to all Members'. The TBT Agreement does not explicitly define the term 'international standard' but it refers to the International Standardisation Organisation ('ISO') and notes that international standards are adopted by consensus by bodies open to the relevant organisations of all WTO members.[135]

Further clarification as to the meaning of this term can be derived from a recent ruling of the AB in a resurgence of the *Tuna-dolphin* dispute.[136] In this case, Mexico complained about the requirements imposed, *inter alia*, by the US Dolphin Protection Consumer Information Act ('DPCIA'), as subsequently interpreted by US Courts, for the labelling of imported tuna as 'dolphin safe'. According to the US regulation, the granting of the 'dolphin safe' label for tuna harvested in the area of the Pacific Ocean where the Mexican fleet operated depended upon the harvesting method used (specifically, tuna harvested by setting purse-nets that might also trap dolphins in that area – but not in other areas – could not be thus certified). Significantly, a treaty to which Mexico and the US were parties (the 'AIDCP') conditioned the granting of the 'dolphin safe' label on other – quantitative – criteria (the level of mortality and serious injury to dolphins, and not on the harvesting method). The dispute led to a finding of breach of Article 2.1 of the TBT Agreement but, for present purposes, the most relevant part is the discussion of what constitutes a 'relevant international standard' under Article 2.4 of this Agreement. The Panel found that the AIDCP could set relevant international standards, but the AB reversed this finding on the grounds that the AIDCP was not an international standardising organisation for purposes of the TBT as it was not open to automatic accession by any WTO member. The decision sets a high threshold for environmental treaty bodies to be considered as capable of adopting TBT-consistent standards.

12.4 Environmental protection and intellectual property rights

12.4.1 Overview

Amartya Sen once noted that it is not necessarily the availability of food but rather the access to it by those in need that must be tackled to prevent famines.[137] A similar argument could be made for technology. However,

---

[135] TBT Agreement, *supra* n. 132, Annex 1, Sections 2 and 4.

[136] *United States – Measures Concerning the Importation, Marketing and Sale of Tuna and Tuna Products*, AB Report (16 May 2012), WT/DS381/AB/R.

[137] See A. Sen, *Poverty and Famines. An Essay on Entitlement and Deprivation* (Oxford University Press, 1981).

unlike food, the very strategies used to steer technological innovation (particularly intellectual property rights or 'IPRs') have implications for the subsequent access to such technology, because of the monopoly IPRs give to inventors, which leads to higher prices and, in some cases, to a refusal to license the technology to potentially competing companies. The development of environmentally sound technologies is therefore not only a technological challenge, but also a policy (how to foster innovation) and a legal one (without severely restricting access).[138]

We have already discussed some aspects of this question in earlier chapters. In Chapter 9, we introduced the debate concerning technology transfer, which is an important component of the principle of common but differentiated responsibilities. In Chapter 6, we analysed the implications of asserting property rights over genetic resources, traditional knowledge and plant varieties, in the specific context of the so-called 'seeds wars'. These are but two manifestations of the broader question addressed in this section: how to foster the diffusion of environmentally sound technologies without hindering their development. As noted in Chapter 9, from a legal perspective the controversy is reflected in the form that technology transfer may take. The main 'forms' identified in economic theory, namely trade (of products manufactured or containing a given technology), licensing (an authorisation to use a technology or a part of it under certain specific conditions) and foreign direct investment (the creation of an entity in the host country with access to the relevant technology),[139] have very different political and legal implications.

The international protection of IPRs is key in the three contexts, although for different reasons. Ensuring basic standards of protection of IPRs, particularly patents (a temporary legal monopoly conferred to an inventor for the production, use and commercialisation of an invention), is important to protect the technologies embedded in products exported to other countries. The very idea of licensing is based on the respect of IPRs. As for foreign direct investment, depending on the specific manner in which it is structured, the protection of IPRs will operate differently. If the components containing the technology are manufactured in the host country, then the technology and know-how must be transferred to the investment vehicle and IPRs protection will play a role in protecting the position of the subsidiary against competitors or the host State. Alternatively, the components may be produced in the home country and sent to the subsidiary to be assembled. This is a case of intra-firm trade where, although less exposed, the components will benefit, as other traded products, from IPRs protection in the host country.

---

[138] For a recent study surveying legal techniques to strike a balance, see S. Chuffart, *Optimising Environmental Technology Diffusion under Intellectual Property Constraints: A Legal Analysis* (PhD dissertation, The Graduate Institute, Geneva, 2014).

[139] See K. Keller, 'International Technology Diffusion' (2004) 42 *Journal of Economic Literature* 752.

In the three hypotheses, the protection of IPRs is useful not only for the development of technologies but also to facilitate their diffusion. Yet, such diffusion is only facilitated because right holders enjoy better protection of their invention. But as any holder of a monopoly, right holders can significantly increase the price of their products and even refuse to enter into license agreements. This power may become an important obstacle to diffusion and prevent the emergence of similar industries in developing countries. It can also discourage innovation more generally by limiting access to technologies that are a necessary stepping-stone for other technologies to be developed. Thus, much like with investment and trade, the relationship between environmental protection and IPRs can be analysed through the prism of synergies and conflicts.

12.4.2 Synergies

12.4.2.1 Approaches to international patent protection

The foregoing observations are useful to understand the role of international law in protecting IPRs. Although there is a vast web of multilateral treaties addressing different aspects of IPRs,[140] the most relevant ones for present purposes are the Agreement on Trade-Related Aspects of Intellectual Property Rights ('TRIPs'),[141] the Paris Convention for the Protection of Industrial Property ('Paris Convention'),[142] and the Patent Cooperation Treaty ('PCT').[143]

The latter two are specifically devoted to expand, albeit to a limited degree, the geographical scope of patent protection. Although such protection remains territorial, these instruments attach some international effects to the filing of a patent application in a State party. Thus, under the Paris Convention, the date of the first filing will count for all other filings submitted in other States parties within twelve months. More importantly, under the PCT, an international filing can be made which, provided some conditions are met, will count as simultaneous filings in all the States parties. As such, this system is an attempt to foster innovation, including for environmental purposes, as it greatly reduces the transactional costs of seeking patent protection in many countries.

The TRIPs takes a different approach. It requires WTO Members to provide a basic level of protection of IPRs in their legislation. Patent protection standards are particularly developed (Articles 27–34). Broader and deeper

---

[140] For an introduction, see F. M. Abbott, T. Cottier and F. Gurry, *International Intellectual Property in an Integrated World Economy* (New York: Wolters Kluwer, 2011).

[141] Agreement on Trade-Related Aspects of Intellectual Property Rights, 15 April 1994, 1869 UNTS 299. On this treaty, see C. Correa, *Trade-Related Aspects of Intellectual Property Rights. A Commentary on the TRIPs Agreement* (Oxford University Press, 2007).

[142] Paris Convention for the Protection of Industrial Property, 20 March 1883, available at: www.wipo.org (last visited on 20 May 2014).

[143] Patent Cooperation Treaty, 19 June 1970, 1160 UNTS 231 ('PCT').

than previous international attempts to protect patents, the agreement also sets parameters for domestic enforcement (Part III) and provides access to the WTO DSB (Article 64). Such protection provides a clear incentive for innovation, as it greatly enhances the position of rights holders. In addition, the TRIPs specifically refers to the question of technology transfer. Article 7 provides indeed that:

> The protection and enforcement of intellectual property rights should contribute to the promotion of technological innovation and to the transfer and dissemination of technology, to the mutual advantage of producers and users of technological knowledge and in a manner conducive to social and economic welfare, and to a balance of rights and obligations.

This obligation is taken up in Article 66(2), which requires developed States to provide incentives to their own companies to transfer technology to least developed countries. Yet, except for some symbolic steps, such as the creation of a 'mechanism' to monitor the implementation of this provision,[144] little concrete action has been taken.

Aside from the general incentives provided by these treaties, other instruments have been developed in the last several years to specifically encourage environment-related technological innovation. In the following sections we discuss two of them, namely the fast-tracking of environmental patents and the efforts to create IPRs markets.

12.4.2.2 Fast-tracking of environmental patents

In the last years, a number of national patent offices, such as those of the UK, China, South Korea, the United States or Australia, have granted preferential treatment to patent applications concerning environmentally sound technologies.[145] The majority of these applications relate to renewable energy technologies and the fast-tracking programmes can significantly expedite review, reducing the time required to obtain the patent by half or even more.

The experience at the domestic level has led to a discussion regarding the possibility of generalising such preferential treatment through an amendment of the PCT.[146] The options considered include accelerated processing of applications, lower fees and enhanced diffusion of green applications. The type of synergy sought is therefore a further reduction of the transactional costs entailed by the filing of a patent application. Not only would this filing, through the PCT, be simultaneously submitted to all the offices of State

---

[144] See TRIPs Council, Implementation of Article 66(2) of the TRIPs Agreement, 20 February 2003, IP/C/28 (this decision requires the submission of reports by developed countries detailing steps taken to comply with Art. 66(2)).

[145] See A. Dechezleprêtre, 'Fast-tracking Green Patent Applications: An Empirical Analysis, ICTSD Programme on Innovation, Technology and Intellectual Property: Issue Paper No. 37' (2013).

[146] See Meeting of International Authorities under the Patent Cooperation Treaty, *Preferential Treatment for International Applications Relating to 'Green' Technologies*, 21 January 2010, Doc. PCT/MIA/17/5.

members but, in addition, it could be given preferential treatment in all of them. However, so far, progress on this front has been slow at the international level, largely as a result of the significant changes that such a system would require in domestic patent laws and the challenges involved in identifying the type of patent applications that would be eligible.

12.4.2.3 IPRs markets

An innovative tool to strike a balance between protecting IPRs and enhancing their diffusion is the use of IPRs markets.[147] Such markets may take different forms, from the mere linking of technology providers and recipients, to the organised sale of patents (e.g. through auctioning) to the creation of markets where licence rights are exchanged more or less freely.

The first instrument can be illustrated by reference to the WIPO Green platform,[148] which is in fact a database of green technologies posted with the agreement of the provider and searchable by a variety of actors interested in acquiring the technology. The purpose of this platform is to provide a market-place where supply and demand meet, without intervening in subsequent transactions (e.g. the licensing of a technology). This tool has the advantage (and disadvantage) of preserving the rights of technology providers, including the ability to grant a licence or not to a potential acquirer or to negotiate its terms.

Another instrument is the organised sale of IPRs, particularly patents, through an auction process. Examples include the patent auctions held in 2005 and 2006 in California, where a portfolio of patents was sold for several million dollars.[149] The interest of this instrument to strike a balance between IPR protection and technology diffusion is, however, limited because the seller (e.g. a bankrupt company) loses the ownership of its IPR and the acquirer has to pay the market price of the patent.

The third type of instrument is more sophisticated. Like the first instrument it provides a regular marketplace for supply and demand to meet and, like the second instrument, it operates transfers of IPRs. Yet, the object exchanged in these markets is not a patent but a 'licence' right to use a patent or a technology (based on several patents). In one case, the GreenXchange launched in Davos in 2010,[150] the seller can choose whether to license the technology to a potential acquirer or not. Thus, the reduction of transactional costs comes mostly from the standardisation of the process. However, in another case, the IPXI,[151] the licence rights exchanged in the market ('unit licence rights') are offered on a non-discriminatory basis and, therefore, a technology provider cannot participate in the market unless it has agreed to license its technology to

---

[147] See A. H. B. Monk, 'The Emerging Market for Intellectual Property: Drivers, Restrainers, and Implications' (2009) 9 *Journal of Economic Geography* 469.
[148] See webaccess.wipo.int/green/ (last visited on 15 August 2014).
[149] See Chuffart, *supra* n. 138, pp. 134–5.   [150] *Ibid.*, pp. 135–6.   [151] *Ibid.*, pp. 137–9.

any acquirer participating in the market. Although IPXI is not specifically concerned with environmentally sound technologies, it does encompass some of them, e.g. energy efficient appliances.

12.4.3 Conflicts

12.4.3.1 The TRIPs and environmental protection

The TRIPs places important constraints on the ability of countries to limit IPRs protection to facilitate diffusion, particularly as a result of its patent protection standards. It provides, however, for some narrowly defined exceptions, under which a country can exclude the patentability of an invention or limit the scope of protection. Three of them are relevant for environmental protection.

First, a country may exclude patentability of an invention when that is necessary to protect *ordre public* or morality ('including to protect human, animal or plant life or health or to avoid serious prejudice to the environment') (Article 27(2)). Second, countries can also exclude the patentability of 'plants and animals other than micro-organisms, and essentially biological processes for the production of plants or animals other than non-biological and microbiological processes' but only on the condition that they protect plant varieties either through patents or through 'an effective *sui generis* system or by any combination thereof' (Article 27(3)(b)). Third, the exclusivity or monopoly enjoyed by patent holders can be limited under certain conditions, which has paved the way for the development of the so-called 'compulsory licensing' of certain technologies (Articles 30–31).

This system has come under criticism in connection with its implications for public health policies[152] as well as, more recently, the diffusion of climate change technology.[153] Over time, the provisions of the TRIPs have been interpreted so as to provide some flexibility to developing countries (12.4.3.2). Many problems remain, however, as suggested by the current attempts at amending the TRIPs and other instruments to balance patent protection with the protection of entitlements over genetic resources and traditional knowledge (12.4.2.3).

12.4.3.2 Interpreting the TRIPs

12.4.3.2.1 Compulsory licensing and public health

As noted in the previous section, the TRIPs allows for some flexibility in its standards regulating the granting and the protection of patents. Article 31 allows States to include in their legislation the possibility, in certain cases, of

---

[152] For an overview of the debate, see R. Love, 'Corporate Wealth or Public Health? WTO/TRIPS Flexibilities and Access to HIV/AIDS Antiretroviral Drugs by Developing Countries' (2007) 17 *Development in Practice* 208.

[153] *Contribution of Intellectual Property to Facilitating the Transfer of Environmentally Rational Technology. Communication from Ecuador*, 27 February 2013, IP/C/W/585.

authorising a third party to use a patent without the authorisation of the right holder. Normally, such authorisation may only be granted if the third party has first tried to obtain a licence from the right holder. However, this requirement may be waived 'in the case of a national emergency or other circumstances of extreme urgency or in cases of public non-commercial use' (Article 31(b)).

This exception, called 'compulsory licensing', has been used for the production of generic drugs (for HIV/AIDS and other diseases) in some countries. Such possibility was specifically endorsed by a 2001 Declaration on the TRIPs Agreement and Public Health, according to which 'the Agreement can and should be interpreted and implemented in a manner supportive of WTO members' right to protect public health' and, accordingly:

> Each member has the right to determine what constitutes a national emergency or other circumstances of extreme urgency, it being understood that public health crises, including those relating to HIV/AIDS, tuberculosis, malaria and other epidemics, can represent a national emergency or other circumstances of extreme urgency.[154]

A remaining obstacle, arising from Article 31(f) of the TRIPs (which requires that the production under compulsory licensing be used mainly for domestic consumption) was lifted in 2003, when a Decision of the General Council recognised that the generic drugs thus produced could be exported to countries in need that do not have the capacity to produce them locally.[155]

This system provides a good illustration of how potential conflicts, when openly recognised and circumscribed, can be effectively addressed through authentic interpretation before reaching the dispute settlement stage.

12.4.3.2.2 *Sui generis* protection of plant varieties

Article 27(3)(b) of the TRIPs gives States some flexibility as to the patentability of plant varieties. As discussed in Chapter 6, the protection of plant varieties is controversial, as many developing countries and indigenous groups see it as a formal acknowledgement of 'stolen' genetic resources or traditional agricultural knowledge. In this context, the TRIPs agreement favoured breeders over farmers requiring States to protect plant varieties through patents or through other *sui generis* means.

The extent of the flexibility allowed by Article 27(3)(b) entirely depends upon the meaning of the expression 'effective *sui generis* systems'. Despite several attempts, the question is still being discussed within the TRIPs Council, with wide disagreements as to what should qualify as an admissible system. Underlying the discussion is the extent to which the rights of breeders to

---

[154] 'Declaration on the TRIPs Agreement and Public Health', 14 November 2011, WT/MIN(01)/DEC/2, paras. 4 and 5.

[155] 'Implementation of paragraph 6 of the Doha Declaration on the TRIPS Agreement and public health', 1 September 2003, WT/L/540 and Corr.1.

receive protection for their plant varieties can be balanced with the rights of farmers, particularly the right to replant parts of the seeds derived from a harvest.

According to UNEP's Handbook on *Trade and Green Economy*,[156] the system established by the International Convention for the Protection of New Varieties of Plants ('UPOV Convention')[157] would typically qualify as an effective *sui generis* system. Like the TRIPs, the UPOV Convention is mainly intended to protect the rights of breeders and it has come under criticism, including from the UN Special Rapporteur on the Right to Food, for its adverse implications for the survival of traditional systems of seed-saving and exchange as well as for the conservation of biodiversity.[158] A different matter is whether the regional or domestic schemes currently under elaboration in a number of developing countries in an attempt to provide additional protection to farmers' rights would also benefit from the exception in Article 27(3)(b).[159]

12.4.3.3 Genetic resources and traditional knowledge: proposed amendments

The discussion of genetic resources and traditional knowledge in Chapter 6 introduced the context in which efforts to reform the TRIPs must be assessed. One objective pursued by developing countries, where most biodiversity is found, in adopting the Convention on Biological Diversity ('CBD')[160] and the Nagoya Protocol[161] was to regulate access to genetic resources and traditional knowledge. Such regulation was deemed important to prevent these resources from being used by multinational companies to develop and patent drugs and plant varieties without sharing the benefits.[162] The question has been brought before two main forums.

One strand of the discussion has taken place in the context of the TRIPs Council. Paragraph 19 of the Doha Declaration entrusted the Council with the clarification of the relations between the TRIPs and the CBD. The Council's Secretariat has prepared briefing notes summarising major steps in the negotiation.[163] The main initiative so far has been the 2006 proposal

---

[156] Handbook, *supra* n. 86, Section 4.5.2.

[157] International Convention for the Protection of New Varieties of Plants, 2 December 1961, 815 UNTS 89 (subsequently revised, particularly in 1991).

[158] See Seed Policies and the Right to Food: Enhancing Agrobiodiversity and Encouraging Innovation. Report presented to the UN General Assembly, 23 July 2009, UN Doc. A/64/170.

[159] Handbook, *supra* n. 86, Section 4.5.2.

[160] Convention on Biological Diversity, 5 June 1992, 1760 UNTS 79 ('CBD').

[161] See *supra* n. 72.

[162] See S. Safrin, 'Hyperownership in a Time of Biotechnological Promise: The International Conflict' (2004) 98 *American Journal of International Law* 641; J. Curci, *The Protection of Biodiversity and Traditional Knowledge in International Law of Intellectual Property* (Cambridge University Press, 2009).

[163] The Relationship between the TRIPs Agreement and the Convention on Biological Diversity: Summary of Issues Raised and Points Made, 8 February 2006, IP/C/W/368/Rev.1. ('Summary Note').

tabled by several developing countries to amend the TRIPs so as to add a disclosure requirement in patent regulation. Specifically, States would have to introduce a requirement that an applicant seeking a patent relating to biological materials or traditional knowledge disclose the source of the materials used and provide proof that it has been lawfully accessed, i.e. in accordance with the prior informed consent and benefit sharing requirements.[164] The proposed amendment could take different legal forms, such as an additional exception to patentability in Article 27 (patentable subject matter), an additional paragraph in Article 29 (conditions on patent applicants) or an entirely new provision (Article 29*bis*).[165] A violation of the proposed disclosure requirement could have serious consequences, going as far as the revocation of the patent.[166] So far, however, these efforts have been unsuccessful. The situation could change if an important group such as the EU lends its support to the amendment proposal. An indication that this is not unrealistic is the adoption by the European Parliament of a resolution calling on the Commission to instruct its negotiators to take the Nagoya Protocol as a starting point for the introduction of disclosure requirements.[167]

Related discussions have also taken place within the context of the World Intellectual Property Organisation ('WIPO') and, specifically, of the Intergovernmental Committee ('IGC') on Intellectual Property and Genetic Resources, Traditional Knowledge and Folklore established in September 2000. In the last years, the Committee has negotiated three texts, which, although heavily bracketed, constitute full drafts introducing disclosure requirements in connection with genetic resources,[168] traditional knowledge[169] and traditional cultural expressions.[170] The first draft (genetic resources) contemplates, *inter alia*, an amendment of the PCT and the Patent Law Treaty[171] requiring or authorising States to introduce disclosure requirements into their legislation. At the time of writing, these drafts had been forwarded to WIPO's General Assembly for subsequent negotiations.

---

[164] *Ibid.*, para. 71.   [165] *Ibid.*, para. 79.   [166] *Ibid.*, para. 75.

[167] European Parliament Resolution of 15 January 2013 on Development Aspects of Intellectual Property Rights on Genetic Resources: the Impact on Poverty Reduction in Developing Countries, 2012/2135(INI), paras. 32–4, available at: www.europarl.europa.eu (last visited on 20 April 2014).

[168] Consolidated Document Relating to Intellectual Property and Genetic Resources, Rev. 2 (7 February 2014), available at: www.wipo.org (last visited on 10 August 2014).

[169] The Protection of Traditional Knowledge: Draft Articles Rev. 2 (28 March 2014, 8:00 pm), available at: www.wipo.org (last visited on 10 August 2014).

[170] The Protection of Traditional Cultural Expressions: Draft Articles, Rev. 2 (4 April 2014, 3.00 pm), available at: www.wipo.org (last visited on 10 August 2014).

[171] Patent Law Treaty, 19 June 1070, 39 ILM 1047.

Select bibliography

Abbott, F. M., T. Cottier, and F. Gurry, *International Intellectual Property in an Integrated World Economy* (New York: Wolters Kluwer, 2011).

Asteriti, A., *Greening Investment Law* (PhD dissertation, Glasgow, 2011).

Bodansky, D. and J. Lawrence, 'Trade and Environment', in D. Bethlehem, D. McRae, R. Neufeld and I. Van Damme (eds.), *The Oxford Handbook of International Trade Law* (Oxford University Press, 2009), pp. 505–38.

Boisson de Chazournes, L. and M. Mbengue, 'A propos du principe de soutien mutual. Les relations entre le Protocole de Cartagena et les Accords de l'OMC' (2007) 111 *Revue générale de droit international public* 829.

Brown Weiss, E. and J. Jackson (eds.), *Reconciling Environment and Trade* (Ardsley NY: Transnational Publishers, 2001).

Charnovitz, S., 'The WTO's Environmental Progress', in W. J. Davey and J. Jackson (eds.), *The Future of International Economic Law* (Oxford University Press, 2008), pp. 247–68.

Chuffart, S., *Optimising Environmental Technology Diffusion under Intellectual Property Constraints: A Legal Analysis* (PhD dissertation, The Graduate Institute, Geneva, 2014).

Cordonnier Segger, M.-C., M. W. Gehring and A. Newcombe (eds.), *Sustainable Development in World Investment Law* (Alphen aan den Rijn: Wolters Kluwer, 2011).

Correa, C., 'Innovation and Technology Transfer of Environmentally Sound Technologies: The Need to Engage in a Substantive Debate' (2013) 22 *Review of European, Comparative and International Environmental Law* 54.

   Trade-Related Aspects of Intellectual Property Rights. A Commentary on the TRIPs Agreement (Oxford University Press, 2007).

Curci, J., *The Protection of Biodiversity and Traditional Knowledge in International Law of Intellectual Property* (Cambridge University Press, 2009).

Dechezleprêtre, A., *Fast-tracking Green Patent Applications: An Empirical Analysis, ICTSD Programme on Innovation, Technology and Intellectual Property: Issue Paper No. 37* (2013).

Di Benedetto, S., *International Investment Law and the Environment* (Cheltenham: Edward Elgar, 2013).

Dolzer, R. and C. Schreuer, *Principles of International Investment Law* (Oxford University Press, 2013).

Douglas, Z., J. Pauwelyn and J. E. Viñuales (eds.), *The Foundations of International Investment Law: Bringing Theory into Practice* (Oxford University Press, 2014).

Dupuy, P.-M. and J. E. Viñuales (eds.), *Harnessing Foreign Investment to Promote Environmental Protection: Incentives and Safeguards* (Cambridge University Press, 2013).

Esty, D., *Greening the GATT: Trade, Environment, and the Future* (Washington DC: Institute for International Economics, 1994).

Frankel, J. and A. Rose, 'Is Trade Good or Bad for the Environment? Sorting out the Causality' (2005) 87 *Review of Economics and Statistics* 85.

Gordon, K. and J. Pohl, 'Environmental Concerns in International Investment Agreements: A Survey' (2011) *OECD Working Papers on International Investment* No. 2011/1.

Henry, G., *Technologies vertes et propriete intellectuelle* (Paris: LexisNexis, 2013).

Love, R., 'Corporate Wealth or Public Health? WTO/TRIPS Flexibilities and Access to HIV/AIDS Antiretroviral Drugs by Developing Countries' (2007) 17 *Development in Practice* 208.

Miles, K., *The Origins of International Investment Law* (Cambridge University Press, 2013).

Monk, A. H. B., 'The Emerging Market for Intellectual Property: Drivers, Restrainers, and Implications' (2009) 9 *Journal of Economic Geography* 469.

Mortenson, J. D., 'Meaning of "Investment": ICSID *Travaux* and the Domain of International Investment Law' (2010) 51 *Harvard International Law Journal* 257.

Pavoni, R., 'Mutual Supportiveness as a Principle of Interpretation and Law-Making: A Watershed for the "WTO-and-Competing-Regimes" Debate?' (2010) 3 *European Journal of International Law* 649.

Petersmann, E. U., *International and European Trade and Environmental Law after the Uruguay Round* (The Hague: Kluwer, 1995).

Robert-Cuendet, S., *Droits de l'investisseur étranger et protection de l'environnement: Contribution à l'analyse de l'expropriation indirecte* (Leiden: Martinus Nijhoff, 2010).

Romson, A., *Environmental Policy Space and International Investment Law* (PhD dissertation, Stockholm, 2012).

Safrin, S., 'Hyperownership in a Time of Biotechnological Promise: The International Conflict' (2004) 98 *American Journal of International Law* 641.

Streck, C., 'The World Summit on Sustainable Development: Partnerships as New Tools in Environmental Governance' (2002) 13 *Yearbook of International Environmental Law* 63.

United Nations Environment Programme, *Trade and Green Economy: A Handbook* (Geneva: UNEP, 3rd edn 2014).

Viñuales, J. E., *Foreign Investment and the Environment in International Law* (Cambridge University Press, 2012).

Von Moltke, K., 'The Last Round: The General Agreement on Tariffs and Trade in Light of the Earth Summit' (1993) 23 *Environmental Law* 519.

Vranes, E., *Trade and the Environment. Fundamental Issues in International Law, WTO Law, and Legal Theory* (Oxford University Press, 2009).

Watson, J., *The WTO and the Environment* (London: Routledge, 2013).

Zaelke, D., R. Housman and P. Orbach (eds.), *Trade and the Environment: Law, Economics and Policy* (Washington DC: Island Press, 1993).

Index